"Sjursen has written the definitive history of our imperial entanglements dating back to the pre-colonial era. Hiswriting is an indispensable companion to Howard Zinn's classic unmasking of the perpetual fraud of American innocence."

— **Robert Scheer, author of** *How the United States*
Got Involved in Vietnam, **journalist, and co-founder**
and editor of *Truthdig.com*

"Nobody fuses together two time-honored cliches: 'those who do not learn from history are doomed to repeat it' and the West Point Academy motto of 'Duty, Honor and Country' better than retired US Army Major Daniel Sjursen."

— **Coleen Rowley, retired FBI Special Agent, 9/11 and Iraq War**
whistleblower, and *Time* **magazine 2002 Person of the Year**

"Sjursen knows how to inform, provoke, and inspire. Even better, he knows how to be equal parts tough-minded and open-minded. *A True History* is for anyone wishing to be pushed beyond their comfort zone in the service of forming a more perfect union in America."

— **William J. Astore, historian, retired lieutenant colonel (USAF),**
and author of *Hindenburg: Icon of German Militarism*

"General Ulysses S. Grant felt the US war with Mexico, 1846–1848, was wrong. In the judgment of real historians like Sjursen, Grant was right. In *A True History of the United States*, Sjursen explains why such historical candor and accuracy are critical by giving us the reason he taught West Pointers not only that Grant was right in his assessment of our war of aggression and aggrandizement in Mexico but also why historical truth in general is a necessary antidote to the hypocrisy of patriotic nationalism: 'Exposure to the historical myths and flaws . . . of the country they might very well die for seemed appropriate. Anything less would have felt obscene.' Read this book to discover why."

— **Retired US Army Colonel Lawrence Wilkerson, former chief**
of staff to the secretary of state, and professor of government
and public policy at the College of William and Mary

T0038314

A TRUE HISTORY OF
THE UNITED STATES

A TRUE HISTORY OF THE UNITED STATES

Indigenous Genocide, Racialized Slavery,
Hyper-Capitalism, Militarist Imperialism,
and Other Overlooked Aspects
of American Exceptionalism

DANIEL A. SJURSEN

TRUTH TO POWER
an imprint of
STEERFORTH PRESS
LEBANON, NEW HAMPSHIRE

Copyright © 2021 Daniel A. Sjursen
ALL RIGHTS RESERVED

An earlier version of this volume's contents appeared in serialized form at the
truthdig.com website under the title "American History for Truthdiggers."

For information about permission to reproduce
selections from this book, write to:
Steerforth Press L.L.C., 31 Hanover Street, Suite 1,
Lebanon, New Hampshire 03766

Cataloging-in-Publication Data is available from the Library of Congress

ISBN 978-1-58642-253-0 (Paperback)

Manufactured in the United States of America

3 5 7 9 10 8 6 4 2

CONTENTS

PREFACE

Poll after poll demonstrates that year after year Americans' basic historical knowledge reaches newly obscene lows. This trend takes on increasing urgency when we observe political leaders and senior policy makers direct foreign and domestic affairs in the apparent absence of knowledge of relevant historical context. Frankly, it is embarrassing to watch, and often tragic in its human consequences.

I was first struck by the severity of this problem when I returned to my alma mater, the United States Military Academy — West Point — to teach freshman ("plebe") American History 101. I was straight out of graduate school, my sense of the decisive importance of the subject heightened by my tours in Iraq and Afghanistan where I fought in wars begun and waged seemingly without the faintest sense of the region's history. That the cadets would likely, almost inevitably, form the increasingly militarized vanguard of future US foreign policy only added urgency.

Most cadets entered West Point having been taught — and thus understanding — a rather flimsy brand of US history. These otherwise gifted students' understanding of the American past lacked substance or depth and pivoted on patriotic platitudes. Such young men and women hardly knew the history of the country they had volunteered to kill and die for. *That*, I thought to myself, is how military fiascoes are made.

Throughout my teaching tenure I set myself the task of bridging — in some modest way — the gap between what scholars *know* and what students *learn*. That process and its challenges motivated me to write this book: an enthusiastic attempt to bridge the perhaps unbridgeable — academic and public history. No doubt the project will be found wanting, but there's inherent value in the quest, in the very struggle. The skeletal geneses of the chapters that follow were the thirty-eight lesson plans I crafted to impart the broad contours of US history to future leaders of an army at war.

That the often censorious (some will say downright un-American) analyses herein were introduced to presumably patriotic and conservative West Point cadets may seem shocking. That many other history instructors on the faculty presented not altogether dissimilar concepts may be more surprising still. Nonetheless, as Martin Luther King Jr. often warned: We should not confuse dissent with disloyalty. In today's politically and culturally tribal times, unfortunately, this seems the reflexive response to any manner of disagreement.

I make no apologies for having presented combat-bound cadets with undeniable dark facts and some critical conclusions common among esteemed scholars. Exposure to the historical myths and flaws — in addition to the well-worn triumphs — of the country they might very well die for seemed appropriate. Anything less would have felt obscene.

———

I write this preface amid both a deadly pandemic and widespread demonstrations in communities large and small inspired by the Black Lives Matter movement that have shaken many Americans' perceptions of the nation's political and economic systems to the core. Whether these historically unprecedented events will translate into structural or lasting change is unclear, but there's no better time to translate the version of American History 101 that I taught at West Point to a public audience and to pose the salient question: *What, exactly, is exceptional about the United States?*

America *is* exceptional — not always in ways that should engender patriotic pride, but rather often in ways that should cause us to reflect, take stock, and strive to do better. Plenty of other countries, for instance, sport equally (if not more) free and democratic societies; dozens are healthier and provide superior medical care; some are even more affluent.

Hardly any, however — particularly in the wealthier "developed" world — have such vast wealth gaps, disparate health services and outcomes, or traditionally weak left-labor parties. Essentially none imprison quite so many of their citizens, militarily garrison the globe, or fight even a fraction as many simultaneous far-flung wars. Even if we were to set aside any associated value judgments, it bears asking why — historically speaking — this is the case.

Why does the United States have income inequality rates equivalent to those of its Gilded Age more than a century earlier?

Why didn't its citizens insist upon, or achieve, universal public health care before — and especially after — the Second World War, when most of its Western allies and even adversaries did?

Why was there, at least in comparative terms, never a viable socialist or serious labor party alternative in mainstream American politics?

Why has an unprecedented class- and especially race-based mass incarceration regime developed in the nation that most loudly proclaims its dedication to freedom?

And why is it the United States wages undeclared warfare across the planet's entirety?

Many of the answers actually lie in the past, in the historical development of US politics and society. These aspects of the darkly exceptionalist present can only be understood through — and partly explained by — a better understanding of four ghastly themes underpinning American history but largely glossed over in standard, introductory survey classes: indigenous genocide, racialized slavery, hyper-capitalism, and militarist imperialism.

Many people loudly claim to hate history, at least as a subject in their schooling. Given the uneven quality of its teachers and consequent presentation, that's quite understandable. Still, distaste for the history *class* hardly tempers the inordinate value nearly all Americans place on the *concept* of history, at least as they choose to understand it. Most people understand themselves, their family, their community, and their nation through the prism of history. The stories we tell about ourselves and our forebears inform the sort of country we think we are, the public policy we craft, and even what we imagine possible.

ORIGINAL SIN — AMERICAN SLAVERY, AMERICAN FREEDOM

Origins matter. Every nation-state has an origin myth: a comforting tale of trials, tribulations, and triumphs that form the foundation of "imagined communities." The United States of America — a self-proclaimed indispensable nation — is as prone to exaggerated origin myths as any society in human history. Most of us are familiar with the popular American origin story: our forefathers, a collection of hardy, pious pioneers, escaped religious persecution in England and founded a New World — a shining beacon in a virgin land. Of course, *that* story, however flawed, refers to the Pilgrims, and Massachusetts, circa 1620. But that's not the true starting point for English-speaking society in North America.

Painting by National Park Service artist Sydney King

The first permanent colony was in Virginia, at Jamestown, beginning in 1607. Why, then, do our young students dress in black buckle-top hats and re-create Thanksgiving each year? Where is the commemoration of Jamestown and our earliest American forebears? The omission itself tells a story: that of a chosen, comforting narrative — the legend of the Pilgrims — and the whitewashing of a murkier past along the James River.

The truth is, the United States descends from both origin points — Massachusetts and Virginia — and carries the legacy of each into the twenty-first century. So why do we focus on the Pilgrims and sideline Virginia? A fresh look may help explain.

The Age of "Discovery"

When it comes to history — like any story — the starting point is itself informative. The cadets to whom I taught freshman history at West Point were required to take only one semester of US history. So where to *start*? The official answer — as in so many standard history courses — was Jamestown, Virginia, 1607.

That, of course, is a fascinating, perhaps absurd, choice. Such a starting point omits several thousand years of Native American history, of varied, complex civilizations from modern Canada to Chile. Time being short, 1607 remains a common pedagogical starting point. As a result, from the beginning our understanding of US history is Eurocentric and narrow, covering only the past four hundred or so years. Consider that Problem No. 1.

Next, contemplate the language we use to describe the founding of new European colonies. This is, say it with me, the "Age of Discovery." In 1492, Columbus *discovered* (even though he wasn't first) America. Now, that's a loaded term. Isn't it just as accurate to say that Native Americans discovered Columbus — a lost and confused soul — when he landed upon their shores?

When we say Europeans *discovered* the New World, we're — not inadvertently — implying that there was nothing substantial going on in the Americas until the Caucasians showed up. Europe has a dated, chronological history, reaching back at least to the ancient Greeks, which most students learn in elementary school and later on in Western Civilization classes. Not so for the Native Americans. Their public history starts in 1492 — or, for Americans, in 1607. What came before, then, hardly matters.

Inauspicious Beginnings

Englishmen came neither to escape religious persecution nor to found a New Jerusalem. Not to Virginia, at least. No, the corporate-backed expedition — by the Virginia Company, a joint-stock venture — sought treasure (think gold), to find a northwest passage to India, and to balance the rival Catholic Spaniards. But first and foremost, they pursued profit.

The expedition barely survived. That should come as little surprise. They chose a malarial swamp for a home. The first ships carried mostly aristocrats — "gentlemen," as they were then labeled — with a few laborers and carpenters for good measure. Gentlemen didn't work or deal with the dirty business of farming and settling. But they did like to argue — and there were too many "chiefs" on this voyage. The first party did not include any farmers or women. Only 30 percent survived the first winter. Two years later only sixty out of five hundred colonists survived the "Starving Time." Over the first seventeen years, six thousand people arrived, but only twelve hundred were alive in 1624. One guy ate his wife.

So why the disaster? Why the poor site selection and early starvation? First, the colonists had chosen a site inland on the James River because they had feared detection by the more powerful Spanish. But mainly the disaster came down to colonial motivations. Jamestown was initially about profit, not settlement. Corporate dividends, not community. This was the *private sector*, not a permanent national venture. In that sense matters in early Virginia were not unlike modern American economics.

Saved by Tobacco, the First Drug Economy

They never did find much gold or, for that matter, a northwest passage. Then again, they didn't all starve to death. Rather, the venture was saved by a different sort of "gold" — the cash crop of tobacco. Tobacco changed the entire dynamic of colonization and control in North America. Finally, there was money to be made. The Englishmen shipped the newest vice eastward and pulled a handsome profit in return. Our beloved forefathers were early drug dealers. More migrants now crossed the Atlantic to get in on the tobacco windfall.

The plentiful gentlemen of Virginia sought to re-create their landed estates in England. Despite significant early conflict with the native Powhatan Confederacy, large tobacco plantations eventually developed along the coast. Who, though, would work these fields? Certainly not the landowners. The burgeoning aristocracy had two choices: lower-class English or Scots-Irish indentured servants, who worked for a fixed period in the promise of future acres, and African slaves. Whom to choose? Unsurprisingly, ethics played little role, and cost was the defining factor.

When mortality was high in the colony's early years, plantation owners favored the cheaper, mainly white, indentured servants. But as more families planted corn, kept cattle, and improved nutrition, death rates fell and slaves became more appealing. After all, though expensive in upfront costs, slaves worked for *life*, and the slave owners got to keep their offspring. Nevertheless, for the first several decades an interracial mix of slaves and servants worked the land in Virginia.

Bacon's Rebellion and the American Future

The problem with the tobacco economy was one of space. To be profitable, cash crops require expansive acreage, and in Virginia this meant movement inland. This expansion set the Englishmen on a collision course with local Native Americans. Furthermore, what was plantation society to do about those indentured servants who survived and matriculated? Land would have to be found somewhere

— though not near the coasts and early settlements. The gentlemen weren't about to divide up their own large estates. To maintain their chosen societal model — landed aristocracy, in which the wealthiest 10 percent possessed half the wealth and the bottom 60 percent held less than 10 percent of accumulated wealth — new land would have to be found farther west, in "Indian territory."

The thing is, after some bloody, early wars with the Powhatan, most gentlemen preferred a stable, secure status quo. Not another war. That'd be bad for business. However, falling tobacco prices, increased competition from nearby colonies, and the relentless search by the former indentured class for more land brought frontier Virginians into conflict with an easy scapegoat: nearby Native Americans. Frustrated lower-class men — both white and black — rallied behind a young, discontented aristocrat, a firebrand named Nathaniel Bacon. Bacon led his interracial poor people's army in attacks on local natives and, eventually, on Governor William Berkeley and the establish-ment gentlemen. In 1675 and 1676, Bacon's throng destroyed planta-tions and even burned Jamestown before Bacon died of disease (the "bloody fluxe") and the rebellion petered out.

Bacon's Rebellion was one of the foundational — and most misunderstood — events in American history. Here, a populist army savagely assaulted hated Native Americans and aristocrats alike. A mix of black and white former indentured servants demon-strated the fragility of Virginian society. The planter class was terri-fied. To avoid — at all costs — a repeat, the landed gentry made a devil's bargain. To ensure stability, they realized they must co-opt some of the poor without ceding their own privileged status.

Enter America's original sins: racism and white privilege. Plantation owners simply hired fewer indentured servants and became more reliant on black African chattel slaves for their labor force. The plant-ers also threw a bone to the middling whites, lowering some taxes and allowing more political representation for white male Virginians.

The implications were as disturbing as they were enduring. White unity became the organizing principle of life in colonial Virginia. To be fair, poor whites lived difficult lives and always outnumbered their

aristocratic betters. Nonetheless, these lower-class Caucasians benefited from the new, racialized social system. Pale skin became a badge
of honor — life may not be optimal, but "at least we are white." Black
freemen became a thing of the past, and soon "blackness" became
inseparably associated with slavery and the lowest of social classes.
Black skin became a brand of slavery, and runaways could no longer
blend into colonial society. Slaves were easily spotted by virtue of their
color.

Bacon's Rebellion linked land, labor, and race in nefarious ways.
Landownership remained the path to freedom. Labor remained essential to profiting from the land, and race came to define the relationship
between land and labor. After 1676 a class-based system morphed into
a race-based system of labor and social structure. The demand for
African slaves rose, and a triangular trade developed among North
America, Africa, and Europe. It seemed that everyone benefited from
slave labor — it became an Atlantic system. The American South had
transformed from a society with slaves into a slave society. It would
remain so for nearly two centuries. Race became a prevalent fact of
life in the Americas — and it still is, more than three hundred years
later.

———

There's nothing simple about America's origins, and it is good that this
is so. In this way the United States is like most other modern nation-
states. Leaving behind exceptionalist rhetoric and exploring uncomfortable truths signify intellectual maturity. Should this country wish
to move forward, be its best self, and fulfill the dream of its finest
rhetoric, then the citizenry must dispense with reassuring myths and
grapple with inconvenient truths.

What, then, do Jamestown and early Virginia have to tell us in the
twenty-first century? Perhaps this: American slavery arose alongside
and intertwined with American freedom. Our society descends from
a sinister original sin: the development of a race-based caste system
along the banks of the James River. Race, class, labor, and slavery were
inextricably linked in our colonial past. They remain so today.[1]

2

ROOTS IN RELIGIOUS ZEALOTRY

It is the image Americans are comfortable with. The first Thanksgiving. Struggling Pilgrims — our blessed forebears — saved by the generosity of kindly Native Americans. Two societies coexisting in harmony. If colonial Virginia was a mess, well, certainly matters were better in Massachusetts. Here are origins all can be proud of.

Our children re-create the scene every November, and we watch them with pride through the lenses of our smartphones. But is this representation of life in colonial New England an accurate portrait of Anglo–native relations at Plymouth or, for that matter, in the larger Massachusetts Bay Colony? Of course it isn't, but nonetheless the impression — the *myth* — persists. That's a story unto itself.

Consider this: How many Americans even know there was a difference between Pilgrims and Puritans? The distinctions matter. The

The First Thanksgiving, 1621, by J. L. G. Ferris

Pilgrims, of course, arrived first. Calvinists of humble origins, the Pilgrims were Protestant separatists who believed the mainstream Church of England was beyond saving. They fled England for the Netherlands in the early seventeenth century, and then, in 1620, about a hundred boarded the *Mayflower* to go to North America. It was they who landed on Plymouth Rock.

The far more numerous Puritans were also pious, dissenting Protestants, but they initially believed the Church of England could be reformed from within. They were generally wealthier, more prominent citizens. In 1630 or so about a thousand Puritans formed the first wave to settle the area claimed by the Massachusetts Bay Colony. They were, indeed, fleeing the persecution of King Charles I, but — unlike the Pilgrims — they received a royal charter for their colony. They hoped to found a "New Jerusalem" in the New World.

Stark Contrasts: Virginia Versus New England

These weren't the gold-hungry aristocrats of colonial Virginia. The Puritans and Pilgrims came as families — they included women. The Massachusetts climate and natural population growth made for far lower mortality than that experienced at early Jamestown. Everyone was willing to work, and the productive family units made, eventually, for bountiful harvests. This was not a land of gentlemen and cash crops, as in Virginia, but of dutiful families tilling the land.

The motivations and origins of the two English colonies affected the social structure of each. Differing goals set the tone from the start. Virginians sought to exploit the land, mine its resources, compete with the Spanish, and turn a quick profit. Not so the Puritans. They strove to settle, to put down roots and thrive in an idealized community. Their middling origins combined with communal goals resulted in familial plots with widespread landownership — another contrast with the tobacco plantations of Jamestown. All this translated into a rough economic equality, at least in the early years. There was also a near-total absence of chattel slavery: the climate didn't support the most common cash crops, and so there was little incentive to import Africans to New England.

God Wills It: The Motivations of the Puritans

It all sounds harmonious, idyllic even. Yet something lurked below the surface, something dark and unpleasant to modern eyes. These were fundamentalist zealots! These insufferable, millenarian Calvinists held themselves in shockingly high esteem. They were *chosen*; they would transform the world by their example. If the Pilgrims sought separation from a world of sin, the Puritans meant to create a *New* World, an example for all to emulate. It briefs well, and makes for an agreeable origin narrative, but isn't there something disturbing about such a people, about such overbearing confidence?

Ponder the words of John Winthrop, an early governor of the Bay Colony:

> . . . we shall find that the God of Israel is among us, when ten of us shall be able to resist a thousand of our enemies, when he shall make us a praise and glory, that men shall say of succeeding plantations: the Lord make it like that of New England: for we must Consider that we shall be as a City upon a Hill, the eyes of all people are upon us. . . .

These were people on a mission, the Lord's mission, come what may. Such people would seem to be on a collision course with the region's natives and Anglo nonconformists. And this would soon come to pass.

The Puritans' motivations and goals raise some salient questions. What does such colossal self-regard say about a society, and what are the implications for that society? Is it, ultimately, a good thing? That's certainly a matter of opinion, but the questions themselves are instructive. Americans must make such queries to get an honest sense of themselves and their origins. This much is hard to argue with: here

in Massachusetts we find the genesis of American exceptionalism —
the blessing and curse that has shadowed the United States for more
than three centuries, driving domestic and especially foreign policy.
Divergent modern political figures, from Ronald Reagan to Barack
Obama, stuck carefully to an American exceptionalist script, in rhetoric if not in deed. Is this "City on a Hill" metaphor, on the whole, a
positive one? This author, at least, tends to doubt it. Perhaps we should
mistrust such pride and conceit, even in their most American forms.

Stifling Dissent: Life in Colonial New England

Could you imagine *living* with these people, comporting with their
way of life? It sounds like a nightmare. Yet we Americans hold these
antecedents in high esteem. Perhaps it's natural, but this much is
certain: Such veneration requires a certain degree of willful forgetting, a whitewashing of inconvenient truths about Puritan society.

Sure, Massachusetts avoided the worst famines of Jamestown's early
years, but life in colonial New England was far from serene. It rarely is
in repressive religious societies. Remember, the Puritans constructed
exactly what they said they would, a theocracy on the bay. The
Massachusetts Bay Colony may indeed have more in common with
modern Saudi Arabia — executing "witches" and "sorcerers" — than
it does with contemporary Boston. Our ancestors were *far more* religious than most Americans can fathom. But there's also a problem of
framing; we've omitted the uncomfortable bits to fashion an uplifting
origin narrative.

There were many subgroups that certainly didn't enjoy life in early
colonial Massachusetts: religious dissidents, agnostics, freethinkers
and, well, assertive *women*. We've all heard of the infamous Salem
witch trials, but nearly four decades earlier the widow Ann Higgins
was executed, hanged for witchcraft, after having had the audacity to
complain that hired carpenters had overcharged her for a remodeling
job on her house.

All told 344 citizens were accused of witchcraft in seventeenth-
century Massachusetts. Twenty were executed. The accused had

commonalities that are indicative of the nature of gender relations in the Bay Colony. Seventy-five percent were women. Most of those women were middle-aged or older and demonstrated some degree of independence. Many were suspected of some sort of sexual impropriety. The point is that colonial New England was inhabited by zealots — conformist and oppressive fundamentalists who strictly policed the boundaries of their exalted theocracy. Forget the Thanksgiving feast: this was Islamic State on the Atlantic!

If life was as idyllic as the settlers intended in hail-the-Protestant-work-ethic Massachusetts Bay, then why were so many colonial "heroes" kicked out? Roger Williams, for example, founder of Rhode Island, promoted religious toleration and some separation of church and state and asserted that settlers ought to *buy* land from the native inhabitants. His thanks? A ticket straight out of Massachusetts. Slightly less well known was Anne Hutchinson. She had the gall to organize weekly women's meetings to discuss theology and even contemplated the concept of individual intuition as a path to salvation. She, too, was banished. There was simply no room for dissent in Puritan society.

"We Must Burn Them": Puritan and Native Relations

This, naturally, brings us to the native peoples of New England. If nonconformist Englishmen fared so poorly in Massachusetts, then what of the Indians? You can probably guess.

Once again, as in Virginia, the Native Americans did not, or could not, wipe out the nascent colonial community, even though, initially at least, there were fewer soldiers among the settlers in Massachusetts. The explanation for the settlers surviving among the Native Americans is far more complex than the simple myth of the noble, benevolent savage. The Puritans were the beneficiaries of catastrophe, for New England native communities had recently been ravaged by infectious European diseases that spread up and down the coastline. The thinned-out native populations thus posed less of a demographic threat to Massachusetts.

Far from the serene images of Thanksgiving amity, Anglo–Indian relations quickly turned from bad to worse. Land was a factor, but not the only one. A permanent settler community such as that of the Puritans would rapidly grow and require expansion, to be sure. As in Virginia, landownership cohered with "freedom" — *Anglo* land and *Anglo* freedom, that is. Still, in New England ideology was as much of a stimulus for war as land, wealth, or further economic motives. Native tribes, the swarthy and "unbelieving" Pequot, Wampanoag, Narragansett, and others, simply did not fit into the Puritans' messianic worldview. Conquered or converted were the only acceptable states for local Indians.

Early colonial wars in Massachusetts were as brutal and bloody as wars anywhere else on the North American continent. Here there was a direct connection between the Puritan religion and the cruelty seen in the Pequot War and King Philip's War. In the Pequot War, Massachusetts militiamen attacked a native fort at Mystic, Connecticut, and through fire and fury burned alive four hundred to seven hundred Indians, mostly women and children. The survivors were sold as slaves.

The militia relied on allied native scouts. Observing the ruthlessness of the Puritan fighting men, one native auxiliary asked Captain John Underhill: "Why should you be so *furious*? Should not Christians have more mercy and compassion?" Underhill's reply was as instructive as it is disturbing:

> I would refer you to David where, when a people is grown
> to such a height of blood, and sin against God and man . . .
> sometimes the Scripture declareth women and children
> must perish with their parents; some-time the case alters:
> but we will not dispute it now. We had sufficient light from
> the word of God for our proceeding.

Should, from time to time, a tinge of doubt betray the Puritans' devout certainty, faithful zeal quickly assuaged the guilty conscience. Consider the words of another participant in the "Mystic Massacre,"

William Bradford: "It was a fearful sight to see them thus frying in the fire . . . and horrible was the stink . . . but the victory seemed a sweet sacrifice, and they gave the praise thereof to God."

Nearly simultaneous to the Virginian Bacon's Rebellion, the Puritans fought King Philip's War in Massachusetts. Mercilessly executed on both sides, this was a war of survival that forever broke native power and independence in New England. Nearly one in fifty colonists were killed in what was by far the bloodiest war in American history, with eleven times the death rate of World War II. The native leader Metacom, known to the settlers as King Philip, was betrayed by an informer and killed, and his head was displayed on a pole in Plymouth, Massachusetts, for decades.

When it came to Native American affairs, the Puritans hardly set the "City on a Hill" example. Or did they? After all, John Winthrop believed that the God of Israel — a jealous, smiting deity if ever there was one — was among the Puritans, guiding their every move. As noted here earlier, Winthrop claimed that this God provided the colonists such strength that ten of their number could "resist a thousand enemies." Viciousness and intolerance toward racially distinct, heathen natives were actually at the heart of "City on a Hill" teleology from the start. What Americans now decry in the Greater Middle East is but an echo of their colonial past. That much is worth remembering.

Not So Different: What Virginians and New Englanders Shared

When considering the two origin-societies of Virginia and Massachusetts, the differences are stark and effortlessly leap forth. More difficult, but just as relevant, are their significant commonalities. For it is in the overlap that we find our shared heritage, that which is universal in the American past and, perhaps, the past of all settler-colonial societies.

Anglo dominance — and arrogance — acutely pervaded both colonial civilizations. In Massachusetts, as in Virginia, conflict with and brutality toward the native peoples were regular features of settler life. In each setting, though to differing extents, a fever for land combined with exceptionalist ideology to conquer slave and native alike. For Englishmen property ownership corresponded with liberty, but all along the eastern seaboard Anglo liberty portended native death and displacement.

———

If colonial Virginian society was fundamentally based on white unity at the expense of African slaves, then perhaps Puritan Massachusetts was founded upon Anglo zealotry at the expense of a "savage" Indian "other." As proud descendants — some literally, most figuratively — of these twin settler-colonial enterprises, Americans must grapple with their inconvenient past. Here there's much work left to be done.

The exceptionalism and chauvinistic Protestantism of the Massachusetts Puritans long influenced the American experiment. From the "City on a Hill" it is but a short journey to Manifest Destiny and the conquest of a continent — native inhabitants be damned!

Again, origins, and origin stories, matter. They inform who we were, and who we are, in stark contrast with who we'd like to *think* we were and are. America is its best self when it searches its soul and reforms from within. When, that is, it confronts its demons and seeks a better, more inclusive and empathetic future.[2]

3

WHOSE EMPIRE?

If Americans have heard of the Seven Years' War — a truly global struggle — it is most certainly under the title "the French and Indian War" (1754–63). Popular images of the conflict are likely to stem from the 1992 movie *Last of the Mohicans* starring Daniel Day-Lewis. When Americans think of this war at all, or discuss it in school, they generally situate the central theater of the conflict in northeastern North America. Yes, the savage Indians and their deceitful French allies were beaten back along the wooded frontier, allowing pacific English — soon to be American — farmers to live in peace. Ending in 1763, and saddling Britain with debt, the French and Indian War is often remembered as a prelude to a coming colonial revolt over excessive taxation. Perhaps it was, but not in a direct, linear sense. Nothing historical is preordained. Chance and contingency ensure as much.

Though the fighting began in North America — western Pennsylvania to be exact — the American theater, like other global imperial battlegrounds in India, Africa, and the Caribbean, was often a sideshow to the main event unfolding in Europe. The Seven Years' War was a global war, fought on several continents between Britain and Prussia on one side and France, Russia, and Austria on the other. It's important to remember that events in America — then and now — did not unfold in a vacuum but rather shaped and were shaped by global affairs. And while it is true that the American Revolution kicked off just a dozen years after the Treaty of Paris ended the Seven Years' War, nothing about the revolt was inevitable. In fact, in 1763, at the close of the French and Indian War, the vast majority of colonists saw themselves as Englishmen and Englishwomen, invested in and proud of their British Empire.

How to Kick Off a Global War

It started over land and money. The "Ohio Country," just west of the Appalachian Mountains, covered much of what is today the states of Ohio, western Pennsylvania, and West Virginia. Rich in lumber, with fertile farmland and plentiful game, the Ohio Country presented a tempting find. Though mainly inhabited by native tribes, the region also just happened to sit on the contested border between France's and Britain's empires in North America.

Both sides (and, no doubt, the native inhabitants) coveted this land. The French saw the Ohio Country as a strategic buffer against the encroaching Brits, and to the Indians, well, it was home. The English settler population of the thirteen colonies was, however, rapidly expanding westward. The stage was set for conflict. All it took was the right spark. Count on the profit motive as a reliable catalyst.

A few decades earlier some prominent Virginia families, including those of both the royal governor and a young militia officer named George Washington, established the Ohio Company of Virginia. It was at heart a property speculation outfit; the company's investors hoped to claim land in the Ohio Country, buy it cheaply from the Crown, and sell at a profit to westward-bound settlers. Buy low, sell high, enrich the already wealthy plantation families of Virginia — same old game!

So when the time came to seize and hold the land in western Pennsylvania once and for all, guess who Robert Dinwiddie, lieutenant governor of Virginia — himself an Ohio Company investor — sent in? That young lieutenant colonel of the militia, George Washington. Washington took a militia company and some allied Mingo Indians and headed toward Fort Duquesne, a French installation near present-day Pittsburgh. The French command sent out from the fort a smaller party under Joseph de Jumonville, with strict orders to avoid a fight unless provoked.

What happened next is contested in the few existing accounts. The most credible sources agree that Washington's force surrounded the French party and opened fire, killing several. Most surrendered, at which point Washington's native counterpart, known as the Half King, wielded a tomahawk to Jumonville's head, killing the Frenchman. This was supposed to have been as much a diplomatic as a military mission, and no state of war had been declared. Washington's choice to open fire was strategically and ethically questionable; however, his inability to control his native allies and the assassination of a prisoner must certainly constitute a war crime.

Early Setbacks, Stillborn Unity

Things didn't go so well for the British early on. Despite exponentially outnumbering the military and settler population of New France, the Brits and their colonists suffered some disconcerting early defeats. Soon after the "Jumonville Affair," the French dispatched hundreds of troops and allied natives to dislodge Washington's force, which had built a ramshackle defense known as Fort Necessity. A military novice in his twenties, Washington placed his fort in an indefensible location and was forced to surrender in humiliation.

Soon after, a large British column commanded by General Edward Braddock was ambushed and nearly destroyed, and Braddock was killed. Washington, barely escaping several near misses, would experience his second consecutive defeat in battle. For the next few years the British knew mostly defeat and the colonists suffered under brutal French and Indian raids up and down the western frontier.

As the settlers' confidence deteriorated under the weight of defeats and frontier insecurity, some leaders began to argue for increased colonial unity as a desperate, defensive panacea. Representatives from the various colonies met in Albany, New York, to discuss the prospect of confederation. The result was disappointing. Although it is true that the first colloquial usage of the term *American* seems to have begun in this period, the diverse and fiercely independent colonies were — despite the vicious frontier attacks — not yet ready for unification. Little was settled, less was agreed to. Contrary to the deterministic interpretations of the French and Indian War as a prelude to the American Revolution, the fact is that individual colonial identities were far too strong and the threat from France far too uneven to prompt any meaningful confederation.

Celebrating Empire

By 1759 the tide had begun to turn. The British, under the governmental leadership of William Pitt, changed strategy and responded to French onslaughts in clever ways. The British already had massive advantages in colonial manpower and naval power. Now they began to follow the French lead and recruit their own Native American allies. The British bankrolled the Prussians under Frederick the Great to do the heavy lifting of ground battle on the European continent and shifted resources to the colonial theaters in India, the Caribbean, and North America. The Brits also imposed an effective naval blockade on New France (roughly analogous to modern Canada) to cut off French reinforcements.

After General James Wolfe famously defeated the French on the Plains of Abraham outside Quebec, momentum clearly shifted to the British. Though this is indeed remembered as the seminal battle of the French and Indian War, we could just as plausibly argue that

The Death of General Wolfe, 1770, by Benjamin West

the French actually lost Canada — and the Seven Years' War — in a battle fought in modern Poland on the European continent. Such was the global, interconnected nature of warfare, even in the eighteenth century.

How then did the English colonists view themselves and define their identity in the wake of British victory? Were they indeed the unified *Americans* on the cusp of independence, as is so often remembered? Hardly.

Sometimes a painting, a period work of art, has much to impart to the observant historian. The artist who created *The Death of General Wolfe*, Benjamin West, was a colonist, an "American," from Pennsylvania, in fact. West's painting was a hit, paraded around the London Royal Academy after its completion. So what exactly did West hope to communicate with his famous painting? Pride. In victory and in *empire*. In the sky he depicts the light of British conquest overcoming the dark clouds of French rule in Canada. A Native American, clearly of a British-allied tribe, crouches in stereotypical dress and in the reflective pose of a truly "noble savage." At center is the martyred General Wolfe, held by his comrades in the ubiquitous Christ-like "lamentation" pose of so many famous Western religious depictions. Here was the new Christ, a general, a *British* general who sacrificed so America could be free (of the French and their native allies, that is).

West, the Pennsylvania colonist, memorialized the French and Indian War not as a prelude to independence but as a *celebration* of British empire. At the close of this brutal, costly war (2.5 percent of the men of Boston had been killed), West and most other American colonists did indeed share a common identity of sorts: as proud *Britons*.

An Unhappy Peace: Conflicting Lessons, Divergent Expectations

The colonists and metropolitan Britons emerged from the long, vicious conflagration with contrasting expectations. As is so often the case, many of these desires ran at cross purposes. The British imperial officials wanted, most of all, to consolidate their gains — France had ceded all of Canada and the Ohio Valley — and ensure stability.

Above all, this meant protecting the newly gained territory and separating English settlers from the native tribes west of the Appalachian Mountains. Toward the end of the war a confederation of Ohio Country Indian tribes realized that the French were losing and they would probably soon find themselves alone to check the expansionist Brits. The crisis of extended war and impending French defeat begot a spiritual awakening among the natives led by a holy man named Neolin.

Neolin's call for native unity influenced an Ottawa war chief known as Pontiac to attack British forts up and down the frontier in a conflict that took his name, Pontiac's Rebellion. Though the British eventually prevailed, they incurred heavy casualties, and the demonstration of native unity had spooked imperial officials. To avoid a repeat rebellion and preserve the status quo, the British announced the Proclamation Line of 1763, which ceded land west of the Appalachians to the Ohio Country tribes and forbade further settler expansion. They also hoped to raise funds from the (presumably grateful) colonists to help pay down Britain's crippling war debts. That meant taxes — and taxes, eventually, meant discord.

None of that jibed with colonists' expectations. They had *started* the war — for land, for expansion, for profit! How could their British protectors deny them their destiny: ample farmland and security from native savages across the Appalachians? They, too, had fought in the key battles of the conflict, as militiamen alongside the British redcoats. Nor did most colonists expect to bear the burden of debt relief for the Crown: Hadn't they already borne the brunt of a war fought adjacent to *their* land and endured Indian raids on *their* homesteads? The stage, so to speak, was set for future confrontation.

The Real Losers: Dwindling Hope for Native Empowerment

If colonial and metropolitan Britons emerged from the war with divergent lessons and expectations, so did the local native tribes. The Ohio Country, which the French had ceded without native permission, was the tribes' home. Pontiac's Rebellion demonstrated just

*General Johnson Saving a Wounded French Officer From the
Tomahawk of a North American Indian,* 1764-68, by Benjamin West

how serious the Indian claims were. Nonetheless, unsurprisingly, the
natives proved to be the war's great victims.

For years, decades even, native tribes had counted on the imperial rivalries among British, French, and Spanish claimants to North
America as a way to divide, conquer, and *survive*. Though the Indians
were generally weaker than the great European empires, they had
become adept at balancing between the differing poles of imperial
power and played the part of spoiler in countless colonial wars. Now,
with New France vanquished and the Spanish Empire increasingly
anemic, the native tribes could no longer rely on tried-and-true past
strategies. They stood alone in the face of a powerful, populous, and
insatiably expansionist British Empire. Pontiac's Rebellion was a
desperate response to the new reality, but the more prescient chiefs
could see tragic times to come.

Some Indians must no doubt have felt expendable as the French abandoned them to their fate. Could natives ever truly trust any Europeans? In the end were these white men all cut from the same cloth, as they arrogantly traded Indian land as spoils in a deadly imperial game?

Consider the painting by colonist Benjamin West in which a "civilized" British officer restrains his "savage" ally from killing their ostensibly common enemy. The message is instructive: yes, the French were their foes, but both (European) sides at least adhered to common rules of gentlemanly warfare. View this painting out of context and it is far from obvious that the red- and white-clad Caucasians are actually *enemies*. Viewed through the lens of Benjamin West, it seems the real enemy of civilization is the "savage" — that anachronistic native who most certainly has no place in the North American future. Though many Native Americans surely couldn't yet foresee it, they were already doomed. It was they, not the French, who had truly lost the Seven Years' War!

———

In 1763, American colonists felt little sense of — the term was yet to be coined — common nationalism. Despite contemporary memories to the contrary, in the coming revolution against Britain the colonists hardly rebelled against the concept of empire itself. Rather, they desired a new, expansive *American* empire, unhindered by London and stretching west over the Appalachians and deep into native lands. If the Seven Years' War was the first conflict for North American empire, it helped set the stage for the second: the American War for Independence.

Of course, all attempts by historians — this author included — to periodize and categorize the past run the risk of determinism and distort the inherent contingency of events. Still, a fresh look at the Seven Years' War raises profound questions about the course of early American history. It is, perhaps, appropriate to exchange the standard narrative of these events for something at once more accurate and, for many, more disturbing. Instead of a simple prelude to the coming revolution, couldn't it be that the Seven Years' War was itself a pivotal turning point in American history — the moment when the balance shifted and native power irreversibly waned? If so, it is long past time to replace the comforting American narrative of a transition from British Empire to liberal republic with a more accurate and complex progression: from empire to revolution to a new *American* empire. We live in it still.[3]

4

PATRIOTS OR INSURGENTS?

"Who shall write the history of the American Revolution?" John Adams once asked. "Who can write it? Who will ever be able to write it?"

"Nobody," Thomas Jefferson replied. "The life and soul of history must forever remain unknown."

Compare the tarring-and-feathering scene with the 1770 painting *The Death of General Wolfe* by colonist Benjamin West. The earlier work shows North American colonists among those devotedly and tenderly attending the mortally wounded British general, who lies in a Christ-like pose. How did (at least some) North American colonists evolve from a proud celebration of empire into the riotous, rebellious, tar-and-feather mob? It's an important question, and it deals with an issue hardly mentioned in standard textbooks. Even rebellious "patriots" saw themselves as *Englishmen* right up until July 4, 1776. Others remained loyal British subjects through the entire Revolutionary War.

Most of the lay public tends to view the coming of the American Revolution as natural, predetermined, even inevitable. After all, "we" are the descendants of patriots with a special, anti-monarchical destiny. The British Crown, with its intolerable taxation, merely stood in the way of American providence and thus was of course shunted aside in a glorious democratic rebellion. At least that's the myth — the comforting, preferred narrative.

The reality of the pre-revolt era was far more complex, influenced by diverse forces, motives, individual agency, and contingency. The truth, as often the case, is messy and discomforting. Still, simplicity sells. Want to earn a bundle in royalties? Avoid publishing an intricate analysis of lower-class colonial motivations. No one reads that stuff! It's easy — just write another flattering biography of a "Founding Father."

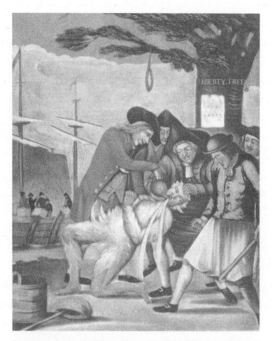

Bostonians Paying the Excise-Man, or Tarring and Feathering, 1774, by Philip Dawe

But just who were these "patriots"? What motivated them to seek open conflict with a powerful empire? How pure were their motives? Did they even represent a *majority* of colonists? And what of their tactics — did the ends justify the means? Only a fresh, comprehensive examination of this untidy, chaotic era promises satisfactory answers to these questions, the questions at the root of the United States' origins. Still, rest assured: the lead-up to the American Revolution has been, and will always be, a contested history. Perhaps Jefferson was right after all, and the soul of this history must remain unknown.

A Reassuring Tale: Common Explanations for the American Revolution

Americans hate taxes with a unique national passion. After all, ours was a nation founded in opposition to insufferable, imperial taxation. Wasn't it? One group certainly thinks so. If you see the American Revolution as only a relic of the past, please note that in 2009, soon after the election of Barack Obama, a new conservative political movement arose and brought its version of history to the public square. The "tea party" was suddenly everywhere. Its support-ers, mostly Republicans, even liked to dress up as colonists, adorn-ing themselves with tricornered hats and carrying signs with anti-tax slogans. For these Americans the past was immediate, and President Obama was the new King George. However, as historian Jill Lepore has written, the Tea Party Revolution was more about nostalgia than serious scholarship. In the tea party's telling — which coheres with the popular understanding — the revolution was *all* about taxes.

Monarchy is equally anathema to the citizenry and inextrica-bly tied to authoritarian taxation. Surely our revolution was also a Manichaean battle between tyranny and democracy, between royalty and republicanism. Despite generations of critical scholarship, some version of these basic, twin explanations pervades Americans' collec-tive memory of revolution and independence.

We all know the basic economic and political chronology of the rebellion. It's usually told in a nice, neat sequence: Stamp Act, Boston Massacre, Tea Act, Boston Tea Party, Intolerable Acts, Lexington and Concord. New tax, colonial protest, British suppression, next tax, et cetera. This is an altogether linear, cyclical narrative, and it emphasizes the anti-tax and anti-monarchical components of colonial motivation. We hardly consider the British side, and it appears self-evident that *all* colonists were patriots. Who wouldn't be? The Brits were "intolerable."

It's not that taxation didn't factor at all into rebel motivations — it most certainly did. Still, there are some awkward questions worth raising: If taxes directly caused the war, then how do we explain that just about every new tax was repealed before 1775? Besides, the colo-nists paid far lower taxes than metropolitan Britons. In fact, the Sugar Act of 1764 actually *lowered* the tax on molasses — it simply sought to more stringently enforce it. The Tea Act didn't upset colonists so much for the economic cost as for the mandated monopoly it granted the British East India Company.

Surely other political and cultural factors must have contributed to a rebellion that men were willing to die for. An honest analysis of the coming of revolution must grapple with the varied, complex motives of individual "patriots." Indeed, the rebellion was as much social revolution as political quarrel.

What Makes a "Patriot"?

There's just one problem: probably no more than one-third of all colonists were actually anti-imperial "patriots." Our Founding Fathers and their followers weren't even in the majority. That's not so democratic! Furthermore, the motivations of the patriots were multifaceted, diverse, and — largely — regional.

If only one in three colonists became dyed-in-the-wool patriots, then what of the others, the silent majority, so to speak? Well, most historians estimate that another third were outright pro-empire loyalists. The rest mostly rode the fence, too engaged in daily survival to care much for politics; those in this group waited things out to see which side emerged on top.

That story, that reality, is — for most Americans — rather unsatisfying. Maybe that's why it never caught on and is hardly taught outside of academia.

As discussed, this was much more than just a quarrel between Americans and Britons; it was an intense debate over what British identity meant for those residing outside the home islands. The slogan "No taxation without representation!" has caught on as a prime explanation for rebellion, but even that reality was far more complex. It wasn't just colonists who were taxed and had no proper voice in Parliament, it was also many urban Britons within the United Kingdom. Tiny, rural, aristocratic districts — so-called rotten boroughs — could count on a seat in the assembly while densely populated towns like Sheffield and Leeds went without representation. Metropolitan Englishmen no doubt had rights that were denied to their colonial cousins, including a free internal trade market and the right to do business with foreign countries. However, colonists had benefits unknown in Great Britain, such as lower property taxes. In addition, there was slavery, from which some colonists profited handsomely via the suffering of fellow humans.

The varied class-based and regional motivations for patriot or loyalist association could be seen in New York's Dutchess County, to consider one example. In many cases the primary motivation was the desire of middling tenant farmers to oppose their oppressive land-lords. Thus the battle lines of tenant riots in the 1760s became the dividing lines between patriot and loyalist a decade later. In Dutchess County's south, the landlords were loyalists, and, consequently, the tenants became avid patriots. Conversely, just a few miles north at Livingston Manor, the landlord was a member of the Continental Congress. Unsurprisingly, his tenants bore arms for the British.

Why We Fight — The Complex Motives of Colonial Rebels

Ideology or economics? This question about the primary cause of the American Revolution has raged among scholars for the better part of a century. There is persuasive evidence on both sides. Still, the strict binary is itself misleading. Patriot sentiment emerged for countless individual and communal reasons. Some colonists were avid readers of John Locke or British commonwealth men like Thomas Gordon and John Trenchard. For them, it was all about ideology and independence — life, liberty, and property. They were also obsessed with alleged conspiracy and corruption at the top ranks of Parliament and the monarchy.

Another group, especially in the northern urban centers, abhorred what they saw as unfair taxation or imperial mercantilism that suppressed both free trade and a lucrative smuggling economy. Indeed, no less a figure than John Hancock himself was a famous smuggler! Still others, mainly in the Chesapeake region, desired more land and westward expansion beyond the Appalachian Mountains into "Indian country." This had, after Pontiac's Rebellion, become ille-gal due to the British Proclamation of 1763, which granted these lands to various native tribes.

Nor can we underestimate the class component of protest and rebellion. Merchants, artisans, and laborers in northern cities, such as Boston, tended to identify with the protest movement. These working- and middle-class urbanites were egged on by firebrands like Samuel Adams — the failed tax collector and sometime brewer of beer. Adams founded a newspaper, the *Independent Advertiser*, that overtly pitched to the laboring classes the notion that "[l]iberty can never subsist without equality." In the South, conversely, the landed gentry tended to be patriots, and it was the smallholders who were often loyalist. Still, any description of patriot motivations can hardly ignore class and the impulses of the uncouth urbanites, those whom historians have labeled "the people out of doors."

———

Standard interpretations of the American Revolutionary movement generally make no mention of religion. This is strange consider- ing the profound religiosity of eighteenth-century colonists. While prominent Founding Fathers such as Thomas Jefferson and Thomas Paine were deists or agnostics, the vast majority of the population was devoutly Christian. Part of what accounts for the dearth of reli- gious analysis among historians is no doubt the secular bias within the academic community. Still, religious fervor in the wake of the mid-eighteenth-century Great Awakening certainly had influence over the rebellion. In comparing the religious proclivities of metro- politan Britons and English colonists in North America, one distinct difference stood out. While most Britons in the United Kingdom were members of the state's Anglican Church, the preponderance of colo- nists were Protestant dissenters — Presbyterians, Baptists, Quakers, and Congregationalists — who had broken with the Church of England. We would be right to expect this inverse religious situation to influence colonial protests in the 1760s and 1770s.

New Jersey stands out as a representative example, at least among the northern and mid-Atlantic colonies. Most yeoman farmers were highly influenced by the Great Awakening's revivalist teachings and became Protestant dissenters. The landed gentlemen, on the other hand, stayed loyal to the hierarchical Anglican Church. The messages of revivalist preachers were distinctly anti-authoritarian and anti-materialist, resonating among the smallholders who felt threatened by landed proprietors. When imperial taxes increased and British officials sought to assert increased control, the battle lines, unsurprisingly, cohered with religious preferences.

Colonists were fiercely chauvinistic Protestants with an intense hatred of Catholics. Thus, when Parliament passed the Quebec Act in 1774, allowing religious freedom to French Canadian *habitants*, many colonists threw a fit! The Crown, they assumed, must be beholden to a papist, Catholic conspiracy. Such religious tolerance was unacceptable and convinced many patriots that perhaps independence was the preferred path. The old spirit of intolerable Puritan zealotry was alive and well.

———

Some colonists simply resented military occupation. The British decision to send uniformed regular army troops to rebellious hotbeds like Boston had an effect opposite to what was intended. This is an old story. American soldiers in Vietnam, Afghanistan, and Iraq have learned this lesson again and again as foreign military presence angered the locals and united disparate political, ethnic, and sectarian groups in a nationalist insurgency. Nor were British troops — generally drawn from the dregs of English society — held in high esteem by the colonists. Most Bostonians were appalled by the uncouth manners of soldiers they described as rapists, papists, infidels, or, worst of all, "*Irish!*"

The presence of thousands of soldiers also worsened a pervasive economic depression. Back then, off-duty soldiers and sailors were allowed to seek side work in the local economy to supplement their meager wages. They thus flooded Boston's job market. Protests against the occupation sometimes got out of control when soldiers, thousands of miles from home in a strange land, made mistakes or overreacted. In one incident an eleven-year-old Boston boy was shot dead by a trigger-happy trooper. Sound familiar? A local journal wrote of the

British occupation: "The town is now a perfect garrison." It was not meant as a compliment.

However, no incident so inflamed the local consciousness — and our own historical memory — as the so-called Boston Massacre of 1770. In popular remembrance, and in countless paintings, the event is depicted as a veritable slaughter perpetrated by heartless redcoats against peaceful patriot protesters. But hold on a moment. Was this really an accurate label? Do five dead men a massacre make? And what prompted the "slaughter"?

What started as snowball and rock throwing at British sentries quickly escalated into a raucous crowd shouting insults, a crowd armed with clubs and, in the case of one man, a Scottish broadsword. Some protesters grabbed at the lapels of a British officer's uniform; several other rebels screamed, "Fire, damn you!" — no doubt confusing the enlisted soldiers. Finally Benjamin Burdick, he with the broadsword, swung the weapon with all his might down upon a grenadier's musket, knocking him to the ground. The soldier climbed to his feet and fired his musket at the crowd. Several fellow troopers did the same. The rest is history.

The soldiers and their officer were put on trial, certainly a strange allowance from a supposedly tyrannical regime. None other than local lawyer John Adams defended the British troops and, taking mitigation into account, won their freedom. Adams took the case at great risk to his reputation, but he believed in equal justice for all, even redcoats. This narrative, no doubt, complicates the entire episode, and well it should. The Revolutionary fairy tale to which we've grown accustomed is in distinct need of some nuance.

No one explanation exists for patriot motivations. Individual preferences, incentives, and decisions are difficult to unpack. These were diverse peoples divided among themselves by class, religion, and region. How can we synthesize their countless motives? The historian Gary Nash offers an apt summary. The coming of the revolution was a "messy, ambiguous, and complicated" story of a "seismic eruption from the hands of an internally divided people . . . a civil war at home as well as a military struggle for national liberation."

Revolutionary Tactics: Venerable Protest or Mob Rule?

When I patrolled the mud villages of southwestern Kandahar province in Afghanistan, we sought to "protect" the population from the local Taliban insurgents. It was a difficult task. When our soldiers retired back to base camp, Taliban fighters owned the night and infiltrated the rural hamlets. A popular Islamist tactic was to leave threatening notes on the doors of suspected Afghan collaborators who dared so much as to speak to the American invaders. We labeled them night letters, just another terror tactic, and reported their prevalence to our higher command. Few of my troopers, of course, knew that colonial patriots left the same sorts of threatening notes on the doors of alleged loyalists in Boston and Philadelphia. Is there really any difference?

Coercion has always been central to revolutions. Like it or not, the American variety was no exception. The patriot minority used threats and violence to enforce their narrative and thrust their politics on the loyal and the apathetic alike. There was little that was democratic about it. Discomforting as it may be, the patriot movement was hardly a Gandhi-like campaign of peaceful civil disobedience. Patriots were passionate, they were relentless, and they were *armed*. Firearms were ubiquitous in the colonies, more so, even, than in Britain. Guns are as American as apple pie. So is street violence.

This was a barbaric world. Colonists slaughtered natives, beat slaves, and publicly executed criminals, often leaving their bodies to rot in the town square. Alcohol abuse was endemic, and drinking men regularly settled tavern disputes with fists and knives. The patriot crowds abused tax collectors, loyalists, and their social betters across the urban North. Tarring and feathering, a favored and famous tactic, was far from the playful embarrassment of our imaginations. Rather, the act of putting molten tar onto human skin left many an unlucky loyalist in unimaginable pain and physically scarred. Many of the government bureaucrats so tortured were simply doing their jobs and sought only to make a living for their families. This was *terrorism*.

Arson and looting were often rampant as the mobs took on a life of their own. In 1765 a patriot crowd tore down the home of loyalist politician Thomas Hutchinson. In New York City another rabble pillaged carriage houses and theaters. The motive: opposition to a relatively modest tax increase. In our collective memory, of course, such rebels are heroes. This is strange, as modern-day racial protests — in Ferguson and Baltimore — are regularly pilloried as riotous criminal actions. Our patriot forebears were morally ambiguous, complex figures. Their tactics straddled the line between resistance and riot. The same could be said of the Los Angeles riots of 1992 and other urban racial outbursts. Of course, the irony is lost on us.

The Other Americans: Rebellion Through the Eyes of Loyalists, Indians, and Blacks

How is it that we hear the loudest yelps for liberty among
the drivers of Negroes?
— Samuel Johnson, English writer (1775)

Further tarnishing the heroic narrative of patriot ascendancy is one inconvenient fact: Most slaves preferred British to colonial rule, and most slaveholding planters were themselves patriots, especially in the South. As was the case in early colonial Virginia, American slavery and American freedom grew side by side in the late eighteenth century, a contradiction at the very heart of the colonial and early republican experience. This pattern endured as colonial patriots moved from resistance to rebellion against imperial authorities. Many modern apologists for our slave-owning founders insist that these men were merely a reflection of their time and place; a time, we are to suppose, when *everyone* supported slavery. Thus we cannot critique the motives or point out the inconsistency in our esteemed forebears. Yet an honest look at the Revolutionary era complicates the apologist narrative.

Indeed, the ostensibly tyrannical British practiced very little chattel slavery within the United Kingdom itself. In fact, in the *Somerset v. Stewart* case of 1772, England's highest common-law court ruled that chattel slavery was illegal. This judgment spooked many southern colonial gentlemen, who began to fear that the British metropolitan authorities were "unreliable defenders of slavery," and this convinced many to join the patriot cause.

The slaves also asserted themselves and contributed to the fears of white planters. Although slave revolts were extraordinarily rare, the very threat of uprising terrified gentlemen in the Chesapeake and Deep South. In one sense the fear was justified. In South Carolina, for example, slaves constituted 60 percent of the colony's population. During the pre-Revolutionary protest movements, some slaves met in secret to discuss ways to take advantage of the growing rift between patriot and loyalist colonists. Slaves also recognized the contradiction in planters clamoring for liberty while these very same men enslaved thousands of Africans. Richard Henry Lee, of a prominent Virginia family, explained to the House of Burgesses why the slaves would not support the patriots: "from the nature of their situation, [the slaves] can never feel an interest in our cause, because . . . they observe their masters possessed of liberty which is denied to them."

Adding insult to injury, in early 1775, soon after the first shots were fired in Massachusetts — at Lexington and Concord — the royal governor of Virginia, Lord Dunmore, threatened to, and eventually did, offer freedom to the slaves as a punishment to rebellious planters. This confirmed the worst fears of the landed class. Ambivalent slave owners were thereby pushed into open rebellion, and already patriot-inclined owners — such as George Washington, Thomas Jefferson, and Patrick Henry — became even more radicalized.

While slavery was statistically more prevalent in the South, the peculiar institution was still a continent-wide phenomenon. Even Benjamin Franklin of Philadelphia published advertisements in his newspapers for the sale of slaves and printed notices about runaways. Though Franklin spoke out against slavery, he himself owned five slaves, which, unlike George Washington, he never freed.

Colonial unity trumped abolitionist sentiment, even in New England. The patriots of Boston knew they needed the support of slave-saturated Virginia to win concessions from British authorities. Thus in 1771, when an anti-slavery bill came before the Massachusetts Assembly, it failed. As James Warren wrote in his explanation to John

Adams, "if passed into an act, it should have [had] a bad effect on the union of the colonies." The first generation of Americans had an opportunity to grant basic human dignity to hundreds of thousands of chattel slaves; instead they chose their own "liberty."

———

Just as hunger for land had sparked off the French and Indian War two decades earlier, so did land speculation motivate many patriots to oppose the Crown. The gentlemen of Virginia, including Washington, Jefferson, and Henry, were heavily invested in large tracts of trans-Appalachian land. Jefferson alone claimed five thousand acres. Their plan was to sell, at a profit, their holdings to small farmers. Thus when the British authorities drew the Proclamation Line of 1763 and ceded land west of the mountains to placate native unrest and avoid costly frontier wars, the planter class felt betrayed. How could the Crown accede to Indian "savages" occupying *their* God-given lands?

There was also a class component to planter frustration. The Proclamation Line was, of course, an imaginary border, and the British had neither the inclination nor the military manpower to police it. Despite the law, lower-class farmers jumped the line and set up homesteads across the mountains. From the point of view of gentlemen speculators, these squatters were stealing their land. And because the Proclamation Line made such settlements illegal, the speculators could not claim title to the land and demand recompense.

Native Americans recognized the threat to their tribal lands and saw the British authorities as their best chance to hold back the settlers. Indeed, in hindsight we can see that the Proclamation of 1763 might have represented the last chance for genuine native autonomy in North America. These tribes were also far from isolated, backcountry actors. In fact, their trade in deerskins actually tied them to the commercial Atlantic economy to a larger extent than most middling Anglo farmers. Recognizing their leverage, the Ohio Country tribes sought confederation in an anti-British coalition, the better to threaten imperial officials and gain concessions for continued autonomy and protection from the colonists. It worked. The last thing that the deeply indebted British needed was another Indian war.

The Virginians, however, could not care less what the Crown wanted. In the fall of 1774 the land speculators tried one last time to obtain the native land. Using a minor Indian raid as the pretext, the colonists launched a devastating attack on Shawnee and Mingo settlements in an attempt to conquer present-day Kentucky. In the short term an army of two thousand Virginians achieved its goals and forced the tribes to grant territorial concessions. However, recognizing that the tribes had signed away the land under duress, the Crown authorities refused to recognize the land grab.

Like the black chattel slaves of the coastal plantations, the native tribes of the frontier felt no loyalty to the patriot cause. In fact, the imperial status quo better served slave and Indian interests than the faux liberty of colonial rebels. The fact that the *most* vulnerable populations of colonial America opposed revolution and eventually sided with the British most certainly challenges the triumphalist, egalitarian patriot narrative. Indeed, on the issues of slavery and native relations, the British appeared far more liberal than the colonists who were, themselves, seeking their own — in Jefferson's phrase — "empire of liberty." That empire would prove far more tyrannical for slaves and natives than what King George had offered.

———

The story of the rebellion that became a revolution, a history of 1763–75, is nearly impossible to synthesize in one essay, one chapter, or even one book. What, then, can we say? Perhaps only this: the revolution was made by a "coalition of diverse social groups," motivated by a range of individual grievances, often at odds with one another. The patriots were by no means always democratic, and the loyalists were hardly all tyrannical monarchists. Slaves and Indians were no fans of colonists' hypocritical, exclusivist notions of (white) liberty and freedom and often favored the Crown. There is much to be proud of in the colonial revolt and very much to be ashamed about as well. Indeed, in the truest sense, we historians are best served when we dutifully and agnostically describe the past in all its diverse, even ugly, manifestations.

Sometimes the myth is more powerful, more influential, than reality. No doubt this has been true of the lead-up to the American Revolution. To critique the motives and tactics of the patriots or our Founding Fathers is to invite rebuke and passionate defensiveness. This is, perhaps, understandable. After all, if the Pilgrims and Plymouth Rock represent our first chosen origin myth, then, most certainly, the American Revolution must stand as the *second*. Who we are, at least who we think we are, is acutely wrapped up in the revolutionary narrative. To question that account is to question *us*. Yet that is what intellectual honesty and the challenges of the present demand of us — to examine America's founding origins, warts and all, and strive toward a truly more perfect union.[4]

5

INDEPENDENCE AND CIVIL WAR (PART ONE)

The war [of independence] was not just about home rule, but about who would rule at home.

— Historian Carl Becker

What sort of revolution was it? Radical or conservative? Military or social? Earnestly democratic or hypocritical farce?

Perhaps a bit of them all. What it most certainly was not was what is presented in the comfortable, patriotic, grade school yarn to which we've all grown accustomed. Yet neither was it something out of a fable of white privilege that can be dismissed outright.

Let us begin with the famous painting on the facing page, commissioned by the US Congress and displayed in the Capitol Rotunda. This rendering prompts some questions: *Who*, exactly, won the war and what sort of war was it? What's not depicted? And why? The artist captures the moment of British surrender after the Battle of Yorktown in 1781. It's all so neat, so symmetrical, with regular Continental army soldiers mounted and standing at right and equally spiffy French troopers, replete with clean white uniforms, at left. The humbled redcoats stand beneath an American officer and offer their surrender as a mounted General George Washington observes from the rear, at right.

Were this the only portrait available for posterity, the viewer might assume the War of Independence was a rather conventional *military* affair, waged tidily between two gentlemanly armies. The popular image is something like this: the Continental army — with some help from the French — vanquished the Brits and won a new, independent nation. There was no dirt, no grime, nothing messy or complex. There were no women, no blacks, no Native Americans, certainly no loyalists or uncouth colonial militiamen involved.

The Surrender of Lord Cornwallis, 1819, by John Trumbull

Perhaps this is how Americans *like* to remember the Revolution, how elementary schoolteachers transmit this epic past.

As we've seen in previous chapters, the way we remember the past is as fascinating and instructive as the reality of events. This is particularly true of the American Revolution, which, I would suggest, is America's *second* origin myth, a saga of colonial liberty smiting British tyranny once and for all, a story topped only by the initial settlement of the colonies. Would that it were so simple.

When evaluating the American Revolution, we must essentially parse out comprehensive answers to the following questions: How and why did rebels — whose army never won a battle in the open field — defeat the most powerful empire in the Western world? How was the social and military experience of revolution lived and experienced by a diverse colonial population? And finally, what did it mean to "win," and who exactly *were* the war's winners and losers? In seeking to answer these questions, we may not always like what we find, or we may become confused by the cluttered conglomeration of the Revolutionary experience. Still, perhaps we will also unearth something profound about who we were as Americans, who we strove to be, and how far we've come in achieving our great revolution.

Blood Has Been Shed: From Lexington to Bunker Hill

In chapter 4 we left our anguished — and hopelessly divided — American colonists on the verge of rebellion, just twelve years after the defeat of France in the Seven Years' War. With the benefit of hindsight, revolution appears all but inevitable, yet nothing was predetermined. Some spark was needed to engulf the continent in bloodshed. It would come in Massachusetts.

On the eve of war the British, like so many regular imperial armies before them, believed they could intimidate the rebels with a display of impressive uniforms, lockstep marching, and a basic show of force. In and around Boston the British sought to seize large stores of colonial arms and, in that strategic vein, marched out of the city toward the village of Concord in April 1775. They bet wrong: the overt show of military force actually raised tensions, radicalized the populace, and caused conflict.

Besides, seizing centralized armories would not in itself work in America, due to one characteristic of the colonists: they were armed. Consider, for a moment, the radical ramifications of an armed populace. The Americans were unique in that, unlike Englishmen, Scots, or Irishmen, nearly all white men were gun owners. The tools were there. It seemed war would come eventually; it was a matter of when and where.

At about 4:00 a.m. on April 19, 1775, the British regulars, on the road to Concord, ran into a paltry *colonial* show of force: seventy or so militiamen had gathered — with muskets — on the Lexington town green. A British officer ordered them to disperse. They did not. No one knows who fired first, but it was the seasoned British regulars who fired last, at least for the moment. When the smoke cleared, several colonists — English subjects — lay dead, more were wounded, and the rest had fled. The road to Concord lay open, and the British took it.

Then, on the way back to their base in Boston, something happened. Colonists from neighboring towns, using hit-and-run tactics on home turf they knew thoroughly, inflicted hundreds of casualties on the withdrawing British redcoats. It was a bloody day, and it changed the course of American history.

The Death of General Warren at the Battle of Bunker Hill, 1815, by John Trumbull

After Lexington and Concord, both sides sought to use the day's events as propaganda to drum up support. Both told lies. Some colonists claimed that marauding redcoats had slaughtered women and children in their path. Some Britons told tales of rebel colonists scalping — and in some cases cannibalizing — surrendered prisoners.

And so, as is often the case, matters after this first draw of blood took on a chaotic momentum. Many formerly lukewarm patriots from the other, less zealous colonies now stood with their firebrand cousins in rebellious Massachusetts. It was to be war. A war among, and for, the loyalty of the people — the sort of war that doesn't end well.

The conflict centered in Boston for the next several months, and the once-overconfident British learned their lesson again in the famous Battle of Bunker Hill — which was actually fought on Breed's Hill — in June 1775. Observe the painting above, like the Cornwallis painting, the work of John Trumbull, essentially the official artist of the Continental army. In this romanticized depiction, which has become visual gospel of the patriot cause, the brutal Brits — accompanied by dark clouds — charge the hill and attempt to bayonet a dying General Joseph Warren. Warren, of course, is clad in virgin white and lies in the Christ-like lamentation pose so popular in paintings of the time.

In the battle the attacking British chose a frontal assault, rather than General Henry Clinton's preferred flanking maneuver, and eventually dislodged the colonists. In a sense the British won — they held the field — but it was a Pyrrhic victory. More than a thousand British and four hundred Americans were killed or wounded. Though it occurred just two months after the fighting commenced, Bunker Hill would prove to be the bloodiest single-day encounter of the entire war.

This, before the colonies had even declared independence! Indeed, that was to come much later, some thirteen months afterward, in July 1776. Just one month after the combatants soaked Breed's Hill with blood, the colonists sent the famous "Olive Branch" petition to King George III, seeking a negotiated solution to the conflict. Most colonists still viewed themselves as both American and British. Few expected outright detachment from the empire. Only the timing was poor. The king, having received word of the bloodshed in Boston, ignored the petition and instead declared the colonies in rebellion in August 1775. The king may, in fact, have passed up an opportunity to de-escalate the rebellion and divide the colonists. Instead the patriots among them moved irrevocably toward independence.

The Decision for Independence, the Issue of God-Given Equality

All men are created equal. They are endowed by their Creator with certain unalienable rights; among these are life, liberty, and the pursuit of happiness.

— Thomas Jefferson (1776) and Vietnamese revolutionary Ho Chi Minh (1945)

It was in these fiery times, after Lexington/Concord and Bunker Hill, that Thomas Paine penned *Common Sense*. This wildly popular tract — it sold a hundred thousand copies in a single year, estimated to be the equivalent of twelve million copies today — was concise and accessible, written in a plain language that spoke to a widely literate

American population. In a sense Paine was a strange messenger for eighteenth-century colonists. A Briton who had recently arrived in America, Paine had, until January 1776, been largely a failure. And for the times, he was a radical; an atheist who called for abolition of slavery and an early form of universal health care, Paine had one more seemingly radical idea: American independency.

Paine's *Common Sense* described the logic of division from Great Britain and dramatically extolled the virtue of the American Cause:

> There is something exceedingly ridiculous in the composition of monarchy . . . so far as we approve of monarchy, that in America the law is king . . . but there is something very absurd in supposing a continent to be perpetually governed by an island.
>
> The Cause of America is in great measure the cause of all mankind. . . . The sun never shined on a cause of greater worth. . . . We have it in our power to begin the world over again.

What it did, besides motivate the patriots, was logically bridge the gap to a declaration of full independence from the British Empire. Within months the Continental Congress in Philadelphia would come to the same conclusion, and a young Virginian planter — and slaveholder — named Thomas Jefferson would be nominated to pen the proclamation.

What sort of document was this? For one thing, the decision to *write it* was itself radical. This was, at root, an act of treason to which dozens of men courageously signed their names. It was a lengthy list of grievances against the king himself, an explanation for their decision to rebel. But it is the document's preamble that we remember, and this, of course, was a thorny matter. The preamble speaks of all *men* being created equal, and certainly the Founding Fathers did not mean to extend political rights to women. But *which* men? White ones, of course, perhaps with a little property or, in the more progressive colonies, perhaps even the landless. Slaves or free black men (one-fifth of the population) didn't count; nor did the "savage" Native Americans beyond the Appalachian frontier. A simple, and not altogether incorrect, conclusion would be that the Declaration of Independence was, at root, a hypocritical document. But there is much more to it.

The preamble and main prose of the declaration tell us many things. Here is one: this was a war about ideas more than territory, and ideological wars tend to be long and brutal in their prosecution. It is — as my experience in America's intractable twenty-first-century Mideast wars demonstrated — a very difficult thing indeed to defeat an enemy fighting fundamentally for ideas.

As noted above, Ho Chi Minh, the Vietnamese revolutionary communist and sworn enemy of the United States, directly quoted the line from Jefferson's preamble in his own country's declaration of independence from the French Empire in 1945. Ho's embrace of Jefferson's language demonstrates that the meaning and interpretation of words and sentiments change through the ages. A non-Christian Asian would certainly have found himself excluded from the fruits of America's eighteenth-century revolution. And yet, perceiving a universalism in the document's preface, Ho was inspired by Jefferson's words nearly two centuries later. This, perhaps, is the American Revolution as its imperfect best.

The Civil War of 1776: Loyalists and Patriots in Revolution

Upon the whole, if we allow [at most] two-thirds of the people to have been with us in the revolution, is not the allowance ample? Divided we have ever been, and ever must be.

— John Adams (1813)

Benjamin Franklin was, perhaps, along with George Washington, the most famed and avowed patriot of them all. For all that, Franklin's own family divided over the Revolution, and one of his most harshest critics was his own son: the royal governor of New Jersey and a staunch loyalist. If even the Franklin family could be torn asunder in the tide of revolution, then certainly something profound was afoot in the colonies.

In addition to being a war for independence, the American Revolution was, and at the time often was referred to as, an American civil war. This was a revolutionary war in the most basic sense, full of armies, guerrillas, militias, local strongmen, and counterinsurgents. While quite eighteenth-century in its flavor and makeup, it was not unlike twenty-first-century events in Iraq or Syria. Though rarely thought of in this way, as a proportion of the population, nearly as many Americans fought *one another* in the Revolution as in the Civil War of 1861–65.

To understand this, we must consider the extent and power of loyalism of one stripe or another. A bit of mental math is in order. We'll stick with the men. Let us assume that 50 percent of white men were patriots. The fifth of the population that was black mainly sided with the British. That takes our calculation of patriots down to only 40 percent of the male population, and of course that excludes the Native Americans (who were, admittedly, not considered in colonial censuses) — who were also, as we'll find, generally allied with the British. In other words, whether in the lead up to or in the midst of the Revolution, the male patriots probably did not constitute a majority.

We often imagine the loyalists to the British cause to have been ultraconservative aristocrats, but in reality they came from all social ranks, classes, and races and had varied levels of devotion to the imperial cause.

There were many reasons to remain loyal: devotion to king and Crown, business connections with the imperial bureaucracy, caution, apathy, and, sometimes, frustration with the excesses of the patriot masses. We must remember that no more than half the (white) colonists were outright patriots. Yet rebel crowds (or mobs, depending on your point of view) from that fraction took it upon themselves not just to protest but to take up arms, to engage in acts of violence, and, frankly, to enforce adherence to their own cause. This drew the ire of many a loyalist — or even neutral — observer. Consider a brilliant satire penned by New York loyalists in 1774 and titled "At a Meeting of the True Sons of Liberty." The authors mock the patriot penchant for dramatic proclamations and list fifteen farcical "resolutions." The fifteenth, and final, is instructive:

> RESOLVED, lastly, that every Man, Woman, or Child, who doth not agree with our Sentiments, whether he, she, or they, understand them or not, is an Enemy to his Country, wheresoever he was born . . . and that he ought at least to be tarred and feathered, if not hanged, drawn and quartered; all Statutes, Laws and Ordinances whatsoever to the contrary notwithstanding.

The loyalists and the many fence-sitters — the latter group surely had sizable numbers — found the patriots exhausting and intrusive. Some took up arms for the British cause, others disseminated loyalist pamphlets, and many held their tongues until it was all over.

Often, neutrality or conscientious loyalism was seen by the patriots as unacceptable. With British regulars pinned down and concentrated by the mere existence of Washington's Continental army, patriot militias policed allegiance to the rebellion in unoccupied towns and villages. It is not that there weren't plenty of loyalists; it's that the British always overestimated the number prepared to throw in their lot militarily with the fleeting, ever-on-the-move British army. By trying hard to raise such loyalist units, the British ended up fomenting a civil war, while lacking the troop numbers and mobility to back their colonial allies in the distant cities and hamlets.

Even in the South, where it was believed (correctly, to some extent) that loyalism ran strong, the British could only capture territory and then move on, leaving the task of securing it to local loyalists. Consider it an "Americanization" strategy on par with the US Army's "Vietnamization" strategy in the Vietnam War, in which US forces sought to hand off territory and responsibility to their local allies in South Vietnam. Once the British (or later, the US military in Vietnam) left an area, however, trouble arose in the rear — rebel terrorism was often met by loyalist retaliation as a cycle of civil war gathered its own chaotic inertia.

Brutal it was, and bloody it could be, but it might have been much worse. Part of the ultimate explanation for British defeat must lie with the generals' decision — as gentlemen — not to unleash many of the most vicious and violent loyalist militias on the patriot populace in a sort of total war. The British, even late in the hostilities, continued to see the colonists as misguided countrymen and hoped at some point to reconcile, not shatter, American society.

Still, in the South in particular, the addition of revolting slaves into the civil maelstrom ushered in the nastiest phase of the war. More Americans died in this communal aspect of the conflict than in conventional British–American battles. Indeed, in the Deep South the Continental army had serious recruiting troubles, as southern patriots were more concerned with policing and protecting against rebellious slaves than with directly fighting for the gallant cause of American independence.

What then are we to make of these *other*, forgotten Americans: the slaves, the Indians, the women? How did they perceive this revolution or, more aptly, this civil war? The next chapter will deal with these questions and ponder an issue at the center of the conflict: Exactly whose revolution was it?[5]

6

WHOSE REVOLUTION? (PART TWO)

The History of our Revolution will be one continued lie
from one end to the other.

— John Adams (1790)

Just how radical *was* the American Revolution? Historians have
debated that question for the better part of a century. A true consensus still escapes us. Nonetheless, the debate itself is instructive and
tells us something of the nature of this experience.

No doubt the American version of revolution lacks many of the
standard symbols of *radical* revolution as we've come to perceive
them, with neither the guillotines of France (1789–94) nor the gulags
and purges of Russia (1917–23). Still, there was an eighteenth-century
radicalism all its own to the American experience.

Pennsylvania was one hotbed of radical egalitarianism. As early
as 1775, radicalism erupted in the Philadelphia militia. The radicals
labeled themselves the Associators and proclaimed an agenda for
(armed) social reform in the colony. Six decades before Karl Marx
began writing, they sought to curb the individual accumulation of
excess wealth and called for universal white male voting (regardless of
financial status) and a general opening up of economic and political
opportunity to the masses.

The power of the impassioned masses (or mob) continued throughout the war, especially in its early phases. After being read the
Declaration of Independence, New York City patriots used a rope to
pull down an equestrian statue of King George III at Bowling Green.
The crowd then demolished the statue, cutting off the head and
mutilating the face. The scene calls forth memories of the toppling
of Saddam Hussein's statue in Baghdad's Firdos Square in 2003. As a
final radical act, the patriots melted down the statue into forty-two

thousand musket balls for the Continental army to fire at the king's soldiers.

It must be remembered that simultaneous with and subsequent to the drafting of the Articles of Confederation for the United States, each individual state tackled the serious business of crafting its own new constitution. Some were rather conservative documents, others quite radical and egalitarian. Indeed, in only two states — Virginia and Delaware — did the initial Revolutionary constitutions maintain property requirements for voting (though many postwar constitutions later reinstituted property restrictions). In the excited frenzy of revolution, many elites "lost control" of the masses. This made many leaders, John Adams among them, uncomfortable.

States such as Pennsylvania experienced what historian Gary Nash called "a revolution within a revolution," instituting universal male suffrage, a powerful unicameral legislature, and early steps to abolish slavery. Thomas Paine's hand was again at work in this business, seeking to make Pennsylvania "the most advanced democracy in the world." Vermont, too, had a radical trajectory, becoming the first state to ban slavery outright, in 1777. New Jersey even extended voting rights — however temporarily — to *women*, something no other state would achieve until Wyoming did so nearly a century later, in 1869.

Furthermore, the *civil* aspect of this war, as we saw in the previous chapter, added to the radicalism of the Revolution. Though there were no guillotines in Philadelphia or Boston, there were, by war's end, more land cessions and flights by loyalists (mostly to Canada), per capita, than in the later French Revolution.

Still, for all this evidence — and much more like it — there remains something ultimately unpersuasive about the "highly radical revolution" argument: it ignores the experience of non-white males. It must be remembered that while in a sense the Revolution had quite radical components for those white men — even those without property — the experience and outcome of the war appeared far less radical, and more conservative, when seen through black or Indian eyes. That, ultimately, explains the geographic (focused on the northern colonies), racial, and patriarchal (whites and males in the narrative foreground) limitations of historian Gordon Wood — made famous by a memorable scene in the film *Good Will Hunting* — and his esteemed book *The Radicalism of the American Revolution.*

The Forgotten Fifth: When Freedom Wore a Red Coat — The Slave Revolution

Your 4th of July is a sham; your boasted liberty, an unholy license . . . your shouts of liberty and equality, hollow mockery.

— Frederick Douglass (1852)

Examine the fragment of the painting on the facing page. In it a proud, dashing black soldier (with a plume in his cap) fights on the British side against the French in a 1781 battle in Europe. In the American War of Independence, too, African and African American slaves often took up arms with the British against the colonists. Many were members of the 1st Ethiopian Regiment, raised in November 1775 by the royal governor of Virginia, Lord Dunmore, in a famed proclamation that bore his name. Stitched into the uniform of each member of the Ethiopian Regiment were three words: LIBERTY TO SLAVES.

There is a scene in the (terribly inaccurate) 2000 movie *The Patriot*, starring Mel Gibson, in which a black man and former slave joins the *Continental* army and by the final battle wins the respect of even the most bigoted soldier in the Gibson character's unit. It's a touching moment, and, indeed, some five thousand black men — slave and free — would fight on the patriot side. The film, along with many other popular depictions of the Revolutionary War, gives us the impression that however imperfect American society was, most black people fought on the colonists' side. Nothing could be further from the truth. In proportion to their numbers in the population, black men *were* more likely than whites to serve as combatants in the Revolution, only by and large they fought *against* the side that had proclaimed all men were created equal.

The Death of Major Peirson, by John Singleton Copley

This is a dizzying, inconvenient fact for some. It complicates and potentially sullies the Revolutionary effort. But it is a fact we must know to describe the totality, warts and all, of our Revolution. Lord Dunmore raised eight hundred to a thousand slave volunteers by offering freedom to those who would flee their masters and gather under his banner. Word of Dunmore's proclamation spread rapidly through the colonies, giving hope to slaves and striking fear in planters throughout the Americas. It convinced many fence-sitting slaveholders that there could now be no reconciliation with the Crown. As Edward Rutledge, a South Carolina signer of the Declaration of Independence, wrote, the Dunmore proclamation effected "an eternal separation between Great Britain and the colonies . . . more than any other expedient."

Indeed, across the colonies, especially in the South, slaves escaped their plantations and sought refuge wherever and whenever the British army passed by or occupied a sizable locale. One military historian, Gregory Urwin, penned an influential article on this phenomenon, aptly titled "When Freedom Wore a Red Coat." Think on that for a moment. Most runaways sought their liberty by joining the British cause, not that of the patriots. What might that say about our Revolution? Was it thus no more than a contradiction, *counter-revolutionary*, and a farce? Perhaps, but once again matters are not clear-cut.

At war's end the British actually sailed away from America with many thousands of slaves. No doubt they left behind some who had helped the British cause, and they sold or returned others, but by and large — and to their great credit — most British generals refused the demands of local colonists to return all of their slaves. At least a few of the slaves who left with the British had belonged to George Washington. Ouch. And consider the further irony that for two decades white patriots had regularly used the terms *enslavement* and *slavery* to describe their treatment by Britain's Parliament and tax collectors.

Among the blacks who had fought alongside the British, many earned a new life after the war. Some fifteen hundred families settled in Birchtown, Nova Scotia, in Canada. Disease and a harsh climate decimated the former slaves, but at least they were free. Some years later, in 1792, more than a thousand set out for the west coast of Africa, where they founded a new city, the aptly named Freetown, now the capital of Sierra Leone.

These stories are inspiring and give us valuable insight into the two sides of the Revolutionary struggle. Still, we have to be careful not to overstate the benevolence of British actions toward the slaves. These were at root military, not humanitarian, gestures, and we cannot ignore the opportunism and self-interest in Lord Dunmore's procla-mation. It's important to note that Dunmore extended the promise of freedom only to those slaves who were owned by rebellious *patriot* masters. Loyalists could keep their human property, and, indeed, many did bring their chattel slaves along into prolonged exile in Canada. Compared with Carolina, Canada was free, but it was by no means a slave utopia.

Still, viewed broadly, the vast majority of slaves either favored, served with, or fought for the British rather than the patriots during the war. And the enraged planter class never let them forget it. Though this is almost entirely lost to modern readers, the Revolution was also the *greatest slave rebellion* in American history. It terrified the owner class and tightened an increasingly brutal slave system. The tragic irony, as historian Ira Berlin has shown, is that the great slave revolt of 1775–83 spooked southern planters into developing a more stringent, controlled, and vigorous antebellum slave system than that which existed before the Revolution. Millions of blacks would come to live under the lash of that slave society — the image of which we've grown accustomed.

The Other America: The Revolution Looking East from Indian Country

> Lay waste all the [native] settlements around . . . that the country may not be merely overrun but destroyed. . . . Rush on with the war whoop and fixed bayonet.
>
> — George Washington, official orders
> to General John Sullivan (1779)

In 2001 an excellent historian by the name of Daniel K. Richter penned a comprehensive native history of early America, with the paradigm-shifting title *Facing East from Indian Country*. Perhaps facing east is what a historian must do when considering Native Americans in American history, including the Revolution: To view Indian experiences, face eastward, rather than starting from the Atlantic coast and viewing the unfolding of history solely in a westward direction. How different the situation must have appeared to the Creek tribe southwest of the colonies or the Iroquois to the northwest of New York.

Just as the slaves realized that their interests were better served with the redcoats, the Native Americans recognized that their autonomy had a better chance of being preserved if they allied with the supposed imperial tyrants and against those who ostensibly extolled the inalienable human right to liberty. Native life, liberty, and happiness could, they believed, be maintained only by standing in opposition to the purported patriots.

And so it was that most Indians fruitlessly waged war while allied with one imperial power — the British — to stave off the encroachment of a new, more dangerous, *colonial* empire, what Thomas Jefferson once called an "empire of liberty." The outcome was tragic.

As we saw during the Seven Years' War, the list of southern colonial patriots is also a who's who of land speculators in early America. Washington, Jefferson, Patrick Henry: They all were in on it at one time or another. Now, in the desperation of war, the speculation game changed again. Recruiting for the Continental army — a miserable, long, thankless duty — became difficult as the war dragged on. Recruiting officers, as ever, needed some way to entice enlistees. It became necessary to promise volunteers land, often Indian land, beyond the mountains, a total of ten million acres. Native land was thus promised to future settlers without the permission, or even the knowledge, of the tribes.

On the long frontier stretching from Georgia to New England, war with the British intermingled with smaller wars against British-backed native tribes. This was often the most vicious fighting the Revolution would produce. Take the example of frontier warfare in northwestern New York State. One historian, Page Smith, called the American campaign in western New York "the most ruthless application of scorched-earth policy in US history." Here General Washington unleashed General John Sullivan with orders to destroy the great Iroquois Confederation, and shatter it he did. The Iroquois mostly sided with the British, though the Revolution kicked off an internal Iroquois civil war when one tribal branch, the Oneida, allied with the Continentals.

It got ugly, fast. Washington called the devastation of the Iroquois "the main American military effort of [1779]" and detached one-third of his army to accomplish the task. Villages were razed, 160,000 bushels of corn burned, and thousands of fruit trees destroyed. Sullivan reported back to Congress that "except one town situated near the Allegheny . . . there is not a single town left in the country of the

Five Nations [of Iroquois]." An Onondaga chief later summed up the experience thusly: "They [Sullivan's troops] put to death all the women and children, excepting some of the young women, whom they carried away for the use of their soldiers and were afterwards put to death in a more shameful manner." (Admittedly, of course, native atrocities along the settler frontier were also common.)

In the end the war — and especially American victory in it — proved, as in the Seven Years' War, to be yet another tragedy for Indians east of the Mississippi River. American colonists, millions that they were, were always more dangerous than a few thousand redcoats and a few hundred imperial bureaucrats spread thinly along the frontier. The United States of America was an existential threat to the native way of life.

None of the affected tribes were included in negotiations toward the Treaty of Paris, which ended the Revolutionary War. No one consulted the Indians before the British saw fit to sign away millions of acres of native land to the new United States. Most native tribes would never accept such claims to their lands, which, to them, were predicated on the white man's conception of international law, something that had little meaning to those living in Indian country.

This situation set up what would become a decade of on-again, off-again war between the armies of the new American republic and the allied tribes of the Ohio Country in the years following the signing of the Treaty of Paris. The last barrier, the infamous British Proclamation Line of 1763, had been breached, and the settler tide would never recede. In just over fifty years that incessant tide would reach the Pacific Ocean. Within a century all overt native resistance was subdued, as tribes chose between genocidal extermination and a life on reservations.

Who Shall Fight for Liberty: The Continental Army at War

The insults and neglects which the army have met with
beggars all description . . . they can endure it no longer. I
am in rags. . . . I despise my countrymen. I wish I could

say I was not born in America. I once gloried in it but
am now ashamed.

> — Lieutenant Colonel Ebenezer Huntington, Yale
> graduate and veteran of battles in Boston,
> Long Island, and Yorktown (July 1780)

When you picture an American Revolutionary soldier, what do you see? A minuteman, of course, a logo of the New England Patriots, perhaps. In reality, though the militia and Massachusetts minutemen played an important role, especially early in the conflict, most of the major fighting was done by Continental army regulars, long-term volunteers filling Washington's ranks. Who fought the war and how it affected them is a story unto itself. War changes society. As John Shy wrote, "the incidence of military service reflects and affects social structure." That was never more true than during the Revolutionary era.

To understand the challenges and tribulations of waging an eight-year war through the combined efforts of thirteen diverse colonies, we must understand a key but often overlooked fact: Contrary to the linear, triumphalist fairy tales, support for the war and enthusiasm for military service actually consistently *declined* in the years leading up to the victory at Yorktown in 1781. Of course, we must remember that even as late as 1780 few would have predicted that victory was likely at all, let alone so near. In this environment of protracted war, in truth it was Continental regulars who performed much of the fighting because militiamen — men of property and some substance — were tied to their farms, families, and villages.

This is not to degrade the importance of the militia. They performed vital, short-duration, local service at key points in the war. Furthermore, it was the militia that waged a micro-revolution at the village level, enforcing patriot conformity in the townships and waging a civil war among neighbors.

Since the propertied militias were often unavailable or unwilling, it was to a considerable degree the dregs of society who filled the ranks of the Continental army. These were the poor, the landless, the immigrants — mostly German and Irish — the former criminals, the wayward youths; those, to be frank, who were most expendable in respectable colonial society. It was the lowest among them who eventually won for the American side. In times since, it has always been thus.

Even so, it was only a tiny fraction of the population that actually experienced extended military service, and these poor souls were paid, if at all, in a currency — Continental dollars — that was soon nearly worthless. Due to rampant inflation and the doubtful prospects of an often failing war, between 1777 and 1781 the value of $100 Continental fell to less than $2 in gold specie. The poorest of men were fighting for nearly worthless slips of paper. The frustration and resentment were palpable. In May 1780, just one year before victory was at hand, Private Joseph Plumb Martin, a seasoned veteran of the Connecticut Line regiments, observed that "the men were exasperated beyond endurance. They could not stand it any longer . . . here was the army starved and naked, and their country sitting still and expecting the army to do notable things."

In the winter of 1780–81 matters spiraled out of control, and Washington had a veritable crisis on his hands. In January the Pennsylvania Line mutinied, shot some of the officers, and marched on Philadelphia to demand back pay from Congress. Washington and Congress folded and negotiated a settlement. Days later the New Jersey Line mutinied, and this time Washington sought to create an example. He ordered executions; though, in passive protest, all six members of the appointed firing squad purposely missed their targets. By this point some one in four of Washington's soldiers were in revolt. The army held together, just barely, and would march south to Yorktown, Virginia, and climactic victory just months later.

———

The American war is over, but this is far from being the case with the American Revolution. On the contrary, nothing but the first act of this great drama is closed.
— Dr. Benjamin Rush (1786)

Sometimes, in hindsight, we readers know *too much*, are too informed of the outcomes to appreciate the contingency and emotional drama of what unfolded. In this case, the messy experience of an eight-year revolution and war of independence shaped the new American republic. Through this crucible did thirteen colonies cohere, sometimes fragment, and ultimately unite. As the historian Carl Becker wrote, the War of Independence was about more than "home rule"; it was also about "who would rule at home." John Shy has called the Revolution a "political education for the masses," and indeed it was.

The war itself was messy and brutal. The stats are instructive: 150,000 to 200,000 colonists performed some military service, about 10 percent of the population; 25,000 Americans perished in the war (about 8,000 in battle, 8,000 of disease, 8,000 on filthy British prison barges), or more than 2 million in today's terms; 100,000 citizens chose exile over residence in the new republic (60,000 loyalists and 40,000 slaves), or some 8 million in contemporary measures.

So how did it actually happen — the victory, the colonial victory, that is? How and why did a rabble of patriot colonials ultimately triumph over the British Empire? There are many reasons. The British faced three thousand miles of ocean to compound their significant logistic and communicative challenges. Limited guerrilla warfare contributed to their anguish. General Washington, though he rarely won, managed to keep the Continental army in the field and in existence.

In a sense the rebels won because they did not lose. By virtue of their survival they prevailed. This is often the case in popular uprisings, and why it was — and still is — so difficult to pacify a rebellious population with military force. Still, Americans mustn't forget that there might be no United States without the French, and eventually the Spanish, entry into the war on the patriot side. To a large extent, larger than most Americans are comfortable with, the United States owes its independence to France. Without the French army, and more vitally the French navy, transforming our revolution into a global war, the conflict couldn't have ended when and how it did — with a British army encircled by land and sea on the Virginia coast at Yorktown.

Maybe the Americans could have won without the French, or maybe not, or perhaps it would have taken several more years and the war would have done even more damage to society. What is certain, as John Shy tells us, is this: "a protracted war, especially one so reliant on popular, more or less voluntary military service, is itself a kind of revolution." In fighting the war, the fighting men and their families experienced a revolution of their own.

What then, in the final sense, can we make of the American Revolution? This much, at least, I'd submit: The founders were neither the infallible demigods depicted by the contemporary political right, nor, for that matter, pure villains to be pilloried, as some on the left would have it. These were imperfect human beings — men, mostly — striving toward independence and tenuously remaking a society.

Taking into account women, slaves, and Indians, the patriot founders excluded probably 60 to 70 percent of the American population from their dreams of life, liberty, and happiness pursued. This does not, in itself, erase the beauty of the founders' aspirations, words, and actions. Rather, I take these salient facts as a warning against all forms of rigid originalism, legal or otherwise — as a warning against the notion that our revolution and forebears ought to remain frozen in their eighteenth-century moment.

Instead the imperfection and ambitions of the founders might remind twenty-first-century Americans to beware the misuse of the past and to always seek the gradual improvement of society and the achievement of a more perfect union. In that sense, this author agrees with Benjamin Rush that, as he said in 1786, the American Revolution is not over, that naught but a few acts of the great drama have closed. We today are waging revolution still.

7

FLOWERING OR EXCESS OF DEMOCRACY

The evils we experience flow from the excess of democracy. The people do not want virtue, but are the dupes of pretended patriots.

— Elbridge Gerry, delegate to the
Constitutional Convention (1787)

The Brits Are Gone: Now What?

It has become by now American scripture. We all know the prevailing myths, history as written by the winners. Virtuous American patriots, having beaten the tyrannical British, set out to frame the most durable republican government in the history of humankind. The crowning achievement came when our Founding Fathers met in Philadelphia in 1787 to draft an American gospel: the Constitution. The war had ended, officially, in 1783.

Have you ever asked yourself why popular versions of America's founding begin with the Declaration of Independence in 1776, or with the defeat of the British at Yorktown, Virginia, in 1781, but skip past the black hole of the mid-1780s to the Constitutional Convention of 1787? What happened in those critical years? What is it that remains hidden in plain sight? Who does the prevailing narrative serve?

Well, in recent years most serious historians finally began studying marginalized peoples, such as slaves, Indians, and women. It is good that this is so. However, the decisions first to draft the Articles of Confederation and then, later, to move toward a new constitution and a more centralized federal government — the key events of the 1780s — were actions that mostly benefited the elites. A top-down structure was imposed on an only partly willing citizenry. This sort of story no longer appeals to academic historians busy drafting a "new" history from the bottom up.

General George Washington Resigning His Commission, 1824, by John Trumbull

From grade school through university survey courses, we are fed the same tale. The victorious colonists — the first generation of *Americans* — briefly organized under a weak governing framework: the Articles of Confederation. This unwieldy government quickly floundered in an era of stagnation and chaos, to be replaced, wisely, by our current Constitution. There is, of course, some truth to this. The Articles of Confederation, the law of the land and America's first constitution, from 1781 to 1789, did grant precious few powers to the national government. Power was dispersed to the *state* governments. In a sense we should probably think of the early thirteen states as separate countries, held together in a loose alliance more similar to today's European Union than to our current US nation. Many states did, indeed, suffer under a period of economic stagnation, and there were several agrarian revolts of one sort or another.

However, it behooves us to consider why the Revolutionary generation chose a weak central government. When thinking about the past, we must avoid determinism and remember that no one in history woke up on a given day and *planned* to fail, to draft an incompetent governing structure. Perhaps the men of the 1780s had good reasons; maybe there was wisdom in such a loose confederation. Was the later constitution *actually* a superior document? This chapter reconsiders that forgotten era, seeks to redeem aspects of the Articles of Confederation, and asks inconvenient questions about just how democratic our later constitution would really be.

The Critical Period: Defending the Articles of Confederation

Each State retains its sovereignty, freedom, and independence, and every power, jurisdiction, and right, which is not by this confederation expressly delegated to the United States in Congress assembled.

— Article II of the Articles of Confederation

It had been a brutal, long, destructive war — the longest war the United States would fight until Vietnam, two centuries later. Tens of thousands died, infrastructure was damaged, state governments were loaded with debt, and many thousands became refugees. Given this reality, we must consider what lessons American leaders learned from the Revolution. Certainly they feared powerful executives (the Articles would have no president), distant aristocratic legislatures (there would be no House of Lords or upper house in the Continental Congress), and standing armies (the Revolutionary army was demobilized, and state militias would provide for the common defense).

The real work of government was seen as occurring at the *state* level, and it was the state constitutions that truly mattered. Each state varied, of course, with Maryland's government being the most conservative and Pennsylvania's the most democratic and egalitarian — by some measures the most democratic in the world. Most states had learned lessons from the late war: they had weak (or in some cases no) executives, powerful — sometimes unicameral — legislatures, and militias rather than professionalized armies. After all, these were post-*Revolutionary* governments, terrified of tyranny and imbued with common conceptions of classical republicanism.

The foundation of republicanism was rather simple and had three pillars — liberty, virtue, and independence. To have liberty, we need to understand that all power tends to corrupt and must, therefore, be checked by virtuous government. Virtue required that representatives always act according to the public interest and not self-interest. Such virtue was possible only when representatives were independent entities not beholden, economically or otherwise, to others. All too often, this required the possession of some degree of wealth, property, and leisure time to study politics.

The problem is that so much of this classical republicanism stood in tension with the democratizing tendencies of all revolutions. In elections for the state legislatures, more men could vote than ever before. Some states, like Pennsylvania, had universal male suffrage and dropped all property requirements for political participation. Common farmers and artisans in the 1780s had increasingly democratic, progressive impulses. They still hated taxation — which had been *increased* after 1783 to pay off state war debts — and they weren't afraid to use the tried-and-true tactics of the Revolution to express their dismay. Farmers and laborers of the 1780s were reform-minded and employed methods consistent with the "Spirit of '76" — petitions, boycotts, even armed insurrection — to pressure their new state governments.

The 1780s were a period in which common folk called for the extension of the franchise (voting rights), the abolition of property requirements, and more-equal representation for distant western frontier districts. Indeed, you could argue that this critical period saw a veritable flowering of democratization, at least among white males. This stood in stark contrast with the sometimes overstated image of depression and stagnation commonly depicted by popular historians.

The Articles are so often derided that we forget that there were real accomplishments in this era. After all, the Articles of Confederation was a *wartime* document and, so governed, the Americans managed to achieve victory over the most powerful empire in the world. This, in itself, was a miraculous accomplishment.

Though there were many problems for the new American republic — which is perhaps best compared to a post-colonial twentieth-century African or Asian state — we must dismiss the chaos theory for why the Articles were eventually replaced by the Constitution. Consider, for a moment, all the things that *didn't* happen to the new republic in the 1780s. There were no interstate wars, no external invasions, no general rebellion. In fact, in many respects, according to the historian Merrill Jensen, there was a spirit of optimism and a sense of an improving humanity within the new country.

Confederation or Empire: The Northwest Ordinance and the Fate of Native Peoples

Another often forgotten accomplishment of US government under the Articles of Confederation was the passing of the Northwest Ordinance, the plan for the occupation and subdivision of the territories ceded by Britain north of the Ohio River and east of the Mississippi. Have you ever noticed how when traversing Midwest "flyover country" on a modern airliner the farmland below appears divided into neatly square plots of similar size? For that we have the Northwest Land Ordinance of 1785, passed into law under the Articles, to thank. The new law divided and subdivided the acres of unsettled (at least by Anglo farmers) land into neat squares for future sale and development.

The British had signed over ownership of this territory to the new United States in the Treaty of Paris (1783), which ended the War of Independence. They did so, of course, without securing permission from or, often, even notifying the land's actual inhabitants, numerous native peoples. This, as we've seen in previous chapters, was a recipe for trouble. The Indians had no intention of ceding their land simply because certain white men across a vast ocean had signed a few papers.

The land granted to the new United States in the Ohio Country was extraordinarily important to the new government under the Articles. Lacking the power of direct taxation of the people, the Congress expected the sale of these lands to private citizens to earn the government ample income to pay down the national war debt and fund wartime bonds issued during the Revolution. It might have worked, too, if those lands were empty. Unfortunately for the land speculators and would-be pioneers, the various tribes of the region had formed a massive coalition and would fight hard for their territory. In fact, in the 1780s and early 1790s two separate US Army forces were defeated by the Ohio Country native confederation. These defeats, and the inability to sell and settle the new lands, helped fuel the depression and fiscal crisis facing the Articles of Confederation–era republic. It was all connected, east with west, domestic with foreign policy.

As a future charter, though, the Northwest Ordinance was profound and shaped the settlement and organization of the ever-expanding United States. The new lands, once settled by a requisite number of farmers, would become federal territories and, eventually, states. This, of course, upset many of the original thirteen states, which had long claimed vast tracts to their west. The ordinance did something else that was rather consequential: It outlawed the institution of slavery north of the Ohio River. This reflected growing post-Revolutionary sentiment in the northern states, which would see nearly all their governments gradually outlaw the "peculiar institution" over the two coming decades. What the ordinance now set up, however, was a growing North–South societal divide over the institution of slavery that would eventually play out in the American Civil War.

The Northwest Ordinance, even if it was premature in signing away and organizing highly contested territory, did achieve two things. First, it increased the probability that land speculators and other factions would call for a more centralized government than the Articles could provide. Only a strong federal government, they would argue, could raise, fund, and field an army capable of defeating the formidable native confederation in the Ohio Country. Second, the ordinance ultimately doomed the native peoples inhabiting this fertile land to either conquest and subservience or expulsion. Before the first waves of settlers crossed the Appalachian Mountains, this outcome was nearly inevitable. The new republic's government had made plans for, divided up, and begun to sell off the Indian land without the consent of the native tribes.

Let us remember that when the British and Spanish agreed to cede everything east of the Mississippi River to the new United States, they were transferring a vast *empire* to the American republic. You could argue, then, that the American tension between republic and empire was already in full swing when the ordinance passed. Furthermore, one of the reasons the stronger future federal constitution appealed to so many eastern elites was that they knew a centralized government was now necessary to manage what Thomas Jefferson famously called "an empire of liberty."

Perhaps the truth is that a confederation of small republics could never manage an empire unless it had a stronger constitution. As we will see in the next chapter, it was under our current Constitution, not the Articles, that we grew into a full empire, one that we retain to this day.

Excesses of Democracy: Elite Responses and Criticisms of the Articles

I dread more from the licentiousness of the people, than from the bad government of rulers.
— Virginia congressman Henry Lee Jr. (1787)

Not all Americans saw the 1780s as a time of hope, experimentation, and increased egalitarianism. For many, especially wealthy, elite citizens, the entire decade, along with the Articles of Confederation that presided over the new republic, was a nightmare. The chief complaints of those who wished to strengthen the federal government were that chaos reigned, the commoners had gained too much confidence and power, and the state legislatures were too beholden to their constituents. The result, as these men — who would become the framers of the Constitution — saw it, was *bad governance.*

Finances played a major role. On this subject neither side of the great debate was happy.

Poor and middling sorts were upset that heavily indebted state legislatures were levying taxes many times higher than this class of Americans had had to pay under imperial rule. Most taxes were collected in gold and silver, resources to which few backcountry farmers had access. These citizens were also aghast at the potential for increased *federal* taxing power, which, indeed, many elites later proposed.

Creditors, financiers, large landholders, and even some genuinely principled republicans saw things differently. In their minds the Revolution had unleashed a popular torrent of excessive democracy, egalitarianism, and a new spirit of "leveling," or what would today be called premodern socialism. Farmers, artisans, and laborers had forgotten their proper place in society and gained too much confidence with respect to their social betters. To the better off, the Revolution had unintended, not altogether positive, second- and third-order effects. As one New Englander declared in the fall of 1786, "men of sense and property have lost much of their influence by the popular spirit of the law."

As the eminent historian Gordon Wood has pointed out, we must understand that a majority of the Articles' most famous critics — and the later constitutional framers — were basically aristocrats in the pre-industrial, pre-capitalist sense of the word. They feared inflation, paper money, and debt relief measures because they modeled their social and economic world on the systems and tendencies of the English gentry. Their entire societal and agrarian order was at risk during the 1780s — in fact it would later collapse in the increasingly commercial northern states, only to live on in the plantation life of the antebellum South. Much of their complaint about "excessive democracy" in the new American state governments may ring hollow to modern ears, but they believed in their position most emphatically.

Let us forget what we know about popular government in the twenty-first century and remember that in the 1780s, especially among the elites, the term *democracy* was still generally used as a pejorative. And to the founding elites, it was high time to stuff the democratic genie — unleashed by the Spirit of '76 — back in the bottle. By *excess democracy*, the elites, who would become Federalists in later political parlance, referred specifically to the ability of commoners to pressure popularly elected state legislatures to print paper money and pass debt relief bills. If creditors couldn't expect prompt repayment in full, they surmised, the social order itself would break down. Many of these elites were themselves creditors or speculators and often were wealthy.

Still, it would be too simple and cynical to ascribe their political beliefs simply to personal, pecuniary interests. Rather, their critique of democracy and the state governments' policies under the Articles was generally consistent with their particular brand of republican worldview. Liberty and order must be balanced in the American republic, or republics, and, they believed, strict libertarianism had gone too far since the outbreak of revolution. But were they right? The centralizing elites' favorite example of unbridled democratic chaos has been passed down in American history under the title Shays's Rebellion.

The Last Act of the American Revolution: Shays's Rebellion

The late rebellion in Massachusetts has given more alarm than I think it should have done. . . . I hold that a little rebellion now and then is a good thing . . . as necessary in the political world as storms in the physical. Unsuccessful rebellions, indeed, generally establish the encroachments on the rights of the people which have produced them. . . . It is a medicine necessary for the sound health of government. . . .

— Thomas Jefferson, writing from Paris in a letter to James Madison, regarding Shays's Rebellion (January 30, 1787)

Every History 101 textbook presents the same narrative about the fall of the Articles of Confederation and the rise of the infallible Constitution. The "people" got out of hand with all that revolutionary fervor, and in Shays's Rebellion in Massachusetts, matters boiled over. In response to the chaos unleashed by these rebels, "respectable" patriots — such as George Washington, Benjamin Franklin, James Madison, and Alexander Hamilton — decided to find a remedy that balanced liberty and order. The result, of course, was the Constitutional Convention of 1787.

But what if our common understanding of Shays's Rebellion is incomplete, perhaps even wrong? What if Shays and his Regulators — they did not call themselves rebels — had a point, genuine grievances, and a coherent worldview? Since this singular event is given so much weight as the supposed catalyst for the American Constitution, it deserves a closer look.

For starters, we have to review the grievances of many American farmers in the 1780s. Remember that the wartime Continental Congress and individual colonies had to raise money and take on debt to fund an eight-year war. Soldiers, when they were paid at all, received paper notes, and merchants, who all too often found their goods requisitioned by the patriots, also received paper currency, essentially IOUs from a broke, fledgling Revolutionary government.

After the Treaty of Paris in 1783, the confederation Congress asked the thirteen states — the Articles of Confederation provided no mechanism for direct federal taxation — to raise money to pay off federal war bonds; furthermore, the individual states had to raise enough gold and silver to redeem their own state currencies. The result was state-level taxation that was on average two or three times higher than in the colonial era. This is ironic, given our common understanding of the American Revolution as a revolt against excessive taxes!

The problem is that the mass printing of paper currency, combined with low confidence in Congress's future ability to pay its debts, led to massive inflation and devaluation of the credit notes. Most creditors and merchants stopped honoring the face value of Continental dollars, and some would accept only gold or silver specie — of which there was an exceeding shortage in the Revolutionary era. By war's end $100 Continental often had a market value of less than $1 in hard specie. If a returning veteran wanted to feed or clothe himself, he needed to exchange his paper pay slips for gold or silver. Indeed, in one of the great crimes against American military veterans in this country's history, poor, desperate, discharged soldiers had little choice but to sell off their nearly worthless currency for a pittance in gold or silver.

Such was the case in rural western Massachusetts in 1786. The state government in Boston imposed a high property and poll tax on the farmers and insisted it be paid in hard currency — gold or silver. As noted earlier, most farmers did not have access to such specie. What they did have was land, animals, tools, and, perhaps, if they were war veterans, Continental paper dollars. If they couldn't pay in gold, the local sheriff could seize their land. And if the sheriff was sympathetic to the farmers and did not enforce the evictions, laws passed by the state government in Boston allowed authorities to seize *his* property.

What, asked many western Massachusetts farmers — a great number of them war veterans — did we just fight a revolution for? To suffer unreasonable taxation and lose our land to our own state government? The sense of injustice was palpable and, in hindsight, understandable. One such smallholder, named Daniel Shays, became a leader of the disgruntled western farmers and would head what eventually became an armed revolt intent on closing the courts and saving their property.

Shays was a former Continental army officer, a wounded veteran of the Battles of Bunker Hill and Saratoga who left the army a pauper. Later taken to court over debts stemming from his time away from his farm, Shays was forced to sell his sword, a gift from the Marquis de Lafayette, to come up with the money. By 1786 he, like many of his compatriots, had nothing left to give when the taxman again came calling.

Almost all the Continental army veterans had by 1786 sold off their paper currency and war bonds to rich speculators for a fraction of the face value. Now the states, and the federal Congress, imposed taxes to pay either the interest on, or the face value of, the very war bonds the veterans had desperately sold off. It all seemed utterly unjust.

Few of the speculators were veterans. Most possessed fortunes and a willingness to play the futures market. One of the reasons Shays's Rebellion occurred in Massachusetts was that the state government in Boston had begun taxing land with the intent to pay off the face value of all state banknotes no later than 1790. Worse still, by 1786 just thirty-five men — nearly all of whom lived in the state capital, Boston — owned 40 percent of all the banknotes. They stood to make a killing when the tax windfall came in.

After Shays and his Regulators refused to pay the tax, armed themselves, closed several county courts, and marched on the federal weapons arsenal at Springfield, the eastern elites panicked. Without a standing federal army, and with the state militia unreliable or sympathetic to Shays's cause, the Massachusetts governor — himself a large bondholder — enlisted other wealthy creditors to hire a private army to put down the growing rebellion.

There was a remarkable overlap between large holders of banknotes and those who contributed to hiring the mercenary force. One wealthy donor, who contributed $500 in gold for the mercenaries, held as much as $30,000 in unredeemed banknotes. When the private militia eventually was successful in suppressing Shays's Rebellion, contributions of this kind turned out to be money well spent.

The dividing lines in Shays's Rebellion were as much regional as class based. This was a battle between the western hinterland and the hub city of Boston, a political tension that exists in Massachusetts to this day. In many colonies the farmers had successfully lobbied to move the capitals out of the commercial hub cities — for example, from New York City to Albany and from Philadelphia to Harrisburg, Pennsylvania. Massachusetts was the anomaly in that Boston remained both the commercial *and* political capital of the state.

Shays and his compatriots wanted the capital moved westward, the aristocratic state Senate abolished, and the stipulated $1,000 in assets of prospective gubernatorial candidates to be lowered or eliminated. So as we can see, class and region certainly complicate this narrative.

Shays's Regulators saw themselves as patriots waging perhaps the final act of the American Revolution. When they were defeated, many "rebels" — including Shays — fled across the border to safe haven in what was then the independent republic of Vermont. This should be unsurprising, since Vermont was itself founded by agrarian "rebels" like Ethan Allen and his Green Mountain Boys, who had clashed with New York State landowners and seceded to form their own country.

Although Shays's Rebellion was put down, we must take a harder look to determine the local winners and losers. Governor James Bowdoin and many anti-Shays legislators were soon voted out of office, and debt relief was passed in the next session of the Massachusetts legislature. Shays was pardoned and eventually even received a pension for his Continental army service. It was the perceived *success* of the rebels — along with the military impotence that forced creditors to hire a private army — that would have a profound effect on Massachusetts, the elites, and the young republic itself.

Shays's movement was only one of many rebellions or threats of rebellion in the 1780s. Thus, one motive of the framers of the Constitution was to create a new federal government with the power, funds, and professional army capable of suppressing unrest. This was ironic, since the American Revolution had been fought, in part, in opposition to the presence of a standing British army.

The true importance of Shays's Rebellion was the fear it struck in the hearts of American elites. Shays's most prominent critic was George Washington. Before he read of Shays's agrarian revolt, General Washington was happily retired at his estate in Virginia. It was his fear of further rebellions — which, according to a favorite analogy, were like snowballs, gathering weight as they rolled along — that convinced Washington to take part in the Philadelphia convention to reform the Articles of Confederation.

In a letter to Henry Lee, Washington expressed his horror regarding the revolt in Massachusetts and, furthermore, revealed his pessimism about the ability of the common man to practice self-government. He wrote:

> The accounts which are published of the commotions . . . exhibit a melancholy proof of what our trans-Atlantic foe has predicted; and of another thing perhaps, which is still more to be regretted, and is yet more unaccountable, that mankind when left to themselves are unfit for their own Government. I am mortified beyond expression when I view the clouds that have spread over the brightest morn that ever dawned upon any Country. . . .

No doubt Washington believed this, and truly feared for the fate of the new republic. But was he *right*?

Can we in good conscience say that Shays and his ilk were nefarious rebels or chaotic brigands? Could it not be said that Shays was correct and a patriot? If Shays and his men were indeed patriots, then what does that say about the motivations of the wealthy men of substance — including Washington — who later gathered in Philadelphia to rein in what they called "the excesses of democracy"? At least this: that these framers were rather dissimilar from Daniel Shays and his fellow men-at-arms; that they did not represent the constituency of farmers and veterans who fought for what Shays certainly believed was their own lives, liberty, and happiness.

This is not to say the Articles were not flawed, or to smear the motives of every founder. Rather, a fresh look at Shays's Rebellion and the elite reactions to it ought to complicate our understanding of who the framers were and were not, whom they did and did not represent, and what they hoped to achieve in Philadelphia. True histories can omit neither the George Washingtons nor the Daniel Shayses of our shared past. The republican experiments of the 1780s and the new constitutional order after 1787 both reflected, to varying degrees, the hopes, dreams, and perspectives of Shays's Regulators and Boston creditors alike. We might even say that America's ongoing experiment, here in the second decade of this twenty-first century, still reflects this tension.

The Road to Philadelphia: From the Spirit of '76 to a New Constitution

What, then, should we make of the turbulent and critical 1780s? Certainly it was a time of transition, of political and constitutional experimentation in the fledgling republic and within each of the still very independent states.

Maybe this too: while imperfect, life under the Articles was not as tumultuous as most students have been led to believe. Thus, at least to some extent, we must see the establishment of a more centralized system under the 1787 Constitution as the fulfillment of the dreams of more *conservative* delegates, increasingly tepid revolutionaries — men of wealth, men of "good standing" — not, necessarily, as consistent with the hopes of an American majority.

A new look at the transition from the Articles to the Constitution, which we will take on in the next chapter, presents a very different backdrop to the Philadelphia convention. A more thorough understanding of the inspirational, if messy, 1780s helps explain what some historians have argued the Constitutional Convention really was: the *counter*-revolution of 1787, a repudiation of the Spirit of '76.

As the historian Woody Holton noted, the 1780s deserve attention and remain relevant because "the range of political possibilities was, in numerous ways, greater than it is today." We must be cautious in how we remember this period, careful not to read history backward from a post-1787 constitutional world, and avoid writing off the Articles of Confederation as somehow doomed to failure.

Political leaders and common folk alike spent the decade after the Revolution asking and answering many seminal questions: What sort of nation would the United States be? Would it even *be* a nation in the modern sense of the word, or instead would be it a collection of states? Should the national government be centralized, federal, or essentially nonexistent? An empire or a confederation? Progressive and egalitarian or socially and fiscally conservative?

Elites and commoners, top-down agendas and grassroots movements — all of these played roles in the 1780s to help define the contours of post-Revolutionary America. They, the then living, could hardly know they were deciding, at that moment, which founding myth later generations would revere as American gospel.

As 1786 turned to 1787, the levelers and progressives, it seemed, would lose out, at least for a time. The 1780s and the Articles of Confederation may have represented their high tide of hope, but the pendulum was about to reverse course, moved backward by patriot elites who were intent on a counter-revolution. The framers, men you know and revere as "democrats" — George Washington, Alexander Hamilton, James Madison, and Benjamin Franklin — would soon craft a document that would curtail what these men actually saw as the "excesses" of democracy in America. This document would soon become their, and our, republican scripture: the US Constitution.[6]

8

COUNTER-REVOLUTION OF 1787? — NEW CONSTITUTION, NEW NATION

> Some men look at Constitutions with sanctimonious reverence, & deem them, like the Ark of the Covenant, too sacred to be touched. They ascribe to the men of the preceding age a wisdom more than human, and suppose what they did to be beyond amendment. I knew that age well: I belonged to it. . . .
>
> But I know also that laws and institutions must go hand in hand with the progress of the human mind . . . we might as well require a man to wear still the coat which fitted him when a boy, as civilized society to remain ever under the regimen of their barbarous ancestors.
>
> — Thomas Jefferson in a letter to Samuel Kercheval (July 12, 1816)

The US Constitution stands almost as American scripture, deified and all but worshipped as the holy book for the American civil religion of republicanism. The painting on the facing page captures the spirit of modern memories, and mythology, surrounding the Constitutional Convention, which was held in Philadelphia. The sun shines through windows, which are conspicuously open, and delivers a halo of light upon the figure of the tall, erect George Washington. He stands on what resembles a religious altar, presiding over the delegates as they sign the sacred compact of American governance. Ben Franklin, himself an international celebrity by that time, sits prominently in the center as the influential young Alexander Hamilton whispers in his ear; meanwhile, the "father" of the Constitution, James Madison, sits just below the altar, on Franklin's left.

Signing of the Constitution, 1940, by Howard Chandler Christy

This is an illustrative depiction of the convention: glorious, dramatic, and mostly inaccurate. In reality the shades were drawn and the windows locked. The delegates — at least those who were there on any given day — conducted their business in total, purposeful secrecy. Fifty-five elite delegates, representing only twelve of the thirteen colonies (Rhode Island refused to send a representative), took it upon themselves to secretly craft a new formula for government that they decided to be in the best interest of "We the People."

In the intervening years, the Constitution has become sacred indeed, an influential foundation used by politicians on all sides of the ideological spectrum to bolster their arguments and justify all number of decisions. In our modern age of hyper-partisanship, to disagree with one side or the other is to hold beliefs that are *un*constitutional, if not treasonous. Still, Americans rarely consider the actual events surrounding the convention or try to understand the text of the document itself. Nor do they bother to question the very peculiarity of a two-hundred-plus-year-old document informing the organization of the modern political and societal space.

The founders, or in the case of the Constitution the framers, are now held in the esteem of veritable deities, a pantheon of American civic saints. Many active citizens, especially on the conservative political right, argue for originalism: the need to follow and understand the Constitution as it was written, back in the late eighteenth century. Indeed, originalism, in one form or another, seems ascendant in post-Reagan America. This is curious, given that many — though not all — founders were skeptical about such thinking way back when.

Thomas Jefferson, though not in attendance in Philadelphia (he was then ambassador to France), remained a powerful intellectual influence on the framers, especially on his friend James Madison. Jefferson, at that time and even more fervently as the years passed, was unimpressed by the growing veneration of the founding generation. He was increasingly persuaded that "the earth belonged to the living," that each generation must reassess its governing structure, and that to submit to the reasoning of our "barbarous ancestors" was a form of tyranny.

Jefferson and his tradition — among those then pejoratively labeled Anti-Federalists — fervently believed the Constitution must be open to amendment and regularly reassessed as the human mind and society progressed. Others, then and now, led by ardent nationalists such as young Alexander Hamilton, actively disagreed, preferring a fixed foundation of governance for "millions yet unborn." That debate, of centralizing Federalists versus skeptical and fearful Anti-Feds, was a tumultuous legacy bequeathed to us all, one that is still raging.

To take a side, or even understand the dialogue, we must look backward, must shed the patriotic yarns taught in public schools from time immemorial and understand the truth of events in the crucial post-Revolutionary years of 1787–89. Hard questions must be asked: Why did so many Americans adopt a more powerful government so soon after revolting against another? Did the Constitution serve to expand or limit American liberty? The answers might surprise you.

As always, we must remember that nothing was inevitable — not the ratification of the Constitution, the presidency of George Washington, or even the continued union of the thirteen individual republics (or states). A deeper look at the actions and motivations of the framers uncovers certain darker forces at work, complicates blind veneration, but leads the modern reader closer to truth and context. That story begins with fifty-five prominent men and a Philadelphia summer.

The Coup d'État of 1787?

> Genuine liberty requires a proper degree of author- ity. . . . All communities divide themselves into the few and the many. The first are the rich and well born, the other the mass of the people. . . . [The masses] seldom judge . . . right. Give therefore to the first class a distinct, permanent share of government.
>
> — Alexander Hamilton

> Liberty may be endangered by the abuses of liberty as well as the abuses of power.
>
> — James Madison

Many Americans, especially coastal elites, believed the Revolutionary spirit had gone too far, especially among the middling folk and commoners. Shays's Rebellion, state-level debt relief (seen almost as a form of modern welfare spending), and the apparent weaknesses of the Continental government, convinced many — often famous — elites that something had to be done. The problem, as Hamilton boldly labeled it, was one of how to rein in "an excess of democracy." That, of course, doesn't sound all that revolutionary; sounds rather contrary to the beloved Spirit of '76.

Hamilton and Madison, among other nationalists (those who believed in a more powerful central government), led the fight to amend the existing constitution of the allied states, the Articles of Confederation. They believed the state-level legislators were too close to their constituents, and too lenient on debt and taxation. This, they believed, explained the postwar recession of the 1780s. Madison, Hamilton, and even Washington, among others, believed the state legislatures to be too susceptible to popular pressure — too *demo-cratic*, one might say.

Other nationalists — or, as they would begin to call themselves, Federalists — sought external security through internal union. Think, then, of things in a new way: the 1787 convention was essentially an *international* meeting with envoys from twelve of thirteen independent states, or *countries*, seeking to strengthen a loose confederation into one nation. Thus, some hoped, the US could elude both internal and external diplomatic dangers. There would, necessarily, be trade-offs. As the authors of the essay "Federalist Number 7" would write: "to be more safe, [we] must risk being less free." Seen in this light, security, as much as politics or economics, motivated the drive toward centralization.

This of course was all rather strange. Had not the very purpose of the Revolution been to demand local representation and dispute governance from a distant body (in London)? Local rule, local decisions — the Spirit of '76! How different, then, was centralized rule from (also distant) New York or Philadelphia? In an era when, as historian Joseph Ellis has reminded us, the average person strayed no more than twenty-six miles from his or her birthplace in an entire lifetime, a convention in Philadelphia was, for all intents and purposes, as far away as a parliament in London.

Still they met, these rather few delegates, in Philadelphia in 1787. Their mandate, specified by the legal governing body of the day — the Confederation Congress — was simply to discuss and recommend changes to the Articles. And it is here, in the forthcoming decisions of the fifty-five delegates, where matters got complicated.

Whatever else the Philly convention and the final drafted Constitution was, it was *unconstitutional*, the Articles then being the law of the land. Almost immediately, these unelected delegates — chosen by the state legislatures and not "We the People" — decided unilaterally to ignore Congress and scrap the entire Articles of Confederation. They would, instead, write an entirely new constitution and present it to the states and the people. It should not surprise us that they decided thus. For the most part the deck was stacked.

Only Federalist-inclined men generally sought to attend, and most skeptics — including the state of Rhode Island — refused to take part.

Immediately the delegates voted to conduct all their actions in secret. The doors would be locked and the windows cloaked, and no letters about the proceedings or public proclamations would be allowed. This, they believed, would allow the men (and they all were men, and white) to speak freely and frankly. Still, this sort of secrecy hardly seemed to jell with truly republican principles. Yet so it would be, as a few dozen, unelected, nationalist-inclined, prominent men secretly — and one could argue illegally — decided to ignore their charter and craft a new, more centralized government on behalf of the people of America. Furthermore, while the Articles of Confederation required unanimity among the states to be amended, the framers unilaterally decided to change the very rules of the game: ratification of the new constitution, they said, would require the consent of only nine out of the thirteen state legislatures.

What an odd foundation, what dubious circumstances, for a document so revered by succeeding generations. Little wonder then that some have taken to calling the Constitutional Convention the Framers' Coup. Seen in a certain light, the sentiment rings true, even if the simplicity of this alternative reading is itself flawed. Of course, few Americans know this more complex history of the Constitution. How, then, could they not blindly revere the resultant document? Perhaps that's the point. The history that is written, the history that is widely taught, represents a conscious decision; a decision that is, more often than not, *politically* motivated.

Qui Bono? An Economic Interpretation of the Constitution

The convention of Philadelphia is to consist of members of such ability, weight and experience, that the result must be beneficial.

— John Adams in a letter to John Jay (May 8, 1787)

> The protection of [property] is the first object of government.
>
> — James Madison, excerpt from "Federalist Number 10"

In 1913 the historian Charles Beard, an intellectual leader of the Progressive movement and US liberalism, wrote one of the most influential and controversial books in US history: *An Economic Interpretation of the Constitution of the United States*. In his bombshell Beard argued that the primary motive for most framers was to establish a strong central government that would protect their financial interests and enrich them personally. His narrative turned the founding myth on its head and shocked the academic world.

To understand why Beard thought this way, we must examine just who these fifty-five delegates were. First off, remember what they *weren't* — common farmers or small shopkeepers. No, these were elites, individuals of wealth and, in some cases, fame. As mentioned earlier, all were male and white. More than half were college educated at a time when less than 1 percent of the population was. Fifty-eight percent were lawyers, 31 percent owned slaves, and 22 percent boasted large plantations. This will not surprise most readers. But there was something else. Twenty percent were securities speculators or major bondholders. Eleven percent speculated in western land and hoped to turn a profit west of the Appalachians. Remember Shays's Rebellion. That revolt kicked off when small farmers were heavily taxed and required to pay in gold and silver to fund war bonds and continental paper money, both of which were at that point owned by wealthy speculators to a large extent.

Most of the Continental IOUs began in the hands of Revolutionary War soldiers and their suppliers, but amid rampant inflation and in desperate need of hard currency, most veterans sold off their bonds and their paper money to speculators for a fraction of the face value. Daniel Shays was one of them; another was fellow military veteran Joseph Plumb Martin. Martin went to his grave bitter about his lack of pay and overall treatment by the national government. He described how at war's end the men in his unit who had paper bills sold them off "to procure decent clothing and money sufficient to enable them to pass with decency through the country [on their way home]."

By the time of the Constitutional Convention, only 2 percent of Americans — very few of them former soldiers or the original recipients — owned bonds. Nevertheless, in the years to come, a huge portion of the state and federal tax revenue would go to servicing and paying interest on those bonds. There was just one problem: In the minds of the wealthy, the Articles of Confederation was insufficient to enforce debts. After all, it had no power to tax, and the state legislatures were proving too responsive to clamors for debt relief from their constituents. Bondholders, creditors, and speculators — including many of the framers — were terrified of the new post-Revolutionary power of uneducated, indebted farmers in their local governments. These men of wealth feared for their positions and power. After all, hadn't the framers believed that their class was best suited to govern society?

Many credit-holding elites feared they would never be paid and recoup debts owed unless a strong federal government could collect taxes and had the power to enforce contracts. Beyond their personal interests, they also believed that only a strong central government could ensure a prosperous economy. Indeed, for many economic nationalists the two key provisions of the Constitution fell under Article I, Sections 8 and 10. These clauses gave the federal government the power to tax and prohibited the states from rescuing debtors or printing paper money. Some said that even if *just those two* provisions made it into the new Constitution, it would still be well worth voting for.

But was it that simple? Certainly, self-interest seemed to play a role, and no doubt the framers were mostly moneyed elites. Madison himself stated that the new federal government ought "to protect the minority of the opulent against the majority."

Without a doubt, the interests of the wealthy were front and center in the new Constitution. Still, Beard's overly simplistic economic determinism erases the agency of framers who were often enthusiastic nationalists and true believers. Indeed, Madison and Hamilton — thought of as "fathers" of the Constitution — were not themselves major creditors or bondholders. Besides, in the minds of these eighteenth-century elites, only property and wealth could render a man politically independent, out of reach of bribery and economic intimidation. This, they believed, was the surest path to public virtue.

Compromised by Compromises: The Emerging Constitution

> No mention was made of negroes or slaves in this Constitution . . . because it was thought the very words would contaminate the glorious fabric of American liberty.
>
> — Dr. Benjamin Rush in a letter to
> Dr. John Lettsom (September 1787)

American children, children who grow up to be politically active adults, are led to believe — and they usually do so with all their hearts — that the Constitution was, from the first, an inherently *democratic* document. But what if it wasn't? What if, instead, it represented an attempt to drive a wedge between the people and their government and was ultimately little more than a compromise between factions? To understand the Constitution thus is not to forever tarnish its legacy but rather to know it in its own context and to maintain a critical eye in contemporary political debates. That, of course, is a dangerous road, one sure to upset originalists and the powerful.

There are, in fact, three distinct ironies about the American Constitution that emerged from the Philadelphia convention. First, the framers intended to write a *less* democratic document, and — though it took generations — ended up with one of the more democratic countries on earth. Second, the delegates were responding to problems (state legislative excesses and economic anxiety) that were inflated and exaggerated. Nonetheless, they proceeded as though their biased opinions were self-evident truths. The document reflects that. And finally, as we shall see, Americans have the *Anti*-Federalist opponents of the Constitution to thank for the democratic, civil libertarian protections found in the cherished Bill of Rights.

Most arguments, and eventual compromises, centered on three key debates: over representation, the presidency, and slavery. Most in the stacked deck of Federalist framers desired a legislative branch that was less responsive than that of the local state governments. Larger districts and fewer total representatives (each congressman would now represent ten times the constituents of an average state assemblyman), Madison believed, was the best way to shield the federal government from too much popular pressure. It was necessary, he said, to "extend the sphere" of governance and create more distance between representatives and citizens.

Some wanted senators to serve for life. Six-year terms was the compromise, but this was still a very long tenure in a time of annual elections at the state level. Madison thought that the Senate should be able to veto any state law. Charles Pinckney of South Carolina argued that "no salary be allowed" for senators because the Senate "was meant to represent the wealth of the country." There were debates and disagreements on these points, but most framers agreed with the basic premise of distant, less-responsive representation.

The more difficult matter was how the legislative seats ought to be divided among the states. Large, populous states, backing the Virginia Plan, wanted a bicameral (two-house) Congress with proportional representation in both chambers. Smaller states backed the New Jersey Plan and equal representation among each of the sovereign states. Eventually the two sides came to a compromise, by Connecticut, and agreed on proportional representation in the House and two senators for each individual state. It remains so today. Furthermore, senators would *not* be elected by the people but rather by state legislatures. This would not change until the early twentieth century. When it came to representation, the Constitution crafted a legislature far less responsive than those of the states.

Other debates surrounded the figure of the executive branch — the president. Under the Articles there was no executive. After all, the states had just rebelled against a king! Many, like Hamilton, wanted a sort of "Polish King," an executive elected for life. This was blocked, but the eventual outcome was a presidency vested with significant powers (vetoes, commander-in-chief authority, and pardons) and not constrained by term limits. Washington *chose* to set a precedent of stepping down after two terms — one that more than thirty consecutive presidents would follow — but he was not obliged to do so. Not until the 1950s was the two-term limit written into a constitutional amendment.

More interesting, the people would not directly elect the president. Rather, here, too, there would be distance between the government and the citizenry. The people would vote for electors who would then select the chief executive. Furthermore, elections would be an all-or-nothing game with the electors from each state voting to give all the state's electoral votes to a candidate of choice, no matter how close the vote. The Electoral College still stands, and its existence explains how and why certain presidents (John Quincy Adams, Rutherford B. Hayes, Benjamin Harrison, George W. Bush, and Donald Trump) have been elected despite losing the popular vote.

Original Sin: The Three-Fifths Compromise — A Road to Civil War?

> [This Constitution] is a better security [for the institution of slavery] than any that now exists. No power is given to the general government to interpose with respect to the property in slaves now held by the states.
>
> — James Madison in a speech reassuring delegates to the
> Virginia Constitutional Ratification Convention (June 1788)

Perhaps the most infamous decision in the Constitution was the Three-Fifths Compromise. This representation arrangement was a concession to southern states and their wealthy planters. According to the three-fifths rule — in force until the Civil War — each black slave would be counted as 60 percent of a person when calculating the number of House representatives allotted per state. Not that the slaves could *vote*, of course — they just counted.

The three-fifths clause had momentous, often disastrous, consequences. The math spoke for itself. The vote of one planter with one hundred slaves would carry as much weight as that of *sixty* voters in the increasingly slave-free North. Southern states would punch above their weight in electoral politics for nearly a century, protecting and expanding slavery every step of the way. The Three-Fifths Compromise helps explain why five of the first seven presidents were slaveholding southerners.

It also played a role in the agreement of the framers not to restrict the slave trade — the forcible and brutal importation of more Africans — until 1808. The result: in the intervening twenty years more than 170,000 Africans were shipped across the Atlantic and into bondage in the southern United States. The prolific descendants of these slaves, those who survived, had populated the South when civil war finally came in 1861. Because of the three-fifths rule, the very existence of slaves lent more power and authority to their masters. The irony, according to historian Woody Holton, was that "in this instance, slaves' interests would have been better served if they had not been considered persons at all."

Nor can we explain away the Three-Fifths Compromise as merely a "sign of the times," for many Americans were, indeed, appalled by this clause in 1787. One New Englander opposed to the Constitution wrote that "[the United States] had to remain a collection of republics, and not become an empire [because] if America becomes an empire, the seat of government will be to the southward . . . empire will suit the southern gentry; they are habituated to despotism by being the sovereigns of slaves."

Even an eventual supporter, and framer, of the Constitution, Philadelphia's Gouverneur Morris, disliked the Three-Fifths Compromise and was horrified by the idea that

> [t]he inhabitant of Georgia and South Carolina who goes to
> the Coast of Africa, and in defiance of the most sacred laws
> of humanity, tears away his fellow creatures . . . and damns
> them to the most cruel bondages, shall have more votes

instituted for protection of the rights of mankind, than the citizen of Pennsylvania or New Jersey.

When it came to the Constitution as a final product, we must understand that the whole document was a compromise. Invisible common citizens were present in that room in Philadelphia. Left to their own devices, the framers would have produced a government even less responsive and more aristocratic, but as they wrote the document they knew they would have to eventually get it ratified by the people. Hence, they softened the harshest clauses and generated the Constitution we all know — messy, flawed, and ever-changing.

Forgotten Founders: The Anti-Federalists and American Freedom

A powerful and mighty empire is incompatible with the genius of republicanism.
— Anti-Federalist Patrick Henry

The very terms of the debate that followed, that of ratification, were flawed. Federalists and Anti-Federalists waged a semantic battle above all. As historian Pauline Maier reminds us, "[t]he words we use, especially names, shape the stories we tell." Anti-Federalist was a *pejorative* term used by the Feds and never accepted by most opponents of the Constitution. It was also illogical. *Anti-*Federalists were actually more in favor of federalism, in the traditional sense of the term, and local autonomy. Perhaps Pro-Rats (ratification) and Anti-Rats would be a more accurate, if conversely depreciative, pair of labels.

It was also never a fair fight. The history we know and are taught is a *Federalist* history, a history (spoiler alert) of the victors. The Federalists wrote most of the documents (like the famous Federalist Papers) on which historians depend. Back at the time, they owned most of the newspapers in the new nation. They tended to live in big cities and trading hubs, along key transportation routes. They were also *for* something tangible — a new, written Constitution — rather than *against* such a document and internally divided as to the right course, like the Anti-Federalists.

Still, there were ever so many Anti-Federalists of one stripe or another during the period of ratification (1787–89). They lived mostly in the West, or upstate (as in New York), far from the bustling cities and wealthy commercial elites. Historians estimate that about half the citizenry opposed the Constitution at the outset. Indeed, the Feds often got enough votes to ratify only by solemnly promising to immediately *amend* the Constitution. New Yorkers gave in only after (Federalist) New York City threatened to secede, and Rhode Island capitulated only after the other states imposed a trade boycott on the little state.

There were also some rather famous citizens among the Anti-Feds. Patrick Henry of Virginia (he of "Give me Liberty or Give me Death" fame) was opposed to the end. So was Virginia's George Mason (a future university namesake). Others initially opposed the Constitution but finally acquiesced (in however lukewarm a fashion), such as Samuel Adams, John Hancock, and Thomas Jefferson.

The ratification debates were intense, and it was years before all thirteen states adopted the Constitution. Some votes were close: Massachusetts's was 187–168, New Hampshire 57–47, Virginia 89–79, New York 30–27, and Rhode Island 34–32. In other words, adoption of the Constitution we now revere was a near-run thing. And as close as these votes were, we must note who actually got to do the voting: white, free men. In some states it was only those who owned property. Women, slaves, and Indians weren't consulted — a good thing as far as the Federalists were concerned. As we'll see, odds are they would have opposed an empowered national government.

So just what did they fear, these various opponents of the Constitution? Simply put, they dreaded what the rebellious colonists had so feared: a president who becomes an executive monarch (a concern that has been partly vindicated given the increasingly imperial powers of today's presidency in foreign affairs); an aristocratic Senate, which was understandable given that the people didn't directly elect senators until 1913; a distant, unresponsive House with the power of federal taxation, like Parliament (this is still an issue for libertarian conservatives in the modern tea party movement); and, of course, a standing national army — this, no doubt, was an outgrowth of bad memories from the Revolutionary era. Indeed, consider the text of the Declaration of Independence: the gripe that King George had "kept among us, in times of peace, a standing army without the consent of our legislatures." A prominent Anti-Federalist in Virginia, John Tyler, asked at his state's ratifying convention whether "[we] shall sacrifice the peace and happiness of this country, to enable us to make wanton war?" Contemporary Americans, seventeen years into an undeclared "war on terror," might think it time to revisit Tyler's question.

The point is that the Anti-Federalists were neither history's villains nor simply its losers. They represented the political inclinations of a significant segment of eighteenth-century Americans, which inclinations, some might argue, remain even in the twenty-first century.

———

> The Constitution proposed . . . is designed not for your-selves alone, but for generations yet unborn. The princi-ples, therefore . . . ought to be clearly and precisely stated, and the most express and full declaration of rights have been made — But on this subject [the Constitution] is silent.
>
> — Robert Yates (pen name: Brutus)

Historian Woody Holton has recommended a teaching experiment, one I used with my cadets when I taught at West Point. I'd end my class on the subject by asking random cadets to name their favor-ite right or privilege guaranteed by the Constitution, which cadets had sworn to "support and defend." Inevitably a hulking male Texan would offer "the right to bear arms!" Others would chime in with free speech, a free press, and freedom of religion. Then I'd ask how many of those rights were contained in the document approved at the Constitutional Convention. Met by blank, confused stares, I'd level the answer: *zero*.

It's a trick question, of course. The Constitution, as first drafted and ratified by the states, was solely a structure-of-government document. All our most treasured protections are found in the first ten *amendments* to the Constitution, what became known as the Bill of Rights. Most staunch Federalists, in fact, insisted that the Constitution be ratified "as is" and opposed a Bill of Rights. This, of course, raises a salient, if uncomfortable, question: If the motive for the Constitution wasn't to safeguard liberty, what does that say about the document?

Actually, it was the Anti-Feds who insisted on, and strong-armed a promise for, a Bill of Rights during the contested ratification conventions. Do you enjoy freedom of speech, of assembly, the right to bear arms? Well, thank the oft-forgotten Anti-Federalists. It's possible, in fact, to argue that it was actually the Anti-Feds who hewed closer to the republican principles of the Revolution, to the Spirit of '76. Taking a fresh look at the Constitution's opponents also reminds us that there is value in studying our conflicts and, sometimes, focusing on history's "losers."

A Roof Without Walls: The Legacy of the Constitution

I suppose to be self-evident, that the earth belongs to the living; that the dead have neither powers nor rights over it . . . every constitution, then, and every law, naturally expires at the end of [each generation]. If it be enforced longer, it is an act of force and not of right.

— Thomas Jefferson in a letter to
James Madison (September 6, 1789)

Barely a decade after revolting against an empire, the thirteen former colonies of America made the conscious decision — no doubt egged on by their prominent elites — to graft a powerful federal government onto their separate states and, in Woody Holton's memorable words, "launch an empire of their own." Why and how it happened, as we've seen, is rather complex. Of this much we can probably be sure: without the experience of the war, it is unlikely that there would have been any call for a centralized government. As Peter Onuf has noted, "revolutionary war-making and state-making were inextricably linked." Wars demand powerful bureaucracies, and failures are unforgiving in the storm of conflict. The weaknesses and shortfalls of the Confederation Congress convinced many rebel leaders that something sturdier was necessary. But they did not convince them all.

A powerful opposition to the Constitution and the national government persevered and fought centralization at every turn. These resisters would not vanish after ratification but rather would form a new faction to oppose what they saw as the excesses of centralized power.

There is irony, in a sense, in our contemporary deification of the Constitution across the political spectrum. Perhaps this can be explained by the ethnic, religious, and regional diversity of the early republic (and our present nation). American nationalism was peculiar and was largely *constitutional* for a century or more (based on a document rather than a common ethnicity) — a condition that perhaps exists even until today. It is the Constitution that has come to bind us. This, of course, is strange because in the 1780s and 1790s it was that very Constitution that *divided* Americans.

What is more, modern Americans forget that, in the end, the Constitutional Convention constructed a new federal government "considerably less democratic than even the most conservative state constitutions." As delegate Robert Morris said at the time, the new government was meant to "suppress the democratic spirit." In a further irony, despite finishing a revolution against the British Crown just five years earlier, Hamilton and other, like-minded framers believed that a respectable United States would have to become more, not less, like Britain.

And still something was lost in the movement toward a stronger constitution. Annual elections, congressional term limits, grassroots voting instructions from constituents, and popular control of the money supply: all these democratic measures — most of which dated back to the colonial era — were gone forever. We might wonder whether this was truly for the better.

There was still another motivation for the Philadelphia convention: elite fear. Shays's Rebellion and other grassroots revolts convinced many wealthy leaders that a strong central government, with a standing army, was necessary to quell future unrest. Seen in this light, the Constitution was meant to *suppress*, not safeguard, liberty, at least from the perspective of certain parties. The southern planters, too, were gripped with fear. They remembered well that the greatest slave revolt in American history — a part of the American Revolution — had recently occurred when many thousands of slaves flocked to the British lines. The new federal army would also, they surmised, be used to deter or quash future slave rebellions.

Those new government powers quickly translated into action as, from 1789 to 1795, US Army manpower increased fivefold, its budget threefold, and the size of the navy by a factor of sixty! In a sense this establishment of a standing army, though modest by today's measures, appears counter to the Revolutionary spirit and a repudiation of the values of 1776.

The Constitution, and the new army it helped to create, also spelled doom for native tribes and unleashed a veritable bonanza in land sales in what was then the West. Sadly, the power of the post-Revolutionary native confederation north of the Ohio River may have inadvertently signed the Indians' death warrant. Indian resistance had stymied land sales (which, it was hoped, would fund the Confederation budget) and helped motivate the centralization instinct among prominent speculators — many of whom became framers. They supported a powerful central government that could secure the land from Native Americans and ensure ample profits to boot.

———

Perhaps a fresh, nuanced look at the Constitution's ratification ought to lead us to restructure our understanding of the era. Maybe rather than a simple revolution-to-republic narrative there were actually numerous revolutions: one revolution surrounding independence, followed by a social, democratic revolution during the Confederation, then a different transformation — a *constitutional* revolution that sought to centralize power, ensure "security," and work toward the creation of an American nation-state. *That* revolution has endured, but we must remember that, at least in its own day, it was a revolution *against* the "excesses of democracy" — an *un*-democratic counter-revolution of 1787!

How then can the Constitution be, as so many Americans today insist it is, an infallible, divinely inspired document? It has, after all, been amended dozens of times. Furthermore, after seventy-four years, it ultimately failed; with the nation torn asunder by civil war, the original sin of slavery came home to roost. The death of hundreds of thousands of citizens was required to update and reimagine the Constitution. And so, as John Adams reminded his contemporaries, long after the Revolution: "divided we have ever been, and ever must be."

Years after the Constitution became the law of the land, establishing a new powerful federal government, Fisher Ames, a staunch Massachusetts Federalist, described the new American political mood:

> The fact really is, that . . . there is a want of accordance between our system [of government] and the state of our public opinion. The government is republican; opinion is essentially democratic. . . . Either, events will raise public opinion high enough to support our government, or public opinion will pull down the government to its own level. They must equalize.

We Americans are still thus divided between democratic sentiments and republican, indirect governance — how else could someone who received three million fewer votes than his opponent have won the Oval Office in 2016? Conservatives and liberals alike are still playing out this old debate. It remains to be seen if the United States can be both democratic and republican, to find a balance; or, for that matter, in these highly divided times, whether we can maintain the union itself.

In its own way, the turmoil of the eighteenth century is with us still.[7]

9

GEORGE WASHINGTON'S TURBULENT ADMINISTRATION

What a stupendous, what an incomprehensible machine is man! Who can endure toil, famine, stripes, imprisonment & death itself in vindication of his own liberty, and the next moment . . . inflict on his fellow men a bondage, one hour of which is fraught with more misery than ages of that which he rose in rebellion to oppose.

— Thomas Jefferson in a letter to John Adams (1816)

Close your eyes and imagine America as it was under the administration of President George Washington. No doubt most readers would envision a heroic, tranquil time, when all was right and the great founders ruled the United States as they had intended. It's a comforting myth and, to be sure, a reflection of a closely held nationalist narrative: America may have faltered, may even have been off track at times, but once, under the steady hands of men like Washington, all was as it should be. How then are Americans to process the *reality* of the first president's tenure — an age of turmoil, violence, and division? Perhaps this: as Billy Joel sings, "The good old days weren't all that good," and as John Adams wrote, "Divided we ever have been, and ever must be."

When Washington became president, no one was surprised. No other man had the fame, confidence, or esteem to preside over the early American republic. Still, the former general inherited a fiercely riven nation, a republic that had only barely ratified the controversial Constitution. Anti-Federalists — opponents of the Constitution — hadn't simply disappeared, and a significant mass of Americans distrusted the growing power of the central government.

President Washington would rule a union of states wildly different from the modern United States. The West remained generally unsettled

— populated and contested by still-powerful Indian confederacies, led by the Miami in Ohio and the Cherokees/Creeks in the South. The nation was still mainly rural, with 80 percent of the population engaged in farming. Most farmers (including many Indian tribes) engaged in semi-subsistence agriculture, consuming much of what they grew but also relying on local trade and barter, as well as the purchase of products such as sugar, salt, and coffee. On the Atlantic coast, of course, and in the larger cities, a sizable minority of Americans was increasingly tied to the national and international commercial economy. These two competing visions of the American Dream — rural versus more heavily populated areas — would remain in tension for decades to come.

A Question of Fairness: Alexander Hamilton's Economic Program

> [I have] long since learned to hold popular opinion of
> no value.
>
> — Alexander Hamilton

No one better reflected the commercial and national centralization mind-set than the West Indian–born bastard (and notably self-made man) Treasury Secretary Alexander Hamilton. It is curious that one of such humble circumstances would not only rise to such prominent heights but also espouse such an aristocratic agenda. Nonetheless, for better or worse, Hamilton — now the title character in an acclaimed Broadway hip-hop production — would dominate the economic (and political) policies of the Washington administration.

Oddly, however, the state (and economy) that Hamilton envisioned for the United States was most similar to that of *Britain*, which he called "the best [government] in the world." Sure, America had revolted against the mother country, but now, according to the treasury secretary, it needed to model itself after the old empire. Hamilton promoted banks, federal power, and, most controversially, the funding and assumption of state debts.

Remember back to the Revolution when soldiers and merchants were paid in near-worthless Continental paper currency. For fear of starvation and penury, most veterans had little choice but to sell their bills and bonds to wealthy speculators at just a fraction of face value. Now, said Hamilton, the new federal government should assume all state debts — thereby eliminating the need for most state-level taxation — and fund, or pay out, the full face value of the bonds and Continental currency in speculators' hands. Though the states were grateful for the debt relief and citizens appreciated the steadily decreasing rates of local taxation, the plan for funding and assumption was controversial from the start.

It is easy to see why. Economics is rarely a simple matter of dollars and cents, of reason and records. There is also a moral component — even today — along with a sense of the need for justice in public economy. Why, many former soldiers and farmers asked, should already affluent speculators and stockjobbers receive such a windfall from the government? Why should hard-earned tax dollars pay the printed value, rather than the fair market value, of the inflation-prone Revolutionary currency? Shouldn't, as now Hamilton opponent James Madison argued, the government make a distinction between the original holders of the notes and the speculating elites now in possession of most outstanding bonds?

To modern, especially populist ears, these questions seem reasonable — just, even. Nonetheless, Hamilton argued that to develop confidence in the market and earn international credit and standing, the United States must fund the bonds at face value and not distinguish between current and original owners. The funding dispute that arose may seem a slight matter to modern readers, but an understanding may be gained by comparing it with the argument over the Wall Street bank bailouts of 2008 and 2009 at the start of the Great Recession. Furthermore, to understand the passion of the funding debate, consider that upward of 40 percent of federal revenue in the 1790s went to pay interest on the funded debt.

Hamilton's position came to reflect that of most Federalists — mostly wealthy, urban types who were early proponents of the Constitution. To succeed, Hamilton believed, the government must primarily associate and concern itself with the wealthy, commercial elites. Hamilton held a strong belief that human nature was fundamentally selfish and thus there was no other course for a successful government than to fix its hopes on the affluent. Hamilton, of course, was on shaky constitutional ground. But he never wavered. The treasury secretary argued that the Constitution granted the federal government *implied* as well as *enumerated* powers, manifested in the "necessary and proper" clause.

Not everyone agreed. Secretary of State Jefferson and many rural, former Anti-Federalists felt that the Constitution did *not* explicitly authorize Hamilton's program and that federal powers should be strictly limited for the protection of the masses. After all, they exclaimed, didn't we just wage a revolution against such policies? The opponents of Hamilton and his centralizing fiscal programs crafted an identity similar to the "country" Whigs of Britain and began to label Federalists with the notorious pejoratives *Tory* and *loyalist*.

Indeed, differing *economic* interests often linked to *political* interests and factions in the new republic. The commercial world of urban, coastal elites required an efficient transportation network and new roads for the rapid movement of goods into and out of the interior. Taxes, banks, and the funding of debt would be required to generate the requisite investment. Those living in the semi-subsistence, rural world feared central power and were suspicious of "city values," and most of these folks wished mainly to be left alone. Sound familiar? Indeed, this rural-versus-urban and cosmopolitan-versus-provincial conflict is still waged today.

Aftershocks of Revolution: Explaining the Whiskey Rebellion

An insurrection was announced and proclaimed and armed against, and marched against, but could never be found.

— Thomas Jefferson in a letter to
James Monroe (May 26, 1795)

Consider the sketch and the photo on the facing page. The drawing depicts a riotous mob brutalizing and terrorizing a tax collector via the tried-and-true, all-American tactic of tarring and feathering. The

Famous Whiskey Insurrection in Pennsylvania, 1882, by R. M. Devens

A tea party protester in colonial garb, 2009

image is similar to many depicting the struggle against British imperial taxation during the Revolutionary era. However, the scene depicted in *this* illustration is in Pennsylvania and occurs a decade *after* the end of the War of Independence. The taxman is an *American*, a citizen of the United States, being tortured during the Whiskey Rebellion.

The photograph below the drawing depicts a modern American's protest against the perceived excesses of federal taxation in 2009. Indeed, in what would come to be known as the tea party movement, many thousands of Americans — often in colonial-era garb — took to the streets in that most American of public rituals: an anti-tax protest.

Anti-tax and anti-federal sentiment is as American as apple pie and still very much with us. But let's return to the 1790s. Remember that Hamilton's economic program, especially funding and assumption of state debts, would require significant federal revenue, even to pay the requisite interest. Where would this money come from? Customs revenues, mainly, from taxes on imported goods entering the many natural harbors of the East Coast, and also from land sales, which would soon become possible with the conquest of Kentucky and Ohio. Still, neither source of income was sufficient, and thus Hamilton recommended an excise tax on distilled whiskey.

The western farmers along the Appalachian frontier — who often distilled their excess grain into whiskey for barter and sale — would bear the brunt of this new taxation. And with a dearth of hard currency, these rural folk were perhaps the least equipped to pay it. Still, over the vigorous protests of the westerners, the Washington administration levied the tax in 1790.

The affected parties did not acquiesce easily. Most simply ignored the legislation and refused to pay. In western Pennsylvania, however, farmers in four counties openly defied the law, forming "committees of correspondence" (like the earlier anti-British patriots), terrorizing excise officers (in another rerun of the 1760s and '70s) and closing the federal courts (as in Daniel Shays's Rebellion). To the rebels, the far-away Congress had no more right to tax them than had the Parliament in England. They sent petitions to Congress, formed local opposition assemblies, and referred to the feds as "aristocrats" and "mercenary merchants." Here was a semantic struggle for the soul of a new nation.

In other words, matters in western Pennsylvania and up and down the frontier weren't unprecedented. Nevertheless, something had changed. Those protested *against* were now Americans, and the states were now governed by Washington's post-constitutional administration, based just a few hundred miles to the east in Philadelphia. President Washington and the Federalists, fearing that the whole constitutional order might collapse, responded forcefully. In August 1794 the president donned his uniform and led an army of thirteen thousand federalized militiamen — a force larger than any he had commanded in the Revolution — and marched west. This was the first and last time a US president would directly and personally command troops in a time of war or rebellion. How difficult it is, indeed, to picture a contemporary president leading a similar procession toward battle.

The Whiskey Rebellion was the single greatest incident of armed resistance to federal authority until the Civil War, yet the rebels dispersed as quickly as they had gathered once faced with Washington and his massive army. What matters, however, is that it happened at all; that rural unrest remained a powerful force — one that would be reaped by later political parties. Also significant was Washington's response. The first president took the threat of rebellion and fracture very seriously. He knew the shakiness of the new republic and sought to send a message to the rebels. And send one he did, a rejoinder that Revolutionary War–era protests were no longer acceptable, that there would now be severe limits on public opposition to federal policies, and ultimately that the government in Philadelphia, and later Washington, DC, was *the* supreme law of the land.

Conquering Ohio: The US Army, "Mad" Anthony Wayne, and a Doomed People

Civilization or death to all American savages!
— A popular military toast of the 1790s

A great portion of early federal revenue was allotted to interest payments on the funded debt associated with Hamilton's economic program. Most of the rest, however, paid for the US Army to wage war on Indians in the Ohio Country. Indeed, the first half of the 1790s saw some of the most vicious and contested native warfare in American history. Strangely, few Americans now know of the battles of this era.

The United States' hold on the western territories (between the

Appalachian Mountains and the Mississippi River) granted to the new republic in the Treaty of Paris (1783) was extremely tenuous. Spain closed the Mississippi River at New Orleans to American traffic and also tried to attract the loyalty of settlers in Kentucky and Tennessee to the Iberian Crown in Madrid. The British army refused to vacate forts in the Ohio Country and continued to arm and support a growing native confederation still (understandably) hostile to American expansion.

However, in the face of these facts and despite the best, if paltry, efforts of the federal government to regulate and organize the settlement of the fertile lands north of the Ohio River, land-hungry pioneers flooded the territory, often refusing to pay for property and setting off conflict with the local native tribes. It was a mess, as hasty expansion often is. In order to sell the land, systematize the settlement, and attract respectable, law-abiding colonizers, the Washington administration realized it would have to force peace — through conquest or surrender — on the Indians.

The natives, some hundred thousand of them in the trans-Appalachian West, had other ideas. *They* had not been present in Paris or acceded to Britain signing over their homelands to the nascent American settlers' republic. They would not capitulate easily or bargain away their independence. They had taken notice when the US Senate ratified a treaty (the nation's first) with the Southern Creek Indians, and then the corrupt Georgia legislature promptly broke it. In Ohio it was to be war.

The problem for Washington was the diminutive, untrained, ill-disciplined army at his disposal. Though growing under the policies of Hamilton, the army proved feeble in early efforts to bring the natives to heel. In 1790, General Josiah Harmar led some fifteen hundred regulars and militiamen into the northwest Ohio Country. They were defeated in several small skirmishes, with heavy casualties, in the vicinity of present-day Fort Wayne, Indiana. The next year General Arthur St. Clair led some fourteen hundred troops and militia to a disastrous fate. On November 4, 1791, his unprepared troops were surprised and vanquished by a thousand Indians commanded by the Miami chieftain Little Turtle. Six hundred soldiers were killed in by far the largest defeat in the US history of Indian wars. To mock the Americans' land hunger, the natives stuffed soil in the dead men's mouths. It was a national humiliation.

Washington proceeded to build a professional standing army of five thousand troops and doubled the military budget. A Revolutionary War hero, General "Mad" Anthony Wayne, then took two full years to train his newly dubbed "American Legion" before decisively defeating the Indian confederation at the Battle of Fallen Timbers in 1794, near the site of present-day Toledo, Ohio. The British refused to save their Indian allies, as they were not willing to risk war with the American republic (they were already busy combating revolutionary France). The defeat and lack of external support sealed the fate of Ohio Country Indians and broke their resistance for another two decades.

The results of Wayne's victory were immediate and profound. Native tribes submitted or moved westward, and the white settler population exploded. What had been decidedly *Indian* land just a few years earlier quickly resembled the white man's land of the East Coast. Between 1790 and 1820, Kentucky's population grew by a factor of eight. Ohio's population also grew rapidly. Still, something far more fleeting was lost: the age of eastern Indian independence, an era when native tribes had often been able to play one European empire against another. The frenzied Americans' desire for land ultimately posed a greater threat to native autonomy than that of any of the other European imperialists. The growth of the United States — a nation purportedly devoted to the equality of man — spelled the end of a very old and unique Native American culture.

Better Hell Than Party: The Development of Federalist and Republican Factions

> If I could not go to heaven but with a party, I would not go there at all.
>
> — Thomas Jefferson (1789)

> Nothing could be more ill-judged than that intolerant spirit which has, at all times, characterized political parties.
>
> — Alexander Hamilton (1787)

Everyone, it seemed — including President Washington — opposed and feared the formation of political parties, or "factions" as they were often called. Still, the development of political blocs should have come as little surprise. Just as the republic remained divided between proponents and opponents of the Constitution, so Washington's own cabinet was split. The secretary of the treasury, Hamilton, desired that the United States become a centralized, British-style fiscal-military state; meanwhile, Secretary of State Jefferson had become the unofficial leader of numerous skeptics who feared and distrusted the federal government. Neither was initially willing to admit it, but these two foes quickly became the de facto heads of the Federalist and Republican Parties, respectively.

The two emergent political parties had both a domestic and international component. Domestically, the Federalists represented wealthy, urbane holders of proprietary wealth and sought centralization of debts, finances, and power in the federal capital. Hamilton was their intellectual muse, even if the staunchly *anti*-party George Washington emerged as their leader. The Republicans, under the de facto direction of Jefferson, represented more southern, rural, and agricultural interests and sought low taxation and minimal government interference. Jefferson, in fact, portrayed the contest as being not between two discrete political parties but between "aristocrats" (Federalists) and republican "defenders of the Revolution."

The battle was both public and personal. The two men could not have been more different, and, given their divergent backgrounds, we might regard each as more suited to the opposing faction. Instead, in a bit of historical irony, the lowborn son of the Caribbean, Hamilton, brought the poor man's chip on his shoulder to the leadership of the more elitist party. Jefferson, on the other hand, a classically aristocratic gentleman of the South, crowed on about the "common man" and radical republicanism. History, indeed, is often stranger than fiction. Still, despite the underlying animosity, neither Hamilton nor Jefferson can be considered party leaders in the modern sense. In the world of the late eighteenth century, true gentlemen stood *above* politicking or campaigning and relied on sometimes subtle literary attacks and the backing of allies and less prominent partisans.

The contours of this schism — of a kind still seen in our own day — would soon set off a few decades' worth of political combat. Less remembered is the international component. The United States, after all, was never, and will never be, an island unto itself. In the early 1790s just about all of the European Western world became embroiled in what would become a two-decade war with revolutionary France — which had ousted a king and declared a republic in 1789. Jefferson's Republicans favored France in the ensuing global war, and, indeed, many staunch advocates of the revolutionaries argued (not without some merit) that America's 1779 alliance with France obligated the United States to aid the burgeoning republic in its wars.

Thomas Paine, the famous author of the American Revolutionary tract *Common Sense*, considered himself an early-stage "citizen of the world" and, being the professional revolutionary he was, went to serve in the new French National Assembly. Jefferson, too, was remarkably radical — at least in correspondence — in his support for France. Even after the French Revolution executed the king and beheaded tens of thousands of counter-revolutionaries, Jefferson remarked:

> The liberty of the whole earth was dependent on [the French Revolution] . . . and . . . rather than it should have failed, I would have seen half the earth desolated. Were there but an Adam and an Eve left in every country, and left free, it would be better than as it is now.

The Federalists, though initially sympathetic to their old allies and brother republicans, were soon more circumspect. They feared the radicalism and resultant bloodshed of the French Revolution and, if anything, began to favor their British cousins. Essentially, the wars of

Europe polarized political factions across the Atlantic. Passions ran high and partisan divisions deepened.

We should, perhaps, be unsurprised that political parties quickly formed in the United States. This was a highly literate and literary culture, with widespread property ownership, a broad franchise for white men, and many newspapers. These were litigious people, concerned with law, governance, and societal mores. In that sense, despite the politicians' regular proclamations to the contrary — so common in the eighteenth century — America was the *perfect* place for parties and factions to form. This was, in a way, the unintended consequence of the colonists' revolution. Rebellion is messy!

Vital Precedents: The Critical (if Flawed) Character of George Washington

> The alternate domination of one faction over another, sharpened by the spirit of revenge natural to party dissension . . . is itself a frightful despotism . . . sooner or later the chief of some prevailing faction more able or more fortunate than his competitors, turns this disposition to the purposes of his own elevation, on the ruins of Public Liberty.
>
> — George Washington

Washington owned slaves (though he freed them upon his death), had ordered mutineers shot during the war, and was by some measures the wealthiest man in all of America. Still, it is doubtful that any other citizen could have held the early republican experiment together. In his day Washington epitomized public virtue and selflessness. Notoriously thin-skinned and ever cognizant of his reputation, Washington worked hard to bolster this image. Though he had become affiliated with the Federalist faction while serving as president, Washington aspired to be the disinterested arbiter of national affairs. He was certainly seen that way by most Americans; even his critics were loath to publicly disparage the president. It was often said that Washington was denied children of his own so that he could be the "father" of his country. And indeed, he was.

It was assumed that Washington, like Polish kings of the era, would be elected but serve for life — an elective monarch. When the new president appeared in public, bands often played "God Save the King." Washington *was* an aristocrat of sorts, a self-styled gentleman. He believed in the social hierarchy and mores of the colonial era and firmly held that some men were born to rule, others to obey.

Nonetheless, it is to Washington that the US republic may owe its greatest thanks. This man, this figurehead and celebrity of the Revolution, set many precedents as chief executive that have stood the test of time. Few of his successors dared to defy the unwritten codes Washington had set. He did not accept a crown though there were moments he might well have become a king; he stood apart from much legislative business and respected the prerogatives of Congress; he kept the United States out of foreign wars and, indeed, warned against entanglements in fixed alliances or other nations' conflicts.

Most important, however, he *left*. After two terms, though he was not legally obliged to do so, Washington chose to step down, retire, and allow for a new presidential election. Had he not, it is doubtful that any of his successors would have done so; the United States may very well have mutated into a British-style constitutional monarchy. As it was, thirty consecutive executives followed the Washington precedent, and only after Franklin D. Roosevelt broke with the tradition in 1940 did a later Congress amend the Constitution to include presidential term limits. We cannot overestimate the significance of Washington's decision.

––––––

Be that as it may, Washington would pass along to his successors a divided nation; a nation cleaved into increasingly oppositional factions of Federalists and Republicans; a nation at the brink of war with Britain, France, Spain, or some combination of the three; a nation still engaged in westward conquest and fierce combat with Native Americans; and, of course, a nation uncertain as to its future.

Though Washington has lent his name to currency, schools, cities, and parks, it is a sadly ironic truth that most of the stoic warnings from his farewell address were quickly ignored. Within four years of his retirement bitterly oppositional political parties brought the nation close to revolution. By 1812 the United States would wage an indecisive war with Britain, and in the twentieth century it would sign on to multiple, permanent foreign alliances of precisely the sort Washington feared. What, then, would the first president think of NATO, or of modern America's relationship with Israel or Saudi Arabia?

If Washington held the new country together, it was only just so — a near-run thing. The American experiment is precarious still.[8]

10

LIBERTY VERSUS ORDER

Liberty, once lost, is lost forever.

— John Adams in a letter to his wife, Abigail (1775)

[A social division exists] between the rich and the poor, the laborious and the idle, the learned and the ignorant. . . . Nothing, but force, and power and strength can restrain [the latter].

— John Adams in a letter to Thomas Jefferson (1787)

Two quotes from the same person. Barely a decade between them. How can a man be so seemingly conflicted? John Adams, who helped lead the revolution against British tyranny, would later become a president apt to suppress dissent and restrict a free press at home. Adams was a complicated man, and the United States was — and is — a complicated nation.

As John Adams succeeded the quintessential American hero, George Washington, becoming the second president of the United States, division pervaded the land, and a debate raged in both the public and private space: Shall we have liberty or order? Could a people expect a measure of both?

Adams, though an early patriot leader and the nation's first vice president, had neither the notoriety nor the unifying potential of George Washington. And he knew it. Ill tempered, insecure, and highly sensitive, Adams appeared unsuited for the difficult task at hand. The body politic was fracturing into opposing factions — his own Federalists and the Jeffersonian Republicans — while the country itself was swept to the brink of war, first with Britain and then with revolutionary France.

Looking back, the ending seems preordained: *of course* the republic could never have failed, we are prone to believe. Only this was far from a certainty, and the outcome was a near-run thing. America nearly came apart in the crisis of 1798–99.

Divided at the Onset: Republicans, Federalists, and Conspiracies Against Liberty

Even a quick glance at the electoral map from 1796 demonstrates not only how close the contest was but also how divided the various regions were. Indeed, even in this first truly contested election (Washington's two terms seemed predestined) one notes an emerging sectional division between a Federalist North and a Republican South. Remember that this was an era in which most northern states had begun to phase out slavery, whereas the South developed an increasingly slave-dependent society. The Federalists dominated in the North, especially along the coast. John Adams was a Massachusetts man, Jefferson a Virginia planter. The division is striking — as though the next century's Civil War was fated from the start. It wasn't, of course; nothing truly is, but no doubt the seeds were there.

The North, in addition to having a smaller enslaved population, was highly commercial and increasingly urbanized. The South remained an agrarian slave society. Still, slavery was not the main division in the second half of the 1790s. Liberty itself was the defining concern — liberty's exact contours and the limits of dissent.

Not that the election of 1796 bore much resemblance to our modern contests. Both candidates stayed home, neither actively campaigned, and each left it to friends, allies, and sympathetic newspapermen to make their respective cases. Nonetheless, Adams and Jefferson — once and future friends — epitomized exceedingly divergent governing philosophies.

Adams lacked the vigor and extremist positions of some Federalists (notably Alexander Hamilton) but believed fervently in the need for a strong, central government to calm and control the tempers of the states and the public alike. Once an ambassador in London, he tended to favor the British in their ongoing worldwide war with France.

Jefferson, conversely, distrusted centralized power and never overcame his youthful Revolutionary hatred for all things British. It was Jefferson, recall, who remarked during Shays's Rebellion in Massachusetts that "a little rebellion" now and again was "a good thing." He had been ambassador to Paris and remained faithful in his support of revolutionary France.

So divided were the American people over this ongoing, destructive war in Europe that ardent Republicans took to wearing liberty caps — stocking-like headgear favored by French republicans — and French-style tricolor cockades on their hats. Federalists, usually sympathetic to the former mother country, responded in kind by adopting a black cockade with a white button to differentiate themselves from the Francophile Republicans.

And in a system that may seem farcical to modern readers, Jefferson — who was narrowly defeated — would therefore become Adams's *vice president*. Until the later adoption of the Twelfth Amendment, the Constitution stipulated that the second highest vote-getter would serve as vice president. Imagine Hillary Clinton serving beside President Trump. The expectation in the day was that country would — for good gentlemen, at least — precede party loyalties. That assumption was wrong more often than not.

The political culture was also absurdly different from our own day. Personal honor was a deadly serious matter, and dueling (sometimes, though rarely, to the death) constituted an elaborate political ritual to protect reputations. Fistfights broke out on the floor of Congress. It all made sense in an odd way. In the tumultuous 1790s neither side saw the opposition as possessing a credible dissent. Rather, the fight appeared *existential* — with the other side representing a threat to liberty or order itself! Federalists used the once-pejorative, but gradually more acceptable, term *democrat* to describe their unseemly, anarchic Republican foes. To Jefferson's Republicans, Adams and his ilk were not "federal" in any sense of the word; rather, they were monarchists, aristocrats even, and the enemies of liberty!

Such was the volatile setting when outright war with France nearly broke out.

The First War on Terror: Immigration, Sedition, and the Quasi-War

> The time is now come when it will be proper to declare that nothing but birth shall entitle a man to citizenship in this country.
>
> — Federalist congressman Robert Goodloe Harper

> [The Alien Act] is a most detestable thing . . . worthy of the 8th or 9th century . . . dangerous to the peace and safety of the United States.
>
> — Vice President Thomas Jefferson (1798)

Imagine a nation at war with a revolutionary ideology. Not a full-fledged, declared war, but a seemingly endless conflict against an amorphous entity thought to imperil the very fiber of the republic. Fear abounds — fear of foreigners, of subversives within. Elected leaders begin to restrict immigration, to deport aliens, and to police the untrustworthy media. Nothing short of avid patriotism is acceptable in the midst of the ongoing crisis. Americans are at one another's throats.

In 1798 revolutionary France — to which Americans arguably owed their independence — and the United States were brought to the verge of war. The French seized US ships on the high seas en route to trade with Britain, still a top commercial partner for American merchants. When President Adams sent envoys to discuss the matter, they were belittled and dictated to by three French agents. The agents were later described by the envoys as Mr. X, Y, and Z, and each had demanded humiliating apologies and bribes as a precondition to even *begin* negotiations. Adams recalled his envoys, and the American people seethed with anger. The bribery demand was particularly gall-

PROPERTY PROTECTED à la Françoise.

A British satirical depiction of French-American relations in 1798 after the so-called XYZ Affair

ing, and one American envoy, according to a later newspaper account, declared that the United States would spend "millions for defense, but not one cent for tribute!"

The Federalists felt vindicated. Indeed, the party would win elections up and down the Atlantic Coast in this period. Alarmist factions within the Federalist ranks began to question the very patriotism and loyalty of the "fifth column" of Republicans. Riots broke out in Philadelphia between pro-French and pro-British factions, and Republican newspaper editors were attacked. Conspiracy theories and exaggeration of threats abounded. As tensions rose, President Adams called for a day of prayer and fasting as a show of national unity. One particularly onerous rumor spread during the fast: Republican insurgents, so said the scaremongers, planned to burn the US capital.

As the war drums beat, Adams asked Congress to sanction a Quasi-War with France, what Adams called "the half war," and indeed the resolution passed. Merchant ships were armed, and the military budget soared, though hysteria spread faster than actual combat at sea. Hard-line Federalists feared civil war and seemed to spy treasonous French agents around every corner. Nativism and fear pervaded the land, as is likely to happen during a war scare.

What followed was a veritable constitutional crisis — perhaps this nation's first. Fear of foreign French intriguers, and their *Irish* allies, expanded like wildfire. In response, Congress first passed the Naturalization Act, which extended the wait before applying for citizenship from five to fourteen years. Then the Alien Friends Act gave the president the extraordinary power to expel, without due process, any alien he judged to be "dangerous to peace and safety." It must be said that no aliens were actually expelled by Adams, but the accumulation of so much discretion and power in the executive branch terrified Republicans.

Even more worrisome were the subsequent attacks on the "disloyal" press — meaning Republican or non-Federalist newspapers. This was a remarkable power to grant the federal government, seeing as newspapers were the central medium of communication and the glue that held together partisan factions of the day. The actual text of the Sedition Act, read today, is chilling. The legislation declared it a crime to

> [w]rite, print, utter or publish . . . any false, scandalous, and malicious writings against the Government of the United States, or either House of the Congress of the United States, with the intent to defame the said government, or either House of Congress, or the President, or to bring them . . . into contempt or disrepute, or to excite against them . . . the hatred of the good people of the United States.

How could it be, the modern reader might ask, that an elected body could so restrict the beloved freedom of the press less than two decades after a revolution was waged in defiance of tyranny? And, indeed, the vote on the matter was highly contested and narrow: 44–41 in the House of Representatives.

Vice President Jefferson, a fierce opponent of the bill, no doubt took notice that the defamation of the *vice* president was conspicuously absent from the text of the Sedition Act. He saw the bill for what it

was: a thinly veiled "suppression of the Whig [Republican] presses."
What, after all, many Republicans asked, had we *just fought a war for,*
if not for freedom of speech and of the press?

This time, unlike in the Alien Act, the legislation was quickly put to
use by Federalist courts. Twenty-five people were arrested, seventeen
indicted, and ten convicted (some jailed). Most were neither spies
nor traitors, but rather Republican-sympathizing newspapermen.
The government even arrested Benjamin Franklin Bache (grandson
of the esteemed founder), who died of yellow fever before his trial.
The Sedition Act expired at the end of Adams's administration, but its
specifics were not declared unconstitutional until a case was brought
forward by *The New York Times* in the 1960s!

This was politics, not national security, and the Republicans knew
it. Some of those jailed styled themselves martyrs of liberty. One,
Matthew Lyons, successfully ran for Congress from within his prison
cell. Partisan loyalties had divided an administration and brought the
nation to the verge of civil war.

Seeds of Secession: Jefferson, Madison, and the Virginia/Kentucky Resolutions

> A little patience, and we shall see the reign of witches
> pass over, their spells dissolve, and the people, recover-
> ing their true sight, restore the government to its true
> principles.
>
> — Vice President Thomas Jefferson referring to the
> Sedition Act in a letter to John Taylor (1798)

The beleaguered Republicans would not go down without a fight.
Despite the suppression of the press, the actual number of Republican-
leaning newspapers exploded. And though the resurgent Federalists
controlled the Congress in Philadelphia, prominent Republicans
turned to the state legislatures to oppose the Alien and Sedition Acts.
As the tensions rose, so did the rhetoric. Many opponents of the bills

took to referring to the federal government as a "foreign jurisdiction." This is not dissimilar to the language employed today by some libertarian ranchers in the American West and some militiamen.

Jefferson himself believed that the federal government — of which he was vice president! — had become "more arbitrary, and [had] swallowed more of the public liberty than even that of England." James Madison, an old and true Jefferson ally, left retirement and entered the Virginia legislature. Now Jefferson the disgruntled vice president and Madison the lowly state representative set to work making the case for the unconstitutionality of the Alien and Sedition Acts.

They did not, interestingly, turn to the federal courts. These they saw as Federalist dominated, and besides, the modern conception of judicial review was not yet established. Instead, in a far more devious — though potentially problematic — way Madison and Jefferson drafted state resolutions for Kentucky and Virginia, which made the extraordinary claim that *state* governments could rightfully declare federal legislation they deemed unconstitutional to be "void and of no force." Essentially, states could nullify federal law because, as the resolutions asserted, the Constitution was but a "compact" among the many states.

Kentucky and Virginia urged the other states to pass similar resolutions, though none saw fit to do so. Still, this was a remarkable moment that set a dangerous precedent. Furthermore, unfortunately, Jefferson's and Madison's attempts to protect civil liberties blazed a perilous path. The concept of nullification and, finally, of southern *secession* would spring from the same lines of argument the two esteemed founders set forth in the Virginia and Kentucky Resolutions. Civil war, of course, was the unforeseen result.

Good Men, Bad Politicians: John Adams and the Peace That Ended a Presidency

Armies, and debts, and taxes are the known instruments
for bringing the many under the domination of the few.
— James Madison (1795)

In addition to legislation meant to ensure order, Adams and the Federalists actively prepared the nation for war. Adams, for one, was doubtful that France could or would ever invade, but he preferred that the nation be prepared. Other ultra-Feds, like Hamilton, saw opportunities for the power and expansion of the federal government during the war scare.

More naval funding was authorized in one year than in all previous congresses to date. And ultimately, a country that had once vehemently opposed standing armies now raised a "New Army" twelve thousand men strong. Pushing for this rapid expansion was Alexander Hamilton, who more than any other founder desired a European-style fiscal-military state. In fact, Hamilton wanted to *lead* said army, though he settled for second in command to the largely ceremonial leadership of George Washington, again called out of retirement.

War hysteria quickly got out of hand. Republicans feared, not without some merit, that the true purpose of this New Army was to suppress the political opposition. Indeed, most of the officers appointed to the new force were of Federalist leaning. But Hamilton had even more grandiose notions than domestic oppression. He saw opportunities aplenty in the case of a war he seems to have truly desired. War with France, he argued, would allow the seizure of Louisiana, Florida, and maybe even distant *Venezuela* from France and Spain!

President Adams, though, had far more common sense and retained enough of the Revolutionary Spirit of '76 to deny Hamilton the supreme command and the empire that the man so desired. "Never in my life," Adams later recalled, "did I hear a man [Hamilton] talk more like a fool." In a letter to a colleague, Adams went so far as to declare Hamilton "the greatest intriguant in the World — a man devoid of every moral principle — a Bastard."

George Washington too quickly lost interest in the military expansion and soon returned to Mount Vernon, and eventually tensions and the war scare eased. But the main catalyst for peace was President Adams himself. Adams retained some of his fear of standing armies, loathed Hamilton, and knew that war was the last thing the new nation needed.

Thus, without consulting his cabinet and in opposition to his own party agenda, Adams sent a peace mission to France. This action cooled the Quasi-War and averted a civil crisis. It was not, however, a prudent *political* move. The actions of Adams inadvertently divided his once-ascendant Federalist Party just before the election of 1800 — when he would again face off against his vice president, Jefferson.

A (flawed) patriot more than a politician, Adams dismissed the Hamiltonians in his cabinet and secured the Treaty of Mortefontaine, bringing to an end the Quasi-War with France. Unfortunately for Adams the paltry politician, word of this diplomatic coup did not reach American shores until he had been defeated in the 1800 balloting.

Liberty or Order: The Eternal Debate

> The Federalists of the 1790s stood in the way of popular democracy as it was emerging in the United States, and thus they became heretics opposed to the developing democratic faith.
>
> — Historian Gordon Wood (2009)

It never ends, the debate. Even now, it is as though Adams and Jefferson were still alive, battling for the possession of our American souls. The relevant issues from the 1790s are as plentiful as they are astounding. So many of the questions of yesteryear are precisely those with which Americans grapple in the twenty-first century: How free should the press be? What constitutes libel? How should government treat leakers and whistleblowers? And what of immigration? Are foreigners a threat to the body politic?

The Patriot Act, warrantless surveillance, torture, race, ethnicity, the bounds of protest (see the NFL kneeling dispute), the biased media, drones, Guantanamo, the scope of federal and executive power. It's all there, isn't it? Adams and Jefferson, if suddenly brought back to life in today's United States, would not be able to fathom an iPhone but would no doubt be ready to weigh in on debates regarding searches and seizures of those devices. On one level we've come so far, on another . . . not so much.

The common denominator in all of this seems to be war — or the fear provoked by war and the threat of it. It matters not whether the United States wages a Quasi-War with France on the high seas or fights a shapeless enemy like "terror" across the Greater Middle East. The questions remain, the passions flare. We divide into camps, armed — sometimes literally — and oriented on our domestic enemies. Today's "liberals" are not seen as misguided although valued countrymen but as traitorous weaklings ready to sell out America. "Conservatives" aren't folks standing for time-tested values but instead are fascist authoritarians bent on tyranny.

It all seems so far off the rails. And it is dangerous.

Through modern eyes, we are apt to see this division as a unique and exceptional feature of contemporary politics. But, oh no, it was always thus.

11

THE JEFFERSONIAN ENIGMA

The "revolution of 1800" . . . was as real a revolution in
the principles of our government as that of [17]76 was in
its form; not effected indeed by the sword, as that, but
by the rational and peaceable instrument of reform, the
suffrage of the people.

— Thomas Jefferson in a letter to
Judge Spencer Roane (1819)

We tend today, in our hyper-partisan moment, to imagine that politics have *never* been worse, more tribal, more contentious than they
are now. But is that true? The United States was born of revolution,
fought a bloody civil war, and has changed time and again throughout its history. And in 1800 the nascent republic would experience
its first-ever electoral transition to a president of the opposing party.
That election and its aftermath would have profound implications
for the young republic and ensure some degree of Jeffersonian legacy
for generations to come. Jefferson's words — the output of his pen —
were often beautiful, but some darkness lurked beneath the surface of
his self-proclaimed republican, agrarian utopia.

The Revolution of 1800: John Adams, Thomas Jefferson, and the Partisan Rancor of an Election

The insults, untruths, and outright verbal attacks during the 2016 election season shocked the American conscience and rattled the republic. Still, even the worst of exchanges between twenty-first-century
politicians hardly compare to the pejorative language slung in both
directions by supporters of rivals John Adams (the sitting president,

seeking reelection) and Thomas Jefferson (the sitting vice president, seeking the presidency) in the election of 1800.

Jeffersonian newspapermen called President Adams and the Federalists "loyalists," "monarchists," "Tories," and the "British faction." Essentially, so the thinking went, these Federalists, led by Adams, were traitors, and loyal Republicans needed to "turn out [to vote] and save [their] country from ruin!"

Of course, the fierce rhetoric ran both ways. One Federalist paper predicted that, should Vice President Jefferson be elected president, "murder, robbery, rape, adultery, and incest will be openly taught and practiced, the air will be rent with the cries of the distressed, and the soil will be soaked with blood." With the ad hominem attacks running at that fever pitch, it is little wonder that the country seemed to be on the verge of civil war after the election results were so close that the matter had to be sent to the Congress for adjudication. Rumors and conspiracies flourished, and many armed themselves for the expected chaos.

It never came. After dozens of tied votes in the House between Jefferson and his preferred vice president, Aaron Burr, a number of Federalists relented and handed victory to Jefferson. In the convoluted system of the day, presidential electors in the Electoral College did not designate which of the two men running on a given ticket (Federalist or Republican) was preferred as president and which as vice president. Therefore, when Jefferson bested Adams in a rather close election, both he and his running mate, Burr, had the same electoral vote count. Loathing Jefferson deeply, some Federalists threatened to throw their support behind Burr, but, after dozens of tied votes, a few Federalists — ironically under the direction of Jefferson's sworn enemy, Alexander Hamilton — gave in and ensured Jefferson's election.

Did this constitute a revolution? It is hard to say. Certainly Jefferson thought so, and indeed the governing theories of the Federalists and the Jeffersonian Republicans were almost diametrically opposed. The two parties even celebrated different holidays marking the birth of the nation, with the Republicans focused on the more egalitarian celebration of Jefferson's Declaration of Independence (July Fourth), while the Federalists favored a celebration of Washington's birthday. This was, truly, a country divided.

What *is* certain is that the United States had (just barely) survived its first peaceful transfer of elected power from an incumbent president to an opposition successor. Think of all the recent European, African, and Asian countries that have struggled so mightily, and often failed, to pass that vital democratic test.

Still, there remained something disturbing about the 1800 (and 1796) election map. The nation was clearly dividing into opposing sections. Nearly the entire South voted Republican, and absolutely all of New England went Federalist. The division was about more than the peculiar institution of slavery — though that played a part — and came down to conflicting worldviews of what republican, post-Revolutionary society should be. For the Jeffersonians, the future was agrarian, expansive, ultimately dominated by the "people," the yeomanry. Its future lay westward. The Federalists were often commercial elites with proprietary wealth and aristocratic ambitions. They looked to the east, to the sea, and to Europe for the country's future.

It is all so bizarre in hindsight: Jefferson — a textbook planter aristocrat with some two hundred slaves — sought to represent small farmers in the South and what was then considered the West, and middling artisans in the North. Adams, though a successful lawyer and proponent of powerful federal governance, owned no slaves and lacked the plantation lifestyle of Jefferson the gentlemen.

Republican Reforms: The Jeffersonian Utopia

> But every difference of opinion is not a difference of principle. We have called by different names brethren of the same principle. We are all Republicans, we are all Federalists.
>
> — Jefferson's first inaugural address (March 4, 1801)

There are no red states or blue states, just the United
States. . . . [T]here is not a liberal and a conservative
America — there is only the United States of America.
            — Senator Barack Obama speaking at the
              Democratic National Convention (2004)

Ultimately Jefferson, the wealthy planter who claimed to speak
for the lowliest laborer, emerged victorious in the presidential
election of 1800. Knowing how close the nation had come to civil
strife, Jefferson, not half the public speaker that he was a writer,
used his inaugural address as a call for unity. Not everyone bought
it. Jefferson's two terms were highly partisan, antagonistic, and
controversial. The Federalists could hardly stomach the man; most
Republicans worshipped him.

Nevertheless, whether or not his victory constituted a "revolution," Jefferson's America underwent profound changes, democratizing certain aspects of society and of the civic culture. Staying true,
initially, to his principles, Jefferson began slashing federal spending
and federal departments. Hamilton's old Department of the Treasury
was eviscerated. Jeffersonians believed in a small, unobtrusive government and sought to create one.

An early target for the Jeffersonians was the Federalist-dominated
army. Defense spending was cut, troop numbers decreased, and —
somewhat counterintuitively — a new federal military academy, at
West Point, was begun in 1802. But a closer look indicates that even
this had political motivations. West Point was to be a training ground
for *Republican*-inclined officers, an antidote to the many Federalist
officers in the ranks.

Political changes translated to social changes as (at least white
male) society democratized. In referring to those higher on the socio-
economic ladder, workers and servants ditched the titles *master* and
mistress for *Mr.* and *Mrs.*; the more colloquial and less deferential
Dutch term of *boss* often served as a substitute for *master* as well.
Indeed, if, as Jefferson famously wrote, "all men were created equal,"

then why adhere to any hierarchy at all? The Federalists were aghast at the comeuppance of these unfettered masses and pined, ironically, for a pre-Revolutionary society.

Empire of Liberty: Jefferson and the West

We shall . . . add to the empire of liberty an extensive and fertile country.

> — Thomas Jefferson in a letter to
> George Rogers Clark (1780)

I infer that the less we say about the constitutional difficulties respecting Louisiana the better, and what is necessary for surmounting them must be done.

> — Jefferson to James Madison (1803)

Suffice to say, it wasn't exactly "street legal" — the famous Louisiana Purchase, that is. Could it really be constitutional for federal agents, appointed by the government, to purchase an immense tract of land and double the size of the country without explicit authorization from the president or Congress? The envoys were supposed to buy only New Orleans and ended up paying a bargain price for a vast continent. You would think the small-government, constitutionally constructivist Republicans would be appalled at such an expansion of federal power. And yet Jefferson and many of his followers thought it vital and in America's interest.

It's ironic, really. After all, vast new territories inevitably meant a groundswell of government officials: surveyors, marshals, and soldiers to garrison the frontier; Indian agents to negotiate treaties; and so on. Still, Jefferson saw the expansion of his famed "empire of liberty" as pragmatic as well as idealistic, because the new nation had a small army and feared the presence of French and Spanish lands to the south and west and British power to the north. Acquiring Louisiana would make America a continental power once and for all and keep Napoleon's France from threatening the young republic.

Still, Jefferson was motivated by much more than that. He always looked westward, was veritably *obsessed* with the West all his life (though he never traveled there). He was awestruck by native peoples but contributed greatly to their eventual expulsion and destruction. The Louisiana Purchase, after all, spelled disaster to the then independent Native American nations that actually lived there. Still, Jefferson thought the extension of republican modernity would lift Indian living standards and turn Native Americans into modern, democratic farmers.

That was the point, Jefferson believed. The United States must not look to the sea or to Europe when modeling society. Europe, the Old World, remained monarchical and hierarchical to the core. For the American republic to blossom, it must remain a nation of small, independent farmers. Landownership and self-sufficiency made for the best republican citizens. By this logic, and given America's exploding population, expansion was not only desirable but also *necessary* — an existential matter, indeed.

To the end of his life, Jefferson seems to have believed that he could organize and rationalize the settlement of the New West and thereby save Native Americans. Ultimately, however, the slipshod tide of settlement inundated the tiny federal bureaucracy, leading to squatting, overdevelopment, and the stealing of native lands. Violence begat violence, and the outnumbered Indians were overwhelmed. Jefferson, perhaps the most expansion-minded president in American history, summed up the triumph thusly: "No constitution was ever before so well calculated as ours for extensive *empire* [emphasis mine] and self-government." Of course, he meant an empire and self-government for *white* Americans. The natives hardly stood a chance.

American Sphinx: The Unknowable Character of Thomas Jefferson

[Jefferson], the philosophical visionary, may be ideally suited to be a college professor, but is not suited to be the leader of a great nation.

— Alexander Hamilton in a letter to Rufus King (1802)

Jefferson's idealism regarding Indian policy was just one of many contradictions at the heart of his life and political philosophy. So much has been written about this fascinating, ingenious, and deeply flawed founder that he almost appears unknowable.

The native enthusiast who opened western land and the path to Indian expulsion. The opponent of federal power who agreed to keep the national bank, waged a naval war with Barbary pirates, and nearly shut down the American economy through the severe restrictions of his Embargo Act, meant to gain leverage over the feuding British and French by cutting all trade with both. The lifelong critic of standing armies who funded a national military academy.

Furthermore, he was an opponent of slavery, at least in certain writings, who himself owned more than two hundred human beings. The man obsessed with the supposed evils of racial mixing who himself fathered several children with his slave Sally Hemmings. That story, more than all the others, may best personify the complexity of Jefferson the man.

Jefferson's wife, Martha, died at age thirty-three after suffering difficult childbirths and several months after the birth of her last child. Jefferson, who was heartbroken, was thirty-nine at the time. From his wife he inherited many slaves. One, the teenage Sally Hemmings, was one-fourth black and — because she was the child of Martha's father — was Martha's *half sister*. It was common for slave owners, through rape, to impregnate women they owned. According to some reports, Sally and Martha, sharing a father, looked alike. Jefferson would eventually father a number of children with Hemmings. These children, one-eighth black, remained enslaved on Jefferson's plantation to the end of his life, often working in the house. Visitors to Monticello were known to remark on the resemblance of some of Jefferson's slaves to their master.

This was the family of Jefferson, of the man who penned "all men are created equal" and clamored about the evils of racial mixing. Though rumors of Jefferson's miscegenation were common even at the time (see the cartoon on the following page), most historians refused to believe the Hemmings story until, in recent decades, it was incontrovertibly proved, in large part through DNA testing. It seems that

A PHILOSOPHIC COCK

1804 caricature

generations of historians, enamored by this Founding Father, second in esteem only to George Washington, could not bring themselves to accept his hypocrisies.

We'll never know for sure, but I tend to believe that Jefferson loved Sally, that her resemblance to his dead wife comforted a grieving and lonely man. This does not excuse Jefferson's blatant hypocrisy but does, I think, illustrate the complexity of humans, then and now.

Between Freedom and Slavery: Jefferson, Free Blacks, and Republican Slaves

The rights of human nature [are] deeply wounded by this infamous practice [of importing slaves] and the abolition of domestic slavery is the great object of desire in those colonies where it was unhappily introduced in their infant state.

— Thomas Jefferson (1774)

Jefferson was not alone in walking a tense and fine line between freedom and slavery. Indeed, the entire republic toed that line throughout the Jeffersonian era and until the Civil War. Society, especially in the North, was democratizing. Larger and larger segments of the population could vote, and they called for more rights and less social deference. In the post-Revolutionary period of idealism and excitement, many — North and South — began to predict the coming end of slavery. They were horribly mistaken.

In fact, southern plantation chattel slavery was about to enter its golden era. Eli Whitney's invention of the cotton gin meant that the demand for this new cash crop would explode, requiring more hands to pick and carry it. Slavery also expanded into the new southwest territories gained in the Louisiana Purchase. Furthermore, fear — visceral white fear — drove planters to tighten the proverbial leash and institute a slave culture even more reliant on terror.

In the 1790s and 1800s another New World possession, a former colony, became just the second country to gain its independence from colonial masters. We might imagine that the United States would be thrilled to embrace this kindred spirit of a nation. But this was a *black* country: Haiti. The Haitian slaves and free blacks had waged a brutal war of independence with France for more than a decade. There was slaughter on both sides, and many white planters were murdered or became refugees. This newly independent black republic was the absolute talk of the town, and news of its brutality spread widely.

The very existence, and example, of the Haitian overthrow of the French terrified southern planters in the United States. They knew that even their own slaves had heard talk of the black victory in Haiti. Thus when a Virginia slave named Gabriel plotted a similar, though smaller, uprising in 1800, the uncovered conspirators were dealt with harshly: dozens were hanged. Jefferson's American republic, in fact, so feared the Haitian rebels that the United States would not recognize the independence of this sister republic in the Western Hemisphere until the American Civil War.

Still, due to manumission — grants and purchases of freedom — and free black immigration, a class of independent African Americans began to grow, especially in the North. The presence of these free, sometimes educated black people caused unease among northern *and* southern whites. Fears sparked by the role of free blacks in the Haitian Revolution, and by Gabriel's conspiracy, led northern and southern states alike to move backward and further restrict the rights of free black people. Northern states developed segregated communities, took away or banned black people's right to vote, and otherwise restricted their freedom. Southern states passed "black codes" similar to those of the later Jim Crow era and eventually expelled most or all free black people to the north of the Mason-Dixon Line.

Consider the irony: Jeffersonian America, while a substantially democratizing white, male society, actually restricted the freedom of free black people and hardened the institution of slavery (even though slavery *was* gradually ending in the northern states) into its most brutal manifestation in American history. As such, a free black man in New York or Boston tended to have *more rights* in 1790 than in 1808 — at the end of Jefferson's second term.

———

As with Jefferson the man, so it was with Jeffersonian America writ large. A mess, a mass of contradictions; a darkness lurking beneath and tottering the nation's very foundations. Already northern society and southern were diverging. Already the contradictions of liberty for some (white men) and slavery or destruction for others (blacks and natives) were shaking the nation.

It was the burden of our American society to bear this inconvenient and uncomfortable fact: our most ardently democratic founder, with a pen of gold and ideas so beautiful they can move us to tears, was also a slave owner who signed the death warrant of many thousands of Indians and of an entire way of life.

Still, Jefferson — for all his flaws — remains forever bound up in the fabric of America's past and also of its present. His democratizing instincts, agrarian glamorizing, and distrust of federal power are alive still in the American psyche and within the platforms of modern political parties. Jefferson's contradictions are America's too. Then, and now.[9]

12

THE FORGOTTEN AND PECULIAR WAR OF 1812

> Strange indeed did it appear to me to find so many names, familiar household words, as enemies — the very names of officers in our own army.... How uncomfortably like a civil war.
>
> — British lieutenant John Le Couteur upon visiting a US Army camp (1813)

Americans, sadly, know little of our own history. Who among us recalls anything about the War of 1812? Few, if any. What those few *do* tend to remember are patriotic anecdotes from a long-ago war: Andrew Jackson mowing down foolish redcoats at the Battle of New Orleans; Dolly Madison saving the portrait of George Washington just before the British burned down the capital; Francis Scott Key penning "The Star Spangled Banner" as he observed the bombardment of Fort McHenry.

These are carefully selected snapshots in an otherwise hazy war. None of this comes together — except in the minds of academic historians — into anything resembling a coherent tale. Why did we fight? Was it necessary? Did we *win*? The cherry-picked anecdotes of jingoism answer none of these vital questions, but ask them we must. The decision to take a nation to war, to send young men into combat, is a solemn one indeed. And the War of 1812 is one of only *five* wars the United States has officially declared.

The conflict deserves our attention for the last reason alone, but also because the war and its complexities are instructive to today's engaged citizen. Though it is rarely remembered this way, in some ways this was a *civil* war, fought between men who spoke the same language, practiced the same religion, and had remarkably similar customs. It was also a war of conquest, suffered worst by the native peoples of the Ohio Country and Upper Canada. It was, too, a side-show theater of the broader Napoleonic Wars (1792–1815); as historian Gordon Wood wrote, "The US was *born* amidst a world at war."

This much is certain: It was a peculiar war, full, in equal measure, of paradox and farce. Thousands died, but little was gained. In some cases brother fought brother. And in a strange irony, the side that best championed liberty was not always American. For all its complexity, perhaps *because* of it, the War of 1812 deserves a fresh look.

An Unnecessary War? The Strange Path to Conflict

[The War of 1812 was] a metaphysical war, a war not for conquest, not for defense, not for sport, [but rather] a war for honour, like that of the Greeks against Troy.
— Republican politician John Taylor of Virginia

Why fight another war with Great Britain? Why fight it in 1812? These are, and were, important questions for the leaders of the nascent American republic. Most histories, and most rhetoric of the day, focused on British insults inflicted upon the American state. Much of the controversy was naval and involved the American struggle to protect its neutral rights to trade with any and all of the warring parties in Europe. Impressment — the British practice of boarding US merchant ships and capturing or forcing the enlistment of American sailors (the Brits claimed they were all British navy deserters) — was considered the most heinous affront of all.

Still, this was an odd grievance over which to start a war. After all, the British Empire had a massive army and unparalleled naval strength. The young American republic was unprepared for war and nearly defense-less. Besides, the British had a point. Though they often captured genuine American citizens, America's own secretary of the treasury estimated that up to one-third of American sailors were indeed British deserters. And it makes sense: the United States paid more, had lower standards of discipline, and wasn't at war! The British were engaged in an existential struggle with French Emperor (and continent conqueror)

Napoleon Bonaparte. They *needed* those deserters back to man the navy that protected the British Isles. Stranger still, soon after the United States declared war, Britain repealed the Orders in Council, the very policy that resulted in impressment. Once President James Madison received word of this reversal, the United States might have rescinded the declaration and saved thousands of lives. It did not.

Part of the reason is this: the War of 1812 was about honor as much as anything else. The ancient Greek historian Thucydides claimed that nations go to war for either "fear, honor, or interest." Wars fought primarily for honor rarely appear in the course of history, but this was one such case. The Americans felt the British had disrespected them and were trying to maintain the United States as a de facto colonial dependency. Many Republican leaders became avid "war hawks" — adding that term forever to the American lexicon — and believed that war with Britain would be a regenerative, purifying, and unifying act. They would be proved wrong, but not before thousands perished in two and a half years of combat.

There were other motives for this war besides the affirmation of neutral rights and the reclamation of national honor. Many westerners (who tended to be avid Republicans) had long coveted Canada, then a British colony. In fact, the Continental army had previously attempted, unsuccessfully, to conquer Canada during the Revolutionary War. And strikingly, the first American constitution, the Articles of Confederation, claimed the province of Canada as a future state within the expanding American union. In 1812, "Free Canada!" became a rallying cry, and the United States would spend most of the war in this fruitless endeavor. *We* were the invaders!

Other American westerners, especially in the Ohio and Michigan Country, feared and loathed the Native Americans who had the gall to demand autonomy. Ever-expansive settlers wanted all land east of the Mississippi and saw war with Britain as a means to that end. The Brits, after all, were allegedly arming and funding the very native peoples who had the propensity to raid American settlements. The powerful native confederation — recently brokered by the Shawnee chief Tecumseh — had to be broken. War would make that possible.

Seen through a wider lens, the American declaration of war is discomfiting. By attacking Britain, the young republic was now tacitly allied with the dictator Napoleon Bonaparte of France in his ongoing war with the United Kingdom — a hypocrisy the British relished pointing out.

There were many other ironies to this war. The British didn't want it, and the weaker Americans insisted upon it. The war didn't unite the country: it fiercely divided the Federalist (which dominated in New England) and Republican (powerful in the South and West) political factions. Indeed, the Senate vote on the declaration of war was the closest in American history. The paradoxes piled up. To wage this war, Madison and the Republicans would have to restrict trade, build a military establishment, and coerce obedience — the very actions most abhorred in Republican ideology.

This would prove to be a strange conflict indeed.

David or Goliath: The Myths of 1812

Many nations have gone to war in pure gayety of heart, but perhaps the United States were the first to force themselves into a war they dreaded, in the hope that the war itself might create the spirit they lacked.

— Henry Adams, great-grandson of
President John Adams (1891)

In Americans' collective memory, then and now, the United States played David to Britain's Goliath. Our fragile little republic, so the story goes, stood up to the bullying British and — just barely — saved our independence from the imperial enemy. But is it so? Just who was David and who was Goliath? That, of course, depends on your point of view.

The British were busy and spread thin. They had been at war with the powerful French on a global scale for some nineteen years. The only British force within striking distance of the United States was in Canada, and this — in a stunning reversal of the popular myth — represented a stunning mismatch. There were barely five hundred thousand citizens in Canada, compared with about eight million in the United States. The British had only a few thousand regular troops to spare for the defense of this massive Canadian landmass. The Americans might be unprepared, and might prove bad at war, but by no means was the initial deck stacked against the large and expansive American republic.

The myth of American defensiveness is also belied by a number of other inconvenient facts. The *United States* declared this war, a war that Britain had no interest in fighting. Furthermore, despite the exaggerated claims of war hawks and patriots of all stripes, this was not a Second War of Independence. There is no evidence that the British sought to reconquer and colonize the mammoth American republic. Any land seizures were planned to be used only as bargaining chips at an eventual peace settlement. Tied down in an existential war of its own, Britain had neither the capacity nor the intent to re-subjugate their former colonists.

Free Canada: Civil War in the Northern Borderlands

The acquisition of Canada, this year, as far as the neighborhood of Quebec, will be a mere matter of marching.
— Thomas Jefferson (1812)

People speaking the same language, having the same laws, manners and religion, and in all the connections of social intercourse, can never be depended upon as enemies.
— Baron Frederick de Gaugreben, British officer (1815)

The United States had long coveted Canada. In two sequential wars, the US Army invaded its northern neighbor and intrigued for Canada's incorporation into the republic deep into the nineteenth century. Here, on the Canadian front, the conflict most resembled a civil war.

Canada was primarily, though sparsely, populated by two types of people: French Canadians and former American loyalists — refugees from the late Revolutionary War. Some, the "true" loyalists, fled north just after the end of the war for independence. The majority, however, the "late" loyalists, had more recently settled in Upper Canada between 1790 and 1812. Most came because land was cheaper and taxes lower north of the border. Far from being the despotic kingdom of American fantasies, Canada offered a life rather similar to that within the republic. Indeed, this was a war between two of the *freest* societies on earth. So much for modern political scientists' notions of a "Democratic Peace Theory" — the belief that two democracies will never engage in war. Britain had a king, certainly, but also had a mixed constitution and one of the world's more representative political bodies.

In many cases families were divided by the porous American-Canadian border. Loyalties were fluid, and citizens on both sides spoke a common language, practiced a common religion, and shared a common culture. Still, if and when an American invasion came, the small body of British regular troops would count on these recent Americans — these "late" loyalists — to rally to the defense of mother Canada.

And the invasion did come, right at the outset of the war. Though the justification for war was maritime and naval, the conflict opened with a three-pronged American land invasion of Canada. The Americans, for their part, expected the inverse of the British hopes — the "late" loyalists, it was thought, would flock to the American standard and support the invasion. It never happened. Remarkably, a solid base of Canadians fought as militiamen for the British and against the southern invaders. Most, of course, took no side and sought only to be let alone.

It turned out that the invading Americans found few friends in Canada and often alienated the locals with their propensity for plundering and military blunder. Though the war raged along the border — primarily near Niagara Falls and Detroit — for nearly three years, the American campaign for Canada proved to be an embarrassing fiasco. Defeats piled up, and Canada would emerge from the war firmly in British hands. In the civil war along the border, the Americans were, more often than not, the aggressors and the losers.

Indians, Britons, Slaves, and the Real Losers of the War of 1812

[The Indians] have forfeited all right to the territory we
have conquered.

— General Andrew Jackson

My people are no more! Their bones are bleaching on the
plains of the Tallushatches, Talladega, and Emuckfau.

— Creek chief Red Eagle

The United States was a republic, Britain a monarchy. Thus in
Americans' collective memories the United States *must* have been
fighting for liberty, for democracy. But was it? Britons saw matters
rather differently. They argued that their mixed constitution, providing for a king and the Houses of Lords and Commons, best protected
liberty and stability at home and abroad. The British actually believed
(not without some merit) that only *they* protected Europe, and by
extension America, from the expansive tyranny of Napoleonic France,
and that the Americans were ungrateful for this sacrifice.

Furthermore, when it came to treatment of black people and Native
Americans, it seems the British better upheld our modern conceptions of liberty and equality. Most Americans felt a mix of fear and
hatred for the local Indian tribes. Settlers perceived the threat of
Tecumseh's Indian confederation to be existential. These westerners
called for a conquest of Canada to remove British support for the
tribes and exterminate the Indians once and for all.

The British viewed the Native Americans in a completely different
way. And the natives saw the Brits as much less of a threat than the
more populous and encroaching Americans. The British supplied,
funded, and generally respected the autonomy of the Canadian and
Ohio Country tribes. With so few English settlers in the colony,
British leaders counted on native allies to defend Canada and were
more than happy to accept and recognize an Indian buffer state on
the frontier. They did so, no doubt, out of self-interest but were still far
more congenial to the tribes than the hated American settlers.

Therefore, in a replay of the Revolutionary War, the vast majority of natives actively sided with, and often fought for, the British. This would prove to be a fateful mistake. Tecumseh's confederation was eventually defeated (and Tecumseh himself killed) at the Battle of the Thames, and the Creek Indians were devastated by the brutal tactics of Andrew Jackson in the South. The Indians emerged from the war defeated and without the reliable support of the British, who quickly sold them out at the peace conference. Never again would native tribes maintain any autonomy east of the Mississippi or prove able to stand up to the far more numerous Americans. The War of 1812 was, for the native peoples, an unmitigated disaster.

In yet another replay of the Revolution, black American slaves deeply rejected American proclamations of a war for liberty and equality. The ascendant American Republicans running the country were powerful in the South and respected the fears of slaveholders in that region. Though desperately short of recruits, the Americans refused to enlist free or enslaved black people into the army. On the contrary, many slaves escaped their plantations and either ran to British lines or, in many cases, swam to British ships — places where they were much more likely to find the liberty that the Americans falsely professed for all. The British offered freedom, an enlistment bounty, and free land to runaways who joined up. Some six hundred American blacks became Royal Marines!

If the War of 1812 was a war for freedom, it was for a very narrow and limited freedom indeed. Republicans extolled their commitment to liberty and equality, but those sentiments extended only to the white men of the young republic. Britain, which had already abolished slavery, would prove the better beacon of liberty for black people and Indians.

Treason at Home? Federalists, Republicans, and the Politics of War

The War of 1812 also constituted a *political* civil war at home between the ruling Republican Party and the opposition Federalist Party. The

The Hartford Convention, or Leap no Leap, 1814 pro-Republican political cartoon

Federalists had much to lose and little to gain from the war. They predominated in New England and in coastal ports and relied on trade with Britain to earn a decent living. They had few visions of grandeur about western land annexations or a conquest of Canada. Furthermore, the more aristocratic Federalists favored Britain in its war with revolutionary and then Napoleonic France, seeing Britain as a rock of stability against a tide of chaos and conquest from dictatorial France.

Many Federalists continued to illegally trade with the Brits, smuggled goods to Canada, and seemed to actively oppose the war. Republicans dubbed them traitors, while the Federalists saw themselves as prudent realists. Some Federalists even considered secession from the union and the formation of an independent New England republic. Most, however, never went that far.

Still, in 1814, after two years of indecisive war, the Federalist Party would unknowingly sign its own death warrant. New England Federalists sent delegates to a convention in Hartford, Connecticut, that meant to oppose the war and recommend new amendments to the Constitution. And in truth, these amendments weren't all bad.

They called for the repeal of the Three-Fifths Compromise, which counted slaves as partial humans for representation's sake and gave extra political weight to the South. They also sought to require a (sensible?) two-thirds majority in Congress to declare future wars and to limit presidents to a single term in office.

Was this, as some claimed, tantamount to treason during a period of active hostilities? Indeed, some Federalists actively discouraged military enlistment and the withholding of federal taxes to fund the war, and some New England governors refused to send their state militias on offensive campaigns. But was this treason or principled opposition to an ill-advised war? The country was divided in answering the question, similar to some issues that remain with us.

The Federalists might have been right, in fact, both ethically and constitutionally, but the Hartford Convention's luckless timing destroyed them politically. Just as the delegates were meeting, the Republicans were securing a status quo peace treaty and General Andrew Jackson was winning a staggering victory over the British at New Orleans (a few weeks *after* the treaty had been signed but before word of the peace reached the Americas). The Republicans waved the bloody shirt and painted the Hartford Convention as a treasonous betrayal. The Federalists would never again gain a majority in either house of Congress or run a viable presidential candidate. Perhaps opposition to war, even a less-than-popular war, never pays politically.

Ironic Outcomes: A Costly Draw

> The War of 1812 is the strangest war in American history.
> — Historian Gordon Wood (2009)

Certainly it was no American victory that forced the British to the peace table. By 1814 the war had become a debacle. Two consecutive American invasions of Canada had been stymied. Napoleon was defeated in April 1814, and the British finally began sending thousands of regular troops across the Atlantic to teach the impetuous

Americans a lesson — even burning Washington, DC, to the ground! (Though in fairness it should be noted that the Americans had earlier done the same to the Canadian capital at York.) The US coastline was blockaded from Long Island to the Gulf of Mexico; despite a few early single-ship victories in 1812, the US Navy was all but finished by 1814; the US Treasury was broke and defaulted, for the first time in the nation's history, on its loans and debt; and 12 percent of US troops had deserted during the war.

The Americans held few victorious cards by the end of 1814, but Britain was exhausted after two decades of war. Besides, they had never meant to reconquer the United States in the first place. A status quo treaty that made no concessions to the Americans and preserved the independence of Canada suited London just fine.

So who were the winners and losers of this indecisive war? American land speculators and frontiersmen, to be sure, for they had broken Indian power and opened up millions of acres for western settlement. The biggest losers, of course, were those very Indians, who saw their last hopes for autonomy fade away. They were now, once and for all, a conquered people. The Federalists lost, too, as a political party and as a viable ideology. Republicans would remain ascendant — with no serious opposition — for some two decades after the war. So if New England and the natives lost, the Republicans, southerners, and westerners emerged victorious.

Nor is it clear *which* side truly fought for anything resembling (our modern conception of) liberty. And in the end, after thousands had died (more from disease than combat) on both sides, Canada remained British and nothing had been done about neutrals' rights on the high seas. Indian power had been broken and the Federalists disappeared, but little else changed.

Perception and Reality: Remembering the War of 1812

[The War of 1812] has revived, with added luster the renown which brightened the morning of our independence: it has called forth and organized the dormant

resources of the [American] empire: it has tried and
vindicated our republican institutions . . . which consists
in the well earned respect of the world.

> — "A Republican citizen of Baltimore"
> writing in a newspaper (1815)

Still, perhaps inevitably, both sides would claim a victory of sorts.
Nationalist sentiment exploded among ascendant American Republicans, who claimed they had won a "second revolution" and smitten
an empire. The decisive victory at the Battle of New Orleans, fought
after the treaty had been negotiated, gave Americans the *impression*
of victory. Since the end of the Napoleonic Wars made the issues of
impressment and neutrals' rights moot, the Republicans could also
claim victory on the seas — even though the British agreed to nothing
of the sort in the Treaty of Ghent. To a fervently patriotic American
majority, the war seemed to vindicate both the nation's independence
and its republicanism. Indeed, more American towns and counties
(fifty-seven) are now named for President Madison than any other
president — including George Washington!

Canadians, too, claimed a victory and developed a new nationalism
and origin myth around their collective defeat of the American invaders. Americans may know and care little about the War of 1812, but
not so the Canadians. In Canada the war is widely seen as a pivotal,
patriotic event, a noble defense of the northland against marauding
American invaders. The British, well, they were mostly just glad all
these wars were over; they never gave much attention to the American
sideshow in the first place. From their perspective, they had punished
the petulant Americans (even burning their capital!) and conceded
nothing at the negotiating table.

So ended and so was remembered an utterly peculiar conflict.

———

It was a dumb war, in retrospect: unnecessary and ill advised. At best
the War of 1812 resulted in a draw that cost the lives of many thousands; a draw that destroyed any hope of Indian autonomy east of the

Mississippi. Still, like most wars, this conflict stirred up patriotism and jingoism, among Americans *and* Canadians. War, many politicians (usually miles away from the fighting) believe, can be a regenerative act, renewing the spirit of patriotism and uniting competing factions. That is a myth. It is almost never this way. Wars tend to be messy, divisive, and inconclusive, and that was especially true of this conflict. Things are lost when a nation embarks on combat: civil liberty at home, human empathy at the front, all sense of realism and proportion in the combatants' capitals.

American mythmakers — two centuries' worth of them — have spun the War of 1812 into a nationalistic yarn. They have focused on the victories of Andrew Jackson, ignored the US debacles in Canada, and turned an obscure song set to the tune of a British drinking ballad — "The Star-Spangled Banner" — into a national anthem. How ironic, then, that the anthem, a *war song* — which recently stirred up so much controversy on football Sundays — emerged from a conflict that should never have been fought and that we didn't really win.[10]

13

BIRTH OF AN ERA OF REVOLUTIONS

It was a time of great change. And as always, a picture — or in this case a painting — is worth a thousand words. In the portrait below, Patrick Lyon of Philadelphia is depicted as a blacksmith hard at work at the forge. He wears an apron and a shirt that shows his muscular forearms. This portrait was commissioned by Lyon himself, and it depicts a man proud of his labor and strength. Here was a *workingman* — blue-collar chic!

Pat Lyon at the Forge, 1826–27, by John Neagle

This is stranger than it may appear to modern eyes. After all, in the eighteenth and early nineteenth centuries, men who could afford to commission such paintings usually preferred to be portrayed in formal dress, adorned in powdered wig and leggings, and surrounded by the expensive objects that implied an aristocratic status. Something had changed.

Lyon may appear to be the quintessential workingman in this painting, but he was also something else: one of the wealthiest men in Philadelphia. He was a leading businessman, an inventor, and, long before, a blacksmith. Pat Lyon possessed more than the requisite means to commission the ubiquitous aristocratic portrait, yet instead he chose to be represented as a simple — yet proud — blacksmith. In contrast with his aristocratic peers and forebears, Lyon explicitly told the artist, John Neagle (1796–1865), that he did "not wish to be represented as what I am not — a gentleman."

There was something profound afoot in American society in the three decades following the War of 1812, a veritable revolution of revolutions — massive changes in economics, politics, and society. Neagle's portrait of Pat Lyon in many respects depicts them all. The United States was becoming more commercialized, more egalitarian (at least for white males), and, to a certain extent, *populist*. The Federalists, seen as the party of aristocracy, had faded from the political scene, and new factions of the Republican Party would lead America through this time of turmoil.

Technology, infrastructure, government investment, and communications: these would all permanently change. Quality of life for most Americans increased, but others, as always, were left behind — victims of a society moving too far too fast.

Lessons of War: Madison, Republicans, and the Hypocrisy of New Nationalism

The War of 1812 was at best a draw, at worst an embarrassing debacle. It demonstrated the unpreparedness of American arms, government, and infrastructure for conflict with a major world power. The United

States, despite major efforts, couldn't even conquer *Canada* and was lucky to maintain its own territorial integrity.

Nonetheless, James Madison (in the presidency from 1809 to 1817) and most Americans, especially Republicans, decided to publicly rebrand the war as a decisive victory, a Second War of Independence. What we know as nationalism — a term not in use until the 1830s — exploded in the aftermath of this indecisive war. If America could defeat mighty Great Britain *again*, what couldn't it do? The entire continent seemed ripe for the taking and, in due time, for the improving. In time Spanish Florida would be illegally invaded by General Andrew Jackson and eventually would be sold to the United States by a Spain that did not have much choice in the matter. The Pacific Northwest would be divided and shared between Britain and the United States, making America a two-ocean power and cutting the Spanish and Russians out of the deal. All, it seemed, was part and parcel of America's unmistakable destiny.

Yet the men who had stood atop the federal government throughout the war privately knew better. They were aware of the debacle that had ensued and how near disaster had been. The war had been fought on a shoestring and, generally, under the republican ideology of limited government. The Republicans, from Thomas Jefferson to James Madison, had espoused a minimalist approach to federal power, but that would change.

Soon the only party that had any real power — the Republican Party — began to fragment into opposing factions and eventually would become nearly unrecognizable. Suddenly Madison and the "new nationalists" began calling for internal improvements (canals and roads), military preparedness (this time the army would not be completely demobilized), a protective tariff to benefit manufacturers, and even a rechartering of the national bank. Every one of these demands had recently been anathema to the doctrinaire Republicans, including the father of the party, Jefferson. What's amazing is how quickly most — including the sage of Monticello — embraced the changes and accepted the increase in federal power and jurisdiction.

Wars change societies; they always have and always will. Things are gained — efficiency, technological innovations, and federal power — but things are also lost, such as civil liberties, ideological purity, and, in the case of America, modesty.

A Society Forever Changed: The Transportation and Commercial Revolutions

> We are under the most imperious obligations to coun-
> teract every tendency of disunion. . . . Let us, then, bind
> the republic together with a perfect system of roads and
> canals. Let us conquer space.
>   — Congressman John C. Calhoun of South Carolina

It is ironic how many modern conservatives tend to blame government action for all problems and extol the virtue of private entrepreneurship and innovation. How rarely are those two sections of society so discrete. The transportation and commercial revolutions that unfolded in nineteenth-century America did forever alter (usually for the better) life in these United States. Commodity costs dropped, travel became affordable, information proliferated, and living standards rose. This — under the sixteen years of Madison's and Monroe's administrations — was possible only through the combination of Republican governmental investment and prioritization of private innovation. The once laissez-faire Republicans ever so quickly pivoted from small government to the funding and application of technological inventions in cooperation with the private sector.

This was a team effort, and it forever altered life in America. Nearly everyone was affected by the proliferation of steamboats, canals, roads, and technological advances. Everyone, even Native Americans, became more tied to the commercial economy. Fewer farmers were needed, and other occupations and professions opened up. There were now both more wage laborers and more commercial entrepreneurs. This meant that property ownership — once the signal indicator of wealth and status — became less influential in economic and political life. It wasn't long before most states eliminated property qualifications for voting.

A prime example of innovation, government investment, and societal change unfolded in New York. In the 1820s, after years of work, the Erie Canal was completed. Running 363 miles from the Hudson River to Lake Erie, the forty-foot-wide canal connected the farms of the Great Lakes and Midwest with the trading port of New York City. Almost overnight the population of that city, and of western New York State, exploded. New York became, forever, the singular commercial hub of the United States. Local farmers and merchants were now plugged into a nationwide and international economy. As the historian Daniel Walker Howe noted, "New York had redrawn the economic map of the United States and placed itself at the center."

The commercial and transportation revolutions set off a communications revolution that sped up time and the flow of information. Mail traveled exponentially more quickly and so did newspapers, the primary items of mail in those days. The number and diversity of papers expanded, bringing politics and international affairs into the daily lives of more and more Americans. But there was, undoubtedly, a dark side to this information propagation. Most newspapers in this era were little more than organs of particular political parties or factions rather than objective news sources. These papers relied, oftentimes, on wealthy benefactors or government printing contracts from the party in power. The next time someone complains about the *unprecedented* partisanship and corporate influence on today's media space, remind them of this era of the Market Revolution, the period of intense economic and communication revolutions in the years following 1815.

Winners and Losers: The Uneven Effects of the Market Revolution

And if we look to the condition of individuals what a proud spectacle does it exhibit! On whom has oppression fallen in any quarter of our Union? Who has been deprived of any right of person or property?

— President James Madison

The crazy part is Madison probably *meant* it. As the chief executive waxed eloquently on the triumphs of technology and his own administration in the above quote, he seemed truly and honestly unaware of how obtuse a statement this was in the second decade of the nineteenth century. This was, however, a time when few would respond to the president by pointing out the hypocrisy of holding some 1.5 million blacks in chains, keeping several million women trapped in the paternalistic home, and having stolen the lands of hundreds of thousands of Native Americans.

Such was the spirit of the times that a "republican" such as President Madison would scoff at such critiques — after all, *those* folks didn't count in his visions of democratic utopia. And so, left behind in this great rising market tide were natives, blacks, many women, and some impoverished white workers.

Native Americans, once again, can be seen as some of the great losers in the Market Revolution era. More roads, more canals, and quicker transportation meant, simply, more white settlers expropriating their tribal lands even faster. The technology and transportation were *not for them.*

In some cases even natives living beyond the borders of the United States were affected by American triumphalism. The "hero" of the War of 1812, Andrew Jackson, had during the conflict seized lands from the Creek Indians, even those who had fought on his side. This opened Alabama and Mississippi for immediate settlement. Only this wasn't enough. In 1818, President James Monroe sent him on a punitive expedition (with unclear orders) into Spanish Florida to punish natives and allied runaway slaves who had exploited the international border to raid American settlements. The weakened Spanish Empire was powerless to stop him.

Jackson's main opponent was a breakaway sect of Creeks who had moved south and intermixed with runaway slaves and marooned blacks to form the famous Seminole tribe. Jackson burned settlements, chased the warriors south, seized some Spanish forts without a fight, and then refused to leave! He even arrested and executed two British traders as "spies" in contravention of international law and caused a diplomatic scandal. Eventually, of course, the Spanish ceded the Floridas to the United States, and native power was forever broken in the old Southwest (the present states of Alabama, Mississippi, and Louisiana).

Enslaved black people *fed* the new market economy; they rarely benefited from it. Contrary to popular conception, Eli Whitney's invention of the cotton gin (short for "engine") did not lessen the burden of enslaved pickers but instead increased their expected yield and workload. Now that the seeds could be separated from raw cotton more quickly, the cotton demand exploded. Furthermore, the temperate climate and limitless land in what was then considered the Southwest (stolen from the Creek and other native tribes) made the United States the top producer of cotton in the world by 1820. It was cotton that made America, and the South, "king." It fed the textile factories of England and Massachusetts alike, and the demand seemed insatiable.

Slaves were expected to work harder, rest less often, and produce more. Worse still, the massive migration southward and westward (one of the most significant in American history) of farmers and planters from Virginia, Maryland, and the Carolinas to Alabama and Mississippi also meant the concurrent shift of slaves. With Virginia tobacco less profitable, Chesapeake planters had less need for their slaves. Thus, over the proceeding decades — and up until the Civil War — men from the Upper South sold slaves, broke up their families, and fed the "Alabama fever," as it was known. The black experience, of forced migration and family separation, cannot be detached from the triumphs of the Market Revolution.

———

> I went in among the young girls [at the Lowell Mills in Massachusetts] . . . not one expressed herself as tired of her employment, or oppressed with work . . . all looked healthy . . . and I could not help observing that they kept the prettiest inside. . . . Here were thousands . . . enjoying

all the blessings of freedom, with the prospect before them
of future comfort and respectability.

> — Colonel and Congressman Davy Crockett,
> on visiting the Lowell Mills textile plants

Crockett, the veritable "King of the Wild Frontier," was right about one thing in the quote above. In Lowell, Massachusetts, and other urban (usually northern) settings, women were, increasingly, leaving the home and entering the workplace. What is interesting, and instructive, is the language this frontiersman used to describe the toiling women. They were, he said, *free*! This seems an odd way for a man of the wilderness, of the vast hardy western frontier, to describe the life of dirty, cramped factory workers held to a rigorous dictatorship of the clock.

In the era of market and transportation revolutions, there was indeed now more economic opportunity, but there also grew a greater disparity between rich and poor (sound familiar?). For all the talk in this era of "self-made men," most white males still toiled as small farmers or wage laborers. Only a tiny fraction accumulated immense wealth.

Some small farmers, often those who found themselves unluckily located away from the roads and canals, saw their business dwindle as the revolutions of commerce, transportation, and economics literally passed them by. Many parts of New England and upstate New York became littered with ghost towns and abandoned farms. Many merchants and artisans went bankrupt, unable to deal with the competition of goods shipped in from afar.

There was also, some felt, a loss of independence, community, and fulfillment produced by the market shift. Jefferson's utopian dream of small, independent farmers from the Atlantic to the Pacific simply hadn't panned out, as Jefferson woefully acknowledged late in his life. This, as we will see later, led to an explosion of religious, social, and temperance revivals — attempts to reconnect a world on the move with the cherished values of the "old way." This, too, seems a natural outgrowth of all such economic and political revolutions in American history.

———

It was a strange time: one of speed and change; of winners and losers; of growth and pain. It was the time of Pat Lyon — the rich man who had himself painted as a blacksmith — and of dislocated slaves pushed ever harder in the cotton fields. This was the era of a rising tide of wealth but also of child labor and the crowded women at the Lowell Mills.

What's certain is that the economic, political, and societal revolutions of 1815–45 cannot be studied in isolation. This was an *era* of revolutions that interacted to forever change antebellum American society. Some prospered as others withered, but all were affected in kind.[11]

14

ANDREW JACKSON'S WHITE MALE WORLD AND THE START OF MODERN POLITICS

> ... When the right and capacity to do all is given to any authority, whether it be called people or king, democracy or aristocracy, monarchy or a republic, I say: the germ of tyranny is there. ...
>
> — Alexis de Tocqueville, *Democracy in America*

There are precious few presidents, indeed, who can claim to have an entire era bearing their name. Andrew Jackson is one. Historians have long labeled his presidency and the years that followed it as Jacksonian America. This is instructive. Whatever else he was, this man, General — later President — Jackson, was an absolute tour de force. He swept to power on a veritable wave of populism and forever altered the American political scene. We might argue, plausibly, that we live today in the system he wrought.

Born to modest means in the Carolinas, Jackson led a hard life and somehow found prosperity. Orphaned as a child, he volunteered as a courier for the Continental army when he was just thirteen years old. Captured by the British, he refused to shine the boots of a captor and was struck on the head with the officer's sword. Jackson would bear the scar, and his hatred for all things British, throughout his life. He became a lawyer, moved west to Tennessee, and eventually amassed a fortune and many enslaved people. As a general in the War of 1812 he stood out as the only real hero of that costly draw of a conflict. Called *Old Hickory* by his troops, Jackson is perhaps the first president to bear a catchy nickname. By the 1820s, Jackson was a household name and a staunch Democratic politician. He sought power for himself and, ostensibly, the "common man."

Politics and presidential campaigning were forever changed by

Jackson. This was a man who knew how to win — no matter the cost. Before Jackson, although many early presidential elections were highly contested, the tradition among candidates was to eschew personal campaigning. These were refined *gentlemen* and they thought themselves above rank electioneering. They sought to evoke a disinterested and modest persona and left it to newspapers and partisans to make arguments on their behalf. Not so Andrew Jackson. Here was a man who exuded confidence and personal popularity. His was the era of the first political party conventions and of outright campaigning. Democrats were prouder of their *candidate* than of their policies, and they ran on Jackson the man.

All of this is ironic because it is unclear that the Founding Fathers actually intended for democratization in the way Jackson and his backers envisioned it. In fact, the United States was established as a republic, not a direct democracy, and institutions such as the Senate and the Electoral College were designed to curtail popular rule. Probably, given human nature and the tendencies of the systems the founders created, the Revolutionary generation misunderstood where their republic would lead — toward greater democratization. Still, it is interesting and worth pondering the fact that Jackson, and the Democrats, stood in *contrast* with the visions of most founders.

Indeed, America's contemporary political culture owes more to Jackson than to George Washington or Thomas Jefferson, which, admittedly, is an uncomfortable truth. As you read this chapter, take a moment to consider whether democracy really is the best possible form of government. Think on the winners and losers inherent in the Jacksonian political revolution and ask whether a better alternative path existed. We live in the political world Jackson created.

A Corrupt Bargain: The Opposing Personalities of John Quincy Adams and Andrew Jackson

Jackson faced off against the son of President John Adams, John Quincy Adams, in two consecutive elections, in 1824 and 1828. These were among the dirtiest and most contested campaigns in US history.

Jacksonians portrayed Adams as an aloof aristocrat, out of touch with the average American. And in a sense he was. Adams lacked the "common touch" or charisma of Jackson. That said, Adams was arguably the most well-prepared and qualified presidential candidate in history. He had been a Harvard professor, senator from Massachusetts, ambassador to Prussia, Russia, Britain, and the Netherlands. He negotiated the treaty to end the War of 1812 and served as President James Monroe's secretary of state. He spoke several languages.

Still, the most qualified candidate lost the popular vote in the 1824 election. Due to the peculiarities of the Electoral College, the election went to the Congress for adjudication. Horrified by the prospect of an uncouth Jackson serving as president, Speaker of the House Henry Clay threw his support behind Adams and won him the presidency. Soon after, in a move with terrible political optics, Adams appointed Clay as secretary of state, a position then considered the fastest road to the presidency. Jackson and his followers — now calling themselves Democratic Republicans, as opposed to Adams's National Republicans — were aghast and labeled this move a "corrupt bargain." Clay probably was one of the most qualified candidates to lead the US Department of State, but the charge stuck and would haunt Adams and Clay for years to come. Consider it an early example of political branding.

As president, Adams sought internal improvements (road, canal, and communications infrastructure) led by an activist federal government so as to improve Americans' quality of life. Clay labeled this the "American System," and it would be funded and fueled by revenue from a national tariff and federal land sales. This became the core of the National Republican ideology. It was a grand ambition and, unfortunately, would never fully come to fruition. For this reason, Adams's one-term presidency was long considered a failure. Still, a fresh look may rehabilitate Adams the man, if not Adams the politician.

John Quincy Adams's National Republican ideology was forward thinking and presaged many later implemented federal improvements. He was a generation or two ahead of his time. He also had rather humanitarian impulses, at least for the age. He protected the Creek

Indians from expulsion and a corrupt treaty and would not countenance Native American removal under his watch. Adams also developed strong anti-slavery sentiments during his long career of public service and would die as something of a full-fledged abolitionist.

Only America wasn't ready for Adams. Voters would decide they didn't *want* a man like Adams or care much for his progressive, activist policies. Jackson was a war hero, a man of action, a man of violence: a man like them. He and his many followers wanted the opposite of Adams and his National Republicans. They wanted cheap western land, rapid settlement, state and local sovereignty, and less — not more — federal intervention in their lives. The southerners, who tended to be staunchly Jacksonian, also feared federal power. They wanted low or no tariffs so they could sell cotton in lucrative overseas markets. Furthermore, if the feds could enforce a tariff, could they not someday ban slavery? In this sense, white supremacy — in the form of slavery and Indian expulsion — stood at the heart of the Democratic agenda.

Adams would lose the 1828 election by a landslide. He wasn't made for the new politics of the era. He was uncomfortable personally campaigning, especially since the election of 1828 essentially began on his Inauguration Day and lasted four years! Adams tried to make the election about *issues*, about his enlightened American System. His followers argued that the very aspects of Jackson's personality that so endeared him to voters actually disqualified him as a viable president. Jackson, they said (not inaccurately), had a violent temper, he was "ruled by his passions," and he had "lived in sin" with a married woman, now his wife, Rachel — she had an estranged husband when she and Jackson were first betrothed.

The charges never really stuck. Jackson was a natural "winner." His supporters rarely talked policy and focused instead on the appealing qualities of the candidate himself. Jackson personally campaigned against Washington insiders and elites. This resonated with many voters (as such campaigns still do). The Jackson campaign also played dirty, dirtier than nearly any candidate before or after. His supporters falsely claimed that Adams was a heretic or an atheist (he was actually a Unitarian) and that while an ambassador he had sold an American girl to the czar of Russia. Adams wanted to talk platforms and policy; Jackson wanted to wage a popularity contest, and that's what Americans got. The Jackson campaign broke down into what we would now call soundbites, as in the popular Democratic ditty that the election was "between J. Q. Adams, who can write / And Andy Jackson, who can fight." The fighter won, as usual.

Jackson won some 56 percent of the popular vote, but the results were highly sectional. The Northeast was strong for Adams while the South and the West of that day swung to Jackson. Southerners and westerners (Jackson himself lived west of the Appalachian Mountains, the first president to do so) trusted the Democratic candidate to better protect their system of slavery and satisfy their hunger for Indian land. The electoral map of 1828 was remarkably similar both to that of Civil War America in 1860 and to those of elections in 2012 and 2016. The South and West favored one candidate, the North and East another.

In the end the election of 1828 was best summed up in the words of one contemporary newspaperman, Thomas B. Stevenson, who declared that the Adams campaign had "dealt with man *as he should be*," while the Jackson campaign had "appealed to him *as he is*." There was no love lost between the two competitors. Jackson declined to pay the traditional courtesy call to the outgoing president, and Adams responded by conspicuously not attending the Jackson inauguration. Regardless, the Age of Jackson had begun.

The Democracy Paradox: Linking the Market and Political Revolutions

In 1800 most states limited the right of even white males to vote. Some had taxpaying provisions; others had property ownership qualificati-ons for the franchise. By the end of Jackson's presidency, most such restrictions were a thing of the past. This can only partly be explained by Jackson's explicit championing of the "common man." Indeed, the democratization of the United States was very much tied up with the concurrent market and communications revolutions of the era.

Capitalism and its cyclical economic panics, or recessions — the last of which had occurred in 1819 — led more and more Americans to believe that politics directly affected their lives. Furthermore, an increase in media outlets (newspapers) and communications technology garnered more exposure to political tracts. The changing economy, especially early industrialization, also provided new economic opportunities to accumulate wealth. Earlier, vast landownership and farming were the main paths to prosperity. Now a man with only moderate amounts of land could earn a fortune through commerce and/or entrepreneurship. These newly rich men chafed under the arcane property qualifications of the day and demanded a fair say in government through the right to vote. In the process rich and poor alike — at least among white males — would soon gain voting rights.

The increase in voters, especially among commoners, meant that politicians like Jackson now had greater incentive to please, and pander to, the masses. In other words, market and communications advancements constituted a social revolution that forever altered concepts of citizenship. Jackson understood this and seized his opportunity. Men like John Quincy Adams were unprepared for, and uncomfortable with, this seismic change.

There was, however, an irony to all this radical democratization. At the same time as millions of poor whites were gaining the franchise, their newly empowered political class quickly denied those very rights to other men, mostly black men. Before 1820 free blacks could actually vote in many northern states and a few southern ones. Unfortunately, some of the first actions of these new poor white voters restricted free black voting. From 1821 to 1842 New York, New Jersey, Pennsylvania, Connecticut, and Rhode Island passed laws curtailing black civil rights. And in new constitutional conventions (common during the 1830s), North Carolina and Tennessee took the vote away from free blacks. Indeed, in 1834, one Tennessee delegate at the convention insisted that "We, the People" meant "we the free white people of the United States and the free white people only."

The conventions in North Carolina and Tennessee eliminated the last vestiges of free black political rights in the South before the Civil

War. Nonetheless, this was an *American*, not a southern, phenomenon. White supremacy was popular among the masses, and they enshrined its callous values the moment they received the vote. We may be poor, they seemed to declare, but at least we're *white*. In this sense America developed an identifiable *caste-* rather than *class-*based system of social hierarchy. The results would linger for generations.

Man of the People? The Character of Andrew Jackson

It was easy, at the time, to see Jackson as something of a throwback to Jeffersonian agrarianism. And by some measures, he was just that. Nonetheless, Jackson's popularity had more to do with personality than platform. Jefferson possessed the grandest library in the United States, Jackson the grandest ego. Jefferson was professorial, Jackson a man of action. Though the two men agreed on certain issues of state sovereignty, the aging Jefferson loathed Jackson and couldn't imagine him as president. Dying on July 4, 1826, Jefferson would just miss seeing what he feared most: Jackson in the White House.

But Jackson was a celebrity: a genuine war hero and hearty frontiersman, and he possessed a charismatic demeanor. He was a violent, coarse man, but he epitomized common notions of nineteenth-century masculinity. He drank, gambled, fought, and never apologized. He fought duels (which were illegal in most states) and bore the scars and bullet wounds to prove it. Indeed, Jackson probably counts as the only president in history to have, as a nongovernmental civilian and in cold blood, personally killed a man. (This occurred in an 1806 duel.) Adams thought these characteristics disqualified Jackson for the office, but the Democrats *loved* these traits. He's tough, he tells it like it is . . . he's just like us!

To demonstrate his "common touch," Jackson opened the White House to the public for his inaugural celebration. The crowd tore out the furniture and nearly rioted. The "man of the people" was nearly trampled by his people. Still, Jackson was undeterred. Throughout his presidency he continued to equate (in what can be a dangerous construct) his *own* will with the "will of the people." But it worked for him and earned him two terms as president. The "people" could not have cared less that Jackson owned a stately mansion, The Hermitage, in Tennessee, replete with Greek columns and French wallpaper. Jackson successfully cultivated a specific anti-elitist and anti-intellectual public persona, and millions loved it. He was also paranoid; he saw conspiracies around every corner and was certain that what President Trump would label nearly two hundred years later the "deep state" was out to destroy him.

That never happened, and Jackson's people remained ever loyal. They barely flinched at the contradictions in his presidency — such as how he doubled spending for internal improvements while in office, despite running against such projects. But if Jackson was president for the "common man," he was certainly only thus for the *white* common man. Jackson was a bigot and a brutal slave owner. In one advertisement for a runaway slave, he promised "ten dollars extra" for "every hundred lashes" the captor inflicted on the fugitive black in question. Jackson undoubtedly played on the fears and prejudices of poor whites to win their support. These people hated, or feared, Indians, enslaved black people, and "uppity" free blacks. Jackson knew that implicitly and pursued policies amenable to this sizable part of the electorate throughout his administration. His "democratization" may have been real, but it was for whites only.

To the Victor Go the Spoils: Jackson the Chief Executive

Like nearly every modern presidential candidate, Jackson ran on a reform platform. Only *he* could, or would, take on corruption and fix DC. Yet in another bit of paradoxical irony, Jackson would make famous a tradition — his "spoils system" — that would lead to an outsized increase in corruption. We have Jackson to thank for the platitude "to the victor belong the spoils." But despite the shock feigned by those who opposed his new policy of appointing friends and allies to nearly every federal position, no one should have been surprised. He had told Americans exactly what he planned to do! During the campaign itself, the editor of the Jacksonian *United States Telegraph* announced boldly that Jackson would REWARD HIS FRIENDS AND PUNISH HIS ENEMIES. He did indeed, and used patronage to do so.

Until 1828 most presidents — including John Quincy Adams — ran the federal bureaucracy as a fairly meritocratic organization. The custom was to leave most mid- and low-level employees in place when administrations switched. The idea was to maintain expertise and professionalism in the various federal departments. Jackson turned that system on its head and produced our modern system of political turnover in Washington. Jackson replaced 919 officials in his first year — more than all presidents combined in the previous forty years.

The result: Rapid turnover meant less experience in the federal agencies, which equated with *diminished* competence in and decreased prestige of the federal civil service. Corruption actually *increased* among these favored political appointees. And in a final bit of irony, the diminished competence of the federal agencies only bolstered the very Jacksonian argument that the government was inefficient and should be weakened! That strategy, employed with great skill to this day, has proved a winning combination for two centuries. The losers: the customers — the American people.

King Andrew I: Jackson's Battles for Supremacy

Most of the controversies of Jackson's presidency revolved around issues of presidential authority. Indeed, many of Jackson's opponents took to calling the president King Andrew I and in the 1830s renamed their political party the Whigs, a title taken from an earlier British party that had opposed royal rule. While not actual royalty, Jackson did display some authoritarian tendencies. He believed strongly in the power of the presidency and reshaped the executive branch forever. While in office he vetoed twelve congressional bills, more than all his predecessors combined (ten). By way of contrast, in four years John Quincy Adams didn't veto a single bill. Jackson never shied away from a challenge and never doubted the importance and preeminence of his office.

Jackson reacted boldly to two of the major crises of his administration: the Bank War and the nullification crisis. It is ironic that Andrew Jackson has long graced the $20 bill since he hardly understood economics and single-handedly destroyed the national banking system of his time. Jackson thought the Bank of the United States (BUS) — something analogous to our Federal Reserve — was both a challenge to his authority and an unconstitutional, elitist curtailment of states' banking rights. So in 1832, in what has been called "the most important veto in US history," Jackson followed through on his promise and killed the bank.

The president had once again demonstrated his authority and smitten the elites, but he simply didn't understand finance or the ramifications of his decision. The bank — and its unelected head, Nicholas Biddle — may well have had too much influence over the national economy, but at least the BUS regulated the system and avoided major financial panics. In its place, Jackson injected chaos and corruption. He withdrew federal money from the BUS and invested it in numerous Democratic-controlled "pet banks," led by his own political allies. For the most part these banks were less stable, less regulated, and more prone to irresponsible lending. The economy would suffer, and this instability contributed to the Panic of 1837, the worst recession to occur between the founding and the Civil War. Of course, by then Jackson was safely out of office. Jackson never apologized and believed to the end that he had done the right thing.

In removing federal money from a solvent bank and transferring these public funds to "pet banks," Jackson had violated the spirit, if not the letter, of the law. As a result he became the first and only president officially censured by the US Senate. It hardly mattered. Jackson may not have known economics, but he did know people. He capitalized on populist resentment of what was perceived as a corrupt and overly powerful federal bank. This played well with his base and the strong strand of anti-elitism that still exists in American culture. Sure, he ultimately would crash the economy, but despite his behavior and policies he remained popular and won a second term.

The disestablishment of the BUS empowered New York City's Wall Street and forever moved the financial capital of the United States from Philadelphia to Manhattan. In the end the people generally lost — even if they didn't blame their hero, Jackson. Without federal controls and regulation, there was no way to mitigate the cycles of capitalism, and Americans would suffer fairly regular "panics," or recessions, for generations to come.

The other major supremacy controversy arose over the federal tariff and its unpopularity in South Carolina. Before the Second World War, the vast majority of federal income came from land sales and the tariff. The tariff on foreign imports was rather high in the 1830s (ranging from 25 to 45 percent) and a key part of Henry Clay's American System. The tariff protected the nascent northern manufacturing industry and helped pay for the promised federal internal improvements. But the tariff was hated in the cotton-growing South. Reliant on the sale of cotton overseas and the import of foreign goods to fuel the southern economy, South Carolina, in particular, feared (correctly) that Britain would retaliate with tariffs of their own — notably on southern cotton. After a particularly high import tax rate passed Congress (the Tariff of Abominations, as it was labeled), South Carolinians dusted off an old states'-rights concept: nullification.

Vaguely resembling Jefferson and James Madison's Virginia and Kentucky Resolutions of the 1790s, nullification represented South Carolina's belief that an individual *state* could declare a federal law unconstitutional and thereby nullify it. This was about more than tariffs, however. Slavery, as always, was the elephant in the room. If the feds could force a tariff on southern states, could they not also someday abolish slavery and upend the entire southern social and economic structure? Ironically, one leading South Carolina spokesperson for the theory of nullification was Jackson's own vice president, John C. Calhoun. Talk about divided government. South Carolina went so far as to call a convention to debate and implement nullification of the tariff, and the stage was set for an epic power struggle — the sort of fight a man like Jackson never backed down from.

Jackson may have supported states' rights on issues as dark as slavery and Indian removal, but he ultimately *loved* the union he had fought and bled for and would not countenance secession or any challenge to his own supremacy. Whatever his motivations, Jackson's response to the nullification crisis must stand as his finest hour. Jackson mobilized the army and threatened to don a uniform and personally lead an invasion of South Carolina. When a man like Jackson — who had killed before — threatened violence, he was seen as deadly serious.

He even told a departing South Carolina congressman to take a message to the convention in that state: tell them, he said, that "if one drop of blood is shed there in defiance of the laws of the United States, I will hang the first man of them I can get my hands on to the first tree I find!" South Carolina would ultimately back down, and Jackson the savvy politician helped broker a tariff reduction so the state could save face. Through strength of purpose, Jackson had preserved the sanctity of the union and averted civil war.

Abuse of Power: Jackson's Indian Removal Policy — An American Tragedy

. . . No man entertains kinder feelings towards Indians than Andrew Jackson.

— Democratic congressman Wilson Lumpkin of Georgia

Build a fire under them [the Cherokee]. When it gets hot enough, they'll move.

— Andrew Jackson in conversation
with a congressman from Georgia

On other matters, Jackson showed far less political courage and succumbed to his own bigotry and the supposed states' rights of the South. If nullification was his shining moment, Indian removal must stand as Jackson's darkest. White settlers in the Ohio Country and, especially, in the old Southwest of Alabama, Georgia, and Mississippi had long resented the presence of Native Americans and the federal

Depiction of the Trail of Tears, 1942, Robert Lindneux

treaties that granted the tribes land they had lived on for centuries. Down south this was prime cotton country seen as wasted on "savages." Gold was even found on some native lands. Worse still, other tribes traded with free blacks and occasionally harbored runaway slaves. The truth, of course, is that the tribes of what was then the Southwest — the five "civilized" peoples, as they were known (Cherokee, Choctaw, Chickasaw, Creek, and Seminole) — were increasingly assimilated and lived mostly as farmers in the vein of white society. Some even owned slaves.

Still, as far as southerners and westerners were concerned, the Indians had to go. Georgia and Alabama, in particular, had long lobbied for the removal of the Cherokee and Creeks, respectively, but President Adams blocked these desires. Andrew Jackson was another matter. To Jackson this was a states'-rights and sovereignty issue. Besides, he had fought Indians all his life and held rather paternalistic views of the "savages." He *sympathized* with the Georgians and other southerners. Georgians, for their part, wanted the Cherokee gone despite past federal guarantees, even though the Constitution clearly granted the right to deal with Indians to the national government. Indeed, a popular song of the day was illustrative of southern views:

All I want in this creation
Is a pretty little wife and a big plantation
Away up yonder in the Cherokee nation.

In 1830, in another highly sectional vote (the Northeast tended to sympathize with the natives), the Congress barely passed (102–97) the Indian Removal Act. Without the Three-Fifths Compromise granting extra representation to southern states in the House of Representatives, the bill would never have passed. Many historians have held the simplistic view that the act authorized Jackson and the federal government to forcibly remove the tribes. That's not exactly true. The Indian Removal Act provided funds for voluntary (if highly encouraged) migration to Oklahoma but clearly stated the rights of Native Americans to stay on their land if they so chose. Seen this way, Jackson's later actions in the Indian removal process constituted an extreme abuse of power.

Georgia responded to the protections granted by the Indian Removal Act by stating that, yes, natives could stay if they so insisted, but they would then have to submit to state laws. Of course, under existing Georgia racial statutes, this would have meant that Cherokees couldn't vote, sue, or own property. Essentially, they would be relegated to slavery. And so in one last desperate attempt the Cherokee took their grievance to the courts. In *Worcester v. Georgia*, a rather complicated case, the Supreme Court in a decision led by Chief Justice John Marshall ruled that the Cherokee must be protected on lands granted to them by federal treaty. Once again, Jackson saw a challenge, a conspiracy even, against his presidential authority.

Jackson flouted the ruling. He claimed the federal government didn't have the power (ironically) to protect the five tribes. It was a state issue, he said. Furthermore, he removed sympathetic Indian agents from the territories and refused to use force to prevent mobs from attacking the natives. When the Cherokee pleaded with Jackson he responded, "You cannot remain where you now are. Circumstances that cannot be controlled, and which are beyond the reach of human laws, render it impossible that you can flourish in the midst of a civilized community. . . ." That, of course, was patently false. In the Bank

War and the nullification crisis, Jackson demonstrated his total willingness to take a stand and use the levers of government to enforce his mandates. Had Jackson chosen to, he could have protected the tribes and enforced the existing statutes.

Instead Jackson simply defied the law and snubbed the Supreme Court. Scoffing at Justice Marshall's ruling in *Worcester v. Georgia*, Jackson supposedly retorted that "John Marshall has made his decision; now let him enforce it!" This shocking statement constituted a veritable challenge to the very notion of separation of powers enshrined in the Constitution.

The results for the five tribes were tragic. By 1838 the last Cherokee holdouts were evicted by federal troops and marched in harsh weather along the Trail of Tears to Oklahoma. It is estimated that four thousand out of twelve thousand Cherokee died en route. As for the less well-known case of the Creeks, perhaps 50 percent died during their deportation. Many of the Seminoles of Florida refused to leave and escaped to the Everglades. The US Army would spend decades at war with this hardy tribe, lose thousands of men, and spend ten times more money fighting the Seminoles than it had spent deporting the other four tribes combined.

Indian removal was a bleak chapter in American history. It constituted what we would today term "ethnic cleansing." Still, apologists remain who claim that we today cannot judge the people of the nineteenth century because "they didn't know better," or "that was the culture back then." This is easily refuted by pointing out the millions of Americans who opposed the evictions even then. Consider the contemporaneous words of just two of their spokespersons. Henry Clay stated that the Indian Removal Act "threatens to bring a foul and lasting stain upon the good faith, humanity, and character of the nation." Former president and then congressman John Quincy Adams went further, declaring that Jackson's program was "among the heinous sins of this nation, for which God will one day bring [those responsible] to judgment."

Cues from Above: The Mob in the Age of Jackson

> The President is the direct representative of the
> American people. He was elected by the people and is
> responsible to them.
>
> — Andrew Jackson

President Jackson regularly violated American law, violated basic civil
liberties, and unleashed a storm of public turmoil. He empowered
his coarse supporters and (one hopes inadvertently) stoked domestic violence on a massive scale. Jackson was pro-slavery and usually
pro-states'-rights, and abhorred the then small abolitionist movement. He called anti-slavery abolitionists "monsters" who stirred up
"the horrors of a servile war" and deserved to "atone for this wicked
attempt with their lives." He asked a session of Congress to authorize federal censorship of abolitionist mail and even went so far as to
order the federal postal service to leave southbound abolitionist mail
undelivered. Historian David Walker Howe has referred to this as "the
largest peacetime violation of civil liberty in US history."

Jackson's policies empowered anti-abolitionists (North and South)
and helped unleash a storm of mob violence against these activists
and, indeed, all anti-Jackson political groups. In 1834 a Jacksonian
New York mob drove Whig Party observers away from a polling place.
The next day a Whig parade was physically attacked. These events
augured three years of such mob violence. Ethnic, racial, and religious
animosities influenced these attacks, but free blacks and abolitionists
were the most common targets. William Lloyd Garrison, a famous
abolitionist, was nearly lynched and was saved only when the authorities held him in jail for his own protection. In New York City there
was a three-day riot in response to an African American celebration
commemorating the date of slavery's abolition in the state. The mob
violence was so pervasive that urban centers responded by forming
the first modern police forces. (These men initially lacked uniforms
and were identifiable only by a copper badge — hence the nickname
cops.) This is a vital point. Most American police forces were formed

not in response to a crime wave but rather on the heels of *white* urban riots!

These mobs were made up of Irish and German Catholic immigrants. The members of these groups tended to be staunch Democrats and were registered to vote by Democratic operatives as soon as they debarked their ships. Though poor and stigmatized, these immigrants *learned* to be white — were informed of their "whiteness" — and passionately enforced the system of racial caste in America. They may have been poor, they may have been Catholic, but at least they were *white*; it was not the first time a sentiment of this kind had been held in America.

The riots were deadly, especially in the South. In 1835 seventy-nine southern mobs killed sixty-three people; sixty-eight northern mobs killed eight. Thousands more were injured and millions of dollars in property damage inflicted. President Jackson didn't personally order this violence, of course, but the perpetrators were nearly always Jacksonians. He had whipped his supporters into such a fervor through his rough, often violent rhetoric that he must bear some responsibility for what followed. He also did little to squelch the violence. During the 1835 Washington, DC, race riot, he called out federal troops but did not instruct them to protect free blacks, who were the main victims of the attacks. Jacksonian mobs reflected their leader and the era. All this represented the democratic tyranny of a white, male majority over weaker minorities and their social activist allies.

Forever Altered: The Second Party System and the Rise of Modern American Democracy

> Give the people the power, and they are all tyrants as much as kings.
>
> — Federalist Noah Webster, a critic of Jacksonian democratization

By 1834, Jefferson's Republican Party was permanently shattered. Jackson's Democratic Republicans took to calling themselves

Democrats, while Clay and Adams's National Republicans chose to take the title of Whigs. The so-called Second Party System had formed, the first system having been the split between Federalists and Republicans in the 1790s. It would last until the Civil War. The Whigs were an interesting lot, truly a coalition of many factions. What really held the Whigs together, though, was their abiding hatred of Jackson.

It was during this Second Party System that modern notions of political partisanship developed. The two sides loathed each other, and Americans were just about evenly split in their loyalties. Both the Whigs and Jacksonian Democrats had long-term effects on the United States' political culture. Jackson's legacy was his party's public electioneering and the *five* Supreme Court justices he appointed. These Democratic judges — including Chief Justice Roger Taney (who would later author the infamous Dred Scott decision) — would move the court in a pro-slavery, states'-rights direction for a full generation.

It's hard to judge these two parties by modern standards, as their positions were paradoxical. The Jacksonians did favor more white, male democratization but were completely illiberal on race and gender. The Whigs distrusted the will of the people and probably preferred the exclusion of some men from the political process; yet they were more tolerant in other ways and willing to protect the political rights of free blacks. Which was the better position? It's hard to know. Perhaps the Whig tendency toward the exclusion of poor whites was inexcusable; then again, given the outcomes, perhaps they were *right* to fear the masses.

What's certain is this: in the end the Jacksonian method of politics and campaigning had won out. Desperate to win the presidency, by 1840 the Whigs had begun trying to "out-Jackson" the Jacksonians. They held party conventions, publicly campaigned, and even sought to appeal to the "common man." Indeed, in 1840 the Whigs succeeded in running a Jackson of their own. The victorious Whig candidate, William Henry Harrison, was himself a war hero, a veteran of the Battle of Tippecanoe, a successful engagement with Indians in the old Northwest. He even had a catchy slogan: "Tippecanoe and Tyler too!" — a reference to John Tyler, the Whigs' vice presidential candidate. Furthermore, Whig cartoons labeled Harrison the "hard cider" (a popular alcoholic beverage) candidate and pictured him in front of humble, rustic log cabins. Here was the Whigs' own "self-made man." It was a deception, of course. Harrison came from a wealthy planter family in Virginia and lived in a mansion. No matter; it worked, and the Whigs won their first election.

———

Looking back from the twenty-first century, it is scary that the contemporary system of two major parties so closely resembles the fierce partisan divides of the Jacksonian era. After all, the division of American loyalties and inability of the two parties to work together led, within three decades, to a horrendous civil war. Jackson, like Donald Trump, was a remarkably divisive figure. He remains divisive among historians who *still* debate his legacy.

Though Jackson was a compelling and popular figure, and counted numerous achievements — he was the first and only president to ever pay off the entire federal debt — his flaws were many. Try as apologist historians may, we cannot disentangle Jackson's white democratization from his legacy of Indian removal, slavery, racism, and mob violence. Indeed, white supremacy stood at the very center of Jacksonian democracy; by design, the "many" wore their skin color as a badge of honor and mark of superiority over the "few," the lesser souls of America. In that way, ironically, Jackson and his acolytes achieved the dream of which wealthy southern elites had dreamed since the founding of Jamestown: to tie the loyalties of poor whites with the prosperity and fortunes of their social betters. Most whites were now united behind a new identity of whiteness-as-Americanism and excluded women, blacks, and natives from the collective community.

In the twenty-first century, as the US body politic continues to grapple with issues of race, immigration, gender, and sexual orientation, and as this country elected to the presidency a man with a character remarkably similar to Andrew Jackson's, perhaps the time is right to assess the triumphs and ills of our great democratic experiment. But here's a word of warning: What you find in reassessing the American past may be disturbing.

Andrew Jackson famously claimed that we should "never believe that the great body of the citizens can deliberately intend to do wrong." Observing the reality of his time, and of our own, I'm not so sure. This much, however, is true: Jackson was many things, but he was dangerous. So, potentially, are all powerful presidents . . . even, maybe especially, the popular ones.[12]

15

THE FRAUDULENT MEXICAN-AMERICAN WAR

The United States of America conquered half of Mexico. There isn't any way around that fact. The US regions most affected by "illegal" immigration — California, Arizona, New Mexico, and Texas — were once part of the Republic of Mexico. They would have remained so if not for the Mexican-American War (1846–48). Those are the facts, but they hardly tell the story. Few Americans know much about this war, rarely question US motives in the conflict, and certainly never consider that much of America's land — from sea to shining sea — was *conquered*.

Many readers will dispute this interpretation. Conquest is the natural order of the world, the inevitable outgrowth of clashing civilizations, they will insist. Perhaps. But if true, where does the conquest end, and how can the United States proudly celebrate its defense of

Resaca de la Palma, Texas, 9 May 1846. Painting commisioned by the US Army

Europe against the invasions by Germany and the Soviet Union? This line of militaristic reasoning — one held by many senior conservative policy makers even today — rests on the slipperiest of slopes. Certainly nations, like individuals, must adhere to a certain moral code, a social contract of behavior.

In the mid-nineteenth century American politicians and soldiers manufactured a war with Mexico, sold it to the public, and then proceeded to conquer their southern neighbor. They were motivated by dreams of cheap farmland, California ports, and the expansion of the cotton economy along with its peculiar partner, the institution of slavery. Our forebears succeeded, and they won an empire. In the process they lost something far more valuable in the moral realm.

(Mis)Remember the Alamo: Texas and the Road to War

We all know the comforting tale. It has been depicted in countless Hollywood films starring the likes of John Wayne, Alec Baldwin, and Billy Bob Thornton. "Remember the Alamo!" It remains a potent battle cry, especially in Texas, but also across the American continent. In the comforting tale a couple hundred Texans, fighting for their freedom against a dictator's numerically superior force, lost a battle but won a war, inflicting such losses that Mexico's defeat became inevitable. Never, in this telling, is the word *slavery* or the term *illegal immigration* mentioned. There is no room in the legend for critical thinking or fresh analysis. But since the independence and acquisition of Texas caused the Mexican-American War, we must dig deeper and reveal the messy truth.

Until 1836, Texas was a distant northern province of the new Mexican Republic, a republic that had only recently won its independence from the Spanish Empire, in 1821. The territory was full of hostile Indian tribes and a few thousand mestizos and Spaniards. It was difficult to rule and harder to settle — but it was indisputably Mexican land. Only, Americans had long had their eyes on Texas. Some argued that it was included (it wasn't) in the Louisiana Purchase, and Old Hickory himself, Andrew Jackson, wanted it badly. Indeed, his dear friend and protégé Sam Houston would later fight the Mexicans and preside as a president of the nascent Texan Republic. Thirty-two years before the Texan Revolution of Anglo settlers against the Mexican government, in 1803, Thomas Jefferson had even declared that the Spanish borderlands "are ours the first moment war is forced upon us." Jefferson was prescient but only partly correct: war would come, in Texas in fact, but it would not be forced upon the American settlers.

Others besides politicians coveted Texas. In 1819 a filibusterer (one who leads unsanctioned adventures to conquer foreign lands), an American named James Long, led an illegal invasion and tried but failed to establish an Anglo republic in Texas. Then, in 1821, Mexico's brand-new government made what proved to be a fatal mistake: it opened the borders to legal American immigration. It did so to help develop the land and create a buffer against the powerful Comanche tribe of West Texas but stipulated that the Anglos must declare loyalty to Mexico and convert to Catholicism. The Mexicans should have known better.

The Mexican Republic abolished slavery in 1829, more than three decades before its "enlightened" northern neighbor. Unfortunately, nearly all the Anglo settlers, who were by now flooding into the province, hailed from the slaveholding American South and had brought along many chattel slaves. By 1830 there were twenty thousand American settlers and two thousand slaves compared with just five thousand Mexican inhabitants. The settlers never intended to follow Mexican law or free their slaves, and so they didn't. Not really anyway. Most officially "freed" their black slaves and immediately forced them to sign a lifelong indentured servitude contract. It was simply American slavery by another name.

After Santa Anna — Antonio de Padua María Severino López de Santa Anna y Pérez de Lebrón, an authoritarian but populist president — seized power, his centralizing instincts and attempts to enforce Mexican policies (such as conversion to Catholicism and the ban on slavery) led the pro-autonomy federalists in Texas (most of whom were Americans) to rebel. It was 1835, and by then there were even more Americans in Texas: thirty-five thousand, in fact, outnumbering the Hispanics nearly ten to one. Many of the new settlers had broken the law, entering Texas after Santa Anna had ordered the border closed, as was his sovereign right to do.

What followed was a political, racial, and religious war pitting white supremacist Protestant Anglos against a centralizing Mexican republic led by a would-be despot. The Texan War of Independence (1835–36) was largely fought with American money, American volunteers, and American arms (even then a prolific resource in the United States). The war was never truly limited to Texas, Tejanos, or Mexican provincial politics. It was what we now call a proxy war for land waged between the United States and the Mexican Republic.

Furthermore, though Santa Anna was authoritarian, certain Texans saw him as their best hope for freedom. As Santa Anna's army marched north, many slaves along the Brazos River saw an opportunity and rebelled. Most were killed, some captured and later hanged. And while slavery was not, by itself, the proximate cause of the Texan Rebellion, it certainly played a significant role. As the Mexican leader marched north with his six thousand conscripts, one Texas newspaper declared that "[Santa Anna's] merciless soldiery" was coming "to give liberty to our slaves, and to make slaves of ourselves." So once again — as in America's earlier revolution against Britain — white Americans clamored about their own liberty and feared to death that the same might be granted to their slaves. When Santa Anna's army was eventually defeated, the Mexican retreat gathered numbers as many slave escapees and fearful Hispanics sought their own version of freedom south of the Anglo settlements.

Surely the most evocative image of the Texas War of Independence was the heroic stand of 180 Texans at the Alamo. *Alamo* has entered the American lexicon as a term for any hopeless, yet gallant, stand. And no doubt the outnumbered defenders demonstrated courage in their doomed stand. The slightly less than two hundred defenders were led by a twenty-six-year-old failed lawyer named William Barret Travis and included the famed frontiersman Davy Crockett, a former Whig member of the US House of Representatives. All would be killed. Still, the battle wasn't as one-sided or important as the mythos would have it. The defenders actually held one of the strongest fortifications in the Southwest, had more cannons than the attackers, and superior cannons, and were armed mainly with rifles that far outranged the outdated Mexican muskets. Additionally, the Mexicans were mostly underfed, undersupplied conscripts who often had been forced to enlist and had marched north some one thousand miles into a difficult fight. Despite inflicting disproportionate casualties on the Mexicans, the stand at the Alamo delayed Santa Anna by only four days. Furthermore, despite the prevalent "last stand" imagery, at least seven defenders (according to credible Mexican accounts long ignored) — probably including Crockett himself — surrendered and were executed.

None of this detracts from the courage of any man defending a position when outnumbered at least ten to one, but the diligent historian must reframe the battle. The men inside the Alamo walls were pro-slavery insurgents. As applied to them, *Texan*, in any real sense, is a misnomer. Two-thirds were recent arrivals from the United States and never intended to submit to sovereign Mexican authority. What the Battle of the Alamo did do was whip up a fury of nationalism in the United States and cause thousands more recruits to illegally "jump the border" — oh, the irony — and join the rebellion in Texas.

Eventually, Santa Anna, always a better politician than a military strategist, was surprised and defeated by Sam Houston along the banks of the San Jacinto River. The charging Americans yelled "Remember the Alamo!" and sought their revenge. Few prisoners were taken in the melee; perhaps hundreds were executed on the spot. The numbers speak for themselves: 630 dead Mexicans at the cost of 2 Americans. It is instructive that the Mexican policy of no quarter at the Alamo is regularly derided, yet few north of the Rio Grande remember this later massacre and probable war crime.

Still, Santa Anna was defeated and forced, under duress and probably pain of death, to sign away all rights to Texas. The Mexican Congress, as was its constitutional prerogative, summarily dismissed this treaty and would continue its reasonable legal claim on Texas indefinitely. Nonetheless, the divided Mexican government and its exhausted army were in no position (though attempts were made) to recapture the wayward northern province. Texas was "free," and a thrilled — and no doubt proud — President Jackson recognized Houston's Republic of Texas on Old Hickory's very last day in office.

Thousands more Americans flowed into the republic over the next decade. By 1845 there were 125,000 mostly Anglo inhabitants and 27,000 slaves — that's more enslaved blacks than Hispanic natives! One result of the war was the expansion and empowerment of the American institution of slavery. Because of confidence in the inevitable spread of slavery, the average sale price of a slave in the bustling New Orleans human-trafficking market rose 21 percent within one year of President John Tyler's decision to annex Texas during his final days in office in 1845. According to international law, Texas remained Mexican. Tyler's decision alone was tantamount to a declaration of war. Still, for at least a year, the Mexicans showed restraint and unhappily accepted the facts on the ground.

American Blood upon American Soil? The Specious Case for War

It took an even greater provocation to kick off a major interstate war between America and Mexico. And that provocation came. In 1844, in one of the more consequential elections in US history, a Jackson loyalist and slaveholder, James K. Polk, defeated the indefatigable Whig candidate Henry Clay. Clay preferred restraint with respect to Texas and Mexico; he wished instead to improve the already vast interior of the existing United States as part of his famed American System. Unfortunately for the Mexicans, Clay was defeated, and the fervently expansionist Polk took office in 1845. His election demonstrates the contingency of history: if Clay had won, war might have been avoided, slavery kept from spreading in the Southwest, and America spared a civil war. It was not to be. Just before Polk took office, a dying Andrew Jackson provided his protégé — even nicknamed Young Hickory — the sage advice that would spark a bloody war: "Obtain it [Texas] the United States must, peaceably if we can, but forcibly if we must."

In the end it was Polk who would order US troops south of the disputed Texas border and spark a war. Still, the explanation for war was bigger than any one incident. A newspaperman of the time summarized the millenarian scene of fate pulling Americans westward into the lands of Mexicans and Indians. John L. O'Sullivan wrote, "It has become the United States' manifest destiny to overspread the continent allotted by Providence for the free development of our yearly multiplying millions." There was an American sense of mission, clear from the very founding of Puritan Massachusetts, to multiply and inhabit North America from ocean to ocean. Mexico and the few remaining native territories were all that stood in the way of American destiny by 1846. As the historian Daniel Walker Howe has written, "'Manifest Destiny' served as both label and a justification for policies that might otherwise simply been called . . . imperialism."

Polk was, at least in terms of accomplishing what he set out to do, one of the most successful presidents in US history. Two of his administration's declared "great measures" involved expansion: "the settlement of the Oregon territory with Britain, and the acquisition of California and a large district on the coast." Within three years he would have both and more. Interestingly, though, Polk wielded different tactics for each acquisition. First, Oregon: Britain and the United States had agreed to jointly rule this territory, which at that time reached north to the border with Alaska. Expansionist Democrats who coveted the whole of Oregon ran on the party slogan "54°40' or Fight!," a reference to the latitude at the top of the Oregon of that day, a line that marks today's southern border of the state of Alaska. In the end, however, Polk would not fight Great Britain for Canada. Instead he compromised, setting the modern boundary between Washington State and British Columbia.

In his dealings with the much less powerful Mexicans, however, Polk took an entirely different, more openly bellicose approach. Here, it seems, he expected, if not preferred, a war. Was his compromise in Oregon reflective of great-power politics (Britain remained a formidable opponent, especially at sea) or tainted by race and white supremacist notions about the weakness of Hispanic civilization? Historians still argue the point. What we can say is that many Democratic supporters of Polk delighted over the Oregon Compromise, for, as one newspaper declared: "We can now thrash Mexico into decency at our leisure."

War it would be. In the spring of 1846, President Polk sent General Zachary Taylor and four thousand troops along the border between Texas and Mexico. Polk claimed all territory north of the Rio Grande River despite the fact that the Mexican province had always established Texas's border farther north at the Nueces River. Polk wanted Taylor to secure the southerly of the two disputed boundaries — probably in contravention of established international law. No one should have been surprised, then, when in April a reconnaissance party of US dragoons was attacked by Mexican soldiers south of the Nueces River. Polk, wily politician that he was, acted shocked upon hearing the news and immediately began drafting a war message — even though, in fact, his administration had been on the verge of asking Congress for a war declaration anyway! In the exact inverse of his negotiations with Britain over Oregon, Polk had made demands — that Mexico sell California and recognize Texan independence — that he knew would probably be rejected by Mexico City, and then sent soldiers where he knew they would probably provoke war. And oh, how well it worked.

Indeed, Polk's administration had already set plans in motion for naval and land forces to immediately converge on California and New Mexico when the outbreak of war occurred. The US Army and Navy complied and within a year occupied both Mexican provinces. Lest the reader believe that the local Hispanics were indifferent to the invasion, homegrown rebellions broke out, and were swiftly suppressed, in both locales. Polk got his war declaration soon after the fight in South Texas. In a blatant obfuscation, Polk announced to the American people that "Mexico has passed the boundary of the United States, has invaded our territory, and shed American blood upon American soil. War exists, and notwithstanding all our efforts to avoid it, exists by the act of Mexico herself." He knew this to be false.

So did many Whigs in the opposition party. Still, most obediently voted for war, fearing the hyper-nationalism of their constituents and remembering the drubbing Federalists had taken for opposing the War of 1812. In cowardly votes of 174–14 in the House (John Quincy Adams, the former president, was one notable dissenting vote) and 40–2 in the Senate, Congress succumbed to war fever. The small skirmish near the Nueces River was just a casus belli for Polk; America truly went to war to seize, at the very least, all of northern Mexico.

General Winfield Scott and the Defeat of Mexico

On the surface, the two sides in the Mexican-American War were unevenly matched. The US population of seventeen million citizens and three million slaves dwarfed the seven million Mexicans, four million of whom were local Indians with minimal loyalty to the young republic. Their respective economies were even more lopsided, for America had emerged strong from its market and communications revolutions. Mexico had only recently gained its independence in 1821, and its political situation was fragile and fluctuating. The United States had existed independently for some sixty years and already had fought two wars with Britain and countless battles with Indian tribes. America was ready to flex its muscles.

Many observers assumed the war would be easy and short. It was not to be. Most Americans underestimated the courage, resolve, and nationalism of Mexican soldiers and civilians alike. That the United States won this war — and most of the battles — was due primarily to superiority in artillery, leadership, and logistics. The US Military Academy at West Point in New York had trained, and numerous Indian wars had seasoned, a generation of junior and mid-grade officers. Many of the lieutenants and captains who directly led US Army formations in Mexico (think of Robert E. Lee, Ulysses S. Grant, William T. Sherman, and James Longstreet, to name only a few) would serve, either for the North or the South, as general officers in the US Civil War. Some of these officers involved in the Mexican-American War relished the glory of exotic conquest; others were horrified by a war they deemed immoral.

It must be remembered that the US Army that entered and conquered Mexico represented a slaveholding republic fighting against an abolitionist nation-state. Many southern officers brought along slaves and servants on the quest to spread "liberty" to the Mexicans. Some of the enslaved took the opportunity to escape into the interior of a non-slaveholding country. The irony was astounding.

President Polk's army was also highly politicized during the conflict. While the existing regular army officers tended to be Whigs in favor of internal improvements and centralized finance to the benefit of the military, all thirteen generals that Polk appointed were avowed partisan Democrats. Polk's biggest fear — which would indeed come to fruition in the election of General Zachary Taylor as president in 1848 — was that a Whiggish hero from the war he began would best his party for the presidency.

When it became clear in 1846 that General Taylor's initial thrust south into the vast Mexican hinterland could win battles but not the war, General Winfield Scott, a hero of the War of 1812, was ordered to lead an amphibious thrust at the Mexican capital. Indeed, Scott's militarily brilliant operational campaign constituted the largest American seaborne invasion until D-Day in World War II. It took months of hard fighting and several more months of tenuous occupation, but Scott's attack effectively ended the war by late 1847.

Still, conducting this war was extremely hard, indeed more difficult than it should have been, on both Taylor and Scott. This was due to President Polk's decision (reminiscent of George W. Bush's decision during the Iraq War) to cut taxes and wage war simultaneously. Indeed, General Scott became so short on troops and supplies that he decided to cut off his line of logistics and live off the land. This was a clever but risky maneuver that his subordinates — U. S. Grant and William T. Sherman — would remember and mimic in the US Civil War.

There was plenty of room for courage and glory on both sides of the Mexican-American War. It is no accident that the contemporary US Marine Corps Hymn speaks of the "Halls of Montezuma," or that several grandiose rock carvings of key battle names in Mexico unapologetically adorn my own alma mater at West Point. On the other side, the Mexican people still celebrate the gallant defense, and deaths, of six cadets — known as *Los Niños Héroes* — who manned the barricades of their own national military academy.

Nevertheless there was, as there always is, an uglier, less romantic side of the conflagration. Nine thousand two hundred seven men deserted the US Army in Mexico, or some 8.3 percent of all troops — the highest ever rate in an American conflict and double that of the Vietnam War. Hundreds of Catholic Irish immigrant soldiers responded to Mexican invitations and not only deserted the US Army but joined the Mexican army, as the San Patricio (Saint Patrick's) Battalion. Dozens were later captured and hanged by their former comrades.

America's military also waged a violent, brutal war that often failed to spare the innocent. In northern Mexico, General Taylor's artillery pounded the city of Matamoros, killing hundreds of civilians. Indeed, Taylor's army of mostly volunteers regularly pillaged villages, murdering Mexican citizens for either retaliation or sport. Many regular army officers decried the behavior of these volunteers, and one officer wrote, "The majority of the volunteers sent here are a disgrace to the nation; think of one of them shooting a woman while washing on the banks of the river — merely to test his rifle; another tore forcibly from a Mexican woman the rings from her ears." In the later bombardment of Veracruz, American mortar fire inflicted on the elderly, women, or children two-thirds of the thousand Mexican casualties. Captain Robert E. Lee (who would later lead the Confederate army in the US Civil War) was horrified, commenting that "my heart bled for the inhabitants, it was terrible to think of the women and children."

It should come as little surprise, then, that when the US Army seized cities, groups of Mexican guerrilla fighters — usually called rancheros — often rose in rebellion. Part of the US effort in Mexico became a counterinsurgency. People rarely take kindly to occupation, and the mere presence of foreigners often generates insurgents. All told, the American victory cost the US Army 12,518 lives (seven-eighths of the deaths because of disease, due largely to poor sanitation). Many thousands more Mexican troops and civilians died. This aspect of the war, events that tarnish glorious imagery and language, is rarely remembered, but it would be wise if it were.

Courageous Dissent: Whigs, Artists, Soldiers, and the Opposition to the Mexican-American War

War, as it does, initially united the country in a spirit of nationalism, but ultimately the war and its spoils would divide the US, nearly to its breaking point. Few mainstream Whigs — those of the opposition party — initially demonstrated the courage to dissent. They knew, deep down, that this war was wrong, but also remembered the fate of the Federalist Party, which had been labeled treasonous and soon disappeared due to its opposition to the War of 1812. Other Whigs were simply dedicated nationalists: the United States was their country, right or wrong. But there were courageous voices, a few dissenters in the wilderness. Some you know; others are anonymous, lost to history. All were patriots.

Many were politicians: those entrusted with the duty to dissent in times of national error. Though only a dozen or so Whigs had the fortitude to vote against the war declaration in 1846, a few were vocal. One was Representative Luther Severance, who responded to President Polk's "American blood on American soil" fallacy by exclaiming that "[i]t is on Mexican soil that blood has been shed" and that Mexicans "should be honored and applauded" for their "manly resistance."

Another was former President John Quincy Adams, who at the time was a member of the US House from Massachusetts (he was the only person to serve in Congress after being president). It was Adams, we must remember, who as secretary of state in 1821 had presciently warned Americans against foreign military adventures. "But she [America] goes not abroad in search of monsters to destroy," he wrote, for "[were she to do so] the fundamental maxims of her policy would insensibly change from liberty to force . . . she might become the dictatress of the world." Adams had seen the Mexican War coming back in 1836, when his avowed opponent, President Andrew Jackson, considered annexation of the Texan Republic. Then, Adams had said, "Are you not large and unwieldy enough already? Have you not Indians enough to expel from the land of their fathers' sepulchre?"

Another staunch opponent of the war was a little-known freshman Whig congressman from Illinois, a lanky fellow named Abraham Lincoln. As soon as he took his seat in the House, Lincoln rebuked President Polk's initial explanation for declaring war. "The President, in his first war message of May 1846," Lincoln told his audience, "declares that the soil was ours on which hostilities were commenced by Mexico. . . . Now I propose to try to show, that the whole of this — issue and evidence — is, from beginning to end, the sheerest deception." The future president would later summarize the conflict as "a war of conquest fought to catch votes." And indeed it was.

Prominent artists and writers also opposed the war; such people often do, and we should take notice of them. The transcendental-ist writers Henry David Thoreau and Ralph Waldo Emerson each took up the pen to attack the still quite popular conquest of Mexico. Thoreau, who served prison time, turned a lecture into an essay now known as "Civil Disobedience." Emerson was even more succinct, declaring that "the United States will conquer Mexico, but it will be as a man who swallowed the arsenic which brings him down in turn. Mexico will poison us." He couldn't have known how right he was; arguments over the expansion of slavery in the lands seized from Mexico would indeed take the nation to the brink of civil war in just a dozen years.

One expects dissent from artists. These men and women tend to be unflinching and to demonstrate a willingness to stand against the grain, against even the populist passions of an inflamed citizenry. But . . . soldiers? Surely they must remain loyal and steadfast to the end, and so, too, often, they are. Not so in Mexico. A surprising number of young officers — like Lee at the bombardment of Veracruz — despised the war. More than a few likely suffered from what we now call post-traumatic stress disorder (PTSD). One lieutenant colonel, Ethan Hitchcock, even attacked the justification for war. He wrote, "We have not one particle of right to be here. It looks as if the [US] government sent a small force on purpose to bring on a war, so as to have the pretext for taking California and as much of this country as it chooses." Perhaps the most honest and self-effacing critique of the war came from a young subaltern named U. S. Grant (who would square off against his then comrade R. E. Lee as commander of the Union army in the Civil War). Grant, a future president and West Point graduate, wrote that he "had a horror of the Mexican War . . . only I had not the moral courage enough to resign."

Finally, let us return to the powerful and unwavering dissent of John Quincy Adams, for the Mexican War, not his presidency, may constitute his finest hour. On February 21, 1848, the Speaker of the House called for a routine vote to bestow medals and adulation on the victorious generals of the late Mexican War. The measure passed, of course, but when the "nays" were up for roll call a voice from the back bellowed "No!" It was the eighty-year-old former president. Adams then rose in an apparent effort to speak, but his face reddened and he collapsed. Carried to a couch, he slipped into unconsciousness and died two days later. John Quincy Adams was mortally stricken in the act of officially opposing an unjust war. That we remember the victories of the Mexican-American War but not Adams's dying gesture surely must reflect poorly on us and our collective remembrances.

A Long Shadow Cast: The "Peace" of 1848

From the war's start there was never any real question of leaving Mexico without extracting territory. Indeed, by late 1847 there was considerable Democratic support for taking the whole country. That the United States did not is due mainly to Polk's peace commissioner ignoring orders and his own firing to negotiate a compromise. But there was something else. Many Democrats from the South — who had applauded the war from the start — now flinched before the prospect of taking on the entirety of Mexico and its decidedly brown and Catholic population. There was inherent fear of racial mixing, racial impurity, and heterogeneity. John Calhoun, the political stalwart from South Carolina, even declared, "Ours is the government of the white man!" And in 1848, Calhoun was right, indeed.

Even the Wilmot Proviso, an attempt by a northern congressman to forestall any conquest in Mexico, was tinged with racism.
Representative David Wilmot called his amendment a "White Man's
Proviso," to "preserve for free white labor a fair country, a rich inheritance, where the sons of toil, of my own race and own color, can live
without the disgrace which association with Negro slavery brings upon
free labor." Wilmot's proposal, unsurprisingly, never passed muster.
But it nearly tore the Congress asunder, with northern and southern
politicians at each other's throats. Northerners generally feared the
expansion of slave states and of what they called "slave power." The
Whig Party itself nearly divided — and eventually would — into its
northern and southern factions. Arguments about what land to seize
from Mexico and what to do with it (should it be slave or free?) would
shatter the Second Party System — of Whigs and Democrats — and
take the nation one step closer to the civil war many (like John Quincy
Adams) had long feared. The "peace" of 1848, known to history as the
Treaty of Guadalupe Hidalgo, would cast a long shadow.

———

In the end the United States expended more than twelve thouand lives
and millions of dollars to make a new colony of nearly half of Mexico
— an area two and a half times the size of France and including parts
or all of the current states of California, Nevada, Utah, Colorado, New
Mexico, and Arizona. Much of the land remained heavily Hispanic
for decades and effectively under military government for many years
(New Mexico until 1912!). The real losers were the Indian and Hispanic
people of the new American Southwest. The United States gained a
hundred thousand Spanish-speaking inhabitants after the treaty and
even more Native Americans. Under Mexican law both groups were
considered full citizens! Under American stewardship, race was a far
more detrimental factor. The results were (despite supposed protections in the treaty) the seizure of millions of acres of Hispanic-owned
land and, in California, Indian slavery and decimation as 150,000
natives dwindled to less than 50,000 in just ten years of US control.
During the postwar period, California's governor literally called for

the extermination of the state's Indians. This aspect of the war's end is almost never mentioned at all.

Words matter, and we must watch our use of terms and language. Mexico hadn't invaded Texas; Texas *was* Mexico. Polk manufactured a war to expand slavery westward and increase pro-slavery political power in the Senate. Was, then, America an empire in 1848? Is it today? And why does the very term *empire* make us so uncomfortable?

So what, then, are readers to make of this mostly forgotten war? Perhaps this much: it was as unnecessary as it was unjust. Nearly all Democrats supported it, and most Whigs simply acquiesced. Others, however, knew the war to be wrong and said so at the time. Through an ethical lens, the real heroes of the Mexican-American War weren't Generals Taylor and Scott but rather artists such as Henry David Thoreau; a former president, John Quincy Adams; and Abraham Lincoln, then an obscure young Illinois politician. There are many kinds of courage, and the physical sort shouldn't necessarily predominate. In this view, the moral view, protest is patriotic.

Let me challenge you to think on this: Our democracy was undoubtedly achieved through undemocratic means — through conquest and colonization. Mexicans were just some of the victims, and, today, in the American Southwest, tens of millions of US citizens reside, in point of fact, upon occupied territory.[13]

16

A BROKEN UNION

Shall I tell you what this collision means? They who think that it is accidental, unnecessary, the work of interested or fanatical agitators . . . mistake the case altogether. It is an irrepressible conflict between opposing and enduring forces, and it means that the United States must and will, sooner or later, become either entirely a slaveholding nation, or entirely a free-labor nation.

— Senator William Seward of New York (1858)

It is difficult to achieve a full realization of how Lincoln's generation stumbled into a ghastly war. . . . To suppose that the Union could not have been continued or slavery outmoded without the war . . . is hardly an enlightened assumption. If one questions the term "blundering generation," let him inquire how many measures of the time he would wish copied or repeated if the period were to be approached with a clean slate and to be lived again.

— Historian J. G. Randall (1940)

The debate may *never* end. Was the coming of the American Civil War the result of some irrepressible conflict between North and South or the result of a blundering generation of politicians? In other words, was the Civil War inevitable, or could it have been avoided? This historian, trained to eschew absolutes such as "inevitability," still understands the pull of an "irrepressible conflict" argument. After all, slavery and its expansion had dominated much political debate ever since the Missouri Compromise of 1820. Furthermore, it is hard to imagine the United States remaining half slave and half free indefinitely. Then again, an intersectional two-party system *had* prevailed

Tragic Prelude, 1937, by John Steuart Curry

for decades and avoided war through compromise after compromise. Besides, truth be told, few northern whites were actual humanitarians; abolitionists remained a fringe movement, and most whites above the Mason-Dixon Line were themselves highly racist and unconcerned with black rights. Seen in this light, perhaps war wasn't preordained.

The only certainty is this: millions of human decisions — contingent, contextual actions — led this nation into a near-suicidal civil war, the largest conflict ever fought in this hemisphere before or since. Americans' penchant for conspiratorial thinking, concern for their own rights and liberties, and capacity for political tribalism made such a bloody conflict possible. Slavery was, undoubtedly, the proximate cause of the divide — the core issue at hand. Nonetheless, it was never so simple as an argument over the ethics or morality of the institution of slavery. The inconvenient truth is that the vast majority of whites — North or South — couldn't give a hoot about black civil rights in the 1850s. Outright abolitionists were often considered wacky extremists, out on the fringes of American politics. The issues at hand, though they centered on questions of slavery in one way or another, were often about *power*. Which way of life and labor would triumph in the West? Would slavery expand or slowly wither and die in the contained space of the Old South? Who would dominate the Congress — northern or southern, free or slaveholding representatives?

Slavery, indeed, must be understood as America's "original sin," a ticking time bomb sneaked into our Constitution for future generations to defuse. And for nearly a century political leaders succeeded in delaying the explosion through combinations of compromise and collective avoidance. If the fuse hadn't been finally lit in the 1850s, perhaps it would have a decade or two later; we cannot be sure. What seems apparent, though, is that after the massive conquests by the United States in the Mexican-American War, increasingly bellicose southern leaders — out of fear of loss of their plantation way of life — pushed too far, too fast, and collapsed the existing two-party system. Then, like a phoenix rising from the ashes, a new Republican Party would form in opposition to the further expansion of slavery. For southerners this was too much, and they made clear their intention to secede should a Republican win the presidency. Bluffs were called. Neither side flinched. Perhaps a million would die.

A Slave Empire: The Obsessive Calls to Expand the Peculiar Institution

Ever since the Age of Jackson, the two primary political parties — Andrew Jackson's own Democrats and the opposition Whigs — were intersectional. In other words, they had southern and northern wings. Most arguments centered on banks, tariffs, federal improvements, and westward expansion. The peculiar institution of slavery was *always* an important issue, but it rarely tore the parties apart along sectional lines. Northern Democrats would usually side with their slaveholding southern compatriots, and many southern Whigs were slave owners themselves. The matter of the Mexican "Cession" — the land conquered from America's southern neighbor — and what to do with it would help shatter the intersectional system into increasingly regional political factions. Most northerners — Whig and Democrat — were uncomfortable with the westward expansion of slavery. They thought such a spread would further empower southerners in the Senate and compete with free labor in the western territories. Southerners — Whig and Democrat — believed that slavery must "expand or die." Cotton defined their economic system, and they feared that the slavery on which it depended would, if contained, eventually die or be outlawed by an increasingly populous North.

Each side was scared of the other, but the southerners were absolutely terrified by the prospect of loss of property, the overturning of their caste system, and racial mixing. That fear drove an obsessive penchant for slave expansion and fed the northern narrative of southern despotism. Southern overreach and overreaction led to the formation of a new pro-slavery ideology and a southern chauvinism unparalleled in American history. Whereas many founders were themselves slave owners, most believed the institution to be a necessary, temporary evil that would eventually disappear. By the 1850s a new generation of planters turned this ideology on its head. Slavery, they said, was a necessary *good* and was superior to the "wage slavery" of northern factory workers. James Hammond, a South Carolinian and a US senator from 1857 to 1860, famously espoused the sheer power of the American slave South, boasting that "the slaveholding South is now the controlling power of the world. Cotton, rice, tobacco, and naval stores command the world. . . . No power on earth dares . . . to make war on cotton. Cotton is king."

Southerners were so desperate to spread slavery that they took international law into their own hands, raising filibusterer (illegal and unsanctioned) armies to forcibly seize new territory. Many southerners had long been obsessed with Spanish Cuba and its plentiful slave society. In 1851, William Crittenden, the prominent nephew of the federal attorney general, led some four hundred volunteers in an unsuccessful invasion of Cuba. Fifty filibusterers, including Crittenden, were captured and executed in Havana. Furthermore, the line between official and unofficial policy was less than clear. The administration of President Franklin Pierce had long expressed a desire to annex Cuba. In fact, in the wake of Pierce's election in 1852, young enthusiastic Democrats led torchlight parades while holding banners reading THE FRUITS OF THE LATE DEMOCRATIC VICTORY — PIERCE AND CUBA.

In an even more ambitious series of adventures, William Walker, perhaps the most famous filibusterer of all, sought, unsuccessfully, in 1853 to conquer Baja California and Sonora from Mexico, and then from 1855 to 1860 led several bloody invasions of Nicaragua in Central America. At one point, in spring 1856, with Walker at the helm of a Nicaraguan army that included two thousand — primarily southern — Americans, the Pierce administration even temporarily granted diplomatic recognition to Walker's Nicaraguan government. Slavery, of course, had already been abolished in most of Latin America by this time. No matter, Walker soon legalized it again, in September 1856. Walker's invasion became a cause célèbre for southerners desperate to increase the number of slave states (and hence slave-state *senators*). One newspaper even proclaimed that "in the name of the white race [Walker] now offers Nicaragua to you and your slaves, at a time when you have not a friend on the face of the earth." By 1860, though, Walker's luck had run out, and he was executed by a Honduran firing squad.

Pierce, though not himself a slaveholder, appeared to be totally controlled by the pro-slave South and capable of colluding with wild, illegal adventurers. Northerners in both major political parties were appalled by what they saw as madness — a veritable obsession to add more slave states to the union. Northern Democrats faltered, southern Whigs stood by their region, and the two-party system of old bent. And later, as official US government policy began to appear to be under the control of the "Slave Power," the system would break once and for all.

The Slave Power Conspiracy: Truth and Fiction

Each side, North and South, was by the 1850s convinced that the other was out to suppress its way of life and trample on its liberty. "Free Soil" northerners — those who wished to avoid the expansion of slavery and its damage to their own free labor — believed that a Slave Power sought to dominate the federal government. In this line of thinking, influential southern aristocratic slaveholders wished to expand their slave labor system into the new western territories and even into the North itself, where the institution would compete with the small farming and wage labor system that provided most northerners' very livelihood. The minority Slave Power, it was believed, would accomplish this through domination of all three branches of the federal government and impose its will on the nation's northern majority.

At the same time, southerners, whether slaveholding or not, seemed to sincerely believe the polar opposite: that "black Republicans" were out to immediately abolish slavery, seize their chattel property, and impose racial equality and mixing on southern society. Poor whites, most of whom had not a single slave, feared the latter as much as the largest plantation owners. After all, their white skin was a badge of honor in a racial caste system and gave them a leg up in highly stratified southern society. Firebrands on either side whipped up their followers and encouraged conspiratorial thinking — this being, perhaps, a highly *American* propensity then and now.

To the northerners it appeared that each of the separate branches of federal power, one by one, had fallen under the sway of the Slave Power. It began with Congress. In 1850 a Democratic coalition pushed through the Fugitive Slave Act, requiring northern authorities to turn over runaways to southern slave owners. The irony of this struck deeply for northerners, especially Whigs. For three decades or more, Democrats had argued *against* the expansion of federal power on one issue after another. Now, suddenly, they demanded what can be considered one of the most blatant expansions of federal authority in US history. After all, under the conditions of the Fugitive Act, federal marshals could (and would) deputize any northern citizens into slave-snatching posses.

Then in 1854 the Democrats — with the help of the remaining southern Whigs — passed the Kansas-Nebraska Act, which overturned the thirty-year-old Missouri Compromise. In that famed system Missouri would be admitted as a slave state, but no further slave states could exist north of the 36°30' line of latitude. This essentially excluded slavery from the northwestern parts of the Louisiana Purchase, most of which had not yet been settled or admitted as states. Now, in the new act, "popular sovereignty" would reign and the inhabitants of these new territories could decide on their own if a state should be slave or free. The Missouri Compromise was dead, and, when all was said and done, so was the Whig Party — fractured for good between southern and northern factions on opposing sides of the bill. After the Kansas-Nebraska Act became law, Senator Truman Smith of Connecticut announced that "the Whig Party has been killed off effectually by that miserable Nebraska business." Smith resigned from the Senate in disgust, but southerners cheered the law!

A new party would be formed, slowly at first, and then with a vengeance by a coalition of northern Whigs, Democrats, and even contemptible Know-Nothings, anti-immigrant nativists. Kansas-Nebraska was a key tipping point. Abraham Lincoln, the former antiwar Whig, declared that "the moral wrong and injustice" of the act opened territory once closed to slavery and thus put the institution "on the high road to extension and perpetuity." Lincoln was more radical than most, admitting that "the negro is a man," but he and the vast majority of Republicans were decidedly *not* calling for the outright abolition of slavery, or for fully extending rights to blacks. They simply wished to limit the practice and keep a competing, slave-based economic system (and in some cases *all* blacks) out of their states. Furthermore, they feared the Slave Power minority that seemed to rule the government. So when the courts seemingly decided to sanction slavery in *all* states, yet another branch of government appeared subservient to the slave faction.

———

Dred Scott lived most of his life in obscurity. But when he sued for his freedom on account of his having spent years with his former owner in free-state territory, he was propelled into the spotlight and the history books. Looking at the composition of the Supreme Court, it should have been obvious that Scott never stood a chance. The court, thanks to the many appointments of President Andrew Jackson years before, had an unelected southern majority. Eighty-year-old Chief Justice

Roger Taney, a Jacksonian devotee, thus wrote a 7–2 opinion that has gone down as probably the court's worst decision in its history. Taney could have just said that as a slave Dred Scott had no right to sue in federal court. That would have been deplorable enough. Instead he went further — much further — and, in the style of his generation of southerners, ultimately overreached.

Taney and six other justices ruled that Scott wasn't a citizen, then implied that *no blacks*, even freemen, could be considered American citizens. Then Taney spent twenty-one pages eviscerating the Missouri Compromise, arguing that Congress never had the right to prohibit slavery in any territory, North or South. It now seemed that owners could take their slaves and settle anywhere, spreading the institution across the breadth of the nation. And of course southerners did little to reassure their northern colleagues. One newspaperman wrote that "Southern opinion upon the subject of Southern slavery . . . is now the supreme law of the land." Among opponents who felt compelled to speak out was Abe Lincoln, a rising star in the new Republican Party. After the Dred Scott decision, he quoted Jesus, stating, "'A house divided against itself cannot stand.' I believe this government cannot endure, permanently half slave and half free." Advocates, he warned, sought to "push [slavery] forward, till it shall become lawful in all the States . . . North as well as South."

The executive branch seemed the last hope for northerners opposed to the Slave Power. But thanks to the Three-Fifths Compromise giving greater weight to southerners in the Electoral College, many early presidents had themselves been southerners. Ten of the first sixteen owned enslaved human beings, eight while in office. Furthermore, many other northern Democratic presidents proved to be at least as pro-slave as their southern compatriots (who often dominated the party). Pierce and his successor, James Buchanan — a Pennsylvanian Democrat congenial to southern desires — would prove more than willing to use the executive branch to enforce the will of the Slave Power. Indeed, in one of many such incidents, in May 1854, after a federal deputy was shot by a Boston mob opposed to the seizure of a runaway slave, Pierce would send companies of marines, cavalry, and artillery to enforce the Fugitive Slave Act. The sight of federal regular troops marching solitary black men back into chains deeply offended many northerners, and they now lost faith in the institution of the presidency.

This was politics, passionate and no doubt sometimes violent. However, in the backdrop of all this debate on congressional legislation and Supreme Court decisions, blood spilled in the remote territory of Kansas. Pro-slavery marauders from Missouri were invading the territory and willing to kill. When it appeared that yet another pro-southern president — Franklin Pierce — was unwilling to put a stop to the Slave Power madness in Kansas, ever more northerners gave up on traditional politics and the old two-party system. Some looked to form a new party firmly against slavery's expansion (this would become the Republican Party); others took up arms and headed west.

Bleeding Kansas, Bleeding Nation

> To put it bluntly, without Kansas, Abraham Lincoln would never have been president of the United States. Moreover, if were not for Kansas, Lincoln would not just have lost the 1860 election — he wouldn't even have been a candidate.
>
> — Professor Jon Earle

I live in Lawrence, Kansas, a uniquely progressive city on the prairie and home of the University of Kansas. There are about ninety thousand year-round residents and some thirty thousand students when school is in session. Just a few miles down the road is the tiny town of Lecompton, which has a population of less than a thousand. Once — some 150 years ago — they were the poles (one pro- and one anti-slavery) of a guerrilla war. Arguably, it is in *Kansas*, in 1854, that the American Civil War began.

When Kansas opened to new settlement, with the Kansas-Nebraska Act and concept of popular sovereignty in place, conflict was nearly certain. Pro-slavery men, desperate to spread the practice (and avoid their state being surrounded on three sides by free states), flooded over the border from Missouri and brought slaves — and guns. Though eastern abolitionists from the New England Emigrant Aid Society, led by Amos Lawrence (the city's namesake), promoted anti-slavery settlement, at least initially the flood of Missourian "bushwhackers" into Kansas was stronger in numbers. As time went on, though, both sides realized that free-state anti-slavery men would predominate among the wave of new settlers. Knowing this to be the case, the Missourian "border ruffians" tried to push through a pro-slavery territorial delegate to Congress and to enshrine a pro-slavery state constitution.

They used tactics that were legal, extralegal, and even violent to win the early rounds of this political conflict. The Missourians simply *hated* the free-staters, especially the devout abolitionists among them, whom they saw as sanctimonious Yankees unhinged by their love for blacks. The pro-slavery men had no qualms about taking up arms. One of their early leaders instructed the Missourians to "mark every scoundrel among you that is the least tainted with free-soilism, or abolitionism, and exterminate him."

By the fall of 1855 the bona fide free-state residents outnumbered the anti-slavery men. No matter, the Missourians created their own territorial legislature in Lecompton (standing in contrast with an unofficial free-state legislature in Topeka) and sent five cannons and fifteen hundred men to lay siege to the free-state stronghold of Lawrence. Though the territorial governor initially cooled tensions, months later the posse entered Lawrence and burned it to the ground. The "Sack of Lawrence" resonated eastward and inflamed passions on both sides. In the minds of northern Republicans, the Pierce administration had proved itself impotent and unwilling to enforce the law or majority rule in the territory.

One loquacious senator, Charles Sumner of Massachusetts, made a two-day-long address titled "The Crime Against Kansas." He excoriated the Pierce administration, the Missourians, and his southern colleagues who defended them. He named names and criticized individual congressmen. Two days later Representative Preston Brooks, the cousin of one of those Sumner had denounced, approached Sumner in the nearly empty Senate chamber and battered him over the head more than thirty times with a gold-headed cane. Southerners applauded! Braxton Bragg, a former army officer and future Confederate general, wrote that the House should vote a thanks to Brooks because "you can reach the sensibilities of such dogs only through their heads and a big stick." From all over the South, Brooks was sent notes of congratulation, along with dozens of new canes. His only real punishment was a $300 fine levied by a district court.

Sumner's injuries were serious. His head was split open, and his injuries, along with mental wounds left by the beating, would keep him away from the Senate for most of the next four years. Even before the attack on the Senate floor, Republicans had taken to calling the war out West "Bleeding Kansas." Now "Bleeding Sumner" joined the list of wrongs the northerners counted against their southern neighbors. The Congress was now, quite literally, divided into two armed camps as members took to carrying pistols to work.

After Bleeding Sumner and the Sack of Lawrence, the guerrilla war in Kansas escalated and the free-staters struck back. Living in Kansas was John Brown, a fifty-six-year-old radical abolitionist with twenty children, many guns, and an Old Testament temperament. He declared that the time for passivity was over, that free-staters must "fight fire with fire . . . and strike terror in the hearts of the pro-slavery people" and that "something must be done to show these barbarians that we, too, have rights." Brown had a plan in mind.

Calculating that five free-staters had thus far been murdered by the bushwhackers, he and four of his sons abducted five pro-slavery men (who had nothing to do with the murders) from their cabins near the Pottawatomie Creek and proceeded to split open their skulls with broadswords! It is hard, no matter how sympathetic his cause, not to compare John Brown and his followers — Bible in hand along with broadsword — to the ghastly showmanship of Islamic State executioners. Certainly, pro-slavery settlers saw Brown as a radical extremist.

Not everyone agreed, and the entire country divided on the case of

Brown — who would be captured, tried, and, on December 2, 1859, hanged — and the Bleeding Kansas conflict. Ralph Waldo Emerson went so far as to say after Brown's sentencing that he was "a saint, whose martyrdom will make the gallows as glorious as the cross." The war didn't end with Brown's execution — not by a long shot. A guerrilla war that took hundreds of lives raged on and off for the next four years. In fact, once the Civil War began outright in 1861, the fighting would continue along the borders of Kansas and Missouri until 1865, a decade's worth of combat.

History, at least superficially, is alive in Lawrence. A customer can order John Brown ale from a local brewery or drink a cocktail at the John Brown Underground bar. University of Kansas students have been known to display images of John Brown holding an NCAA championship trophy instead of a Bible. Even the university mascot, the fabled Jayhawk, is a reference to the anti-slavery "jayhawker" guerrilla militia. Across the state line, University of Missouri sports fans can purchase T-shirts that say QUANTRILL IS MY "HOMEBOY," a reference to the Confederate bushwhacker leader responsible for the burning of Lawrence and execution of most of its male, anti-slavery population. As it recedes into history, the Bleeding Kansas or "Border War" issue that so inflamed the passions of an entire nation in the 1850s still resonates in this regional pocket of America.

John Brown, a veritable hero in Lawrence, would leave his Kansas stomping grounds and bring his guerrilla war to a climax in Virginia. He always had millenarian, if fatalistic, aspirations. He, along with some of his sons and a few other supporters, seized the federal army arsenal at Harpers Ferry, Virginia, where, under Brown's scheme, they would distribute the weapons to foment a slave uprising up and down the East Coast. This was a crazy plan, more dream than reality — and of course it failed miserably. In the attempted seizure the local slaves did not revolt, and the white townspeople violently turned on Brown's band. Eight of his party, including two of his sons, were killed, and the survivors, including Brown, blockaded themselves in a thick-walled building to make a last stand. That night a company of US Marines led by two army officers, Robert E. Lee and Jeb Stuart (both future

Confederate generals), used battering rams to storm the building. Losing one of their own, the marines killed two of the attackers and captured the rest, including a wounded John Brown.

It was as though Brown knew all along that he would fail and die as a result. He seemed stoic before the court, stating, "If it is deemed necessary that I should forfeit my life for the furtherance of the ends of justice, and mingle my blood further with the blood of my children and with the blood of millions in this slave country whose rights are disregarded by wicked, cruel, and unjust enactments, I submit; so let it be done!" He was, of course, found guilty. As he was led to the gallows, Brown handed a scribbled note to a guard. It read, "I, John Brown, am now quite certain that the crimes of this guilty land can never be purged away but with blood." He would be proved correct.

The Electoral Revolution of 1860:
Abraham Lincoln and the Coming of War

The Republican Party was ever so young at the time of the presidential election of 1856. Its candidate, a famed western adventurer named John C. Fremont, would lose to pro-South Pennsylvania Democrat James Buchanan. Americans voted largely according to the region in which they lived, and maps showing the results of the 1856 election foreshadowed the full sectional split to come. The rhetoric of the opposing sides had been extremely polarizing. Democratic papers published articles claiming that Fremont's "Black Republicans" would "turn loose . . . millions of negroes, to elbow you in the workshops, and compete with you in the fields of honest labor." Another group of Democrats paraded girls in white dresses holding banners that read, FATHERS, SAVE US FROM NIGGER HUSBANDS.

It was a less-than-conclusive election, even though the electoral vote wasn't very close. Fremont received 33 percent of the popular vote but carried all of New England and much of the Upper Midwest. The Republican Party was a non-factor in the South, sometimes not even appearing on the ballot. Buchanan received 45 percent of the popular vote — the anti-immigrant Know-Nothings garnered 22 percent and split much of the middle states' vote — but carried the South. When the Know-Nothings dissipated and the Republicans strengthened their party, it was certain the election of 1860 would be formative, perhaps even revolutionary. It was uncertain whether the union could hold.

In the 1860 campaign, the Deep South Democrats played the same game they had rolled out for 1856 — arguing that (1) the "black" Republicans would unleash their slaves and a regime of misogyny; and (2) if Lincoln were elected the slave states would be "forced" to secede. This tactic had worked in 1856, scaring many northern Democrats (and former Whigs) into supporting Buchanan. Then again, most Republicans didn't take seriously the southern threats of secession. They should have.

Something was profoundly different in 1860. The southern Democrats once again overreached, insisting that the Democratic Party platform include a slave code for the western territories that would enshrine forever their right to expand slavery as an institution. When the northern Democrats refused, the southerners walked out and formed a new Southern Democratic Party, which nominated Vice President John C. Breckenridge of Kentucky as their presidential candidate. The northern Democrats stuck with Illinois's Stephen Douglas, and, in a desperate attempt to forestall crisis, old Whigs and conservatives in the Upper South formed a Constitutional Union Party (nominating John Bell of Tennessee), which took *no stand* on the slavery question and instead pleaded for caution and preservation of the union.

With the Democratic vote split three ways, it became a possibility that Lincoln could win by simply carrying the northern states in a straight sectional vote. And indeed he would. He didn't even appear on the ballot in the Deep South. Before Election Day, however, the Southern Democrats pounded the Republicans with propaganda and leveled threats of secession and racial revolution. Lincoln was elected by men who were northern and white. The Republicans actually took pains to present themselves as the "White Man's Party," for it was they, they said, who wanted to exclude slavery — and by extension blacks — from their states and territories.

Thus, no matter how hard we try, it would be inappropriate to paint the 1860 election as one between civil rights Republicans and slave/ segregation Democrats. What actually happened was this: An honest, incorruptible candidate (Lincoln), who was somewhat more progressive on race and slavery, won only 40 percent of the popular vote but carried an electoral majority by winning the entire North. The southerners, then, acted the sore loser and seceded without even giving Lincoln a chance to govern. From their perspective, the three candidates who were more amenable to slavery had won a majority (60 percent) of the popular vote and thus Lincoln lacked a mandate. True enough, but he had won a *constitutional* majority, and, in the end, we must remember that it was the South that seceded, the South that insisted on the evacuation of federal military installations, and, ultimately, the South that fired the first shots on their American brothers in Fort Sumter, South Carolina. By early 1861 it was clear: there would be war. John Brown had been right.

———

It is impossible to know if war could have been avoided. What seems certain is that there were many blunders committed on both sides, though more by the insecure, alarmist, and chauvinistic South. Believing the Yankees would back down, the southerners pushed and pushed and pushed again, wanting to have their cake and to eat it too. The call for a slave code, though, would prove to be a step too far.

In the 1850s the functions of the federal government all became highly politicized and regional, crippling the bureaucracy and the sense of national union. By 1860 all three branches of government were seen as highly suspect. Congress became deadlocked on key votes between northern and southern factions that were increasingly fanatical; at times the armed parties nearly came (or did come) to blows on the floors of the House and Senate. Two weak presidents (Pierce and Buchanan) refused — despite their constitutional prerogative — to enforce federal law in Kansas. They folded to the South time and again, derelict in their duty. And of course the Supreme Court lost the trust of at least half of the population (the northern half) when the Dred Scott decision made it appear tainted by partisanship.

It is difficult not to feel a similar foreboding about our national divisions in the modern day. If the 1850s teach us nothing else, it is that terrible things happen when tribally divided political factions bring the mechanisms of federal rule to a standstill.

17

THE SECOND AMERICAN CIVIL WAR — THE SLOW, PERILOUS SHIFT TO EMANCIPATION

> My paramount object in this struggle is to save the Union, and is not either to save or to destroy slavery. If I could save the Union without freeing any slave I would do it, and if I could save it by freeing all the slaves I would do it; and if I could save it by freeing some and leaving others alone I would also do that. What I do about slavery, and the colored race, I do because I believe it helps to save the Union.
>
> — President Abraham Lincoln in a letter to the abolitionist Horace Greeley (August 22, 1862)

It is nearly impossible to illustrate the magnitude of the American ordeal of civil war. It is not just the hundreds of thousands of soldiers and civilians killed, but the fact that *this war* — perhaps more than any other — utterly transformed the United States. The bookshelves simply overflow with fascinating military histories of the conflict, and I'll leave that part of the story to their distinguished authors. Rather, let us here examine how, in the course of just four years, the war moved from being dedicated solely to the preservation of the Union to becoming a war of liberation to emancipate slaves.

How, in other words, did President Lincoln move from his above quote — declaring that he would do nearly anything with the slaves (including leaving them in bondage) to preserve the Union — to the Emancipation Proclamation of 1863 and, eventually, the Thirteenth Amendment constitutionally abolishing slavery in 1865? What's certain is that Lincoln himself may have transformed — for both tactical and moral reasons — as a brutal war moved him squarely into the abolitionist camp. This is perhaps the most profound tale of this horrific war: the one with the most transformative effects.

The Myth of Union Invincibility

It's often said that the North held all the strong economic, political, and military cards at the start of this war. And indeed it did — on paper. The Union states had the vast majority of the white population, nine-tenths of the manufactured goods, seven-tenths of the miles of railroad tracks, nine-tenths of the merchant ships, and seven-tenths of the grain production. The North also received most of the country's annual immigration and had eight-tenths of the nation's banking flow. By these measures it seemed the South didn't stand a chance.

But a closer look narrows the gap between the two belligerents. The North had essentially *no army* — its paltry regiments were mostly spread across the vast western interior fighting Indians. Furthermore, some of the most able US Army officers —think of Robert E. Lee, T. J. "Stonewall" Jackson, and James Longstreet — quickly resigned their commissions and joined the new Confederate army. *That army*, of course, was mobilized rather quickly because it had a head start. After John Brown's raid on Harpers Ferry in 1859, spooked southerners from Virginia to Texas formed militias to stave off perceived threats of slave rebellion. Many of these local militiamen would form the core of the future Confederate armies.

Perhaps the biggest equalizer, however, was the matter of opposing war aims. The Union could win only if it *conquered* and occupied much of the South. A win for the South, on the other hand, meant simply not losing. This is a much easier, and defensive, task. The Union could count on long supply lines (which had to be guarded) and frequent guerrilla attacks by the Confederates at its rear. The South fought on familiar turf and with much shorter supply lines. And the population numbers were themselves deceptive. Though the North counted seven-tenths of the white population, the South counted nearly four million slaves. These laborers kept the southern agrarian economy churning and freed up millions of potential soldiers for the Confederacy. Conversely, northerners, out of fear of crippling their economy, couldn't mobilize nearly so high a percentage of the workforce.

Many residents of the South also argued that its rural population was more martial and effective than the supposedly effete Yankees. Some even claimed that just a single southerner could "whoop 10 Yankees!" Though the South met early battlefield success and was generally better led during the war's early campaigns, such conceited proclamations would be proved wrong. It turned out that there was enough (often foolhardy) valor on *both sides*, as men killed and died with a discipline that is shocking to the modern reader. In the end nothing was inevitable, neither Union victory nor Southern defeat, but by 1862 one thing seemed certain: It was to be a long, hard war.

For Union: Lincoln Walks the High Wire (1861–62)

President Lincoln was obsessed with Kentucky. He had been born there, but there was far more to it. After all, not *every* slave state had seceded. Missouri, Kentucky, Maryland, and Delaware stayed in the Union — in some cases only just. Lincoln knew he needed to keep the so-called border states on the Union side, or at least neutral. Many lateral (east–west) railroad lines ran through the western border states and would be vital to shifting troops from theater to theater. Maryland and Delaware, along with already seceded Virginia, surrounded the Union capital, Washington, DC. The president's very safety was at stake.

So it was that Lincoln's desire to keep the border states in the Union informed the president's strategic thinking in the war's first year. Lincoln had to downplay the abolitionist sentiments of his Republican Party and reassure Northern Americans — most of them wildly racist — that this war was for *union*, not a crusade against slavery. In keeping with this strategy, in the war's early months most Union commanders were ordered to return runaway slaves and enforce the Southerners' rights to their "property."

Lincoln didn't want and, he thought, couldn't afford a crusade. What was needed was a quick victory, and a limited war that didn't too badly damage Southern property or increase border state sympathy for the Confederacy. Initially, Lincoln called for only seventy-five thousand three-month volunteers, and this is telling. One grand victory and the seizure of the Confederate capital in nearby Richmond, Virginia, might just end the war in one fell swoop. Of course, it was not to be. The green Union army was outled and, ultimately, outfought at the July 1861 Battle of Bull Run, near Manassas Junction, Virginia, and fled back to the District of Columbia in disarray.

In Tennessee and Mississippi an unknown, disheveled general named Ulysses S. Grant — who had failed in most of life's endeavors and been cashiered from the regular army years before for drunkenness — met with more success. Still, the rebels had generally acquitted themselves well in the war's early years. It was to be a long war. Union strategy would have to change. As Lincoln wrote, "We must change tactics or lose the game." It was time to strike the economic and cultural heart of the Confederacy: the institution of slavery.

"As He Died to Make Men Holy, Let Us Die to Set Men Free": Emancipation Comes at Last

Lincoln was stuck between political forces. The opposition Democrats in the North were decidedly against emancipation of the slaves, as was much of the Northern population (especially Irish immigrants). His own Republicans — especially the "radical wing" — on the other hand, were becoming frustrated with Union military defeats and Lincoln's unwillingness to attack slavery. But Lincoln was personally edging ever closer to the "radical" position, for reasons of "military necessity." Congress, in July of that year, had passed the Confiscation Act of 1862, which held that Union military officers were no longer obliged to return runaways to Southern slaveholders. Congress knew, as did Lincoln and his commanders, that slavery was the core of the Southern war machine. Slaves dug trenches, built forts, raised crops, and enabled millions of white men to head to the battlefront. Something *had* to be done to strike a blow to the South's war-making capacity. An attack on slavery seemed to be just the thing.

Unfortunately, Lincoln felt he first needed a battlefield victory before issuing an Emancipation Proclamation. And for a year his armies in the vital Eastern Theater had known nothing but defeat: at Bull Run, the Peninsula Campaign, the Shenandoah Valley, and Second Bull Run. Then in September 1862 the effective, victorious Confederate general Robert E. Lee took his Army of Northern Virginia northward and invaded Maryland. He hoped to turn Maryland into a rebel state, gain international recognition for the Confederacy, and, perhaps, end the war. On September 17, 1862, at Antietam Creek, Lee was just barely defeated and forced back into Virginia. Though the ever-cautious Union commander General George B. McClellan had failed to trap and destroy or at least meaningfully pursue Lee's army despite having found a misplaced copy of the Confederate battle plan, Lincoln had the "victory" he needed.

Soon afterward, he issued probably one of the most profound, questionably legal, and consequential executive edicts of all time: the Emancipation Proclamation. It declared that on January 1, 1863, all slaves held in the rebellious states were "then, thenceforward, and forever free!" So, how many slaves did Lincoln free in January 1863? *Zero*. The edict didn't touch the slaves in border states — Lincoln still needed to keep these states in the Union — and applied only to slaves in regions actively in rebellion. Of course, the Confederates reigned in these areas and weren't about to free their slaves. In the end the proclamation was a *war* measure not a humanitarian decree. But it did change one thing: the Union army would transform overnight into an army of liberation wherever it marched.

This much, too, is certain: there would have been no Emancipation Proclamation had the war not lasted so long and turned so bloody. It was the death of whites by the tens of thousands that convinced the Union to free the blacks. The irony, of course, was that if the Union had won at Bull Run, or if General McClellan had seized Richmond in July 1862 (as he nearly did), then the war might have ended with slavery *intact*. After all, emancipation was not yet a stated war aim, and it is likely that a coalition of Southerners, border-staters, and Northern Democrats would have negotiated reunion without emancipation. Who knows how long slavery might then have persevered in the American South.

Who (Really) Freed the Slaves?

Ask an American on the street today "Who freed the slaves?" and nine times out of ten the answer will be "Abe Lincoln, of course." But that's not strictly true. Lincoln did claim to generally abhor the institution of slavery, but he was extraordinarily cautious in its abolition. His Emancipation Proclamation didn't free a single slave on the day it took effect. And it wasn't just "military necessity" that had provoked the decision. From the earliest days of the war, the slaves, if not the Northern whites, were totally sure this was a war for abolition. By the tens of thousands they risked their lives to escape to Union lines. They placed the question of emancipation — of what exactly was to be done with these "contrabands" of war, as the slaves were termed — on the agenda of the Union army and, by extension, the US government.

How this process worked can be made clear with a simple vignette, undoubtedly repeated thousands of times during the war. A family

The Emancipation of Negroes, 1863, by Thomas Nast

of runaway slaves — man, woman, and child — escapes a plantation and enters Union-held territory. They meet a lowly private on guard duty. The soldier is no abolitionist; heck, he has probably never met many black people. He certainly doesn't see them as his equal. Still, he catches the look in the poor child's eyes and doesn't want to be responsible for turning these slaves away. So he asks his lieutenant what to do, who asks the captain, who asks the colonel, who asks the general, who . . . eventually asks President Lincoln. What exactly *is* the policy of the US government toward these human "contrabands"? The question becomes public, is debated in Congress, on the streets, in countless taverns.

Most standard histories ignore this facet of the war and deny agency to the millions of enslaved black people, most of whom are portrayed as victims and then grateful beneficiaries. Only they were so much more. Seen in this light, it was the slaves, through their many thousands of dangerous escapes, who freed themselves, by flooding the Union army lines both before and after the famed Emancipation Proclamation.

Whither Civil Liberties?

The Civil War probably did more to expand federal and presidential power than any other war in American history. Although both the Union and Confederacy were republics and ostensible democracies, each soon found that exigencies of war would force them to curtail civil liberties and centralize governance. The latter was particularly ironic in the states'-rights-obsessed South. Lincoln, in response to anti-conscription and antiwar riots, called out the army in more than a few cities, suspended habeas corpus, and imprisoned many antiwar figures. He even banished one Ohio politician to the South! Some of these measures have been, rightfully, criticized by later scholars.

But context matters. Lincoln had a war to win, political enemies at his rear, and an army that had known mostly defeat for two full years. Furthermore, the draft riots were a genuine threat and a reflection of Northern racism (and unhappiness about fighting for black freedom), especially among the Irish. For example, in the New York riots of July

1863, angry mobs attacked blacks throughout the city, killing more than a hundred and prompting Lincoln to call in federal troops fresh from the Battle of Gettysburg to suppress the five-day melee. Lincoln's critics, who took to calling him "King Abraham," "a Caesar," and a tyrant, remained angry throughout the war. They resented the implementation of a military draft (the first of its type), his transformation of the war into one of emancipation, declarations of martial law, and his suspension of civil liberties. However, the American people, by and large, stood by Lincoln and gave him a surprising victory in his bid for reelection in 1864.

The actions of Confederate president Jefferson Davis were even more ironic. His was a republic supposedly founded on states' rights and in opposition to centralized control. And yet it was the Confederacy that first passed a conscription law and drafted its white population into military service.

Interestingly, a "Twenty-Negro Law" exempted substantial slaveholders from conscription, resulting in opposition by some to what was called a "rich man's war and poor man's fight." The government in Richmond could temporarily commandeer slaves for war labor. Furthermore, high taxation (which the Southern Democrats supposedly abhorred) combined with food shortages to cause notorious "bread riots" in Richmond and mass desertions from the South's armies. In some regions deserters and draft dodgers formed armed militias that essentially ruled certain counties as independent nations.

The story was the same, North and South, as it often is: "military necessity" and a long, bloody war curtailed individual freedom.

Carnage: Waging the Civil War

It was a bloodbath. From start to finish thousands upon thousands of Americans — clad in blue or gray — fell dead or maimed on the field of battle. Few had predicted such a massive bloodletting; after all, this was to be a ninety-day war. Instead it lasted more than four years. The American Civil War was by far the costliest in American history. Some six hundred thousand died, if not more — equivalent to more than the American fatalities of the two world wars taken together. On a single day at the Battle of Antietam (September 17, 1862), more men were killed and wounded on both sides than in all previous American wars. More Union men became casualties that day than the number that would fall on D-Day in 1944.

The primary cause of all this death and destruction, besides the devotion of both sides, was the rifled musket. In previous wars the United States and other belligerents generally used smoothbore muskets, which were far less accurate. Rifling a musket increased its range and accuracy fourfold and made defense the far stronger tactical position. The rifle also decreased the offensive value of artillery, as gunners could now be picked off when the cannons were brought forward. Furthermore, traditional cavalry charges became a thing of the past, since bullets took down horses and riders long before they could reach the infantrymen's lines.

Still, there was more to it than mere technology. The *tactics* of this war had not yet caught up with the technological advances. Most officers on both sides, trained in Napoleonic tactics at West Point, preferred the offensive to the defensive. They were taught to be aggressive and to seek out and destroy the enemy's main force. Few recognized the transformational power of the rifle soon enough to stray from the "close-order column" tactics of the Napoleonic Wars, and they marched their men straight into the deadly maelstrom of enemy fire. Though often misguided, these officers *were* brave; there is no question. Colonels and generals led from the front, and in the Civil War a general was more likely to be killed than a private. The inverse has tended to be true ever since. By war's end, after years of failure to recognize the tactical revolution that had been unleashed, both sides had shifted to entrenchments and defensive fortifications. Unfortunately, by then hundreds of thousands had fallen in foolish close-order charges.

We Are Men: Black Soldiers in the Civil War

Once let the black man get upon his person the brass letters US, let him get an eagle on his button, and a

musket on his shoulder, and bullets in his pocket, and
there is no power on earth or under the earth which can
deny that he has earned the right of citizenship in the
United States.

> — A speech by abolitionist and former runaway
> slave Frederick Douglass at National
> Hall in Philadelphia (July 6, 1863)

Few could have imagined it. Most Southerners and plenty of
Northerners couldn't have foreseen the mass arming of blacks and
their service in the armies of the federal republic! But this is exactly
what occurred, as early as 1862, when Congress gave its approval. The
decision was driven by two main forces: (1) military necessity and (2)
the clamoring of blacks and runaway slaves themselves to serve the
Union. And enlist they did, in record numbers. Though just 1 percent
of the prewar Northern population, blacks eventually constituted 10
percent of Union army volunteers. Furthermore, *85 percent* of the
North's of-age black population enlisted.

All told, by war's end 180,000 black soldiers would serve the Union.
They were paid less than white soldiers, treated poorly by many white
troopers, served under white officers, and were initially kept behind
the lines for humiliating menial labor. Still, the valor of the black
troops cannot be overestimated. By 1865, 20 percent of the 180,000
black soldiers had died, a casualty rate much higher than among their
white brothers-in-arms. Many black soldiers came from the border
states, for enlisting in the army was the only sure way to freedom
in regions where slavery remained legal after the Emancipation
Proclamation was issued. Tens of thousands of others were runaways,
only recently held in bondage.

These men knew *exactly* what they were fighting for. The war was no
abstraction for a runaway slave. In the army they could contribute to a
victory they hoped would bring their permanent salvation. They also
found many other things in the army: the dignity of service; a transformation of their self-image; and, among some at least, a new respect
in the collective national opinion. Still, serving in a black regiment was

dangerous for soldier and officer alike. The Confederates were appalled by the sight of blacks armed and in uniform. Some Confederate units refused to take black prisoners and had a policy of shooting captured black soldiers and their hated white officers. Besides, with much to prove on the field of battle, combat could be extraordinarily perilous.

One of the first and most famous black regiments formed was the 54th Massachusetts Infantry. Its colonel was the twenty-six-year-old Robert Gould Shaw, the son of prominent abolitionist parents in Boston. As a Massachusetts regiment, raised partly at the behest of Frederick Douglass and other famous local abolitionists, the 54th was the North's "showcase black regiment." In July 1863 the unit volunteered to lead the assault on the formidable Fort Wagner in South Carolina. In the heroic, and ultimately unsuccessful, attack, nearly half the regiment became casualties and Shaw was killed charging the fort's parapet. Though the attack failed, the exploits of the 54th resonated across the North. The *Atlantic Monthly* declared, "Through the cannon smoke of that dark night [at Fort Wagner], the manhood of the colored race shines before many eyes that would not see."

The Confederates threw the body of Colonel Shaw into the pit of a mass grave along with hundreds of his enlisted men. When a Confederate officer supposedly replied to a request for Shaw's body with the taunt "We have buried him with his niggers," Shaw's proud father replied, "We hold that a soldier's most appropriate burial-place is on the field where he has fallen." Colonel Shaw still lies with his men in that pit on a South Carolina island.

Lincoln's Final Act: The Thirteenth Amendment

Neither slavery nor involuntary servitude, except as a punishment for crime whereof the party shall have been duly convicted, shall exist within the United States, or any place subject to their jurisdiction.

— Section I, Thirteenth Amendment
to the Constitution (1865)

By January 1865 the war was finally nearing its end. More than half a million soldiers were dead, and nearly two hundred thousand blacks wore the uniform of the Union. Still, President Lincoln felt there remained work to be done aside from achieving victory in the war. During a lame-duck session of Congress, he pushed the Thirteenth Amendment through the House of Representatives on its way to ratification. He was advised not to do so. Some thought that it would motivate the South to fight on; others, that it would alienate Lincoln's supporters in the slave-laden border states; plenty just disagreed with the final abolition of slavery.

Nevertheless, Lincoln proceeded. He did so mainly because he feared the war would end before slavery was on its way to abolishment. His Emancipation Proclamation, after all, was an executive *war measure*, sanctioned not by Congress but by presidential fiat. Though the proclamation declared the slaves were "forever free," might not the courts determine after the war that the edict was unconstitutional or no longer in effect? Might then, as Lincoln feared most, the runaway slaves that donned the Union blue be rendered slaves once again at war's end? Here Lincoln demonstrated his true mettle. He and his supporters lobbied for the necessary votes, probably bribed their way to some, and eventually won passage of the amendment. Thus ended slavery everywhere. And ironically, it was in loyal border states such as Delaware that it ended last — long after the Union army had liberated the slaves of Alabama.

Emancipation and the Thirteenth Amendment that followed constituted, by some economic measurements, the largest and quickest forced confiscation of property in world history and were, by their very nature, a major and complex undertaking. The achievement was profound, if unexpected. A war undertaken, by Lincoln's own declaration, for preservation of the Union — regardless of the outcome for the slaves — had within four short years morphed into a conflict that abolished slavery once and for all. It was now the law of the land. It was a long, hard road, but after half a century of effort, the once-mocked abolitionists had achieved freedom for the slaves.

———

On April 14, 1865, just days after Robert E. Lee surrendered his army, Lincoln was assassinated in Ford's Theatre in Washington, DC, by the actor and Confederate sympathizer John Wilkes Booth. Lincoln would not see the Union to final victory. Nonetheless, by April 1865, Lincoln knew that victory was near — though it was not the sort of victory he had initially envisioned. He had hoped to quickly reestablish and *preserve* the Union without resorting to total war.

Instead the carnage of Bull Run, the Peninsula Campaign, Shiloh, and other battles led him to see the bitter truth. Victory demanded that the *old* Union and the *old* South be destroyed and a *new* union reconstructed on its ashes. This would be the task at hand when the Confederacy surrendered. The nation had changed by 1865. The role and scope of federal power had forever increased; notions of race and citizenship had been reformulated. And lastly, a new nationalism formed as Americans started to think of the federal Union as the paramount law of the land. Before the war, most Americans referred to *these* United States. After the conflict, almost all labeled this country *the* United States!

The war appeared to solve many things: the question of union, the legality of secession, even the existence of slavery. Yet so much more, so many unanswered questions, lay before Lincoln's untested successor and the nation as a whole. How shall the Union be pieced together, and how *should* four million souls — recently held in bondage — be integrated into American society? The nation would have to be reconstructed, to be sure, but few knew quite what to do for newly freed former slaves. In the aftermath of civil war there existed an opportunity, a first chance, to legislate and enforce racial equality once and for all. Americans had only to seize the chance. Tragically, they would not.[14]

18

RECONSTRUCTION, A FAILED EXPERIMENT?

The slave went free; stood a brief moment in the sun;
then moved back again toward slavery.

— W. E. B. Du Bois (1913)

It was, perhaps, the greatest betrayal, the ultimate lost opportunity, in all of American history. The failure of Reconstruction — the reunion and reorganization undertaken after the Civil War — was a dark, yet briefly vibrant, moment in our collective past. This was a time of promises made but not kept, mainly promises to the newly freed slaves. The results of this lost opportunity for genuine civil rights and racial equality resonate in the present day.

Most Americans know something about our great Civil War. Lay enthusiasts, historical reenactors, and even otherwise disengaged citizens can recount the basic contours of great battles, horrific casualties, and the sudden freedom granted the slaves. Well, it makes sense: war, when it is not actually unfolding *around* you, is exciting. Conversely, the process of picking up the pieces, rebuilding a nation, and creating new social structures for a forever changed country, the stuff of Reconstruction, is far less well known.

It should be otherwise. The dozen or so years after the American Civil War are among the most consequential in our history and have far more relevance to contemporary affairs than almost any other era. Nearly every issue Americans grapple with today — citizenship, race, terrorism, affirmative action, the scope of federal power, and reparations payments — all have strong roots in the period of Reconstruction. It was in these years that the US government would briefly triumph and ultimately fail in a grand experiment to achieve the twin goals of postwar Reconstruction: justice and reconciliation.

The historiography (the history of historians) of Reconstruction has a long, sordid history. Readers of a certain age, in fact, may recognize some of the older interpretations of this period. In the late nineteenth and early twentieth centuries, historians such as William A. Dunning and his many students at Columbia University — the so-called Dunning school of scholars — dominated this field. According to this highly biased, southern-influenced interpretation, the problem with Reconstruction was that it went too far. The story went something like this: President Abraham Lincoln had a plan for leniency toward the former Confederates, and his successor, Andrew Johnson, attempted to follow the Lincoln vision. He was thwarted, however, by Radical Republicans in Congress who pushed too far too fast and were overly punitive with the former rebels. They sent "carpetbaggers" (outsiders) from the North who worked with "scalawags" (or collaborators) to force racial equality and northern capitalist dominance on the poverty-stricken South. In this view former slaves simply weren't ready for the vote and other civil rights, and the Reconstruction-era governments in the South were massive, corrupt failures. Luckily, by 1877 a compromise was reached, the federal troops left, and heroic former Confederates in the newly formed Ku Klux Klan drove out the Yankee carpetbaggers and restored home rule to their governments.

If that interpretation seems shocking by modern standards, well, it should. What's most disturbing is that some version of the Dunning interpretation remained mainstream and in students' textbooks well into the 1950s; until, that is, the civil rights era. That this vision prevailed so long reflects a culture of white supremacy that existed long after the Civil War and, some argue, still exists today. The whole edifice was premised on the notion that blacks, as former slaves, were incapable of self-government and required the steady, paternalistic hand of their white southern superiors. After the civil rights era a new generation of historians took a fresh look at Reconstruction and rehabilitated the efforts of Radical Republicans, lauding their ultimately unsuccessful attempt to guarantee basic civil rights to newly freed blacks.

What, then, can now be said about Reconstruction? Perhaps this: it was a remarkably idealistic attempt to bring freedom and *equality* to four million souls only recently held in bondage. Some of the brief achievements of this period (such as blacks voting, holding office, and serving in Congress) would not again occur on a broad scale for a century. The failure of these attempts was not due to corruption or the unpreparedness of blacks; rather, the racism and apathy of *white* Americans — both south and north of the Mason-Dixon Line — doomed black Americans to generations of slavery by another name: Jim Crow.

An Enormous Challenge: Reconstruction Begins

If war among the whites brought peace and liberty to blacks, what will peace among the whites bring?
— Frederick Douglass (1875)

Americans began arguing about how best to reconstruct the Union before even winning the war. In fact, various generals and politicians experimented with several methods of reunion and racial reconciliation. Some Union generals treated escaped slaves like lowly laborers, either paying low wages for hard jobs or returning them to the plantations they had fled. This approach was common in the occupied Mississippi Valley and parts of Louisiana during the war. On the Carolina coast, however, the planters fled the approaching Union forces during the war and left behind some ten thousand slaves. Union generals granted land to the slaves and created a remarkable, if brief, experiment in black self-rule. White New Englanders flocked to the Carolina Sea Islands to teach blacks to read, treat them medically, and train them in farming techniques. In another remarkable turn, Confederate president Jefferson Davis's own plantation, Davis Bend, in Mississippi was seized and turned into a "negro paradise," as General Ulysses S. Grant declared it should be. The plantations were settled and worked by the slaves as a collective, and Davis Bend proved remarkably profitable for the rest of the war.

Such experiments, however, dealt only with the relatively few slaves left behind in the wake of Union armies. After the South's surrender, the US government confronted a much larger challenge: What to do for some *four million* former slaves made free by the war? The size of the task was staggering. Six percent of all northern white males had died as a result of the conflict, along with 18 percent of Confederate men. The freeing of the slaves was, by some counts, the largest confiscation of wealth (and "property") in world history. The South was in ruins — it needed to be rebuilt and its surrendered rebels somehow reintegrated into the Union. It would have been a daunting task even if everything had gone right.

Besides, the South may have been beaten on the battlefield, but it was less clear that southerners considered themselves truly defeated. Union general James S. Brisbin wrote to a congressman in December 1865 that "[t]hese people are not loyal; they are only conquered. I tell you there is not as much loyalty in the South today as there was the day Lee surrendered to Grant. The moment they lost their cause in the field they set about to gain by politics what they had failed to obtain by force of arms." The average Confederate soldier may well have turned over his rifle (though often the soldiers kept their firearms) and taken off the uniform, and he may even have accepted the freeing of the slaves; however, he fully expected to maintain the edifice of white supremacy and return to the ways of the antebellum South.

The Worst President in History? Andrew Johnson and the Failure of Presidential Reconstruction

Johnson lacked all the qualities that made Lincoln a great president. He was combative, had no charisma, failed to compromise, and was wickedly racist. When Johnson showed up drunk and gave a rambling, inebriated inaugural address, he was acting completely in character. Johnson was from Tennessee but had remained loyal to the Union, the only southern senator to do so. He hated the planter aristocracy and the secessionists, but he was even less tolerant of blacks, whom he considered uppity, and northern abolitionists. Johnson planned Reconstruction on his own terms. He lavished pardons on any Confederate official who wrote to him or visited Washington, and he insisted that the leadership of the southern states remain in place and that these states should quickly reenter the Union. He had no love for famed abolitionists like Frederick Douglass, of whom he said at the conclusion of a meeting: "He's just like any nigger, and he would sooner cut a white man's throat than not."

Few Confederates, even high-ranking ones, were severely punished. There were no war crimes trials, military tribunals for treason, or mass hangings. Even Confederate president Jefferson Davis spent but two years in prison. The Confederacy's vice president, Alexander Stephens, would rejoin the US Congress within a decade of the war's end and end his career as governor of Georgia. As soon as white southerners were back in charge of local government, the Deep South states quickly enacted "black codes," or laws, controlling every aspect of the freedmen's public lives. As an example, the Louisiana Black Codes read, in part:

> Section 1. . . . No negro or freedman shall be allowed to come within the city limits . . . without special permission.
> Section 2. . . . Every negro freedman who shall be found on the streets after 10 o'clock without a written pass . . . shall be imprisoned and compelled to work five days on the streets.
> Section 5. No public meetings . . . of negroes shall be allowed. . . .
> Section 7. No freedman who is not in the military service shall be allowed to carry firearms. . . .

Indeed, the southern states, with the planter class back in charge, had largely negated the North's achievements of the war and crafted a new version of slavery. All-white police forces and judiciaries, often composed of Confederate veterans still wearing their gray uniforms, enforced the black codes. Union veterans and Radical (meaning more liberal) Republicans in Congress began to wonder, if there was to be no punishment for the Confederates or meaningful freedom for the slaves, what the war had even been for.

The Radical Moment: Congressional Reconstruction

Johnson and his southern compatriots would later argue that "radical" Reconstruction was despotic and unnecessary. Nevertheless, the record demonstrates the opposite. Through presidential vetoes and white southern intransigence, the South brought radical Reconstruction upon itself. When Congress passed the remarkable Civil Rights Act of 1866, Johnson quickly vetoed it. This legislation provided for equality before the law, but not the vote, for the freedmen. Congress overrode his veto with a two-thirds majority — the first time a major bill was passed over a presidential veto in US history. To solidify black rights, the Congress even passed the Fourteenth Amendment to the Constitution, which stated:

> All persons born or naturalized in the United States and subject to the jurisdiction thereof, are citizens of the United States and of the State wherein they reside. No State shall make or enforce any law which shall abridge the privileges or immunities of citizens of the United States; nor shall any State deprive any person of life, liberty, or property, without due process of law; nor deny to any person within its jurisdiction the equal protection of the laws.

And taking matters a step further, the Republican Congress also passed the Fifteenth Amendment, which guaranteed the vote to black men (but not women). In a remarkable turn of events, black men had gained civil and political rights in just three years and over the objections of the president. The Republican Party, which hadn't existed in the South before the war, began winning elections and even placing blacks — often former slaves — in elected offices. Eight hundred black men would serve in state legislatures from 1868 through 1877; a black man was briefly governor of Louisiana; more than a dozen blacks served in the US House, and one in the Senate. White southerners called this "Negro Rule," but in reality it was the first ever attempt at *democracy* in the South. After all, in a few Deep

South states, former slaves constituted an actual majority of the population.

Johnson was appalled by both the Fourteenth and Fifteenth Amendments and the radical changes unfolding in southern society. And by suddenly removing the Radical Republican Edwin Stanton from his position as secretary of war, he violated the recently passed Tenure of Office Act, which required congressional approval of such moves. That was the last straw for an already frustrated Congress. The House voted to impeach President Johnson, and the Senate came within one vote of the two-thirds majority required to remove him from office. Even though he remained president, Johnson had been politically castrated and wouldn't run for reelection in 1868. He would be succeeded by the great Union war hero General Ulysses S. Grant. Grant's Democratic opponents, Horatio Seymour and Francis P. Blair, would play the race card — actually, the racist card — in their failed 1868 campaign. Blair claimed that the Republicans had placed the South under the rule of "a semi-barbarous race of blacks who are worshippers of fetishes and polygamists" and who long to "subject the white women to their unbridled lust."

Though blacks had won remarkable political power in a few short years, they generally lacked any true economic clout. There were early efforts, though, spearheaded by the likes of General William Tecumseh Sherman, to offer forty acres and, apocryphally, "a mule" to freedmen along the southeastern coast. In January 1865, before the war had ended, Sherman enacted Special Field Order 15 from Savannah, Georgia, thereby setting aside such confiscated land for thousands of freedmen. Unfortunately, by September 1865, after the war's end, President Johnson rescinded Sherman's order and mandated that the land be restored to the Confederate owners. Some Union generals publicly opposed the president's decision. General O. O. Howard — head of the new Federal Freedmen's Bureau, designed to support the newly emancipated slaves — was nearly fired and court-martialed after writing to his superiors: "The lands which have been taken possession were solemnly pledged to the freedman. Thousands of them are already located on tracts of forty acres each.

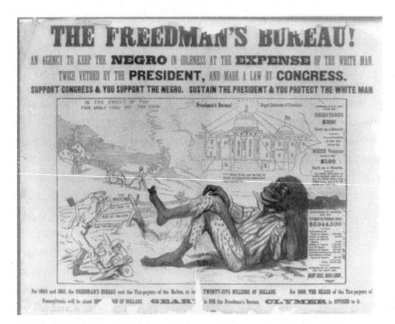

Propaganda poster, 1866

The love of the soil and desire to own farms [is] the dearest hope of their lives."

Howard's Freedmen's Bureau was itself a remarkable institution. Though always small, never having more than nine hundred employees in the entire South, the bureau worked toward the education and betterment of the former slaves in what was the earliest known federal welfare program of any size. Still, opposition cartoons in the South depicted the bureau — which was remarkably successful in most cases — as a haven for freeloaders and lazy black men. (This language rings as remarkably similar to twentieth-century complaints against modern welfare programs.)

Some Radical Republicans — to their immense credit, given the times — wanted to go a step further. Congressman Thaddeus Stevens, chairman of the House Ways and Means Committee, unsuccessfully fought for the confiscation of four hundred million acres of Confederate land and its redistribution to the freedmen. Stevens, in opposition to Johnson's view, believed the federal government ought to treat the southerners as a "conquered people" and reform "the foundation of their institutions, both political, municipal and social," so that "all our blood and treasure [were not] spent in vain." Given the century of Jim Crow laws, lynching, and political disenfranchisement that followed Reconstruction, it appears that men like Stevens were ultimately right and exceptionally ahead of their times. Such a redistribution of land would be radical even today and labeled by some "socialism," "affirmative action," and "reparations." In hindsight the denial of landownership to most freedmen doomed them to labor in the fields and on the plantations of the onetime slaveholders. The terms of work and the social caste system remained remarkably consistent with the prewar "Old" South.

Domestic Terror: The KKK Counter-Revolution

It was a time of great terror. Though pitched battles between armies became a thing of the past, the South was far from pacified and remained an extraordinarily violent place. The federal army — which after the war never counted more than thirty thousand men across the entire South — did what it could to stanch the violence and protect victims, who were almost always former slaves. The most infamous group of revisionist former rebels was known as the Ku Klux Klan, or the KKK for short.

The members of the Ku Klux Klan, formed in Pulaski, Tennessee, by Confederate veterans, wore white sheets over their heads so as to appear "as the ghosts of the Confederate dead." In reality, of course, the Klan was merely a resurrection of the old militias and slave patrols that had enforced white supremacy for centuries. Its tactic was violence; its goal, counter-revolution; its method, terrorism. The Klan was extraordinarily violent, probably killing more innocent black men, women, and children during Reconstruction than the number of Americans killed in the 9/11 attacks of 2001. After all, from 1865 to 1968 in Texas alone, more than a thousand blacks were murdered by whites.

Other statistics and events are equally shocking. In October 1870 bands of whites in South Carolina's Piedmont region drove 150 freedmen from their homes and committed thirteen murders. In Louisiana in 1873 a legally organized and accredited black militia tried to defend the parish courthouse in Colfax against a superior white force of former Confederates armed with rifles and a small cannon. The black militia held out for a time but was ultimately overwhelmed. At least fifty were summarily executed under a white flag of truce.

Furthermore, after northern troops pulled out of the South and turned government over to white locals, the reign of terror continued. Some three thousand blacks were lynched between 1882 and 1930.

Among the reasons given for these murders: "[a black man] didn't remove his hat"; an African American "wouldn't call [a white man] master." In yet another case a white killer simply had "wanted to thin out the niggers a little."

It's not as though the Klan could not be controlled, even though it would be fair to characterize the US Army campaign of 1866–77 as a form of what we would now call counterinsurgency. In fact, whenever the army had the will, leadership, and capacity to suppress the Klan, it did so. After the Ku Klux Klan Act of 1871 was passed at the request of President Grant, the law proved remarkably successful in stymying the power of the KKK throughout much of the South; for the first time ever, a certain class of crimes was brought under federal jurisdiction. Ultimately, it was a question of will, not ability. The simple fact was that northerners had little stomach for more fighting and complained of the expense — in blood and treasure — of continued occupation. In the end the northern public lacked the will necessary to win the peace as it had won the war.

The Lost Cause: Southern "Redemption"

There was a right side and a wrong side in the late war, which no sentiment ought to cause us to forget. . . . [The South] has suffered to be sure, but she has been the author of her own suffering.

— Frederick Douglass in his remarks at Madison
Square in New York City, Decoration Day (1878)

The former Confederates never really accepted defeat or the reorganization of their social system. In reality, they bided their time, waged secret violence, and, perhaps most important, crafted an alternative "Lost Cause" narrative. According to this remarkably resilient yarn, the South had actually outfought the North and was beaten only because it was overwhelmed by northern superiority in numbers and resources. The South hadn't *really* fought for slavery but rather for states' rights and southern honor. In reality, soldiers on both sides — blue and gray — had more in common than they realized when they were killing each other in massive numbers. According to the Lost Cause myth — which still exists — reconciliation between the sections was more important than justice for blacks or punishment for rebels.

Southern generals were rarely punished and rose to prominence rather quickly as Reconstruction wound down in the 1870s. They gave popular speeches, in both the North and South, speaking of the need for reconciliation and reunion, words that tended to serve as code for abandonment of the former slaves to the will of their old masters. In 1877 in Brooklyn, New York, former Confederate general Roger Pryor told a crowd that applauded him:

> The Union is re-established . . . over the hearts of people. . . .
> But slavery was not the cause of secession. For the cause
> you must look . . . to that irrepressible conflict between the
> principles of state sovereignty and federal supremacy. . . .
> Impartial history will record that slavery fell not by effort
> of man's will, but by an act of Almighty God, and so, fellow
> citizens, the soldiers of the late war are brought today to
> fraternize over the graves of their departed comrades, and
> renew their vows of fealty to the Constitution.

Such sentiments were remarkably common and accepted on both sides of the Mason-Dixon Line. As violence and the slow removal of federal troops from the South began to keep blacks from the polls, Southern Democrats began winning statewide elections. By 1875 former Confederate general James L. Kemper, who had been in

Pickett's Charge at Gettysburg, was *governor* of Virginia and gave a speech to unveil a statue of General "Stonewall" Jackson in Richmond. On the occasion, Governor Kemper revealed not only a new heroic statue but also his own version of the rhetoric of Lost Cause and reconciliation. He exclaimed:

> Not for the Southern people only, but for every citizen of whatever section . . . this tribute . . . is to be cherished, with national pride. . . . Stonewall Jackson's career of unconscious heroism will go down as an inspiration. . . . It speaks with equal voice to every portion of the reunited common country . . . to inspire our children with patriotic fervor. . . . Let Virginia demand and resume [its] ancient place in the sisterhood of States.

Considering that Stonewall was a traitor who resigned his US Army commission to fight for a treasonous southern slaveholding secessionist republic just fourteen years earlier, this was remarkable rhetoric. That it resonated among some northerners as well as southerners is more peculiar. But so it was.

The Lost Cause myth took on a life of its own and, eventually, drafted a Reconstruction chapter as well. According to this version, it was actually the *KKK* that was heroic during Reconstruction, protecting rightfully white leadership and the honor of southern white women. As late as the early twentieth century, this was somehow a mainstream interpretation. It was in 1915 that D. W. Griffith's incredibly successful silent film *The Birth of a Nation* depicted the Klan as the heroic savior of the white South from venal northern carpetbaggers and insufferable, lustful black savages. How mainstream was the film? Well, it was a favorite of President Woodrow Wilson, a Virginian, and received a private screening at the White House.

The South may have lost the war, but it most certainly won the peace.

Betrayal: The Retreat from Reconstruction

The abandonment of southern blacks shouldn't have come as a surprise. After all, what did it truly mean to remake the South in the North's image when the North itself was so virulently racist in the mid-nineteenth century? Most northerners had signed up for the army to save the Union and cared little for the enslaved black people. Soon after the war, *The Cincinnati Enquirer* announced, "Slavery is dead, the negro is not, there is the misfortune."

Most northerners were tired of Reconstruction by the mid-1870s. The commitment of troops and money to protect what many saw as corrupt and inefficient "black" administrations just didn't seem worth it. Besides, the economic mismanagement — the Panic of 1873 was the worst financial disaster in forty years — and staggering corruption that plagued the Grant administration only further alienated the northern populace from what seemed a distant and futile task down South. The tragedy of it all, of course, is that when the US government stuck with it, used the army, and enforced the law, the Reconstruction governments achieved remarkable successes — political wins for blacks that most southern states wouldn't see again until *the 1980s!* Unfortunately, most of the white North was fickle and bigoted.

Besides, even if the Republican president and Congress stood by the goals of Reconstruction, the southern-dominated Supreme Court soon eviscerated much of the congressional legislation protecting black civil rights. Indeed, it would take a century for the courts to begin appropriately applying the Fourteenth and Fifteenth Amendments to southern blacks. In 1883 the court would rule that the Civil Rights Act of 1875 was unconstitutional. And after all, it was the Supreme Court of the United States that would later, in 1896, rule in *Plessy v. Ferguson* that segregation was legal!

A lackluster candidate, Rutherford B. Hayes, ran on the Republican ticket for president in 1876. The party was seen as tainted by corruption in the Grant administration and mismanagement of the economy and had lost control of the Congress two years earlier, in 1874. It was almost amazing that the little-known Hayes, a former governor of Ohio, managed to keep the vote close in what turned out to be a disputed election with many abnormalities. It was unclear who had won a few southern states. It appeared, however, that Samuel J. Tilden, the Democratic nominee, had the majority of both the popular and electoral vote. It was at this moment that the Republican Party — for which Reconstruction and justice had become a political liability — struck a nefarious deal.

For the sake of party and power, "Rather*fraud*" B. Hayes, as he was subsequently called, sold out the millions of southern blacks who had loyally supported the Republicans for years. The candidate who had lost the popular vote would become president in exchange for his promise to remove the US Army from the South. And so he did. Ironically, he also turned the South over to Democratic one-party rule for a century to come. Hayes was obviously lacking as a political tactician. The truth is, however, that by the time of the 1876 election the majority of northern whites had tired of Reconstruction. More concerned with economic depression than black civil rights, northerners were ready to throw in the towel and turn the South back over to its traditional white leaders, come what may. The Compromise of 1877 only reinforced what was by then inevitable: the abandonment of the South's blacks. Looking back, a dozen years after General Robert E. Lee's surrender at Appomattox Court House, one could plausibly wonder: What *had* all those men died for in the Civil War?

———

Justice and reconciliation. These were, ultimately, the twin goals of postwar Reconstruction. A century and a half on, though, the keen observer wonders if the two goals were *ever* compatible. To seek justice and equality for the freedmen seemed to inevitably make reconciliation with white former Confederates ever less likely. To prioritize reconciliation with the former rebels seemed to sentence black people to a prolonged bondage of sorts, under the segregationist regime of Jim Crow.

Still, this author sees Reconstruction as an admirable attempt —
however far ahead of its time it might have proved to be — at true
social and political equality in the United States. It is remarkable
that Reconstruction was even attempted in the America of the 1860s
and '70s. If only the US Army had stayed longer, enforced the law
more stringently, redistributed land and wealth more equitably — if,
in other words, the nation had stuck with the Radical Republican
approach — perhaps then the civil rights movement of the 1960s
could have begun a century earlier, thousands of lynchings avoided,
and the riots, violence, and racial upheaval of our own day dodged.

Seen in that provocative light, the real hero of Reconstruction was
the congressional "radical" Thaddeus Stevens of Pennsylvania, the
man who called for free land and civil equity for southern blacks, at the
point of the bayonet if necessary. He would die before Reconstruction
truly got under way, and upon his death in August 1866, Stevens, a
white man, for the last time challenged his countrymen to "rise above
their prejudices." As he wished, he was buried in an integrated ceme-
tery, an action taken, in the words of his self-composed epitaph, "to
illustrate in my death the principles which I advocated through a long
life: Equality of Man before his Creator."

Alas, there would be no such equality in the lives of his countrymen. The American experiment was, at it always seems to be, a step
behind its egalitarian rhetoric. The United States, it turns out, was not
ready for *true* Reconstruction — and more's the pity. Many thousands
of northerners died during the American Civil War, and it would have
been highly satisfying to imagine that they had died for something
more than a century of Jim Crow, slavery by another name. But that
is the real America, warts and all. And that, in the end, was the failed
experiment in Reconstruction.

Still, Reconstruction achieved much and demonstrated what was
possible if, someday, Americans had the moral and political will to see
it through. The brief Republican governments of the South brought
the region its first-ever public school system. They brought more
hospitals, more asylums for orphans and the insane. South Carolina

19

LIES WE TELL OURSELVES ABOUT THE OLD WEST

They [the Sioux Indians] are to be treated as maniacs or wild beasts and by no means as people.

— General John Pope in instructions to his officers during the Great Sioux Uprising in Minnesota (1862)

The West. The frontier. Few terms, or images, are as quintessentially American or as culturally loaded as these. Interestingly, the West — unlike other regions — is often defined as both a time *and* a place. It is also hopelessly shrouded in myth. Americans leaders, from George Washington to Donald Trump, frequently claimed that the West, the frontier, somehow defined us as Americans. It was long seen as a place of opportunity, rebirth even. If a man failed in the East, well, then, "Go West, young man," as one Indiana newspaper declared in the popular phrase it coined.

The truth, of course, is messy. Even focusing primarily on the West's most immortalized era, 1862–90, the serious historian finds a story teeming with less fact than fiction. Some have even questioned whether there is any merit in studying the West as a separate historical discipline. Still, something must be said of the place and the time. Americans, after all, seem to have decided that the frontier does, in fact, define us; that the West is *who we are*. And so it is, for better or for worse.

There are many other compelling reasons to study the West, even if they do not comport with our "cowboys and Indians" cinematic image from mid-twentieth-century movies when the western genre dominated the film scene. First, the American West was an important meeting ground, where Anglo, black, native, Hispanic, and Asian Americans coalesced. Though land and wealth were the main goals of these competing factions, defining the West also became a contest for cultural dominance. The West was a place where the federal government, then much more circumscribed than now, first expanded its role and played a key part as financier, organizer, referee, and lawman. Additionally, the West demonstrated the radical nature, and boom-bust cycle, of American capitalism in the starkest of ways. Finally, of course, the West of the late nineteenth century was the time and place where one version of Native American sovereignty ended and a new phase began. This, truth be told, was one of the great — yet complicated — crimes of the American experiment.

Myth Versus Truth: Reinterpreting the West

Americans have long mythologized the West. From Plymouth Rock, to Manifest Destiny, to the Plains Indian wars, to John Wayne on the twentieth-century silver screen, it all looks the same in the American imagination. Cowboys and Indians, lawmen and villains, soldiers and savages, farmers and miners, and always, ultimately, black hats and white hats. It's remembered for its excitement and mystique, as well as a morality tale — good guys and bad guys. As always, of course, the reality is far more complex, more nuanced.

Still, it's valuable to parse out truth from legend, fact from fiction. After all, the *real* West — to the extent that it can ever be defined — is so much more fascinating and wholly human. Let us, then, address but a few of the defining symbols and myths of America's shared western past.

Gold Rushes

From California to Nevada, from Montana to the Black Hills of South Dakota, the craze for precious metals became a fixture of the western saga. The San Francisco 49ers of the National Football League bear the nickname of those who came in the first major wave of the California gold rush, in 1849. In the common image, any lone man could make his fortune simply by panning for gold and catching some luck. It all fits comfortably within the altogether *American* obsession with the so-called self-made man.

Across the Continent: Westward the Course of Empire Takes Its Way, 1868, by Fanny Palmer

The reality was uglier and less satisfying. Mining *was* an important factor in the West. Miners flooded remote areas faster than farmers. Their presence could cause trouble — as when miners set up settlements in places white people had never before inhabited, often provoking Indian wars. Most important, the essence of mining was extraction, like so much of western culture. In the end, though, only a tiny percentage of miners struck it rich. Mining turned out to be complicated and increasingly technological. The individual panner of gold often arrived too late, after the surface gold had been captured, and found that his mining method was outmoded and inefficient. Soon enough the power shifted to corporations, and most miners worked for a lowly wage in dangerous, dismal conditions.

By the late nineteenth century many mine owners were easterners who had never set foot in the West. They simply added investments in mining to their complex financial portfolios. Miners weren't strictly rugged individualists either. Indeed, few American industries lent themselves so easily to a Marxist analysis of class struggle. Miners unionized, led strikes and sit-downs, and battled (often fatally) with federal troops or National Guardsmen. Seen in this light, the western miner's condition bears striking similarity to that of *eastern factory workers*.

There were legitimate socialists and revolutionaries among the miners. The Industrial Workers of the World (IWW), or "Wobblies," had a strong presence in the mine shafts. The reaction of conservative mine owners and bought-off lawmen was often vicious. In Bisbee, Arizona, hired vigilantes supported by a local sheriff rounded up 1,186 striking copper miners and supporters, forced them onto railcars, and shipped them over the border to New Mexico. Two were beaten to death.

Overall, the horrid social condition of miners couldn't have been more different from the Jeffersonian western ideal of the small, independent farmer setting roots in the soil. Thomas Jefferson, in fact, would have been horrified by the sight of these dirty wage slaves toiling their days away and engaging in debauchery at temporary mining camps at night, totally untethered to place or agriculture. Furthermore, a good number of the miners weren't Jefferson's idealized white men at all: they were Irish *Catholics* or, worse still, Chinese immigrants. Still, in other ways, mining was a defining western experience, involving all the key factors of real western life: class, race, chance, and federal largesse.

Railroads

The "iron horse" steam engine traversing the plains is one of the iconic images of the West. The railroads embodied civilization as much as raw technological advance. Yet contrary to their clean, straight, parallel lines on maps, the railroads were a complicated, inefficient industry. First of all, although Chinese and Irish workers were seldom in the iconic (staged) photographs depicting the meeting of intercontinental lines, they constituted the vast majority of railroad workers. Many thousands died constructing the rail lines that connected the Atlantic and Pacific Oceans.

The corporations that built the railroads were more interested in profit than quality craftsmanship and often had to double back to improve dangerously feeble tracks. The railroad entrepreneurs usually weren't up-by-the-bootstraps individualists either. Rather, the rail-roaders were extraordinary recipients of federal largesse — what we might call corporate welfare. The federal government subsidized the construction of the transcontinental lines with cash and enormous land grant subsidies. In many cases a railroad received two hundred square miles of adjacent land for each mile of track completed. Thus, despite the supposed "free land" granted to willing pioneers by the 1862 Homestead Act, it was actually the railroad companies that owned much of the best (and most valuable, due to its proximity to transportation) land in the West. Where possible, the corporations engaged in speculation and sold the land at a handsome profit.

Railroaders were often highly corrupt, plaguing and embarrassing the Grant administration in scandal after scandal. They bribed politi-cians, set up subsidiaries that robbed the taxpayer, and hired vigilan-tes to intimidate striking workers or nearby Indians. The railroads, as beneficiaries of generous federal welfare, weren't always in tune with supply and demand. Lines sometimes were overextended and had to be abandoned in part because they proved unnecessary and unprofitable. Companies sometimes ran lines into arid areas, like western Kansas, that were hard to settle. Railroad supply, by the late nineteenth century, had far outstripped citizen demand, but the federal dollars kept rolling in. As the historian Richard White wrote, eventually "empty railroad trains ran across deserted prairies to vacant towns." However, one thing the railroads did do was affect the future layout and prosperity of town-ships and cities. Existing settlements unlucky enough to lie distant from a rail line or station eventually withered away, and as a result so-called ghost towns dotted the West. Conversely, a simple bribe from a local politician might motivate railroaders to place a previously unplanned stop in a town. Indeed, the railroads — as much as the later federal highways — defined the geography of the western landscape.

Rugged Self-Sufficiency

One of the more persistent myths holds that westerners were all hardy individualists, opposed to federal intrusion and beholden to no one. Though still pervasive, such a description strikes the serious historian as farcical. From start to finish western territories, states, and citizens were among the largest recipients of federal aid. Indeed, when not accusing the federal government of some slight or infraction, westerners were constantly clamoring for more federal aid. It was in the West, in fact, that the federal government first meaningfully inserted itself into Americans' daily lives. A western region was organized into a territory — under the direct control of a federal governor — before it was, eventually, accepted as a new state. This could happen almost immediately, as in the case of California, or take sixty-four years for states like Arizona and New Mexico.

Still, regardless of when their regions reached statehood status, westerners were reliant on the federal government. They desired, and expected, loans and aid for enterprise and transportation, soldiers for protection (and conquest of Indians), and surveyors to organize and distribute (cheaply!) the land. Politically, though the western states complained of powerlessness, the reality couldn't have been more divergent. Blessed with massive lands, precious natural resources, and comparatively few people, western states still had two senators and at least one congressional representative in the House. Indeed, a state like Wyoming — which still has roughly the population of New York City's least populated borough, Staten Island — has the same number of senatorial representatives as the thirty-times-more-populous state of New York. Then and now, the West was actually proportionally overrepresented in Washington.

Well into the twentieth century, the West received federal assistance disproportionate to its population. The Taylor Grazing Act of 1934 provided for generous leasing of federal land to western ranchers, and Franklin Roosevelt's New Deal created many federal work projects in the western states. In fact, during the New Deal, Wyoming received, on a per capita basis, *three times* the average amount of direct federal financial assistance given to states. So much for rugged independence.

Independent Family Farmers
The vision of the independent, small family farmer was the ultimate Jeffersonian ideal of future western American prosperity. And though

millions of small farmers would settle the West, corporate agribusiness or land speculation was just as often the agricultural norm. Real estate — more than gunfighting or Indian fighting — was the dominant force in the American West. With all that open land, settlement, squatting, and speculation became the name of the game. Moreover, in the minds of many Americans, there was *never* enough land — though, interestingly, the West still hasn't filled up. Americans of the day feared that the United States would run out of land and end up like Europe, crowded and riven by the class structures that develop in the absence of well-distributed landownership.

Though just about all western land was technically owned by the central government, few settlers were willing to wait on federal speculation, division, and allotment. Many simply followed the notion "first in time, first in right" and squatted on available lands. For the government, using the army to remove them rarely seemed viable. Wealthy speculators turned a pretty profit by buying large tracts of the cheap land from the federal government and then selling it to smallholders. From large-scale speculation and massive private landholdings it was but a short step to the twentieth-century mechanized agribusiness that has driven so many family farms into insolvency.

Nor did farm settlement always make sense. Much of the land west of the 98th meridian is semiarid, and rainfall in these areas — western Kansas and Nebraska and eastern Colorado, for example — was insufficient to support agriculture. By the early twentieth century hundreds of thousands of these settlers had failed and retreated eastward. This explains why many towns in western Kansas had a higher population in 1880 than in 1980. Only through analysis of this mix of failed irrigation, land squatting, and high-finance speculation can we begin to understand the byzantine and poorly planned nature of western settlement. Seen in this light, it becomes understandable that many native tribes struggled to understand white notions of property. It hardly made sense to Anglo Americans; why should it seem natural for a pre-Columbian civilization?

Ranchers and Cowboys

There is no more romantic myth in the American West than that of the cowboy. Indeed, the image of the cowboy has come to define the place and time — so much so that men and women in the American South and West still wear the purported clothing styles of the cowboy. So just who were these cowboys and where did they come from? Well, the first were Spaniards, and then Mexicans. It was the Spanish who brought the cattle that cowboys would drive to market in the New World. Indeed, the styles of the cowboys came from Hispanic clothing and culture. Consider the Spanish loanwords that entered the American lingo and mystique of the cowboy: *lasso, rodeo, ranchero.*

Still, the cowboy on horseback driving cattle from Texas to Kansas City or some other railroad town had a heyday of little more than two decades. The beef industry, like farming, was quickly mechanized, and by the end of the nineteenth century the era of the cattle drives was mostly over. Ranching became rather corporate, and the true conflict was usually not between cowboys and rustlers but between ranchers and nearby small farmers. It is important to remember that the cowboy of our imagination was not on the western scene for long and that he didn't always look or act the way we imagine. There were black cowboys and many Mexican cowboys (they had invented the business), and new studies show that there was a fair amount of homosexuality practiced in these all-male communities. If it is thus, one wonders why it is the image of the rugged, white American cowboy that has stuck in the collective national psyche. That it is so might tell us more about the American present than the past.

Gunfighters

The showdown in the dusty street at high noon between two men with six-guns — an outlaw and a sheriff — is one of the great melodramas of the West, especially as depicted in film. The clock strikes noon, each man quickly draws his weapon, and the fastest gun wins! Exhilarating but, sadly, inaccurate. Cattle-town newspapers and other primary sources make no mention of such duels in the streets. Violence *was* rampant in the West, of course. Indeed, the murder rate in Dodge City, Kansas, was about ten times that of today's New York City, and the less well-known mining town of Bodie, California, had a rate some *twenty-two times* the New York rate. Still, less than one-third of the victims died in actual exchanges of gunfire. More than half were unarmed, often shot in the back and at a close distance. This was *murder*, not the martial chivalry of the imagination.

Another interesting point is that many of the romantic outlaws we remember today — such as Jesse and Frank James and John Wesley Hardin — were far less Robin Hood and far more racist than most modern Americans know. Many of these men were unreformed Confederates, angry at the government and ready to do violence to blacks. The James brothers had ridden with Confederate guerrilla leader William Quantrill and his raiders during the Civil War and were probably involved in Quantrill's attack on Lawrence, Kansas, in 1863, in which more than 150 residents were killed. Hardin, perhaps the most prolific killer of the era, thought of *himself* as a victim — a victim of "bullying negroes, Yankee soldiers, carpetbaggers, and bureau agents" in his native Texas. Most of these fabled outlaws were cold-blooded killers and unreconstructed Southern bigots.

The End of Native Sovereignty:
Four Phases of an American Tragedy

It is very hard to plant the corn outside the stockade when the Indians are still around. We have to get the Indians farther away in many provinces to make good progress.

— US Army general Maxwell Taylor comparing
Vietnamese to American Indians (1965)

"Indian Country"
The term has become a military shorthand for any "wild," "unconquered" region the US Army attempts to "secure." The army and the native peoples of America maintain a strange relationship and kinship to this day. Think of it as the ultimate love–hate relationship.

Indian fighting, after all, is what the US military mostly *did* in the periods between the nation's few major wars in its first century or so. At present, all helicopters in the US Army inventory — Iroquois, Apache, Blackhawk, Chinook — bear the names of tribes or leaders the US government once fought and conquered. This author served in modern-day "cavalry" (reconnaissance) units, where each Friday formation meant donning vintage Stetson hats and riding spurs. Each cavalry unit's flag, or guidon, sports dozens of streamers commemorating battles fought long ago with Native American tribes and bands.

The relationship between the modern US Army and its former Indian foes actually mirrors the complexity of the late-nineteenth-century clash of these two forces. The army was often brutal and bloodthirsty. So, too, were many Indians, though they lacked the capacity to exterminate large numbers of whites in the same way. Then again, the real danger to the Native Americans usually came not from soldiers but from white civilian settlers and vigilantes — and in these cases the army was sometimes used to *protect* (however imperfectly) the Indians from pioneer encroachment. One way to frame the era from 1862 to 1890 is as a broad counterinsurgency waged by the army across a large expanse filled with myriad actors and pursuing the ever-changing, often muddled policies of the US government.

The real problem for the Indians was this: the United States never formulated a permanent Indian policy that would guarantee native sovereignty and never had either the will or the capacity to separate the settlers and natives. Unsurprisingly, given the choice between protecting natives and appeasing settlers, the government erred on the side of the white man. In broad strokes US government policy toward the Indians of the Great Plains and Far West went through four phases in the nineteenth century: removal from lands east of the Mississippi; concentration in a vast "Indian territory" between Oklahoma and North Dakota; confinement to much smaller reservations on part of that land; and assimilation of the Indians into white American-style farming and culture, through the allotment of even smaller, individual tracts of barren land. The natives lost at every step, and their territory shrank with each new phase. Still, the

Indians remained active agents during this period, winning victories, suffering defeats, fighting one another, and, often, allying with the US Army. It was a complicated, tragic battle for the Native Americans of the American West.

Removal

This was the policy of President Andrew Jackson. In 1830 he pushed through the Indian Removal Bill, which forced the five so-called civilized tribes to vacate their lands and move west of the Mississippi, and promptly ignored the Supreme Court when it objected on constitutional grounds. He and his successor, Martin Van Buren, went so far as to use the army to evict the tribes at bayonet point and march them — in the infamous Trail of Tears — into modern-day Oklahoma. Thousands of Indians died, but the majority of white southerners who took over the land cheered the presidents' decisions. This was supposed to be a permanent Indian territory, a vast expanse into which the Native Americans would now be concentrated — and sovereign — in perpetuity. It was, of course, not to be. In an early sign of what was to come, when the five civilized tribes made the mistake of allying with the Confederates — from whom they expected more freedom and independence — the US government made them pay: it subsequently confiscated half their lands. Indian territory would shrink and shrink as the years passed.

Concentration

During the period of concentration, roughly 1848 to 1873, the Indian wars never actually ceased. Miners, settlers, and sometimes the army violated supposed native sovereignty and moved onto the land. Furthermore, some tribes and bands refused to accept the white man's overland trails and railroads running through their regions and attacked men and women on the roads. So the wars continued, brutally, even if the fiction of the vast Indian territory technically continued.

In 1862 a Sioux uprising in Minnesota, precipitated by crop failure and game reduction, resulted in the deaths of some five hundred settlers. President Abraham Lincoln ordered the rebellion put down. The militia and army suppressed the Sioux, captured hundreds, executed thirty-eight, and moved the rest to Dakota Territory, into Indian country. In 1864, Colonel John Chivington attacked a village at Sand Creek, Colorado, during a war with the Cheyenne tribe. The massacre of some two hundred Indians, 75 percent of them women and children, should have come as no surprise, since Chivington had announced his intentions beforehand: "I have come to kill Indians and believe it is right and honorable to use any means under God's heaven to kill Indians." It is notable that Chivington's men were local volunteers, not regular army soldiers, and carried the hatred for Indians common to local settlers. The Sand Creek massacre only further inflamed the Plains in war, a state that was almost perpetual until 1878.

The most horrific and genocidal Indian experience came in California, which, because of the gold rush, never truly implemented a concentration or confinement policy. The whites wanted *all* of these rich Pacific lands. Here the 150,000 natives of California were pushed through a truncated version of all four phases in a span of only twelve years. The federal commissioners attempting to broker a treaty in 1851 made clear their expectations: "You have but one choice, kill, murder, exterminate, or domesticate and improve them." Miners, ranchers, and militia murdered thousands, and many more perished from diseases brought by the gold rushers. By 1860 only 30,000 California Indians out of 150,000 remained alive — a record of extermination unparalleled in our troubled history with Native Americans — though few Americans remember this campaign today.

Many in the US Army, too, were full of contempt for the natives. The senior commander in the West, General Philip Sheridan of Civil War fame, declared in 1868: "The only good Indians I ever saw were dead." The Sioux tribes under Chief Red Cloud had given the army a run for its money from 1866 to 1868, defeating just about every force sent against them in the Dakota Territory and Montana. Eventually the US government agreed to destroy its regional forts and signed the Fort Laramie Treaty, which promised the Black Hills of South Dakota and other sacred lands to the Sioux and Cheyenne in perpetuity. Fort Laramie was one of the last treaties signed by the US government with a sovereign Great Plains tribe. That time was passing. The end of war in 1868, in retrospect, was but a truce, during which the settlers and US Army paused briefly but did not give up their hunger for Indian land on the Plains. The great chief Sitting Bull of the Sioux learned that lesson early and proclaimed that "possession is a disease with them [white men]."

The notion that the United States — or more accurately its settlers and prospectors — would actually yield the land between Oklahoma and North Dakota to a so-called concentration of Indians was, in hindsight, baseless. The government always wanted to own all the land between prosperous California and the Missouri River limit of settlement. Besides, land-hungry settlers and speculators had no intention of following federal Indian policy anyway. They knew the army had too few soldiers to police the entire frontier, and that it would be relatively easy to cross the Missouri, find a plot in Indian territory, and squat on the land. Would the federal army have the will or capacity to protect Indians from the settlers? It was never likely.

Senator Stephen Douglas of Illinois, a fierce advocate of a transcontinental railroad through Indian land, captured the common feeling and dispelled any lingering idea of a permanent Indian land. He noted, years before the Civil War, that "the idea of arresting our progress in that direction [West] has become so ludicrous that we are amazed. . . . How are we to develop, cherish and protect our immense interests and possessions on the Pacific, with a vast wilderness 1,500 miles in breadth, filled with hostile savages, and cutting off direct communication. The Indian barrier must be removed." There was, rumor had it, gold and other precious minerals — in addition to millions of acres of fertile land — in that fifteen-hundred-mile breadth of Indian territory. Neither settlers nor federal officials were willing to follow the concentration policy and let the Indians be: "progress," as always, seemed to demand expansion. Some other method of Indian control would have to be found.

Confinement

The answer, many federal officials eventually decided, must be to confine the natives to shrunken parcels of land, known forever as Indian reservations. This strategy was in direct contradiction to and contravention of earlier legal treaties signed with various native tribes and, along with the westward wave of settlers after the Civil War, made Indian war almost inevitable. There was always a fine line between concentration and confinement — both constricted the Indians to certain lands, but the reservations were generally smaller and far less rich in minerals and arable land. Various actors, and branches of government, led the transition from concentration to confinement on the "rez."

In 1870 the Supreme Court ruled that Congress had the power to "supersede or even annul treaties" with Indian tribes. This ruling essentially destroyed the previous system of Indian affairs and emboldened settlers. Soon afterward Congress followed the court's decision, making any future treaty-making with the Indians illegal. The tribes were not, the text of legislation read, "to be acknowledged or recognized as an independent nation, tribe, or power." Next came the ubiquitous settlers. After the "boy general" hero of the Civil War, George Armstrong Custer, led his 7th Cavalry on a "reconnaissance" expedition into the sacred Black Hills, he almost assured a new gold rush by publicizing the news that "from the grass roots down it was 'pay dirt.'" Within two years, there were ten thouand miners in the new town of Deadwood in the Black Hills. Unsurprisingly, miners were attacked by Sioux warriors who refused to countenance their presence.

The exhausted and scandal-ridden Grant administration decided to end the "Indian problem" once and for all. In what he declared his new Peace Policy, President Ulysses S. Grant ordered that all Great Plains tribes and bands no later than January 1, 1876, move onto the truncated reservations outlined by his government or be considered "hostile." Grant knew, of course, that this would mean a war. He probably expected one and had convinced himself that a final showdown was necessary.

January 1 came and went, and nearly ten thousand Sioux, Cheyenne, and Arapaho still roamed the Northern Plains. The army moved in, and once again Custer was in the lead. Following his aggressive, often reckless (if courageous) instincts, Custer divided his force into three parts and converged on the huge combined native village near the Little Bighorn River in southeast Montana. He should have followed orders and waited for reinforcements. He didn't. On June 25, 1876 — just a week before the nation's centennial celebration — thousands of warriors under Crazy Horse and Sitting Bull quickly overwhelmed and destroyed Custer and his wing of 250 or so troopers. The news of Custer's "Last Stand" shocked the nation and entered the American mythology as a "gallant" defeat on par with the Greeks at Thermopylae or the Texans at the Alamo.

Sitting Bull, Crazy Horse, and other chiefs quickly split up. They knew that the defeat of Custer meant the full force of the army would now be unleashed upon them. They were right. Thousands of troops converged and waged a "scorched earth" campaign during a brutally cold winter. Starving, outnumbered, and exhausted, within a year most Indians withdrew to their reservations. Crazy Horse was the last to surrender and was subsequently bayonetted to death in an alleged escape attempt. Sitting Bull led his followers into Canada, where they were given some sanctuary, but within a few years they returned to their reservation because of food shortages. It turned out that Custer's Last Stand was really the last stand of the sovereign Northern Plains tribes. That day's victory by the Indians ultimately ushered in their final removal to reservations.

Assimilation and Allotment

The seeds of forced assimilation of Indians and conversion into farmers had long been planted in the Anglo mind. As early as 1859 an annual report of the Bureau of Indian Affairs noted, "It is indispensably necessary that [the Indians] be placed in positions where they can be controlled and finally compelled by sheer necessity to resort to agricultural labor or starve. . . . There is no alternative to providing for them in this manner, but to exterminate them." Ironically, when the new policy of assimilation and allotment of land plots to individual Indians came to pass in the 1880s, it was ushered in by white eastern-ers who called themselves "Friends of the Indian."

These men — and many women — believed that Indians must be converted from hunters who held land in common into white-style farmers and property owners. If they weren't thus transformed, the reformers believed, the natives would become extinct. One reformer, Carl Schurz, wrote that "[civilizing them] which once [seemed] only a benevolent fancy, has now become an absolute necessity, if we mean to save them." The signal achievement of the assimilation and allotment phase was the Dawes General Allotment Act, which in 1887 broke reservations into multiple tracts to be allotted to individual Indians, ostensibly for farming, which was often impossible due to the choice of barren, arid lands for reservations. The kicker was this: the *millions of acres left over* would then be open for sale to whites.

The Indians themselves, of course, were barely asked what they preferred. When they were, a majority of Indian tribes opposed the allotment policy. The resulting land cession was disastrous. In 1887 Indians held 138 million acres. Over the next forty-seven years, sixty million of those acres were declared "surplus" and sold to whites. Other lands were desperately sold off by Indians or ceded to the government for much-needed cash. By 1934 the Indian tribes held only forty-seven million acres.

There was also a cultural component to the new phase of "Indian policy": assimilation. Consider what followed to be cultural imperia-lism. Indian children were sent to distant eastern boarding schools — most famously the Carlisle Indian School in Pennsylvania — where they were taught in English alone, were told their parents' ways were backward, and were forced to wear American-style clothes and hair-styles. The girls were dressed in Victorian dresses and taught piano, the boys drilled in uniform as military companies. The secretary of the interior summed up the policy: "If Indian children are to be civi-lized they must learn the language of civilization." Clearly, he meant a more holistic transformation than the simple learning of English. Tribal life was upended.

The tragic last hurrah of Indian independence came in 1890. A Paiute holy man in Nevada preached a new sort of nonviolent religion. If Indians gave up alcohol, lived simply and traditionally, and danced a certain slow dance, the Great Spirit would return them their lands and white ways and implements would disappear. By the time the belief reached the Northern Plains and the Sioux tribe, it had garnered a slightly more militant message and spread widely among the hopeless and despondent tribe. The "Ghost Dance" terrified whites and Indian agents, and when a band left the main reservation to dance on the Badlands of South Dakota, the US Army sent in the ubiquitous 7th Cavalry Regiment, no doubt yearning for vengeance. Tribal police were sent to arrest Sitting Bull at his home, and in violence that followed, Sitting Bull and more than a dozen other men — both policemen and supporters of the chief — were killed.

The cavalrymen then set out in the winter snow and surrounded the Ghost Dance band along Wounded Knee Creek. The soldiers began disarming the Sioux when a gun went off. A massacre ensued, and the soldiers fired four new machine guns down into the encampment. One hundred forty-six Indians were killed, including sixty-two women and children. It was more massacre than battle. Twenty-five soldiers were killed, most of them probably shot in crossfire from their own forces. As a tragicomic if instructive coda, the US Army — desperate to depict the incident as a "battle" — awarded no fewer than twenty Medals of Honor to the troopers at Wounded Knee. They have never been rescinded.

Looking back, what happened to the natives of America seems so inevitable. But was it? Could not the United States have settled for just a bit less expansion and allowed a permanent sovereign Indian Territory to develop along its own chosen lines? Couldn't reservations have been placed on more fertile land? And furthermore, could not those yet smaller reservations have *stayed* in Indian hands rather than being "allotted to whites"? Of course. There existed alternative options at every step of the way.

Ultimately the US government always lacked the will and capacity to protect Indian sovereignty. It's an old story, really — something

President Washington had predicted. In 1796 he wrote, "The Indians urge this [policing of a line between whites and natives]; The Law requires it; and it ought to be done; but I believe scarcely anything short of a Chinese Wall or a line of troops will restrain Land Jobbers and the encroachment of settlers." The tale was basically the same from 1796 to 1890. The army was rarely large enough to create that "line of troops," and the government was never willing to meaningfully use the military resources that existed to evict white Americans.

Role Reversal: The Anglicization of the Southwest and California

Just who *were* the "immigrants" in the American Southwest and Pacific Coast? Today there is an easy, if inaccurate, ready answer: the Mexicans. Yet in truth, a Hispanic and mestizo population and culture preceded Anglo-American conquest by some 250 years. Furthermore, Native American peoples had themselves been conquered by the Spanish in the late sixteenth century and antedated European rule by perhaps ten thousand years. What's more, native peoples had fought one another for the land throughout the continent's settled history. This wider view certainly complicates the traditional American political attitudes of our own day and raises as many questions as answers.

As should by now be clear, the West was *never* truly empty — no matter how often the artists of the period romantically depicted it as such. One of the strongest and most embedded communities was that of the Hispanic and mestizo descendants of the Spanish invasion. Spain permanently entered the American Southwest as early as 1598, with Juan de Oñate's conquest of New Mexico from the Pueblo Indians. And yet to watch a classic film or read an old western dime novel is to erase these Hispanic and mixed-race peoples from the story of the West. They were neither the cowboys nor Indians, soldiers nor native warriors, of the traditional tale. They don't *fit*. That this should be the case is fascinating, if tragic. The people we now call Mexicans, Mexican Americans, or Hispanics were present and effusive through the entire "classic" era of the American West. Let us remember their story.

The original, Hispanic residents of California and the Southwest were promised their private landholdings would be protected under the provisions of the Treaty of Guadalupe Hidalgo, created at the conclusion of the Mexican-American War. It was not to be. Swindlers, settlers, and hustlers tricked or bullied thousands of Hispanics off their land in the decades following the war. It wasn't enough that the Yankees had conquered half of Mexico, the residents complained; now their lands were forfeited too. During the California gold rush, a Civil War veteran and forty-niner wrote in *The Stockton Times* that "Mexicans have no business in this country. The men were made to be shot at, and the women were made for our purposes. I'm a white man — I am! A Mexican is pretty near black. I hate all Mexicans."

Yet New Mexico, for example, remained majority Hispanic into the twentieth century (which may help explain why it was not admitted as a state until 1912), but even there Hispanics held minimal political or economic power. In fact, they divided among themselves as many Hispanics sought to "Europeanize or 'whiten' themselves," by claiming Spanish, rather than native, descent. This, some thought, would protect them from the worst of white infractions, though it didn't always work. The victims of lynching, it turns out, were not limited to southern blacks. Mexicans were often extrajudicially murdered for alleged crimes or just to "encourage them to stay in their place."

Still, Mexicans weren't erased from the Southwest. They were needed as agricultural laborers — then and now — just as blacks were in the Old South. Nativists (anti-immigration advocates) fought the local planters (who needed the labor), fearing that migrating Mexicans might "reverse the essential consequences" of the Mexican-American War. Racial lines hardened throughout the twentieth century, and in 1930 the US census form added a separate classification of Hispanics as "Mexican." Before then Hispanics fell under the category of "white."

Culturally the Hispanics often found themselves erased by or amalgamated within an *Anglo* Texan or Californian society and mythology. In the process northern Mexico became the *southwestern* United States; cowboys became homogeneous and white, Indians became a savage red. There wasn't much identity left for those in between.

Whether in the nineteenth century or today, the border between the US and Mexico has been little more than a legal and social fiction. Like the Indians, the Hispanics of the Southwest had been conquered but never truly erased. Texas and California were once northern Mexico. Which raises salient questions today: Are "undocumented" Mexican immigrants "illegal intruders," or are they rightful residents of "Occupied America"?

———

Historians often described this period in western history as another type of Reconstruction — something similar to what was attempted in the post–Civil War South. There are indeed parallels: a military presence, violence, federal impotency, citizen apathy, and racism. Still, the analogy falls short. It is problematic to compare Indians to recently freed slaves or to former Confederates. In the end the US government abandoned the freedmen and turned power back over to the Confederates within a dozen years. In the West, conversely, few attempts were made to reconstruct or restrain the land-hungry settlers, and the government actively backed and abetted the invaders. Furthermore, the Indians permanently lost their land — and for what crime? The Confederates had seceded, thereby committing treason, and received but twelve years of light punishment. Indians had adhered to treaties more faithfully than whites and were rewarded with banishment, theft, war, and extermination.

The legacy, and tragedy, of the American West is with us still. As a classroom exercise on the heels of the 2010 census, I often ended my lesson on this topic at West Point with a slide listing five of the poorest US counties. Then I'd circle four — Buffalo, Todd, and Shannon in South Dakota and Wade Hampton (now Kusilvak) in Alaska — and ask the students what these counties had in common. They are all Indian reservations, of course, or places with major Native American majorities. Buffalo County holds the Crow Creek reservation; Todd, the Rosebud Sioux; Shannon, the Pine Ridge Sioux; and Wade Hampton a population that is 92 percent Eskimo. These counties, each filled with thousands of tragic individual stories, are living relics of our past; of each phase of the US government's calamitous Indian policy — first removal, then concentration, followed by confinement to the reservation, and finally hopeless forced assimilation. Think on it: Within just a few hours' drive of swanky downtown Denver, and just a few hours' flight from hipster enclaves in New York City, there are veritable monuments of American crimes and human suffering — our semi-sovereign, mostly impoverished Indian reservations.

To visit one is to experience the past within the present. Disembark your plane in a crowded metropolitan center and take the long drive. You may cruise past federally owned ranchlands, through federally subsidized mega-farms, past long-abandoned mine shafts, through ghost towns that the railroads bypassed; stop for fuel where a man in a Stetson fuels his luxury pickup truck. Keep driving, past failed family farms that ran short of water on the arid plains, through strip mall after suburban strip mall; through a town with a vaguely Spanish name and past an oil rig. Finally, when the conveniences of modern life seem almost to have vanished, see the passing sign: ENTERING [INSERT TRIBE] RESERVATION, and proceed. You may feel as though you've left one world for another, but it is not so: all that you passed is the West — the legacy, the charm, and the tragedy.

We are Americans: It is our complex inheritance.[16]

20

WEALTH AND SQUALOR IN THE PROGRESSIVE ERA

The Gilded Age. The American Industrial Revolution. The Progressive Era. Call it what you will, but one salient, Dickensian fact about this period endures: it was the best of times, it was the worst of times — depending on your point of view. Industrialization brought immense wealth for some and crippling poverty for others. Mass production might result in savings for the consumer, but working wages remained low. The boom-and-bust cycle of laissez-faire capitalism was in full swing, resulting in national banking panics and, from 1893 to 1897, the worst financial depression up to that point in the country's history.

The key story of this era revolves around various attempts — by rural farmers and urban workers, by women and blacks, Republicans and Democrats, Populists, Progressives, and even socialists — to mitigate the excesses of industrialized American capitalism. It would not prove to be an easy task, and, we could cogently argue, it is a task Americans still grapple with. The two-party system nearly fell apart in this period because neither major political brand seemed to have a viable answer to the key question of day: how to maintain peace and the basic standard of living during a time of massive industrial growth and rising economic inequality.

Were the corporate leaders of the Gilded Age corrupt robber barons or rags-to-riches heroes? Was factory work a long-term good, driving down prices and growing the American economy, or was it soul-sucking wage slavery? Maybe both. What's certain is that the nature of labor changed forever. Systems of efficiency like Taylorism and the assembly line specialized labor and brought much monotony to the workplace. Early American factory life was a nightmare, not unlike contemporary conditions in much of the developing world. The tyranny of the clock, a relatively new addition to the factory floor, dominated life as the average laborer worked six days a week, ten hours a day. By 1900 there were 1.7 million children toiling in the labor force.

Worse still, in the late nineteenth century neither political party supported unions or any sort of modern social welfare system or safety net. The results were barbaric. Unorganized workers lacked health care, safety regulations, and unemployment insurance. From 1880 to 1900 there were thirty-five thousand deaths on the job, *annually* — the equivalent of a Korean War every year for two decades. Beyond the fatalities, an average of 536,000 men and women were injured at work in each of those years.

The coldhearted ideology of the day — in both major political parties and among the wealthy — tended to blame poverty on the workers *themselves*. Except among a tiny (but growing) core of socialists, few Americans who were not directly affected by the plight of workers demonstrated any enthusiasm for federal intervention or poverty mitigation. Indeed, the *Democratic* President Grover Cleveland — a fiscal conservative — declared in 1893: "While the people patriotically and cheerfully support their Government, its functions *do not* include the support of the people." The Republicans were often even less sympathetic.

Most politicians simply reflected the prevailing mores. American elites (and many hoodwinked workers and farmers) clung tightly to belief in the American Dream — that with enough hard work and grit anyone, by pulling on their own bootstraps, could become rich. The empirical statistics, even then, debunked this ideology as little more than anecdotal, but it endured and endures. An academic of that era, William Sumner, summarized this viewpoint: "Let every man be sober, industrious, prudent, and wise and poverty will be abolished in a few generations." Nor did many popular preachers, such as Henry Ward Beecher, show much sympathy for the plight of the poor, with Beecher famously announcing that "no man in this land suffers from poverty unless it be more than his fault — unless it be his sin."

Nonetheless, when the economy finally collapsed in 1893 — due in large part to the corruption and excesses of various corporate monopolies — views on charity, social welfare, and the supposed character defects of the poor began to change. Perhaps the federal and local governments *did* have a role in citizens' welfare. Of this much, many were sure: something had to change.

Populism and Agrarian Revolt: The Good, the Bad, the Ugly

After 1877, when the Republican Party abandoned southern blacks along with any remnants of its old abolitionist sentiment, the GOP became increasingly identified as the party of business, of corporations and the capitalist class. The Democrats, now largely a regional (southern) party, also proved initially conservative on economic issues and stuck with pure free-market capitalism. Neither party, it seemed, appealed to the best interests of small rural farmers or urban wage workers. One result of industrialization was the accumulation of massive wealth in the hands of the very few, mostly northern and eastern corporatists. In 1890 the richest 1 percent of the population owned 51 percent of the national wealth, while the poorest 44 percent owned less than 2 percent. The result of this imbalance was instability, strikes, work stoppages, federal intervention, and, often, bloodshed. Unions formed, shattered, and rose again. Still, at a national level, it was the rural farmers who first revolted.

Farmers felt themselves the perennial victims of a rigged system. They lived by the whims of market prices, of supply and demand. They hated the national tariff — which protected urban manufacturing but caused rising costs in the consumer goods necessary to live on the prairie. Furthermore, the post–Civil War move away from paper currency or "greenbacks" to hard specie, meaning gold, devastated all but the wealthiest farmers. Seeing themselves as the ideal Americans of the Jeffersonian vision — the salt of the earth who tilled the land — they demanded that silver (which was more plentiful) as well as gold be used to back their paper currency. Small farmers simply didn't have much in the way of gold reserves, and the "hard money" policies of the Republicans and urban elites devalued what little cash they had.

Disgusted with two-party politics, and feeling abandoned by both mainstream Republicans and Democrats, a new organization, the People's Party, formed and met with early electoral successes in their western and (sometimes) southern heartlands. The Populists, as they were called, entered American politics and, in one guise or another, have been with us ever since. Theirs was the policy and ideology of "us" versus "them," rich versus poor, West versus East, rural versus urban, and — lamentably — white versus black. The Populists for the most part distrusted the state; then again, they did support federal intervention when it suited *them*.

Riding a tidal wave of rural and agricultural support, William Jennings Bryan of Nebraska managed a veritable takeover of the Democratic Party by 1896, fusing it with the Populists, and ran for president. Bryan was one the great orators in American history. His speeches summoned the tone of evangelical church rallies. At the Democratic National Convention in Chicago, Bryan mesmerized the crowd as he placed an imaginary crown of thorns on his head and pronounced, "We will answer their [the Republicans] demand for a gold standard by saying to them: You shall not press down upon the brow of labor this crown of thorns." Then, stretching out his arms as if on a cross, he hollered, "You shall not crucify mankind upon a cross of gold." Bryan, however popular and however enthralling on a podium, would go on to lose in 1896 (and then twice more). He was defeated by the Republican William McKinley, who ran on a platform of nationalism and status quo prosperity and who labeled Bryan a radical tainted by his party's association with the old Confederate South.

And there was something else: money in politics. McKinley and his corporate Republicans raised $7 million (the equivalent of $3 *billion* today), the Democrats just $300,000. Bryan ran an energetic campaign, riding the rails and giving six hundred speeches in twenty-seven states; McKinley rarely left his home and rested on his financial advantages. In the end money won. McKinley would be president. Lest we become too sentimental and consider Bryan's and the Populists' failed campaign as some sort of moral effort, it is necessary to illuminate the dark side of the Populist Party.

Many Populists demonstrated strong strains of nativism and racism. They railed against "Jew" bankers, "Slavic" immigrants up north, and in the South the "Negro menace." This was not mere rhetoric. As Populists rose in the West and South, blacks were being utterly disenfranchised. Southern states — now back in the hands of many former Confederate leaders — struck almost every eligible black voter from the rolls. Between 1898 and 1910 the number of black registered voters in Louisiana dropped from 130,000 to 730! The Populist Party, in other words, may have been the party of the "people," but it was most certainly only thus for *white* people. Consider the contrast. The very year Bryan ran his crusading campaign, the Supreme Court would hold that segregation was legal when it ruled in the case of *Plessy v. Ferguson*. Few Populists made an effort to craft an interracial alliance of poor people, and thus it was ultimately American *blacks* who were left to writhe on Bryan's proverbial cross of gold.

The Progressive Moment: Social Freedom or Social Control

The Panic and Depression of 1893 was so severe — and the government so unprepared and unwilling to intervene — that millions of families were brought to the brink of starvation, and the "ranks of a tramp army" of unemployed men swelled. Though the Populists never managed to convince or co-opt northern factory workers to join their crusade, many of the sentiments and proposed policies of the People's Party began to infuse a new movement of mostly middle-class "Progressives," as they styled themselves. Progressives weren't exactly radical in the traditional sense — though their wealthy opponents depicted them as such — and they belonged to *both* major political parties. What they most had in common was an abiding criticism of the excesses of American "boom–bust" capitalism, and a sense that regulation of markets and the intervention of government could mitigate the worst aspects of this and future depressions.

Throughout their heyday, 1896–1920 or so, Progressives called for, and often achieved, many of the government programs and policies that exist to this day. They pushed for antitrust and anti-monopoly regulations, the eight-hour workday, an end to child labor and unemployment, and workers' compensation insurance, to name but a few. One problem for the Progressives was their inability to forge lasting alliances with rural Populists, whom they saw as backward country bumpkins. Nor did the rural poor trust the machinations of these seemingly arrogant urban reformist Progressives. The two groups had such divergent cultural values and traditions — as well as different views on immigration and government intervention — that a true union of urban/rural workers and reformists never manifested itself.

Historians long have argued about the ultimate nature of the Progressive movement. Some view the Progressives as genuine reformers with the best interest and freedoms of the working classes at their root. Others sense an overriding aura of social *control* in the Progressive agenda. Though the remarkable achievements of the Progressives should never be ignored, their paternalistic and controlling side bears some analysis. As true believers in the government's ability to reform, regulate, and solve the nation's economic *and* social problems, Progressives sometimes displaced the social justice rhetoric of the Populists "with slogans of efficiency." Indeed, Progressives seemed to "know what was best" for poor farmers and urban immigrants alike — sobriety and moderation. This explains why so many Progressives were also in favor of temperance. Their motto was "trust us," meaning the experts, your social and educational betters.

While Populism pitted the "people" against the state, Progressives believed in the utility of *using* the state, through new theories of social science, to intervene in the economy and reform society. Indeed, the paternalistic impulses of some Progressives were such that they saw the masses — urban or rural — as a threat to democracy, a populace *itself* in need of regulation. Therein lies part of the dark side of the Progressive movement. Sure, Progressives made great, if gradualist, progress on improving working conditions, government regulation, and the right of (white) women to vote. This ought to be rightfully celebrated. Still, many Progressives, both academics and policy makers, believed in the social Darwinist notion of human beings' "survival of the fittest." In that vein a powerful wing of the Progressives backed eugenics programs of forced sterilization laws. Those deemed physically or mentally unfit were to be sterilized for the good of the American "whole." Beginning in 1907, two-thirds of US states would eventually pass forced sterilization laws. Indeed, even the Supreme Court ruled, in *Buck v. Bell* (1927), that compulsory sterilization was fully legal and constitutional. In a disturbing irony, Adolf Hitler and other Nazis would later cite America as a positive example and model of their early racial purity programs.

Progressives had a deep blind spot related to race in general and African Americans in particular. The inconvenient fact is that the "Progressive Era" coincided with the Jim Crow era and the height of racial terrorism in the South. When Progressives talked about easing inequality they meant *white* inequality. The same went for most Populists. Indeed, as *The New York Times* reported on the 1924 Democratic National Convention: "An effort to incorporate in the Democratic Platform a plank condemning the Ku Klux Klan . . . was lost early this morning by a single vote. . . . There [was oratory against the proposal] by William Jennings Bryan, who spoke with his old-time fire and enthusiasm."

"Progressive" Democrats couldn't even agree to condemn the Klan! Perhaps we shouldn't be surprised. The Progressives and Populists had one thing in common: They wanted to win national elections. As a result, they showed a willingness to play the race card and ignore the southern regime of terror that was then at its height.

As most Progressives and Populists remained silent, lynching reached its zenith in this era, and neither party took national action. It didn't take very much for a black man to be lynched in the "Progressive Era" South. In 1889, Keith Bowen was killed for simply entering a room where three white women were sitting. In 1904 a white mob lynched a black man for knocking on a white woman's door. In 1912 Thomas Miles was killed for writing a note to a white woman, inviting her for a cold drink. Multiply this by a thousand and we get a sense of the scale of lynching in this period. And what did a self-described "Progressive" president, Theodore Roosevelt, have to say about all of this? The New York–bred Brahmin lowered himself to the baseness of a southern apologist. He stated that "the greatest existing cause of lynching is the perpetration, especially by black men, of the hideous crime of rape." How's that for victim blaming?

The Wild Election of 1912: Who Was the Real Progressive?

Nevertheless, by 1912 the old notion of a governmental hands-off policy in economics and society was out of style. In that presidential election three men ran on a platform of "Progressivism" — Republican incumbent William Howard Taft, Democratic challenger Woodrow Wilson, and the old stalwart Theodore Roosevelt, who had formed his own third party, the Progressive (or "Bull Moose") Party. In this election, the three main candidates all sought to "out-progressive" the others. In truth, though, the men were, in their policies and platforms, remarkably similar. And they *admitted* it! Wilson stated, "When I sit down and compare my views with those of a Progressive Republican I can't see what the difference is." Roosevelt, ever more succinct and blunt, declared that "Wilson is merely a less virile me."

So who *was* most traditionally Progressive? It's a tough question. Roosevelt was most associated with Progressivism, in theory. He touted his achievements as a "trust-buster," believed that big *government* could balance big *business*, and had a strong environmental record including an expanded program of national parks. Still, he was socially conservative, feared anarchy, and supported overt imperialism. His racism, and that of his followers, was also a problem — some called the Roosevelt wing of the Republican Party the "Lily-whites." Taft, though portrayed by his opponents as a "business" Republican, actually busted twice the number of trusts as Teddy, mandated an eight-hour workday for federal employees, and pushed for a progressive income tax. Wilson — born to a slaveholding family in Virginia in 1856 — had racist instincts but supported some trust-busting and believed the Constitution to be a "living document" that must change with the times.

In the end Roosevelt, though the most successful third-party candidate in history, split the Republican vote and propelled Wilson into the White House. Wilson followed through on many of his campaign promises, and the 63rd Congress, during his first term as president, was one of the more productive in US history. Under Wilson's watch, Congress lowered the tariff, abolished child labor, and passed a new antitrust act, the eight-hour workday, and federal aid to farmers. Wilson's first term seemed a Progressive dream. But the man also had southern roots and was a product of his era and its hateful culture. The favorite movie of the Progressive Wilson was *The Birth of a Nation*, which depicted the KKK as heroic. Furthermore, he excluded black soldiers from the fiftieth-anniversary observance of the Battle of Gettysburg and ushered in segregation of federal buildings and the federal civil service. On the issue of race, under Wilson, "Progressive America" had taken a step backward.

Why No Socialism in America? Urban, Rural, and Racial Division

It is a question asked time and again by historians on both sides of the Atlantic: Why did a significant socialist movement not rise in the United States as it did in Europe? Indeed, we could argue that *this* is one of the rare things that actually *is* exceptional about America. Indeed, while many liberal Progressives in the United States admired the social programs long flourishing in industrialized Europe, they never managed to implement most of these policies in Washington. One reason they had so much trouble was the power of the courts in America. Through the peculiar United States system of lifetime appointments of judges, the justices — especially on the Supreme Court — were a generation behind contemporary policy makers and tended to strike down social welfare provisions as unconstitutional. It would take decades to modernize the court. European countries rarely had such problems with experimentation and improvisation.

Thus the United States fell way behind Europe on social welfare and remains so today. One dream of American Progressives was universal health insurance, which they proposed back in 1912. More than a century later, the United States holds the distinction of being perhaps the last major industrialized country *not* to have such a program.

The Strike, 1886, by Roger Koehler

Germany had shown the way in 1883, and the United Kingdom passed the National Insurance Act in 1911.

This is not to say that American socialists did not exist. In fact, 1912 was probably the high tide of socialist sentiment in this country. Many socialists, including their party leader, Eugene Debs, a former union man, believed that neither of the two major parties had an answer to the ills and excesses of capitalism. As one union member summed it up, "People got mighty sick of voting for Republicans and Democrats when it was a 'heads I win, tails you lose' proposition." Though it is rarely remembered or spoken of now, in 1911 socialists were elected mayors of eighteen cities, and more than three hundred held office in thirty states. In the 1912 presidential election Debs received a remarkable one million votes, the most ever for a far-left socialist candidate. Clearly, some proportion of voters agreed with Debs that "The Republican and Democratic parties, or, to be more exact, the Republican-Democratic party, represent the capitalist class in the struggle. They are the political wings of the capitalist system."

Still, though Debs's accomplishments were real, it must be said that no serious socialist or social democratic movement ever gathered much steam on this side of the Atlantic. The reasons were as numerous as they were lamentable. The working class in the United States was utterly divided against itself — something the *owners* of this country exploited and perpetuated. Rural Populists wanted lower tariffs, cultural homogeneity, an end to new immigration, and a return to "traditional values." They were never able to make common cause with the urban (often immigrant) working class, despite their obvious common interests. Just as today, the American working and middle classes were then waging a culture war over race, citizenship, immigration, and social "values."

But the main factor was race, specifically the "Negro question." Both urban white immigrants and rural white farmers defined progress and reform along the narrowest of racial contours. They believed in *white* Progressivism and *white* Populism. In the interest of not alienating their parties' southern wings and winning elections and because of their downright bigotry, they left African Americans to suffer economic peonage and physical torment. Progressives and Populists of the period failed to recognize one salient truth: some cannot be free so long as all are not free. When it came to fulfilling the idealistic dreams of populism and progressivism, race, as in so many American matters, would prove to be the nation's Achilles' heel. It would take two generations to even begin to right that wrong.[7]

21

THE TRAGIC DAWN OF OVERSEAS IMPERIALISM

Empire. It is a word that most Americans loathe. After all, the United States was born through its rebellion against the great (British) empire of the day. American politicians, policy makers, and the public alike have long preferred to imagine the United States as, rather, a beacon of freedom in the world, bringing light to those in the darkness of despotism. Europeans, not Americans, it is thought, had empires. Some version of this myth has pervaded the republic from its earliest colonial origins, and nothing could be further from the truth.

According to the old historical narrative, the United States has always been a democratic republic and only briefly dabbled, from 1898 to 1904, with outright imperialism. And indeed, even in that era — in which the United States seized Puerto Rico, Guam, Hawaii, and the Philippines — the United States saw itself as "liberating" the locals from Spanish despotism. This wasn't real imperialism but rather, to use a term from the day, "benevolent assimilation." Oh, what a gloriously American euphemism!

The truth, of course, is far more discomfiting. The United States was an empire before it had even gained its own independence. From the moment that Englishmen landed at Jamestown and Plymouth Rock, theirs was an imperial experiment. Native tribes were conquered and displaced westward, year in and year out, until there were no sovereign Indians left to fight. In 1848 the US Army conquered northern Mexico and rechristened it the American Southwest. Yes, the United States was always an empire, what Thomas Jefferson self-consciously called an "empire of liberty." Only the American empire looked different from the British and Western European variety. Until 1898 the United States lacked the overseas possessions and expansive naval power that have come to define our contemporary image of the term *empire.* That was the British, French, and Spanish model. No, the United States was a great land empire most similar to that of Russia, but an empire nonetheless.

Still, there is something profound about 1898 and the years that followed. For it was in this era that the American people — and their leaders — became sick with the disease of overseas imperialism. With no Indians left to fight and no Mexican lands worth conquering, Americans looked abroad for new monsters to destroy and new lands to occupy. Britain and France were far too powerful and were not to be trifled with; but Spain, the deteriorating Spanish Empire in the Caribbean and Pacific, proved a tempting target. And so it was, through a brief — "splendid," as it was described — little war with Spain, that the United States would annex foreign territories and join the European race for colonies.

The year 1898 is central to our understanding of the United States' contemporary role in the world, for it was at that moment that the peculiar exceptional millenarianism of American idealism merged with the Western mission of "civilization." The result was a more overt, distant, and expansive version of American empire. And though the United States no longer officially "annexes" foreign territories, its neo-imperial foreign policy is alive and well, with US military forces ensconced in some eight hundred bases in more than eighty countries — numbers that by far exceed those of other nations. Furthermore, the remnants of America's first overseas conquests are with us today, as the people of Puerto Rico, Guam, and Samoa are still only partial Americans — citizens, yes, but citizens without congressional representation or a vote in presidential elections. How ironic, indeed, that a nation founded in opposition to "taxation without representation" should, for more than a hundred years now, hold so many of its people in a situation remarkably similar to that of the American colonists before the Revolutionary War.

In retrospect, then, 1898 represents both continuity with America's imperial past and a bridge to its contemporary neo-imperial future. This era is key because it stands as a moment of no return: a pivot point at which the United States became a global empire. One can hardly understand contemporary interventions in Iraq and Afghanistan without a clear account of 1898 and what followed. The Spanish-American War and the occupation of the Philippines are two of America's fundamental sins, and their consequences resonate in our ever uncertain present.

The Closing of the Frontier

In 1890 the distinguished American historian Frederick Jackson Turner combed the latest US census and declared, in a widely read speech, that the American "frontier" was officially "closed." He meant, of course, that there were no longer any uncharted western lands to explore or Indian tribes to fight. The West was conquered and "civilized," once and for all. According to Turner, westward expansion had defined American history and American values. "Civilizing" the West, through hardy individualism and strife, had altered and established the American soul. In his telling, which was very influential in its day, the "loss" of the frontier wasn't necessarily a good thing; in fact, it had the potential to "soften" Americans and rot the foundation of the republic.

It was believed that without new lands to conquer, new space in which to expand, Americans would become a sedentary people riven with the same class divisions and social conflict infecting Europe. Furthermore, without new markets, how would American farmers and manufacturers maintain and improve their economic situation? The West was an idea, mostly, but it spoke to an inherently American trait: expansionism. Ours was a society of more: more land, more profits, more freedom, more growth. In a view widely held — then and now — the United States would die if it ever stopped expanding. From "sea to shining sea" wasn't enough; no two oceans should hem in American markets, the American people, or American ideals. This was, and is, the messianic nature of the American experiment, for better or worse.

Many citizens were riddled with anxiety about the "loss" of the West. This helps explain the widely popular phenomenon of Buffalo Bill Cody's traveling "Wild West" shows, in which he paraded Indians around the cities of the American East and, eventually, around the world. Americans were transfixed at the sight of "savage" natives and "noble" cowboys and cavalrymen. For Americans of the 1890s, the West — and all it entailed — represented both freedom and virile masculinity. As more and more Americans moved to big cities and became factory laborers, many wondered whether American manhood itself was not in crisis. Those with the means (and the inherent insecurity), men like Theodore Roosevelt, the scion of a wealthy patrician New York family, made pilgrimages to western ranches as though they represented the New Jerusalem. It is only thus that we have the image of this future American president, a city boy, adorned in western attire. Such was the inherent unease of the times.

How to Sell an Unnecessary War: William Randolph Hearst and the Media-Militarist Conspiracy

By 1898 the United States was bursting with energy, self-righteousness, and anxiety. The only question was where all that expansionist energy would direct itself. It was then that a coalition of newspapermen and imperialist politicians provided a ready target: Cuba. Spain had, for many years, been engaged in a counterinsurgency campaign against Cuban rebels seeking independence. This would provide the opening that America's burgeoning imperialists longed for. At the same time, none of this interest in Cuban affairs was new. Before the American Civil War, southerners had repeatedly called for the annexation of Cuba as a new slave state.

Now, however, a conglomeration of powerful interests pushed for US intervention on behalf of the Cubans. If that campaign resulted in the seizure of Cuba, then all the better. Historians have long debated which factors or impulses were most responsible for America's overseas expansion and intervention in Cuba. The reality, though, is that it was a confluence of interests that pushed the United States toward war with Spain. Corporate capitalists sought new markets for their goods; missionaries dreamed of Christianizing and "civilizing" foreign peoples; naval strategists coveted bases and coaling stations to

LA FATLÉRA DEL ONCLE SAM (per M. Moliné).

Guardarse l' isla perque no 's perdí.

Satirical drawing, 1896, La Campana de Gràcia

project power across the seas; expansionist politicians — prominent among them Theodore Roosevelt and Senator Henry Cabot Lodge — believed the United States had a mission to expand in order to salvage the virility of the republic; and muckraking newspapermen led by William Randolph Hearst desired nothing more than to sell papers and turn a profit, and the best way to do that was to report, and exaggerate, Spanish atrocities and drum up a new, popular war. War sells, after all.

The key triumvirate, however, was the alliance among Assistant Secretary of the Navy Roosevelt, Massachusetts senator Lodge, and newspaper magnate Hearst. Lodge genuinely hoped for some crisis to precipitate war with Spain. In 1898 he wrote to a friend: "There may be an explosion any day in Cuba which would settle a great many things." How right he was! First, an intercepted letter from the Spanish minister in Washington was found to contain unflattering references to President William McKinley. Hearst's papers exaggerated the story, with his *New York Journal* running the headline, WORST INSULT TO THE UNITED STATES IN ITS HISTORY. This came on top of several years of stories in which the *Journal* writers whipped up chauvinist support for war with Spain.

Then, fatefully, on February 15, 1898, an American naval vessel, the USS *Maine*, exploded in a harbor in Cuba, killing 258 sailors. Without the slightest pause for an investigation, a Hearst headline proclaimed DESTRUCTION OF THE WARSHIP MAINE WAS THE WORK OF AN ENEMY. It wasn't, and experts confirmed later that the explosion was accidental. Even at the time, several policy makers and experts suspected the *Maine* had fallen victim to fluke tragedy. The secretary of the navy wrote that the explosion was "probably the result of an accident"; furthermore, the country's principal expert on maritime explosions — a professor at the US Naval Academy — concluded that "no torpedo such as is known in modern warfare can of itself cause an explosion as powerful as that which destroyed the *Maine*." It hardly mattered. The explosion of the *Maine* provided the casus belli for a nation ready for war.

Crowds gathered to protest at the Spanish embassy; effigies of Spaniards were burned. Hearst, the newspaperman who had long sought war, cabled to one of his correspondents that "*Maine* is a great thing." President McKinley — who had seen the horror of war at the Battle of Antietam — was initially hesitant to rush into action, but he quickly bowed to the pressure of a militaristic public and Congress. He, without international legal sanction, insisted that Spain give up possession of its "ever-faithful isle." The president must have known, of course, that Spain could never bow to such a demand and still maintain its global prestige. Then, on April 11, McKinley delivered a message to Congress arguing that the United States must intervene in Cuba not simply as a result of the *Maine* explosion, but as a humanitarian intervention on behalf of the embattled Cubans. As historian Stephen Kinzer has written, McKinley thus "became the first American president to threaten war against another country because it was mistreating its own subjects." He would not be the last.

Spain declared war on the United States on April 24, and Washington issued a declaration the next day. The military conflict was to last less than four months, ending in a decisive American victory over an empire long past its prime. Secretary of State John Hay called it a "splendid little war," and, indeed, it was by some measures the most popular war in American history. War fever infected the American people. The French ambassador observed that a "sort of bellicose fever has seized the American nation"; the London *Times* called it "the delirium of war"; a German newspaper described it as a "lust for conquest."

Seeking martial glory, Roosevelt resigned his position as assistant navy secretary and raised a regiment of volunteer cavalry, the Rough Riders. He would take it to Cuba as part of the hastily formed American expeditionary force seeking to "liberate" the island. Roosevelt found the combat he so desired when his regiment bravely charged to victory in the Battle of San Juan Hill — which was actually fought on nearby Kettle Hill and involved the often forgotten help of the professional black 9th and 10th Cavalry regiments. Old Teddy was as giddy as a schoolboy, shouting at the height of the battle: "Holy Godfrey, what fun!" He would later call the battle "the great day of my life." After the battle Roosevelt annoyed his professional military peers by shamelessly and uncouthly lobbying for a Medal of Honor for himself (President Bill Clinton would eventually bestow the award eighty years after the future president's death).

The war was far from glorious. The Spanish were dislodged from Guam, the Philippines, Puerto Rico, and Cuba, but deaths from disease outnumbered US battle deaths by some eight to one. Few Americans cared about this fact, so caught up were they in the martial fever of the day.

In early 1899 the US Senate would, by a narrow margin, ratify a treaty in which Spain ceded Guam, Puerto Rico, and the Philippines to America. This moment was, indeed, a point of no return — the instant that the United States became an overseas empire. Cuba technically received independence but, under Congress's Platt Amendment, became essentially a US protectorate; Washington retained the right to intervene at will in Cuban affairs.

And what of the Cubans themselves, on whose behalf the war was supposedly fought? US military and political personnel were, upon arriving on the island, surprised to learn that a significant portion of the population and the rebels were black. After all, the last thing the United States of 1898 wanted was an independent black republic on its southern shores. Furthermore, when it turned out the Cuban revolutionaries had expansive social reformist aims beyond independence, Washington was even less apt to grant full independence. General Leonard Wood, the military governor of Cuba, argued that the United States should maintain an indefinite occupation of the island "while saying as little as possible about the whole thing." Wood was eventually pleased by the text of the Platt Amendment, stating, "There is, of course, little or no independence left Cuba under [the amendment]." This all cohered with Wood's worldview. He considered the Cubans "as ignorant as children," and sought to choose their first president.

The Spanish-American War served another purpose for Americans. The conflict, it was said, would heal the divisions of the Civil War and unite the nation behind a "noble" cause. Newspapers bristled with stories of former Union and Confederate veterans serving together in the American army in Cuba and the Philippines. In one famous anecdote, the former Confederate general Joseph "Fighting Joe" Wheeler — by then an old man — led a charge and seemingly forgot whom exactly he was fighting, rallying his men with the cry "Let's go, boys! We've got the damn Yankees on the run again!" It seemed that the Spanish-American War was all things for all people, except, of course, the Spaniards and the natives of the former colonies.

After the victory, the Americans' goals became ever more expansive. A war waged for Cuba turned into a war of conquest as the United States seized the Spanish colonies of Guam, Puerto Rico, the Philippines, and — for good measure — the independent island of Hawaii, which the Dole corporation coveted as a source of sugar for the American market. In reference to that island, McKinley declared, "We need Hawaii just as much and a good deal more than we did California. It is manifest destiny." And so it was.

Fighting for American Manhood

Modern historians continue to grapple with the puzzle of America's leap into the colonial land grab in 1898. What prompted the sudden bellicosity of American military might? What drove the spirit of the populace to cheer on the war? As usual, there is no simple answer. This much, however, seems certain: the answers to these questions are as much cultural as political. Indeed, one factor that seemingly drove the rush to war was a prevailing American insecurity about the citizens' collective manhood and masculinity. The historian Jackson Lears, in fact, has persuasively argued that "imperialists deployed a mystical language of evolutionary progress . . . celebrating the renewal of masculine will and equating it with personal regeneration."

Why all this gender insecurity? Well, the nation had, with the exception of several small Indian wars fought by the regular army, been at peace since 1865. The younger generation looked up to the martial exploits of their Civil War veteran fathers. The elders feared that the nation's youths, for lack of military service and without a western frontier to conquer, were growing soft. Fewer and fewer Americans of the late nineteenth century did backbreaking farmwork in the fields or ranches of the West as the population shifted toward unskilled "soft" labor in the cities of the East and Midwest.

In this climate of insecurity and toxic masculinity, many Americans and their public leaders began to believe the United States needed a war to rejuvenate the population and retrieve America's collective masculinity. As early as 1895, Theodore Roosevelt — the poster boy for masculine self-consciousness — declared that he "[s]hould welcome almost any war, for I think this country needs one." Because many women, such as the famed social activist Jane Addams, were or would soon be dissenting anti-imperialists, the expansionists depicted their opponents as lacking what Roosevelt declared "the essential manliness of the American character." Furthermore, pro-imperialist political cartoons often depicted their opponents wearing women's clothing.

In perhaps his most famous speech, "The Strenuous Life," Roosevelt referred to America's mission in pacifying the now rebellious Filipinos as "man's work." The speech was littered with socio-sexual language such as his consistent exhortations that Americans must not "shrink" from their duties, and argued that anti-imperialists had an "unwilling-ness to play the part of men." In another speech, in Boston, Roosevelt stated, "We have got to put down the [Philippine] insurrection! If we are men, we can't do otherwise." Of course, gender roles and mascu-line insecurity alone cannot explain the drive for colonies and mili-tary expansion; neither, though, can we discount its role in propelling the nation forward into war and conquest.

White Man's Burden: Race and Empire

The White Man's Burden
Take up the White Man's burden,
The savage wars of peace —
Fill full the mouth of Famine
And bid the sickness cease. . . .
Take up the White Man's burden,
Ye dare not stoop to less. . . .
By all ye cry or whisper,
By all ye leave or do,
The silent, sullen peoples
Shall weigh your gods and you.
Take up the White Man's burden,
Have done with childish days. . . .
Comes now, to search your manhood.

— An excerpt from the Englishman Rudyard Kipling's
poem "White Man's Burden," an inducement for the
United States to occupy the Philippine Islands and
join the other imperialist nations of Europe

Racism is the original sin of the American experiment. White suprem-acy was part of the cultural baggage American troops carried abroad. This was the era of social Darwinism, the notion that "survival of the fittest" applied to man as well as beast, that certain races were scientifically superior to others. It was all snake oil, of course, but it was a predominant ideology — especially since the "higher-level" white race wrote the books and carried the most advanced weapons. It was thus that racism, along with masculinity, would drive American expansionist imperialism at the turn of the twentieth century.

The war with Spain and the much longer conflict with the Filipino rebels occurred in the context of what was the height of racial violence in the American South. Lynching of blacks reached pandemic proportions, what the author and later anti-imperialist Mark Twain described as "an epidemic of bloody insanities." By one estimate, in the period surrounding the start of the twentieth century someone in the South was hanged or burned alive on average once every four days. Racism infected the populace and policy makers on both sides of the Mason-Dixon Line. And that disease would frame America's new wars, which, by no accident, were waged against brown folks. The language of this imperial era, and the prevailing racialized ideology so prevalent in American society, pervaded and justified America's wars, suppressions, and annexations.

Before the wars even began, men like Roosevelt argued that the United States had a racial obligation to get into the imperial game. He wrote, in 1897, that he felt "a good deal disheartened at the queer lack of imperial instinct our people show . . . [it would seem] we have lost, or wholly lack, the masterful impulse which alone can make a race great." Later, as governor of New York, Roosevelt — who dedicated a peculiar amount of his attention to international rather than state affairs — declared that the United States had a "mighty mission" and that it needed a "knowledge of [our] new duties." Where the American flag once flew (in Cuba and the Philippines), "there must and shall be no return to tyranny or savagery."

After the United States seized the Philippines from Spain, a long legislative debate ensued over just what to do with the islands: Should they be granted independence or held as a colony? On the floor of the Senate, the influential Indiana Republican Albert Beveridge summarized the majority opinion. The Filipinos, because of their race, couldn't possibly govern themselves. "How could they?" he exclaimed.

"They are not a self-governing race. They are Orientals." Later, back in Indiana, Beveridge questioned how anyone could oppose the "mission" of American imperialism. After all, he argued, "The rule of liberty . . . applies only to those who are capable of self-government. We govern Indians without their consent. . . . We govern children without their consent." Coarse though his language was, Beveridge was articulating a consistent truth: Americans did have a long history of selectively applying civil rights, regularly denying them to blacks and natives. Why not, then, deny such freedoms to "Orientals"?

Other interest groups agreed with the racialized framing of America's role in the world. Missionaries, for example, flocked to the Philippines to Christianize the natives — apparently, and ironically, unaware that most Filipinos were already Christian (Roman Catholic). American soldiers also used racist language to address the tough counterinsurgencies they found themselves engrossed in and to label and dehumanize their enemies. Just before open warfare broke out between American troops and Filipino rebels in the capital of Manila, one US trooper wrote, "Where these sassy niggers used to greet us daily with a pleasant smile . . . they now pass by with menacing looks." It was, indeed, remarkable how quickly the pejoratives long applied to African Americans were retooled for America's new Asian subjects.

When fighting did break out in the Philippines, the soldier who fired the first shots ran back to his lines and yelled, "Line up, fellows, the niggers are in here, all through!" Years later, another American soldier wrote home from the Philippines that "I am growing hardhearted, for I am in my glory when I can sight my gun on some dark skin and pull the trigger." American soldiers and officers — often veterans of the Native American wars of the past century — also took to mixing metaphors when describing their Filipino opponents. General Elwell Otis urged Filipinos in his district to "be good Indians." General Frederick Funston considered Filipinos "a semi-savage people." Theodore Roosevelt took to calling Filipino insurgents "Apache or Comanche," or otherwise "Chinese half-breeds" or "Malay bandits."

In another twist of irony, many of the army regiments engaged in combat in the Philippines consisted of black enlisted men. Often more sympathetic to the locals, these African American troopers recognized how racism alienated and inflamed the Filipino population. One black soldier, B. D. Flower, wrote home in 1902: "Almost without exception, soldiers and also many officers refer to natives in their presence as 'Niggers' . . . and we are daily making permanent enemies." Analogous situations exist in America's contemporary occupations in Iraq and Afghanistan. Arabs are often called "camel jockeys," "rag heads," or "sand niggers." The temptation and comfortable mental heuristic to lump the enemy together as an inhuman and often racialized "other" all too often only empowers and spreads rebellion. It is a lesson that this author lamentably learned in Baghdad and Kandahar, and that US Army soldiers of the last century learned in Manila.

Nor was it just missionaries and soldiers who employed racial rhetoric to justify the annexation of new colonies and subjugation of the Filipino rebel movement. An editorial in the Philadelphia *Public Ledger* opined, "It is not civilized warfare, but we are not dealing with a civilized people. The only thing that they know is fear and force, violence and brutality, and we are giving it to them." Senior politicians also used racist and pejorative language. President McKinley referred to "misguided Filipinos" who simply couldn't recognize that the United States acted "under the providence of God and in the name of human progress and civilization." In sum, the United States had a racial, religious, and civilizational duty to "benevolently assimilate" those whom William Howard Taft — the civilian governor of the Philippines and future US president — patronizingly called "our little brown brothers."

From the poetry of the day to the crass language of the common soldier to the rhetoric of the missionary to the proclamations of senior politicians, race infected the words and ideas of American imperialists. Armed with the armor of white supremacy, American fighting men and policy makers would, in the conflict that followed in the Philippines, wage war with a savagery they would never have applied to a white European enemy.

Quagmire and Atrocity: The Philippine-American War

> No imperial designs lurk in the American mind. They
> are alien to American sentiment. . . . Our priceless prin-
> ciples undergo no change under a tropical sun.
>
> — President William McKinley in
> speaking of the Philippines (1899)

It has long been inaccurately labeled the Philippine Insurrection or
the Philippine-American War and has been almost lost to history.
Few Americans today even recall what is actually best described as
a long-running Filipino rebellion. In a cruel irony, it was to be the
United States — forged in opposition to empire and occupation
— that would now play King George as the Filipinos struggled for
independence.

There was nothing inevitable about the war in the Philippines.
Sure, the island chain was a Spanish possession, but given that the
war of 1898 was waged allegedly over Cuba, nothing stipulated that
the United States had to invade and occupy the Philippines. Here
again, Roosevelt was front and center. Without consulting his boss
or the president, Assistant Secretary of the Navy Roosevelt issued
preemptive orders to Admiral George Dewey's Pacific fleet to sail to
Manila and sink the Spanish ships there in the event of an outbreak of
war. War began and Dewey followed orders. The result was a massacre. The better-equipped American warships outranged the Spanish
vessels and inflicted 381 casualties while suffering only 6 wounded.
Even then, with the Spanish fleet at the bottom of the harbor, nothing
preordained the American ground occupation of the islands, but a
sort of militaristic inertia ensured that McKinley would indeed sail an
army to Manila to take control of the archipelago.

McKinley, true to his honest nature, later admitted that when he
heard of Dewey's victory at Manila he "could not have told you where
those darned islands were within a thousand miles." Presidential
ignorance aside, before a significant land force could reinforce Dewey,
the naval commander sought all the help he could get in defeating the

Spanish garrison. Dewey went so far as to sail Filipino rebel leader Emilio Aguinaldo — the Filipinos had been in the midst of an independence struggle with the Spanish when the Americans arrived — from Hong Kong to Manila, hoping Aguinaldo's rebels would reinforce American efforts on the islands. Aguinaldo believed that he and Dewey had a deal: that once the combined American-Filipino force liberated the islands, the United States would recognize Philippine independence. It was not to be.

In the end, when the Spanish garrison surrendered Manila, Aguinaldo was not even invited to the ceremony. It was then, under pressure from expansionists in McKinley's own party, that the US president had what he described as a "divine intervention" instructing him to annex the Philippine Islands. Struck by a sudden urge as he walked the corridors of the White House on the night of October 24, 1898, he fell to his knees "and prayed Almighty God for light and guidance," according to McKinley. God told him to seize the Philippines. Later he would declare that "there was nothing left for us to do but to take them all, and to educate the Filipinos, and uplift and civilize and Christianize them by God's grace." (As previously noted, most of these pagans who required Christianization were already Roman Catholics!) Interestingly, this was not the only militaristic divine intervention in US presidential history. Before the 2003 invasion of Iraq, then president George W. Bush famously announced that "God told him to end the tyranny in Iraq!" In both cases God seems to have saddled Americans with dirty, difficult tasks.

At the start of 1899, McKinley imposed official military rule over the Philippines. Aguinaldo, who led his own army, one that was then staring across the lines at the American army, could never accept this arrangement. He declared, "My nation cannot remain indifferent in view of such a violation and aggressive seizure of its territory by a nation [the US] which has arrogated to itself the title, 'champion of oppressed races.' . . . My government is disposed to open hostilities." Before the fighting kicked off, however, the Filipinos, following in the footsteps of the American colonists, nominated members to a newly elected congress and wrote a constitution that drew from the examples of Belgium, France, Mexico, and Brazil. Washington ignored this impressively democratic turn of events.

The war began when sentries from the two opposing armies fired upon each other on February 4, 1899. The day ended badly for the Filipinos. The superiorly armed and trained American army implemented a prepared plan of attack as soon as the first shots were fired, and by day's end three thousand Filipinos lay dead, in contrast with sixty American fatalities. Within weeks thousands more Filipino troops and civilians were killed. The anti-imperialist American senator Eugene Hale then declared in Washington, accurately, that "[m]ore Filipinos have been killed by the guns of our army and navy than were patriots killed in any six battles of the Revolutionary War."

After Aguinaldo's conventional army was mostly defeated, the archipelago settled into years of guerrilla warfare between the US Army and assorted local rebels (or freedom fighters, depending on your point of view). As the war turned into an insurgency, the brutality of both sides — but especially of the Americans — intensified. US soldiers, seeking to gather tactical information from captured insurgents, took to administering the "water cure," a crude form of waterboarding that dates back to the Spanish Inquisition in the sixteenth century. A victim was held to the ground and force-fed water; then his tormentors would stomp on his stomach and repeat the process. Most victims died. A form of this torture would later be employed by the United States at Guantanamo Bay and various secret prisons during the so-called war on terror.

A private wrote in a letter published in a newspaper that after an American soldier was found mutilated, General Loyd Wheaton ordered his forces "to burn the town and kill every native in sight, which was done." By 1901, Secretary of War Elihu Root had formalized the brutality of the war, telling reporters that from then on the US Army would follow a "more rigid policy" in the Philippines. One reporter from a New York magazine, *The Outlook*, went to see this rigid policy for himself. He wrote back a horrifying description of American counterinsurgency. "In some of our dealings with the Filipinos we seem to be following more or less . . . the example of Spain. We have established a penal colony; we have burned native villages . . . we resort to torture as a means of obtaining information." One general, James Franklin Bell, told a reporter that after two years of war "one-sixth of [the main island] of Luzon's population had either been killed or died of disease" — which would have amounted to more than half a million people. Bell was awarded the Medal of Honor for his efforts.

A reporter from the Philadelphia *Public Ledger* observed, "Our men have been relentless, have killed to exterminate men, women, children, prisoners and captives . . . lads of ten and up, the idea prevailing that the Filipino, as such, was little better than a dog."

Reports of high numbers of prisoner executions appear credible. By the summer of 1901 casualty figures showed that five times as many Filipinos were being killed as wounded — the opposite of what is normally seen in wars. General Arthur MacArthur, senior commander in the Philippines and father of the future general Douglas MacArthur, admitted that his men were indeed under orders to use "very drastic tactics." That seems an understatement. Nor was American military violence the only threat to the Filipinos. Around the same time, a cholera epidemic killed more than one hundred thousand people. America's brand of "freedom" came at a high price for the Filipino population.

By late 1901, with the insurgency all but defeated, many Americans had begun to lose interest in the war. Then, on September 28, Filipino rebels on the distant Philippine island of Samar surprised and killed a high percentage of a US Army company, mostly with machetes. Roughly fifty Americans were slain outright or mortally wounded. Labeled by the press as the "Balangiga Massacre," it was immediately compared (inaccurately) to Custer's Last Stand and the Alamo. The real controversy, however, erupted after Brigadier General Jacob "Hell-Roaring Jake" Smith, a sixty-two-year-old vet of the Indian Wars, was sent to pacify Samar.

Reports of extreme abuses and alleged war crimes immediately arrived back home. This time the Congress had little choice but to conduct a pro forma investigation. During congressional hearings, a US Army major testified that General Smith had told him: "I want no prisoners. I wish you to kill and burn. The more you kill and burn, the better you will please me. I want all persons killed who are capable of bearing arms." When the major asked for an age guideline, Smith allegedly replied, "10 years." Smith, called to the hearings, eventually admitted to all this. He was court-martialed but served not a day in prison. His punishment was a reprimand from the secretary of war, with the leniency being justified on the grounds that Smith was driven to crime by "cruel and barbarous savages." For another American general, Frederick Funston, even the reprimand of Smith was too harsh. Funston freely admitted in a speech that he "personally strung up 35 Filipinos without trial, so what's all the fuss over [Smith] dispatching a few treacherous savages?" Asked how he felt about the growing anti-imperialist movement in America, Funston declared that those harboring such sentiments "should be dragged out of their homes and lynched." Reading of this interview, the avowed anti-imperialist Mark Twain volunteered to be the first man lynched.

The final major campaign occurred on southern Luzon in 1902. General James Franklin Bell removed natives from villages and placed them in concentration camps; crops were burned and livestock was killed; a random Filipino was selected for execution each time an American soldier was killed in combat (a certain war crime even by the standards of the day); and an American decree made it "a crime for any Filipino to advocate independence." In three months fifty thousand locals were killed. The war was effectively over, though short spurts of violence and rebellion would occur occasionally for another decade. Untold hundreds of thousands of Filipinos were dead. The water buffalo, the key to rural life in the region, had been made nearly extinct, its numbers diminished by some 90 percent. Indeed, as historian Stephen Kinzer disturbingly noted, "Far more Filipinos were killed or died as a result of mistreatment [over four years] than in three and a half centuries of Spanish rule." This, it appears, was the price of American "liberty" — and the islands would not receive genuine independence until after World War II!

For the Soul of America: The (Mostly) Noble Anti-Imperialist Movement

For all the villains in this story, there were Americans willing to dissent against overseas conquest and imperialism. Indeed, they were a large, diverse, and sometimes peculiar lot. They too are the heroes of the era. From the very start of the Philippine occupation, many prominent citizens publicly opposed the war. This coalition of intellectuals, politicians, artists, and businessmen may have acceded to the conquest of native and Mexican lands but saw imperial expansion overseas as un-American and unconstitutional. Throughout the era they made their voices heard and fought for the soul of the nation.

Early critics of the war pointed out the hypocrisy of fighting for Cuban rights when African Americans at home were still regularly lynched and disenfranchised. A dozen prominent New Yorkers raised the alarm in a public letter before the war with Spain, proclaiming, "The cruelty exhibited in Cuba is no peculiarity of the Spanish race; within the last few weeks instances of cruelty to Negroes occurred in this country which equal, if not surpass, anything which has occurred in Cuba. . . . Our crusade in this matter should begin at home." The most prominent black leader of the era, Booker T. Washington, raised a similar concern in a speech after the Spanish surrender. After praising the heroic efforts of the troops, he called for America to heal racial wounds on the domestic front. He argued, "Until we conquer ourselves, I make no empty statement when I say we shall have, especially in the southern part of our country, a cancer gnawing at the heart of the republic."

It was, however, the annexation of the Philippines that truly kicked off a dissenting movement in the United States. Skeptics across the spectrum of public life would form the Anti-Imperialist League, which, at its height, had hundreds of thousands of members — one of the largest antiwar movements in American history and an impressive achievement in a period of such intense martial fervor. Leaders of the movement included Democratic Party stalwart William Jennings Bryan, the magnate Andrew Carnegie (who offered to buy the Philippines from the US government to set the islands free!), the social activist Jane Addams, the labor organizer Samuel Gompers, the civil rights leader Booker T. Washington, former president Grover Cleveland, former president Benjamin Harrison, and author Mark Twain. What the members of this diverse group had in common was a profound sense that imperialism was antithetical to the idea of America.

Bryan, one of the great orators of the day, summarized this notion when he proclaimed that "the imperialistic idea is directly antagonistic to the idea and ideals which have been cherished by the American people since the signing of the Declaration of Independence." The politician and Civil War veteran Carl Schurz compared the Filipino rebels favorably with the colonial patriots and asked what Americans would do if the natives refused to submit: "Let soldiers marching under the Stars and Stripes shoot them down? Shoot them down because they stand up for their independence?" Of course, that is exactly what the US Army would do, under orders from the president himself.

The Anti-Imperialist League won many moral but few practical victories. Part of the reason for this was the US government's overt suppression of civil liberties. Famously, in what became known as the "mail war," the postmaster general ordered anti-imperialist literature mailed to soldiers in the Philippines to be confiscated. Critics of American foreign policy called it the "rape of the mail." Practically thwarted, artists and cultural critics took the anti-imperial fight to the public. The most prominent and outspoken was Mark Twain, and this, more than his famous books, marked the man's finest hour. He announced his stand in late 1900, stating, "I have seen that we do not intend to free, but to subjugate the people of the Philippines. We have gone there to conquer, not to redeem. . . . And so I am an anti-imperialist." Twain only lashed out harder as the war went on. By 1901 he declared that "we have debauched America's honor and blackened her face" and recommended the Stars and Stripes be changed: "We can just have our usual flag, with the white stripes painted black and the stars replaced by the skull and cross-bones." Some called it treason, others patriotism.

Though the anti-imperialists might appear to be saints, there was a dark element in the movement. Many dissenters' opposition to annexation of foreign lands came not from a moral code but from fear of the racial amalgamation that might result. Some of these men were anti-imperialist senators from the South. One, Senator Ben Tillman of South Carolina, summarized this viewpoint, concluding, "You are undertaking to annex and make a component part of this Government islands inhabited by tens of millions of the colored race . . . barbarians of the lowest type." Furthermore, he stated, "It is to the injection of the body politic of the United States of that vitiated blood, that debased and ignorant people, that we object." This was far from the language of liberty, but remained embarrassingly common in the movement.

This offensive component aside, eventually, and remarkably, genuine anti-imperialist sentiments made it into the official platform of the Democrats, one of the two mainstream political parties. Imagine a major party platform, even today, declaring: "We oppose militarism. It means conquest abroad and intimidation and oppression at home. It means the strong arm which has been ever fatal to free institutions." It was a noble platform, indeed. But ultimately these sentiments and this party lost. Theodore Roosevelt, the national cheerleader of imperialism, easily retained in the election of 1904 the presidency to which he had risen from vice president when McKinley was assassinated in 1901. In a sense, this marked the death knell of an era of anti-imperialism. There had been, in the election, a referendum on the nature of the national soul, and, sadly, the American people chose war, conquest, and annexation.

———

This era remains with us; it is alive in our debates and politics. Consider this: Even now, citizens of Puerto Rico, Guam, and Samoa have no representation in Congress, nor a vote in presidential elections. The status of these territories and their populations is peculiar for a nation that so strongly professes democracy. The situation is a direct result of decisions made in 1898–1904. In 1901 the Supreme Court, by a vote of 5–4, ruled in *Downes v. Bidwell* that "the Constitution does not apply"

22

A SAVAGE WAR TO END ALL WARS, AND A FAILED PEACE

Over there, over there
Send the word, send the word over there.
That the Yanks are coming,
The Yanks are coming . . .
We'll be over, we're coming over,
And we won't come back till it's over, over there.

— An excerpt from George M.
Cohan's song "Over There"

America wasn't supposed to get in the war. When the country finally did, it was to be a war "to end all wars," to "make the world safe for democracy," one in which, for once, the Allies would seek "peace without victory." How powerful was the romantic and idealistic rhetoric of Woodrow Wilson, America's historian and political scientist turned president. None of that came to pass, of course. No, just less than three years after the outbreak of the Great War in August 1914, the working classes of the United States would join those of Europe in a grinding, gruesome, attritional fight to the finish. In the end some 116,000 Americans would die alongside about 9,000,000 soldiers from the other belligerent nations.

Today the American people are quite comfortable with the mythical sense of their role in the second of the two world wars. The Nazis had to be stopped at all cost; the Japanese had deceitfully attacked our fleet; and — in the end — America saved the day. The United States thus became, as a popular T-shirt proclaims, "back-to-back" world war champs. Still, most of the citizenry knows little about the First World War, which was once called the Great War. The issues involved and the reasons for fighting seem altogether murky, messy even. So as a simple patriotic heuristic, Americans tend to frame the First World War as a prelude to the second. Not simply in the sense that one led in some way to the next, but that the German enemy was equally evil in each — that the kaiser in 1917 was only slightly less militaristic than Adolf Hitler in 1941. Germany's race for world domination, we vaguely conclude, really began in the second decade of the twentieth century and wasn't fully thwarted until 1945. None of that is strictly true: The kaiser's government was far more complex than that of Nazi Germany, for example, and a German sense of guilt over the war was more collective in 1914 than 1939 — but the legend of the war and America's role in it can more easily be simplified by use of this mental shorthand.

In reality Europe blundered into war because of a mix of absurd factors that undergirded the entire nation-state and imperial system of the day: jingoistic nationalism, the race for Asian and African empires, a destabilizing series of opposing alliances, and the foolish notion that war would rejuvenate European manhood and, of course, be swift, decisive, and brief. Instead, technological advances outran military tactics and the two sides — Germany, Austria, and Turkey on the one hand and Britain, France, and Russia on the other — settled in for an incomparably brutal war of stagnation and filth. Unable to win decisively on either front, both sides dug in their men, artillery, and machine guns and fought bloody battles for the possession of mere meters of earth. It was to be the war that ultimately "finished" Europe, destroying the long-term power of the continent and ultimately shifting leadership westward to the United States. Not that any of this was clear at the time.

Europe lost an entire generation, killed, maimed, or forever psychologically broken by the war. Many Europeans lost faith in the snake oil of nationalism and turned away from the standard frameworks of monarchy or liberal democracy. Some found solace in socialism, whereas others doubled down on ultranationalism in the form of fascist leaders. Despite nine million battle deaths — a number unfathomable when the war began — World War I solved little and sowed the seeds for the European cataclysm of 1939–45. It is an uncomfortable truth, especially for the United States, a nation that tends to see itself as being at the center of the world; the United States played mostly a late, and bit, part in the drama across the Atlantic. However, the populace believed its own propaganda, crafted a myth of American triumphalism, and learned all the wrong lessons from the war. Instead of being a "war to end all wars," the Great War turned out to be just the beginning of American interventionism — the pivot toward the creation of today's fiscal-military hegemonic state. And it didn't have to be that way.

Getting In: Wilson Takes Us to War

Most Americans were horrified by the brutality of trench warfare in Europe and thanked God for the Atlantic Ocean. A majority in the United States, due to cultural and linguistic ties to Britain, favored the Allies. Still, another segment of the population, German Americans and (the viscerally anti-British) Irish Americans, tended to favor Austria and Germany. So while President Wilson advised the people and his government to be "neutral in fact as well as in name . . . impartial in thought as well as action," genuine neutrality was always a long shot. One of the problems was Wilson himself, who began to see the war as an opportunity for the United States to lead "a new world order." If he could do so as a peaceful arbiter, so be it; if it required America's entry into the fields of fire, perhaps that couldn't be avoided.

Only William Jennings Bryan, Wilson's first secretary of state and three-time Democratic presidential nominee, could be considered a truly neutral voice in the cabinet. "There will be no war as long I am Secretary of State," the legendary firebrand thundered upon joining the administration. He felt obliged to resign barely a year later, and the United States slid toward war. Of course the United States had never been strictly neutral. Close economic ties with the Allies ensured that. Rather than embargo both sides or demand that Britain open its starvation blockade of Germany to US trading vessels, Wilson's government exported hundreds of millions of dollars in goods annually to the Allied nations and funded some of their debts. In just the first eight months of the war US bankers extended $80 million in credits to the Allies, and then, after Wilson lifted all bans on loans, US financial interests would float $10 million per day to Britain alone! By the end of the war the Allies owed $10 billion in war debts to the United States, the equivalent of some $165 billion in today's dollars. Indeed, the US economy had by 1917 come to rely on Allied war orders. How would Wall Street recover these debts if not through Allied victory? And how could the bogged-down Allies defeat Germany without the promise of American troop reinforcements?

Furthermore, Wilson acquiesced to Britain's blockade of Germany. He told Bryan it would be "a waste of time" to argue with Britain about the blockade, but this made the United States, in fact if not in name, a partner of the Allies. German officials, with some sound logic, protested that the United States, if truly neutral, would condemn a British blockade that starved European children. Wilson remained silent.

His voice was quite clear, however, on the subject of German submarine warfare against Allied (namely American) shipping. Though the German navy had been built up in the decades before the war, its battleships and cruisers were still no match for the combined Anglo-French fleets. Therefore, in order to stymie the blockade and attrit the Allied supply lines, the Germans turned to submarine, or U-boat, warfare. Indeed, at certain points during the war, the German U-boats nearly brought the Allies to their logistical knees. It was only American distribution that kept Britain, in particular, afloat. The German government spent much of the conflict at war with itself over whether to sink American merchant ships supplying the Allies. One can, after all, understand the German predicament: Allied naval power was isolating the Central Powers and the Americans were economically allied with Britain and France!

When, however, a German sub sank the British luxury liner *Lusitania* in May 1915, killing more than 120 US citizens, there was a great outcry from Americans. Former president Theodore Roosevelt, always a reliable war hawk, called the attack "murder on the high seas!" He was still a popular figure, after all, so his demand for war in response to German "piracy" was a serious matter. It turned out the *Lusitania*, traveling from the United States to Britain, was carrying 1,248 cases

Without Warning!, 1917, by J. H. Cassel

of three-inch shells and 4,927 boxes of rifle cartridges. The British had put the American passengers at risk as much as the Germans did. In response, in one last plea for "real neutrality," Secretary Bryan called for calm and stated, "A ship carrying contraband, should not rely on passengers to protect her from attack — it would be like putting women and children in front of an army." When Wilson failed to sufficiently curtail warlike rhetoric, Bryan tendered his resignation. With him may have gone any real chance at US neutrality.

The British, to be fair, had also contravened America's "neutral rights" throughout the war. They upheld the blockade, denied the United States the ability to easily trade with Germany, and even went so far, in July 1916, as to blacklist eighty US companies that allegedly (and legally) traded with the Central Powers. Furthermore, key immigrant communities in the United States were appalled by Britain's forceful put-down of Ireland's 1916 Easter Rebellion for independence and the subsequent execution of rebel leaders. Wilson, weak protestations aside, gave in to London at every turn.

Initially Germany promised no further surprise attacks on passenger vessels and American merchant ships, but as the war ground on, German chancellor Theobald Bethmann-Hollweg faced a decision between submission on one hand and utilizing the U-boats to their fullest on the other. Fatefully, the German military forced Hollweg's hand and Berlin declared "unrestricted submarine warfare" in early 1917. This was not the only affront to American prestige. In late February 1917 the British leaked a German message — the famous Zimmerman telegram — seeming to offer an alliance with Mexico and the potential for the Mexicans to "reconquer its former territories in Texas, New Mexico, and Arizona." Despite the truth that Washington had (probably) illegally conquered the region and turned northern Mexico into the Southwest United States in the 1840s, Americans were in no mood for subtleties, and anti-German sentiment exploded across the country. It was to be war.

Still, this outcome was never inevitable. Germany sought not to conquer the world, but to win — or at least honorably extract itself from — a stagnant and costly European war. Nor should we give in to the mostly false notion that Germany was an authoritarian, brutal, Nazi-like dictatorship while the Allies were liberal democrats. Austria was a dual monarchy, but Germany had a mixed government with a royal kaiser but also a parliament and one of the most progressive social welfare systems in the world. Besides, Russia — a key country in the Triple Alliance — was perhaps the most backward, largely feudal, monarchy on the planet. Furthermore, as the famed progressive senator Robert La Follette of Wisconsin reminded Americans when he cast a vote against Wilson's April 2, 1917, call for war, Britain and France possessed their own global empires. In that sense the US merely sided with one set of flawed empires over another. La Follette exclaimed on April 4 that "[Wilson] says this is a war for democracy. . . . But the president has not suggested that we make our support conditional to [Britain] granting home rule to Ireland, Egypt, or India." The man had a point.

Nevertheless, Wilson's request for a war declaration passed Congress and mobilization began. The president stood before the legislature and claimed the United States "shall fight for the things we have always carried nearest to our hearts — for democracy . . . for the rights and liberties of small nations. . . . We have no selfish ends to serve." Wilson was only formalizing a millenarian message he had been spreading for years. In 1916, in a speech one historian has called "at once breathtaking in the audacity of its vision of a new world order" and "curiously detached from the bitter realities of Europe's battlefields," Wilson declared that America could no longer refuse to play "the great part in the world which is providentially cut out for her. . . . We have got to serve the world." And so it was, whether in the interest of "serving the world" or backing its preferred empires and trading partners, that the United States would enter its first war on the European continent. It would not be the last.

Over There: America at War

The United States may have been an economic powerhouse holding most of the financial cards in the deck, but its military was woefully unprepared for war on the scale of what was being waged in Europe by 1917. Though some limited preparations began with the 1916 National Defense Act — which gradually raised the size of the regular army to 223,000 men — the US military remained tiny (only the seventeenth largest worldwide) compared with those of the belligerent nations. After all, the combined German and French fatalities at a single battle — Verdun in 1916 — exceeded the total dead of the US Civil War, still the bloodiest conflict in American history.

Meanwhile the Germans nearly won the war before the United States could meaningfully intervene. After the 1917 Russian Revolution turned communist, the new Russian leader, Vladimir Lenin, made a humiliating peace with Berlin. The Germans now shipped dozens of divisions westward and attempted one last knockout blow against the British and French on the Western Front. And since President Wilson and the leading US Army general, John J. Pershing, insisted that American soldiers fight under an independent command, it took many extra months to raise, equip, and train an expeditionary force.

It took more than a year before the United States could muster even minimal weight at the front. Nonetheless, the British and French lines just barely held in early 1918, and the infusion of 850,000 fresh, if untested, American troops helped make possible an Allied summer counteroffensive that eventually broke the German front lines.

It was all over by November 11, 1918 — once called Armistice Day, now celebrated as Veterans Day in the United States — when the Germans agreed to an armistice in lieu of eventual surrender. Still, when peace came, the German army largely remained on French soil. There was no invasion of Germany, no grand occupation of the capital. The end was nothing like that of the next world war. To many German soldiers and their nationalist proponents at home, it seemed that the army had been sold out by weak civilian officials — especially the socialists and Jews in the government. This belief, along with the later insistence by the Allies on a harsh retributive treaty at Versailles, sowed the seeds for the rise of fascism, ultranationalism, and Hitler in 1930s Germany.

When all was said and done, the US had suffered just 116,000 of the 9 million battle deaths of the war. Despite collective American memories of Uncle Sam going to the rescue, an honest reflection requires admission that it was Britain and France — which together had suffered roughly two million dead — that won the war for the Allies. The United States was a latecomer to the affair, and while its troops helped overrun the German lines, Berlin was cooked as soon as its spring offensive failed in 1918. The United States had hardly saved the day. It was a mere associate to Allied victory. Such humility, though, tends not to suit Americans' collective memory.

Over Here: War at Home and the Death of Civil Liberties

The war that Wilson claimed was being waged to make the world "safe for democracy" forever changed and restricted American civil liberties. It strengthened a fiscal-military federal state that shifted to a war footing. Every single facet of Americans' lives was now touched by the hand of federal power. First off, the war required a mass military mobilization. The era is often remembered for its intense public patriotism, but, when only seventy-three thousand men initially volunteered for the military, the government brought back conscription for the first time since the Civil War and drafted nearly five million men from eighteen to forty-five years old. Some noted progressives got carried away with the idea of federal power and regulation. "Long live social control!" one reformer enthusiastically wrote. Another wing of antiwar progressives wasn't so sure. The longtime skeptic Randolph Bourne — who noted with distaste that "[w]ar is the health of the state" — worried that most progressives were allying themselves with "the least democratic forces in American life." He concluded, "It is as if the war and they had been waiting for each other." And throughout history, so often they have been.

The government first sought to control the economy and ensure that American business was placed on a war footing. The War Industries Board (WIB) regulated the production of key war matériel through a combination of force and negotiation with the "captains of industry." Though the WIB quickly transitioned the United States to a war economy, one the organization's own leaders, Grosvenor Clarkson, described the potential dark side of such a system: "It was an industrial dictatorship without parallel — a dictatorship by force of necessity and common consent which . . . encompassed the Nation and united it into a coordinated and mobile whole." Additionally, Wilson's government needed to get control of the country's proliferating labor unions to ensure a smooth economic war machine. His National Labor Relations Board (NLRB) attempted to mediate disputes between capital and labor. It never really worked. Strikes continued and even grew throughout the war years, and the NLRB — with the backing of police, militia, and federal troops — worked overtime to quash workers' demands. The result was a sense of national need over individual freedom. George Perkins, a top aide to financier J. P. Morgan, caught the mood when he exalted that "[t]he great European war . . . is striking down individualism and building up collectivism." It would do so in industry, and also in culture and politics.

Though waves of patriotism and anti-German anger swept the nation, many Americans — especially the ethnic Irish and Germans and a broad swath of midwesterners — remained skeptical of the war. Furthermore, this was an era of strong antiwar socialist power in American politics. Eugene Debs, had, after all, won nearly a million popular votes in the 1912 presidential election. As surprising as this sounds at present, twelve hundred socialists held political office in the United States in 1917, and socialist newspapers had a daily readership of some three million citizens. For all his external rhetoric about peace, liberty, and democracy, President Wilson wasn't taking any chances at home. He and his congressional supporters delivered a propaganda machine and civil liberty curtailments unparalleled in the annals of American warfare. Indeed, Wilson was obsessed with sedition and disloyalty, warning, "Woe be to the man or group that seeks to stand in our way." And he and his Congress were willing to back up such threats with action.

In 1917 and 1918, Congress passed the Espionage and Sedition Acts. In a sweeping violation of Americans' constitutional rights, for example, the Sedition Act declared illegal "uttering, printing, writing, or publishing any disloyal, profane, scurrilous or abusive language about the United States government or the military." Apparently this applied to any criticism of the draft. Thus when Eugene Debs spoke critically, and peaceably, about the war outside a conscription office, he was arrested and later sentenced to ten years in federal prison. Standing before the judge at his sentencing, Debs made no apologies, asked for no leniency, and uttered some of the most beautiful words in American history: "Your honor, years ago I recognized my kinship with all living beings, and I made up my mind that I was not one bit better than the meanest on earth. . . . I say now, that while there is a lower class, I am in it; while there is a criminal element, I am of it; while there is a soul in prison, I am not free."

Debs was not alone. Some nine hundred people were imprisoned under the Espionage Act — which is still on the books — and two thousand more were arrested for sedition, mainly union leaders and radical labor men such as members of the Industrial Workers of the World. Appeals to the Supreme Court failed; all branches of government, it seemed, were complicit in the curtailment of standard civil liberties. Interestingly, the now aged Espionage Act was used extensively by the Obama administration to charge journalists, as well as Chelsea Manning and Edward Snowden. What's more, more than 330,000 Americans were classified as draft evaders during World War I, and thousands of them, mostly conscientious objectors, were forced to work in wartime prison camps, such as the one at Fort Douglas, Utah, for the duration. Finally, even the mail was restricted, with the postmaster general refusing to deliver any socialist or antiwar publications and materials.

Wilson also needed a government propaganda machine to drum up support for the war, especially among apathetic midwesterners, socialists, and so-called hyphenated Americans. He found his answer in the Committee for Public Information (CPI), which, led by the journalist George Creel, employed social scientists and greatly exaggerated German atrocities to motivate the public. The CPI employed seventy-five thousand speakers and disseminated over seventy-five million pamphlets during the war years. One social scientist bragged that wartime propaganda was designed to create a "herd psychology," and philosopher John Dewey referred to the methods as "conscription of thought." Fact, it seemed, was secondary to results, and the preferred outcome was a united, anti-German public ready to fight and die both in the trenches abroad and for "patriotism" at home.

Not all Americans were willing to acquiesce to this state of affairs, and some wrote critically of the wartime climate in the United States. One Harvard instructor complained, "With the entry into the war our government was practically turned into a dictatorship." Furthermore, the journalist Mark Sullivan maintained that "[e]very person had been deprived of freedom of his tongue, not one could utter dissent. . . . The prohibition of individual liberty in the interest of the state could hardly be more complete." The effect fell worst on German Americans and southern blacks.

The problematic results of all this were altogether predictable. Hyper-nationalist Americans, treated to lies and exaggerations about their German enemies, began to take matters into their own hands and to police "loyalty" at home. Across the country 250,000 citizens officially joined the American Protective League (APL) while many more joined informal militias. APL members opened mail and bugged phones to spy on suspected "traitors." These excesses also infected the culture and language in a number of ludicrous ways. German-sounding words were Americanized or renamed. Hamburger became Salisbury steak, sauerkraut was changed to "liberty cabbage," and the German measles was rechristened the "liberty measles." One is reminded of french fries being renamed "freedom fries" when France refused to back the United States' 2003 invasion of Iraq.

Such farce aside, the actions of the APL and unofficial militias quickly got out of hand and often turned violent. Americans suspected of disloyalty were taken to public squares and forced to kiss the flag or buy liberty bonds. Others were brutally tarred and feathered or painted yellow. One German American, Robert Prager, was hanged by a mob in Illinois. In response to the incident the supposedly liberal *Washington Post* reported, "In spite of the excesses such as lynching, it is a healthful and wholesome awakening in the interior of the country."

African Americans also, predictably, suffered during the war, in terms of both humiliation and physical attacks. The famed civil rights leader W. E. B. Du Bois predicted at the start of the war that "[i]f we want real peace, we must extend the democratic ideal to the yellow, brown, and black peoples." That proved to be a bridge too far. In the army blacks served in segregated units and found wartime France much more hospitable and egalitarian than the American South. Many never returned home. Those who did so returned to a country beset with race riots. Dozens of blacks and others were killed in riots in Chicago, East St. Louis, and twenty-five other cities. At the same time a new manifes-tation of the Ku Klux Klan — now concerned with not only blacks but also immigrants, Jews, and Catholics — grew in numbers. This expan-sive version of the Klan operated publicly and even controlled many political offices during the period. Lynching exploded across the South: thirty black men in 1917, sixty in 1918, seventy-six in 1919 — including ten war veterans, some still wearing their uniforms. It seemed that the American South could not bear the sight of "uppity" blacks returning home as "men" wearing the uniform of the US Army.

The war's end also broke the back of the then-powerful American Socialist Party. After the Bolshevik Revolution in Russia, the US government helped foment a veritable "Red Scare," an illogical fear of all speech and action on the American left. One observer noted, "Not within the memory of living Americans, nor scarcely within the entire history of the nation, has such a fear swept of the public mind." During the scare, which reached a peak in 1920, Attorney General A. Mitchell Palmer created the General Intelligence Division, led by a young and zealous J. Edgar Hoover, later the longtime head of the Federal Bureau of Investigation. In the federal counterattack that followed, four thousand supposed "radicals" were arrested and hundreds were stripped of their citizenry and shipped to the Soviet Union.

It was the death knell not only of American socialism but also of the more liberal and skeptical brand of progressivism. Randolph Bourne would see the future clearly in the midst of the war. "It becomes more and more evident that, whatever the outcome of the war, all the opposing countries will be forced to adopt German organization, German collectivism, and [to indeed shatter] most of the old threads of their old easy individualism," he wrote, continuing on to say that "[Americans] have taken the occasion to . . . repudiate that modest collectivism which was raising its head here in the shape of the progressive movement." Bourne was right: Progressivism — for now — was dead. It, along with 116,000 American men and a handful of American women, was killed by the war.

Men like Eugene Debs and Randolph Bourne, along with other skeptics, were ahead of their time. They realized a universal truth that applied then as well as now. Things are lost in war — freedom, liberties, individualism. Some are never recovered. That, along with battlefield triumphs, must define the American experience in the Great War.

The Seeds of the Next War: Wilson, Versailles, and the Road to World War II

The manner in which the First World War ended helped sow the seeds for a second world war. Though Wilson personally brought his sense of America's special destiny to the peace conference at Versailles, France, and despite his wide popularity among the masses of Europe, he was unable to craft the treaty and postwar world he desired. Indeed, his idealistic, and perhaps naive, sense of American duty and interventionism, which has ever since been labeled Wilsonianism, has never really left the scene in America. The realpolitik-minded Allied leaders of Britain, France, and Italy were in no mood for lectures on democracy and human rights from Mr. Wilson. Given his personal popularity and America's latent power, they appeased him to some extent, but that was all.

Even though he stayed in Europe for six full months, Wilson's preferred peace would not come to pass. Despite the romantic liberty-rhetoric of his so-called Fourteen Points, the president was forced to accede to the Allies on key elements that would poison the well of peace. Germany, in the "war guilt" clauses of the treaty, was held solely responsible for the outbreak of war. Berlin was also saddled with a crippling war debt and forced to compensate the victorious Allies with territory and enormous sums of cash for decades to come. Adolf Hitler would play on Germans' (sometimes legitimate) grievances regarding these matters to rise to power decades later. So much for "peace without victory."

On issues of colonialism, too, Britain and France were never willing to play ball. They sought perpetuation and even expansion of their empires — at the expense of Germany, of course — in Asia and Africa. So died Wilson's promises of a war for the "rights of small nations." Britain and France carved up the old Ottoman Empire and redrew lines in the Middle East that to this day contribute to disorder and civil war. When the Allies rejected Japan's proposal for a "racial equality" clause in the treaty, the ministers of that nation — a member of the Allied war against the Central Powers — nearly walked out. Eventually they did leave, with lasting resentments that would come back to haunt the US and the other Allies in the Pacific.

Many representatives from colonial nations had placed an enormous amount of trust in Wilson. Never trusting the tainted imperial governments of Britain and France, these unofficial peace delegates hoped that Wilson's Fourteen Points would save them. A young French-educated Vietnamese man named Ho Chi Minh was unable to even gain entrance to the proceedings. He would not forget, and forty years later he emerged as an anti-colonial guerrilla leader. Furthermore, when it became clear that the European colonies would not receive postwar home rule, riots and protests erupted in India, Egypt, and China. Observing this, and commenting on the failures of the Treaty of Versailles, a young library assistant named Mao Zedong — later the leader of China's communist revolution — protested, "I think it is really shameless!"

Russia, because it was communist, was excluded from the conference. In fact, in an episode lost to US, but not Russian, history, twenty thousand US troops joined many more other Allied soldiers in an occupation of parts of Russia, backing the non-communist "White" Russian armies in their failed attempt to overthrow "Red" power. The Soviet government and its successor state, the Russian Federation, now led by Vladimir Putin, would never forgive the West for this perceived transgression.

Still, President Wilson hoped that the new League of Nations — the deeply flawed precursor to the United Nations — would achieve what the basic contours of the treaty could not. Wilson took these matters personally and embarked on a nationwide tour of American cities to sell the treaty and league to a citizenry (and Congress) increasingly skeptical of international involvement. Wilson asked the people: "Dare we reject it [the treaty] and break the heart of the world?" But Americans did reject it, as would their representatives in the Senate, where it lost by seven votes. The United States would sign a separate peace treaty with Germany and declined to join the now weakened League of Nations. By this time Wilson, having suffered strokes including a final one that paralyzed half his body, was nearly an invalid. His advisers and wife would keep his medical condition a secret from the American public, remarkably, nearly to the end of his second term.

Perhaps a more equitable, or Wilsonian, peace treaty would have assuaged German shame and avoided the rise of Hitler. Beyond that, we must wonder whether a swift, limited German victory — along the lines of the Franco-Prussian War — might also have avoided the catastrophe of Hitler and the Second World War. And then there is the matter of America's "retreat" from Europe after declining to join the League of Nations. Could US involvement and leadership have avoided the rise of fascism and outbreak of conflict in Eastern Europe and the Pacific? In truth, these questions are unanswerable. Still, they are important to consider. What is certain is that Allied imperialism survived for forty to fifty years, leading to outbreaks of left-leaning guerrilla wars in the 1950s and '60s; European nationalism remained a major factor, contributing to the rise of its most extreme form, fascism; and American "Wilsonianism" emerged from the war as a still-powerful force in US foreign policy, guiding a full century's worth of (ongoing) American worldwide military interventionism.

———

Historians continue to argue whether the Great War was the culmination or the death knell of progressivism. In a sense it was both. Indeed, the use of an activist, empowered federal government to rally the populace and control the people whom World War I personified was always the dream of one strand of progressives. Yet in the end we must conclude that war — and its domestic excesses — destroyed the foundation of the progressive movement. The citizenry had tired, temporarily at least, of big government and federal interventions at home and abroad. The progressive push for a stronger, European-style social democracy withered just as swiftly as the Treaty of Versailles itself. In the election of 1920 the Republican Warren G. Harding swept to victory on a platform of a return to "normalcy," and two straight conservative, business-friendly Republican administrations followed. As the progressive warrior Jane Addams had warned when the United States entered the war, "This will set back progress for a generation." How right she was.

Those three presidents — Harding, Calvin Coolidge, and Herbert Hoover — would, it must be said, keep the United States out of any major international war, but they would also crash the economy and dismantle the social safety net, paving the way for the Great Depression.

And though the policy of isolationism, which actually personified the views of George Washington and more than 150 years of American tradition, briefly flourished between the wars, it would eventually become a pejorative term. When war again brewed in Europe, partly because of the way the Allies mishandled their "victory" and negotiation of the "peace," most Americans and their leaders were able to fall back on their comfortable myth of the United States having "saved the day" in 1917–18. Forgotten were the last war's horrors, the domestic excesses of the warfare state, and the once-prevalent, if vanquished, antiwar movement that had flourished not thirty years in the past.

Americans believe their own lies — the lies they are told and those they themselves craft. And the United States has failed to see through its falsehoods about the Great War even though a century has passed since it ended. Its sense of messianic destiny and unparalleled accumulation of military power is such that, even after the celebration (or mourning) of the hundredth anniversary of the end of World War I, the United States alone still views that conflict in heroic terms. Americans, at least the 1 percent willing to volunteer to go to a war and the numerous policy makers ready to send them off, still stand ready, as the song said, to go "over there." Only now everywhere is "over there," and American hubris appears to know no bounds. And, we could argue, it all began with the fictions we told ourselves about America's experience in World War I — and more's the pity.[19]

23

THE DECADE THAT ROARED AND WEPT

The Jazz Age. The Roaring '20s. The Flapper Generation. The Harlem Renaissance. These are the terms most often used to describe America's supposedly booming culture and economy during the 1920s. No doubt there is some truth in the depiction. Real wages did rise in this period, and the styles and independence of certain women and African Americans did blossom in the 1920s — at least in urban centers. Still, the prevailing visions and assumptions of this era mask layers of reaction, racism, and retrenchment just below the social surface. For if the 1920s was a time of jazz music, stylishly dressed flappers, and lavishly wealthy Wall Street tycoons, it was also one infused with Protestant fundamentalism, fierce nativism, lynching, and the rise of the "new" Ku Klux Klan. How, then, should historians and the lay public frame this time of contradictions? Perhaps as an age of culture wars — vicious battles for the soul of America waged between black and white, man and woman, believer and secularist, urbanites and rural folks.

The term *culture war* is familiar to most twenty-first-century readers. Indeed, many are likely to remember the common use of the term to describe the politics of the 1990s, when politicians and common citizens alike argued about cultural issues such as abortion, gay marriage, and prayer in schools. Those divided times have arguably continued into our present politics with a new fury. Something similar happened in the often mischaracterized 1920s. Few eras are truly one thing. Thus, the juxtaposition is what matters and, perhaps, what links the past to the present. As such, if we are to label the 1920s as a Jazz Age, or a vividly black Harlem Renaissance, then we must also admit that the era was an age of lynching, nativism, and Prohibition. If the '20s brought modernity and human rights to some, it also suffered from the reaction of Protestant fundamentalism and sustained gender inequality. If the 1920s economy began with a roar, we cannot forget that it ended with a crash.

It is in the contrasts that the historian uncovers larger truths. Cheeky labels and generalizations conceal as much as they reveal. An honest assessment of the vital, if misunderstood, 1920s might lead the reader to a variety of intriguing notions, not the least of which is the uncanny — if imperfect — conclusion that the period is connected to our own politically tribal twenty-first-century moment and the symptomatic election of Donald Trump.

The Jazz Age or the Age of Lynching?

In no era, it seems, has the United States been able to overcome its original sin of slavery, racism, and racial caste. It most certainly failed to do so in the 1920s. There were, of course, early signs that the renaissance of black culture following the First World War had strict geographic and temporal limitations. Indeed, the hundreds of thousands of African American soldiers who deployed overseas during 1917–18 found that the racial and social norms in France were far more open and accepting than those of the United States — especially those in the American South. Some never left France, forming a robust and creative black expatriate community in Paris. When most black soldiers did return home, proudly adorned in their military uniforms, they faced political violence and the threat of lynching at record levels.

Still, for all these grim intonations, the 1920s was a vibrant era for black culture. Jazz, made popular in the period, is arguably the only true, wholly American art form. The Harlem Renaissance formed by black writers, musicians, poets, and critics in New York City would become legendary. The 1920s, in the wake of World War I, was also the start of the First Great Migration of African Americans from the rural South to the urban North — one of the largest and fastest internal movements of a population in modern history. This shift created the racial pattern and mosaic that modern Americans take for granted.

In 1900, 90 percent of American blacks still lived in the South. They left to seek war-industry jobs and postwar urban industrial work. Others hoped to escape the racism, violence, and suffocating caste system of the South. Most settled in urban centers in the Midwest and Northeast. Detroit, for example, counted some 6,000 black residents in 1910, but more than 130,000 in 1930.

Blacks still suffered violence and discrimination in their new northern settings. For the most part, though, they faced isolation. White families simply moved away when blacks filtered into a neighborhood. Though tragic and racially repugnant, this isolation did indeed usher in a period of African American cultural rebirth in pockets of the 1920s North, Harlem being the most famous. Jazz performers such as Fats Waller, Duke Ellington, and Louis Armstrong perfected their craft, and jazz poets such as Langston Hughes — whose work pioneered and presaged the rap scene of the late twentieth century — paved the way for a new, vibrant black literature. In perhaps the biggest surprise of all, African American artists, musicians, and writers became wildly popular with white American audiences and respected on an international level. Whites devoured black music and culture in a manner, and with a cultural appropriation, that would continue into the present day.

Even so, the Harlem Renaissance had strict racial and spatial limits. The most famous jazz venue, New York City's Cotton Club — which boasted a house band fronted by Duke Ellington — remained whites-only throughout the era. While well-to-do white audiences flocked to the club nightly, the African American talent was forbidden to drink in the club, linger, or interact with the white guests. They had to relax and seek their pleasures in neighboring buildings and other clubs in Harlem.

Black political leaders were divided, and they often clashed with one another. Some followed Booker T. Washington in claiming that blacks must temporarily accept segregation in exchange for education and community improvement. Others favored W. E. B. Du Bois, who argued that a "talented tenth" of black leaders must lead the masses in a fight for civil rights. Du Bois helped cofound the National

Association for the Advancement of Colored People (NAACP), which would play a prominent role in the black struggle for equal rights for the next century. Still another segment of blacks supported Marcus Garvey, who preached "Africa for the Africans" and cultural/political separation from white America.

Ultimately the black civil rights movement of the 1920s stalled. Though the NAACP managed to convince the House to pass the Dyer Anti-Lynching Bill in 1921, this seemingly simple legislation was rejected by the Senate on more than one occasion and never became law.

If the 1920s was an age of jazz and flourishing black cultural expression, it was also an age of racial reaction. Unsettled by the growth and popularity of black culture, and incensed by the return of "uppity" uniformed blacks from the war, some whites unleashed a new wave of lynching during the decade. Indeed, the 1920s was also the high tide of popularity for a new manifestation of the Ku Klux Klan. The "new" or "second" KKK emerged in 1915 after a long dormancy after the end of Reconstruction in 1877. This Klan expanded its message of hate from a sole focus on African Americans to a preoccupation with and aversion to Jews, Catholics, and certain immigrants. The new Klan was also larger and more public than its earlier secretive southern manifestation. By 1924 it had perhaps five million members nationally and undoubtedly many more sympathizers.

The 1920s Klan also expanded geographically, becoming extraordinarily powerful and popular in the North. Indeed, during the 1924 Democratic National Convention in New York — a convention that refused to include an anti-lynching plank in the party platform — thousands of uniformed KKK members marched in the streets of the city. The Klan was particularly powerful in the Midwest, in Indiana alone counting more than 250,000 members, including the governor. Local Klan chapters operated like fraternal orders or social clubs and held public barbecues and rallies throughout the country. The new KKK was also more politically palatable, winning control of several statehouses — Indiana, Texas, Oklahoma, and Oregon — north and south of the Mason-Dixon Line, and with some public officials openly flaunting their Klan affiliation.

Perhaps it should come as little surprise that the Klan's numbers exploded during a period of negative eugenics, social Darwinism, and scientific racism. Best-selling books like Lothrop Stoddard's *The Rising Tide of Color Against the White World-Supremacy* posited that the discontent and malaise in America and Europe were due to the influx of the darker races. Many white Americans, and not only those belonging to the KKK, were highly influenced by these pervasive arguments. Indeed, when Stoddard debated W. E. B. Du Bois on a stage in Chicago, thundering that "[w]e know that our America is a White America," his words carried much popular weight. Thus, while Du Bois handily won the intellectual debate — presciently asking Stoddard: "Your country? How came it yours? Would America have been America without her Negro people?" — it became increasingly clear that philosophical blacks such as himself were definitively not winning the popular contest for the racial soul of the country.

Racializing America: The Immigration Acts of 1917–24

The power of the new Klan, the most substantial social movement of the 1920s, was apparent in the strict immigration restrictions imposed throughout the decade. This was something new. For more than a century open immigration — especially from Europe — had been the avowed policy of the United States, a nation that had long prided itself on accepting the world's "tired, poor, and hungry." The Klan, which was at root a backward-looking organization pining for a time when America was "great," influenced a significant segment of the nonmember population, which agreed that the United States should be — and allegedly always was — a white Protestant nation. In response to a recent influx of "lesser" Catholic and Eastern Orthodox Southern and Eastern Europeans, WASP America sought to shut the immigration valve — at least for some types of immigrants. This restriction, disturbingly, was wildly popular and easily passed a sympathetic Congress, making the 1920s one of American history's most intense eras of nativism and immigration control.

Political cartoon, 1921

White Protestants of the time, and their elected representatives, became obsessed with a cultural program known as Colonial Revival. This movement celebrated the nation's distant past — a time, supposedly, when Anglo-Saxon Protestantism was the dominant force in American life. Colonial Revival was more than an architectural and fashion phenomenon, and became linked with nativism and anti-immigration sentiment. As the esteemed historian Jill Lepore has noted, both the style and political nativism of the era "looked inward and backward, inventing and celebrating an American heritage, a fantasy world of a past that never happened." Such reactionary social and political frameworks remain potent forces even today.

Politically, the nativists were victorious and the outcome was a series of increasingly stringent immigration laws, along with the introduction of a new legal category, the "illegal alien," into the national discourse. All told, the immigration acts of 1917, 1918, 1921, and 1924 reduced the overall level of immigration by 85 percent, slowed immigration from Southern and Eastern Europe to a trickle, and virtually eliminated migration from Asia and Africa. Then, as now, according to historian Gary Gerstle, immigration "became a policy site onto which Americans projected their fears." The first act, in 1917, began by excluding any immigrant who could not read — a backhanded method of targeting and limiting the so-called new immigrants, primarily Catholics and Jews from Southern and Eastern Europe, who tended to have lower literacy rates than Northern European migrants. The next act, in 1918, shut out "radical" immigrants — socialists, communists, and anarchists — who also tended to make up a larger portion of the "new" immigrants. As Democratic US representative Charles Crisp of Georgia put it, "Little Bohemia, Little Italy, Little Russia, Little Germany, Little Poland, Chinatown . . . are the breeding grounds for un-American thought and deeds."

Much of the new nativist sentiment was also openly anti-Semitic, as Jews were commonly associated with radicalism and communism because Russian Jews were initially overrepresented in the Bolshevik ranks during that country's 1917 "Red" Revolution. One US consular official in Romania described the Jewish refugees in Bucharest as "economic parasites, tailors, small salesmen, butchers, etc. . . . [with] ideals of moral and business dealings difficult to assimilate to our own." Italians, too, were suspected of having radical ties, which helps explain the controversial trial and execution of the Italian-born anarchists Nicola Sacco and Bartolomeo Vanzetti in a robbery-murder case that captured the nation's attention in 1920. They were found guilty even though most of the arguments brought against them were disproved in court. Fear of radicals swept the country, becoming most potent, ironically, among congressmen from the South, which had the fewest "new" immigrants in the entire nation. For example, Democratic senator Thomas Heflin of Alabama told Congress: "You have it in your power to do the thing this day that will protect us against criminal agitators and red anarchists . . . you have it in your power to build a wall against bolshevism . . . to keep out . . . the criminal hordes of Europe."

The result was the Emergency Immigration Act of 1921, the first open attempt to exclude certain ethnic and racial groups from the United

States. The method was to limit annual immigration from any one country to 3 percent of that country's population in the United States as of the 1910 census. By this calculation, which obviously favored Nordics and Anglo-Saxons, there would be an estimated 80 percent reduction of Eastern and Southern Europeans from the prewar average. President Woodrow Wilson, to his credit, refused to sign the bill, but President Warren G. Harding, Wilson's successor, would do so in May 1921. And the act worked. The number of immigrants from Southern and Eastern Europe dropped from 513,000 in 1921 to 151,000 in 1923.

But the nativists running the government weren't satisfied. Still obsessed with the "menace" of Jews, Italians, and Slavs, Congress passed the seminal Immigration Restriction Act of 1924, a bill that openly touted the new "scientific racism" of this social Darwinist era. Indeed, the star witness before the House Committee on Immigration was Harry Laughlin, a prominent eugenicist. The committee asked him to study the "degeneracy" and "social inadequacy" of certain immigrant groups, and Laughlin gleefully did just that. Racialist language permeated the debate in Congress, as when Indiana Republican Fred Purnell exclaimed, "We cannot make a heavy horse into a trotter by keeping him in a racing stable. We cannot make a well-bred dog out of a mongrel by teaching him tricks." West Virginia Democrat R. E. L. Allen doubled down, claiming that the strength of the law lay in "purifying and keeping pure the blood of America."

The new bill changed the relevant census to that of 1890, a time when even fewer Southern and Eastern Europeans had been in the country. Three percent of that number lowered the annual immigration limit of these ethnic groups to just 18,400, down from the prewar annual average of 738,000. Furthermore, the act, and two Supreme Court decisions, held that all Japanese, Indian, and other East and South Asian immigrants must be barred from the United States; the basis of all this was supposedly a 1790 law that "reserved citizenship for 'free white' immigrants." Meanwhile, African nations and colonies were allowed only one hundred immigrants each per year. Interestingly, Mexican laborers were exempt from the restrictions, though not for lack of prejudice against them. Rather, corporate and agribusiness interests lobbied against limiting the migration of Mexican peasants and laborers, who were seen as vital to business.

Political restriction of immigrants also influenced cultural norms and laws. Fearing the scourge of "mongrelization" and "miscegenation," many states hardened laws against interracial marriage. This movement culminated with a 1924 Virginia law that "prohibited a white from marrying a black, Asian, American Indian, or 'Malay.'" Furthermore, this law changed the definition of black from anyone with one-sixteenth African ancestry to any individual with at least one black ancestor, regardless of how remote.

When we imagine the cosmopolitan and open-minded Jazz Age of the 1920s, it is important, too, to recall its hardening of racial lines and the litigious attempts to make America white and Protestant again.

The First Culture Wars: Battles Over the Bible, Alcohol, and Modernity

A prevailing mental picture of the 1920s is that of the flapper, sporting a bob haircut, exposed knees, and a plethora of jewelry. This "New Woman" drove automobiles, smoked cigarettes, and drank alcohol. Surely, we imagine, these female Americans were in every sense modern, and representative of an entire era. Only it isn't so. For every free-spirited flapper, there was a traditionalist wife. And, if there was much imbibing in the '20s, we must remember that this was also the decade of the national prohibition of alcohol manufacture and sales. For every modernist infused with scientific truths, there was more than one Protestant fundamentalist. This, the apposition of the modern and traditional, is the real story of the 1920s — one often omitted from the history books but vital to any comprehensive understanding of the decade.

Prohibition had been a goal of temperance activists, especially women in the movement, for at least three-quarters of a century. The old arguments held that sober citizens — men were the primary targets — were more likely to be diligent workers, faithful husbands, dutiful fathers, and better servants of the nation. By the later part of the 1920s, prohibitionists had the necessary power in Congress and the state legislatures to push through — over President Wilson's veto — the Constitution's Eighteenth Amendment, which outlawed the production and sale, but not the consumption, of alcoholic drinks. This new, powerful wave of sentiment against alcohol spoke to cultural battlefields in America. Pro- and anti-prohibition attitudes tended to cohere with the nation's growing rural–urban divide. Rural folk tended to support the ban while city dwellers found it intrusive. Prohibition also linked directly to religion and immigration. Many temperance activists favored the ban as an attack on the "un-American" values and mores of immigrant communities, which tended to drink more heavily. It was a matter of social control and another way to make the nation great — and white and Protestant — again.

Known as the Noble Experiment, Prohibition created more problems than it solved and lasted only a dozen or so years before its repeal through the Twenty-First Amendment. It was almost impossible to enforce, and bootleggers and speakeasies proliferated around the nation, especially in the urban North. Prohibition — similar to the contemporary "war on drugs" — also turned the production and distribution of alcohol over to criminal elements and syndicates. Organized crime ran rampant in the wake of the Eighteenth Amendment, ushering in a wave of shootings and bombings among rival bootlegging gangs. The most famous gangster was Chicago's Al Capone, who made tens of millions of dollars and ruled with an iron fist. In one famous incident, the St. Valentine's Day Massacre, his men executed nine rival gang members in a busy district in Chicago. The federal government responded, eventually putting Capone away for tax evasion, but Washington never had the resources or ability to enforce the alcohol ban in a meaningful way. The Noble Experiment was ultimately a bloody failure. Still, it, too, reflected the culture wars of the 1920s.

Battles were also fought over the role and scope of women's public sphere in American life. While many mostly urban women shook off the mores of their mothers and embraced the flapper lifestyle, other Americans — generally rural men and women — continued to insist the woman's place was in the home. Though women did finally get the vote in 1920, they did not vote as a bloc — as some had expected or, alternatively, feared — but rather divided along the same political and cultural lines as the male population. Struggles over the role of women were inseparably tied to arguments between country and city, between religion and secularism, and between modernism and traditionalism. So while more women entered the public sphere and altered their styles, they were still constricted by local "decency" laws that could go so far, as in Washington, DC, as to regulate the length of bathing suits and dresses down to the nearest inch. Furthermore, after a wartime surge, there were still relatively few women working outside the home. Indeed, contrary to popular imagination, the women's labor force grew by only 2 percent in the 1920s.

Perhaps the most famous front in the 1920s culture war revolved around the role of religion in American life. Indeed, we can hardly overestimate the power of organized religion in America, from the nation's very inception. Church attendance and religious adherence in the US is, and has always been, among the highest in the world. For all the sweeping social changes of the '20s, that remained a salient fact. During the Progressive Era and in the decade that followed the end of World War I, an increasingly urbanized, modernized, and immigrant population (read: Catholic and Jewish) seemed threatening to many rural, Anglo-Saxon Protestants who saw themselves as the only "real" Americans. In response to the unsettling changes in American society, a new wave of Protestant fundamentalism — specifically the view that the words of the Bible were inerrantly true and were meant to be taken literally — took hold in rural America.

Fundamentalists battled against immigrants, flappers, drinkers, and all sorts of modernists throughout the decade. One of the first and most famous battles — one not yet settled — revolved around the question of public education and whether teachers should impart the scientific theories of Darwinian evolution to the nation's students. The battle lines were drawn; all that was needed was a spark to begin the war, and it came in the little town of Dayton, Tennessee, in 1925. Tennessee had become the first state to prohibit the instruction of evolution in public schools. The American Civil Liberties Union (ACLU), founded in 1917 to defend conscientious objectors, then located a high school biology teacher in Dayton, John Scopes, who was willing to challenge the law and teach evolution. Scopes was charged with a crime, and the ensuing trial gained national attention, perhaps the first such case to be dubbed the trial of the century.

The trial quickly moved beyond the narrow bounds of whether Scopes had violated the law — he clearly had — and became, instead, a battle between the theories of evolution and creationism, between secularism and fundamentalism. And there were other issues, themes, and questions raised by the case. First, there was the strong urban–rural divide that tended to cleave along secular and religious lines. And more saliently, a question of democracy: Could the people of a community ban the teaching of credible scientific theory if a clear majority, such as in most southern states, didn't adhere to that science? The secularists framed the case around a question of free speech: Did a teacher have the right to impart a scientific theory that he or she found credible? These were tough issues and still are.

The "Monkey Trial," as it came to be known, was a national sensation, the first to be broadcast nationwide on radio. Both sides hired celebrity lawyers: for the prosecution, William Jennings Bryan, a three-time Democratic presidential candidate; for the defense, Clarence Darrow, a famed radical litigator who had defended Eugene Debs. For Bryan the trial was all about the "great need of the world today to get back to God," a question of faith and local, especially rural, sovereignty. For Darrow, perhaps the nation's most famous litigator, the case was all about reason, science, and free speech. Darrow explained his reasons for taking on the case by saying, "I knew that education was in danger from the source that has always hampered it — religious fanaticism."

The climax of the trial came when Darrow put none other than Bryan himself on the stand for a cross-examination regarding the Bible itself. Bryan was deeply religious but no theologian. The crafty Darrow peppered Bryan with tough questions about the supposed infallibility of the Bible and asked whether its words were to be taken literally. Bryan, sweating and confused, struggled through the questioning and seemed to contradict himself with some regularity. Consider just one famous exchange from the trial record that demonstrates the conflict between the two men and their worldviews:

> **Darrow:** You have given considerable study to the Bible, haven't you, Mr. Bryan? Do you claim that everything should be literally interpreted?
>
> **Bryan:** I believe everything in the Bible should be accepted as it is given there. . . .
>
> **Darrow:** You believe the story of the flood [Noah] to be a literal interpretation?
>
> **Bryan:** Yes, sir.
>
> **Darrow:** When was that flood? About 4004 B.C.?
>
> **Bryan:** That is the estimate accepted today. . . .
>
> **Darrow:** You believe that all the living things that were not contained in the ark were destroyed?
>
> **Bryan:** I think the fish may have lived. . . .
>
> **Darrow:** Don't you know that the ancient civilizations of China are 6–7,000 [six thousand to seven thousand] years old?
>
> **Bryan:** No, they would not run back beyond the creation, according to the Bible, 6,000 years.
>
> **Darrow:** You don't know how old they are, right?
>
> **Bryan:** I don't know how old they are, but you probably do. [Laughter] I think you would give preference to anybody who opposed the Bible.

Everyone knew that Scopes would be found guilty, and indeed he was; his fine was $100, paid by the renowned journalist H. L. Mencken. Still, the trial had much grander, more consequential results. Modernity and science had battled traditionalism and dogma. Though Darrow seemed to get the better of Bryan in their exchanges, there was no clear winner. The cities and the major national newspapers lauded the "victory" of Darrow, but rural America remained stalwart and resistant to evolution and still is. Evangelical Protestant Christianity, after all, remains one of the most potent forces in American political and cultural life.

Normalcy, Laissez Faire, and the Road to the Crash

For the most part the 1920s are remembered as a boom time, an era of unparalleled prosperity and conspicuous consumption. Even the middle and lower classes are thought to have benefited from the soaring economy. And in a sense, this was true — at least for a while. Between 1922 and 1928 industrial production rose 70 percent, the gross national product 40 percent, and per capita income 30 percent. Still, lurking under the surface were troubling signs that prosperity was uneven and, in many ways, little more than a shiny facade. Throughout the decade, some 40 percent of the working class remained mired in poverty, 75 percent of Americans did not own a washing machine, and 60 percent couldn't afford a radio. Forty-two percent of families lived on less than $1,000 a year. What's more, income inequality reached record highs (which are being matched in the present day), with one-tenth of 1 percent of the families at the top earning as much income annually as the bottom 40 percent of all families.

Furthermore, unions were losing ground throughout the country as newly empowered corporations broke strikes with the backing of government and, sadly, the public. This occurred despite the fact that working conditions remained deplorable in many industries. Each year in the 1920s, twenty-five thousand workers were killed on the job and an additional hundred thousand became permanently disabled for work-related reasons. Given these stunning facts, why was much of the public then so hostile to labor? Partly this reflected an outgrowth of the 1919–21 fear of radicalism known as the Red Scare — the Socialist Party and the Industrial Workers of the World were destroyed in the postwar years — but it also tied to race and ethnicity. Labor issues became associated with immigrant issues and, as demonstrated, nativism and anti-immigration sentiments ran rampant in the Roaring Twenties.

Despite these under-the-surface realities of gripping poverty, enough Americans were doing well to such an extent that they could shut out the picture of struggling sharecropping farmers (black and white) and impoverished immigrant industrial workers in the big cities. These suffering people, then as now, were invisible — so long, at least, as general prosperity was the order of the day.

By the presidential election of 1920, the Progressive Era was dead. Sick of centralized government social reforms and soured by the experience of war, a majority of Americans turned their backs on liberal revisionism. What these citizens wanted most of all was to turn the clock backward to what they imagined was a simpler time, before the war, and even before the progressive turn in American politics — a time, they imagined, of liberty, autonomy, and freedom from government interference. The Republican candidate in 1920, Warren G. Harding, rode to victory on this tide of conservatism and anti-progressivism. On the campaign trail, Harding promised a return to "normalcy," by which he meant the retreat of the federal government from a reform agenda and a reintroduction of laissez-faire economics. In Boston in May 1920, Harding summed up his view of the future by asserting, "America's present need is not heroics, but healing; not nostrums, but normalcy; not revolution, but restoration; not agitation, but adjustment . . . not submergence in internationality, but sustainment in triumphant nationality." And it was precisely this reactionary — and ultimately corrupt — agenda that Harding would pursue in the White House.

Harding and his two Republican successors — Calvin Coolidge and Herbert Hoover — would cozy up to big business and corporations. Harding made clear his intentions in his inaugural address. "I speak for administrative efficiency, for lightened tax burdens . . . for the omission of unnecessary interference of government with business, for an end to the government's experiment in business," Harding proclaimed in a clear repudiation of the progressive agenda. His successor, Coolidge, who famously proclaimed that "the business of America is business," bragged toward the end of his term, "One of my most important accomplishments . . . has been minding my own business. . . . Civilization and profits go hand in hand." An older brand of Republican, Theodore Roosevelt, would have probably been disappointed in his party's new agenda. TR, the famous trust-buster, had always believed that spreading out economic opportunity and avoiding the monopoly of wealth was essential to the long-term prosperity of the nation. But that was a different time; TR was a progressive, of sorts — and most Americans now rejected such government activism. They would pay the price.

Harding appointed Andrew Mellon, the fourth richest man in America, as his secretary of the treasury. Mellon, who served for many years, including under Coolidge, would upend the entire edifice of progressive social and economic reformism. During his tenure, Congress would exempt capital gains from the income tax and cap the top tax rate — an early form of what is now labeled trickle-down economics, in which the wealthiest Americans receive the lion's share of tax cuts. The top income brackets would see their tax rates lowered from 50 percent to 25 percent, while the lowest bracket was given a much smaller cut, from 4 percent to 3 percent. Hoover, who was secretary of commerce before serving as president, believed in voluntary associationalism, the theory that government should encourage corporations to work together and reform working conditions, all absent federal regulation. It didn't work. It rarely does: consider a more recent example, the 2008 financial crash, as exhibit A. What the reign of Mellon and Hoover did do was tie federal power to private corporate interests. *The Wall Street Journal* summed up the situation: "Never before, here or anywhere else, has a government been so completely fused with business."

Indeed, in a contemporary landmark study, *The Modern Corporation and Private Property* (1932), the authors concluded that a "corporate system" had "superseded the state as the dominant form of political organization." Big business liked it that way and launched new publicity campaigns intended to demonstrate that corporations had a "strong social conscience" and that government-provided social welfare was unnecessary and ill advised. With money came immense advertising power, on a scale that could not be matched by working-class interests.

It remained to be seen whether profit-driven corporations could responsibly guide the massive US economy in the absence of federal oversight. It's an experiment that has been tried — and has failed — throughout American history and remains popular among certain political factions.

This spreading political and social gospel of materialism also affected American culture. As historian Jill Lepore wrote, "During the 1920s, American faith in progress turned into a faith in prosperity, fueled by consumption." Americans spent more than they earned, paid with credit, and rode the runaway train of an economy that was sure to crash. Only no one seemed to see it coming. When Hoover accepted the 1928 Republican nomination for the presidency, he predicted — barely a year before the stock market crash — that "[w]e in America are nearer to the final triumph over poverty than ever before in the history of any land." He would soon eat these words. None of it was sustainable — the mushrooming stock market or the growing wealth disparity. In a prescient article, "Echoes of the Jazz Age," F. Scott Fitzgerald captured the absurdity of the moment, writing, "It was borrowed time anyway — the whole upper tenth of the nation living with the insouciance of a grand duc and the casualness of chorus girls." And, as in the first minutes after the Titanic struck an iceberg, the rich carried on just as before.

The depression would be the worst in American history. When the crash came, it came hard and fast. A decade's worth of irresponsible, risky financial speculation — altogether unregulated by the feds — had created a bubble that few had recognized. As the expert John Galbraith wrote in his study of the crisis, "The Great Crash," the 1920s economy was "fundamentally unsound" and the "bad distribution of income" contributed to the onset of deep depression. Over the three weeks following the initial stock market crash, the Dow Jones Industrial Average fell from 326 to 198 and stocks lost some 40 percent of their value. Hoover's initial, and prevailing, instinct was to work with business to right the economic ship. Within weeks of the crash he invited corporate leaders to the White House in an effort to coordinate a response. Nothing of substance was forthcoming; the corporations still clung to the profit motive and were unwilling to bend for the good of the country. As the historians Steve Fraser and Gary Gerstle have concluded, "All in all, the corporate rich failed miserably to meet their responsibilities toward the poor." This fact was readily apparent, but, still, Hoover balked at any strong federal response.

Hoover tried to reassure Americans, but beyond cajoling corporations to take responsible voluntary actions he was unwilling to meaningfully intervene. He believed charity was the best way to ameliorate rising poverty but opposed any form of government relief, arguing that to provide such help would see the nation "plunged into socialism and collectivism." The obtuse and heartless response of a generation of Republican politicians and corporate leaders reads today as cruel farce. When, by 1930, half the 280,000 textile workers in New England — Coolidge's home region — were jobless, the former president commented simply, "When more and more people are thrown out of work, unemployment results." Then, in early 1931, Coolidge again showed his flair for understatement: "The country is not in good condition." Henry Ford, perhaps America's most famous business leader — and, incidentally, an anti-Semitic admirer of Adolf Hitler — claimed in March 1931 that the Depression resulted because "the average man won't really do a day's work unless he is caught and cannot get out of it. There is plenty of work if people would do it." Weeks later, Ford would lay off seventy-five thousand workers.

Only making matters worse, President Hoover fell back on his protectionist instincts and severed the US economy from Europe with a new tariff act in 1930. Other nations, predictably, retaliated with trade restrictions of their own and world trade shrank by a quarter. By 1932, one in five US banks had failed, unemployment rose from 9 percent to 23 percent, and one in four Americans suffered a food shortage. The very foundation of liberal-capitalist democracy seemed to be crumbling. *The New Republic* proclaimed, "At no time since the rise of political democracy have its tenets been so seriously challenged as they are today." The Italian fascist dictator Benito Mussolini predicted that "[t]he liberal state is destined to perish."

These premonitions were understandable at the time. Millions of Americans — out of work and desperate for food and shelter —

gathered in temporary outdoor camps, dubbed "Hoovervilles," and increasingly became radicalized, drawn either to the communist left or the fascist right. One thing seemed certain: the fate of global democracy seemed to hinge on the ability of the United States, the world's largest economy and democracy, to find a middle way that mitigated poverty without a turn toward left- or right-wing totalitarianism. That would require American voters to send the likes of Hoover and his failed ideology packing and elect a different sort of candidate with fresh ideas on how to confront the crisis of the Great Depression. That man was Franklin Delano Roosevelt. When he took power in 1933 it was uncertain whether he, and American liberal capitalism, would endure.

An American Crime: The Bonus Army March on Washington

It is by now the platitude of platitudes: Americans love their military veterans, adulating them today (though vacuously) at every turn. Only it wasn't always so. In fact, one could argue that there exists a long, highly American trend — dating back to the underpaid and underfed Continental Army of the Revolutionary era — of asking the world of our veterans in war and then, predictably, ignoring their postwar needs. There is perhaps no better example than the suppression of the Bonus Marchers in our nation's capital in the spring and summer of 1932. This, to be sure, must count as a great American crime.

The controversy centered on the redemption of the promised federal bonus certificates given to the millions of veterans of the First World War. Most of these bonuses could, by law, be redeemed only far in the future, around 1945. But for hundreds of thousands of jobless, homeless American combat vets, that simply wouldn't do. They were hungry now, they were cold now. A Great Depression was on the land, and many of these vets demanded the payout immediately. Ironically, later Keynesian economists argued that paying out this large sum of money would actually have acted as a stimulus to the depressed American economy — but this was decidedly not the prevailing theory of the day among business-friendly Republicans such as President Hoover. He flatly refused the payout.

In the spring of 1932 some twenty thousand veterans, carrying their bonus certificates, converged on the national capital. They promised to stay put until their demands were met, and they set up makeshift camps across Washington, DC. One observer, the famous writer John Dos Passos, observed that "the men are sleeping in little lean-tos built out of old newspapers, cardboard boxes, packing crates, bits of tin or tarpaper roofing, every kind of cockeyed makeshift shelter from the rain scared together out of the city dump." It was a sad scene and an embarrassing fall from grace for these proud war vets. When the bill to pay off the bonus failed in the Senate — it had passed the House — most of the "Bonus Army" stalwartly stayed put. In response, Hoover coldly ordered the active-duty army to evict them — a potential violation of the Posse Comitatus Act, which prohibits the use of the regular army to suppress disorder within the nation's borders.

The next day four troops of cavalry, four companies of infantry, a machine-gun company, and six tanks gathered near the White House, all under the command of General Douglas MacArthur. MacArthur's aide-de-camp that day was future general and president Dwight Eisenhower, and future general and World War II hero George Patton commanded one of the cavalry troops. This was not their finest hour. MacArthur personally led his troops — all wearing gas masks — down Pennsylvania Avenue as they fired tear gas to clear the vets out of old buildings, some of which were set on fire by the advancing troopers. Thousands of Bonus Marchers, along with their women and children, frantically ran. Soon the entire encampment was ablaze. The whole tragic affair was over rather quickly. The day's toll: two veterans shot to death, an eleven-week-old baby dead, an eight-year-old boy partly blinded, and thousands more injured by the tear gas.

The brutality was swift, and, make no mistake, it was purposeful. Then Major Patton gave the following instructions to his troops before the assault: "If you must fire do a good job — a few casualties become martyrs, a large number an object lesson. . . . When a mob starts to move keep it on the run. . . . Use a bayonet to encourage its retreat. If they are running, a few good wounds in the buttocks will encourage them. If they resist, they must be killed." How quickly Americans would forget this man's despicable role in this national disgrace in favor of memories of his actions in World War II. The vets did not get their hard-earned and much-needed bonuses that day. What they received was the violent rebuke of a government that had abandoned them to poverty and despair. The famed journalist H. L. Mencken captured the moment ever so perfectly, writing, "In the sad aftermath that always follows a great war, there is nothing sadder than the surprise of the returned soldiers when they discover that they are regarded generally as public nuisances." For an impoverished generation of World War I veterans, this was the thanks for their service.

———

Even at the time, not everyone bought in to the mythology and consumerism of the Roaring Twenties. Some cultural critics — artists and writers in particular — saw through the hollow facade of American life and society. These were the men and women of the "Lost Generation," those both damaged and horrified by the horrors of the Great War and disgusted by the materialism of the proceeding decade. Though their prose remains on the curriculum for students throughout the nation, their assessment of the dark underbelly of the decade has not stuck. Americans, it seems, prefer the clichéd labels of Jazz Age and Harlem Renaissance to the inverse realities of the nativism, lynching, Prohibition, fundamentalism and social control so prevalent in the decade that "roared."

Ernest Hemingway, a wounded veteran of the First World War, wrote in his acclaimed novel *A Farewell to Arms*: "The world breaks everyone. . . . But those that will not break it kills. It kills the very good and the very gentle and the very brave impartially." Indeed, Hemingway, like so many others in his Lost Generation, chose exile as an expatriate in Paris to life in consumerist America. His fellow "lost" author, F. Scott Fitzgerald, also critiqued the era and expounded upon the disillusionment of many veterans, writing in *This Side of Paradise*: "Here was a new generation . . . dedicated more than the last to the fear of poverty and the worship of success; grown up to find all Gods dead, all wars fought, all faiths in man shaken."

Indeed, there was among many Americans, especially urbanites of the middle or upper class, a worship of success and materialism infusing the 1920s. This is the way we tend to imagine and reconstruct the decade in our minds — a time of energy and movement toward modernity — forgetting Fitzgerald's rejoinder: that the period carried a loss of faith, a fear of poverty, a battle between ideologies and, yes, competing images of what it meant to be an American. The 1920s gave birth to a national culture war, perhaps America's first. Open a newspaper, flip on the news — no cease-fire yet.[20]

24

FDR AND HIS DEAL FOR A DESPERATE TIME

FDR was neither radical nor conservative, no matter what his defenders and critics have claimed, both then and now. One part "traitor to his class" and another part defender of capitalism, he was both dangerously power-hungry and the savior of American-style liberal democracy. This man was — like his party's cofounder, Thomas Jefferson — an enigma, an unknowable sphinx. And yet he was the man for his moment. Indeed, FDR and his "New Deal," as both a response to economic depression and a reorganization of society, represent one of the most profound transitions in US history. FDR served as president longer than anyone before or since, elected four times by wide margins. His opponents feared the man, and his supporters canonized him with rare and remarkable passion.

First elected in a landslide in 1932, the Democrat entered office loaded with expectations. Seen as the anti–Herbert Hoover (his Republican opponent for the presidency), Roosevelt sailed to a victory that many saw as an electoral rebuke to the conservative Republican regimes of his three immediate predecessors. Though it was difficult to know exactly what his policies and ideology would be, the people placed their hopes and dreams in the thirty-second president: he would, if nothing else, bring change. With the stock market crash of 1929, the economy crumbling, and countless Americans out of work in the early years of the Great Depression, Roosevelt took office with the mandate for change and a public expectation of national salvation. Perhaps no man could live up to such demands. FDR would, over the next dozen years, experiment, tinker, triumph, and fail. He knew the highest of political highs and the lowest of lows. Some historians and political scholars have even wondered, studying the maelstrom of conflicting Rooseveltian policies, whether FDR even had a coherent economic or political ideology. And they have a point.

Migrant Mother, 1936, by Dorothea Lange

What we do know is this: by the end of his second term, Roosevelt had forever transformed his own party, the American economy, the role and scope of federal power, and, it can be said without exaggeration, the nation itself. Whether these changes were for the better remains open to interpretation and debate. Indeed, today's politicians, left and right, continue to battle over the legacy and ideals of this singular man. Perhaps a fresh look at the real Roosevelt — the man, the myth, the inheritance he handed down — will better illuminate the contours of today's political combat.

A New Deal (to Save Capitalism?)

Roosevelt's detractors labeled him a socialist before he ever took office. His partisans deified him ahead of his inauguration and predicted he would save the nation from its economic plight and bring back prosperity. Roosevelt was, in fact, neither a "commie" nor a miracle worker, neither Christ nor Antichrist. What he was, as he took the mantle of executive power in March 1933, was imbued with a mandate for change and determined to do something — not just to end the Depression but to reshape the country. Through fits and starts, periods of immense popularity and stretches in the political doldrums, FDR would improvise and legislate with an energy and passion rarely seen from an American president.

From the very start, both on the campaign trail and in his inaugural address, Roosevelt announced that the train of change was a-coming. Accepting his party's nomination in a Chicago stadium, he exclaimed, "I pledge you, I pledge myself, to a new deal for the American people." Just what that New Deal would mean in practice was initially rather vague, couched in rhetoric more than clear public policy. FDR liked to say that the "New Deal is as old as Christian ethics. . . . It recognizes that man is indeed his brother's keeper. . . . [It] demands that justice shall rule the mighty as well as the weak." To the optimistic leftist and the fearful conservative alike, this rhetoric smacked of socialism. But it was never that.

The New Deal would prove both less ideological and more restrained than its proponents and detractors ever surmised. Experimentation, rather than a coherent Marxist ideology — which some of the president's enemies suspected — defined the New Deal. On the campaign trail in May 1932, FDR said as much, explaining, "The country needs and, unless I mistake its temper, the country demands bold, persistent experimentation . . . take a method and try it: If it fails, admit it frankly and try another. But above all try something." Roosevelt was nothing if not practical and intellectually malleable. Once, responding to the campaign question "What is your philosophy?" he retorted "Philosophy? Philosophy? I am a Christian and a Democrat — that's all." It would prove an accurate self-description throughout most of his tenure.

What Roosevelt was, from the start, was inspiring and comforting. Whether through his soaring public speeches or his soothing radio addresses — the famed "fireside chats" — Roosevelt reassured the American people. In his inaugural address he famously intoned, "This great nation will endure as it has endured. . . . The only thing we have to fear is fear itself." The people found Roosevelt, for whatever reason, to be strangely and uniquely accessible. In his first week in office, FDR received 450,000 letters. The mail continued apace throughout his presidency, and he made time to read a selection daily. He saw himself, and was often portrayed, as the People's President. As such, he repeatedly invoked his deeply held belief that society — and democracy — would fail to function if too many workers and farmers slipped into desperate poverty. Even before his election, he asserted that "[i]n the final analysis, the progress of our civilization will be retarded if any large body of the citizens falls behind."

Assembling a brain trust of mostly progressive advisers — including Labor Secretary Frances Perkins, the first female member of a presidential cabinet — FDR got to work. In his vaunted first "100 Days," Roosevelt would push through emergency legislation meant to ease Americans' suffering and begin the path to economic recovery. The Emergency Banking Act briefly closed the nation's banks — a four-day banking "holiday" — and reopened them only once they had been declared sound. In a following flurry of legislation, he proposed, and Congress passed, the Glass-Steagall Act, which separated investment banking from personal banking, and he created the Securities and Exchange Commission (SEC); the Public Works Administration (PWA), which oversaw ten-thousand-plus infrastructure projects; an agriculture bill that called for direct government payments to farmers who agreed not to produce certain crops, thus controlling overproduction; the Tennessee Valley Authority (TVA), a public corporation that employed thousands to create public improvements in one of the nation's more depressed regions; and the Civilian Conservative Corps (CCC), which hired 250,000 young men for forestry, flood control, and beautification projects. By the time the 100 Days were up, Congress had passed fifteen pieces of legislation.

Perhaps most popular with "his" people was the new Federal Emergency Relief Administration (FERA), which increased, for the first time, direct federal unemployment assistance to the states. This "handout" or "relief" (depending on your point of view) was something President Hoover and his fellow Republicans had fiercely resisted. The result of FERA was profound. Roosevelt, the savvy politician, had artfully transferred the allegiance of the nation's poor from their local leaders to the president and Washington, DC.

Most transformative, though, was probably the National Industrial Recovery Act (NIRA), which abandoned Progressive Era trust-busting for the "cartelization" of major industries. The act would establish federal regulations on maximum work hours and child labor and guarantee the limited right of workers to unionize. The NIRA also empowered the government to oversee and control production in whole industries, and forced price and wage increases. Another component of the NIRA was to be the Public Works Administration, which undertook an ambitious federal construction program meant to get the unemployed back to work. In many ways early New Deal legislation — especially the nationalistic CCC and the self-regulating cartels of the NIRA — would have pleased FDR's boyhood idol, his cousin Theodore Roosevelt. They bore the hallmarks of TR's own economic philosophy so very clearly.

Still, the results of the famed 100 Days were mixed. What historians would later call Roosevelt's "First" New Deal halted a bank panic, authorized the greatest public works program in US history, and granted billions in federal unemployment relief. Most important, it buoyed the hopes of the people and infused them with Roosevelt's own optimism. Nevertheless, it must be admitted that this deluge of new laws lacked any coherent pattern or ideology. The early New Deal also maintained — rather than overthrew — capitalism, regardless of the hopes of some on the far left. And certainly it did not end the Depression, which would rage for many more years.

Expectations of a quick fix were, to be fair, unrealistic. Yet from one (admittedly liberal) perspective, it is good that the First New Deal did not end the economic emergency outright. After all, had prosperity been restored by 1934, the follow-on "Second" New Deal — and the program's more ambitious, transformative reforms — might never have come to pass. Indeed, we could argue that it was only the continued economic crisis that ensured the election of the massive Democratic majority required to pass the rest of FDR's New Deal in 1935–36.

Just before the legislative midterm elections of November 1934, Roosevelt's influential interior secretary, Harold Ickes, recognized that more transformative reform was needed to address the Depression.

He noted in his diary that "[t]he country is much more radical than the Administration. . . . [Roosevelt] would have to move further to the left in order to hold the country." True radicals, both left and right, as we shall see, were gaining popularity, and FDR — about to propose several of his transformative reforms in 1935 — may well have shifted left in response to these fringe threats. From this perspective, Roosevelt did what he later did — ushering in a more leftist Second New Deal — in order not to destroy but to save American capitalism. These new measures, according to FDR's son Elliott, were "designed to cut the ground from under the demagogues." Roosevelt himself explained that he was working "to save our system, the capitalist system [from] 'crackpot ideas.'" In another bold assertion, FDR told a Syracuse, New York, crowd:

> The true conservative seeks to protect the system of private property and free enterprise by correcting such injustices and inequalities as arise from it. The most serious threat to our institutions comes from those who refuse to face the need for change. *Liberalism becomes the protection for the far-sighted conservative. In the words of the great essayist* [Lord Macaulay, not named by FDR], *"Reform if you would preserve." I am that kind of conservative because I am that kind of liberal.* [Emphasis added.]

Still, despite such proclamations, this rather political interpretation of the New Deal's motivation may overstate the case.

Roosevelt was, it must be admitted, at least partly driven by genuine empathy for the poor. As historian David M. Kennedy concluded, it was "solicitude for his country" — a distinct Roosevelt family value — "that lay at the core of his patrician temperament." By this logic FDR was a sympathetic, if paternalistic, person who was always both more and less than the "traitor to his class" that he was quickly dubbed. Indeed, as early as 1939, Raymond Moley observed that Roosevelt "is outraged by hunger and unemployment, as though they were personal affronts in a world he is certain he can make far better, totally other, than it has been." So if FDR's policy was decidedly not communist

subterfuge, it was still in many ways rather idealistic and transformative. By 1935 the president was waging a war of political persuasion
meant to change the public's mind about the role of federal government in poverty reduction and economic stabilization. Roosevelt
recollected that the Constitution was established to "promote the
general welfare" and that it was thus government's "plain duty to
provide for that security upon which welfare depends." It was a battle,
a war really, that FDR would ultimately win, at least until the conservative revival of the 1970s–80s.

Let us, then, surmise that Roosevelt had become a cautious idealist
by 1935. In that year's annual address to Congress, FDR declared that
"social justice, no longer a distant ideal, has become a definite goal."
The common objective in his economic policies, then, seems to have
been both the mitigation of the worst aspects of grinding poverty
and the old progressive dream of stability — "wringing order out of
chaos." To provide this, Roosevelt needed to win over the hearts and
minds of the majority of people to his own view that corporate business interests alone couldn't be counted on to provide the stability
and poverty mitigation needed in a modern industrial society. To this
end, he declared that "[m]en may differ as to the particular form of
government activity with respect to industry or business, but nearly
all are agreed that private enterprise in times such as these cannot
be left without assistance and without reasonable safeguards." By his
third year in office Roosevelt had convinced an unforeseen majority
of Americans of just that — and his policies of government investment and poverty alleviation would rule in Washington for at least
the next thirty years.

From Reform to Disappointment:
The Second New Deal and Its Legacy

After securing record Democratic majorities in the House and Senate,
Roosevelt unleashed his most ambitious and transformative legislation during the fateful 1935 congressional session. Ever more "alphabet
soup" — acronym-laden — agencies and bills would be created and

approved. These included even larger job creation programs, including the Rural Electrification Administration (REA). When the REA first put Americans to work, fewer than two out of ten farms had electricity. A decade later nine of ten did. Even grander was the Works Progress Administration (WPA), which put 8.5 million people to work during its eight-year life span, employing a variety of citizens, from construction workers to artists and authors, on various public projects. In the end the WPA would build half a million miles of highways and almost a hundred thousand bridges. This was a federal investment in infrastructure that was unheard of and unimaginable just a few years earlier.

Still, there was controversy and scandal. Roosevelt was, whatever else he may have been, a savvy, consummate politician. Recognizing the old saw that "all politics is local," the president used the WPA as a "gigantic federal patronage machine," handing out jobs and projects to amenable (mostly Democratic) state- and city-level politicians and administrators. Indeed, in one extreme case, all New Jersey WPA employees were required to "donate" 3 percent of their modest paychecks to the local Democratic Party. Nevertheless, in the short term at least, WPA projects reduced unemployment and provided millions the dignity of honest work.

Perhaps the most substantial, and long-lasting, piece of New Deal legislation was the Social Security Act. It included a program of life-long old-age insurance, as well as institutional federal unemployment insurance. The insurance provisions for the elderly were motivated by both humanitarian considerations and practical economics. Much of America's impoverished community was made up of septuagenarians, but so, too, was much of the workforce. Social Security benefits would both decrease poverty and "dispose of surplus workers" over the age of sixty-five. Providing a marginal retirement fund for the elderly would, by this logic, open up more jobs for younger, able-bodied, unemployed men and women. Originally, Roosevelt and his New Dealers — as his loyal bureaucrats came to be called — wanted to include a national system of health care in the Social Security Act. This provision was doomed to fail and was quickly jettisoned, however, in the face of public, political, and corporate obstacles. America, it seemed — unlike its European counterparts — was not yet ready for universal health care.

Even without the health care provisions, Social Security was a bold measure. Nonetheless, it was far from the socialistic, radical proposition that FDR's enemies feared. Rather than finance the insurance through direct, progressive taxation, Roosevelt insisted that Social Security be based on "private insurance principles," specifically that "the funds necessary . . . should be raised by contribution rather than an increase in general taxation." Social Security was thus, in the words of historian David M. Kennedy, to be "not a civil right but a property right. That was the American way." As such, rather than an income-redistribution program, this was to be a mandatory pension system financed by regressive taxes on the workers themselves. It remains so today.

When his more liberal advisers warned Roosevelt that Social Security would actually initially burden workers, decrease consumer spending, and fail to minimize income inequality, he replied simply that "I guess you're right on the economics, but those taxes were never a product of economics. They are politics all the way through." Progressive New Dealers also wanted Social Security insurance to pay the same amount to everyone, regardless of earned income, thus achieving some limited wealth redistribution. Again, Roosevelt, this time through his labor secretary, explained his opposition to such measures. "The easiest way would be to pay the same amount to everyone," Frances Perkins concluded, "but that is contrary to the typical American attitude that a man who works hard, becomes highly skilled, and earns high wages 'deserves' more on retirement." And so it would be. Here again, the Roosevelt administration based Social Security on the private insurance model, rather than the European income-redistribution model that prevailed (and prevails) in just about every other industrial nation.

Nevertheless, despite the moderation underlying most of his Second New Deal legislation, there is no doubt that FDR did tilt leftward in 1935–36. Yet even this was as much rhetoric as reality. In June 1935

Roosevelt pushed for tax reform, telling Congress that "[o]ur revenue laws have operated in many ways to the unfair advantage of the few, and they have done little to prevent an unjust concentration of wealth." Thus he asked for "very high taxes" on the largest of incomes and for "stiffer inheritance taxes." FDR called his proposal a "wealth tax"; his opponents soon dubbed it a "soak-the-rich" plan. Still, in principle, tax reform polled well in Depression-era America.

Motivated by his legislative successes, Roosevelt took his smite-the-rich rhetoric out on the campaign trail when he ran for reelection in 1936. Whereas in his First New Deal, FDR had sought cartelization and cooperation with certain business interests, he now told a frenzied crowd in New York's Madison Square Garden that his "old enemies . . . business and financial monopoly, speculation, reckless banking, class antagonism, war profiteering . . . organized money . . . are unanimous in their hate for me — and I welcome their hatred." At several campaign stops, Roosevelt railed against the supposed cabal of "economic royalists" standing in the way of his reforms. This combative language earned the president standing ovations lasting as long as thirteen minutes!

What motivated this leftward turn, at least in rhetoric, was a desire to cow his socialist-leaning critics and build a wholly new political coalition. The president knew that many years of depression had bolstered the legitimacy of an extreme left wing in American political life, and that this faction — because of its potential to split the 1936 Democratic vote — was the real threat to his power and agenda. As FDR told a reporter during the tax debate in 1935, to combat "crackpot ideas" "[i]t may be necessary to throw to the wolves the forty-six men who are reported to have incomes in excess of one million dollars a year." As David M. Kennedy has concluded, the 1936 campaign rhetoric of "radicalism" was "more bluff than bludgeon." Roosevelt had little to lose, at least politically, in demonizing the far right and the super-rich. What he sought to gain, however, was something far more transformative: a permanent coalition of workers, farmers, union men, minorities, and liberal intellectuals. For these folks, populist bombast sold well. And it worked.

FDR won a record landslide victory in 1936 and appeared to have a stronger mandate than any president since James Monroe. His opponent, Alf Landon, had carried only two states in the Electoral College. Journalist William Allen White stated that Roosevelt "has been all but crowned by the people." Still, if politics informed much of FDR's radical tilt in 1935–36, there can be little doubt that he was also motivated, to some extent, by altruistic concern for the impoverished. In January 1937, in his second inaugural address, he laid out the core of his beliefs and agenda-setting philosophy for his next term. "The test of our progress," he proclaimed, "is not whether we add more to the abundance of those who have much; it is whether we provide enough for those who have too little."

What's more, at the dawn of 1937, the economy had finally begun to show signs of recovery. The Federal Reserve Board's Index of Industrial Production had jumped from a score of 50 (out of 100) to 80 by late 1935. As of November 1936, the unemployment rolls had shrunk by nearly four million from the 1933 high. Then, as soon as recovery seemed imminent, the economy came crashing down again in mid-1937. Within weeks, a "second" depression kicked off; stock values plummeted by a third, and corporate profits dropped nearly 80 percent. By 1938, two million more workers had been laid off, bringing unemployment back up to an astounding 19 percent. Both conservative and radical leftist critics dubbed it the "Roosevelt Recession." Many Americans would ask, both then and later, what had caused this second crash and the resultant economic downturn.

To some extent, the downturn was due to the simple, standard fluctuations of the business cycle in a still firmly entrenched capitalist economy. By this logic, because of the inherent ups and downs of the market, contraction was to be expected after four straight years of economic expansion under Roosevelt. Still, conservatives and laissez-faire economists blamed the recession on a lack of business confidence, arguing that FDR had demoralized corporations with his "radical" campaign rhetoric and relatively progressive tax policies. Though this may have been an appealing narrative for corporate leaders, it crumbles under closer examination.

Later Keynesian economists, and the most dedicated New Dealers in Roosevelt's own administration, probably came closer to the mark. According to these thinkers, the reason for the 1937–38 recession was simple: the New Deal hadn't gone far enough. The government, they claimed, had committed a few key errors in 1936–37. Roosevelt, still trapped in an older school of economic thinking, fretted over balancing budgets — the budget was actually in the black for the first nine months of 1937 — and balked at more sorely needed deficit spending. His Federal Reserve, furthermore, worried about inflation, which can actually benefit a depressed economy, and contracted the money supply despite high levels of unemployment. Finally, the new regressive Social Security taxes took some $2 billion out of the national income without returning any benefits, which would not begin going out until 1940. The cure, according to the most zealous New Dealers, was simple: resume large-scale public spending. It might have worked, but by the middle of Roosevelt's second term, large sections of the public and the resurgent (southern) conservative wing of FDR's own party had lost their stomach for more New Dealing. So it was that the depressed economy would sputter along until a new wave of deficit spending — ushered in by the military buildup for World War II — achieved a full recovery.

Despite all the experimentation inherent in the New Deal, and the energy with which FDR initially championed it, in the end Roosevelt proved to be a reluctant and moderate spender. In a certain sense the president wrought the worst of all economic worlds: insufficient government spending and fear of deficits on the one hand, and, on the other, beating the populist drum at a level high enough to unnerve corporate investment. By 1938, Roosevelt was much weakened as a political leader. The nation entered its ninth year of the Great Depression, and ten million workers remained unemployed. For all that, at least democracy seemed safe in the United States. And Roosevelt remained convinced that some action toward poverty relief remained necessary to maintain that safety. Just a month after Adolf Hitler's Germany gobbled up Austria, FDR declared, "Democracy has disappeared in several other great nations, not because the people . . .

disliked democracy, but because they had grown tired of unemployment and insecurity, of seeing their children hungry . . . in the face of government confusion and government weakness." If his New Deal had not brought recovery, at least it had not produced fascist or communist authoritarianism.

Radicals and Demagogues:
Threats to the New Deal — Left and Right

Was a big high wall there that tried to stop me
A sign was painted said: Private Property,
But on the back side it didn't say nothing —
[That side was made for you and me.]
One bright sunny morning in the shadow of the steeple
By the Relief Office I saw my people —
As they stood hungry, I stood there wondering if
[This land was made for you and me.]
— Politically radical verses from Woody Guthrie's
1940 version of "This Land Is Your Land"

The New Deal, and the entire American democratic and capitalistic system, was always at risk from radicals and demagogues on the left and right ends of the political spectrum. Only through a juxtaposition of FDR and these more radical thinkers can we illustrate the truly moderate character of Roosevelt and his program. Furthermore, to ignore or marginalize more radical voices is to misunderstand the temper and anxieties of many Americans in the midst of the Great Depression. A crashed economy and skyrocketing unemployment are radicalizing triggers in and of themselves. There were, throughout the 1930s, many paths not taken as FDR carefully threaded the needle of restraint.

Some of the left-wing radicals were ideologically consistent socialists or communists, but many others were simply frustrated populists raging against the wealthy elites and their perceived collaborators. For example, in Iowa during April 1933 a mob of mask-wearing farmers

Disgruntled members of the old Eugene Debs–led American Socialist Party had formed the Communist Party USA in 1919, and by 1932 the party ran a black man for vice president of the United States. The Communists received over one hundred thousand votes in '32, an all-time electoral high for the party. Official membership in the party rose by a factor of thirty from 1930 to 1935. Roosevelt recognized this challenge from his far left and ramped up his economically populist and redistributionist rhetoric for the 1936 presidential campaign.

Additionally, popular demagogic figures arose during this period and challenged Roosevelt from the far left and right. Louisiana's popular senator Huey Long created the Share Our Wealth Society in January 1934, with promises to radically redistribute income and make "every man a king." Another famous activist, the progressive novelist Upton Sinclair, won nearly a million votes for California's governorship in running on a utopian "production-for-use communitarian platform." Finally, the eccentric, anti-Semitic "radio priest" Charles Coughlin combined both left- and right-wing policies — just as the German Nazis had — and formed the National Union for Social Justice. This organization had a platform promoting inflation and railing against international Jewry. The power and popularity of these men, as well as their influence on Roosevelt, should not be underestimated.

Long, known as "the Kingfish," was probably Roosevelt's most popular competitor during the early New Deal. He was a shrewd operator and a powerful orator. He attacked Wall Street and corporate barons, utilizing the well-worn language of class resentment and William Jennings Bryan–style populism. Long made no secret of his fanaticism, declaring in 1935 that he "wished there were a few million radicals" in the United States. His zealous dream of economic leveling was apparent even before the Depression, when he won the Louisiana governorship on the slogan "Every man a king, but no one wears a crown." As a senator, Long carried his contempt for the elite political establishment into DC with the swagger of what some called a "hillbilly hero." Though Long was initially a supporter of the New Deal, Roosevelt called him "one of the two most dangerous men in the country." (The other, FDR said, was General Douglas MacArthur.)

Roosevelt's fears and instincts were borne out. By 1934 Long decided that the New Deal had not gone far enough, and his Share Our Wealth Society called for the confiscation of large fortunes, a steep income tax on the rich, and the redistribution of $5,000 to each and every American family. Economists recognized that the dollars didn't add up; as one put it, "confiscating all fortunes larger than a million dollars would only produce . . . a mere $400" per family. Still, neither Long nor and his faithful supporters were daunted for a moment. The Kingfish would announce over the radio that his listeners should "[l]et no one tell you that it is difficult to redistribute the wealth of this land. It is simple." By 1935, Long's organization claimed five million members. Then, in a direct threat to FDR, Long told reporters "that Franklin Roosevelt will not be the next president of the United States. . . . Huey Long will be." In response to these boasts, a worried pro-Roosevelt Democratic senator warned that Long "is brilliant and dangerous. . . . The depression has increased radicalism in this country . . . the President is the only hope of the conservatives and the liberals; if his program is restricted, the answer may be Huey Long."

Long wasn't the only radical challenger to Rooseveltism. Radio priest Charles Coughlin, a naturalized American but Canadian-born, could not directly challenge FDR by running for the presidency himself, but the movement he unleashed pecked at the New Deal order from both the left and right. The Coughlin constituency included largely lower-middle-class ethnics, often only one generation removed from Southern and Eastern Europe, who had found some level of prosperity before the outbreak of the Depression. These dispirited workers were attracted not to Coughlin's religion but to his unique brand of populist politics. Coughlinites denounced international bankers and the gold standard while demanding inflation to mitigate debts. That was the leftist component of the muddled ideology. On the other hand, his supporters also fiercely attacked communism and campaigned against Wall Street, whose machinations they attributed to supposedly sinister Jewish business executives. Coughlin certainly seemed an imminent threat to the Democrats, especially after he declared that some 33 percent. No doubt some New Deal legislation seemed to catalyze this growth. After the passing of the NIRA — which includes a modest right to unionize — the president of the United Mine Workers (UMW), John L. Lewis, took to declaring in radio addresses and speeches that the "president wants you to join a union." Moreover, the 1935 Wagner Act, which officially guaranteed the workers' right to organize and required employers to bargain with union representatives, seemed to bolster Lewis's agenda. With such soaring rhetoric, Lewis rose to the fore of the entire American labor movement, even if his declaration about what the president wanted wasn't wholly factual. In fact, we now know that FDR was lukewarm toward labor, feared its potential radicalism and preferred government regulation and social welfare to union-led collective bargaining. The Wagner Act and the NIRA were actually compromise measures forced on the administration by grassroots activism and the president's urban ethnic constituencies.

No matter, by 1934–35 labor felt it had the wind in its sails, partly because of a popular president. In 1934 unions staged two thousand strikes across almost every industry in every region of the country. Some led to violence and public sympathy for the strikers. Then, in the famous and successful 1936–37 "sit-down" strikes, United Auto Workers (UAW) members occupied several General Motors plants in Flint, Michigan, and refused to move until their demands were met. According to historian David M. Kennedy, this was nothing less than "the forcible seizure by workers of the means of production." And when the Michigan governor refused to call in troops to enforce the court injunction against the strikers, the UAW won most of its demands: recognition of union bargaining rights, a shorter workweek, and a minimum wage. The role of government in all this was actually minimal. Though FDR worked behind the scenes to urge GM to settle, the main contribution of government was, quite simply, staying out of the way. This represented a major turnaround from the violent military and police interventions of earlier decades.

This was the high tide of labor success in the Depression era. The victorious sit-downers emerged from the GM plants full of buoyant energy and waving American flags. They seemed, for once, to have overcome the racial and ethnic divisions that had plagued organized labor in the past. One worker declared, "Once in the Ford plant they called me 'dumb Polack,' but now with the UAW they call me brother." Though stirring, this sentiment was, for the most part, just wishful thinking.

The American labor movement had actually fractured once again. The older American Federation of Labor (AFL), populated mostly by old-stock Anglos, threw all its energy behind skilled tradesmen. Factory workers and unskilled laborers on assembly lines, who were usually newer Italian and Slavic immigrants, were often ignored by AFL leaders. John Lewis of the UMW recognized this fault early on and by November 1935 formed the more radical Committee for Industrial Organization (later known as the Congress of Industrial Organizations). The CIO, in theory, called for ethnic and racial equality in union membership, but this additional hint of radicalism often served to alienate the public, especially in the conservative and labor-unfriendly South.

What's more, despite the victories in the sit-down strikes, the workers themselves lost much public sympathy. Many middle- and upper-class Americans feared the radicalism and effectiveness of the spreading sit-down strikes and quickly turned on organized labor. This was especially the case after various union branches began calling sudden "wildcat" sit-down strikes across the country, copying the successful Flint model. Rumors of communist infiltration — often exaggerated by corporate interests — further hurt the public image of the CIO unions, including the United Mine Workers and the United Auto Workers. At this point Congress jumped in, with Representative Martin Dies of Texas opening the first hearings of the new House Committee for the Investigation of Un-American Activities (HUAC) by calling sympathetic AFL spokesmen to Washington. These opponents of the CIO played their appointed role and attacked the new movement as "a seminary of Communist sedition."

Furthermore, major corporations fought back with a vigor rarely seen before or since. Businesses contributed to anti-labor advertising campaigns and also resorted to subterfuge and force to break the unions. Ford Motor Co. had long suppressed unionism and even built up a paramilitary force of some three thousand armed men to stalk and threaten "disloyal" employees. GM, for its part, invested $1 million to "field a force of wire tappers and [union] infiltrators" to combat the UAW. Radical labor's Waterloo came during a steel strike over Memorial Day weekend of 1937. When a UAW marcher threw a stick toward approaching police, pistol shots rang out and the law enforcement agents essentially rioted. When it was over, ten strikers were dead, seven shot in the back. Thirty others, including a woman and three children, were wounded by gunfire, and nine of them were permanently disabled as a result.

At this point government power intervened in the more traditional way. Pennsylvania's governor imposed martial law in the wake of the steel strike, and Ohio's governor did the same in Youngstown after two shooting deaths of steelworkers there. All told, the summer of 1937 saw eighteen workers killed. Still, public sympathy had by then shifted from labor and moved to the side of business and the police. The radical potential of the sit-down strikes, when combined with an effective corporate propaganda campaign, disquieted a majority of Americans. President Roosevelt was now in a tough spot. He couldn't side with labor without being seen to sanction the increasingly unpopular sit-downers, but he couldn't attack labor without alienating some of his most loyal voters. As was typical, Roosevelt chose the middle path. He declared a "plague on both your houses [business and the union]," and just like that, as historian Irving Bernstein concluded, "A brief and not very beautiful friendship had come to an end."

Despite such disappointments, organized labor did not abandon Roosevelt as he had abandoned it. On the contrary, union workers had, by the end of the 1930s, become reliable Democrats. This destroyed, once and for all, the old labor dream of a separate workers' party, such as existed in much of Europe. Unions abjured calls for the fall of capitalism and became mainstream players in the two-party political system. In this process, as David M. Kennedy noted, "they wrote the epitaph for American socialism."

Affirmative Action, but Only for Whites

The Negro was born in depression. . . . It only became
official when it hit the white man.

> — Clifford Burke as quoted by Studs Terkel
> in an oral history of the Great Depression

At the height of the New Deal, according to the black scholar and
historian W. E. B. Du Bois, some 75 percent of African Americans still
were denied the right to vote. Since at least 1877 blacks could count
on neither major political party to reliably champion their rights.
Nonetheless, it was undoubtedly during the Great Depression that a
supermajority of African Americans moved toward the Democrats.
That this should be so is somewhat odd. The Democratic Party, we
must remember, was the preferred party not only of Civil War–era
Confederates but of postwar segregationists and white supremacists.
Indeed, by the 1930s the Democrats boasted a single-party system —
in which they were unchallenged by Republicans — across the Old
South. Still, there was something about Franklin Roosevelt, a scion
of a northern patrician family, and his New Deal that appealed to
America's largely impoverished black population. Black Americans
saw hope in the man and his policies. Tragically, their faith would
prove misplaced and they would soon find themselves left out of the
New Deal's largesse in a carefully orchestrated system that achieved
nothing less than white "affirmative action."

The main culprits in this epic sellout were powerful southern
Democrats along with FDR himself, who proved all too willing to
compromise with these white supremacists — a decision that the
president saw as politically necessary. The southern wing of the
Democratic Party had long been dominant. This requires some explanation and analysis. Given the peculiar American system of state-
based senatorial representation, the seventeen states that mandated
racial segregation had a combined thirty-four seats in the Senate.
Almost all were Democrats; the Republicans rarely even ran an
opposing candidate, and blacks (who largely favored the GOP, the

party of Lincoln) were disenfranchised. Thus these senators made up the majority of Democrats in the Senate and had undue influence on the party platform and policies. Furthermore, these senators — along with southerners in the House — usually had the most seniority in Congress and thus chaired the key committees, controlling which bills made it to the floor for debate and a vote. Finally, because of the low franchise among African Americans and with blacks counted for representation purposes although they were blocked from voting, each white southerner in Congress had far more statistical sway in Washington than his northern counterpart. Throughout the New Deal era, these dominant southerners would use their power for one primary purpose: to maintain their apartheid system of white supremacy.

The new attraction of northern blacks to the Democratic Party and the apparent sympathy of southern blacks for New Deal socioeconomic reforms were seen very differently by African American leaders and southern white party leaders. Whereas one black preacher in the South hopefully told his flock to "[l]et Jesus lead you and Roosevelt feed you," the attraction of African Americans to Roosevelt and his New Deal was seen as a threat by many whites. As one Georgia relief agent concluded, "Any nigger who gets over $8 a week is a spoiled nigger, that's all. . . . The Negroes regard the President as the Messiah, and they think that . . . they'll all be getting $12 a week for the rest of their lives." Here we see an early manifestation of the belief among white bigots that blacks were lazy and reliant on government welfare by their very nature.

From a neutral perspective, black enthusiasm for the New Deal was wholly understandable. As was, and is, always the case in American history, depressions and recessions tend to have disproportionate effects on the black community. In 1932, for example, black unemployment reached 50 percent, double the national rate. Often the last hired, blacks were usually the first fired. Despite Roosevelt's later sell-out of American blacks, there were reasons for hope upon his first election. First Lady Eleanor Roosevelt would remain a vocal proponent of black civil rights throughout her husband's tenure, even if

FDR often failed to follow her lead. Still, in 1933 the president did consult an informal group of advisers known as his "black cabinet" and appointed the first ever black federal judge.

Nonetheless, the Depression only increased southern anxiety and raised the rates of terror attacks in the region. Lynchings tripled in 1932–33, with twenty-three such killings occurring in a single span of twelve months. This shocking statistic led the Congress to propose, once again, federal anti-lynching legislation. Northern Democrats and African Americans hoped, in vain, that FDR would throw his weight behind the bill. He would not, and the bill failed again in the face of southern intransigence and a marathon six-week Senate filibuster. During the filibuster, Louisiana senator Allen J. Ellender made clear the stance of his fellow southerners, proudly declaring, "I believe in white supremacy, and as long as I am in the Senate I expect to fight for white supremacy." For his part Roosevelt felt he had no choice but to abandon the bill to its inevitable fate. He told the NAACP's Walter White: "If I come out for the anti-lynching bill now, they [southern Democrats] will block every bill I ask Congress to pass to keep America from collapsing. . . . I just can't take that risk." From the president's perspective, civil rights legislation would, once again, have to wait.

By and large, though, the real crime of the New Deal was the way it excluded blacks from the structural social safety net and relief budgets. It was the southern Democrats who ensured this by insisting on — and gaining FDR's acceptance of — local control of federal relief and employment programs. Southern political leaders insisted this be the case as the price for their legislative support. For example, when South Carolina senator Ellison "Cotton Ed" Smith learned that New Deal programs might provide cash relief to black tenant farmers, he stormed into a government administrator's office and exclaimed, "Young fella, you can't do this to my niggers, paying checks to them. They don't know what to do with the money. The money should come to me. I'll take care of them. They're mine." Unsurprisingly, local welfare administrators in the South segregated such programs or rejected them outright on the basis of race.

Then, when Congress passed the Social Security Act — with its substantial old-age insurance and unemployment relief components — the southern Democrats again twisted the legislation to exclude blacks. Though the bill would have no specific racial language, the southerners insisted on, and won, a provision to exclude farm laborers and domestic servants from Social Security coverage. Thus, at a stroke, 9.4 million of the neediest workers — a disproportionate number of them black and brown — were denied these benefits. The results were tragic and far reaching. Whereas white workers benefited from the "affirmative action" of a social safety net and old-age insurance, blacks fell ever further behind. By the twenty-first century white household wealth was on average nine times that of black families.

Roosevelt and the Democratic Party were directly complicit and caught up in this corrupt system of racial exclusion. It's important to understand that the white supremacists in the party were not conservatives in the contemporary sense of the word. The South was largely a dirt-poor region. Its Democratic representatives liked the New Deal and its social welfare programs — so long as the programs didn't upset the region's structural racial caste system. Consider the irony and staggering juxtaposition of FDR and perhaps the most virulently racist in the Congress, Senator Theodore Bilbo of Mississippi. Bilbo proudly declared in 1938 that "[the United States] is strictly a white man's country . . . one drop of Negro blood placed in the veins of the purest Caucasian destroys the genius of his mind." Despite this shocking assertion, Bilbo would proclaim, two years later, "[I am] 100 percent for Roosevelt . . . and the New Deal." And when this deplorable man was reelected by a landslide in 1940, FDR himself sent a letter to Bilbo containing this sentence: "I was so delighted to learn of your splendid victory . . . assuring . . . a real friend to liberal government."

Perhaps the paradox and contradictions appear staggering. And indeed they were. Such were the fissures in the inherently unstable "big tent" of the 1930s Democratic coalition. Roosevelt felt he had to work with the monsters in the South to "save" and "transform" America. This led him into some disreputable bargains that haunt his reputation. So it was, then, that "liberal," yet racist, southern legislators crafted and the economic devastation the Depression wrought in the United States, it is surprising that FDR did not assume the powers of a dictator at some point during his years in office.

Roosevelt did flirt with rule by executive fiat and was seen by many opponents as something nearing a tyrant. We must ask, then, whether FDR was, indeed, a dangerous man and examine the contours — and limits — of his personal power. Many commentators, even liberals and old-time progressives, in fact urged Roosevelt to assume singular power. Even before his inauguration, America's most famous editorialist, Walter Lippmann, wrote to Roosevelt: "You may have no alternative but to assume dictatorial powers [to end the Depression]." And in fact Roosevelt threatened as much in his first inaugural address. Many of his supporters loved it! Today we forget that the biggest applause line in this famous speech wasn't "We have nothing to fear but fear itself." Rather, the crowd roared most loudly when FDR declared that if the legislature failed to act according to his views, "I shall ask the Congress for the one remaining instrument to meet the crisis — broad Executive power to wage a war against the emergency, as great as the power that would be given to me if we were in fact invaded by a foreign foe." This remarkable, if disturbing, statement earned the new president cheers, but his limited moves in that direction would meet with major opposition.

Roosevelt ran into the most trouble and disapproval in response to his so-called court-packing scheme. Fearing that the rather conservative, mostly Republican-appointed Supreme Court would strike down most of his New Deal legislation as unconstitutional (it had already overturned twelve such measures in the preceding months), Roosevelt proposed legislation that would allow him to appoint an additional justice for each justice over the age of seventy who refused to retire. Though a staggering reorganization of the judicial branch and an infringement on its independence, FDR felt the proposal was justifiable. His plan would weaken the power of the most conservative justices on the court — "the Four Horsemen" — all of whom were seventy or older. FDR saw this as a necessity to save the economy. His attorney general, after all, had warned the president that "they [the court] mean to destroy us. . . . We have to find a way to get rid of the present membership of the Supreme Court." And, from Roosevelt's perspective, these septuagenarian conservative justices were out of touch with the needs of a new industrial economy gripped by depression.

However, in this case Roosevelt's political motivations were all too clear. A massive public outcry ensued. The columnist Dorothy Thompson wrote, "If the American people accept this last audacity . . . without letting out a yell to high heaven, they have ceased to be jealous of their liberties and are ripe for ruin." The president's Court Reform Bill opened him to renewed charges of dictatorship, and not just from his traditional conservative opponents. A plurality of Democratic congressmen abandoned him, and a Gallup survey of the public showed that fully 55 percent of the population opposed the court packing. The bill never passed, and Roosevelt's popularity was permanently damaged.

Nonetheless, though the president had lost the battle, he may have won a Pyrrhic victory in the war. Soon after Roosevelt's announcement of the plan, Justice Owen Roberts switched sides and the court began approving each piece of key New Deal legislation. What one commentator called "the greatest constitutional somersault in history" has since been labeled the "switch in time that saved the nine [-justice court]." Though FDR never managed to expand the court, he had, he observed, "obtained 98% of all the objectives intended by the Court plan." True enough, but the court-packing scheme had exposed the deep fissures in the president's own party. Southern Democrats abandoned him and began to fear that if the executive branch could request and gather such federal power on this issue, it might later delve into the South's own "business" of racial segregation. For the rest of his time in office, Roosevelt would face taunts about his dictatorial temperament from these southerners and many others. For example, in the midst of the crisis, the famed H. L. Mencken published a satirical essay on the American Constitution that began: "All government power of whatever sort shall be vested in a President of the United States."

Ultimately, however, despite his flirtations with strongman rule and sometime bending of the rules, Roosevelt never governed by full executive fiat. He, unlike Mussolini or Stalin, accepted the constitutional primacy of legislatures and accepted far less than he proposed through compromise with Congress. In the final analysis, FDR may have been dangerous, but he was not a dictator. His loyalty to the Constitution and his fealty to executive limitations may have been just the thing that saved America's admittedly flawed democratic system. It is hard to know if another man would have demonstrated such humility and restraint when times got tough. Those qualities must remain a significant part of Roosevelt's legacy.

Backlash: Sowing the Seeds of a New Conservative Political Movement

For all that, Roosevelt still alienated large portions of the American electorate and the established power structure. His policies and persona earned him the undying ire of a new conservative movement that formed in response, and in opposition, to all things Roosevelt. Today the resurgence of conservatism and its takeover of the Republican Party are traditionally dated back to Richard Nixon or Ronald Reagan, but in reality its seeds had been sown by 1935. That nascent movement of the 1930s and its anti-FDR bona fides remain a major part of American political life to this day.

By 1934 organized corporate interests felt threatened enough by the New Deal that they worked with conservatives within the president's own Democratic Party to form the American Liberty League, an organization whose birth marked the start of organized opposition to Roosevelt's policies. Then in 1935 the newspaper magnate William Randolph Hearst, after hearing of FDR's "wealth tax," branded the president's proposal "Communism" and took to referring to him as "Stalin Delano Roosevelt." This, despite the fact that the top tax rate of 79 percent on incomes over $5 million covered precisely one individual: John D. Rockefeller. Then, in response to Roosevelt's 1936 campaign attacks on "economic royalists," some employers slipped propaganda into workers' paychecks falsely claiming that the Social Security Act would "require all participants to wear stainless-steel identification dog-tags" and that there was "no guarantee" that workers would ever see a return on their payroll-tax deductions.

Worse still for Roosevelt, at the end of the 1937 special congressional session — in which not a single one of the president's bills had passed — a large, bipartisan group of southern Democrats and northern Republicans released a ten-point "Conservative Manifesto." It attacked union strikers, demanded decreased taxes, defended states' rights, and criticized growing federal power. Historian David M. Kennedy has labeled this document as the "founding charter for modern American conservatism." Then, in the 1938 elections, the Republican Party rebounded, winning more seats than at any other time since 1928. This was a knockout blow to the New Deal, and Roosevelt would pass hardly any social welfare legislation for the remainder of his presidency.

In Congress the new HUAC committee hinted that FDR's program was "communistic," and the panel cultivated ties with right-wing groups and worked closely with FBI head J. Edgar Hoover. Committee members and their public supporters began to claim that the New Deal was a communist conspiracy spearheaded by "new" foreigners who had gotten into the country despite the restrictions of the 1924 Immigration Bill. Some referred to Roosevelt's policies as a "Jew Deal." HUAC chairman Martin Dies promised to wage "relentless war without quarter and without cessation" on 3.5 million — mostly Jewish, Italian, and Slavic — immigrants that he dubiously claimed had entered the country illegally. He even blamed the Depression on these immigrant groups, stating, "If we had refused admission to the 16,500,000 foreign born who are living in this country today, we would have no unemployment problem." Tragically, when German Jews sought refuge in the United States from Nazi rule throughout the later 1930s, it was Dies and his fellow "new" conservatives who mobilized the congressional opposition that stood in their way and relegated many of them to concentration camps and ovens.

That aside, whether for better or worse, Roosevelt's experimental, innovative federal welfare legislation, along with the fact that he was loved among immigrant workers, helped rally to the standard of conservatism a new swath of disgruntled Americans. And not all of them were rich, corporate businessmen. Just as Roosevelt had delivered a new, and for a time dominant, coalition of minorities, urban ethnics, impoverished farmers, and liberal intellectuals, his conservative opponents began forming their own nascent consortium. This grouping would include southern racists, Anglo nativists, business interests, states'-righters, opponents of welfare "excesses," and a stable upper middle class grown ever more fearful of the strength of unions and minorities. That coalition would stem the liberal tide by 1968 and decisively seize power in 1980.

———

What, then, can we conclude about the New Deal and its legacy? Let us start with what it did not do. Roosevelt's flurry of legislation did not end the Depression. It did not meaningfully redistribute the national wealth — America's income profile was, in 1940, much the same as it had been in 1930. Nor did it challenge the system of capitalism or the tenet of private ownership. The New Deal was never as socialistic as its enemies had claimed. What it did do, importantly, was put in place institutional structures that provided security to large numbers of Americans. The New Deal regulated banking, helping prevent a major economic crash until 2008 — after, it must be noted, Glass-Steagall restrictions had been overturned. It stopped an avalanche of bank and mortgage defaults through new systems of federal controls, many still in existence. The New Deal must be said to have put in place a security apparatus for banking and homeownership that facilitated the post-war suburban housing boom of the 1950s and '60s. Most decisively, the New Deal increased the power of the federal government and put to rest, at least temporarily, the notion that the "market" and the goodwill of the private sector were sufficient to sustain a secure economy for all. Thenceforward the US government would play a decisive role in market regulation, poverty relief, and labor practices.

Roosevelt may have been too optimistic when he promised that the New Deal would "make a country in which no one is left out," but the program did take steps in the direction of economic security for most. If the New Deal didn't substantially challenge capitalism, it did upend the role of the federal government in the constitutionally mandated "protection of the general welfare." And notably, it did so without shredding the Constitution. Roosevelt eschewed radicalism and, as David Kennedy concluded, "prevented a naked confrontation between orthodoxy and revolution." This was no small matter.

As the historian Jill Lepore has noted, "FDR's ascension marked the rise of modern liberalism." Indeed, the Democratic Party, strengthened by the new "Roosevelt coalition" — of blue-collar workers, union men, southern farmers, racial minorities, progressive intellectuals, and women — would dominate American politics for nearly three decades after FDR's death in 1945. Still, the new, powerful coalition was always inherently unstable and contained within itself the sources of its own destruction. Southerners and northern white working-class ethnics were always less than comfortable in an alliance with poor blacks, who were seen as a threat both to the prevailing racial order and the job/wage prospects of white workers. By the mid-1960s these undercurrents of tension would explode and the coalition would break over the emotional issues of black civil rights and government-sponsored social welfare programs. The result, we now know, was an empowered conservative movement and Republican Party that has, arguably, commanded American politics ever since. The seeds of all this were in the New Deal and the Roosevelt coalition from the very start.

Whether one reveres Roosevelt and his New Deal or perceives him and his program as the forebears of wasteful spending and an overpowering federal welfare state, on one point perhaps all can agree. What appears most remarkable about FDR, his Depression-era leadership, and his New Deal is this: for whatever reason — be it the president's brilliance or sheer luck — the United States, unlike many other Western nations, avoided the radical and authoritarian turns toward communism or fascism that paved the road to another world war.

Early in Roosevelt's tenure, the soon-to-be-famous British economist John Maynard Keynes wrote the following to the new president:

> You have made yourself the trustee for those in every country who seek to mend the evils of our condition by reasoned experiment within the framework of the existing social system. If you fail, rational change will be gravely prejudiced throughout the world, leaving orthodoxy and revolution to fight it out. But if you succeed, new and bolder methods will be tried everywhere, and we may date the first chapter of a new economic era from your succession to office.

At this, at least, Roosevelt would succeed, in promoting rational change and avoiding excessive radicalism or revolution. FDR threaded the needle between the overpowering currents on the rise elsewhere in the industrial world.

What is less clear is whether Roosevelt's middle path was ultimately best. After all, his relative conservatism on matters of labor, race, and deficit spending — he regularly insisted, contrary to common memory, on balanced budgets — sounded the death knell of socialism in America, ensuring that the United States, alone among highly developed Western nations, would have neither universal health care nor a powerful labor party. By co-opting the poor, the farmers, the urban workers, the intellectuals, and minorities within his new Democratic coalition, he essentially bolstered the American two-party system and slammed the door on any "third-way" policies. FDR was, in the end, no traitor to his class. On the contrary, he saved the wealthy — both the newly rich and his own patrician blue bloods — from what might very well have been the collapse of the capitalist system itself. It was a fact that many of his enemies among the "economic royalists" were too shortsighted to realize.

Through his perhaps unique combination of genuine empathy, paternalist practicality, and political savvy, FDR escaped revolution from either the left or the right. Still, in pursuing a pragmatic path, he left much social justice struggle to future generations and left the conservative movement very much intact. It would fall to others to strive toward racial equality, more far-reaching poverty-reduction programs, and a truly egalitarian wealth redistribution. His Democratic successors would try, falter, compromise, and ultimately fail in this later mission, ceding much political ground to a newly empowered conservative Republican Party. By the twenty-first century, the Democrats, in the interest of winning elections, would tilt so far to the right as to be nearly indistinguishable from the rising Republicans. Democrats could still emerge victorious from time to time, but by the end of the second decade of the new millennium, income inequality would again reach levels unseen since the start of Roosevelt's first term.

Had FDR not gone far enough? Did his middle path doom the New Deal? Today, with wealth disparity again reaching record levels, racism and nativism back on the rise, organized labor on life support, and globalization castrating American manufacturing, it would seem — at least to progressives — that both questions must be answered in the affirmative. Nevertheless, given the time, the stalwart American tradition of individualism, and the power of the conservative opposition, expecting more from Roosevelt may constitute wishful thinking of the highest order. Seen in this light, Franklin Delano Roosevelt — the man, the dream, and his policies — charted both the possibilities and limitations of progressivism in America. As for the United States, a conservative country it was, and perhaps it shall remain.[21]

25

FROM ISOLATIONISM TO A SECOND WORLD CONFLAGRATION

Isolationism. Appeasement. Few words in American history have a more pejorative meaning than these. To this day antiwar political figures are broadly described as naive isolationists ready to let the world burn in chaos; furthermore, current attempts at diplomatic compromise often are likened to British prime minister Neville Chamberlain's perceived appeasement of Germany's Adolf Hitler in 1938. At times such comparisons hold water. Usually they don't. Each era and its prevailing context carry along contingent events and millions of decision makers with agency of their own. Rarely does one period bear any real resemblance to another. Few if any contemporary adversaries constitute the threat and pure evil of Hitler. Few international compromises are as ill fated as that made at Munich in 1938.

Still, we are told, the era between World War I and World War II continues to offer supposedly incontestable truths and lessons to be learned. In 1945 most Americans left the Second World War convinced — for the first time in our national history — that the United States must engage with and lead the world of nations. Never again could a democratic nation compromise with or placate an authoritarian adversary. This, we are told, is the key lesson of the twenty-odd years separating the two wars. In certain instances, perhaps, the internationalists have been proved right. Then again, with the United States now engaged in countless wars and operating military bases around the globe, one must admit that the triumph of interventionism has had its cost, both to the budget and to our republican ideals.

It must be said that there is some truth in the prevailing critique of the Western powers' response to the rise of fascism in the 1920s and '30s. Still, a closer look at the era and the United States' unique role in it reveals the complexity and nuances of an international situation that was exceedingly difficult. The leaders of the 1930s did not have the benefit of the hindsight of today's politicians, historians, and critics. Almost none fully foresaw the horror of the coming war and Holocaust. To grasp the prevailing attitudes of the day, we must explore with open minds, and we must be willing to accept uncomfortable truths and quandaries.

Even after violence among European nations broke out in the late 1930s, most Americans remained highly skeptical of war and somewhat isolationist. Many prominent politicians, writers, artists, and celebrities deeply feared a replay of World War I, a conflict they deemed to have been unnecessary if not outright criminal. Against this tide of isolationism or, perhaps more accurately, anti-interventionism stood a more internationalist collection of politicians and their sometimes wary champion, President Franklin Delano Roosevelt. Elected in 1932 to fix the Depression-era economy, FDR spent his first term focused on domestic issues. Nevertheless, he came from a globally inclined establishment family and had himself been a Wilsonian internationalist progressive and an assistant secretary of the navy during the First World War. FDR saw the seriousness of the fascist threat before most Americans and spent much of his second term and the early part of his third term a few steps ahead of the people in his willingness to intervene against the Axis powers.

Still, being the canny politician he was, Roosevelt was careful in leading the United States to war, moving in fits and starts toward joining the fight. In doing so FDR severely stretched the limits of executive power and secrecy, demonstrating some of the dangerous tendencies he had indicated in his domestic response to the Great Depression. The result was not only a two-front war — which, admittedly, it was probably necessary to eventually fight — but a permanent alteration of the role and scope of federal power. No president since Roosevelt has actually declared war, but every president has wielded the expanded executive powers that FDR unilaterally carved out for himself.

Avoiding the Last War: World War I Memory and Isolationism

Americans and Europeans alike were traumatized by the First World War. The roughly nine million combat deaths, the vast majority suffered by the European belligerents, surely was sufficient reason. Memories of what at the time was called the Great War were heavy on both sides of the Atlantic. Many political and cultural leaders vowed to never again support such a costly and ultimately fruitless nationalist bloodbath. Antiwar movements sprang up in the interwar years even before there was a looming new conflict to protest. The horror and absurdity of World War I nursed a fatalism in Europe, but American perceptions of that contest were more complex. After all, the US military had been a latecomer to the war and suffered only a fraction of the casualties of the original belligerents. Still, Americans themselves were transfixed with the idea that the United States had won the war through its intervention. Some were proud of this, but many others were resentful: they felt the people of the United States had been deceived into becoming involved in an unnecessary war.

American opponents of World War I, who probably constituted a majority of the population in the 1930s, vowed to never again be tricked into intervening in a European war. They fell back on a long tradition of disengagement from foreign squabbles and looked inward. Only later would this popular and inherently American view be pejoratively dubbed isolationist. Martial spirits in general were losing their luster in the interwar period. Throughout 1935, retired marine major general Smedley Butler, a two-time Medal of Honor recipient, traveled the country on a speaking tour for his book *War Is a Racket*. Butler was then the most decorated marine in US history, and his thunderous critiques carried the weight of his credentials. "War is a racket," he declared. "It always has been. It is possibly the oldest, easily the most profitable, surely the most vicious. It is the only one international in scope. It is the only one in which the profits are reckoned in dollars and the losses in lives." Furthermore, he blamed past American interventionism on the influence of big business, exclaiming that he had "spent 33 years and four months in active military service and during that period I spent most of my time as a high-class muscle man for Big Business, for Wall Street and the bankers. In short, I was a racketeer, a gangster for capitalism."

Butler's earthy rhetoric resonated with an American public that was increasingly suspicious of the nation's 1917 entry into World War I. Leading politicians, such as Senator Gerald Nye, argued that the United States had fought in Europe only to secure the debts of Britain and to enrich the domestic arms industrialists — whom Nye termed "merchants of death." When Nye was head of the ultimately fruitless Senate Special Committee on Investigation of the Munitions Industry, he publicly declared what many Americans had long thought: "When Americans went into the fray [World War I] they little thought they were there and fighting to save the skins of American bankers who had bet too boldly on the outcome of the war and had two billions of dollars of loans to the Allies in jeopardy." Not coincidentally, Nye's statement was uttered in the same year that Butler's speaking tour was occurring.

Artists and writers, too, chimed in against future wars in Europe. The novelist John Dos Passos wrote, "Rejection of Europe is what America is all about." Furthermore, Ernest Hemingway's classic anti-war novel A Farewell to Arms was highly popular in the 1930s. Even revisionist academic historians penned influential books arguing that Americans had been duped into war by the British and their Wall Street financiers. So strong was the cultural and political antiwar sentiment that in the first postwar decade Americans rejected the League of Nations proposed by President Woodrow Wilson, a security treaty with France, the World Court, free-trade policies, and the forgiveness of Allied war loans. In the 1920s, in fact, Washington went so far as to negotiate sea-power reductions at the Washington Naval Conference and to technically make war illegal in the Kellogg-Briand Pact. Thus when during the mid-1930s the rise of European fascism and Japanese imperialism became ever more threatening, most Americans — remembering with horror the Great War — had little stomach for a second world war.

By 1935, with Adolf Hitler already securely in power in Berlin, and with the Japanese fighting China over the province of Manchuria, many Americans were holding preemptive peace marches. In April, on the eighteenth anniversary of US entry into the war, fifty thousand veterans held a "march for peace" in Washington, DC. Three days later 175,000 college students nationwide held a one-hour "strike for peace" and demanded the abolition of on-campus ROTC programs. Responding to this popular outcry, the Congress would draft and President Roosevelt would sign the first of what would eventually be five so-called Neutrality Acts. This bill required the president to declare a total arms embargo on all belligerents, should any nations go to war, and to declare that all American citizens traveling on foreign ships did so at their own risk. The core of the legislation was a blatant attempt to avoid the last war's perceived causes — Allied debts and deaths caused by submarines. Only 1939 wasn't 1914, and the nature of the next war would be different, pulling in the United States once again despite its citizens' best efforts.

As noted earlier, the United States was a latecomer to World War I, and the same was true for World War II. It took two years, three months, and seven days from Hitler's September 1, 1939, invasion of Poland before America would unleash its full military might against the Axis powers — primarily Germany, Italy, and Japan. Even then it would take a surprise attack by the Japanese to seal the deal. Indeed, it is rather remarkable that substantial portions of the American electorate and their representatives kept the nation out of both wars as long as they did. That delay was undoubtedly influenced by the tradition of American non-interference in Europe and the specter of the last war. However, bolstered with today's knowledge of history, many commentators and historians of our own time lambaste the isolationist sentiments of 1930s Americans, even blaming them for the rise of fascist leaders and the ultimate horror of Nazi and Japanese policies. This may be unfair, though the hesitancy of the Allies, and especially of the distant United States, did embolden the fascist powers. Furthermore, given the challenge of the ongoing Great Depression, Allied powers often lacked both the capacity and will to meaningfully intervene before 1939.

Still, it must be said that the Allied — and American — response to fascist aggression in the 1930s was not the finest hour in the fight against that malignancy. When in 1931 Japan executed a "false-flag" attack to justify a military invasion of Chinese Manchuria, much of the rest of the world made only a paltry protest. And when Benito Mussolini's Italy invaded Ethiopia in 1935 and the League of Nations, of which the United States was not a part, reacted by imposing an oil embargo, the United States — then producer of half the world's oil — demurred. The US decision and the collapse of the embargo defanged the concept of punishment: a cutoff of oil would have stopped Mussolini's mechanized forces in their tracks. Ethiopia, despite putting up a gallant fight, soon fell to the Italians.

Next came a 1936 fascist coup in Spain, led by General Francisco Franco, that set off a three-year civil war. When the duly elected leftist democratic government appealed to the Allies for help, it received none except from the communist Soviet Union. The US Congress, by a single vote, passed a new Neutrality Act that extended the arms embargo to both sides — the practical effect of which was to deny the Spanish liberals the means to fight. The fascist powers of Germany and Italy had no such qualms and sent arms, planes, and eventually infantry to Franco. More than two thousand Americans, usually idealistic leftists, defied US government policy and enlisted to fight for the Spanish republicans. These American volunteers, who became known collectively as the Abraham Lincoln Brigade, were thrown into battle with almost no training and often were used as shock troops; as a result they took heavy casualties. Such expatriate fighters were immortalized in Hemingway's novel *For Whom the Bell Tolls*. When Franco emerged victorious from the civil war, even President Roosevelt recognized the folly of the US government's decisions, conceding to his cabinet that his Spanish policy had been "a grave mistake."

At this point, America's old allies began to feel they could no longer count on support from the New World. In early 1938, British prime minister Neville Chamberlain declared that "he would be a rash man who based his calculations on help from that quarter . . . the isolationists are so strong & so vocal that [the United States] cannot be depended upon for help if [Britain] should get into trouble." Thus

Anti-isolationist cartoon, 1939, by Theodor Seuss Geisel (Dr. Seuss)

when, later that year, Hitler demanded the cession of the Sudetenland, a German-speaking portion of Czechoslovakia, Chamberlain and his French counterpart negotiated with the German leader in Munich without any meaningful backing from Washington. Not that the British were willing or able to make war in 1938. As Chamberlain himself stated, the Czech crisis was "a quarrel in a faraway country between people of whom we know nothing." Still, it must be said that previous US inaction in Ethiopia and Spain discouraged British and French firmness at the Munich negotiations.

Indeed, Roosevelt appeared to be of two minds about the issues at stake. He feared Hitler's expansive desires, and when the Allies ultimately handed over part of Czechoslovakia to the Germans he privately noted that the British and French had left the Czechs to "paddle their own canoe" and predicted that these two allies of the US would have to "wash the blood from their Judas Iscariot hands." Even so, Roosevelt made clear to the British and French that they were on their own at Munich, declaring that the United States "has no political involvements in Europe and will assume no obligations in the conduct of the present negotiations." Furthermore, when the unbacked Chamberlain did hand over the disputed Sudetenland, Roosevelt was relieved and cabled Chamberlain the simple phrase "Good Man."

Soon after Munich, Hitler — who had actually desired war in 1938 — swallowed up the rest of Czechoslovakia. In the years since the Munich debacle, it has been repeatedly argued that a firmer Allied stance might have staved off war or defeated an unprepared Hitler. Though not without merit, such moralistic proclamations belie certain facts. Hitler, seeking an immediate war with the European allies of the US, was disappointed when he felt obliged — under pressure by his own advisers — to compromise at the Munich Conference. What's more, Britain and France were militarily unprepared and their allied dominions — Canada, Australia, and New Zealand — had made clear they were unwilling to fight for the Czechs. Given that the Allies could not depend on an even less prepared and inclined United States, they had little choice but to compromise. Truth be told, they probably succeeded in buying themselves a year to prepare for war.

Munich, and Germany's subsequent seizure of Czechoslovakia, changed everyone's calculus. Hitler would be sure to get his war next time, and Britain and France vowed to fight for the likely next target of the Nazis — Poland. It was also a watershed for FDR, if not for all Americans. Roosevelt concluded that Hitler was a "mad man" and "a nut," and the president shifted his own (often secretive) policy to "unneutral rearmament" and tacit support for the Allies. Unfortunately, someone else also learned a lesson from Allied weakness at Munich — Soviet leader Joseph Stalin. Certain he could not count on the Allies to check Hitler, Stalin began considering a deal with his fascist archenemy, Hitler. Just before the Nazi invasion of Poland in September 1939, the Soviets would sign a nonaggression pact with Germany, and the two autocracies secretly agreed to divide Eastern Europe between themselves. Still, both Stalin and Hitler were aware that this was a marriage of convenience that would last only until the great ideological war between fascism and communism would begin.

Further proof of American hesitancy could be found in its perfidious response to the Jewish refugee crisis of the 1930s and '40s. When Germany occupied Austria in 1938 without a shot fired, three thousand Jews *per day* applied for visas to the United States in the capital city of Vienna. Unfortunately, due to the harsh restrictions on Jews and East Europeans entering the United States under the 1924 National Origins Act, the US consulates in Germany and Austria could legally process only 850 visas *per month*. Eventually the consulates had a backlog of some 110,000 visa applications. By 1938, of course, it was no secret that the Nazis were persecuting Jews across the Third Reich, stripping them of citizenship and civil rights and even subjecting them to violence. Still, America proved to be little help to hundreds of thousands trying to escape. In a bit of Kafkaesque political tragedy, under German law Jews who left the country could take only a very small amount of money with them. The immigration-restrictive United States forbade granting visas to people "likely to become a public charge" — meaning poor people. Thus, with unemployment raging in Depression-era America, there was little hope this ban would be lifted or that a sizable number of Jews could thread the legal loophole and seek refuge in the Land of the Free.

It's not that the Germans wouldn't let Jews go at that point in time. In fact, Nazi minister of propaganda Joseph Goebbels announced that "if there is any country that believes it has not enough Jews, I shall gladly turn over to it all our Jews." A Nazi newspaper commented, "We are saying openly that we do not want the Jews while the democracies keep on claiming that they are willing to receive them — and then leave the guests out in the cold." And indeed the United States, and the other democracies, largely did. A *Fortune* magazine survey in 1938 indicated that only 5 percent of American respondents were willing to raise immigration quotas for Jews. Even Roosevelt, who would later push the nation toward war with Germany, parroted the popular American line. Asked by a reporter, just five days after the worst Nazi pogrom against Jews to date, whether he would "recommend relaxation of our immigrations restriction," he answered simply: "That is not in our contemplation. We have the quota system." It was not his or the nation's proudest moment.

All in all, the United States alone cannot bear the blame for Hitler's rise or the eventual Holocaust. However, due to a range of factors described, America and its erstwhile allies failed to demonstrate the will or capacity to check the rising fascist states. It would take outright war for the British and French, and the machinations of a rather secretive and increasingly internationalist American president, to halt Nazi and later Japanese aggression.

Getting the War He Wanted:
Roosevelt and Executive Power (1935–41)

Though he so often, and for so long, bent to the political whims of an isolationist public, it now seems clear that from early in his presidency FDR saw the fascist threat and slowly worked to pull the United States toward a de facto — and eventually official — state of war. When in 1935 the US Congress rejected joining the World Court, both Hitler and Mussolini had already risen to power. Roosevelt, surmising that these fascist states may one day have to be checked, lamented to a friend that "we [in the United States] face a largely misinformed public opinion." Roosevelt had once been a supporter of President Woodrow Wilson's League of Nations and was even inclined to partner with the league to punish Italy's invasion of Ethiopia in 1935, but he also knew he was far ahead of isolationist public opinion on such matters.

Domestic politics was always on the president's mind. During the Ethiopia invasion, FDR told Democratic National Committee chairman James Farley that "I am walking a tightrope. I realize the seriousness of this from an international as well as domestic point of view." He feared that if he got too far out in front of Congress at that moment he would hand the isolationists a weapon to use against him in the upcoming presidential election campaign.

Even after his 1936 reelection, when Roosevelt gave a modest speech in Chicago in October 1937 about the threat of fascist aggression in

Europe, he took half measures. Despite strongly illustrating the threat from the new authoritarian regimes, he backtracked with reporters just one day later, declaring sanctions "out of the window" and claiming that the United States was "looking for a program . . . [that] might be called stronger neutrality." After the Chicago speech failed to rally the American people, Roosevelt allegedly stated, "It's a terrible thing, to look over your shoulder when you are trying to lead — and to find no one there."

By the late 1930s — after the fall of Ethiopia, Manchuria, and Spain and the start of German rearmament — the president had privately made it clear to European democratic leaders that he was "with them" but felt the need to be less candid at home. Though he regularly expressed his dismay with many of the more restrictive parts of the five Neutrality Acts, he felt obliged to proceed slowly with any military preparations or diplomatic promises. This, of course, was problematic. Roosevelt's private assurances to France and Britain had little effect on Hitler's policies, since, as historian Donald Watt astutely concluded, "deterrence and secrecy are largely incompatible notions."

Matters came to a head on September 1, 1939, when Hitler unleashed a swift, brutal invasion of Poland. The British and French quickly declared war on Germany but could do little to save the doomed Poles. FDR stayed neutral, of course, but took a view different from the one President Wilson had taken in 1914. Roosevelt admitted his own inclinations when he announced to Americans that he "cannot ask that every American remain neutral in thought." Still, pro-Allied rhetoric was one thing, but tangible support was another matter. Though FDR now knew he needed to try to repeal the Neutrality Acts, he was obliged by law to invoke the acts on September 5. This mandated an embargo on all arms to belligerents on both sides — including Britain and France. British officials told the American ambassador to London that they were "depressed beyond words" that the United States had invoked the neutrality law. Roosevelt began work to weaken the legislation but had to tread carefully, writing that "I am almost literally walking on eggs" in dealing with Congress and public isolationist sentiment.

By November 1939, FDR convinced Congress to repeal certain aspects of the Neutrality Acts, but the legislature still insisted that all transfer of matériel to the Allies be on a cash-and-carry basis and that absolutely no credits be granted to Britain or France. After Hitler took western Poland and began shifting divisions to the French border, Roosevelt confided his deep concern to the journalist William Allen White. "What worries me," the president stated, "is that public opinion over here is patting itself on the back every morning and thanking God for the Atlantic Ocean (and the Pacific)." Declaring that technology made the oceans a less secure barrier than in the past, Roosevelt expressed his quandary and his proposed way forward, writing, "Therefore . . . my problem is to get the American people to think of conceivable consequences without scaring the American people into thinking they are going to be dragged into this war." FDR was walking a tightrope. At the very least, he knew by late 1939 that Hitler must be defeated and that US support for the Allies would be essential to that end, and he may even have realized American entry into the war would eventually be necessary. Still, he couldn't admit all this publicly.

When, after a brief lull dubbed the Phony War in Europe, Hitler struck westward in May 1940 and shattered the British and French defenders in just six weeks, matters became ever more urgent for Roosevelt. France would soon surrender, while the British army barely escaped the beaches of Dunkirk in France. The British, though relieved by the alterations to the Neutrality Acts, still resented American caution and paucity of support. America's Anglo friends feared that the United States would resist war almost to the last Briton and then intervene only at the final moment; as such, a frequently heard complaint among British officials was "God protect us from a German victory and an American peace." Still, the fall of France had again changed the war's calculus and convinced Roosevelt that Britain must endure. He would spend the next eighteen months redoubling efforts, legal and otherwise, to provide Britain's new prime minister, Winston Churchill, with everything he needed to keep his country afloat. It was the beginning of a robust and historic relationship.

Churchill had an American mother and personified Anglo-

American unity. Furthermore, he knew the limitations of British arms and realized his nation's destiny lay with the United States — with American support and, eventually, American intervention. He would work hard to cultivate the strongest of relationships with FDR via letter, telegraph, and telephone. Roosevelt, for his part, decided privately that the new national emergency required continuity of executive leadership. Justifying his decision as a matter of duty rather than ambition, Roosevelt permitted his political allies to arrange a "spontaneous" demonstration in favor of nominating him for an unprecedented third term as president. Simultaneously, FDR took unprecedented steps to win public support for the Allies, using the FBI to monitor "subversive" groups through illegal wiretaps and to secure information about isolationist groups and leaders. Still, while working behind the scenes to move the nation closer to war, Roosevelt regularly proclaimed, disingenuously, on the campaign trail that "I have said this before, but I shall say it again and again. Your boys are not going to be sent into any foreign wars." In just over a year millions of Americans would be sent to fight in Europe and the Pacific. In November 1940, Roosevelt won another convincing political victory and a third term.

The first order of business was to send to Britain fifty World War I–era destroyers that Churchill had requested. Sensing he would lack the necessary support in Congress, Roosevelt slyly — some have argued illegally — proceeded by executive order. First he had the nation's top military leaders declare the ships obsolete, then unilaterally used his powers as commander in chief to dispatch the destroyers across the Atlantic. The next issue was finance. In December 1940, with the Nazi air force bombing London, Britain's ambassador carried a message to the United States that came straight from Churchill. "Britain's broke. It's your money we want," he stated, adding that "the moment approaches when we shall no longer be able to pay cash for shipping and other supplies." Knowing the United States would be in dire straits if Britain were to fold, Roosevelt enunciated a new doctrine that would bear his name. In a stark speech he portrayed a world divided between good and evil and spoke of "an emergency as serious as war itself," calling on the United States to become "the great arsenal of democracy."

To do so meant further alteration of the Neutrality Acts and a new lend-lease bill to overcome the cash-and-carry provisions still on the books in Congress. The theory was that the United States would provide arms and vehicles to the British — and after Hitler's eastward invasion, the Russians too — under the ludicrous pretense that the supplies would be returned after the war. Some sarcastically asked, "How does one return used bullets?" At the time, FDR's earthy analogy was that of lending a neighbor your hose to put out a fire in his house. Clearly lend-lease constituted far more than that. This time Roosevelt knew he had to go through Congress, and though his isolationist opposition mounted one last fervent counterattack, the president got his bill passed by a largely partisan majority. On one point the isolationists were right: Lend-lease was a major step toward war and it shed any lingering pretense of US neutrality.

The anti-interventionists were essentially correct in their prediction that arms shipments to the Allies would lead to American entry into the war. Even before lend-lease, Roosevelt was taking a number of secretive steps to coordinate with the British. He had already authorized a top-secret joint planning exercise between American and British military leaders to coordinate strategy in a future wartime alliance. Other executive orders — without congressional sanction — extended the US naval defense perimeter eastward and authorized naval vessels to patrol the area. FDR then sent soldiers and marines to occupy Greenland and Iceland to deny these islands to the Nazis. By June 1941 the US defense perimeter extended deep into the North Atlantic. Exactly what the isolationists had feared — a clash between German submarines and American shipping — now seemed inevitable, just as it had in 1917.

Roosevelt worked hard to sell his interventionist and increasingly bellicose policies to a still somewhat skeptical public. In one radio fireside chat, the president even divulged the supposed existence of a Nazi map — later proved to be bogus — showing a plan by Hitler to seize Latin America. That he needed to so motivate the public remained obvious when, later in 1941, the extension of the first peace-time draft in American history passed Congress by only one vote.

Churchill may have declared, in the wake of lend-lease, "Give us the tools, and we will finish the job," but in reality the prime minister always expected an eventual US intervention in the war. Furthermore, though the lend-lease bill passed Congress, it included a restrictive clause that "[n]othing in this Act shall be construed to permit . . . the convoying of vessels by naval vessels of the United States." In other words, no armed escorts, no potential for armed naval conflict in the North Atlantic. Astonishingly, just as Roosevelt was publicly denying even considering naval escorts, he secretly advised the military that "the Navy should be prepared to convoy shipping in the Atlantic to England." By mid-1941, despite the president's initial proclamations to the contrary, the US Navy would engage in an undeclared shooting war with German subs. FDR would argue that tactical necessity demanded this course of action. After all, the Nazis were sinking British ships five times faster than the vessels could be replaced. Germany seemed capable of starving the Brits of supplies and thereby winning the war.

Nevertheless, what transpired in the North Atlantic was remarkable and more than a little disturbing. Without congressional authoriza-tion, Roosevelt had armed naval vessels track German subs and call in their positions to British ships and aircraft; eventually the US vessels were ordered to "shoot on sight." By year's end American sailors were killing and dying in a naval shooting war. One proof of Roosevelt's clandestine — if not illegal — intentions was his advice to the British not to announce the change of US naval policy in favor of convoys. He told Churchill that "it is important for domestic political reasons . . . that this action be taken by us unilaterally. . . . I believe it advisable that when this new policy is adopted here no statement be issued on your end." Though some knowledge of the undeclared naval war would eventually come to public attention — especially after the US Navy suffered casualties — it is notable that just two men, Churchill and Roosevelt, were coordinating an extralegal war on the high seas with-out US congressional authorization. Without a doubt, future American presidents would claim equal right to unilaterally deploy US military personnel, though that eventuality could not yet be foreseen.

In one last classified mission, kept secret even from the First Lady, Roosevelt and Churchill met secretly on twin warships in Placentia Bay off the coast of Newfoundland. For three days these two unofficial allies hashed out future wartime coordination and even the contours of a postwar world. The resulting document, known as the Atlantic Charter, assumed victory in a war the United States had not even entered. The executive presumptuousness of both the meeting and the document was truly unprecedented in the annals of American foreign policy. By the fall of 1941 the United States — at least its naval arm — was at war in the Atlantic. On September 11, FDR publicly declared, "From now on, if German or Italian vessels of war enter our waters . . . they do so at their own peril." It was obvious to any serious observer that the United States and Germany would soon be fully at war. However, to the surprise of many Americans, the impetus for formal declarations would occur on the other side of the world, at Pearl Harbor, Hawaii.

Plunging Toward War: The View from Japan (1921–41)

At the end of 1941, the United States and Japan — two nations that did not want war, at least with each other — would lock in monumental conflict. Japan had been a major regional power for nearly a century, having rapidly industrialized in the late nineteenth century and decisively beaten the Russians in the 1904–05 Russo-Japanese War, the first time ever that a Western great power had been defeated by an Asian enemy. However, despite Japan's naval and battlefield victories, the United States — with President Theodore Roosevelt as lead negotiator — had mediated a peace that denied the Japanese most of their land conquests in Northeast Asia. Then, even after Japan allied with Britain in World War I, none of the major participants at the Versailles Peace Conference, including US president Wilson, would acquiesce to a racial equality clause in the treaty. The final straw of racial frustration came with the United States' 1924 National Origins Act, which cut off all immigration from Japan and denied a path to citizenship for many Japanese Americans. As a proud nation with a powerful military machine, and recently victorious in two consecutive wars, Japan resented the second-class status relegated to it by haughty European imperialists. Many Japanese military men felt that these colonial Western nations had set the rules of the game, long benefited from them, and then changed the rules when the newly resurgent Japanese sought to play.

Throughout the 1920s and '30s, increasingly militarized Japanese regimes sought to right perceived past wrongs and carve out an "Asia for the Asians," which meant, in practice, Asia for the Japanese. The primary target was China. After Japan seized Manchuria in 1931, few Western countries expressed more than passing concern. Thus emboldened, the Japanese army next invaded China proper in 1937 and seized much of that country's eastern coast. The Japanese were themselves prejudiced against their fellow Asians and fought a war of terror in China, executing perhaps three hundred thousand civilians in the infamous Rape of Nanking. Despite moral blandishments from Washington — and with Europe fully focused on Hitler's Germany — Roosevelt didn't even invoke the Neutrality Acts. Realizing that the cash-and-carry provisions in the legislation would benefit the Japanese over the cash-poor and disorganized Chinese, FDR avoided that through the strained justification that at that point neither side in the Japanese–Chinese conflict had formally declared war. Though the United States was unlikely to sell arms to the Japanese aggressors, at least overtly, invoking the cash-and-carry provisions of the latest Neutrality Act would have opened that possibility.

Japanese military aggression relied on a vibrant trade with the United States throughout the late 1930s. Even after a Japanese warplane sank the USS *Panay* in broad daylight on the Yangtze River, killing two American sailors and wounding dozens (for which Tokyo did apologize and pay reparations), Roosevelt did not cut off trade. Ironically, due to a dearth of natural resources, the Japanese war machine could run only with ample supplies of American scrap iron and petroleum. In August 1937, at a time when the United States was continuing to provide vital war matériel to the Japanese, *The Washington Post* ran

the headline AMERICAN SCRAP IRON PLAYS GRIM ROLE IN FAR EAST-
ERN WAR.

It was clear by 1940 that Japan was bogged down in an indefinite land war in China and that, despite its early successes, victory
remained a distant prospect. Furthermore, to perpetuate the war,
Japan was highly dependent on certain foreign raw materials, especially oil, 80 percent of which it received from the United States.
This situation seemed to grant extraordinary leverage — in the
form of sanctions — to Washington, but it was a dangerous game
to play with a desperate adversary. As early as the autumn of 1939,
US ambassador Joseph Grew warned the president that "[i]f we
cut off Japanese supplies of oil . . . [Japan] will in all probability
send her fleets down to take the Dutch East Indies," a region rich in
rubber and petroleum. Secretary of State Cordell Hull agreed with
the warning against provoking Japan, arguing that the United States
had already secretly committed to Britain that if America went to
war, Washington would pursue a "Germany First" strategy. Hull,
and senior military leaders, thus argued that armed confrontation
with Japan would "be the wrong war, with the wrong enemy, in the
wrong place, at the wrong time."

Indeed, the United States was only beginning its own rearmament
and had neither the capacity nor the strategic desire for a two-front
war. The plan, in the increasingly likely case of war, was to destroy
Hitler's forces and then, if necessary, confront Imperial Japan. But
it was not to be. The United States had long been a Pacific power,
especially after the 1898 seizure of the Philippine Islands, which US
military planners now considered indefensible. Despite that assessment about the Philippines, United States concern about Japanese
aggression was great enough to prompt Washington to try sanctions
against Tokyo. The result was predictable: both sides sped toward war
through misunderstandings, misreading each other's intentions, and
inaccurately assessing ability to pressure the other party.

In the fall of 1940, after Japan occupied northern French Indochina,
the hawks in FDR's cabinet — Treasury Secretary Henry Morgenthau
and War Secretary Henry Stimson — argued that full-fledged sanc-

tions would force Japan to curtail its aggression. Over the next twelve months the United States would ratchet up sanctions (which have a poor historical track record), first on aviation gasoline, then on scrap iron, and, finally, on oil and most other commodities. Despite dozens of diplomatic engagements between the Japanese ambassador and top US officials, the embargo on oil, especially, placed the two countries on a collision course.

Tokyo and Washington were now running on different clocks. The United States hoped to stave off war with Japan while checking its adversary's most blatant aggression. The Japanese, on the other hand, had only an eighteen-month oil reserve and calculated, based on US rearmament schedules, that it would have only two years' worth of naval superiority in the Pacific. As such, Tokyo had determined — unless Washington lifted the sanctions — to go for broke and pursue a two-pronged attack, on resource-rich Southeast Asia (including the Philippines) and on the main US fleet at Pearl Harbor. The plan was ambitious and ill advised, but not insane. The Japanese hoped to shock the United States into early negotiations by sinking much of America's Pacific navy, an act that would buy Tokyo the time and resources to bring the China war to a successful conclusion. Even the most bellicose Japanese planners realized that an all-out, protracted war with America would lead to strategic defeat. Still, Japan's leaders felt cornered and desperate, so they risked it all.

By late November, FDR and his cabinet knew that war with Japan, though undesired, was likely. Secretary Stimson wrote in his diary that Roosevelt said at a meeting that Japan was likely to soon launch an attack against the United States without warning. "The question," Stimson recounted, "was how we should maneuver [Japan] into the position of firing the first shot without allowing too much danger to ourselves." American code breakers had some forewarning that a Japanese attack was likely but knew neither the time nor the location of the strike. Such statements, information, and newly unclassified documents have created a veritable industry of conspiracy-theory peddlers who — much like the 9/11 "truthers" — claim that Roosevelt had prior knowledge of the Pearl Harbor attack and allowed more than two thousand sailors to die so he could finally bring his unwilling nation into war.

No smoking gun has been, or is likely to be, found. It stretches the imagination to think a sitting US president would allow thousands of sailors and five of the nation's battleships to be lost when a much less costly provocation for war would have done just fine. The conspiracy theorists also ignore the skill of an enemy that executed a well-planned assault. And these charges turn a blind eye to numerous American intelligence failures that led to the disaster. The main American failure, though, was what historian George Herring has called a "failure of imagination." US planners knew an attack was imminent but assumed it would fall in Southeast Asia or in the Philippines (where one eventually would) and underestimated the capacity of the Japanese military to deliver such an audacious blow to Hawaii. At a fundamental level, the most likely explanation for the onset of World War II is this: Having learned in 1938 the dangers of appeasement, the United States spurned cautious expediency and backed a proud Japanese nation into what Tokyo saw as a choice between war or surrender. Japan chose war, and the rest was history.

———

On December 7, 1941, Japanese forces surprised the American Pacific Fleet at Pearl Harbor. In a stunning attack, they sank ships and caused numerous casualties. Four days later Hitler's Germany declared war on the United States. War had finally come to America. Given the machinations of FDR and his internationalist allies, and the perceived provocations against Imperial Japan, perhaps Pearl Harbor shouldn't have been so much of a surprise. Nonetheless, nothing would ever be the same. The United States would mobilize its extensive military might and help win a war across two oceans, becoming, after victory in this "good war," both an Atlantic and a Pacific superpower. It remains to be seen whether this, ultimately, was a net positive for the American republic.

Unfortunately, lost in the triumphalism of world war victory was much memory of the process of US entry into this war. It is, after all, astonishing, given the almost unanimous internationalism of the postwar era, to recall just how reticent about intervention most Americans remained as late as 1941. Also lost is a fair, and perhaps critical, accounting of FDR's secretive and unilateral actions in the years before America's entry. Furthermore, since the reputed lessons of the interwar era have led to a seemingly limitless expansion of US military might around the globe, perhaps there is no better time to contemplate the devious means by which this now canonized president led a great nation to war.

Roosevelt's road to war cleared the way for an unprecedented expansion of the powers of the presidency. His dubious, often illegal, executive measures formed the basis for an increasingly imperial presidency and today's national security state. Nazi Germany, almost all would now agree, had to be stopped. So, perhaps, did Imperial Japan. The cost to the American republic, though, would prove to be grave. Even "good wars," after all, have consequences.[22]

26

JUST HOW GOOD WAS THE "GOOD WAR"?

> For the past 50 years, the Allied war has been sanitized and romanticized almost beyond recognition by the sentimental, the loony patriotic, the ignorant, and the bloodthirsty.
>
> — Former US Army infantry lieutenant
> Paul Fussell, *Wartime: Understanding and Behavior in the Second World War* (1989)

The United States' role in the Second World War has been so mythologized that it is now difficult to parse out truth from fantasy. There even exists a certain nostalgia for the war years, despite all the death and destruction wrought by global combat. Whereas the cataclysm of World War II serves as a cautionary tale in much of Europe and Asia, it is remembered as a singularly triumphant event here in the United States. In fact, the war often serves as but a sequel to America's memorialized role in the twentieth century: as back-to-back world war champ and twice savior of Europe. The organic simplicity of this version suits the inherently American vision of its own exceptionalism in global affairs.

However, there is a significant difference between a *necessary* war — which it probably was — and a *good* war. In fact, *good war* might be a contradiction in terms. The bitter truth is that the United States, much as all the combatant nations, waged an extraordinarily brutal, dirty war in Europe and especially the Pacific. President Franklin Delano Roosevelt cut nasty deals and allied with some nefarious actors to get the job done and defeat Germany and Japan. In the process he and those very allies shattered the old world and made a new one. Whether that was ultimately a positive outcome remains to be seen. Nevertheless, only through separating the difficult realities of war from the comforting myths can we understand not only the burden of the past but also the world we currently inhabit.

For the United States a two-front war was by no means inevitable. Tough talk and crippling sanctions helped push Japan into a fight in the Pacific that probably could have been avoided. And though Roosevelt had been waging an undeclared naval war with Germany in the North Atlantic, Japan's 1941 attack on Pearl Harbor hardly guaranteed that a still-isolationism-prone American public would support war in Europe. This was awkward in light of Roosevelt and British prime minister Winston Churchill's secret policy of "Germany First" as a target in any future war. Lucky for them Germany's megalomaniacal Adolf Hitler spared them the trouble. Within days of Japan's surprise strike on Pearl Harbor, Germany and Italy foolishly declared war on the United States.

Hitler misread American intentions and its military potential. In the wake of Pearl Harbor he declared, "I don't see much future for the Americans. It's a decayed country. And they have their racial problem, and the problem of social inequalities. . . . American society is half Judaized, and the other half Negrefied. How can one expect a state like that to hold together — a country where everything is built on the dollar." While Hitler's analysis of American social problems may have been astute in some respects, he underestimated the very *power* of that American dollar. His foreign minister, Joachim von Ribbentrop, had a more clear-eyed assessment, warning the fuhrer: "We have just one year to cut off Russia from her American supplies. . . . If we don't succeed and the munitions potential of the United States joins up with the manpower potential of the Russians . . . we shall be able to win [the war] only with difficulty." Here Ribbentrop, up to a point, essentially predicted the near future and exact course of the conflict between Germany and its foes.

America's allies were overjoyed by the Pearl Harbor attack and the subsequent German declaration of war. Churchill, whose nation had declared war on Germany in 1939 and who had always pinned England's hopes on American intervention, remembered thinking when he heard of the Japanese attack: "So we had won after all. . . . Hitler's fate was sealed. Mussolini's fate was sealed. As for the Japanese, they would be ground to powder. . . . There was no more doubt about the end." That night, Churchill wrote later, he "slept the sleep of the saved and thankful." China's Chiang Kai-shek was described as being "so happy he sang an old opera aria and played 'Ave Maria' all day." He, too, foresaw his country's salvation. Still, there remained a war to actually fight.

Who (Really) Won World War II?

Ask the average American who won the Second World War and you can count on a ready answer: the US military, of course! Certainly the United States contributed mightily, but the truth is far less simple. By the end, more than sixty million people would die in the war, only about four hundred thousand of them American. Those figures alone point to the magnitude of the roles of nations other than the United States.

There were three fundamental determinants of Allied victory: time, men, and matériel. A longer war favored the Allies because of their manpower and economic potential. Both Germany and Japan pinned their hopes on a short war. But it was British and, even more so, *Russian* men who provided that time for what Britain's Lord Beaverbrook called "the immense possibilities of American industry." In the second half of 1941 alone, Russia had suffered three million casualties, and it would eventually sacrifice some thirty million military and civilian lives in the epic struggle with Nazi Germany. Eight out of ten Germans killed in the war fell on the Eastern Front.

This is not to downplay the role of American might in the war's outcome. As for matériel, the US capacity for mobilization was uncanny. The national income of the United States, even in the midst of the Great Depression, was nearly double the *combined* incomes of Germany, Italy, and Japan. Still, make no mistake, Russian sacrifice and Russian manpower were the decisive factors in Allied victory. That, of course, is a discomfiting fact for most Americans, especially because World War II was so quickly followed by the Cold War between the Soviet Union and the United States. But this doesn't make it any less true. Indeed, a broad-stroke conclusion would be that Russian, and to some extent British, *men* bought the necessary *time* for American *matériel* to overwhelm the mismatched Axis Powers. Such an analysis is far less rewarding for American mythmakers.

The United States was actually rather fortunate. Thanks to timing — it entered the war late — and geography, the United States could choose to fight a war of equipment and machines rather than men. This route would cost the least in terms of American lives and also had the ancillary benefit of revitalizing the Depression-era economy and positioning the United States for future global leadership. All this was possible thanks to the Atlantic and Pacific Oceans and the resultant fact that the US homeland, almost alone among combatant nations, was untouched by the war itself.

US military planning reflected these fortunate realities. Prior to the Pearl Harbor attack, Army Chief of Staff general George Marshall assumed that Russia would fall and therefore victory in Europe would require some 215 American infantry divisions. However, as the war evolved — and especially after Germany's defeat in Russia at the pivotal Battle of Stalingrad — it became apparent that the Soviets would survive. In response, the US military truncated its mobilization to just ninety divisions. This "arsenal of democracy" strategy guaranteed that American industry would combine with Russian bloodshed to win the war. Thus, even though the United States did raise the largest army in its own history, that force remained smaller than Germany's and less than half the size of the Soviet military.

While the untouched American economy expanded throughout the war, the Russian people faced economic contraction and diminishing quality of life in their titanic ground struggle with the Nazis. Due to the brutal German invasion, Soviet food supplies were cut by two-thirds, millions slid into destitution, and many starved to death. In the United States, by contrast, personal wealth grew and the American economy proved capable of producing ample amounts of guns *and* butter. Despite the undoubted courage of US service members in combat, the average American's chance of dying in battle was only one in a hundred, one-tenth the rate of the American Civil War. Furthermore, as a proportion of the total, US military casualties were lower than among any of the other major belligerents in World War II.

By way of comparison, fewer Americans were killed than Hungarians, Romanians, or Koreans. Twice as many Yugoslavians died as Americans, ten times as many Poles, and fifty times as many Russians. This reality was not lost on Joseph Stalin and the often frustrated Russians. Even at its height, only 10 percent of US lend-lease aid went to the Soviets, and, one Russian complained during the war: "We've lost millions of people, and they [Americans] want us to crawl on our knees because they send us Spam." Even Churchill recognized the Russian point of view in early 1943 when he declared that "in April, May and June, not a single American or British soldier will be killing a single German or Italian soldier while the Russians are chasing 185 divisions around." When the British prime minister spoke those words only eight US divisions were in the entire European theater. Given this disparity, one understands Stalin's frustration and his demand for the Western Allies to open a second front in France. Indeed, this concern animated much of the tension in the troubled alliance throughout the war.

The Politics of Alliance: The United States, Britain, and the Soviet Union

The Big Three powers — Britain, the Soviet Union, and the United States — forged what was ultimately an alliance of convenience and necessity, rather than ideology. For all the lip service paid to the liberal principles of the Atlantic Charter, the reality is that a flawed American democracy had little choice but to partner with an unabashed maritime empire (Britain) and a vast communist land empire (the Soviet Union) to fight international fascism. Such an alliance would be messy from the start.

The dynamics of the alliance were ultimately based on the different goals and relative positions of each partner. The United States was distant from the battlefields and endowed with extraordinary economic potential. It sought supremacy in the Pacific, relative stability and balance in Europe, and global economic dominance in the postwar world. Britain hoped merely to survive and then to salvage its still-substantial global empire. The British wanted to maintain clout in Europe and ensure that no one continental power — whether Germany or the Soviet Union — dominated the region. Britain's diminishing manpower and economic output meant that it required help from its larger partners. Stalin engaged in an existential fight with the Nazis and initially feared his nation's utter destruction. Thus the Soviet Union had little choice but to work with — and receive aid from — the Western capitalist powers. Nevertheless, the Soviets still adhered to a revolutionary ideology of communist expansion and, fearing future invasion from the West, hoped to create a friendly buffer zone of protection in Eastern Europe. This directly collided with the wish of the Western democracies to establish capitalist republics in the same region. Clearly the Allied positions and desires were often contradictory and affected the strategies of each power.

The defining issue — and point of contention — in the alliance was the Soviet demand for Britain and America to swiftly open a second front in Western Europe in order to take German pressure off the Russian heartland. This demand ran into limits of time — it would take the US military quite a while to fully mobilize — and British hesitancy. Churchill remembered well the slaughter of trench warfare in the Great War and the embarrassment of the British army's recent defeat in France and evacuation from Dunkirk. The British thus preferred peripheral actions that secured their empire and played to their strengths at sea and in the air. The Americans, however, were willing and eager to quickly strike the heart of Germany to end the war, but they faced the reality that British manpower would form the bulk of troop strength in Europe for at least one or two years as Washington raised its army. Thus, throughout the war, a pattern repeated whereby the Western Allies delayed launching a second front in France and the Soviets expressed increasing frustration and, ultimately, mistrust of their capitalist partners.

In early 1943 some leaders of the Allied Powers met in Casablanca. With the Soviet Union beset with fighting, Stalin declined to attend. At that conference Churchill maintained the leverage required to win the day. He convinced Roosevelt to first invade North Africa and take pressure off the British army, then grapple with German general Erwin Rommel in Egypt. Without a fully mobilized force, Roosevelt had limited means to reassure the Soviet Union that a true second front was forthcoming. So he did his best, announcing a doctrine that called for nothing less than the "unconditional surrender" of Germany and Japan. This strategic straitjacket would eventually have a significant effect on the war's outcome but did little to ease Stalin's legitimate concerns. Roosevelt may have had little choice at the Casablanca conference but to defer to Churchill's peripheral Mediterranean strategy, but American strategists had an additional fear. If the Soviets truly turned the tide of battle in the east — which seemed probable by 1943 — before the Western Allies invaded France, might the Russians not dominate all of the European continent?

US secretary of war Henry Stimson recognized this at an early point, criticizing Churchill and the British plan. In May 1943, Stimson declared, "The British are trying to arrange this matter so that the British and Americans hold the leg for Stalin to kill the deer and I think that will be a dangerous business for us at the end of the war. Stalin won't have much of an opinion [of that policy] and we will not be able to share much of the postwar world with him." Furthermore, US generals — imbued with the unique "American way of war" replete with overwhelming, swift offensives — saw a massive invasion of France as the only logical way to win the war and save the continent. Besides, *any* victory that kept American casualties relatively low required Russian survival. As General Dwight Eisenhower, senior US commander in Europe, emphasized in pushing for a rapid invasion of France, "We should not forget that the prize we seek is to keep 8,000,000 Russians in the war."

As the British and Americans scuffled over the timing for an invasion of France, the date for a true second front was continually delayed. In May 1943, Roosevelt was still assuring Stalin that he "expected the formation of a second front this year," and even added that to facilitate this, American lend-lease supplies to the Soviet Union would be cut by 60 percent. Of course, the reality was that no second front in France was forthcoming until at least spring 1944 so long as the British kept insisting on campaigns in Africa and the Mediterranean and in the air. British hesitancy and intransigence frustrated the American military chiefs to no end, and they recommended to Roosevelt in July 1943 that if the Brits didn't relent "we should turn to the Pacific and strike decisively against Japan; in other words, assume a defensive attitude against Germany." Such a move, in fact, might have been popular with an American populace that was, after the "sneak attack" on Pearl Harbor, angrier with Japan than with Germany.

Nonetheless, Roosevelt refused to back away from the "Germany First" strategy and overrode his military chiefs. Politics played a role here, as they often did for FDR. American mobilization took time, and the president felt he needed to unleash some sort of strike on Germany before the midterm elections. An all-out invasion of France wasn't yet possible, so Roosevelt agreed to Churchill's proposed lesser invasion in North Africa, pleading with General Marshall, "Please, make it before election day." Eisenhower, who would lead the attack, thought the African diversion "strategically unsound" and concluded that it would "have no effect on the 1942 campaign in Russia." If FDR's generals were unhappy, Stalin was livid. The Soviet leader, with good reason, doubted the sincerity and motives of the Western Allies and resented bearing the full brunt of the German army's offensives. At the first meeting of the Big Three leaders, in Tehran, Iran, in November 1943, Stalin reminded Churchill of the millions of casualties already sustained by the Red Army. Indeed, later historians would see this period as sowing the seeds for a divided, suspicious, Cold War world that would emerge soon after the German surrender.

Amid the British hesitancy about an invasion of France, the Americans felt a greater sense of urgency. The United States, unlike Britain, was truly engaged in a two-front war and needed Soviet assistance in the Pacific to avoid massive casualties in the already bloody campaign against Japan. Stalin knew this, and months before the Tehran Conference he had reminded Roosevelt that "in the Far East . . . the USSR is not in a state of war." If the Americans wanted future Russian intervention in the Pacific, Stalin made it clear that FDR had to push the British along and deliver a second front soon.

That second front was also necessary, many American strategists knew, if the United States and Britain were to maintain postwar influence on the continent. One State Department assessment at the time warned, "If Germany collapses before the democracies have been able to make an important military contribution on the continent . . . the peoples of Europe will with reason believe that the war was won by the Russians alone . . . so that it will be difficult for Great Britain and the United States to oppose successfully any line of policy which the Kremlin may choose."

With both these concerns in mind, Roosevelt decided on a relatively sanguine approach to Stalin. Given the strength of the Soviet army, he may not have had much choice. Nevertheless, FDR appeared to acquiesce to Stalin's postwar influence in Eastern Europe, and again played politics in his negotiations at the Tehran Conference. After agreeing to Soviet dominance in the Baltic states, the future of Poland came up. Here, according to official minutes from the conference, Roosevelt explained to Stalin that "there were in the United States from six to seven million Americans of Polish extraction, and, as a practical man, he did not wish to lose their vote." Therefore, while accepting a Soviet sphere of influence in the region, Roosevelt asked Stalin to delay any decision on Polish frontiers and to make some "public declaration in regard to future elections in Eastern Europe." Given that the Second World War erupted over the issue of Polish sovereignty, this was a remarkable concession. Then again, while the United States had approximately ten divisions in Europe at the time, Stalin had hundreds more, some of them even then on the very frontier of Poland. It's unclear how the Western Allies could have stopped him.

In another remarkable exchange, Roosevelt appeared to placate Stalin, much to the consternation of Churchill. When, over dinner, Stalin proposed that fifty thouand German military officers be "physically liquidated" after the war, Churchill rose to his feet and declared, "I will not be party to any butchery in cold blood!" Roosevelt, seeking to lighten the mood, stated, "I have a compromise to propose. Not fifty thousand, but only forty-nine thousand should be shot." Churchill was furious, but such was the nature, and paradox, of the alliance. In the end the leaders left Tehran after agreeing to the opening of a second front in France by May 1944 and for a Soviet entrance into the Pacific war soon after the defeat of Germany.

When next the three leaders met, in Yalta, in February 1945, Germany was on the verge of defeat and Russian troops had fought their way to the outskirts of Berlin. Stalin's divisions dominated Eastern Europe by way of physical presence, and the United States was engaged in an increasingly bloody "island-hopping" campaign in the Pacific. The Japanese showed no sign of relenting and were fighting to almost the last man in every battle. Soviet assistance was thought necessary to shorten the Pacific war. At Yalta the Allies discussed the membership rules for the new United Nations, the partition of Germany, the fate of Eastern Europe, and Soviet participation in the war with Japan.

Here again, Roosevelt appeared to appease Stalin regarding Poland and all of Eastern Europe. The Russian leader made clear that Poland "was a question of both honor and security," even "one of life and death" for the Soviet Union. Roosevelt replied with a personal note that assured Stalin "the United States will never lend its support in any way to any provisional government in Poland that would be inimical to your interests." Such a statement appeared to give Stalin a free hand in Eastern Europe, and many later historians would conclude that FDR — perhaps due to his increasingly feeble health — had sold out to Stalin.

The reality was much more nuanced. Roosevelt knew he held the weak hand in Europe. The Red Army already occupied half the continent, and unless FDR was willing to mobilize a few hundred more divisions and order Eisenhower to fight his way to Poland, there was little the president could do to alter the facts on the ground. When the presidential chief of staff, Admiral William Leahy, demurred about the implications of Roosevelt's note, FDR said, "I know, Bill — I know it. But it's the best I can do for Poland at this time." Soon after, he told another associate that, regarding Yalta, "I didn't say the result was good. I said it was the best I could do." And it probably was, though that was certainly little consolation to Poles.

In exchange Stalin promised, again, to declare war on Japan. Roosevelt saw this as the real prize to be gained at Yalta. He told Stalin that he "hoped that it would not be necessary actually to invade the Japanese islands," if the Soviets attacked in Manchuria, made Siberian air bases available for US bombing of Japan's cities, and otherwise demonstrated the essential hopelessness of Tokyo's cause. This was genuinely vital. The American Joint Chiefs of Staff estimated that a Soviet intervention could shorten the Pacific war by a year or more and thus save many American lives. Besides, a shrewd FDR also hoped that focusing Soviet military strength eastward might actually loosen Stalin's grip on Eastern Europe.

In the final assessment, the Big Three ultimately managed a difficult alliance — built on necessity rather than affinity — to achieve the defeat of both Germany and Japan. This was no small task. The cost of victory was a divided Europe — physically and ideologically. FDR and Churchill weren't feeble but they were rather realistic in their negotiations with Stalin. Perhaps Roosevelt, ever the charmer and the schemer, had something in mind for future policy pressure on the Soviets, but, with his death just two months after the Yalta Conference, we'll never know.

Fighting a World War: Paradox and Contradiction

[The bombing] is inhuman barbarism that has profoundly shocked the conscience of humanity.

> — President Franklin Roosevelt describing
> the German bombing of Rotterdam, Holland,
> in which 880 civilians were killed (1940)

There are no innocent civilians. It is their government and you are fighting a people, you are not trying to fight an armed force anymore. So it doesn't bother me so much to be killing the so-called innocent bystanders.

> — General Curtis LeMay, US Army Air Corps commander
> in the Pacific theater after American planes killed
> approximately 90,000 civilians in Tokyo (1945)

The Second World War surpassed even World War I in its barbarity. In this second global conflict civilians would bear the brunt of the fighting, a significant change from the First World War. As the conflict rolled along, the combatant countries increased in desperation and brutality. This was not limited to the Axis Powers or the communist Soviet dictatorship. To win the war at the least cost in their own people's lives, the Western democracies would continually dial up the cruelty of their tactics and shift the suffering onto enemy civilians. That, perhaps, was the major contradiction of the Anglo-American war effort. Two ostensible democracies agreed in principle to the humanitarian tenets of the Atlantic Charter, then waged a terror war (especially from the sky) on civilians.

There were other paradoxes and realities that deflated many popular myths about America's role in the war. For example, though most Americans remember World War II as a time of extreme patriotism and selflessness, in truth the populace did not race as one to the recruiting stations. A strong strain of isolationism remained even after the attack on Pearl Harbor. Indeed, all but a few of the most anti-interventionist congressmen were reelected in November 1942. Draft deferments were common and coveted from the start. Because married men were exempted from the first draft calls, some 40 percent of American twenty-one-year-olds became betrothed within six weeks! The exemption was later ended, and eventually some 18 percent of families would send a son to the military. Nevertheless, this was a fraction of the commitment seen in other belligerent nations.

The draft itself was controversial and — as in most large, hasty bureaucracies — inefficient and often unfair. The typical GI who liberated Western Europe and the Pacific was twenty-six years old, five feet eight inches tall, and 144 pounds. He had, on average, completed just one year of high school. He took a pre-induction classification test that determined which jobs he was qualified for. Paradoxically, those troopers who were larger, stronger, and smarter usually ended up in the army service forces and army air forces. Thus the typical infantryman who carried a heavy pack and did the bulk of the fighting was shorter and weighed less than his peers in the rear. All told, the US Army's "tail-to-teeth" ratio — the relative number of support to combat troopers — was two to one, the highest of any army in the war. Proportionally far fewer men in the US Army did the fighting than in Allied or enemy armies.

When US soldiers did fight — at least in Europe — they were often outmatched by the Germans and equipped with gear that was inferior. Nothing in the American armored arsenal could stand toe-to-toe with the feared Panther and Tiger tanks of the enemy. What the Americans did have was numbers. They made up for inferior quality with mass production of mechanized vehicles. Still, the rule of thumb was that it took five or more American Sherman tanks to overcome a Panther or Tiger tank. German troops were also more battle hardened and usually more effective in early combat meetings between the two forces. This defies the myth of American superiority and single-handed victory in the war. After all, in late 1944, when the US Army nearly ran out of infantry replacement troops, the Soviets deployed exponentially more divisions' worth of foot soldiers against the Germans.

The Western democracies also fought a war with such brutality that it contradicted their own principles. This, too, is often forgotten. Strategic air bombing of German and sometimes French cities was inaccurate and, beyond the slaughter on the ground, notoriously dangerous for the flight crews. That's why, early on, the British shifted to nighttime "area bombing" over more hazardous but somewhat more accurate daytime bombing. At first, the US Army Air Corps recoiled at these tactics, with one senior US officer deploring "British baby killing schemes" that "would be a blot on the history of the air forces of the [allied] US." However, as the realities of the danger and inaccuracy sank in, the Americans, though sticking to daylight bombing, would succumb to the pressure to bomb civilians. By 1944–45 the Army Air Corps was staging massive raids on major cities. A single attack on Berlin killed twenty-five thousand civilians. Ten days later a combined Anglo-American assault unleashed a firestorm in Dresden that killed thirty-five thousand. All told, the British and American air forces killed many hundreds of thousands of German civilians from the air. The fiction that the targets were "strategic," "military," or "industrial" didn't stand up under close scrutiny.

Did the bombing *work*, though? Airpower enthusiasts are certain that it did and does — that bombing alone can end a war. Nevertheless, in 208 separate postwar studies conducted by the US Strategic Bombing Survey, that military-commissioned organization concluded that bombing had "contributed significantly" but had not by itself been decisive. Even under the heaviest bombing, German economic output tripled between 1941 and 1944, and while the attacks certainly hurt local morale they had "markedly less effect on behavior." In other words, factory employees kept going to work, soldiers kept fighting, and German industrial output actually increased during the war.

The bombing of Japan was even more brutal and more overtly targeted at civilians. When General Curtis LeMay took over the 21st Bomber Command in January 1945, he unleashed a literal firestorm on Japan's mostly wooden cities. "I'll tell you what war is about," he once opined. "You've got to kill people, and when you've killed enough they stop fighting." In that spirit LeMay had his pilots practice and perfect firebombing techniques meant to purposely set off thermal hurricanes that killed by both heat and suffocation as the flames removed oxygen. On the single night of March 9–10, 1945, a massive raid in Japan killed ninety thousand men, women, and children — some boiled alive within the canals where they had sought refuge — and left a million people homeless. In the five months after that night, 43 percent of Japan's sixty-six largest cities was destroyed. About a million people died, 1.3 million were injured, and 8 million lost their homes.

Working as an analyst on LeMay's staff in those days was a young officer, Robert McNamara, who would be secretary of defense during the Vietnam War. His job was to carefully study and increase the efficiency of this mass murder. McNamara remembered that LeMay once admitted they probably would have been tried for war crimes had the United States lost the war. And when asked about this more than sixty years later, McNamara concluded that the general had been correct.

The European Theater: Distractions and a Second Front

America's war for Europe actually began in North Africa. There, in November 1942, General Eisenhower's army rushed ashore on the beaches of the Vichy (Nazi-collaborating) French colonies of Algeria and Morocco. Though US commanders and diplomats tried to convince the French troops guarding those beaches to lay down their arms, it came to pass — paradoxically — that in its first major ground combat in the European theater of operations (ETO), US troops killed *French* soldiers and died at French hands. After forty-eight hours and hundreds of deaths, the United States arranged a general cease-fire with the fascist-sympathizing Admiral François Darlan. An incensed Hitler immediately occupied the remainder of France and forced the Vichy government to "invite" German forces into Tunisia to check the American advance.

In early combat engagements with the Germans, Eisenhower's untested troops were regularly embarrassed by General Rommel's battle-hardened veterans. At Kasserine Pass, the first sizable engagement between US and German troops, the Americans were handily beaten. Nevertheless, by March 1943 assaults of Americans from the west and General Bernard Montgomery's British forces from the east converged to defeat the German-Italian army. The Allies captured some 250,000 Axis prisoners, but many of the best German divisions escaped to Italy. Meanwhile, as the Allies were making this early if feeble effort at a second front, the Soviets still were confronting more than two hundred Axis divisions in Russia.

Though the American military commanders wanted to strike next at France itself, the Brits — who still provided the majority of divisions in the ETO — convinced Roosevelt to target the island of Sicily, followed by the Italian mainland. The Americans insisted, however, that all new divisions sent to the ETO be diverted to Britain in preparation for the invasion of France. Thus the campaign in Italy — which the US commanders didn't want to fight in the first place — would have to proceed on a shoestring. The Germans sent just sixteen divisions to Italy, and that force, under the command of the brilliant field

Germany, 1945

marshal Albert Kesselring, used the peninsula's rugged terrain to tie down two Allied armies in an indecisive battle of attrition for nearly two years. As the historian David M. Kennedy strongly concluded, this was a campaign "whose costs were justified by no defensible military or political purpose," except, perhaps, to assuage Churchill's hesitancy about the France invasion and his career-long obsession with securing the Mediterranean Sea.

When the Allies hit the Italian mainland at Salerno, the US commander, General Mark Clark, unwisely chose to forgo the customary preliminary bombardment — hoping to exploit the element of surprise — and as a result a vicious German counterattack almost drove the Americans back into the sea. Only emergency naval gunfire support saved the beachhead. What followed was five months of grinding attritional warfare. Unable to make any significant northward progress, Clark requested another amphibious assault — which controversially delayed the France invasion again — on the beaches of Anzio, north of the main German defensive lines. Though little resistance was met on the shoreline, General John Lucas hesitated long enough for the Germans to mount another counterattack. Lucas's pathetic force was thus pinned down on a narrow beachhead for months, and the entire Italian campaign again ground to a halt. When, in the late spring, the Allied forces finally broke through the German defense, General Clark struck out for the political prize of Rome rather than cutting off the main German force. This allowed Kesselring to escape and set up a new series of defensive lines to the north. Then the whole process repeated itself for nearly a year.

Kesselring's small force held out until almost the end of the war. The needless sideshow in Italy cost 188,000 American and 123,000 British casualties. All the while, Kesselring held the two Allied armies at bay with fewer than twenty divisions, hardly any of which had been transferred from the Eastern Front. Stalin and the Soviets were enraged by the Allied foray into Italy, especially when the Salerno and Anzio landings further delayed the cross-channel invasion of France. He wrote to Roosevelt that the latest delay "leaves the Soviet Army, which is fighting not only for its country, but also for its Allies, to do the job alone, almost single-handed." Stalin then hinted at how this frustration could presage later (Cold War–style) conflict, adding, "Need I speak of the dishearteningly negative impression that this fresh postponement of the second front . . . will produce in the Soviet Union — both among the people and in the army?" Given the quagmire in the Mediterranean, the Soviet leader had a point.

While the battles raged in North Africa and Italy, the Combined Bomber Offensive (CBO) — strategic bombing from the air — was the closest thing to a second front available in Northwestern Europe. This controversial campaign was both dangerous to airmen — casualty rates for bomber crews were among the highest in the war — and highly destructive to civilians. Nonetheless, both British and American air commanders hoped to prove that their service's contribution could win the war single-handedly. It was not to be so. What *did* occur was a massacre of German civilians. This shouldn't have been surprising. The Italian Giulio Douhet, the principal air war theorist of the 1920s, had long argued that in modern warfare civilian targets should be fair game. As he famously wrote, "The woman loading shells in a factory, the farmer growing wheat, the scientist experimenting in the laboratory" were targets as legitimate as "the soldier carrying his gun." Incidentally, this was the precise argument al-Qaida leader Osama bin Laden would make years later in justifying his 9/11 attacks on the US homeland.

Some of the devastation among civilians was inevitable, given the technological limitations of 1940s aircraft; military decisions growing out of those limitations greatly increased death on the ground. A British bomber command study in 1941 concluded that only one-third of bombers made it to within five miles of their targets. Thus in 1942 the British Royal Air Force (RAF) directed that bombers henceforth focus on targeting "the morale of the enemy civil population." The Brits euphemistically referred to this as "area bombing." It amounted to premeditated murder from the skies. At first the US Army Air Forces (USAAF) shunned the British approach, but soon the Americans were mimicking the RAF tactics. The war had changed the hearts of many leaders. Back in 1940, President Roosevelt may have been horrified by the German air attack on Rotterdam that killed some eight hundred civilians, and which he called "barbaric," but by 1943–44 the RAF and USAAF were sometimes killing thousands of civilians per day.

The airmen of the USAAF faced their own horrors. Accidents took nearly as many lives among American airmen as combat actions. In 1943 the USAAF lost 5 percent of its crewmen in each mission, casualties so appalling that two-thirds of American airmen that year did not survive their required quota of twenty-five missions. Despite this human cost, and despite the optimistic predictions of the airpower enthusiasts, strategic bombing alone could not substitute for a ground-level second front in France.

On June 6, 1944 — D-Day, nearly two years and seven months after the attack on Pearl Harbor — British and American troops rushed ashore on the beaches of Normandy, France. The invasion was coordinated with an even larger Russian offensive, Operation Bagration, which shattered many German divisions and caused 350,000 Axis casualties. Initially, at least, the Normandy invasion met with far less success. Though the Western Allies managed to get tens of thousands and then hundreds of thousands of troops ashore, it took more than a month to break out of the stalemate at the beachhead. Finally, in July–August 1944's Operation Cobra, a massive aerial bombardment followed by General George Patton's armored spearhead, the Anglo-American armies annihilated forty German divisions and inflicted 450,000 casualties. For a moment it looked as though the war would be over by Christmas. The Joint Intelligence Committee in London predicted that "organized resistance . . . is unlikely to continue beyond December 1, 1944, and . . . may end even sooner." It was not to be.

The Allies still had only one functioning French port available to them, and this slowed vital logistics. Fuel and food simply couldn't keep up with Patton and Montgomery's mechanized thrusts. In September 1944, Operation Market Garden, the brainchild of General Montgomery, kicked off with a three-division parachute assault to secure key bridges on the path to Germany. The attack stalled, and Montgomery's tanks couldn't reach the final bridge in time. The long-shot gamble hadn't worked. Market Garden cost thousands of Allied casualties and then petered out, leading to a winter stalemate. The Germans still had a lot of fight in them and held strong for two more months, inflicting twenty thousand American casualties at the indecisive Battle of the Huertgen Forest, which occurred along the Belgian-German border.

In December, Hitler launched one final mad offensive to divide the Allied armies and seize the vital port of Antwerp in Belgium. The Americans were initially pushed back, creating a "bulge" in the Allied lines. Then Hitler's gamble ground to a halt when the skies cleared and Allied planes could again pound the vulnerable Germans from the air. Even though the Battle of the Bulge came as a shock to the Allies and turned out to be the bloodiest single fight for the Americans in the ETO, Hitler had expended his last reserves and suffered a hundred thousand more casualties. By April the Soviets were fighting on the outskirts of Berlin, Eisenhower's troops had breached Germany's Western Wall, and American and Russian troops were linking hands along the River Elbe west of Berlin. In the first week of May, Hitler committed suicide and Germany surrendered. The date, May 8, would be forever known as Victory in Europe, or V-E, Day.

The Pacific Theater: War Without Mercy

The war in the Pacific wasn't supposed to occur at all. Containment and deterrence of the Japanese was supposed to delay, perhaps avoid, a war in the Pacific. "Germany First" was the strategy agreed upon by the British and American senior commanders well before the United States entered either theater of war. Nonetheless, in a calculated, if ill-advised, gamble, the militarists atop the Japanese government decided on an all-out surprise attack meant to destroy the American Pacific Fleet in the hope of forcing Washington into a peace settlement and economic concessions. The architect of the attack, Admiral Isoroku Yamamoto, knew the risks involved. He had studied at Harvard, later served as a naval attaché in Washington, and held a deep respect for America's vast industrial potential.

Yamamoto had, in the recent past, been a voice for moderation and argued against the surprise attack. He knew that Tokyo would have only a small window for victory and that Japan, if the war dragged on, would eventually be overwhelmed by the now roused American "sleeping giant." "If I am told to fight regardless of the consequences," Yamamoto had warned the Japanese prime minister, "I shall run wild for the first six months or a year, but I have utterly no confidence for the second or third year." How prescient the admiral would prove to be.

At first Yamamoto's gamut seemed to pay off. By 10:00 a.m. on December 7, 1941, the day of the Japanese attack, eighteen US ships, including eight battleships, had been sunk or heavily damaged, more than three hundred US aircraft destroyed or crippled, and more than twenty-three hundred sailors and soldiers killed. The Americans were caught by surprise, but — in a stroke of luck — none of the US Navy's aircraft carriers, which would prove more valuable than battleships in the coming war, were at Pearl Harbor that morning. All survived to fight another day.

Still, Yamamoto and the Japanese military did indeed "run wild" in the six months following Pearl Harbor. British, Dutch, and American possessions — Hong Kong, Guam, Wake Island, the East Indies, and Indochina — fell one after the other to the Japanese blitz. On February 15, 1942, in what is widely considered the worst defeat in British military history, a garrison of eighty-five thousand surrendered to a Japanese force barely half its size. The attack on the US contingent in the Philippines, commanded by the implacable, demagogic General Douglas MacArthur, had begun December 8, 1941, the day after the Pearl Harbor attack. Though MacArthur had been warned of the possibility of an imminent Japanese attack, he unforgivably allowed nearly his entire air force to be destroyed on the ground. Without an air corps and with the US Pacific Fleet crippled, the fate of the Philippines was sealed.

MacArthur had been a strong combat leader in World War I, but he gained a reputation as a shameless self-promoter. After the Japanese attack on the Philippines he was given the derisive nickname Dugout Doug, which implied he was making himself safe in his tunnel headquarters while his men were dying under the Japanese assault. He would visit only once with his soldiers during their fierce battle on the Bataan peninsula before Roosevelt ordered him to evacuate to Australia.

On March 12, MacArthur left General Jonathan Wainwright in command of the doomed garrison and left with his family and personal staff on a small patrol boat. In what seemed an obvious PR stunt and face-saving measure, Congress conferred the Medal of Honor on him. By May 6 roughly ten thousand American and sixty thousand Filipino soldiers had surrendered to the Japanese. Dwight Eisenhower, a former subordinate of MacArthur, was less than impressed with the senior general's performance. In his diary that night Ike wrote that "[the Philippine garrison] surrendered last night. Poor Wainwright! He did the fighting. . . . [but MacArthur] got such glory as the public could find in the operation. . . . General Mac's tirades to which . . . I so often listened in Manila, would now sound as silly to the public as they did to us. But he's a hero! Yah."

A tragedy followed. The Japanese army in the Philippines, itself undersupplied and malnourished, wasn't prepared to accept seventy thousand prisoners. Furthermore, in a clash of cultures, the Japanese — who subscribed to a Bushido code that some experts have described as "a range of mental attitudes that bordered on psychopathy" and "saw surrender as the ultimate dishonor" — brutalized the captives. In an eighty-mile forced march, the prisoners were denied water, often beaten, and sometimes bayoneted. Six hundred Americans and perhaps ten thousand Filipinos died on the Bataan Death March. Thousands more wouldn't survive the following four years of captivity in filthy camps.

The Americans and British had surely taken, in the words of General "Vinegar" Joe Stilwell, "one hell of a beating." Even so, as Yamamoto had feared, the tide quickly turned. When the Japanese fleet headed for tiny Midway Island, an American possession to the west of Pearl Harbor, to finish off the remaining US ships, the Americans — thanks to "Magic," their program for cracking the Japanese naval code — were ready. American fliers sank four of Japan's six carriers at the loss of only one US carrier, shifting the momentum of the entire Pacific war in a single engagement. From this point forward US industry would pump out carriers, submarines, cruisers, and aircraft at a rate exponentially higher than Japan's. Whereas the Japanese constructed only six additional large carriers throughout the war, the US fielded seventeen large, ten medium, and a stunning eighty-six escort carriers.

The Americans now went on the offensive, albeit slowly at first. Naval commanders preferred a drive straight across the Central Pacific, island-hopping from one Japanese garrison to the next, but MacArthur insisted on a campaign through the Southwest Pacific from Australia, to New Guinea, and finally to the Philippines — to which MacArthur had famously vowed to return. Roosevelt, the astute politician, split the difference in supplies and troops and decided on a less efficient two-track advance. Admiral Chester Nimitz and the marine corps would lead in the Central Pacific while MacArthur and the Army moved slowly toward the Philippines.

The first stop for Nimitz was the distant Solomon Islands. There, on the island of Tulagi, the marines received their first — but certainly not last — taste of fierce Japanese defensive tactics. Only 3 of Tulagi's 350 defenders surrendered. Others were incinerated when lit gasoline drums were thrown into their concealed caves. On nearby islands, only twenty of five hundred defenders surrendered. All told 115 US Marines died in these fights, establishing the approximately ten-to-one ratio of casualties that would prevail throughout the long Pacific war. Nevertheless, the Japanese still had some offensive potential and in the Battle of Savo Island inflicted the worst-ever defeat of the US Navy on the high seas. Nearly two thousand American sailors were killed or wounded. Still, the Japanese had failed to ward off the US invasion of the island Guadalcanal in the Solomon chain. Thus began one of the strangest campaigns of the Pacific war — perhaps the only such battle in which Americans were *defending* an island and did not enjoy total air and naval superiority. It was a long, tough campaign and stretched the morale and resources of the US soldiers and marines engaged.

The brutality and fanaticism of both sides were again on display. When American marines ambushed an attacking force, eight hundred Japanese died and only one surrendered. After some of the wounded tried to kill approaching American medics, the marines slaughtered every surviving Japanese soldier. By October 1942 the US garrison had been reinforced, expanding to some twenty-seven thousand; by year's end the number would be sixty thousand. The joint army/marine force could then take the offensive. Still, in four more months of bloody fighting the Americans suffered nearly two thousand more casualties. At that rate US casualties could grow to cataclysmic levels if every Japanese island garrison were assaulted. It was thus decided to "hop" the islands, bypassing most and securing only vital platforms for airfields and logistics hubs. Most of the other Japanese garrisons were left to rot, their supply lines to Tokyo severed.

In the Southwest Pacific, MacArthur first helped the Australians defend Papua, though the ever-charming general won few friends there when he described the more than six hundred Australian dead on that island as "extremely light casualties," indicating "no serious effort." MacArthur's own force suffered heavy casualties when he recklessly wasted troops to seize Buna and Gona, but it did, by December 1942, end the Japanese threat to Australia. In March 1943, MacArthur's air chief, General George Kenney, successfully organized his planes in a spectacular attack on a Japanese reinforcing convoy of ships. After the bombers sank the troop transports and a few destroyers, American fighter planes and patrol boats strafed and machine-gunned the floating survivors in a veritable war crime. Such was the mercilessness of the Pacific war. Then in April 1943, when the "Magic" code showed that Admiral Yamamoto intended to fly in and visit his troops at the front, US Navy fliers intercepted his airplane, sending the admiral to a warrior's death.

For the rest of the war US Marines and soldiers hopped from one island to the next, suffering horrific casualties whenever they needed to seize, and not bypass, a stronghold. Early on, US commanders began to worry about the potential catastrophe of invading Japan itself, since with each step to the home islands the defenders fought even more tenaciously. For example, on the tiny island of Tarawa — about the size of New York City's Central Park — five thousand Japanese defenders inflicted three thousand casualties on the attacking marines. That attrition rate was simply unsustainable for the Americans. The resolve of the Japanese soldiers was demonstrated on island after island. Almost none became prisoners, partly because US troops decided to stop taking any, but mainly because to surrender was to the Japanese the ultimate dishonor. Indeed, the Japanese army's Field Service Code contained *no instructions* on how to surrender, stating flatly that troops should "[n]ever give up a position but rather die."

So it was that Nimitz drove straight west across the Central Pacific and MacArthur hopped to the northeast of Australia. When Nimitz's troops reached the island of Saipan, the final three thousand desperate Japanese defenders, some wielding only knives tied to bamboo poles, suicidally rushed the American lines screaming the battle cry "Banzai!" They were wiped out. Then on Marpi Point, at the northern tip of the island, Japanese women and children leaped to their deaths off the 250-foot cliffs. The horrified American interpreters shouted through bullhorns in an attempt to coax at least some to choose surrender over suicide. Still, thousands jumped, and when the battle finally ended, the Americans had suffered an additional fourteen thousand casualties.

In July 1944, President Roosevelt visited his two Pacific commanders — Nimitz and MacArthur — in Hawaii to discuss strategy. When Nimitz and members of the president's staff suggested that it was perhaps best to bypass the well-defended Philippines, MacArthur loudly objected. Should their Filipino "wards" not be liberated, MacArthur boldly warned FDR, "I dare say that the American people would be so aroused that they would register most complete resentment against you at the polls this fall." Only a man like MacArthur would dare serve up such an overt political threat. Nonetheless, the president made another "non-decision": both Nimitz and MacArthur would drive forward as planned, and the Philippines remained on the target list.

The war had permanently turned against the Japanese by late 1944. The issue was settled, and only the final casualty counts were in question. US submarines cut Japanese oil and other supplies to a trickle. Japan was in danger of being starved. Then, in the epic Battle of Leyte Gulf, the Japanese fleet was all but destroyed. When US rescue vessels approached the thousands of floating Japanese survivors, most submerged themselves and chose drowning over capture. Leyte Gulf marked the end of an era of ship-on-ship gunnery duels. Naval airpower was now the dominant force, and no nation would ever again build a battleship. Moreover, though the Japanese fleet was forever crippled, it was at Leyte that the remaining Japanese naval aircraft began their suicidal "kamikaze" attacks, purposely flying into American ships.

On January 9, 1945, MacArthur landed more than ten divisions in the Philippines. Yet as predicted his opponent, General Tomoyuki Yamashita, along with a large garrison, put up a stout defense. Retreating into the jungles and mountains of the vast Philippine interior, Yamashita executed a costly delaying action for months in a campaign that resembled the tough fight in Italy. In the end the Philippine invasion was a costly operation that historian David M. Kennedy has concluded "had little direct bearing by this time on Japan's ultimate defeat."

In the Central Pacific theater, the next stop was the volcanic island of Iwo Jima. Here, despite seventy-two days of aerial bombardment and three days of naval gunfire, the twenty-one thousand Japanese defenders managed to inflict twenty-three thousand casualties on the US Marines. Almost none of the defenders surrendered, and more than twenty thousand died — many incinerated in their bunkers by tank-mounted flamethrowers. The final battle in the Central Pacific was on the island of Okinawa. Though the locals were racially distinct, the Japanese considered them part of the home islands. As had Yamashita's force in the Philippines, the seventy-seven thousand Japanese defenders decided not to contest the landing sites and chose to wage a lengthy battle of attrition inland. The Japanese knew they couldn't win; they merely hoped to buy time so their brethren could better fortify the homeland.

On Okinawa the American invasion force rivaled the numbers put ashore in Normandy, France. So intense was the combat that the senior American commander, General Simon Bolivar Buckner, was himself killed. Toward the end of the desperate, doomed defense, Japanese volunteers — in an early form of suicide bombing — would rush the Americans with satchel charges strapped to their bodies. The US soldiers and marines referred to them as "human bazookas." The suicidal tactics also proliferated offshore, where waves of kamikaze aircraft sank 36 ships, damaged 368 more, and inflicted some 10,000 casualties.

In June the final six thousand Japanese defenders, armed with sidearms and spears, made a final "Banzai" charge. The Japanese commander ordered an aide to behead him once he had ritually thrust a hara-kiri dagger into his own belly. When it was all over, seventy thousand Japanese soldiers were dead along with a hundred thouand Okinawan civilians. The Americans suffered thirty-nine thousand combat casualties and twenty-six thousand more non-combat injuries, for a total casualty rate of 35 percent. Thus, with Okinawa and

Iwo Jima secured, Hitler dead, and Germany having surrendered, nervous American generals and admirals wondered what sort of carnage awaited them in Japan itself. The question was whether such an invasion would be necessary.

Original Sin: Race Rears Its Ugly Head at Home and Abroad

I'm for catching every Japanese in America, Alaska, and Hawaii now and putting them in concentration camps. . . . Damn them! Let's get rid of them now!

— US representative John Rankin of Mississippi (December 15, 1941)

Their racial characteristics are such that we cannot understand or trust even the citizen Japanese.

— Secretary of War Henry Stimson (1942)

Racial caste and racism constitute, undoubtedly, the original sins of the American experiment. In each overseas war that the United States has waged, that sin didn't halt at the shoreline. Rather, America's racist baggage was and is always along for the trip. This was especially true during the Second World War, a war ostensibly waged for democracy. Both at home and abroad the United States failed to live up to its values and treated African Americans and the Japanese in particular with a brutal form of racial animus.

No description of the American home front in World War II is complete without a brief account of the internment of Japanese Americans on the West Coast, many of them native-born citizens. Essentially, more than one hundred thousand of these people were uprooted from their homes, turned into internal refugees, and then imprisoned in sparse inland camps for the duration of the war. This treatment of the Japanese Americans, ostensibly motivated by fear of internal subversion — of which almost none was eventually found — was unique to this Asian minority. Even though Nazi Germany was considered the greater global threat and the first military priority in the stated "Germany First" strategy of the Allies, no substantial class of German Americans or Italian Americans was interned. That only Japanese were so treated should not come as a surprise. There had long been racial hatred of the Japanese in California, and all immigration from Japan was shut off through the federal Immigration Act of 1924.

So it was on February 19, 1942, that Roosevelt signed Executive Order 9066, sealing the fate of 112,000 Japanese Americans, 79,000 of whom were citizens. They were first placed under a curfew, and then, with only what they could carry, they were moved to camps in a number of states. There they lived under guard behind barbed-wire fences for years. In many cases those who were interned had sons fighting for the country that had imprisoned them. Indeed, the 442nd Regimental Combat Team, an all-Japanese-American unit, was one of the most decorated outfits in the entire war.

Plenty of Americans were appalled by internment, even at the time. The famed photographer Dorothea Lange took photos of the removal process. She had been commissioned to do so by the War Relocation Authority, but once the photos were developed the government chose to lock them away for decades in archives labeled IMPOUNDED. Lange herself disagreed with the president's executive order, and, according to her assistant, "She thought that we were entering a period of fascism and that she was viewing the end of democracy as we know it." Despite personal appeals from sympathetic citizens, Japanese Americans found no relief from the US Supreme Court, which, in an infamous 1944 decision, *Korematsu v. United States*, upheld the order in a 6–3 decision.

Unlike the war in Europe, the Pacific war was a *race* war, one that cut both ways. In the Pacific theater, Japanese troops and civilians were treated far worse than America's German or Italian enemies. Some of this mistreatment may be explained by the unwillingness of Japanese troops to surrender, Japan's mistreatment of American prisoners of war, and the ongoing anger over the surprise attack on Pearl Harbor. Still, generations of anti-Asian racism did seem to play a role in the unique animus toward the Japanese enemy. The hatred on both sides of the Pacific conflict was so intense that the esteemed historian John Dower called it a "war without mercy." Neither side saw the other as fully human. As one marine on Guadalcanal lamented, "I wish we were fighting against Germans. They are human beings, like us. . . . But the Japanese are like animals." Indeed, it was not atypical for the Japanese people as a whole to be depicted, especially by war's end, as vermin to be exterminated. Nor were the Japanese above perpetuating their own intra-Asian philosophy of racism. They too were a proud, chauvinist people with a great deal of racial nationalism animating their wartime actions.

Still, there was something unique about the fighting in the Pacific. Though most Americans loathed the Nazis, it was only in the Pacific theater that it became commonplace for US servicemen to shoot prisoners, strafe lifeboats, mutilate bodies, make necklaces out of ears or teeth, and fashion letter openers from Japanese bones (one of which was mailed to FDR, who refused the gift). As historian John Dower wrote, "It is virtually inconceivable that teeth, ears, and skulls could have been collected from German or Italian war dead and publicized in the Anglo-American countries without provoking an uproar." Prisoner mistreatment also defined the Pacific war. Some 90 percent of captured Americans reported being beaten, a typical prisoner lost an average of sixty-one pounds, and more than a third died in captivity. In Europe, by contrast, 99 percent of imprisoned Americans survived the war. In response to this mistreatment and especially after several groups of Japanese attempted ambushes in surrender ruses, US troopers turned to an informal policy of shooting all prisoners.

Propaganda on both sides depicted the "other" as racially inferior and subhuman. Japanese schoolbooks instructed students that they, as Japanese, were "intrinsically quite different from the so-called citizens of Occidental countries," who were depicted as weak and overly materialistic. In the US wartime cartoons — including animated cartoons by leading filmmakers such as Warner Bros. — portrayed the "Japs" as buck-toothed savages and bespectacled lunatics. And in Frank Capra's famous Why We Fight film series — which was mandatory viewing for all soldiers in basic training — the narrator instructed the viewer that all Japanese were like "photographic prints off the same negative." Furthermore, the senior navy admiral, William "Bull" Halsey, publicly defined his mission as to "Kill Japs, kill Japs, and kill more Japs," vowing that after the war the Japanese language would be spoken only in hell. Overall, while the US government depicted war with Germany and Italy as a war against fascism or Nazis, in the Pacific the war was distinctly waged against the Japanese as a people. This alone surely contributed to the brutality of the fighting.

————

> *Dear Lord, today*
> *I go to war:*
> *To fight, to die,*
> *Tell me what for?*
>
> *Dear Lord, I'll fight,*
> *I do not fear,*
> *Germans or Japs;*
> *My fears are here.*
> *America!*
>
> — "A Draftee's Prayer," a poem in *The Afro-American*,
> a black newspaper (January 1943)

The America that went to war in December 1941 was still a Jim Crow America. The United States fielded a Jim Crow military, manufactured with a Jim Crow industry, and policed the home front with Jim Crow law enforcement. Ironically, a nation that purported to fight against Nazi racism and for human dignity did so at the time in which nearly all public aspects of American life remained segregated. The war did, however, begin to change America's racial character, setting off one of the great mass migrations in US history as blacks left the South for northern industrial plants or induction into the military.

Throughout World War II blacks served in segregated units led by white officers. In the army they were usually relegated to support duties and menial labor. They were at first denied enlistment in the army air corps or US Marines altogether. In the navy they worked only as cooks and stewards — the naval academy at Annapolis had yet to have a single black graduate. Northern blacks had to deal with the double indignity of serving under white officers in primarily *southern* mobilization camps. In such locales it was not uncommon for black troops to be denied service in restaurants that gladly served German and Italian POWs. And as in World War I, many uniformed African Americans, seen as "uppity blacks," were lynched.

The vibrant black press recognized all this as a problem from the very start and pushed hard for racial integration and equality in public and economic life. *The Crisis* newspaper editorialized that "[a] Jim Crow Army cannot fight for a free world." While philosophically correct, this proved to be practically untrue. Some African Americans, under-standably, refused to serve. One black man from the Bronx wrote to President Roosevelt that "[e]very time I pick up the paper some poor African-American soldiers are getting shot, lynched, or hung, and framed up. I will be darned if you get me in your forces."

Some progress was made when FDR mandated equal employment practices in war industries in the face of black labor leader A. Philip Randolph's threat to march one-hundred-thousand-plus African Americans on Washington. Eleanor Roosevelt, well known as a civil rights proponent, had arranged for Randolph to meet with the pres-ident, and the result was Executive Order 8802, which prohibited racial discrimination in defense-related industries. On other issues, however, Roosevelt caved in to his southern Democratic supporters. During the 1944 presidential election progressive congressmen hoped to guarantee black soldiers the right to vote, something they were denied in their mostly southern home states. However, FDR — always politically conscious — acceded to his party's southern wing and left enforcement of voting laws, even for soldiers, to the individual states, with obvious consequences. So huge numbers of black draftees were fighting and dying for a country in which they could not vote.

Many blacks pointed to the hypocrisy of such measures and orga-nized to press for reform. They took to calling their goals the "Double V" Campaign, meaning victory over the Axis and victory at home against segregation and Jim Crow. The Double V philosophy also often had international components, demonstrating solidarity with black and brown colonized peoples around the world. As the black sociologist Horace Cayton wrote in the *Nation* magazine in 1943, "To win a cheap military victory over the Axis and then continue the exploitation of subject peoples within the British Empire and the subordination of Negroes in the US is to set the stage for the next world war — probably a war of color." Indeed, quite a few such wars of colonial independence did break out in the decades following the surrender of the Axis.

Violence also plagued military camps and cities on the home front. When blacks attempted to move into a Detroit public housing project, whites barricaded the streets. A riot broke out and six thousand federal troops marched on the city in June 1943. That August another race riot broke out in response to rumors of police violence in Harlem in New York City. Six people were killed and six hundred were arrested. Riots cut both ways. In Mobile, Alabama, white shipyard workers rioted over the influx of black workers and the promotion of some African American welders. Eleven blacks were seriously injured. In Beaumont, Texas — a town plagued by housing and school shortages — white mobs rampaged through black neighborhoods, killing two and wounding dozens.

In the face of the domestic violence and prejudice against blacks in the military, some African American troops served with great distinction in the war. One such decorated unit, the all-black 761st Tank Battalion, fought in Normandy under General Patton. The fiery Patton sent them straight to the front with dignity, exclaiming, "I don't care what color you are, so long as you go up there and kill those Kraut sonsabitches." No doubt such unit actions, combined with black migration to the North and home-front activism, did, slowly, shift the needle on civil rights in America. Though a meaningful civil or voting rights bill would have to wait for two decades, President Harry Truman in 1948, three years after the war's end, finally ordered full desegregation of the US armed forces. It was a small victory, but a victory nonetheless.

Dropping "The Bomb": The Atomic Weapons Debate

> Killing Japanese didn't bother me very much at that time. . . . I suppose if I had lost the war, I would have been tried as a war criminal. . . . But all war is immoral and if you let that bother you, you're not a good soldier. . . .
>
> — General Curtis LeMay, US Army Air Force commander in the Pacific theater

One of the greatest and most terrible projects of World War II was the production of the atomic bomb and the ushering in of the Nuclear Age. In the end, for better or worse, the United States won the race to harness atomic energy. That it did so was at least in part due to Hitler's persecution of German Jews, including Jewish physicists, dozens of whom fled to America and worked on the secret Manhattan Project to build and test the bomb. German racial biases also derailed their own (eventually canceled) atomic program after Hitler took to calling nuclear physics "Jew physics." By 1945 the US military had developed atomic bombs capable of destroying entire cities. The scientists involved — many of whom actually were pacifists — had unleashed upon the world a destructive weapon that could not be stuffed back into Pandora's box.

The question now, with the Pacific war still raging, was whether to use the A-bomb on Japanese cities. In the generations since the decision to drop the two bombs, a great debate has occurred among scholars and laypeople alike over whether it was necessary or right to do so. After all, many Americans find it disturbing to note that the United States is the only nation ever to use such a weapon in war. The debate centers on the purported justification, or motive, for dropping the bombs. Most agree that the prime motivation was to avert the massive American (and Japanese) casualties expected in an invasion of the Japanese home islands. Some analysts have overestimated the supposed casualty projections — throwing around numbers of up to one million American soldiers — to argue that the no-warning atomic bombings were ethically excusable. However, estimates by top military authorities varied from General Marshall's low of 63,000 to Admiral Leahy's 268,000. Whichever estimate one chooses, there is no doubt that one deciding factor was fear of high casualties — especially after US troops had suffered a killed/wounded rate of 35 percent against Japanese defenders on Okinawa just months before.

But were the only options the A-bomb or an invasion? This question hinges on Roosevelt's earlier proclamation that the Allies would accept only the "unconditional surrender" of the Axis Powers. This unqualified demand limited American options for closing the Pacific war and made an invasion of the home islands seem inevitable. Still, even at the time there were dissenting voices on the issue. Roosevelt's chief of staff, Leahy, expressed "fear . . . that our insistence on unconditional surrender would result only in making the Japanese desperate and thereby increase our casualty lists." Assistant Secretary of War John McCloy added, "We ought to have our heads examined if we don't explore some other method by which we can terminate this war than by just another conventional attack." McCloy listed as alternatives giving the Japanese a warning (or demonstration) of the bomb prior to dropping it, and modifying the unconditional-surrender demands. In fact, the latter might not have proved too difficult.

In reality, by June 1945, Emperor Hirohito had asked his political leaders to examine other methods to end the war besides a fight to the finish. As it turned out, within Japan serious consideration was given to such peace entreaties, and Tokyo reached out through Soviet interlocutors to propose a qualified peace. The main Japanese demand — to which the United States would eventually accede! — was to maintain the emperor as the head of state.

Either way, by summer 1945 the Japanese were beaten. They were confined to their home islands, could barely supply their main army in China — an army that would soon be attacked by the Soviets — and had no navy left to speak of. To be clear, they no longer posed any serious offensive threat to the United States. Therefore, couldn't an invasion be avoided and a simple naval blockade be continued until Japan surrendered? Perhaps. Then again, given the extreme defense put up by Japan's soldiers throughout the war, it's also plausible that mass starvation might set in before the enemy capitulated. It's difficult to measure the potential casualty rates and ethical considerations of this alternative to dropping the bomb.

All of this amounts, in the end, to counterfactual speculation. The reality, as historian John Dower has convincingly demonstrated, is that the eventual choice to drop two A-bombs on Japan amounted to a "non-decision." Besides one petition against the no-warning use of the bomb initiated by some prominent scientists who had worked on the Manhattan Project, there's no evidence that any senior policy makers with real decision-making authority or influence — including Truman — ever seriously considered *not* dropping the weapon on civilians. Secretary of War Stimson and Manhattan Project leader General Leslie Groves each remember that the final meeting to discuss dropping the bomb lasted less than forty-five minutes. Truman later wrote, "Let there be no mistake about it, I regarded the bomb as a military weapon and never had any doubt that it should be used." Here we must understand that these officials and decision makers led a nation at war that had fire-bombed women and children from the sky as a matter of course. This, they felt, was necessary and proper. By the time the final decision was made, nearly one million Japanese and several hundred thousand German civilians had already been killed in conventional bombings. The dropping of the two atomic bombs was in a sense a non-decision; however, it is one with which the world has had to live forever after.

None of this should read as ethical relativism or historical apologetics. There were plenty of senior officials then and soon afterward who opposed or lamented the use of the A-bombs. Former ambassador to Japan Joseph Grew argued that the United States should agree both to retention of the emperor and to eliminate the demand for unconditional surrender. Secretary of War Stimson thought that contrary to public misconception "Japan is susceptible to reason" and might soon surrender if the United States agreed that the emperor would remain. Key military figures from the war also opposed the bomb's use. Admiral "Bull" Halsey — never known as a soft man — wrote, "The first atomic bomb was an unnecessary experiment. . . . It was a mistake ever to drop it . . . [the scientists] had this toy and they wanted to try it out, so they dropped it. . . . It killed a lot of Japs, but the Japs had put out a lot of peace feelers through Russia long before." General Eisenhower, meanwhile, wrote in his memoirs: "[Upon hearing the bomb would be dropped] I had . . . a feeling of depression and . . . voiced . . . my grave misgivings, first on the basis of my belief that Japan was already defeated and that dropping the bomb was completely unnecessary, and secondly because I thought that our country should avoid shocking world opinion by the use of a weapon whose employment was . . . no longer mandatory . . . to save American lives."

Nevertheless, Truman did drop atomic bombs on the Japanese cities of Hiroshima (140,000 dead) and Nagasaki (70,000 dead) before Emperor Hirohito declared to his advisers: "I swallow my own tears and give my sanction to the proposal to accept the Allied proclamation." Japan surrendered soon afterward, and, under direction from the emperor himself, there was no resistance to military occupation from a populace that quickly took on pacifistic qualities. Meanwhile, the emperor was allowed to keep his ceremonial position. The American people had reached V-J Day.

———

> The problem after a war is with the victor. He thinks that
> he has just proved that war and violence pay.
> — A. J. Muste, a noted pacifist (1941)

World War II altered the planet forever. It was the bloodiest war ever fought between human beings. It built the foundation for a new world, for better or worse. Yet there are tragic ironies inherent in the Allied endeavor. The Western democracies went to war in response to the invasion of Poland, way back in 1939; still, at war's end the Allies grimly acceded to the domination of that same Polish state by one of the Allied Powers, the Soviet Union. Their willingness — even if they had no real choice — to substitute an authoritarian Soviet state for a German Nazi state in Eastern Europe demonstrates what should have been obvious all along: Britain and France didn't really fight for democratic sovereignty but, rather, for self-interest, for the balance of power. The Allies ended the war with a divided Europe, half of which would be undemocratic after all, setting the stage for a new and deadly Cold War.

Allies who purportedly fought for the freedom agenda of the Atlantic Charter never lifted a finger to stop the Holocaust or accept substantial Jewish refugees. The British still dominated an empire full of brown people, while the Americans carried Jim Crow across the seas. National-liberation struggles against European colonial rule would proliferate in the decades following the war, when local populations made Japan's earlier obtuse slogan "Asia for the Asians" a reality. As for the Jews, after suffering six million deaths amid a stunning global silence, the world's guilty conscience would soon shift the burden of past European sins to the Palestinian Arabs of the Middle East — establishing a Jewish state, Israel, in a complex region without the permission of the local inhabitants. That, of course, would set off a new intractable conflict, one that has raged ever since the end of the Second World War.

As for the United States, the war — despite its cost of four hundred thousand American lives — proved a boon. Deficit spending and stimulus brought the Great Depression to a close, and the destruction of the world economy, while the US homeland remained untouched, positioned America to lead with increasing industrial and financial strength. American bankers would run the International Monetary Fund and the World Bank. American diplomats would lead politically in the new United Nations.

The United States, which had harbored traditions of isolationism or at least anti-interventionism in world affairs since the time of George Washington and right up until December 7, 1941, would now flex its political and diplomatic muscles the world over. Never again would the US military retire to its home bases after a war; instead it would sprout new outposts the word over. Today the United States has some eight hundred overseas bases while China and Russia combine for fewer than a dozen. The full mobilization of the war economy to defeat the Axis Powers wouldn't disappear so easily either. What emerged was a powerful military-industrial complex that influenced members of Congress and benefited the arms manufacturers, so that by the late twentieth century the United States, of all countries, would be the number one global arms dealer. No less a figure than General, then President, Eisenhower would eventually warn the nation about this nefarious nexus known as the military-industrial complex.

The war changed forever the moral calculus of combat, altered what was acceptable, sometimes in the span of precious few years. Roosevelt in 1940 decried German terror bombing of Dutch cities but in 1945 sanctioned his own air forces incinerating ninety thousand Japanese civilians in a single night. All this would set the stage for a world in which both the Americans and the Soviets could confidently craft nuclear war plans with the potential for barely imaginable destruction. Nuclear weapons would spread, of course, until a day — our own day — in which the world lives a hair trigger away from the annihilation of humanity. The US president alone, or at least among a very few global leaders, holds the power to press the proverbial button and set off a war that would dwarf the cataclysm of World War II. Now, *that's* a power beyond the dreams of either Hitler or Mussolini.

When I was teaching future army officers at West Point, I often concluded my lesson on the Second World War with a purposely provocative question. What is the moral difference, I'd ask, between flying passenger jets into the World Trade Center and the Pentagon — thereby killing almost three thousand (mostly) civilians — on the one hand, and sending hundreds of airplanes to firebomb, incinerate, suffocate, and boil ninety thousand civilians on a single night in Tokyo, on the other? This question inevitably set off a firestorm of its own, as cadets yelled and debated with one another (and me) until the bell rang. The general conclusion of most cadets was simple: since the United States had actually declared war on Japan, those air strikes — even though they targeted exponentially more civilians — were more acceptable than al-Qaida's attack on the United States. That's a fair point, and one worth parsing out, but it, too, ultimately falls flat. After all, Osama bin Laden did declare, in writing, war on the United States back in 1996.

27

A CRUEL, COSTLY, AND ANXIOUS COLD WAR

Nothing is inevitable. Not war, not peace. Those writers and politicians who tell readers or constituents otherwise are selling snake oil. So it is, oftentimes, with proclamations about the Cold War. Americans have been taught, programmed even, to believe that a permanently bellicose nuclear standoff with the Soviet Union was inescapable — such was the diabolical nature of global communism. There were no alternatives, we have been told, to a firm military response to Soviet aggression in the wake of World War II. This myth of inevitability serves to explain the seemingly unexplainable: how Soviet Russia, America's valued ally in World War II, so quickly transformed, almost overnight, into a national bogeyman. You're not supposed to ask tough questions or draw nuanced conclusions; to wit: Weren't the United States and the Soviet Union ideological enemies long before they were allies, even if they were only allies of convenience? And couldn't different American policies have assuaged Soviet fears and lessened the atmosphere of tense standoff after 1945? To answer yes to either, of course, is to commit national heresy, but honest history demands that the scholar and student do exactly that.

It is long past time for popular, digestible lay histories to reexamine the causes of the Cold War, to reassess the level of US culpability in the outcome, and to demonstrate the nefarious international and domestic effects of the resultant militarized standoff. Though far from inevitable — if probable — the Cold War remains highly prominent in US history, not only because the world for more than four decades lived one press of the proverbial button away from nuclear annihilation, but also because the country that Americans now inhabit — its government, military, foreign policy, and shrinking liberties — was forged in the immediate postwar years.

US government pamphlet, 1942

America's foremost enemies have changed since World War II, but over time they have come full circle. There were the Russians, then the Russians/Chinese, then terrorists and Iraqis, and, today, the Russians and Chinese once more. The United States has never ceased, in the postwar era, to have an allegedly existential enemy. Such mortal foes serve a momentous purpose for governments. They focus and unite the populace in fear of the foreign "other" and distract from growing wealth disparity and deindustrialization. They foster trust in ostensibly informed intelligence and defense officials and draw the public gaze away from increasingly dissipating civil liberties. The ever-growing and all-embracing military-industrial complex demands — counts on — a combination of communal apathy and fear. Fervid consumerism and outward-looking trepidation are musts for the militarist welfare state to function.

It has long been so. Nonetheless, something profoundly changed in the aftermath of American triumph in the Second World War. The

United States, until then mainly hesitant about overseas intervention and empire building, became — and remains today — a globalist hegemon. In a sense, 1945 stands as the pivotal turning point in American foreign and domestic policy. The "sleeping giant" of North America woke and transformed into an ever-vigilant militarist colossus, dotting the earth with hundreds of its armed bases and ready to intervene anywhere, anytime, at a moment's notice.

Seen in this light, rather than ushering in that which the common American GI of World War II had hoped for — an era of relative peace and tranquil prosperity — victory over Nazi Germany and Imperial Japan only brought forth a new insecurity, new fears. In US government rhetoric and, to some extent, technical reality, the Soviet and communist behemoth loomed as an altogether more profound threat — one that could bring about the extinction of the human race. Be that as it may, few Americans saw then (or now) the ominous position that their government held in that apocalyptic reality: that one false move or misunderstanding by an American president could just as easily destroy humankind. As we rewind, then, to mid-1945, let us reassess, with fresh eyes, the role of the early Cold War and its effect upon the United States. Seen with clear vision, it makes for a hell of a story, one that ultimately is absurd.

Broke World, Rich America: 1945 in Retrospect

When Germany and later Japan surrendered, much of Europe, Asia, and North Africa was in rubble. Societies had collapsed right along with the buildings; economies were devastated; tens of millions were dead. Only the United States, alone among industrialized powers, stood largely untouched. Its homeland unscathed, its casualties relatively light, and its economy booming, America stood proudly and powerfully astride a broken world. The United States faced a monumental choice: How would it wield its unsurpassed strength now that the guns had fallen silent? The fate of a people, and a planet, rested on America's fateful decision.

Wars, it turns out, are good for business, stimulating the domestic economy and generating something close to full employment. They are especially so when fought as away games, distant from the homeland, ensuring that all the downsides — death, destruction, psychological depression — occur elsewhere. In that sense, the Second World War was a boon for the US economy, lifting the nation out of the Great Depression in a way that President Franklin D. Roosevelt's modest stimulus programs could not. Almost all of the rest of the world, however, was broke, allies and enemies alike. American lend-lease aid had kept the partners of the United States afloat, but newly inaugurated president Harry Truman put an end to the program soon after Japan's surrender. Both the Soviets and the British suffered. The Brits, humiliatingly, had to come to Uncle Sam with hat in hand for a $3.75 billion loan. Washington drove a hard bargain with its "special" ally, insisting that the cash be spent on American goods and that the British Empire be opened up for free trade with the United States.

Still, rich though America was, many senior policy makers feared that with the end of the war the domestic economy might once again slide into depression. As a preventive, they decided, international markets would have to be found for America's manufactured goods, including those of the booming weapons industry. In an unprecedented move, the state, war, and navy departments formed a committee in 1947 that concluded "it is inescapable that, under present programs and policies, the world will not be able to continue to buy United States exports at the 1946–47 rate." America's old ways — limited intervention and limited interaction with the rest of the world — would have to be altered. New markets for American defense and consumer goods would need to remain open during the coming "peace," and, if necessary, US cash would initially have to be infused into Europe to increase foreign purchasing power. Seen in this light, later loans and overseas grants — think of the Marshall Plan, which in 1948 provided more than $15 billion to rebuild Western Europe — were as much about self-interest as humanitarianism.

Whether this was ultimately a tactical or a moral move, the fact remained that only the United States was capable, in the late 1940s, of such largesse. For all the later propaganda about the scope of the Soviet threat, the two sides' wealth and economic potentials — the true measures of modern power — were never close. This was especially true in 1945, when the United States, with just 7 percent of the world's population, possessed 40 percent of global income, half the world's manufacturing output, and three-quarters of the world's gold reserves. America also proved that it could field, supply, and deploy a massive military — a real achievement considering that just seven years earlier the US Army was smaller than that of Romania.

Fellow belligerents in the late war held an understandable resentment for the power and position of the pristine United States. After all, only four hundred thousand Americans, nearly all of them members of the military, died in a conflict that took sixty million lives worldwide. The country generally believed to have had the greatest loss of lives was the Soviet Union, which suffered more than twenty million military and civilian fatalities; in addition, it bore the brunt of the Nazi war machine — eight-tenths of Germans killed in the war died fighting Russians. After taking such blows, it saw its lend-lease aid cut off by the Americans almost as soon as the guns fell silent.

While the people of Europe and Asia scrounged and starved in the immediate aftermath of a devastating war, America's consumer economy boomed. And as tens of millions of foreign military veterans flooded into weakened domestic economies, the United States thanked its veterans with the generous GI Bill, financing higher education and low-interest home loans for countless demobilized service members. Though the cost of the GI Bill constituted 15 percent of the federal budget by 1948, it paid for itself ten times over through increased future tax revenues. As the rest of the combatant countries struggled, America was building a new middle class. It was the envy of the world. How the United States would wield its new, unprecedented power remained to be seen.

Contested Origins: The Outbreak of Cold War in Myth and Memory

> Russians, like the Japanese, are essentially oriental in
> their thinking . . . and it seems doubtful that we should
> endeavor to buy their understanding and sympathy.
> We tried that once with Hitler. There are no returns on
> appeasement.
>
> — Secretary of the Navy James Forrestal (1945)

The standard American tropes about the origins of the Cold War are so much malarkey, little more than comforting patriotic yarns designed to raise morale and bolster mythologies of American exceptionalism. Reality was far less simplistic than this propaganda. In truth, the United States and Soviet Russia shared responsibility for the outbreak and perpetuation of an unnecessary and highly dangerous Cold War. Analyzing this era, and parsing out fact from legend, requires holding two dissonant truths simultaneously: that Soviet premier Joseph Stalin was indeed a monster and mass murderer, yet at the same time he, and Russia, possessed justified fears and grievances with respect to an often aggressive United States.

When Germany surrendered in May 1945, the massive Soviet armies were, by force of arms, ensconced in all the former sovereign nations of Eastern Europe. The Soviets had bled on a level unfathomable to an American to "liberate" all the territories east of the Elbe River in Germany from Nazi control. The British and Americans, by contrast, held France, the Low Countries, and Italy, plus Germany west of the Elbe. These were the military realities on the ground, the tyranny of operational maps. As such, this situation set the stage for serious questions about the future boundaries of Europe, the degree of local sovereignty, and the economic systems that would prevail. While not inevitable, the Cold War does appear to have been likely given the seemingly binary division of Europe between two powerful but ideologically distinct allies, the Soviet Union and the United States.

The United States was, despite its smaller army, much more powerful than its later Soviet foe. A generation of Russian men and women was dead, the country had been ravaged by the Nazi invaders, and the Soviet economic potential paled in comparison with that of the United States. The Americans, by contrast, had sole possession of atomic weaponry, control of nearly half the world's economic resources, naval/air supremacy, and a pristine homeland thousands of miles from the nearest Russian soldier and protected by two giant oceans. To paraphrase FDR, all that Americans had to fear, in this moment, was fear itself. Still, it appears that US foreign-policy elites craved fear, craved an enemy. Thus developed the traditional narrative that the Soviet army under the direction of "Crazy Joe" Stalin had intended to conquer Western Europe and, perhaps, the world. According to this notion, they, the "Asiatic" Russians, were to blame for kicking off the Cold War.

Before pressing on, it's important to recognize that there is some truth in the standard, prevailing narrative. The Soviets, under Stalin, were deeply cynical. When "Uncle Joe" realized after Munich that the Western Allies were unlikely to stand up to Hitler, he cut a deal with the Nazis, signing a nonaggression pact with Hitler in 1939. Taking matters a step further, upon the outbreak of war, the Soviets gobbled up eastern Poland and the Baltic States and invaded Finland. This was blatant, opportunistic expansionism. Furthermore, since World War II officially started when Britain and France decided to fight Germany over its invasion of Poland, it might be said that the Soviet Union was a tacit enemy of the Allies at the outset of conflict. Stalin, terrified of what he saw as an impending war with the fascists, wanted friendly, docile buffer states on his western border. To cripple Polish nationalist opposition, Soviet troops were ordered to secretly execute thousands of Polish military officers and dispose of the bodies in the Katyn Forest. This war crime was the norm for a regime that murdered its own people, especially dissenters, as a matter of course.

Furthermore, after Stalin joined the Allies in reaction to being invaded by Nazi forces, he continued to operate duplicitously regarding Eastern European sovereignty as a whole and the Polish question in particular. At the Allies' Tehran, Yalta, and Potsdam Conferences, despite agreeing to limited language of "sovereignty" and "elections,"

Stalin made quite clear that he intended for the Soviets to maintain preeminence and a sphere of influence in the regions "liberated" from the Germans. Even President Roosevelt, who always held out hope that he could "deal with" Stalin and hold the wartime alliance together after the Axis countries surrendered, seemed, ultimately, to realize this. In March 1945, three weeks before his death on April 12 and less than six months before the war's end, he complained privately: "We can't do business with Stalin. He's broken every one of the promises he made at Yalta." Nonetheless, Roosevelt thought it imprudent to stop working with the Soviets, and we probably can never know how he would have proceeded if he had lived longer. One final point: There is no doubt that Stalin sought to maintain a powerful ground army and to prioritize the development of nuclear arms, submarines, and long-range bombers after the war with the specific intent to strike at the US homeland if necessary.

Still, we must now ask why. Why, that is, did Stalin and the Soviets operate as they did? The answer is security, not hegemony. Stalin's Russia, though espousing a powerful evangelist communist ideology, operated much the same as czarist Russia had before the 1917 revolution. As such, the Soviets pursued powerful — but not unmanageable or hegemonic — foreign-policy goals familiar even to nineteenth-century European observers: access to the Dardanelles Strait, a warm-water port for its navy, and influence over the Iranian plateau on its southern border, as well as clout in friendly states on its western border with Europe. Looking westward from a Soviet's point of view, we can understand the obsession with "buffer states" in Eastern Europe. After all, much of Russia had been devastated by three invading armies — two German, one French — that spilled across its borders along that very axis of approach. Padding its western border with client, buffer states seemed good policy. Security, plain and simple, was the primary goal.

As for Poland, the two great powers viewed that beleaguered state quite differently. For Britain and the United States a democratic, sovereign Poland cohered with their global rhetoric and postwar preferences. However, their inclinations were far from existential. To

Stalin, conversely, Poland was a "matter of life and death for the Soviet state." It was, for Stalin, "a question of the security of the [Soviet] state, not only because we are on Poland's frontier but also because throughout history Poland has always been a corridor for assaults on Russia." Besides, Stalin could argue, hadn't Roosevelt himself acquiesced to Russia's predisposition? FDR had said, at Yalta, "I hope that I do not have to assure you that the US will never lend its support in any way to . . . a government in Poland that would be inimical to your interests." To Stalin that meant a friendly, and by definition communist, Poland. Besides, what leverage, ultimately, did the US president have to change Poland's already de facto status? Little to none.

Conquest, whether of the European continent or of the entire globe, was beyond Russia's reach or intent. After all, Stalin the paranoid megalomaniac was also a rational realist and a cool customer at the game of geopolitics. Some serious American policy makers ultimately knew this, including George Kennan, the preeminent US diplomatic expert on the Soviets. As early as July 1946, Kennan explained that "[s]ecurity is probably their [the Soviets'] basic motive, but they are so anxious and suspicious about it that the objective results are much the same as if the motive were aggressive." Here, Kennan accidentally summarized the problem set: the United States and the Soviet Union viewed the post-surrender world through two different lenses — that of a nation recently ravaged and invaded (Russia) and that of another largely untouched by what was ultimately an overseas intervention (America). Each side projected motives onto the other, and most Americans concluded that Soviet goals were nearly limitless. But Stalin knew, better than anyone else, the limits of Soviet power and potential. As a result, he would push only so far and no further. There was no serious consideration of conquest of Europe or global empire in the late 1940s. That fear, as is so often the case, was in Americans' collective heads — projection rather than reality. It was to remain so for nigh on fifty years.

Until the late 1960s even most academic historians bought the traditional Soviet-blaming narrative. However, as American culture shifted with the disaster of the Vietnam War, a new generation of scholars — "revisionists" — began analyzing American culpability in the early Cold War. Their argument built on the security-centric analysis above and argued that, at root, Soviet postwar policies were defensive rather than aggressive. After all, much of the Soviet Union had only recently been demolished, with seventeen hundred towns, thirty-four thousand factories, and a hundred thousand collective farms destroyed. The revisionist historians, including this author, drew further practical conclusions. For example, whereas Soviet-blamers decried FDR and Truman's unwillingness to defend Eastern European sovereignty, a more prudent analyst questions exactly what the Americans could have done about that in 1945–46. Just as Western armies were in control of Western Europe, the many millions of Stalin's soldiers claimed squatter's rights in Eastern Europe. Short of a cataclysmic World War III, it's unclear what leverage the US and Britain had to change the facts on the ground.

Furthermore, the expanded Soviet sphere in Eastern Europe must be viewed in context; it was little different from US dominance in the Caribbean and South and Central America. Why should the victorious and powerful Soviets not demand the kind of clout that America already had? What's more, Stalin proved far more flexible and cautious than most American leaders — then and now — were willing to admit. He had serious economic problems at home, and, though he was a publicly vocal proponent of worldwide communist revolution, he lent only limited support to burgeoning communist parties in the 1940s. He left rebellious Finland some autonomy, gave marginal aid to Greek communist rebels, put only intermittent pressure on Iran and Turkey (quickly backing down when pressed by the United States in 1946), and, most important, gave minimal military or moral support to Mao Zedong's successful communist revolution in China.

Add to this Russian caution and elasticity the genuinely threatening United States policies that heightened Stalin's fears. He simply never trusted the West, just as the West never truly trusted him. Throughout the war, Britain and the United States delayed opening a meaningful second front in France, despite Stalin's pleas, and let millions of Soviets die in taking the brunt of the Nazi onslaught until the last eleven months of a six-year war. Then, immediately after the war, President Truman suddenly refused to extend loans and aid that the Soviets desperately needed. Indeed, American ships carrying aid were ordered to reverse course when they already were en route to Russia. Stalin called these actions "brutal," executed in a "scornful and abrupt manner." Such behavior furthered the Soviet view that the West harbored a capitalist plot to bankrupt and destroy the relatively young communist state of Russia, then the only such nation in the world. Further feeding Stalin's paranoia was the United States' unwillingness — despite the pleas of Soviet diplomats and American scientists — to share nuclear secrets with its ostensible ally. This was most certainly read by Stalin's conspiratorial mind as a not so surreptitious threat. Who can blame him?

We must conclude, then, that both sides bore some responsibility for the eruption of the Cold War — that misunderstanding and misinterpretation of each power's respective motives contributed to the strife. Still, given the objective power imbalance between the two sides, the early US nuclear monopoly, the facts and limitations on the ground, and legitimate Soviet security fears, it is the United States, primarily, that must bear the larger share of responsibility for early escalation of the Cold War. Even so, however, from the often ignored Polish perspective it is paradoxical — and tragic — that a war begun over the question of Polish sovereignty would end with that nation still in proverbial shackles. Only the occupier had changed. This stands as a disconcerting fact, one that turns the whole premise for World War II on its head, but there's not much, in the end, that the West could have done to change this reality.

Such is the truth, and tragedy, of realism in foreign affairs. It remains so today. Many serious intellectuals saw this back then. Even the highly respected, and anti-communist, theologian Reinhold Niebuhr recognized the futility of American bellicosity or attempts to change the world as it was. In September 1946, Niebuhr wrote in *The Nation* that the United States should end its "futile efforts to change what cannot be changed in Eastern Europe, regarded by Russia as its strategic security belt." Indeed, he continued, "Western efforts to change conditions in Poland, or in Bulgaria, for instance, will prove futile in any event, partly because the Russians are there and we aren't. . . . Our copybook versions of democracy are frequently as obtuse as Russian dogmatism." Finally, "If we left Russia alone . . . we might actually help, rather than hinder, the indigenous forces which resist its heavy hand." This wisdom, essentially, defined the road not taken in the postwar years. Instead the United States became quickly determined in its reflexive anti-communism, and both sides settled down in their own armed camps. The result would be a world held hostage to the threat of nuclear annihilation for decades to come, and, in the end, none of the millions of "hot war" deaths in an era of "cold war" would ever change that reality. Nations, just as people, are capable of dying in vain.

American Action, Soviet Counteraction: The Early Cold War (1946–54)

One of the first major crises broke out in little Greece. It was here, oddly, that the United States would take its stand; here where an inexperienced, insecure President Truman would plant his anti-communist flag; where the United States — for better or worse — would self-consciously avoid another "Munich," another "appeasement." But was it the right place, and was it necessary? With hindsight, this appears unlikely. By 1946–47, Britain, a traditional protector of Greek independence, informed the United States that the British economy could no longer support military aid to the provisional capitalist government of Greece. The implication: the mighty USA should step in.

Yet the conflict in Greece was a civil war, and though there was a communist faction, Stalin actually did little to bolster that group. Besides, the right-wing government in place may have been notionally capitalist but it was also highly corrupt and monarchical. Indeed, a US envoy to Greece returned to the States with the following conclusion: "There is really no state here in the Western concept. Rather we have a loose hierarchy of individualistic politicians, some worse than others, so preoccupied with their own struggle for power that they have no time, even assuming capacity, to develop economic policy." He continued, claiming that Greek government activities were distinguished by "an almost complete deterioration of competence." That Greek capitalist factions were superior to the communists was the big lie. Nonetheless, Truman — always crafting an image of toughness — decided to get the United States indirectly involved in the fight on the basis of that lie and granted $400 million in military aid to the Greek government, some 1 percent of the entire US federal budget.

He went further still. Greece, Truman decided, would provide the model for future American interventionism. An obtuse, misguided report from the US State, War, and Navy Departments had already concluded in apocalyptic terms that "[t]here is, at the present point in world history, a conflict between two ways of life [Western capitalist and Soviet communist]." Truman agreed — he liked simplistic heuristics — and developed a shallow sort of "domino theory" that if Greece fell to the communists, so, too, would Turkey, then France, and on and on. What the new president needed, he determined — perhaps to ensure his historic legacy — was a doctrine, a Truman doctrine. Such a credo must be brought to and sold to the American people, of course. To convince a populace weary of war, Senator Arthur Vandenberg advised Truman, there was "only one way to get" what the president wanted: "That is to make a personal appearance before Congress and scare the hell out of the American people." And so he would. Before a joint session of Congress, Truman would present an unsophisticated binary picture of the world. To achieve a peaceful world, "it must be the policy of the US to support free peoples who are resisting attempted subjugation by armed minorities or by outside pressures." He should have been more specific. After all, he meant Soviet outside pressures, not American compulsion, which continued as heartily as ever. Still, hypocrisy aside, most Americans bought his line — hook, line, and sinker.

By taking over responsibility for stability and anti-communism in Greece from the British, the United States, under Truman, invariably militarized a regional, actually local, ideological conflict and applied this model the world over. To do so was an American choice, an unnecessary one at that — and against the advice of George Kennan, the supposed architect of Cold War "containment" of Russia. Even as the government official and respected scholar of the Soviet Union decried the Russian danger, he always believed, according to historian James Patterson, that the "West should not overreact by building up huge stores of atomic weapons or making military moves that would provoke a highly suspicious Soviet state into counter-actions." This, through the Truman Doctrine and intervention in the Greek civil war, was exactly what the United States had done, and less than two years after the war in Europe had ended! The consequences were severe, ushering in an ever-escalating Cold War.

Truman had taken the United States on a wayward path for little, irrelevant, corrupt Greece, in the process overturning one of the most sacred and long-standing American traditions in international relations: non-entanglement in peacetime affairs of countries across the seas. This had been the policy, and philosophy, of George Washington, of Thomas Jefferson, yet Truman reversed 150 years of custom over Greece. From the Truman Doctrine, matters easily flowed on a course of peacetime military alliances — the very approach that had sleepwalked the nations of Europe into the cataclysmic First World War. So it was that in 1949, long before the Soviets (few remember this) crafted their own Warsaw Pact alliance, the United States signed onto the North Atlantic Treaty Organization (NATO), the articles of which obligated America to rise to the defense of any allied partner, say . . . Belgium. This was profound, and traditionalists in the Senate, such as Robert Taft of Ohio, balked. Hadn't George Washington, Taft noted, declared it was "our true policy to steer clear of permanent alliances"? Had not Jefferson called for "peace, commerce, and honest friendship with all nations, entangling alliances with none"? Well, Harry Truman — the accidental president and product of corrupt Kansas City machine politics — had decided otherwise, and a compliant Congress and populace would follow him blindly.

Senator Taft — known as Mr. Republican — knew he would be on the losing end of the vote but made sure to say his piece and raise questions about the nature of the NATO alliance that continue to resonate to this day. "By executing a treaty of this kind," he told his colleagues, "we put ourselves at the mercy of the foreign policies of eleven other nations." True. Those eleven nations billed NATO as a defensive alliance, but, asked Taft, would the Russians see it that way? Hardly. Taft then took the concept of the alliance to its slippery logical conclusion. "If the Russian threat justifies arms for all of Western Europe," he declared, "surely it justifies similar arms for Nationalist China, for Indochina, for India, and ultimately for Japan; and in the Near East for Iran, for Syria, and for Iraq. . . . There is no limit to the burden." Right again.

Taft received a standing ovation for his soaring, sensible rhetoric but won only thirteen votes from his colleagues. His assertions would ultimately be proved right on many levels. NATO marked the end of the dream — manifested in the United Nations — of internationalism and signaled a return to power politics. Taft saw that a hardening of either side in the Cold War would severely limit the potential of the infant UN. The NATO alliance, he thundered, was a violation of "the whole spirit of the United Nations charter . . . it necessarily divides the world into two armed camps." Indeed it did. And the division remains. Because of NATO — to which the United States is still obligated by treaty — America could be drawn into a war, perhaps a nuclear war, over Lithuania, a country few US citizens could locate on a map. That is Truman's legacy.

It didn't have to be this way. There were prominent dissenting voices at the time, though they were quickly "red-baited," silenced and ushered to the political margins. One such figure was FDR's former vice president, Henry Wallace. Wallace, then serving as Truman's commerce secretary, wrote a long letter to the new president in 1946.

> How do American actions since V-J Day appear to other nations? I mean by actions concrete things like $13 billion for the War and Navy Departments . . . tests of the atomic bomb and continued production of bombs . . . and the effort to secure bases spread over the globe from which the other half of the globe can be bombed. I cannot but feel that

these actions must make it look to the rest of the world as if
we were paying only lip service to peace. . . .

Then Wallace took it a step further. The United States should offer
"reasonable . . . guarantees of security" to the Soviets "and allay any
reasonable Russian grounds for fear, suspicion, and distrust." We
"must recognize . . . there can be no 'One World' unless the US and
Russia can find some way of living together." Truman and probably
most Americans — (by then) brainwashed — were in no mood for
such idealism, which was fantasy as the president saw it. He mostly
ignored the former vice president, and when Wallace took his views
public at Madison Square Garden, Truman demanded his resignation
from the cabinet. From then on the Democratic Party establishment
worked tirelessly to paint Wallace, who himself was a Democrat, as a
"pinko" and a "commie" and banished him from the limelight.

And so the war drums beat on, catapulting the United States and the
never-so-innocent Soviet Union from one crisis to another. In June
1948, Russians blockaded US-occupied West Berlin. In the standard
American version of events, the Soviets did so as an act of outright
aggression, a test of Truman's manhood and fortitude even. The story at
the center of the American public's attention was the subsequent "Berlin
Airlift" of supplies into the city by aircraft of the US military, an effort
that went on round the clock until Stalin backed down. What is forgotten is the cause of the Soviet blockade. Mainly Stalin was frightened by
Western plans under way, against earlier agreements, to unite the three
occupation sectors of Germany — French, British, American — into a
strong, coherent, independent West German state. The Russians, from
this perspective, had genuine cause to fear a reunited German entity,
especially since Germany's west held most of the country's industrial
capacity. But Stalin backed down in the face of stunning American airlift
capacity — something the Soviets could not have pulled off then — and,
just as he had feared, West Germany did become an independent republic, rearmed, and soon joined the anti-Soviet NATO military alliance.

Then, to bolster Western Europe's purchasing power and stabilize local economies, Secretary of State George Marshall announced

his plan — the Marshall Plan — to provide substantial financial aid to the European continent. This was, in fact, a remarkably generous and successful program; we need only look to the relative prosperity of Europe today for proof. The aid was even offered to the Russians and their Eastern European clients, but with so many strings attached that the Soviets, perhaps unwisely, turned it down. Stalin correctly smelled a capitalist rat. The Marshall Plan did have ulterior motives, mainly to discredit and undermine the collectivist narratives of Western Europe's then-powerful communist political parties and to establish a capitalist monopoly on the continent west of Berlin. These motives were unmistakable even back in 1947, when future secretary of state Dean Acheson proclaimed to fellow Americans in a State Department publication that "these measures . . . have only been in part suggested by humanitarianism. . . . Your government . . . is carrying out a policy of relief and reconstruction chiefly as a matter of national self-interest." National interest over internationalist solutions was to be the story of the Cold War.

Next, in 1949, China fell to its local communist insurgency. This was a disaster for men like Wallace who had dared imagine an "other" world, "One World." Having already foolishly divided the globe between two ideological camps, Truman — and his critics on the right, who were even more hawkish than he was — could not see this turn of events as anything other than a "win" for the Soviets and a supposed (but not actual) monolithic global communism. It mattered not that Stalin had offered scant support to Mao's communists, that Russia and China were historically natural enemies (and would spill blood on their borders by the 1960s), or that Mao's foe, the Nationalist opposition headed by Chiang Kai-shek, was corrupt, brutal, and somewhat dictatorial in its own right. Those were seen as mere details, "egghead" intellectual hogwash. The most populous nation on the planet had "turned Red," and that called for anti-communist "toughness" at home and abroad. In a sense, the Republicans and conservative Democrats would never forgive Truman for "losing China" — as if it ever was ours to lose — a sentiment that inflicted a psychological wound far deeper than any actual strategic wound on the capitalist West.

So it was, as the middle of the twentieth century arrived, that Truman and the United States became trapped in a bind of American making. After the fall of China, it was clear that the president — having described the world in binary, Manichaean terms — had laid an enormous, perhaps impossible, task before the nation: to check and balance now Eurasia-wide communism and prevent its further spread by any means necessary. This expensive, dangerous, and ultimately hopeless policy combination of "containment" and "rollback" would characterize the next forty years of US foreign relations. A bloody war in Korea was the first — though far from last — result of Truman's bifurcated world vision. We will consider the Korean War in more detail later, but no doubt the horror of that unexpected military clash both influenced Truman's decision not to run for reelection and helped bring about the triumph of national hero Dwight Eisenhower as a Republican in the 1952 presidential election.

Ike, as General Eisenhower was known, was actually skeptical of big government spending and aggressive international interventionism. After all, he served as president in another time, an era of more limited foreign engagement. Still, as a Republican and a product of his moment, Ike was constricted in his choices and vision. So it was that, in 1953, when Stalin died and his seemingly more amenable heirs came to power, the US president would squander an opportunity to defuse tensions and substantially reduce defense expenditures and the growing arms race. When the Kremlin leadership called for a new summit meeting, Ike ignored the advice of his old comrade, Britain's usually uber-hawkish prime minister Winston Churchill, and declined. He was a newly inaugurated president, after all, who had run his election campaign on the premise that Truman and other Democratic leaders were soft on communism. As a Republican dependent on conservatives in Congress, he could not politically risk another Yalta Conference that carried the stigma of compromising with the "enemy." It was the ultimate lost opportunity.

Eisenhower did, however, devise a unique way to lower defense expenditures and balance the budget (a pet project of his) during his two terms as president. He decreased America's reliance on conventional ground forces and expanded the nation's nuclear arsenal and capabilities. Letting the Soviets know about this new strategy was key. Rather than duke it out with communists in the mud of Korea or some other meaningless locale, the United States would declare a right to "massively retaliate" against any perceived Soviet aggression with nuclear weapons. This was genuinely scary talk. Though such a policy might have made some sense in 1946 — when the United States held a nuclear monopoly — it seemed suicidal in the 1950s, a time when the Soviets, too, possessed nuclear arms. It raised serious logical questions: Would the US sacrifice London or New York to save Seoul or Berlin or some other border-nation metropolis? We'll never know the answer.

The reliance of Eisenhower's strategy on nuclear retaliation often created political momentum for the use of such weapons. On a number of occasions — such as when the French garrison was besieged by communist insurgents in Vietnam, and when Mao's Red Chinese shelled the small Nationalist-held coastal island of Quemoy — serious policy makers in the administration advised Ike to use nukes. And in the Chinese islands crisis, when the chairman of the US Joint Chiefs of Staff publicly asked "what America's nuclear weapons were for, if not for use in such crises," the rightfully freaked-out British sought assurance from Eisenhower that nuclear war wasn't actually on the table.

"Massive retaliation," as it was dubbed, actually represented a scary escalation of apocalyptic rhetoric. Still, there is doubt that Eisenhower the man ever seriously considered using the bombs. The former general hated war, had been horrified by the sight of battlefields in Europe, and may have been bluffing in order to avoid future Korea-style regional wars. Ike's defenders, then and now, argued just that. Certainty on this question, of course, is unattainable, but we do know that throughout the Eisenhower administration no more than a handful of US soldiers died in combat the president had initiated. How many US presidents — before, but especially since — could boast such an accomplishment?

This is not to imply that Ike's hands were clean or that he didn't contribute to the militarization of the amped-up Cold War. Indeed, just as Senator Taft had predicted, the NATO alliance would expand and be further militarized during Ike's tenure. When war broke out in Korea under Truman in 1950, rather than focus more on Asia, the Western European powers became convinced that this local war was just a distraction for an impending Soviet invasion of Germany and France. No such plan or intention existed, of course. Nonetheless, throughout the 1950s the NATO allies demanded, and received, ever more US Army infantry and armored divisions in Europe. In an even more controversial move, NATO even decided to form an independent Federal Republic of (West) Germany, arm it with $4 billion in American loans, and welcome it into the alliance!

Only a decade had passed since Nazi Germany unilaterally conquered the mainland of Europe, and Russia was understandably horrified when the country of West Germany suddenly appeared in 1949. NATO, going a step further, even formed its own integrated army! Once again Senator Taft read the expansion of NATO as an unnecessary propellant for Cold War tensions. The creation of an armed German rump state and a NATO army, Taft declared, was a mistake, and he concluded:

> I believe that the formation of such an army, and its location in Germany along the *Iron Curtain* line . . . is bound to have an aggressive aspect to the Russians. We would be going a long way from home, and very close to the Russian border. . . . The formation of this army is more an incitement to Russia to go to war rather than a deterrent.

Taft, in still another defeat, was right again. Nine days after the formal acceptance of West Germany into NATO, the jittery Soviets guided the hands of East German leaders and other Eastern European states to sign a counterbalancing Warsaw Pact alliance. It was the West, not the Soviets, that started the world on the road to dichotomous military alliances.

If Eisenhower detested conventional wars and the deaths of American soldiers, he showed no such concern for the sovereignty, liberty, or lives of foreigners. The president remained determined to combat communist "aggression" wherever it should rear its ugly head, and his tool of choice was not the US military but the newly formed Central Intelligence Agency (CIA). Operating in the shadows, under Ike's orders, the CIA funded rebels, masterminded coups, coordinated air strikes, and took any other actions necessary to topple left-leaning figures — often democratically elected — across the globe. "Successful" (in the short term) though most of these operations were, the United States still lives with the consequences of such international illegal operations.

———

When populist, elected prime minister Mohammad Mossadegh of Iran threatened to nationalize his country's foreign-exploited oil resources in 1953, the CIA and British intelligence (MI6) helped to overthrow him. A dictatorship ensued under the Western-friendly but brutal shah of Iran. The United States, a nation formed in opposition to monarchy, had installed a king in a distant land.

Soon afterward in Guatemala, the elected, reformist, somewhat leftist president Jacobo Arbenz nationalized 250,000 acres owned by the US corporation the United Fruit Co. In reaction the CIA trained and supplied a small army of insurgents to topple him. When the US-sponsored ground attack stalled, planes piloted by Americans bombed the capital, Guatemala City. Arbenz fled, and a murderous but pro-American general, Carlos Armas, took over.

The American track record of foreign meddling only worsened as the 1950s wore on. When Ike ordered General James Doolittle of World War II fame to review the activities and goals of the CIA, the resulting report summarized the spy-infused spook-thinking of the Eisenhower-era Cold War. Doolittle concluded, "It is now clear that we are facing an implacable enemy whose avowed objective is world domination. . . . There are no rules in such a game. *Hitherto acceptable norms of human conduct do not apply*" (emphasis added). As if to prove Doolittle correct, US propaganda broadcasts encouraged Hungarian rebels in 1956 to fight the Soviets. The rebels died by the thousands in the streets of Budapest when the expected American aid never arrived.

Under Ike, US cash bought votes in Syria; US advisers illegally intervened to elect a Philippine president; US operatives gave financial and logistical support for an uprising that toppled the government of Indonesia, after which Suharto, the successor president, would later be responsible for hundreds of thousands of deaths; and, in a demonstration of vicious absurdity, the CIA planned to assassinate the popular Congolese president Patrice Lumumba. His own domestic enemies got to Lumumba first, but not for lack of CIA effort. The agency's director, Allen Dulles, had cabled the CIA's local station chief: "We conclude that his [Lumumba's] removal must be an urgent and prime objective." This was as good as a death sentence for the Congolese populist. Had he not been killed by his domestic opponents, he may well have met an even more gruesome death — the CIA's biological warfare bureau was in the process of selecting a pathogen to knock Lumumba out of action.

By the middle of Eisenhower's two terms in office, most countries had been pressured to line up on one side of the geopolitical and ideological fence or the other. And the dirty truth was the United States found itself backing nearly as many crackpot despots as the Soviet Union. This included American backing for such royalists as the shah of Iran and the king in Saudi Arabia, elected autocrats in South Korea and Taiwan, and military coup artists who ruled in Thailand, Pakistan, and much of South America. This, to be sure, was not the postwar world that FDR and Churchill had ostensibly dreamed of aboard their ships in the North Atlantic as they signed the Atlantic Charter. Still, fifteen-odd years later this was the world as it was, and in many ways remains.

Korea: The First Forgotten War

Korea came along and saved us.

— Secretary of State Dean Acheson referring
to his successful effort to convince Congress
to adopt his recommendation of an
increased military budget

Here's a contentious assertion: the military conflict in Korea was an absolute bloodbath and an unnecessary waste that never would have continued as long as it did if television technology had been available then to project the ghoulish images of war into American homes every day. To say this is not to deny that, today, South Korea is a far more vibrant, open, and preferable environment than contemporary North Korea, which is dominated by an unhinged dictatorial regime. Rather, it is a statement that some sixty-five years ago such a war could have been avoided and, if not, certainly limited in scope and duration. That it was not is an indictment of leadership decisions made at the time, in Moscow, Beijing, and Pyongyang, to be sure, but also in Washington, DC.

At the end of World War II, just after the Russians had intervened in the Pacific theater at the eleventh hour in Manchuria, a tacit agreement was reached for Soviet troops to occupy the northern half of the Korean Peninsula, above the 38th parallel, while US troops occupied and administered the southern half. As Cold War tensions rose, each party backed a communist or capitalist regime in its own sector. Still, by 1950 it was unclear that the division of Korea would be permanent. In fact, US and Soviet troops had already left the peninsula, and — in an unwise public statement of defense strategy — Secretary of State Acheson left South Korea off his list of countries within his defined American "defense perimeter" in Asia. This may have been an oversight, but the gaffe undoubtedly encouraged the North Korean communists to consider an invasion of the south.

When the North Korean army rolled across the border in late June 1950, a de facto state of war — often forgotten now — already existed on the peninsula. Partisan attacks from both sides of the parallel cost some one hundred thousand Korean lives between 1945 and 1950. At the time of the invasion, however, US officials were convinced that global communism was a monolith and that Stalin was directly behind the action. Once again, American leaders misread Stalin's role. President Kim Il Sung of North Korea masterminded the invasion himself, fearing — with some cause — that Syngman Rhee's autocratic southern statelet might soon invade the north and hoping a North Korean invasion would spark a national communist revolution. It didn't. Stalin, in fact, had initially resisted Kim's plans to attack, assenting only at the last moment, and never provided the level of Soviet arms and air support that Kim thought had been promised to him. Still, in President Truman's binary world, the North Korean attack was read as a direct provocation from Stalin. If the United States didn't stand tall in Korea, Truman feared, his domestic political opponents would brand his administration with the odious terms *Munich* and *appeasement*.

So, though Kim's supposed revolution never erupted, North Korea's Soviet-supplied tanks did initially roll over the surprised South Korean defenders. The capital of Seoul soon fell, and total conquest of the peninsula seemed likely. At this point Truman made two monumental decisions: to commit US ground forces to fight on the Asian mainland to engage in combat not five years after the Second World War had ended; and to not seek congressional approval or a declaration of war. The first decision sentenced tens of thousands of GIs to die in Korea's rugged terrain; the second decision set a dangerous, unconstitutional precedent, that executive war powers were so broad that Congress had almost no role to play in war making outside an advisory and financial capacity. Read backward from the present, with US troops engaged in several undeclared wars, it is the second decision that looms larger and turned out to be more fundamental.

Truman, at first, wouldn't even call it a war; rather, he termed it a "police action" in front of reporters. Four days into the invasion, with American air and naval support already engaged, and GIs twenty-four hours away from spilling ample blood in Korea, Truman foolishly announced in a press conference: "We are not at war." Still, despite his horrifying precedent and early mismanagement of the war, the American people — patriotic as ever — initially rallied to the president's cause. Congress, too, was acquiescent. When Truman announced his unilateral deployment of troops to combat he received a standing ovation in the legislature. Congress then authorized him to call up the reserves and extended the draft.

For all that, the US Army did not perform well early in the war. Douglas MacArthur, America's celebrity general, had poorly trained and prepared his occupation soldiers stationed in Japan. The units were ill equipped and ignorant of Korea's terrain, and their commander, known as Mac, had utterly underestimated his adversary. In the first two weeks, the United States and its allied forces suffered 30 percent casualties and were pushed into the small "Pusan Perimeter" on the far southeast of the peninsula. Eventually, as reinforcements poured in, MacArthur pulled off a military masterstroke, a risky, enveloping, amphibious invasion behind the North Korean lines at the port of Inchon. Almost at once North Korean resistance collapsed, and the invaders fled northward in disarray. This was Mac's last miracle, however. In reality the "general in chief" was a walking problem.

Known to be arrogant, self-important, and often foolhardy, MacArthur wasn't popular even among those who had been his fellow senior officers in the late world war. Omar Bradley thought him vain and domineering. Eisenhower felt the same way; once asked whether he knew MacArthur, Ike had said, "Not only have I met him . . . I studied dramatics under him for five years in Washington and four in the Philippines." President Truman too thought little of the ambitious general. Truman referred to him in his journal as "Mr. Prima Donna, Brass Hat." However, after Inchon, MacArthur's optimistic theatrics would encourage Truman to make his worst, and most fateful, decision of the war: to go beyond the original United Nations mandate and attempt to unify the entirety of Korea under the capitalist Rhee regime. From the Soviet perspective, and especially that of the nearby Chinese, this escalation understandably read as Western aggression. Still, at the time, for Truman it seemed a non-decision. Public opinion clamored for it, MacArthur demanded such a strategy, and the Pentagon dare not defy the president. It was a recipe for disaster.

The Chinese, meanwhile, had given ample warning they might intervene, especially if US troops approached their border along the Yalu River. From their rather rational perspective, US intervention in the distant Korean War was little more than a pretext for renewed intervention in China in the wake of the recently concluded civil war there. You can see why the Chinese thought this way. Truman had ordered the US fleet into the narrow strait dividing mainland China from the final Nationalist stronghold and rump state on the island of Taiwan. What's more, recently the United States had refused — in its capacity as a permanent UN Security Council member — to seat Mao's Chinese delegation, instead maintaining the official charade that Chiang's tiny island redoubt was the real China. This fiction would endure for a few more decades. Finally, as US troops — under MacArthur's own foolish orders — did approach the Yalu River, the Chinese were not unaware of American boasting about military successes in Korea and the calls from congressional conservatives to "smash the Chinese revolution." In this setting the Chinese, it appears, genuinely feared for their safety.

So it was that even with MacArthur predicting the troops would be home by Christmas, and having told Truman there was "very little" possibility of Chinese intervention, hundreds of thousands of Chinese troops poured across the Yalu River. In bitterly cold weather, Mao's battle-hardened veterans of the Chinese civil war drove through and around the surprised and flat-footed Americans. Though extraordinary heroism would save most American units from destruction, MacArthur's earlier carelessness and exuberance had contributed to their tactical woes — he had left massive gaps between the two main Western armies on the peninsula. The average GI, not MacArthur in his gold-brimmed hat, would suffer the consequences. In a humiliating retreat the Americans lost Seoul before stabilizing the lines. It was the second time enemy forces had taken the city.

Mortified by the setback, MacArthur lashed out and demanded — publicly — the crazy, the impossible: atomic bombing of Chinese industrial targets (cities), the unleashing of Chiang's army into the fight, and a complete blockade of the massive Chinese coastline. Truman fumed over this frantic insubordination but kept cool publicly. After all, the Democratic president had domestic political opponents to deal with — and they, mostly Republicans, were encouraging him to follow Mac's advice and extend the war into China.

After Christmas, a new tactical commander under MacArthur, General Matthew Ridgway, led a successful limited counterattack that regained Seoul and established fixed front lines generally along the 38th parallel. There the lines of a stalemated war would basically remain for the next two years. Then MacArthur, finally, perhaps inescapably, committed career suicide once and for all. He, a serving US general in the field, sent a critical anti-Truman letter to the opposition Republican leader in the House of Representatives, Joseph Martin. An elated Martin read the letter on the floor, including one bit where MacArthur declared that the "[Truman] administration should be indicted for the murder of American boys." This display of staggering insubordination was the last straw for Truman, who, with the assent of the Joint Chiefs, summarily fired Douglas MacArthur, the American hero.

Truman's decision was the right, really the only, one for an American president. MacArthur had not only tested the very limits of civilian control of the US military, he had also been dead wrong in his increasing unhinged counsel and demands. His preferred course of accepting "no substitute for 'victory'" — a concept still taught at West Point — would have utterly trashed relations with terrified NATO allies, killed untold millions in a prolonged ground war with China, murdered countless Asian civilians under American atomic bombs, and potentially set off a cataclysmic global nuclear war with the Soviet Union. All that aside, MacArthur, it seems, got the last word.

Mac was welcomed back to the United States — his first time home from Asia in thirteen years — as a conquering hero. It's no wonder MacArthur's most famous biographer titled his book *American Caesar*. Within weeks the general addressed a joint session of Congress and was interrupted by applause thirty times in a thirty-four-minute speech. After the booming oratory MacArthur rode triumphantly down Pennsylvania Avenue, with bombers and fighters flying in formation overhead, as a crowd of three hundred thousand cheered him on. The next day New York City threw him a ticker-tape parade. Some estimates placed the crowd at seven and a half million. A Gallup survey indicated that 69 percent of the American people sided with him over Truman. Within twelve days Truman received more than twenty thousand letters about the general, and they ran twenty to one in favor of MacArthur. Some letters were so overtly hostile and threatening that they were shown to the Secret Service.

Given all this madness, it's difficult to know who really won the epic battle between MacArthur and Truman. One surmises that MacArthur won the popularity contest, but Truman and the senior generals got their way when it came to policy. Finally standing up to the now dismissed MacArthur, Chairman of the Joint Chiefs Omar Bradley announced that he had always supported the president and believed that MacArthur's recommendations "would involve us in the wrong war, at the wrong place, at the wrong time, and with the wrong enemy."

What we can say is that the war that already existed continued, just as before; only now it played out as a grueling stalemate. The grand theatrics over, war dragged on and on. Though there was no organized antiwar movement to speak of in the pre-Vietnam era of 1950s patriotism, the war became wildly unpopular with the American people. Dubbed "Truman's War," and with thousands of GIs — 45 percent of US casualties occurred in the stalemated final twenty-eight months of war — dying on meaningless pieces of high ground like Heartbreak Ridge and Pork Chop Hill, the populace began to wonder what it was all for.

Still, peace talks that began in July 1951 had their own stalemate, eventually two years long, before the exhausted Chinese and North Koreans came to terms. During the stalemate, the frustrated American public, desperate to end the war — but not willing to simply quit the fight — began again to consider MacArthur-like solutions. According to one November 1951 poll, 51 percent of Americans favored using the Bomb on "military targets" (whatever that meant in practice). When peace came, in July 1953, it was far from clear exactly what had changed. Some writers point to Stalin's death and surmise that the new Soviet leaders pressured the Chinese and North Koreans to back down and accept the terms. Hawkish historians often imply that newly elected Ike had secretly threatened to use nuclear weapons upon his ascension to office. This is unproved. Most likely, the Chinese and the Koreans of the north were exhausted, just as the Americans and the Koreans of the south were by mid-1953. In the end, perhaps, it took a Republican president and former general like Eisenhower to bring the war to a conclusion. Eisenhower accepted terms for the cease-fire without gaining any major concessions from the enemy. Had Truman accepted such an armistice, he would have been attacked from the right, but Ike was a newly elected Republican and his party now controlled the legislative branch as well. As the historian H. W. Brands wrote, "If anyone could end the awful stalemate, it was Ike." That may ultimately have been the case.

Contrary to many later assertions that US entry into the Korean War was humanitarian in nature, it must never be forgotten that America waged a vicious campaign. US planes dropped 635,000 tons of bombs on the small peninsula, more than the combined total dropped in the Pacific theater of World War II. The bombing only contributed to a land-based "scorched earth" policy in which US, South Korean, and other allied troops wiped thousands of villages off the map and destroyed irrigation systems that fed the land. Thousands of Koreans starved to death. These were but a tiny fraction of the two million Korean civilians who perished under the bombardment and seesaw land invasions — some 10 percent of the prewar population of the entire peninsula.

The war in Korea ended as a draw, with the front line running along the 38th parallel line. The peninsula wasn't to be unified either by communists or capitalists. Neither the Americans, Soviets, or Chinese appear to have had it in their power to achieve this. And so, for the accomplishment of basically nothing, the United States suffered thirty-three thousand combat deaths and the Koreans took four million casualties killed, wounded, missing, most of them civilians. For all that, the supposedly invincible United States did avoid the communist takeover of the south. Still, the shift early in the war's first year to an offensive strategy to reunify the entire country for capitalism provoked Chinese intervention, and once the war settled into a stalemate the United States could not agree to an acceptable armistice for more than two bloody years. That mostly Korean blood must rest, at least partially, on America's hands.

Commies on Every Corner: The Postwar Red Scares

Foreign enemies, real or imagined, are by nature the friend of centralized government and the foe of civil liberty. America's hyper-opposition to communism in the 1940s and '50s demonstrates this truth as clearly as any other national scare in US history. Some of the fear was genuine, a grassroots civilian response to a scary nuclear--armed world; still, it must be said that much of the panic was artificial, sown externally by senior government elites with political and economic motives to pursue through an external "Red Scare." Much was lost — social goals not sought, art not crafted, and individual liberties not protected — amid anti-communist hysteria. We may be tempted to conclude that the Cold War existed most fervently in the heads of America and Americans, more real there than along the divided frontier of East and West Berlin. War, as the progressive intellectual Randolph Bourne once wrote, "is the health of the state." But wars — the finite type that governments declare and wage — end. Cold wars, on the other hand, can conceivably last forever, to the glee and forever health of the state and its arms-manufacturing oligarchs. This is the power of perpetual militarism at home and militarized standoffs abroad. The 1940s and '50s manifested as an Orwellian world — one Americans still inhabit today. Global communism is gone, but global "terror" quickly replaced it; Stalinist Soviet "aggression" is dead, but the Russian bear in the form of Vladimir Putin is alive and well. Let us think on that in analyzing the Red Scare of the early Cold War.

The wave of fear that gripped the nation during the early Cold War showed itself politically as well as socially. It affected a variety of American institutions, from Hollywood to the legislature to the living room. In the political realm, conservative Democrats and newly resurgent Republicans manipulated anti-communist sentiment to attack even modestly liberal opponents, thereby temporarily closing the book on FDR-style social welfare. Everyone, it seemed, played the red-baiting game, but few did it better than rising Republican star Richard M. Nixon. Running for a US Senate seat in California,

Nixon labeled his opponent, Helen Gahagan Douglas, "Pink right down to her underwear." He called her the "Pink Lady"; she dubbed him "Tricky Dick," a nickname that stuck. Covering the campaign, a columnist at *The Nation* remarked upon Nixon's "astonishing capacity for petty malice." Right the author was, of course, but Nixon won the Senate seat and went on to be one of the most hawkish Cold Warriors in Washington before serving as Eisenhower's vice president.

If Nixon was just beginning his career-long campaign of malice, the real heavyweight of hysterical anti-communism on Capitol Hill was Wisconsin's Republican senator Joseph McCarthy. His was the most virulent, damaging, and ultimately absurd brand of red-baiting. The wildly delusional McCarthy seemed to see commies on every corner. He rose to prominence when he delivered a now famous speech to a Republican women's club in Wheeling, West Virginia, in which he thundered, "I have here in my hand a list of 205 names that were made known to the Secretary of State as members of the Communist Party and who nevertheless are still working and shaping the policy of the State Department." He had, of course, no list. Time and again over the years, doubters demanded to see this list or other such documents that the senator allegedly held, but McCarthy regularly brushed them off and never produced one. What's more, the number of "known communists" on McCarthy's list changed, from 205 to 57 to 81, over just a few months.

Boisterous public theatrics masking personal fraud was the name of the game for McCarthy. Running for office in 1946, his campaign relied on his supposed World War II record as a combat flier in the Marine Corps, dubbing him "Tail Gunner Joe." Joe was a blatant liar. He claimed to have flown thirty combat missions; in fact, he had gone on none. Later, he would walk around Washington with a limp that he said was caused by "ten pounds of shrapnel" that earned him a Purple Heart. Actually he had hurt his foot in a fall down a set of stairs at a party. In addition to being a pathological liar, the senator was a drunk, a braggart, and a bully. He carried bottles of whiskey in a dirty briefcase that he claimed was full of his famous "documents" and bragged that he could put away a fifth of whiskey a day. Most of all, McCarthy loved hyper-masculine bravado. He referred to some supposed subversives as "homos" or "pretty boys"; those who opposed him were "left-wing bleeding hearts" or "egg-sucking phony liberals"; he leered at and otherwise sexually harassed attractive women who appeared before his many committee hearings.

McCarthy was a loose cannon and rarely, if ever, backed up his hyperbolic claims. He almost never followed up on his charges, and he never identified a single subversive by name. Eventually Democrats and some sober Republicans tried to investigate and refute the man. A committee led by Democratic senator Millard Tydings exposed a litany of lies and exaggeration surrounding McCarthy. The majority report concluded that, taken as a whole, McCarthy's claims were "a fraud and a hoax perpetrated on the Senate of the United States and the American People." Still, McCarthy survived the hearings and continued on his crusade. He wasn't down yet. Indeed, between 1951 and 1954 he led no fewer than eighty-five committee investigations into domestic communist influence.

Eventually, however, as much of his deceit came to light, McCarthy went too far. In what became known as the Army-McCarthy hearings of 1954, the senator questioned General Ralph Zwicker — holder of a Purple Heart and a Silver Star medal — and told the man that he had "the brains of a five-year-old child" and was "a disgrace to the army." After that incident McCarthy was eviscerated on television by the legendary CBS anchor Edward R. Murrow. Later in the hearings the army's chief counsel, Joseph Welch, interrupted McCarthy to famously ask, "At long last, do you have no decency, sir?" Welch received a standing ovation. McCarthy was bewildered; he didn't realize his public career essentially had ended. After that, President Eisenhower — who, even though he found it politically expedient to stay silent on McCarthy's antics, had never cared for the man — removed McCarthy from the list of welcome guests at the White House. "It's no longer McCarthyism," Eisenhower declared, "it's McCarthy-wasm." That December the Senate voted 65–22 to censure McCarthy. (Senator John F. Kennedy, whose brother Bobby worked as an aide to McCarthy, and whose father staunchly supported the

Wisconsin Republican, was the only Democrat not to publicly support the censure. In fact, when still a member of the House, the future president once claimed that "McCarthy may have something.")

Three years later the chronic alcoholic died at age forty-eight. Yet his legacy and spirit lived on. Students of the era should never forget how popular McCarthy was among significant segments of the American people, or how small was the number of Republicans — and even Democrats — who would defy him in the early days. If McCarthy lost the practical battle to prove a vast conspiracy — which never really seemed to be his true motive or priority — he succeeded in pulling American politics and culture to the right and popularizing an anti-communist frenzy and tactics that outlived the man himself. The era of McCarthy, even today, is far from dead.

The fact that McCarthyism eventually fizzled out and in the end the man was disgraced does nothing to minimize the damage caused to the senator's victims. Though the State Department didn't find any truth in McCarthy's initial allegations of communist infiltration, at least ninety employees of the US foreign service were fired as "security threats." This was in an era when to be gay was equated with anti-Americanism and vulnerability to blackmail. Indeed, the hunt for government-employed gays became a national priority in some powerful minds. Roy Black, then the head of the District of Columbia vice squad, called for a national task force because, he claimed, "There is a need in this country for a central bureau for records of homosexuals and perverts of all types."

Congressional legislation also reflected the worst instincts of McCarthyism during this and earlier periods. Truman's 1947 Executive Order 9835 set up "loyalty boards" in all federal government agencies, which employed some two and a half million people. The loyalty boards played it fast and loose with regard to civil liberties protections, denying accused government workers the right to know the identity of their accusers — often undercover FBI agents — or to confront them in court hearings. Indeed, many of those employees investigated were guilty of little more than belonging to vaguely liberal organizations. In 1948, Truman's administration went further, actually prosecuting the senior leadership of the American Communist Party on trumped-up charges.

The national legislature also got in on the game. In 1950, Congress passed the Internal Security Act — over Truman's courageous veto, it must be said — which required all American communists to "register" with the attorney general. A year later the Supreme Court in a 6–2 ruling upheld the Smith Act, which held that the First Amendment protections of free speech, press, and assembly did not apply to communist citizens. One of the two voices of reason on the court, Hugo Black, delivered a pained dissent, writing, "There is hope, however, that in calmer times, when . . . passions and fears subside, this or some later Court will restore the First Amendment liberties to the high preferred place where they belong in a free society." It is important to keep in mind, also, that support for anti-communist political legislation was never limited to Republicans. Democrats and various establishment leftists, especially after the "loss" of China, jumped on the commie-bashing express — some out of genuine agreement, others out of a sense of self-preservation within the prevailing winds.

These dubious bills may have been a lot of things, but what they were not was a proportional response to the actual threat of communism in America. By 1950 membership in the US Communist Party — never very high — was at its lowest level since the 1920s. Out of a population of 150 million, the United States counted only some 30,000 members. The party actually received little support from Moscow and had never been a very potent force in American politics. Ongoing pressure and prosecution of card-carrying Communist Party members were so intense that by 1957 membership plummeted to about five thousand members. So many of them were FBI agents that bureau chief J. Edgar Hoover considered massing his men to take over the party at a key leadership conference. Also, for all the talk of spies, subversion, and communist trickery in the United States, not a single public official was convicted of spying at any time during the postwar Red Scare. (The case of Alger Hiss, a State Department official, dealt with perjury counts, and the husband and wife convicted of espionage and executed in the infamous Rosenberg case were not government officials.)

Just as in the 1920s Red Scare — in which the bureau was an important player — the FBI played a nefarious role in the anti-communist hysteria of the 1940s and '50s. Using surveillance, wiretapping, and undercover informants — some of them religious figures, such as Cardinal Francis Spellman — agents of Hoover destroyed many a public reputation behind scant evidence. Critics of the FBI included US journalist and writer Bernard DeVoto, who in 1949 publicly decried the FBI leader's use of "gossip, rumor, slander, backbiting, malice and drunken invention, which, when it makes the headlines, shatters the reputations of innocent and harmless people." Such criticism of the bureau was rare, however, especially since it was widely alleged that Hoover kept detailed "blackmail files" on almost every major figure in Washington. Perhaps that's why Truman would complain only privately about the FBI. Shortly after becoming president in 1945, he wrote out this private thought by hand: "We want no Gestapo or Secret Police. FBI is tending in that direction. They are dabbling in sex life scandals and plain blackmail. . . . This must stop." It didn't.

In addition to clearing vile, perhaps unlawful bills, key congressional committees also went on the anti-communist hunt. The most famous was the House Un-American Activities Committee (HUAC), populated by some of the most hawkish and — predictably — bigoted representatives on Capitol Hill. Mississippi senator John Rankin used HUAC as a platform to attack and stymie the nascent black civil rights movement, calling it "a part of the communistic program, laid down by Stalin approximately thirty years ago. *Remember communism is Yiddish*" (emphasis added). Starting in 1947, HUAC's attention turned to probing alleged left-wing activity in Hollywood. Seeing the investigation as an anti-artistic "witch hunt," some famous entertainers courageously fought back. Judy Garland cried, "Before every free conscience in America is subpoenaed, please speak up! Say your piece. Write your Congressman a letter!" Frank Sinatra boldly asked, "Once they get the movies throttled, how long will it be before we're told what we can say and cannot say into a radio microphone. . . . Will they call you a Commie? . . . Are they going to scare us into silence?" However, a big part of Hollywood was sympathetic to the HUAC investigation, and "friendly witnesses" before the committee included

Gary Cooper, Walt Disney, and an actor who later would be spending much time in the nation's capital — Ronald Reagan.

There were serious consequences for some uncooperative members of the movie industry. After ten unfriendly witnesses, dubbed the "Hollywood 10" (including famed screenwriter Dalton Trumbo), refused to testify at committee hearings, they were held in contempt and made to serve prison sentences of between six months and a year. They and hundreds of others were blacklisted by the movie industry.

Among the Hollywood celebrity victims who were damaged severely by red-baiting was Charlie Chaplin. The American Legion led protests against the pacifist message of his 1947 film *Monsieur Verdoux*, and a few years later, while the British-born Chaplin was out of the United States, the government suspended his reentry permit until he agreed to "submit to rigorous examination of his political beliefs and moral behavior." He refused and remained in exile until 1972, when he returned to receive a special Oscar. He died in Switzerland in 1977.

The anti-communist frenzy extended well beyond the realm of public policy and partisan politics. In the education sector, schools and colleges fired faculty members — even those with tenure — who refused to deny they were communists. Estimates place the number of educators who lost their jobs at six hundred, most smeared by accusations of communist sympathies. States and towns, especially after the outbreak of the Korean War, banned communists from teaching, the civil service, and seeking public office. Private citizens built backyard bomb shelters; students across the nation practiced absurd "duck-and-cover" drills that supposedly would offer protection in a nuclear explosion. Pop culture, mainly books and movies, also played on the anti-communist fervor. Between 1948 and 1953, Hollywood produced about two hundred blatantly "anti-Red" features, such as *The Red Menace* (1949), *I Married a Communist* (also known as *The Woman on Pier 13*, 1950), and *I Was a Communist for the FBI* (1951).

America's Red Scare was no single thing. Red-baiting and anti-communist crusading served many purposes for many groups and individuals in the United States of the 1940s and '50s. The Red Scare manifested as politics more often than as genuine fear for national security. Republicans, mostly out of instinctive partisanship, needled Democrats for their alleged "softness" on communism. Segregationist southern Democrats stifled any talk of civil rights reform by equating the racial equality movement with communism. Religious populists pushed Christianity as an answer to "godless" global communism. Business leaders busted unions back down to size by overstating union connections to far-left political movements. Social conservatives and homophobes whose real agendas were to destroy elitism or promote social homogeneity scapegoated intellectuals, nonconformists, and gays as red sympathizers or worse. Finally, corporate leaders and unreconstructed laissez-faire economic theorists bashed FDR's welfare state — that old enemy — as socialistic and un-American.

Communism, communism, communism! The term was everywhere, all things to all people, serving many diverse interests. During the Truman and Eisenhower years, the Cold War became, at root, just another tool to bludgeon one's social, economic, and political enemies. And it worked like a charm.

Seen in context, the American Red Scare was unique in the Western capitalist world. Though the communist parties of Italy, France, and Britain were far stronger than the one in the United States, none of those countries experienced a major Red Scare in the 1950s. Indeed, in 1954, the famously anti-communist Prime Minister Winston Churchill refused when asked to establish a royal commission to investigate British communism.

The postwar Red Scare in America was politically and culturally destructive, narrowed the window for dissent, and ultimately harmed US foreign policy by shutting off existing pathways to detente with the Soviet Union. Still, it bears mention that during this same period Soviet Russia underwent its own anti-capitalist scares, imprisoning millions and killing countless thousands. Of course there is little comparison to be made between the American and Russian experiences. The United States, after all, never had a gulag! Even so, the American Red Scare was a major blot on the national experiment in representative government and open society. The forced homogeneity, hyper-patriotism, and domestic militarism of the era demonstrated the capacity for cruelty and repression among American leaders and people alike. What is international is ultimately national; wars — even "cold" wars — come home and poison societies. The greater tragedy is this: whereas most wars usually end in a few years, the Cold War, as mentioned earlier, dragged on and on until it morphed into a comfortably equivalent "war on terror." As such, the propensity for "scares" on the home front pervades; America hasn't heard the last of these recurring outbursts of public fearmongering.

Upon a Cross of Iron: Forging the Military-Industrial Complex

The domestic arms industry had long held significant power in the United States, as in every other developed country. However, in the wake of World War I these "merchants of death" were publicly castigated by special congressional investigators and much of the public at large for allegedly causing — and then profiting from — America's military intervention in Europe. Still, in retrospect, that was an era of "small ball" for the domestic weapons trade. During the Second World War the US economy, and those of Allied powers, came to rely on corporate defense contractors at unseen levels. Though many lost such contracts in the immediate postwar years, these corporate titans had, during the war, amassed incredible power and leverage in Washington, especially on Capitol Hill. Furthermore, unlike in the first war, the arms industry was never heavily villainized in patriotic post-1945 America. After the war, they spent enormous sums on lobbying, campaign financing, and advertising to "sell" the supposed, and quite profitable, need for the maintenance of extraordinary defense budgets. They required a threat to make their case, of course, and the Soviet Union fit the mold perfectly. So it was that within just a couple of years of the wartime alliance between government and industry, the corporate arms dealers partnered with congressional and executive-branch hawks to peddle the gospel of Cold War.

The alliance, what President Eisenhower would later dub the military-industrial complex, was wildly successful, laying the foundations for the militarized garrison state we still inhabit. Though wartime defense spending levels initially plummeted in 1946–47, the announcement of the Truman Doctrine and outbreak of the Korean War were a godsend for both the Pentagon and its civilian suppliers. Defense spending, at an annual $13.1 billion in 1950, jumped to $50.4 billion in 1953, a Korean War high, and leveled off between $40 billion and $47 billion during rest of the peacetime 1950s. The cost came not only in the tax burden but also in cuts to nonmilitary government (social welfare) spending, which dropped from $30 billion in 1950 to $23.9 billion in 1952. By the mid-1950s three-fourths of the federal budget went to military spending. Much of that money went — you guessed it — to the conservative southern states that competed to host military bases and production facilities. Thus it came to pass that America, in the early Cold War, spent far more on its projectiles than its people.

Working together, civilian defense hawks in the Truman and Eisenhower administrations would feed policy solutions — in the way of papers and speeches — that justified, demanded even, the expansion of military budgets. Just before the war in Korea, senior policy makers wrote a "blueprint" for Cold War, NSC-68, that asserted, "The Soviet Union is seeking to create overwhelming military force." Accordingly, the United States must embark on "a rapid and sustained build-up of the political, economic, and military strength of the free world." This included an increase of "several times present expenditures" on national defense. At first Truman, some congressmen, and much of the public were skeptical. Then came Korea — which, as NSC-68 proponent Dean Acheson exclaimed, "saved" the campaign for higher spending. The war was a justification for enormous military spending, spending that stayed high indefinitely.

In academia and in key research and development laboratories, federal military backing dominated. By 1949 the Department of Defense and the Atomic Energy Commission accounted for 96 percent of all federally funded university research grants in the physical sciences. Two scientists, representing many others who feared for the fate of academic freedom, warned that "[i]t is essential that the trend toward military domination of our universities be reversed as speedily as possible." It wasn't reversed.

Instead of FDR's dream of a welfare state, the United States — unlike all the developed nations of Europe — built a national security state. In Senate hearings on the future of national defense, military contractor witnesses, including representatives from Lockheed, successfully argued that in the aftermath of World War II what the nation still required was "adequate, continuous, and *permanent*" (emphasis added) funding for military production. Lockheed and its many counterparts won both the emotional and economic public arguments again and again. The novelist William Faulkner observed, during this era, that "[o]ur economy is no longer agricultural. Our economy *is* the Federal Government" (emphasis added).

Faulkner, in the end, was right. The military-industrial complex had "won." Indeed, even today its reign continues. Nonetheless, the complex could never fully win over the leader of the 1950s-era free world. Eisenhower, though he did not possess a "clean" Cold War record, had always been plagued with doubts about the rivalry with the Soviets, war in general, and the defense industry in particular. Ike, after all, despite his top-level military bona fides, was nevertheless the child of Kansas pacifists. Though the nuclear arms race definitively ramped up during his administration, Ike privately questioned the efficacy of using the Bomb or the ability of the nation to survive an atomic war. "There just aren't enough bulldozers to scrape the bodies off the street," he said darkly. Eisenhower famously ended his second term with a televised farewell address warning of the dangers of the military-industrial complex, the first time most Americans would hear the term. He had dedicated his first major address as president to reckoning the cost of the ongoing arms buildup. Invoking William Jennings Bryan's long-ago, populist "Cross of Gold" speech, Ike declared:

> Every gun that is made, every warship launched, every rocket fired signifies in the final sense a theft from those who hunger and are not fed, those who are cold and not

clothed. . . . This world in arms is not spending money
alone; it is spending the sweat of its laborers, the genius of
its scientists, the hopes of its children. . . . This is not a way
of life at all in any true sense. Under the clouds of threatening war, it is humanity hanging from a cross of iron.

It was, undoubtedly, Eisenhower's best speech. Nonetheless, if
even such a credentialed, trusted, and respected figure as General
Dwight David Eisenhower could not, ultimately, stem the power of
the military-industrial complex or the profits of the corporate arms
dealers, what chance, really, did his successors have? What chance
have we today?

———

Though the Cold War–Red Scare steamroller appeared to flatten all
before it in the 1940s and 1950s, rational dissenting voices and other
possibilities did exist. Take the nation's top scientists. After the war,
they, especially the nuclear physicists, were among the loudest proponents of international cooperation and sharing of nuclear technology.
Soon after the war, the newly formed Federation of Atomic Scientists
attached a rider to a congressional bill calling for civilian, rather than
military, control of atomic power. Seeking to enlist public support,
America's most famous scientist, Albert Einstein, declared, "To the
village square we must carry the facts of atomic energy. From there
must come America's voice." A group of scientists, including Leo
Szilard, J. Robert Oppenheimer, and Einstein himself, published the
edited collection *One World or None: A Report to the Public on the Full
Meaning of the Atomic Bomb*. In the essay he wrote, Einstein argued
for general "de-nationalization" of atomic weaponry.

There is something else, something ever more profound. It is a cruel
and, for Americans, uncomfortable reality. Russia and the United
States have followed remarkably similar national paths with respect to
their historical foreign affairs. Both formed and initially expanded as
settler-colonial entities that grew into land-based empires. Throughout
the nineteenth century the United States drove westward; meanwhile,

Russia swelled eastward. Once the two powers ran out of space for territorially contiguous expansion, they gazed covetously at the same region — the great Pacific Ocean, Russia's east, America's west. Long before separate economic ideologies — capitalism and communism — developed as coherent, opposing systems, the stage was set for international rivalry between the two behemoths.

Then, when the Great War and, later, World War II broke out, both Russia and the United States were drawn into the fray. The Old World now became a contested space for two new powers on the rise. Unable to reconcile their seemingly opposing interests and ideologies, the result would be decades of precarious — sometimes deadly — Cold War. Americans, of course, see themselves as exceptional — so do the Russians, by the way! — as above realpolitik or outright imperialism. To an American, after all, the national interest naturally coheres with the global interest. Washington's goals and actions are always mostly benevolent; conflict, on the other hand, results when nefarious actors don't realize what's good for them, don't play by the (American) rules. It is through this twisted prism that the US citizenry views its history and its conflicts. The Cold War was no exception.

Like it or not, the record demonstrates that much of the blame for the outbreak and continuation of the Cold War rests with the United States. No less fervently than the Soviet Union did with communism, America sought to export its own, often self-serving, brand of capitalism the world over. The United States was the more powerful of the adversaries. It began with an atomic monopoly and maintained nuclear superiority for most of the Cold War. Its economic dominance was unprecedented in 1945 and remained supreme for the next forty years. The Soviet Union never posed the potential threat to the West that the United States and its allies presented to the East.

The truth is, the United States and the Soviet Union were never truly allies during World War II. They fought together as a temporary necessity despite unbridgeable ideological and economic differences. Seen in a broader, more holistic, view, America had been a mortal opponent of Russian communism since the outbreak of the Bolshevik Revolution in 1917. The United States punished and isolated the Soviets, even sent troops onto Russian soil in the early 1920s to back the old-regime opponents of the revolution. As in the 1950s, so it had been in the Roaring Twenties; both decades boasted domestic Red Scares at home and anti-communist aggression abroad. The Soviets, unlike uninformed Americans, hadn't forgotten the events of the 1920s — not by a long shot. Today's Russians still haven't.

The Cold War that the two sides waged was never as "cold" as it was touted to be. More than a hundred thousand US soldiers died in various local hot wars; so did millions of mainly Asian civilians caught in the crossfire. At home, the economy and society took on a pervasive warlike tone, even if this manifested below the surface of American life. In both the United States and the Soviet Union, the Cold War took on an institutional life of its own — as a way of life. The range of political, economic, and social possibilities narrowed during the second half of the twentieth century as governments closed ranks, suppressed liberties, and established "patriotic" norms. Dissent and "strangeness" were punished in both societies. It was to be the world's, and ultimately humankind's, loss.

Trillions in wealth and countless hours of energy and thought were wasted on potential wars and on actual wars that need never have been fought. As such, the opportunity cost was as staggering as it was unknowable. In the wake of the most bloody and devastating war in human history, the great powers — led by the United States — might have embarked upon building a more equitable and peaceful world; they might have exclaimed and lived the cry of "Never again!" Instead they sought global leverage. Security, rather than serenity, remained the currency.

Remember that there were options, paths not taken. Our leaders, and we as individuals and a people, possessed agency. History is contingent on the actions and inactions of countless billions. In the Cold War, tragically, the sum of those actions and inactions brought the earth to the brink of destruction, killed millions, and bequeathed to us a militarized, dangerous, precarious world. Such is the power of tribalism, nationalism, ideologies — whether capitalist or communist.

History, as we ought to remember, is both more and less than some litany of simplistic lessons learned, to the chagrin of many modern military historians. Still, if there is meaning to a serious, fresh study of the early Cold War, perhaps it is this: When the government presents the next ostensibly existential enemy — whether Mexican, Muslim, Russian, or Chinese — we must question the very premise of binary duality. Carefully interrogate the supposedly inevitable, imagine alternative courses, and help live the not-impossible dream of peace. To do otherwise is to acquiesce to an eternity of repeating "cold" wars. The odds may seem stacked against such individual thought, but violence or perpetual standoff isn't the only way.[24]

28

JFK'S COLD WAR CHAINS

Among the American people — if not historians — John F. Kennedy regularly ranks as one of the best presidents in various opinion polls. There is, undoubtedly, something magnetic about the Kennedy administration, dubbed "Camelot" by the president's wife, Jacqueline, soon after his assassination. However, one wonders if sentiments like this are little more than postmortem nostalgia for a young, handsome president. JFK memorialization and mythology are such that it seems the memories contain something for everyone. Today mainstream liberals tout his efforts on civil rights; defense hawks laud the toughness of his Cuban Missile Crisis stand; conversely, antiwar types insist that Kennedy was about to pull the US troops out of Vietnam when his presidency was ended by an assassin's bullets. To the scholar, however, much of the passionate praise for JFK seems unwarranted for a short administration that boasted so few tangible accomplishments.

A detached, probing view of the Kennedy years elucidates a generally popular president who was nevertheless a conventional Cold Warrior, a tool of the military-industrial complex, forever stalled on domestic legislation and reactive rather than proactive on black civil rights. This Kennedy — the human president — was also a highly political creature, motivated as often by partisan rancor and opinion polls as by the national interest. It is this Kennedy who fell into the Cold War-era trap that ensnared all Democratic presidents since and including Harry Truman; ever since Truman was accused of having "lost China," a string of Democratic executives that by no means ended with JFK became obsessed with conveying "toughness," avoiding the well-worn "Munich analogy" of appeasement, and out-hawking the Republicans in foreign affairs. It was a highly insecure Kennedy who escalated the doomed American war in Vietnam and terrorized Cuba's popular government throughout his thirty-four-month administration.

Perhaps forever, Americans will remember these words from Kennedy's sunlit inaugural address: "Ask not what your country can do for you; ask what you can do for your country. . . . Ask not what America will do for you, but what together we can do for the freedom of man." It is the final, less famous, clause in this passage that rings as problematic and, ultimately, hollow. From the perspective of a working-class Cuban, a Vietnamese peasant, or an unemployed, disenfranchised black American, JFK was no champion of man's "freedom." Rather, he hedged on African American civil rights, accelerated warfare in Southeast Asia, cut taxes on the wealthiest Americans, and obsessed himself with overthrowing the Castro administration in Cuba.

Our story, though, must not center only on the singular figure of Kennedy. Camelot went far beyond a compelling, photogenic politician, and far beyond his attractive wife and children. JFK assembled a team of youthful, energetic, elite advisers — many of them academics — forever christened the "best and the brightest." Kennedy made a show of crafting this highly educated team, which included Secretary of Defense Robert McNamara, national security adviser McGeorge Bundy, Secretary of State (and Rhodes scholar) Dean Rusk, informal adviser and Harvard professor Arthur Schlesinger Jr., and his brother Robert "Bobby" Kennedy as attorney general. Two of Kennedy's choices might seem peculiar for a supposedly liberal administration — McNamara and Bundy were Republicans. The oddness did not stop at politics: the appointment of Bobby was unashamedly nepotistic, and the vice president, Lyndon B. Johnson, was a rough-hewn — some would say crude — southerner. Despite the odd mix, the glossy aura of the team seemed to stick, especially in Americans' collective memory.

Let us consider, now, how this group of the "best and brightest" led an optimistic generation of Americans into leaving so much undone at home, blundering further into an unwinnable war, and bequeathing an ever more dangerous world.

To rethink Kennedy, as such, is also to normalize and provincialize him. Some will find much left to like about this less glamorous Kennedy, others far less. Regardless, this — the Kennedy of history not fantasy — is the president who must inform America's present moment.

Looks and Charm: Riding Charisma into the White House

It began with a debate with television cameras. Kennedy faced off against Richard Nixon, an anti-communist hawk and Dwight Eisenhower's vice president, in the 1960 presidential election. Theirs was only the second televised US presidential debate in history, and it mattered, as 90 percent of Americans now had a TV set. It was September 26, 1960, and the face-off between the two candidates was broadcast live on CBS, NBC, and ABC. It was an uneven fight. Nixon, though a highly skilled debater, had been sick and hospitalized for twelve days and was less prepared than usual. Nevertheless, most Americans who listened on the radio thought Nixon — trained in high school debate — had "won." The more numerous TV viewers, however, favored Kennedy — freshly tanned and seemingly cool and composed — over Nixon, who appeared unshaven and had refused to wear any heavy makeup.

The common memory of the 1960 election tends to contrast the youthful Kennedy, forty-three years old as of election day, with the old Washington hand Nixon — but the vice president was only three years older than his rival! The coarse, insecure, and petulant Nixon was seen by many as lacking style, making Kennedy seem the much younger man. Nixon had "no class," JFK had said, and a *Washington Post* editor (and Kennedy supporter), Ben Bradlee, claimed that Nixon had "[n]o style, no style at all." In the end the race was tight, one of the closest popular votes in American history, with JFK counting just a thirteen-thousand-vote margin of victory. So close was the election that Nixon believed the vote had been rigged and seriously considered contesting it. He may well have been right: Evidence existed for fraud in Illinois and Texas (Democratic vice presidential candidate Lyndon

Johnson's home state). "We won, but they stole it from us," Nixon would say, and a thirteen-year-old member of the Young Republicans named Hillary Rodham would volunteer to search for such fraud in Chicago.

That Kennedy would ultimately prevail seems obvious to modern readers. He has become, after all, a "liberal" phenomenon. Yet this was less than clear at the time. Indeed, JFK seemed, in 1960, a lukewarm choice for most Democrats in the party's left wing. Progressives distrusted him due to his silence — and at times support — of McCarthyism when Kennedy was a senator. Others, including Eleanor Roosevelt, resented that black civil rights had not seemed a priority for Senator Kennedy. Journalist Eric Sevareid of CBS complained of the Kennedy image itself, noting that Jack and his advisers were all "tidy, buttoned-down men . . . completely packaged products. The Processed Politician has finally arrived." The Massachusetts senator's wealth also drew the ire of some on the left. After losing to JFK in the key West Virginia primary contest, the prominent Minnesota senator, later Johnson's vice president, Hubert Humphrey complained, "You can't beat a million dollars. The way Jack Kennedy and his old man [the multimillionaire Joseph P. Kennedy Sr.] threw money around, the people of West Virginia won't need any public relief for the next fifteen years." This much was certain: The Kennedy of 1960 was no reincarnation of FDR. Such hagiography only came later.

Kennedy also ran a dirty, dishonest campaign. He campaigned against the outgoing incumbent Eisenhower administration from the right. He crowed about a nuclear "missile gap" with the Soviets — which was, by implication, Vice President Nixon's fault as well — even though he had been told by high-ranking defense officials that none existed. Kennedy went with the lie. In reality, the United States then possessed overwhelming nuclear superiority; it counted the equivalent of fifteen hundred atomic bombs and three thousand planes capable of carrying atomic bombs, while the Soviets had only fifty to a hundred missiles and just two hundred long-range bombers. It didn't help that the gentlemanly Eisenhower kept mostly quiet: he refused to divulge the classified information that would have disproved the "gap" — and provided only lukewarm support for his vice president. In truth, Ike never much cared for Nixon.

Beyond Kennedy's red-baiting over the nonexistent missile gap and his composure at the television debate, the candidate's success was bolstered by his image. He inspired frenzy at campaign rallies, where groups of people — mainly women — jumped barriers and chased his car. A prominent journalist at the time, Haynes Johnson, described Kennedy as "the most seductive person I've ever met." It was this mystique, a carefully cultivated portrait, that helped nudge JFK over the finish line. Personal appeal mattered! The historian Jill Lepore has concluded that "Kennedy prevailed, in part, because he was the first packaged, market-tested president, liberalism for mass consumption." Furthermore, she noted that JFK certainly "looked more like a Hollywood movie star than like any man who had ever occupied the Oval Office." So, for better or worse, it was John Kennedy who took the national helm in January 1961.

After the inauguration, the Kennedy family continued to awe the media and refined American elites. As the historian James Patterson noted, many reporters, themselves often liberal, "lavished attention" on the king and queen of Camelot. Jack had "unparalleled access" to the media, and he used it well. He was the first president to allow his press conferences to be televised live, and within six months some 75 percent of Americans had watched one. Among these TV viewers, 91 percent reported a favorable impression of Kennedy's performances. The telegenic First Lady, Jackie, thirty-one years old when her husband was elected president, would also proudly show off to reporters, and eventually America's TV viewers, the elegant ways in which she redecorated the White House. Furthermore, the First Couple made sure to invite famous artists, musicians, writers, and other celebrities into their official home. No doubt this cultivation contributed to the fact that although he had serious political opposition, Kennedy remained personally popular throughout his short tenure. This son of great wealth seemed to represent the hopes, dreams, and sanguine ambition of an entire people. Whether Americans were duped — then and now — is another question entirely.

Great Expectations: A New Frontier at Home?

Although JFK is revered as a specifically liberal icon by most American Democrats and independent progressives, his actual record hardly warrants such a label. On the surface, of course, high expectations for legislative success seemed more than appropriate. The Democrats had captured both houses of Congress and the Oval Office in 1960, after all. *Newsweek* predicted that Kennedy would enjoy a "long and fruitful 'honeymoon' with the new Democratic 87th Congress." Kennedy, *Newsweek* continued, "will find Congress so receptive that his record might well approach Franklin D. Roosevelt's famous 'One Hundred Days.'" Furthermore, the magazine noted that with the capable House Speaker Sam Rayburn in place, and the former Senate Majority Leader Lyndon Johnson on board as VP, matters couldn't have been more favorable for the new administration.

It was not to be, and such dramatic and hyperbolic predictions would seem foolish within precious few years. Sure, the fervent Kennedy would count some modest early accomplishments. His creation of the Peace Corps encouraged a spirit of selflessness and international service in a hopeful young generation. Speaker Rayburn also ushered through Congress a small bump in the federal minimum wage and modest public funding for job training in depressed areas such as Appalachia. But that's about it for "liberal" social and economic legislation. Most of the rest of Kennedy's agenda was either blocked by Congress's many conservatives, both Democrats and Republicans, or proved to be far more amenable to the political right than to the left. Furthermore, the supposedly enlightened Kennedy administration actually appointed fewer women to high-level federal postings than did his predecessors. His cabinet, in fact, was the first since Herbert Hoover's not to include a single woman. JFK, in short, was no political reincarnation of Franklin Roosevelt.

When it came to economics, Kennedy was rather centrist and — for the times — right of center. His tax cut dropped the top marginal rate on individuals from 91 percent to 70 percent, and corporate rates from 52 percent to 48 percent. His predecessor, the Republican

Eisenhower, had maintained higher taxes. Observers noted that the tax cut, though sold otherwise, mainly benefited the most well-off Americans. The only thing particularly Keynesian about Kennedy economics was the deficit-spending largesse he rained upon the military-industrial complex. Rapid increases in defense spending, as they usually do, provided a short-term bump for the health of the economy and lowered unemployment.

Kennedy's domestic failures can be attributed to a combination of factors. First, Jack was never very enthusiastic about "kitchen-table" issues. Even when he was in Congress, where he was known as a less-than-average senator and not particularly hardworking, his passion was for foreign policy over domestic issues. As president, Kennedy quickly tired of domestic affairs and never much cared for the more liberal lawmakers, referring to them as "honkers" and refusing to court them personally. This was apparent from the outset. As his adviser Theodore Sorensen diligently worked on the inaugural address, JFK burst in and exclaimed, "Let's drop the domestic stuff altogether." And he did! This famous speech is notable for almost completely ignoring home-front issues. This focus continued throughout his presidency. Kennedy, in fact, once noted to Nixon — of all people — that "[f]oreign affairs is the only important issue for a president to handle, isn't it? . . . I mean, who gives a shit if the minimum wage is $1.15 or $1.25, compared to something like Cuba?" No doubt millions of US workers did.

Congress, as it existed in the early 1960s, was stacked against the new president. The Democratic caucus was far from united. Indeed, the party was already coming apart — even if it would take later developments in civil rights and the Vietnam War to irrevocably break it. Conservative southern Democrats continued, as they had since the latter part of the New Deal, to form reactionary coalitions with far-right Republicans. This alliance was usually strong enough to either vote down or fatally filibuster a liberal bill. And since almost all leadership assignments in Congress were based on seniority and southerners generally faced no Republican challengers in elections, the powerful committees were usually chaired by conservative southern Democrats. These committee heads often buried progressive — especially civil rights — legislation and refused to bring bills to the floor for open debate and voting. It was this coalition between southern conservative Democrats and their Republican colleagues that killed all the potential laws favored by Kennedy's progressive base, including health insurance for the aged and the creation of an urban affairs department.

Finally, Kennedy, though seen as tough on foreign affairs, didn't demonstrate much courage on seminal domestic matters. He usually hedged bets and avoided controversy in order to bolster his image and avoid political losses for himself or for his party at the ballot box. Raised in a highly competitive family, JFK hated to lose. Pressured by liberals in his party to fight for key legislation, he said, "There is no sense in raising hell, and then not being successful. There is no sense in putting the office of the presidency on the line on an issue, and then being defeated." Only in the "manly" matters of foreign affairs would Jack go all in. As such, whatever the claims of his defenders, JFK's legislative record was weak. Just ten days before the assassination, *The New York Times* noted that "[r]arely has there been such a pervasive attitude of discouragement around Capitol Hill. . . . This has been one of the least productive sessions of Congress within memory." Kennedy's politicized caution in legislative decision making had real consequences for certain desperate constituencies in America — none more prominent than African Americans fighting for civil rights.

Hope and Despair: Kennedy and Civil Rights

The partisans and apologists for the mythical Kennedy and his post-humous promoters cling to the false belief that as a northern "liberal," JFK was some sort of civil rights crusader. That he was not. Though Kennedy was, at times, genuinely horrified by the most overt southern bigotry — and particularly shocked by images of young black protesters being attacked by police dogs in Birmingham, Alabama — for the most part the president hedged his bets and treated civil rights like any other political issue. He rarely stuck his neck out for the

cause, and he took the side of righteousness only when it was politically palatable, or absolutely necessary, to do so.

The story of Kennedy and civil rights began with his 1960 presidential campaign. During the run-up to the 1960 election, the young
civil rights leader Martin Luther King Jr. was imprisoned in Georgia
for a minor traffic violation and sentenced to four months at hard
labor. This draconian punishment was an obvious attempt to stifle the
black civil rights movement, and African Americans and northern
liberals led a large public outcry. Both major-party presidential candidates felt the need to take action. Nixon worked behind the scenes to
quietly intervene with Georgia's governor but said nothing publicly.
Kennedy, however, after receiving a telephone call from King's wife,
Coretta, decided to publicly express sympathy while brother Bobby
telegraphed the judge and demanded King's release. The move
succeeded, and King was soon out on bail. The Kings and their backers were thankful and seem to have urged some black voters to back
Kennedy in the November election. Whatever the cause, black voters
chose the Democrats by a margin seven points higher than they had
in 1956, potentially swinging a few key northern states to Kennedy.
Indeed, Eisenhower was later quoted as attributing the Republican
defeat to "a couple of phone calls."

But what motivated the Kennedys? That would remain to be seen.
Civil rights activists, by the early 1960s, were becoming angrier about
the slow pace of social and political change in America. The author
James Baldwin summed up the feeling in 1961: "To be a Negro in this
country and to be relatively conscious is to be in a rage all the time." In
that spirit, an increasing number of black students affiliated with the
Congress of Racial Equality (CORE) took "freedom rides" on interstate buses throughout the South in order to test the recent court integration orders. In Alabama and Mississippi the riders were brutally
attacked time and again. Their leaders pleaded to the new Kennedy
administration for federal protection. Such protection wasn't initially
forthcoming and arrived only slowly. Attorney General Robert
Kennedy would later defend his slow reaction by blatantly lying, stating that he had not been notified beforehand about the protests.

In response to the freedom rides and other ongoing civil rights protests, the Kennedys generally remained in a cautious reactive mode. After all, though their hearts were — partly — sympathetic to the movement, they were still Democrats in the 1960s. As such, they feared the ire of the prominent and powerful southern faction within the party and the loss of its votes. Jack would, no doubt, make many symbolic moves that improved on the civil rights record of the proceeding administration — hiring more blacks in federal jobs, appointing five African Americans as federal judges including Thurgood Marshall, and instructing the Justice Department to heavily increase its oversight of voting rights cases. Nonetheless, more often, political considerations stifled Kennedy's action on civil rights. He worried about formidable southerners in Congress such as Senator James Eastland of Mississippi, chair of the important Judiciary Committee. In fact, as a favor to Eastland, Kennedy would appoint four ardent bigots to federal judgeships in the Deep South. One of these judges once described African Americans in his courtroom as "niggers" and compared them to chimpanzees.

Furthermore, JFK took precious little tangible executive or legislative action during his first two years in office. He refused to introduce a civil rights bill — part of the 1960 Democratic platform — in 1961–62 and reneged on his campaign promise to declare an executive order to integrate federal housing. He would wait, he decided, until after the 1962 midterm elections before issuing the housing order or introducing a civil rights bill. The bottom line remained the same as ever: Kennedy lacked passion for any domestic affairs, including civil rights, and moved forward only ever so cautiously on these issues.

Indeed, at times the president and his attorney general were concerned that the civil rights movement was moving too fast, and they sought to slow down racial unrest. During the height of the freedom rides, President Kennedy yelled to an aide: "Tell [the riders] to call it off!" When the riders refused, Kennedy called for a "cooling-off period." This wouldn't do for the activists, and CORE chief James Farmer retorted that African Americans "have been cooling off for 150 years. If we cool off any more, we'll be in a deep freeze."

Nor would Kennedy protect Martin Luther King Jr. from the obsessive hatred and harassment of FBI chief J. Edgar Hoover. Hoover, convinced that King was a Soviet-run communist (he wasn't), asked Attorney General Robert Kennedy to allow the bureau to tap the civil rights leader's phones. Bobby acquiesced, and Hoover developed a "blackmail file" full of King's sexual infidelities, but ultimately the FBI found that King and his staff had little to no connection with radical socialists. Historians still speculate over why the Kennedys acquiesced to Hoover's unwarranted harassment of King. What seems clear is that Hoover — who assiduously acquired dirt on all Washington figures — had one heck of a file on JFK. He knew about Kennedy's extramarital affairs, including one with Judith Campbell — also the mistress of a Mafia gangster — and about the president's concurrent collusion with the US mob to assassinate Cuba's Fidel Castro.

When Kennedy did worry about civil rights he did so cautiously and mainly out of foreign-policy concerns. He feared that the United States could not lead the "free world" effectively if the Soviets could point to a hypocritical America that mistreated its black citizens. It was here that the issues of the Cold War and civil rights collided. So it was, then, in the aftermath of the police chief of Birmingham, Alabama, unleashing dogs and water cannons on peaceful black protesters that Kennedy finally gave the order to prepare a civil rights bill and gave his most inspiring speech on race.

> The heart of the question is whether all Americans are to be afforded equal rights and equal opportunities. . . . If an American, because his skin is dark, cannot eat lunch in a restaurant . . . if he cannot send his children to the best public school available, if he cannot vote . . . if, in short, he cannot enjoy the full and free life which all of us want, then who among us would be content to have the color of his skin changed and stand in his place?

This was, no doubt, a powerful and persuasive bit of oratory, but even after the speech Kennedy remained cautious and sought to temper the movement. Indeed, many rights activists thought Kennedy's bill was too late and didn't go far enough — in fact, it did only cover desegregation of public facilities without addressing voting rights. It dealt, too, only with de jure segregation while ignoring de facto housing denials, police brutality, and employment discrimination. Thus, when the bill went forward — and got caught up in the expected filibuster of southern congressmen — civil rights activists continued, against the president's will, to take direct actions.

Most famously, in May 1963 a coalition of civil rights leaders organized what they dubbed a massive March on Washington for Jobs and Freedom (in their historical memory, Americans tend to, instructively, omit the "jobs" portion of that title). The march was designed to force legislative action by shutting down the capital through prolonged sit-ins by many thousands of demonstrators. Young radicals, such as John Lewis of the Student Nonviolent Coordinating Committee (SNCC), also planned to join seasoned leaders like MLK on the stage and make fiery addresses. Kennedy and his brother were panicked, and they labored to tone down the march. Older black moderates compromised under pressure from the president, and, in line with an agreement reached between the administration and the organizers of the protest, the march was limited to one day, liquor stores were closed, and demonstrators were required to dress in "respectable clothing." Kennedy aides even read the proposed speech of the firebrand Lewis and forced other black leaders to seek to soften the SNCC leader's message and tone at the last moment. Lewis was furious but agreed. Had he not, administration officials stood ready to disconnect the public address system. Still, the march would go down as an important event in American history. It is celebrated by centrist "liberals" to this day.

Nonetheless, at the time many young black activists felt stifled and were frustrated by the lack of tangible results from the event. It didn't change intransigent southern opinions on Capitol Hill, and according to Senator Hubert Humphrey of Minnesota, "had not affected a single vote" on the proposed, and stagnated, Civil Rights Act. To the more radical demonstrators, the event had been a sellout of the movement:

its leaders, they charged, were little more than "Uncle Toms." The fiery Black Muslim Malcolm X labeled it the "Farce on Washington" and declared:

> It was the grass roots out there in the street. It scared the white man to death, scared the white power structure in D.C. to death. . . . They [the Kennedys] called in these national negro leaders that you respect and told them, "Call it off!" And Old Tom [MLK] said, "'Boss, I can't stop it because I didn't start it. . . . I'm not even in it, much less at the head of it." And that old shrewd fox [JFK], he said, "If you ain't in it, I'll put you in it. I'll put you at the head of it. I'll endorse it. . . ." This is what they did with the March on Washington . . . they joined it . . . they took it over. And as they took it over it lost its militancy. It ceased to be angry. It was a sellout. It was a takeover.

Malcolm X may have been hyperbolic and impassioned, but he wasn't exactly wrong, either. The march had been, on some levels, precisely as he described. Kennedy's adviser and later biographer Arthur Schlesinger Jr. admitted as much when he described Kennedy's civil rights strategy and achievements in the wake of the march. "So in 1963," he wrote, "Kennedy moved to incorporate the Negro revolution into the democratic coalition." To some extent he did, but at what cost? Undoubtedly, this co-opting of existing civil rights efforts contributed to sanitizing and de-radicalizing a vibrant grassroots movement.

So it was, when an assassin took the president's life, that his proposed Civil Rights Act — like JFK's entire record on this moral issue — remained in political deadlock on Capitol Hill. It would take a new president and ever more public sacrifice from grassroots black activists to get the act through. Kennedy could, and ultimately would, only do so much for racial equality in segregated America.

To the Brink: Kennedy's Cold War

In his abbreviated administration, Kennedy would fulfill his dream of being an ardent Cold Warrior, pressing the Russians and combating communism the world over. In this way, whatever his defenders later surmised, Kennedy was little different from — and was perhaps more hawkish than — his predecessors and successors. He regularly escalated crises and, along with the foolish Soviet premier Nikita Khrushchev, brought the planet to the brink of destruction. JFK would leave behind an ever-colder Cold War, and he did little to usher in even a modicum of détente with the Soviets. The tragic part, the disturbing bit, is that Kennedy — an astute student of foreign affairs — seems to have known better; to have known that communism was no global monolith, that the Soviets and Chinese were actually enemies, that, in fact, the United States had a nuclear program far superior to the Soviets'. Even so, with such knowledge in hand, Kennedy went ahead anyway — whether due to his insecurity, political fortunes, or toxic notions of masculinity — and faced off against the Russians at every turn and in many places.

Kennedy had already presented his simplistic views on the campaign trail. "The enemy," he said, "is the communist system itself . . . increasing in its drive for world domination. . . . It is also a struggle for supremacy between two conflicting ideologies: freedom under God versus ruthless, godless tyranny." Despite the obvious flaws, hyperbole, and factual inaccuracy of this Manichaean worldview, Kennedy would use his often quoted inaugural address to lay out America's resultant plan of action. "We shall pay any price," he exclaimed, "bear any burden, meet any hardship, support any friend, oppose any foe to assure the survival and success of liberty." And in a sense Kennedy would have American troops, diplomats, and spies do just that. What was less clear was whether the targets and victims of America's liberty burden had desired US intervention in the first place. Individual and collective notions of freedom and liberty are often complex, subjective, and prisoners of context. In Kennedy's public view, at least, there was no room for such nuance.

British political cartoon, 1962, by Leslie Gilbert Illingworth

The Cold War only heightened under JFK for a number of reasons. One was his personal style as a competitive, aggressive statesman unwilling to back down. Another was the continued and growing power of a military-industrial complex that stepped up its demands for more contracts, more weapons, and more cash throughout the administration. Finally, there was the provocative and often foolish behavior of Kennedy's counterpart, Soviet premier Khrushchev. Perhaps bolstered by recent successes in nuclear and space technology, or due to Kremlin readings of Kennedy's youth and inexperience, Soviet policy during the Kennedy years was particularly combative, especially in the so-called Third World.

Kennedy took some of his action based, no doubt, on political considerations. In the election campaign he had run to the hawkish "right" of the Republican Eisenhower — whom he painted as too timid, especially when it came to military interventionism. Thus the new president rolled out a strategy, known as flexible response, as a rebuke of Ike's notion of massive retaliation — reliance on nuclear weapons over conventional war. Flexible response simply meant that the United States would maintain the capability and stated intent to check the Soviets anywhere, on any level, from diplomacy to espionage to limited war to outright land war to an apocalyptic nuclear exchange. In truth, however, the new strategy was little more than a gift to the Pentagon and arms industry. To wit, a pre-inaugural task force on national security determined that significant defense spending increases were both desirable and necessary. Such spending, even if it weren't necessary, the task force concluded, would be a boon to the national economy — a defensive Keynesianism or military welfare state. The report concluded that "[a]ny stepping up of these [defense] programs that is deemed desirable for its own sake can only help rather than hinder the health of our economy." Over the next three years the military budget would grow 13 percent, from $47.4 billion to $53.6 billion. Defense spending for defense spending's sake was to be the mantra of the Kennedy years.

If JFK loved and was enamored with the military — he famously formed the Green Berets army special forces unit to conduct counterinsurgency missions, keeping a beret on his desk — he could barely stomach diplomats. For him, the diplomats at the State Department were little more than "striped-pants boys" who did little but shuffle papers. Indeed, as an undersecretary of state in the Kennedy administration complained, the president and his team were "full of belligerence" and "sort of looking for a chance to prove their muscle." Kennedy and Khrushchev would ensure there was opportunity for that to happen. JFK also funded many other expensive ventures related to national security, such as the Apollo program — announced in response to the Soviet launch of its Sputnik satellite — to put US astronauts on the moon. Though celebrated in retrospect, the US space program cost $35 billion before an American set foot on the lunar surface in 1969 but produced, according to historian James Patterson, "relatively little scientific knowledge." As a competition with the Russians, however, Apollo proved quite popular with the American people, and Kennedy knew it.

In his Cold War adventures, Kennedy — like many politicians of his postwar generation — became obsessed with the vague notion of "credibility," the idea that anything that smacked of compromise with the Soviets displayed only "weakness," or "softness," and was comparable to Britain and France's ignominious Munich deal with Hitler in 1938. In preparing for a May 1961 summit meeting with Khrushchev, he said, "I'll have to show him that we can be as tough as he is. . . . I'll have to sit down and let him see who he is dealing with." For JFK, it was a toxic vision of a face-off between alpha males on a world stage . . . with nukes. This flawed and simplistic thinking grounded just about every Kennedy decision in world affairs from 1961 to 1963. It would eventually bring the world to the brink of destruction in the Cuban Missile Crisis and suck the US military into a disastrous, unwinnable war in Vietnam.

Kennedy's first disaster came in Cuba. Fidel Castro, a popular communist insurgent leader, had — in a direct threat to American business interests — overthrown the dictatorial US-backed Batista regime in 1959. At that time US corporations controlled 80 percent of Cuba's utilities, mines, and oil refineries, 40 percent of its mainstay sugar industry, and 50 percent of its railways. Furthermore, the Italian American Mafia controlled many lucrative Cuban casinos. Once in power, the populist Castro confiscated millions of acres from the American United Fruit Co. and set up national systems of housing, education, and land redistribution. These programs were highly popular among Cuban peasants, many of whom had suffered greatly under the US-backed dictatorship. In response, the Eisenhower and Kennedy administrations pressured the International Monetary Fund not to lend much-needed money to Cuba. Unsurprisingly, in response, Cuba signed trade agreements with the Soviets, who agreed to buy all of the sugar crop — a crop that previously had gone mostly to the United States and that the United States was now refusing to buy.

So it was that Eisenhower and the even more Castro-obsessed Kennedy decided to destabilize and eventually overthrow the revolutionary Cuban government. All this, particularly the later US-sponsored mercenary invasion, was a violation of the law. President Harry Truman's earlier treaty with the Organization of American States had proclaimed that "[n]o state or group of states has the right to intervene, directly or indirectly, for any reason whatsoever, in the internal or external affairs of another state." And for the public record, the new American president — though he knew of ongoing plans to invade Cuba — seemed to admit as much. Kennedy told a press conference that "there will not be, under any conditions, any intervention in Cuba by United States armed forces." It is true, of course, that when the Bay of Pigs invasion came it was mostly conducted with dissident Cuban mercenaries. Nonetheless, Americans piloted the supporting attack planes, armed the fighters, and served as CIA spy liaisons leading up to and during the invasion. When four Americans piloting those planes were shot down and killed, the US government refused to tell the families the truth about how their loved ones had died.

In addition to approving the disastrous Eisenhower plan to invade Cuba at the Bay of Pigs, Kennedy's administration had actually considered even more drastic, immoral action. The Joint Chiefs of Staff proposed Operation Northwood — a plan to conduct "false flag" terror attacks killing American civilians and then blame the deaths on Cuba — in order to drum up support for war. Kennedy and other civilian leaders refused to back the outlandish plan. However, its existence and acceptance by the top military service chiefs demonstrated the paranoia, frenzy, and Cuba-obsession of the era.

Kennedy should have known better than to go through with the invasion. He hadn't planned it himself, first of all, and had been given much dissenting advice from within his own administration. Arthur Schlesinger was against it, as was the liberal Adlai Stevenson, a two-time Democratic presidential candidate and Kennedy's ambassador to the United Nations. So was the marine corps commandant, who warned that Cuba was eight hundred miles long and hard to conquer. As was the respected Senator J. William Fulbright, who presciently predicted in a memo to the president that "[t]o give this activity covert support is of a piece with the hypocrisy and cynicism for which the US is constantly denouncing the Soviet Union." So, too, was Undersecretary of State Chester Bowles, who wrote Secretary of State Dean Rusk that "[o]ur national interests are poorly served by a covert operation. . . . This would be an act of war." And so it was.

Though Cuban nationals would serve as ground troops in the

ill-fated invasion, US Navy destroyers escorted the landing crafts and US-piloted planes provided the preemptive bombing raids. It wasn't enough. Castro was tipped off by spies and even US press reports and was prepared. Furthermore, the Cuban civilians living near the landing site were highly supportive of the generally popular Castro; there would not be — as the CIA and dissidents had wrongly predicted — an uprising around the Bay of Pigs. Within twenty-four hours Cuban fighters and Soviet-made tanks operated by Cubans checked the invasion and inflicted heavy casualties on the attackers. Most surrendered; many were killed.

When the dissidents realized they were in serious trouble they requested additional air strikes, and a stoic but rattled Kennedy balked. For this some US military leaders would never forgive him. The chairman of the Joint Chiefs, General Lyman Lemnitzer, called the decision "reprehensible" and "almost criminal." This was an overstatement. What the military brass seemed unable to comprehend was that Cuba's new leader was popular, and no token force of a mere fourteen hundred dissidents, only a hundred or so of them trained soldiers, could overthrow Castro. That would have required a direct US military commitment and a risk of war with Russia. In reality Kennedy was, not for the last time, poorly served by the assessments of his Pentagon and CIA spymasters. The Bay of Pigs fiasco was their failure as much as that of the actual invaders.

Still, Jack and Bobby Kennedy wouldn't quit. The brothers seemed genuinely obsessed with Castro and determined to save face and win back the ever-vital "credibility" they had lost in the Bay of Pigs. Jack would put Bobby, the attorney general, personally in charge of the secretive Operation Mongoose, a CIA-coordinated program to damage the Castro regime. "My idea," Bobby said, "is to stir things up on the island with espionage, sabotage, general disorder." And indeed he did, as agents contaminated Cuban sugar exports, bombed factories, led paramilitary raids, and attempted — thirty-three times — to assassinate a sovereign head of state, Castro. All of this was illegal under the Truman-era treaty or any standard application of international law, and it constituted state terrorism.

The unintended consequences of US bellicosity toward Cuba were manifold. The Bay of Pigs failure heightened tensions with the Soviets and added a personal pugilism to the rivalry between Kennedy and Khrushchev. The US neo-imperial invasion whipped up Cuban nationalism and increased Castro's popularity. Both Cuba's leader and his ally Khrushchev were now certain the Kennedy administration intended to invade the island with US forces and depose the government. Castro pleaded for help and got it. Soon after the Bay of Pigs action, the Soviets began sending thousands of military personnel to the island and by the spring of 1962 had armed Cuba with missiles, some of them nuclear. A new, ever more dangerous crisis would result.

It must be said, first, that Khrushchev, ultimately, had foolishly blundered in secretly stationing nuclear missiles just ninety miles from Florida. The net gain to his ability to strike the United States homeland was far too negligible to warrant the risk of a US invasion, an air strike, or even an accidental escalation by either side of the conflict. He was placing Soviet credibility on the line, on the global stage, with neither an effective exit strategy nor the willingness and intent to actually wage nuclear war. For these and other perceived failures, eventually, the Soviet Politburo would remove the premier and replace him in 1964.

Still, we can — given the context — understand Khrushchev's motives. The United States had been the illegal aggressor in the failed invasion of Cuba and seemed intent on overthrowing a Soviet ally; besides, the US-led NATO military alliance had long encircled the Soviet Union with nuclear-armed bases adjacent to Russian territory. Should the United States really go berserk over one such base in the Caribbean? As Khrushchev stated before the Cuban Missile Crisis, "The Americans surrounded our country with military bases and threatened us with nuclear weapons. Now the Americans will learn what it feels like to have enemy missiles pointed at you." He wasn't wrong, but that didn't make his move in Cuba a smart play.

Kennedy would later be memorialized for his cool handling of the ensuing Cuban Missile Crisis, and it must be admitted that he did ignore his more bellicose advisers and ultimately avoid a nuclear war.

Still, he operated within rather narrow bounds of imagination, and must bear some of the responsibility for how close the world came to destruction. In many ways he got lucky. First, JFK never even seriously considered early advice from liberals in his own party like Adlai Stevenson, who recommended immediate, reasonable compromise: foreign demilitarization in Cuba, a no-invasion pledge by the United States, a removal of Soviet missiles followed by a concurrent removal of similar US missiles in Turkey. After all, Stevenson asked, why risk nuclear war over a few missiles in Cuba when both great powers already possessed enough long-range ICBMs to destroy the other many times over? But the Kennedys would have none of it. They wouldn't "appease" the Soviets.

Besides, there were political considerations. Congressional midterm elections were imminent, and JFK couldn't have the Republicans attacking him from the right for being "soft" on Russia. No, he decided, there would be no secret tit-for-tat deals — he would publicly denounce the Soviet move and place a naval quarantine around the island. There would be no further shipments of Soviet military equipment, and Khrushchev would have to be the one to back down. It ultimately worked out, of course, despite many close calls — the shooting down of a US spy plane pilot, and the timely refusal of a Soviet submarine captain to fire a nuclear torpedo when a US Navy destroyer targeted his vessel with what turned out to be non-lethal depth charges — and thus we forget how dangerous a move Kennedy had made. Absolute terror gripped the world before the Soviet ships approaching the quarantine turned around and Khrushchev eventually folded. The famous American evangelist Billy Graham even preached about the "end of the world" during the crisis. America's NATO allies were terrified equally by the escalatory moves of the United States and the Soviet Union.

To the president's credit, Kennedy was not taken in by the staggering lunacy of many of his advisers, especially some in the military. His national security adviser and his vice president called for immediate no-warning air strikes on the Cuban missile sites. So, eventually, did every single member of the military's Joint Chiefs of Staff. Jack opposed them, as did Bobby, who astutely noted, "We've talked for 15 years about a first strike, saying we'd never do that." To launch such a strike would make his brother the "Tojo of the 1960s," Bobby said in referring to the official who was Japan's prime minister and head of the military at the time of the surprise attack on Pearl Harbor in 1941.

What's interesting, in retrospect, is that eventual agreement hashed out between the Soviets and the Americans ultimately resembled the early deal that the "dovish" Stevenson had proposed. The Soviets would pull out all the nuclear weapons, and the United States would lift the quarantine and promise not to invade the island — though, the record shows, it did continue its espionage and harassment. That was the public end of the deal, the one that made the USA look strong and allowed Kennedy to boast that he had "cut his [Khrushchev's] balls off!" But secretly, Kennedy had actually opened negotiations to remove US mid-range missiles from Turkey — which were becoming obsolete anyway. The weapons were indeed removed by April 1963.

Kennedy's military advisers in particular were incensed by the deal. Air force general Curtis "Bombs Away" LeMay crowed, "We've been had!" to the president's face and banged on the table. The deal was, he exclaimed, "the greatest defeat in our history. . . . We should invade [Cuba] today!" It wasn't — by any stretch of the imagination — but for LeMay and an entire generation of military intellectual mediocrities groomed in the early Cold War, the deal was a personal defeat, a lost chance to use their "toys" in a once-and-for-all shootout with the Russkies! As for the mainly civilian deaths that would ensue if the great powers did go to war over Cuba, that mattered not, according to another air force general, Thomas Power, who thundered to the president: "Why are you so concerned with saving their lives? The whole idea is to kill the bastards. . . . At the end of the war, if there are two Americans and one Russian, we win." It was this level of absurdity from some of his most senior advisers that Kennedy had to deal with. This, too, helps explain history's kinder view — in hindsight — of JFK's crisis leadership.

The president, even if his blunders and aggression toward Cuba had ultimately caused the crisis he "solved," did seem to learn one valuable lesson from the standoff: don't trust the military! The military and CIA had called for open invasion and escalation during both the Bay of Pigs and the Cuban Missile Crisis. They, along with many of Kennedy's civilian advisers, seemed genuinely prepared to fight it out with the nuclear-armed Soviets over a relatively small Caribbean island. Speaking about the Joint Chiefs' unanimous advice to bomb and invade Cuba, Kennedy curtly remarked, "These brass hats have one great advantage, if we . . . do what they want us to do, none of us will be alive later to tell them they were wrong." And finally, late in his presidency, JFK also had something important in mind that he never got the chance to impart. "The first thing I'm going to tell my successor," he explained, "is watch the generals, to avoid feeling that just because they're military men, their opinions on military matters are worth a damn." He was an intelligent man, Jack Kennedy, capable of complex thinking and great achievements. His flashes of brilliance and lucidity — such as this appraisal of his military leaders — demonstrate his potential.

Unfortunately, as substantiated in both the Bay of Pigs and the Cuban Missile Crisis, he was just as apt to cause as to solve a crisis. He avoided escalation of the ill-advised mercenary invasion he green-lighted; he called off the military attack dogs when they sought to start a war over a missile crisis he and his flawed Cold Warrior mentality helped cause. Such were the tragedies and triumphs of John F. Kennedy — stuck in the Cold War box and unable to escape his outdated conceptions of masculinity and toughness, as well as his competitiveness and insecurity.

———

Kennedy's blunders included the escalation of the war in Vietnam. He would continue to back a corrupt South Vietnamese regime that lacked legitimacy and funnel ever more military advisers into the country until there were some sixteen thousand on the ground. He even tacitly backed an illegal military coup that overthrew and murdered the formerly US-backed president of South Vietnam. In essence Kennedy's Cold War bellicosity and flawed Manichaean worldview would — just as they almost sparked a nuclear war over

Cuba — lead the United States inexorably deeper into its greatest military fiasco and defeat in a place few Americans could find on a map: Vietnam.

What, then, must we conclude about Kennedy? Perhaps a comparison is in order. Like a later young president who promised hope and possessed both a handsome family and cultivated taste — Barack Obama — Kennedy seemed the polite, enlightened choice for the self-styled elites. His knack with the media, his pop-culture chic, and his propensity to surround himself with the famous and the celebrated invoked praise and admiration from America's supposed cultured class. This style, this image, allowed many Americans to ignore his relative lack of substance. What, truly, did Kennedy do to improve life for impoverished peasants in the Third World, disenfranchised and terrorized blacks tilling sharecrop soil or suffering in urban ghettos, for the long-oppressed people of Cuba, for anyone in real need? The answers can be argued. What is clear is that it is time to reevaluate Kennedy and hold him to the same standard as presidents who were not martyred. His death was a tragedy among America's population, but for countless millions across the world, so was his presidency.[25]

29

VIETNAM, AN AMERICAN TRAGEDY

It is the war that never dies. *Vietnam*: The very word is shrouded with extraordinary meaning in the American lexicon. For some it represents failure; for others, guilt; for yet more, anger that the war could have and should have been won. Americans are still arguing about this war, once the nation's longest. For those who lived through it — the last war the United States fought partly with draftees — it was almost impossible not to take sides; to be pro-war or antiwar became a social and political identity unto itself. This tribal split even reached into the ranks of military veterans, as some joined antiwar movements and others remained vociferously sure that the war needed to be fought through to victory. Indeed, today even the active-duty US military officer corps is rent over assessment of the Vietnam legacy.

Regarding America's role in the Vietnam War, the mythmaking began long before North Vietnamese tanks overran US-backed South Vietnam in April 1975. Indeed, myths and exaggerations pervade the entire collective memory of this brutal war. Some believe that the politicians and antiwar protesters sold out the US military and that a "liberal" press was complicit in this treason as well. Neither was the case. Others claim that with more military force, more bombing, and more patriotic backing, the US military would have marched away as the victor. This, too, is patently false. Without destroying North Vietnam in a genocidal fury and thereby risking world war with China and the Soviet Union, it is unlikely the US Army and Marine Corps could have forced the communists to capitulate. The communists actually led a coalition of nationalists fighting a civil war that was ultimately about independence. Such wars are difficult to "win" in any traditional sense. Then there's the common belief that all veterans were treated terribly upon their return. While some were indeed

US Marines move against the enemy in Vietnam in 1968

abused, the historical record demonstrates that the scale and pervasiveness of the mistreatment have been exaggerated.

Each of these myths carries political baggage and serves some political purpose. So divided was Vietnam-era American life that one's stance on the war framed almost all social and political thinking. For some it still does. People on opposite sides of the debate often draw conclusions and "lessons learned" from the Vietnam War and apply them to contemporary US military and foreign policy. This has proved dangerous and disruptive. Starkly applicable "lessons" from the past rarely translate into coherent contemporary policy. Still, today, with the US military again ensconced in seemingly never-ending armed conflict, the truth about America's tragic foray into Vietnam is more vital than ever.

A careful study of the informational sources and the works of the most respected historians of the conflict demonstrates some important truths: that the United States lost the Vietnam War both politically and militarily; that the United States may have been on the "wrong" side and acted far more like a European colonial power than most Americans are apt to admit; that the United States engaged in wanton destruction of a rather poor society in its fruitless quest for "victory" over the communists; that global communism itself was no monolith and that although Hanoi gladly accepted support from Russia and China, this remained very much a Vietnamese war; that the press, protesters, and skeptics had not sold out their country but, rather, were on the right side of history. The Vietnam War, in sum, should never have been fought — the distant country was never a vital national security threat to the United States; American intervention was, ultimately, a national crime and tragedy.

A Long Backstory

The Vietnam War, in its entirety, lasted thirty years, from 1945 to 1975. Though the United States was always somewhat involved, the American combat actions were only one part of a prolonged Vietnamese civil war and struggle for independence. The war never revolved around the United States. The American military meddled, struggled, and gratuitously killed Vietnamese for over a decade, but the outcome was always destined to be decided among the native population itself. When it did intervene, the United States was rarely a source of stability. Indeed, America merely took over where imperial France had left off, and it set back Vietnamese sovereignty. As such, the US role was shady and nefarious from the first.

During the Second World War the Japanese "liberated" Vietnam from French colonial rule and proceeded to rule as Asian imperialists themselves. In response Ho Chi Minh led a nationalist guerrilla independence movement that — from the American perspective — was tainted by his communist ideology. But Ho was always a nationalist first and a communist second. His men endured heavy losses against the Japanese occupiers in the hope of gaining independence for Vietnam at the end of World War II. One can understand the aspiration: after all, the United States and Britain had seemed to promise as much in 1941 in the Atlantic Charter, in which they vowed to "respect the right of all peoples to choose the form of government under which they will live."

World war quickly turned into Cold War, and the United States, once nominally opposed to European imperialism, quickly performed an about-face and backed the British, French, and Dutch attempts to regain their empires in Asia. This was particularly unfortunate for Ho and his nationalist-communist alliance. He would have to wait and fight longer to gain independence for his nation. At the end of World War II his hopes had been high. When the Japanese evacuated in 1945, Ho's revolutionists held a celebration with a million people on the streets and read a declaration of independence that included verbatim sections from the US Declaration of Independence and the French Declaration of the Rights of Man. Ho would soon find that such principles applied only to white Westerners.

Still, as the United States was switching over to a pro-imperial policy, Ho desperately wrote eight letters to President Harry Truman begging for American support based on the superpower's own promises in the Atlantic Charter. Truman ignored him. Thus the Vietnamese waged a guerrilla war against the French army from 1946 to 1954. By 1954, though not yet committed on the ground, the United States — obsessed with stifling world communism — was footing 80 percent of France's bill for the war. The French lost anyway, and at a peace conference in Geneva they agreed to evacuate their army so long as South Vietnam was temporarily split from the north; the nation was to be divided until national elections were soon held. The elections never came because theUnited States called them off, choosing instead a Vietnam divided by economic and political ideology. When the two-year deadline to hold elections arrived in 1956, a US Joint Chiefs of Staff memo explained they could not occur because "a settlement based on free elections would be attended by almost certain loss [for the opponents of communism]." So the "arsenal of democracy" would stifle that very condition in Vietnam.

The United States would essentially create a new state in the south, and it backed an unpopular Catholic supporter of the large landlords — most Vietnamese were Buddhists and peasants — named Ngo

Dinh Diem, who had only recently been living in New Jersey. Diem was corrupt, authoritarian, and averse to social and economic reform. By 1960 the National Liberation Front (NLF) formed in the south and, with North Vietnamese support, waged a new guerrilla war against Diem's regime. Early reports from US government analysts saw, even then, just why the NLF movement flourished and the Diem regime floundered. One analyst, Douglas Pike, traveled to Vietnam and observed that "[t]he Communists have brought to the villages of South Vietnam significant social change and have done so largely by means of the communication process." The later Pentagon Papers — a comprehensive study of US involvement in Vietnam conducted by the Department of Defense — said of this early phase of the war that "[o]nly the Vietcong [guerrillas] had any real support or influence on a broad base in the countryside."

Meanwhile, back in Saigon, the South Vietnamese capital, Buddhist monks began setting themselves aflame in the streets, committing suicide in protest of Diem's corruption and authoritarianism. Diem responded by having troops raid Buddhist pagodas and temples and kill nine protesters demonstrating on behalf of the Buddhists. This was the government that the United States would soon go to war for, the government for which more than fifty-eight thousand American soldiers would give their lives.

The "Best and the Brightest" Blunder: Kennedy's Vietnam

After the departure of the French, US president Dwight Eisenhower offered economic aid and a limited contingent of US military advisers (685 in 1960), but he avoided any major American escalation. His successor, John F. Kennedy, as a firm believer in the modernization schemes and philosophies of contemporary intellectuals, would commit more American resources to Vietnam. By October 1963, just before Kennedy's assassination, there were sixteen thousand US "advisers" in the country. The very next month Kennedy's government tacitly supported a South Vietnamese military coup that left Diem dead and the country even more disorganized and demoralized.

The militarization of the Vietnam War fit rather neatly with Kennedy's overall view of communism and his subsequent foreign and defense policy. Communism had to be stopped, now and everywhere — even in remote Vietnam. The US military was, for the most part, on board. Kennedy's chief military adviser, General Maxwell Taylor, took to calling Vietnam a "laboratory" for US Army development in the counter-commie fight. In addition, Kennedy would stifle suggestions — made by some of his more liberal advisers — to enter into negotiations with North Vietnam and set the stage for the promised (by treaty!) elections. Afraid he would look weak on communism, the president ensured that the election plan was stillborn.

Before he dropped the feckless and unpopular Diem, Kennedy had long known that the South Vietnamese government was corrupt. In response to the Senate majority leader's suggestion that Saigon use American aid for social reform, the president simply said, "Diem is Diem and the best we've got." Kennedy persisted, ignoring important dissenting counsel he received from key advisers and agencies. The CIA warned that to save Saigon the United States would need to commit at least two hundred thousand troops; this proved to be a low estimate. The CIA, admittedly, had been wrong before, and Kennedy ignored the warning.

In the years since the murder of Kennedy, many of his defenders have pointed to a few late-stage actions to argue that had the president lived, he would have pulled the United States out of the quagmire. Their Exhibit A is a speech Kennedy gave in September 1963 in which he declared, "Unless a greater effort is made by the government of South Vietnam, I don't think the war can be won out there." He then ordered the removal of some one thousand US troops. Kennedy mythmakers tend to ignore much evidence to the contrary, however. They omit, for example, that Kennedy had added in the speech that he did not "agree with those who say we should withdraw. That would be a great mistake. . . . This is a very important struggle." The defenders also fail to mention that most of the withdrawn troops were from an engineer battalion that had completed its work and was already scheduled to leave. Those troops were also to soon be replaced by others after Christmas.

Kennedy's closest advisers have also weighed in and given us probably the best indication of the president's thinking at the time. He told close friend Charles Bartlett in 1963 that although "[w]e don't have a prayer of staying in Vietnam . . . I can't give up a piece of territory like that to the communists and then get the people to reelect me." Furthermore, Kennedy's own secretary of state, Dean Rusk, added later that he "had hundreds of talks with John F. Kennedy about Vietnam, and never once did he say anything [about withdrawal]." We'll never know for sure if JFK would have de-escalated the war had he lived to win reelection in 1964, but it seems unlikely. Military escalation and counterinsurgency were entrenched in Kennedy's Cold Warrior ideology, and he remained a prisoner of the worn-out playbook of stopping communism wherever it reared its ugly head. Here, as in several other policy areas, Kennedy emerges as more politician than statesman.

LBJ's War: Escalation and Stalemate

Vice President Lyndon B. Johnson inherited a stalemated war and Kennedy's legacy on Vietnam when an assassin's bullets put him in the Oval Office in November 1963. As a consequence, he could not and would not reverse the foreign-policy course of his martyred predecessor. Johnson, like Kennedy, was a Democrat stricken with the self-compulsion to look "tough" against communism. LBJ held much the same binary worldview as Kennedy and Truman. Just after the assassination, LBJ told Henry Cabot Lodge Jr., the US ambassador to South Vietnam, that "I am not going to lose Vietnam. I am not going to be the president who saw Southeast Asia go the way China went [in 1949]." With Johnson afraid to look weak, the conflict became "LBJ's War."

Still, despite the breakdown of the South Vietnamese army and government, LBJ was at first cautious about escalating the US military role. Unlike Kennedy, LBJ loved domestic policy and was more interested in promoting his Great Society liberal social legislation than in pursuing a big war in Southeast Asia. This tension defined Johnson's administration. Nevertheless, in the end he underestimated the will of the North Vietnamese and the Vietcong, who continued to fight and escalate. It seemed they would never give in unless pummeled by American military might. Tragically for all, as Johnson would discover, even a massive application of US force would not work.

Unlike Truman's war in Korea, LBJ's war would be fought almost unilaterally by the United States. There was no grand coalition this time. Australia and South Korea sent troops, but Asian allies other than South Korea did not — the Philippines wouldn't even allow the US Air Force to bomb from its bases there. NATO allies sat out the war. LBJ would ultimately escalate and Americanize the war based on lies and omissions. After two incidents in which Vietnamese naval vessels allegedly attacked US ships (it seems the second incident never happened) in the Gulf of Tonkin, LBJ pushed through a resolution — but not a declaration of war — in Congress authorizing American military reinforcement and an enlarged combat role. It passed 416–0 in the House and 88–2 in the Senate. This demonstrated the power of the Cold War consensus of the time. A nation would, with a spirit of unity, blunder into a war.

Then, in 1965, after his landslide presidential victory as an incumbent in 1964, Johnson hedged. He approved a sustained bombing campaign and sent in a hundred thousand more US troops but refused either a general mobilization, which conservatives wanted, or a negotiated withdrawal, which the left demanded. LBJ also lacked a legitimate stable partner. The generals running South Vietnam were corrupt and unpopular — what State Department Asia expert William Bundy called "absolutely the bottom of the barrel." The bombing made the US appear a bully and, inevitably, inflicted heavy civilian casualties. In a span of just two years, 1965–67, American planes would drop more bombs than the combined US total in both theaters of the Second World War. Furthermore, enough toxic defoliant, Agent Orange, was dropped on the countryside to destroy half of the south's total timberlands. It is estimated that in all the years of American intervention some 415,000 civilians were killed and one-third of all South Vietnamese became refugees.

Johnson's incremental strategy pleased no one, and although by avoiding national mobilization he mitigated the war's political impact, his escalation exponentially increased casualties borne by the US Army, a hybrid of draftees and professional soldiers. Escalation led to further escalation, and the United States became progressively mired in Vietnam. By 1967 there were half a million American troops on the ground and the US government had spent $25 billion — and in that year alone nine thousand Americans were killed. It is true that American troops "won" most tactical engagements, but the heavy losses suffered by the North Vietnamese and the Vietcong were far from fatal to the communist cause. With a growing, young, and nationalistic population, North Vietnam could count on two hundred thousand young men coming of age annually! Besides, Ho was receiving arms and cash from both the Soviet Union and China, Vietnam's historic enemy.

By 1967 the war was on track to become America's longest and most unpopular. It depleted the government's coffers, caused deficits and inflation, transferred resources to the growing military-industrial complex, and escalated the arms race. The war's length and brutality also unnerved European allies and tarnished the United States' standing in the so-called Third World, the developing regions. And Johnson knew all this. He later wrote that he "knew from the start that I was bound to be crucified either way I moved. If I left the woman I really loved — the Great Society — in order to get involved with that bitch of a war on the other side of the world, then I would lose everything at home. All my programs. All my hopes to feed the hungry and shelter the homeless. All my dreams to provide education and medical care to the browns and the blacks and the lame and the poor."

In an effort to save the Great Society, Johnson would equivocate and hide the extent of US military involvement from the American people in the early years. He would also conceal the dissent growing among even the Kennedy cabinet appointees who were most loyal to him, including Defense Secretary Robert McNamara. As early as December 1965, McNamara told Johnson he didn't believe public support for the war would persist long enough to achieve victory. The president asked, "Then, no matter what we do in the military field there is no sure victory?" McNamara replied, "That's right. We have been too optimistic." Two years later McNamara was so distraught that he was found pacing his office and weeping. Johnson too agonized over the war, wept when he signed condolence letters, checked casualty figures in the operations room at four in the morning, and sneaked away to pray at a local Catholic church (he was a Protestant).

Still Johnson persisted, and — contrary to later myths — in this he had the broad support of most Americans until well into 1968. Furthermore, by keeping Kennedy's defense officials and policies in place, he would show those communists just how tough he, and America, was. At one point he even told Ambassador Lodge to "[g]o back and tell those generals in Saigon that Lyndon Johnson intends to stand by our word [and win]!" Johnson ignored conflicting evidence and even realized that Vietnam — what he called a "little piss-ant country" — wasn't itself of great strategic value. He would fight on and escalate because he was insecure in foreign-policy matters and a firm believer in the "domino theory." As for the military, most senior officers demanded more, not less, American involvement.

The US Army that fought the Vietnamese — unlike that which had won World War II — was unrepresentative of the American people. Draft exemptions and deferrals ensured that about 80 percent of US soldiers came from poor or working-class backgrounds. More were African Americans relative to the percentage of black Americans in the population as a whole. This was true particularly in the combat units, as disproportionate casualty statistics revealed early on. America's troopers were also younger than in previous wars, the average combat soldier just nineteen years old as opposed to twenty-seven in Korea and World War II. While some units and leaders adapted to the counterinsurgent nature of this war, many brought conventional tactics and training to the fight. Famously, one army major explained after obliterating the village of Ben Tre, "We had to destroy the village to save it." General Curtis LeMay, the chief of the Air Force, urged that the United States "bomb North Vietnam back to the 'Stone Age.'" And so the brutal war slogged on.

By late 1967 the senior US commander, General William Westmoreland, made ever more optimistic predictions and was paraded around back home by Johnson to "sell" the war. Yet even LBJ had questions and doubts. Westmoreland claimed victory was near but also kept requesting more troops and regularly underestimated the numerical strength of the enemy. In mid-1967, after yet another troop request, Johnson replied, "Where does it all end? When we add divisions, can't the enemy add divisions? If so, where does it all end?" It was a fair question, and LBJ should have gone with such skeptical instincts. Still, as 1967 turned to '68, Westmoreland was telling the domestic press that there was "light at the end of the tunnel" and that he was "absolutely certain that whereas in 1965 the enemy was winning, today he is certainly losing."

Then, in January 1968, despite all the proclamations of imminent victory, the Vietcong and North Vietnamese unleashed a nationwide offensive, attacking Saigon, nearly every other major city, and most US military bases. Though taken by surprise, the United States actually won a strictly military victory, but it suffered a political and strategic defeat. In March, James Reston of *The New York Times* summarized the situation well: "The main crisis is not in Vietnam itself, or in the cities, but in the feeling that the political system for dealing with these things has broken down." And so it had. Despite the tactical successes and the high casualties inflicted on the enemy in what came to be known as the Tet Offensive, the South Vietnamese government was as corrupt and illegitimate as ever and victory was nowhere in sight. It certainly wasn't "around the corner."

It was clear that the Johnson administration and the generals had been lying or equivocating all along. The famous CBS anchorman Walter Cronkite was so appalled by the Tet Offensive that he exclaimed, "What the hell is going on? I thought we were winning." He then journeyed to Vietnam and returned to pronounce on air that "[i]t seems more certain than ever that the bloody experience of Vietnam is to end in a stalemate." And so it would, but not for a long while, and not without many more deaths.

The war would now become far more unpopular and shatter the Democratic Party. On March 31, Johnson announced a limited escalation to the American people but denied the larger military requests and shocked the nation with the following words: "There is division in the American home now. . . . I do not believe I should devote an hour of my time to any personal partisan course. . . . Accordingly, I shall not seek, and will not accept, the nomination of my party for president." LBJ was emotionally exhausted and resigned himself to opening peace negotiations. His speech was important because it marked the president's first admission that his policy of continued escalation had failed. Ultimately, antiwar candidates like Eugene McCarthy and (latecomer to the opposition) Bobby Kennedy would battle each other in a tough Democratic primary campaign, at least until June 4, 1968, when Kennedy, like his older brother, was assassinated. At the ensuing Democratic National Convention in Chicago — while police rioted against the gathered protesters and beat many senseless — a relative moderate, Vice President Hubert Humphrey, emerged as the nominee, despite not having competed in any primaries. The left-wing contingent of the party was demoralized.

Cynical Denouement: Nixon's Vietnam

Humphrey and the Democrats would ultimately lose in the 1968 presidential election, to none other than Richard Nixon and his cynical brand of conservative politicking. Nixon was helped into office by actions that approached the level of treason. During the campaign, Johnson was concurrently trying to negotiate a cease-fire and potential peace between North Vietnam and South Vietnam. The key was getting the south to agree to talk with National Liberation Front representatives. Nixon, however, knew that good news in Vietnam wouldn't bode well for his political stakes. Thus he and his future national security adviser, Henry Kissinger, appear to have arranged for a prominent woman at the peace conference to promise the South Vietnamese that they would get a better deal should Nixon be elected. The South Vietnamese pulled out and the deal fell apart. LBJ even confronted Nixon at the time, who subsequently lied about the trickery.

Nixon claimed throughout the campaign to have a "secret plan" to end the war. Soon after he was elected, he even proposed, in private, his infamous "madman theory," telling an aide that he "wanted the North Vietnamese to believe I've reached the point where I might do anything to stop the war. We'll slip the word to them that . . . you know Nixon is obsessed about communists. We can't restrain him when he's angry — and he has his hand on the nuclear button — and Ho Chi Minh himself will be in Paris in two days begging for peace." This, of course, hardly transpired.

In reality Nixon would prolong the war not through escalation, per se, but by "Vietnamizing" the war: training and more heavily using Vietnamese troops while savagely bombing the north and south. Nixon was a cunning dealer. He knew that the growing antiwar movement would taper off if fewer Americans and more South Vietnamese were dying in the war. What he really desired was what he called "peace with honor," to save American face by delaying the defeat of South Vietnam. In fact, it is unclear if he ever truly believed that the United States could "win." Nixon, just like Johnson, personalized the conflict, stating that he "will not be the first President of the United States to lose a war." So in the short term he would extend the ground war into Cambodia and Laos, and he secretly and illegally bombed both countries for years. So the south held on, just barely, as US troop numbers declined and the monthly draft calls fell back at home. Thus Nixon divided and stifled the antiwar movement and gained time and space to bomb his way to "peace with honor." South Vietnam's President Nguyen Van Thieu was furious, sensing that the cynical Nixon would ultimately abandon him — though the US president denied it all the while.

By the time Nixon came into office in 1969 the US Army in Vietnam was demoralized and nearing a breaking point. Until 1969, most units had fought with great courage and maintained discipline. Still, as it became clearer that the United States would Vietnamize and not really win the war, some units broke down. No trooper wanted to be the last man to die in Vietnam. Small units started "coasting" and avoiding danger, some enlisted men increasingly refused to follow orders, and in a thousand incidents in 1969–72, soldiers attempted to kill, or "frag," unpopular and aggressive officers. Racial conflicts tore through the ranks. So did drug abuse; by 1971 it was estimated that 40,000 of the 250,000 American men in Vietnam were heroin addicts. Seven out of every hundred soldiers deserted, and double that number went AWOL — absent without leave.

As discipline slowly diminished, American brutality only escalated. In one highly publicized and polarizing incident, Lieutenant William Calley ordered his platoon to murder hundreds of civilians, including babies, in the village of My Lai. Though Calley was convicted of murder and sentenced to life in prison, his sentence upset many pro-war advocates. Under pressure, Nixon changed Calley's sentence to house arrest and the former officer was ultimately released without serving a day of his original prison sentence. A popular song at the time, "The Battle Hymn of Lt. Calley," actually lauded this war criminal. Such was the tribal division of American society during the war.

By 1972 the gradual withdrawal was such that only ninety-five thousand American troops remained in Vietnam. Thus when the North Vietnamese took the offensive that spring it was the Vietnamese who did most of the dying. However, the assault was checked with massive American bombing. Nixon exclaimed, "The bastards have never been bombed like they're going to be bombed this time." Approximately a hundred thousand North Vietnamese troops were killed, and South Vietnam survived, for the moment. However, with US troops filtering out it was clear Nixon's policies had only delayed the inevitable.

That Christmas, Nixon ratcheted up the bombing even more in an attempt to gain concessions from the North Vietnamese at the Paris peace talks. Thousands died as a result, but in the end Nixon and Kissinger ended up accepting a peace that was remarkably similar to the one that had long been on offer. The "Christmas bombing" hadn't been necessary and didn't change the terms of peace. In fact, in exchange for the release of Americans held captive, Nixon agreed to quite a concession of his own — to allow North Vietnam's soldiers to stay in South Vietnam after the cease-fire. This probably doomed the Saigon regime, and, indeed, in April 1975 — a bit more than two years after a peace treaty had been signed — North Vietnamese tanks overran the capital. By then Nixon had resigned in the Watergate scandal. The war was over. It took thirty years and the defeat of two imperial foreign powers, but Vietnam was independent and united.

What then can be said about Nixon's handling of the Vietnam War? Later pro-war apologists claim that it was Nixon's heavy bombing of the north that forced its leaders to sign the peace treaty that generally was ignored by the Vietnamese contending in the war but did offer political cover to the Americans for their pullout. This is ahistorical. Nixon's expansion of the war into Cambodia and Laos and terror bombing of both of these countries and North Vietnam accomplished nothing besides a temporary survival of the South Vietnamese regime. It was Nixon, not the North Vietnamese, who ultimately gave the greatest concession; it was Nixon who gave in to the most important and controversial demand of the communists — that North Vietnamese troops be allowed to remain on the ground in parts of South Vietnam. Vietnamization and all the bombing prolonged a doomed war and delayed the inevitable. During Nixon's term in office, the United States lost 20,553 servicemen killed and the Vietnamese suffered hundreds of thousands of deaths. These soldiers and civilians, many of them women and children, did not have to die. Nixon's insecurity and obsession with saving face and not "losing Vietnam" cost hundreds of thousands their lives. Imagine if the president had accepted the eventual peace terms several years earlier. Many lives surely would have been saved and the war's outcome would likely have been precisely the same. Nixon's war was a waste.

War in the Streets: Bringing "Nam" Home

The antiwar protests at home stabbed the American soldiers in the back and snatched defeat from the jaws of victory in Vietnam — such is the pervasive myth perpetuated by pro-war apologists. For this powerful group, which includes many current and former military officers, it was privileged college students and un-American hippies who sold out their country. It simply isn't true. Public support for the war actually remained rather strong until after the Tet Offensive of 1968. Furthermore, while the antiwar protests did eventually swell and put pressure on Johnson and Nixon, they were far from the decisive force of conservative imaginations. The war went on just as before. The protesters represented a genuine, principled grassroots movement and were not, by and large, the tools of the Soviet Union or international communism. With hindsight, in fact, the antiwar movement was ultimately right about the immoral and unwinnable nature of the American war in Vietnam. The protesters have, in a sense, been vindicated from a historical standpoint but pilloried in our collective memories.

Prior to 1968, most of the press and media establishment supported Johnson and his war policies. Even television news programs aired mostly friendly coverage until Tet. And though privileged college students have often been blamed for "stabbing the troops in the back," most campuses were actually rather quiet until the late 1960s. Indeed, between 1965 and 1968 only 2 to 3 percent of students considered themselves activists and fewer than 20 percent had participated in a protest. It's important to remember that the conflict, in general, was far more popular than is often thought. Nearly all major public institutions, such as unions, businesses, Congress, the media, and the churches, either supported the war or stayed silent.

Nonetheless, opposition to the war did slowly grow and eventually reached a fever pitch during the Nixon years. In October 1967 a Catholic priest named Philip Berrigan broke into a Baltimore draft office and doused draft cards with blood. Young Americans also sought out creative ways to avoid the draft and service in Vietnam: getting married, having children, prolonging stays in college, joining the National Guard, and faking illness or injury. The system of deferments ensured that the average soldier in Vietnam would be poorer and blacker than society at large. This scandalous state of affairs was obvious at the time and constituted a national disgrace.

Recognizing the link between racism at home and militarism abroad, and horrified by the high casualty rates among poor black soldiers, many key leaders of the civil rights movement eventually turned against the war. John Lewis of the Student Nonviolent Coordinating Committee (SNCC) publicly denounced the war in 1966. Stokely Carmichael, a SNCC leader and future Black Panther later known as Kwame Ture, encouraged students to burn their draft cards. Heavyweight champion Muhammad Ali refused to be inducted into the army and as a result his boxing title was stripped from him. He asked, "Why should they ask me to put on a uniform and go ten thousand miles from home and drop bombs and bullets on brown people in Vietnam while the so-called Negro people in Louisville were treated like dogs?" Then in 1967, Martin Luther King Jr., probably the most famous and respected civil rights leader, declared that "we are fighting an immoral war" and that his own country was "the greatest purveyor of violence in the world today."

Although support for the war remained strong throughout most of his term, LBJ regarded this movement with an obsession bordering on paranoia. He became convinced that Soviet communists were behind the grassroots movement and, in an illegal program known as CHAOS, ordered the CIA — in defiance of its charter — to spy on protesters. FBI agents also infiltrated and attempted to disrupt the antiwar movement. When they found little evidence of communist collusion, LBJ leaked information saying the opposite to right-wing congressmen in an attempt to discredit the protesters. What's more, the CIA knew that what it was doing was illegal and unethical. Director Richard Helms wrote an internal memorandum explaining that "[t]his is an area not within the charter of the Agency, so I need to emphasize how extremely sensitive [this is]. Should anyone learn of its existence, it would prove most embarrassing."

Nonetheless, there was a powerful student-led antiwar movement brewing, if slowly. Groups such as the Students for a Democratic Society (SDS) organized protests and marches on the Capitol and Pentagon. Their numbers would eventually swell into the hundreds of thousands, dividing the nation. Violence often occurred. When Nixon invaded Cambodia, a hundred thousand marched on Washington and college campuses exploded, with many schools forced to end the term early due to the chaos. Then in Ohio and Mississippi, overly aggressive police or National Guardsmen opened fire and killed peaceful student protesters and bystanders. America, it appeared, was being ripped apart.

Nonetheless, as powerful as the antiwar camp eventually became, the conservative backlash against the demonstrators and "hippies" was just as strong. Nixon actively fomented this backlash in his speeches. And it worked. A *Newsweek* poll after four students were shot dead at Ohio's Kent State University found that 58 percent of respondents supported the National Guard over the students, despite the fact that the students who were killed had not provoked the guardsmen. Furthermore, even in 1970, 50 percent of respondents supported Nixon's invasion of Cambodia while just 39 percent opposed. The protesters may have been loud and attention grabbing, but what Nixon termed a conservative "silent majority" remained strong to the war's end. These voters would, in the aftermath of Vietnam, become a new bedrock in a resurgent Republican Party.

Some pro-war Americans proved willing to take violent action. In New York City some two hundred construction workers attacked a few hundred demonstrators who were commemorating the victims of Kent State. Wielding fists and hard-hat helmets, they beat the peaceful activists. The workers then marched on city hall, bringing along a mob of supporters, and raised an American flag. Seventy protesters were bloodied, yet there were only six arrests. The very next day, the leader of that local construction union traveled to the White House and presented Nixon with an honorary hard hat. The president accepted it as "a symbol, along with our great flag, for freedom and patriotism to our beloved country." Mob violence now had presidential sanction.

———

The notion that a treasonous antiwar movement led by the Soviet Union had pulled the carpet out from under a successful military effort is just one of many later Vietnam myths. Another, particularly powerful among veterans and later military historians, is the "better war" thesis: the suggestion that "new" counterinsurgency tactics implemented by General Westmoreland's successor, General Creighton Abrams, would have, given more time and support, won the war. Such revisionism is nonsense. Others claim that an outright invasion of the north and increased (perhaps nuclear) bombing would have earned the US military a victory, if only those crummy politicians and protesters had allowed such actions.

Neither theory is persuasive. Hawks have always overestimated the value of airpower and bombing as a means of conflict resolution. Furthermore, given the iron will and commitment of the North Vietnamese and Vietcong, it seems that nothing short of sheer obliteration and genocide would have won the war. The real problem was with the corrupt South Vietnamese government. Too few Vietnamese supported or felt any loyalty to the Saigon regime. Every year one-third of South Vietnamese soldiers would desert. Saigon also ceded the popular policy of social and political reform to the communists, who thus gained power and prestige both north and south of the border. The United States could never seal the thousand miles of border from insurgent infiltration without sending more than a million troops to fight in a nation that was, ultimately, peripheral to US interests.

Later right-wing politicians continued to insist that, as President Ronald Reagan declared, the Vietnam War was a "noble cause" and should have been won. However, what's more likely is that Vietnam demonstrated the limits of American military power abroad. It also established the inherent difficulty of defining "victory" in a nuclear age — especially in waging a counterinsurgency. The "better war" thesis also denies agency to the Vietnamese in what was at root their civil war. The war ended as it did because the communist-nationalist alliance simply had more legitimacy and fortitude, and won over more Vietnamese supporters. There was little, essentially, that US military power could do — besides kill by the millions — to alter this salient reality. What Vietnamese called the "American War" was actually only one phase in a thirty-year independence struggle. Seen this way, the United States hardly had a chance of achieving its goals.

Vietnam, like most anti-colonial insurgencies, presented enormous challenges to a foreign army. Consider the strategic geography:

South Vietnam had a long, porous border that was never adequately sealed. The Vietcong boasted safe havens in North Vietnam, Laos, and Cambodia. The north was able to almost continuously provide direct military support to its troops and guerrilla fighters in the south, and supplies from the Soviet Union and China kept rolling in. The United States also faced a tough, historically nationalistic population, one that hated foreign occupation even more than it hated the corrupt regimes in Saigon. The combination of the long border, safe havens, foreign support, and the lack of a legitimate allied host would undoubtedly have been impossible to overcome unless Washington was willing to exterminate the North Vietnamese as a people and risk global nuclear world war.

Taken as a whole, the defeat in Vietnam was a failure of imagination: to imagine a non-monolithic communism, to imagine alternative responses to the domino theory and military intervention. Trapped in a straitjacket of Cold War dogma, US policy makers forgot that the alliance of the historical enemies Vietnam and China was only one of convenience. Perhaps there was no military possibility of checking a dedicated anti-colonial nationalist movement. Nevertheless, as American troops remain mired in nearly two decades of war in the Greater Middle East, it seems that the conservative revisionist school of thinking on Vietnam may have won out. If there are lessons left behind by the tragic conflict in Vietnam, it is unclear that Washington, and the American public, has learned any of them.[26]

30

CIVIL RIGHTS, A DREAM DEFERRED

What happens to a dream deferred?
Does it dry up
like a raisin in the sun?
Or fester like a sore. . . .
Maybe it just sags like a heavy load.
Or does it explode?
   — Langston Hughes, from his poem "Harlem" (1951)

Rosa Parks sat, Martin Luther King Jr. stood up, the Supreme Court overturned school segregation, and the rest, as they say, was history. African Americans, long abused and long thwarted, ultimately won their civil rights in what has become a defining American story. Only that's what this is — a story, a mythologized and sanitized past that fails to engage with the complexity of the issues at hand.

According to what American children are taught, the civil rights activists managed a coherent movement; there seldom is mention of the internal battles within the black and white liberal communities. As it is taught, the movement had a discrete chronology, a beginning and an end. It begins with the US Supreme Court's decision in *Brown v. Board* or Rosa Parks's refusal to give up her seat to a white person on a crowded, segregated bus in Montgomery, Alabama. It ends, usually, with either the signing of the Civil Rights Act of 1964 and the Voting Rights Act of 1965, or with the King assassination in April 1968. The mythologized movement has a distinctly southern geography — lost are the riots, poverty, and persistent de facto segregation of the urban North.

In learning the patriotic gospel of American civil rights struggle, students are instructed that there was a "good" black movement, fronted by MLK and dedicated to nonviolence; conversely, there was a "bad" movement, associated with Malcolm X and the Black Panthers, a supposedly violent and, ultimately, counterproductive crew. Gone, again, is the nuance, the movement's gradations, and the genuine emotional and intellectual pull of black-power politics and culture. In the traditional yarn, the civil rights movement went just far enough — winning civic but not economic rights — and was wildly successful. In the process, Americans are led to believe, the United States conquered its demons and saved its soul. The nation is thus vindicated and its sins are forgiven. White liberals can continue to sleep well.

What if this popular telling conceals as much as it reveals? It's possible, in fact, that the history of civil rights struggle in the America of the 1950s and '60s was always far more contested, angry, and radical than is commonly remembered. Taken as a whole, in this way, the pageantry is removed and we can see the civil rights movement as a campaign begun with the arrival of the first slave ships and still being fought today, sometimes out in the streets. In this more honest, if discomfiting, tale, the movement peaked in the 1960s but began far earlier and never really ended. It unfolded, albeit differently, in the North and the South and included equally strong traditions of both nonviolence and armed self-defense on both sides of the Mason-Dixon Line. In this version of a complex story there are few purely "good" or "bad" activists; indeed, their histories include many gray areas, and much overlap is visible among the traditions of King, Malcolm X, and many influential grassroots characters lost to history. This movement, the real movement, unfolded in the streets and dragged along its leaders, white or black, just as often as it was led by them. President John Kennedy (who did not live to see his proposed Civil Rights Act become law), President Lyndon Johnson, and King were joined by radical, frustrated students, the sons and daughters of sharecroppers, and even armed black nationalists. The real story is messy and best explained through a reevaluation of one Rosa Parks.

Parks is often misremembered as an old lady who was just too exhausted to give up a bus seat. It's the perfect origin story for a prettified movement: an elderly woman — utterly sympathetic — battling unrepentant bigots in the Deep South. Parks, like King — who gained national fame organizing a bus boycott that Parks had started — emerges as a "good," almost grandmotherly activist. In reality Parks was only forty-two years old at the time of the first of her two arrests, was a woman of great purpose, and certainly was not soft or anyone's pushover; she was a lifelong activist and far more radical than most Americans know. She began her career in activism protesting the trumped-up conviction in the 1930s of the Scottsboro Boys — nine black men, one as young as thirteen, charged with a rape they did not commit. She attempted to vote as early as 1943, turned away time and again until she succeeded in registering in 1945. By 1949 she was an NAACP youth leader, then secretary to E. D. Nixon, head of the Montgomery NAACP. Just before the bus incident and subsequent bus boycott, Parks attended a training session for direct-action activists in Tennessee.

Parks, in 1992, challenged the notion that she was meek and harmless, stating, "People always say that I didn't give up my seat because I was tired, but that isn't true. I was not tired physically. . . . I was not old, although some people have an image of me as being old. I was forty-two. No, the only tired I was, was tired of giving in." Rosa Parks was, so to speak, a badass — a social justice warrior in her own right. And her courage and commitment spurred a movement that vaulted a twenty-six-year-old Baptist minister, Martin Luther King Jr., to international prominence. Indeed, as one contemporary claimed, "If Mrs. Parks had gotten up and given that cracker her seat, you'd never heard of Reverend King." That's probably true. Parks, though, was a woman, and even in the civil rights community women often remained second-class citizens. During the famous bus boycott that she had single-handedly kicked off, she mostly answered phones and did secretarial work within activist operations. Also forgotten is that she lost her job and suffered economic insecurity due to her brave stand — demonstrating, importantly, that there always was, and is, an economic component to civil rights activism.

The facts of Parks's long career poke holes in the legend built around her. Years after the Montgomery bus boycott, she and her husband left the South and moved to urban Detroit, where she lived until she died in 2005 at the age of ninety-two. Entering the supposed promised land of the non–Jim Crow North, she found no need to quit fighting for justice. Parks lived out her life as an urban activist, protesting segregation, corporate downsizing, and South African apartheid. She refused to fully rebuke the black rioters of the mid-to-late 1960s. She admired Malcolm X and claimed that he, not MLK, was her hero! She was an early opponent of the Vietnam War and attended black-power conferences in 1968 and 1972. A believer in self-defense, she had kept guns in her home when she lived in Alabama. After King was assassinated in 1968 she attended his planned Poor People's March to fight for economic justice. By the 1970s she had taken to dressing in African-style clothing, and in the decades before her death she would lobby for reparations to black Americans. Parks lived and died a crusader. She, and the movement of which she was a part, was always far more complex, divided, and radical than the picture presented in watered-down accounts.

The "Long" Civil Rights Movement

By the end of World War II, the lot of black Americans had not improved much over the previous seventy years. Abandoned by northern "liberals" at the end of Reconstruction, blacks largely fended for themselves in a harsh world, especially in the systemically segregated Deep South. Still, their struggle and quest for civil and human rights never stopped. Undeniably, progress was slow, and the movement, such as it was, had peaks and valleys. In the hyper-sensitized Red Scares of the twentieth century, black civil rights activism was dismissed or attacked as communistic. The influence of communism on activists was always exaggerated, but many black political and cultural leaders were sympathetic to the reds and the Soviet Union. After all, only the Communist Party insisted on racial justice as part of its platform, and it was the party that became associated with the legal defense of the Scottsboro Boys. In the 1930s the Communists even ran a black man for vice president. In these ways, the Communists were far ahead of the US political mainstream on the civil rights issue. As the esteemed historian Howard Zinn wrote, "The Negro was not as anti-Communist as the white population. He could not afford to be, his friends were so few."

White America was quick to apply the broad brush of communism to black activists. In 1949, after Jewish residents of Peekskill, New York, were deemed responsible for inviting the black singer Paul Robeson, alleged to be a member of the Communist Party, to perform, Gentiles rioted and attacked concertgoers. Robeson was subsequently put under constant government surveillance, and his phone was bugged, his mail was intercepted, and his passport was seized, making it impossible for him to travel abroad. The civil rights movement was also initially linked to the labor movement. From the start, black organizers critiqued the economic system that kept their people largely impoverished and sought allies within the labor movement. They managed some successes, but Operation Dixie, a postwar attempt to unionize the labor-hostile South, faltered under charges of communist infiltration. It was an old, if effective, game: equate civil rights activism with global communism and thus maintain the bigoted status quo. Amid fear of the stigma of communist association, the push for civil rights moved away from unions. By the mid-1950s the churches had become the key institutions of civil rights protest. However, with many churches focusing on the moral aspects of racism, the economic components of the mission often were softened.

After the Supreme Court overturned school segregation and after Rosa Parks and others had won a legal right to keep a seat on a bus, black life in America was disturbingly similar to that of a century earlier. In the South only a token few blacks were permitted to vote, every public institution was segregated, and many newspapers wouldn't even print black persons' names — for example, printing that "Joe and Jane Doe were killed, and two negroes." North and South, black unemployment was double the white average; half of all blacks lived in poverty, even during the boom years of the 1950s. Some key unions even virtually barred blacks from membership. The school systems of the South were the ultimate symbol of inequality. In

1945, South Carolina spent three times as much per pupil on its white schools as it did on black ones; Mississippi was even worse, spending four and a half times as much on white students. Black school years tended to be shorter, and teachers in black schools were paid less. All this put to lie the Jim Crow doctrine of "separate but equal."

Why Now? A Second Reconstruction

After moving along at more or less a steady rate in the first half of the twentieth century, activism and protest exploded in the 1950s and picked up even more energy throughout the 1960s. It's important to consider why this was, for it was no accident. Two factors, above all, contributed to the breakout of civil rights activism in the period: Cold War considerations and the now ubiquitous medium of television, which broadcast across the world the images of black protest and white backlash. The Soviets — though flawed messengers themselves — were correct in their criticism of American race relations and gloried in spreading propaganda on the topic throughout the developing nations. This Soviet effort worked. US hypocrisy on race and the country's regular meddling in post-colonial affairs won Washington few friends in the Global South. Indeed, the US government knew this and was growing concerned, and a bit embarrassed, by the bad press that the Jim Crow South was earning America. President Harry Truman's Committee on Civil Rights concluded, as early as 1946, that "[w]e cannot escape the fact that our civil rights record has been an issue in world politics. . . . Those with competing philosophies have stressed our shortcomings . . . they have tried to prove our democracy an empty fraud." Which it largely was — after all, blacks couldn't even vote in half the country!

Though slavery had ended in 1865 and Reconstruction had initially brought much progress, no blacks had served in Congress between 1905 and 1929. No black southerners served between 1891 and 1987! National security experts and leaders in both the Truman and Eisenhower administrations were becoming seriously concerned that American bigotry was a liability in the global fight against communism. Media images, especially television images, of police dogs attacking black protesters and other atrocities also garnered the sympathy of many white Americans and only further embarrassed the United States on the world stage. Finally, with the accession of Earl Warren as Eisenhower's chief justice of the Supreme Court, the judicial branch of government began dismantling the legal super-structure of Jim Crow segregation, beginning with the ruling against school segregation in *Brown v. Board of Education* in 1954.

Then, in tiny Money, Mississippi, a white posse in 1955 abducted and murdered a fourteen-year-old boy from Chicago for allegedly whis-tling at a white woman. Emmett Till was visiting relatives at the time and received a fatal lesson in the social mores of the Deep South. His mutilated and bloated body, found in a river, was shipped back north to his mother. In a moment of profound courage and consequence, his mother decided on a public, open-casket funeral, displaying for the world what the attackers had "done to her boy." No one was ever convicted of the crime, and the female "victim" of the alleged whistling later would recant, changing her story about Emmett Till's actions in the 1955 encounter. The case was a national and international sensa-tion, and it brought about a major outbreak of protest and activism.

Whose Civil Rights Movement? Top-Down and Grassroots Interpretations

In the standard telling, the civil rights movement was spearheaded by "great men" such as Martin Luther King, Jack Kennedy, and Lyndon Johnson. Understood thus, only the "good," moderate civil rights leaders mattered, and it was they who accomplished great things. In reality the civil rights movement was very much a grassroots program, and anonymous black (and some white) activists more often than not forced national political leaders to countenance change. Major figures, including presidents and judiciary members, often responded to the grassroots activity in the streets and not the other way around. The "great men" were usually behind the curve on civil rights and remained wary of "too much change too fast." It took the sacrifices of the street protesters — who often risked bodily harm and arrest — to force national leaders into action.

Even the court decision in *Brown v. Board* was sparked by the willingness of average black citizens across the country to open lawsuits with the help of the National Association for the Advancement of Colored People, the NAACP. This took courage, and many litigants were threatened in their home communities. In the next major event, the Montgomery bus boycott, Rosa Parks and then MLK may have become symbols of the protest, but it was accomplished only through the activities of thousands of average black citizens who, lacking bus service because of the boycott, organized carpools or walked long distances to work for an entire year. Without this direct-action activism, the court would have been unlikely to rule against segregation on public transportation, as it did in 1956.

An interesting dynamic between the grassroots and top-down interpretations occurred during the school integration controversy in 1957 in Little Rock, Arkansas. When Governor Orval Faubus refused to allow nine black high school students to attend the city's Central High School — he deployed state National Guard troops to block the students — President Dwight Eisenhower and the federal government faced a serious constitutional challenge. Ike, contrary to popular conception, was no friend of the civil rights activists. The president had served out a career in a segregated army and had even opposed Truman's order to desegregate the armed forces after World War II. Eisenhower opposed the Brown decision and the entire notion of using federal law to alter race relations in the South. He stated, "The improvement of race relations is one of those things that will be healthy and sound only if it starts locally. . . . I believe that Federal law imposed upon our states . . . would set back the cause of race relations a long, long time." The flaw in his thinking seems obvious in retrospect: the former Confederate states had shown zero willingness to change for nearly a hundred years, and there was no indication that they would change anytime soon, at least without massive protests.

Eisenhower even sympathized with and normalized southern bigotry. When Ike invited Chief Justice Earl Warren — a liberal on

Little Rock Integration Protest, 1959

race relations — to the White House, he sat him next to John W. Davis, the attorney fighting against integration in the ongoing Brown court case. Eisenhower leaned over to Warren and said of the intransigent southern politicians: "These are not bad people. All they are concerned about is to see that their sweet little girls are not required to sit in school alongside some big overgrown Negro." Civil rights was not a national priority in the 1950s. In the 1956 presidential election neither Eisenhower nor his opponent, Democrat Adlai Stevenson, talked very much about the issue at all. Ike, before the Little Rock crisis, had even stated, "I can't imagine any set of circumstances that would ever induce me to send federal troops into any area to enforce the orders of a federal court, because I believe that the common sense of America will never require it." Just months later, he would be proved wrong about the "common sense" of Americans.

Eisenhower, true to his constitutional duties, eventually did intervene, even if his sympathies never lay with the civil rights movement. When matters spiraled out of control in Little Rock and mobs attacked children, random blacks, and "Yankee" reporters, Ike federalized the Arkansas National Guard and deployed eleven hundred active-duty army paratroopers to protect the nine students and integrate the school. He did so under a "constitutional duty which was the most repugnant to him of all his acts in his eight years in the White House," according to a top aide. Eisenhower was also probably motivated by the international blowback as TV images of innocent black children being harassed by angry mobs flashed across the world. Once again America appeared wildly hypocritical and vindicated the Soviet critique of the United States. The paratroops would, in a remarkable turn of events, stay in place until November, and the National Guard remained on-site for the entire school year. Ike had finally, if reluctantly, acted, but in an oft-forgotten postscript Governor Faubus got the last laugh. He simply closed all Little Rock schools for the following academic year, 1958–59, rather than see desegregation continue. Southern backlash was alive and well despite the ruling of the court and the deployment of federal soldiers.

King and his newly formed — if ill-organized — Southern Christian Leadership Conference (SCLC) would continue to spread headline-grabbing activism around the South after the Montgomery bus boycott, but here again King was very much only a figurehead for a decidedly grassroots movement. It was black college students, many of whom were members of the Student Nonviolent Coordinating Committee (SNCC), who drove the movement forward. They began by conducting sit-ins at segregated lunch counters and eventually rode segregated Greyhound buses throughout the South to protest already illegal but rarely prosecuted segregation in interstate transportation. In these acts the students captured the televised attention of many white liberals, but they also faced extreme violence and received scant protection from a reluctant Kennedy administration. During the rides, a bus was firebombed in Anniston, Alabama, and dozens of freedom riders, as they were dubbed, were arrested and made to serve significant jail time — some at the infamously brutal Parchman Farm Penitentiary's maximum-security wing in Mississippi.

In 1963, King took his movement and growing personal fame to Birmingham, Alabama, one of the most segregated and violent cities in the South. Known colloquially as "Bombingham," the city was the site of more white terror bombings than any other southern locale.

The intensely bigoted local police chief, Bull Connor, played right into the hands of King and the grassroots activists in the city, siccing attack dogs on peaceful black protesters and firing water cannons at the demonstrators. The televised images horrified millions of white Americans, including, reportedly, President Kennedy. Indeed, in the aftermath of Birmingham, Kennedy would feel obliged to introduce a civil rights bill in Congress. Reflecting on the counterproductive role of Connor, JFK stated, "The civil rights movement should thank God for Bull Connor. He's helped as much as Abraham Lincoln."

That same year King helped organize the massive March on Washington to generate pressure for civil and economic rights for blacks. Even here, though, the grassroots found itself in tension with the movement and national political leadership.

Another split between the grassroots and top-down leaders occurred during the 1964 presidential primary season. When the Mississippi Democratic delegation refused to seat any black members — despite almost half of the state population being black — SNCC members and other activists formed their own party, the Mississippi Freedom Democratic Party (MFDP), and crashed the party convention in Atlantic City, New Jersey. Despite impassioned speeches from MFDP leader Fannie Lou Hamer, the delegation was denied seats and forced into a humiliating compromise by President Lyndon Johnson and the party leadership. In reaction, many SNCC and MFDP activists forever lost faith in white liberals, establishment politicians, and even the nonviolent movement leaders such as MLK. Stokely Carmichael, a fiery Trinidadian SNCC leader from the North, complained in 1965 about King and his SCLC. Feeling abandoned by these national leaders, an increasingly radicalized Carmichael stated:

> Here comes the SCLC talking about mobilizing another 2-week campaign, using our base and the magic of Dr. King's name. . . . They're going to bring the cameras, the media, prominent people . . . turn the place upside down and split. Probably leaving us sitting in jail. That was the issue, a real strategic and philosophical difference.

Such tensions within the movement — often based on generational differences — would remain a key factor in an increasingly divided black activist base. Indeed, soon after the MFDP fiasco, SNCC would vote to remove all its white members.

The Civil Rights Act of 1964 did eventually pass, after Kennedy's assassination in November of the previous year, and blacks achieved their goal of desegregation (but not necessarily integration). Still, the bill did nothing to address voting rights, which were still denied to the vast majority of blacks in the South. In response, both the SCLC and the SNCC descended on Selma, Alabama, to protest for a voting rights act. King grabbed the headlines, but it was John Lewis and numerous grassroots activists who bore the burden of police violence when they attempted to ceremoniously march on the capitol in Montgomery. Lewis's skull was fractured by a police baton, and dozens of others also were seriously injured. This was now 1965, a full ten years since the Brown decision, and the intransigence of southern whites remained strong as ever. Still, the horrifying images out of Selma goaded President Johnson into action: He pushed the Voting Rights Act through Congress by year's end.

Most civil rights histories end there, with the achievement of the two key pieces of congressional legislation, but the movement carried on. Legislation was one thing, but actual implementation of integration and voting rights required ever more protest across the South throughout the 1960s and '70s. King kept fighting, even planning a poor people's movement to march on Washington to fight against systemic poverty and for the economic components of civil rights. SNCC leaders went to Mississippi and Alabama to conduct voter registration campaigns in these deepest of the Deep South states. All were met with violence and arrest, yet the grassroots activists kept fighting. In a sense, the true odyssey of civil rights was their story.

Rethinking Black Power

If we must die, let it not be like hogs
Hunted and penned in an inglorious spot. . . .

Like men we'll face the murderous, cowardly pack,
Pressed to the wall, dying, but fighting back!
— From the poem "If We Must Die," by Claude McKay

Black power. Black nationalism. The Black Panthers. The very terms now carry deeply pejorative connotations. The common portrayal in conventional narratives is that as the 1960s progressed, the "good" civil rights movement of Dr. King was overtaken by the "bad" movement of black-power activists such as Carmichael, Malcolm X, and the Black Panthers. These activists are considered violent, reverse racists and counterproductive to the civil rights cause. This is simply untrue. Black power and black nationalism had always been powerful elements of the "long" civil rights movement. Indeed, the twin tracks of the nonviolence of King and armed black self-defense always existed side by side and remained vital twin components of a diverse movement.

To understand the true origins of black power and the complex nature of the Black Panther movement, we must begin in the extremely poor and violent majority-black community of Lowndes County in Alabama. The county first came to the attention of SNCC during the 1965 Selma-to-Montgomery march, which passed through it. The organization quickly traveled to the area to attempt a new approach to protest. In an internal SNCC strategy memo, the group described how it intended to take power in majority-black communities around the South, beginning in Lowndes County. In the memo, SNCC asked:

> When you have a situation where the community is 80% black, why complain about police brutality when you can be the sheriff yourself? Why complain about substandard education when you could be the Board of Education?
> . . . Why protest when you can exercise power?

So it was that SNCC flooded into the poor, majority-black communities of the county and — in the face of loathing by the white-dominated Democratic Party — formed its own political party, the Lowndes County Freedom Organization (LCFO). It chose as a symbol of bold determination the black panther. Encouraged by the results of the Alabama intervention, the later Black Panther Party for Self Defense (BPP) would be formed in Oakland, California, and spread across urban communities throughout the nation.

The LCFO and its Black Panther logo were never about violent aggression, but rather black empowerment, self-defense, and voting rights. The move toward black power was driven, primarily, by white intransigence. Massive violent backlash, local refusal of southern white communities to follow court integration orders, and the unwillingness of establishment political figures to protect or support the movement drove the young activists in radical directions. Carmichael, in a film discovered years later, articulated the frustration among the young activists when he stated, "Dr. King's policy was that nonviolence would achieve the gains for black people. . . . He only made one fallacious assumption: In order for nonviolence to work, your opponent must have a conscience. The United States has none." Once — on stage with MLK — he famously declared, "The time for running has come to an end. You tell them white folk in Mississippi that all the scared niggers are dead."

Lowndes County proved a tough nut to crack. In 1906, W. E. B. Du Bois declared that "outside of some sections of the Mississippi and Red River Valley, I do not think it would be easy to find a place where conditions were more unfavorable to the rise of the Negro." A 1903 report from a US district attorney claimed that "Lowndes County is honeycombed with slavery." Whereas in 1900, Lowndes County had five thousand black registered voters, after the arrival of Jim Crow legislation there were only fifty-seven registered in 1906. Matters had changed little by 1965. Still, Carmichael and SNCC brought enthusiasm into their voting rights campaign. He exclaimed, "We're going to tear this county up. Then we're going to build it back, brick by brick, until it's a fit place for human beings."

Whites fought back ferociously in Lowndes. One white mother declared that "Niggers in our schools will ruin my children morally, scholastically, spiritually, and every other way." White mobs and posses murdered many activists, including the white Reverend

Jonathan Daniels. In response, members of the LCFO armed themselves and prepared to fight back. One resident exclaimed at the time that "[y]ou can't come here talking that non-violence shit. You'll get yourself killed and other people too." It took a few years, and much effort, but the LCFO eventually took power in Lowndes County, even electing a black sheriff! Inspired by the empowerment of rural blacks, the BPP in Oakland adopted the panther logo and the Carmichael doctrine of black power.

Throughout northern urban areas, the Black Panthers armed themselves, usually legally, and followed and observed the police for instances of brutality. They fought against gun control in California, and conservatives, led by Governor Ronald Reagan, were the ones pushing for such legislation! While there were acts of violence committed by the Panthers, their work spanned many areas, including community organizing and the distribution of free breakfasts to black urban children. An outgrowth of black power was a cultural component that sought to convince Americans that "black is beautiful." Black women and men turned their back on white notions of beauty and began wearing their hair naturally in "Afros" and donning Afro-centric clothing. Many, including Carmichael (Kwame Ture) and the boxer Cassius Clay (Muhammad Ali), took Islamic or African names rather than continue to accept their given "slave" names. Black power was an influential movement from the start and gained ever more adherents in the black community — including Rosa Parks — with the arrival of the 1970s. Indeed, it was government backlash and suppression of the Panthers and other black nationalists that ultimately squashed this prominent movement. Black power was then demonized by many history teachers and key political figures and was non-organically stripped away from the "good" civil rights activism of Dr. King. Still, King was never as centrist as his hagiographers had claimed.

The Radical King: Reimagining the Man and the Movement

Martin Luther King Jr. was never as moderate or popular as is commonly remembered. Dozens of US senators, John McCain among them, would vote against designating his birthday a national holiday. King was polarizing in his time, hated in the white South, and demonized as a communist by many conservative northerners. Then something changed. By the late 1980s, King was canonized as the "good" or peaceful leader of the civil rights movement and placed on a national pedestal in juxtaposition with the "bad" activists such as Stokely Carmichael, Malcolm X, and the Black Panthers. In truth, however, there was never as much distance between King and the emboldened black-power activists as is commonly believed. MLK was radical — for his time and even based on contemporary standards. Yet this salient fact has been erased from memory in favor of the de-radicalized King of public memory.

King eventually broke out of his simple, nonviolent image, and even though he never called for violence, he gradually radicalized ever further in opposition to white intransigence. King always had an economic component to his activism. He recognized that official integration alone would never solve the inherent problems of black poverty and unemployment. In 1967 he stated, "Let us be dissatisfied until the tragic walls that separate our outer city of wealth and comfort from the inner city of poverty despair shall be crushed by the forces of justice. Let us be dissatisfied until slums are cast into the junk heaps of history, and every family will live in a decent sanitary home." King also refused to abandon black rioters who exploded with anger toward their generational poverty and police brutality in northern urban cities. In 1968 he declared that "I'm absolutely convinced that a riot merely intensifies the fears of the white community . . . but it is not enough for me to stand before you tonight and condemn riots . . . without condemning the intolerable conditions that exist in our society. . . . And I must say tonight that a riot is a language of the unheard." LBJ's Advisory Committee on Urban Disorder agreed, stating in its official report that "white racism and an explosive mixture which has been accumulating in our cities . . . pervasive discrimination and segregation in employment, education, and housing" were to blame for the riots.

King even criticized capitalism itself. He went on the record, stating, "Call it democracy, or call it democratic socialism, but there must be a better distribution of wealth within this country for all of God's children." MLK had long stated that American society was afflicted by "three evils" — racism, imperialism, and hyper-capitalism. By 1967, King would openly oppose the Vietnam War, which he had long despised privately. In a speech at the Riverside Church in New York City, he referred to the United States as "[t]he greatest purveyor of violence in the world today," adding, "my own government, I cannot be silent." He also stated that he saw the war as "unjust, evil, and futile." When King stepped out of the pure civil rights arena into larger critiques of capitalism and American imperialism, he was lambasted by the mainstream media, including *The New York Times*. At the time of his 1968 death — which occurred when, as few now remember, he was rallying support for the Memphis sanitation company union during a visit to the Tennessee city — close to half of Americans, and nearly all conservatives, had a negative view of him. When MLK was assassinated he was far from the widely adulated figure he would later become.

Opportunities Lost: What the Movement Didn't Address

The civil rights movement's successes were fought and stalled at every moment by intransigent whites both north and south of the Mason-Dixon Line. Ultimately, this white backlash would stymie the largest goals of the movement and ensure that civil rights legislation didn't go far enough. So what did the 1950s and '60s activism achieve? It ended de jure segregation of public facilities — though it would take until 1969 for most southern schools to adhere to 1954's court desegregation order. It gave blacks the franchise in the South. These were real achievements, but they hardly scratched the surface of white supremacy in America.

First, the FBI infiltrated and destroyed black-power movements through the COINTELPRO program, which focused on crippling black radicals. The bureau even tapped the "moderate" MLK's phone and sent him an anonymous letter encouraging him to commit suicide. In an internal FBI memo King was labeled "the most dangerous Negro in the future of this nation from the standpoint of communism and national security." The FBI later colluded with the Chicago police to assassinate the Black Panther leader Fred Hampton, riddling his body with bullets while he lay in bed. This federal backlash combined with white southern backlash to limit the achievements of the civil rights movement.

Also, key figures in the civil rights cause were assassinated in the 1960s, including Malcolm X, John Kennedy, Robert Kennedy, and Dr. King. In addition, northern whites were scared off by the violence of the urban riots of the period and began to culturally and politically shift to the Republican Party.

So where did the movement ultimately falter? Simply put, King and other activists achieved civil rights but never conquered latent racism or economic inequality. That failure ensured that the cause and relative position of American blacks would, ultimately, change very little in the aftermath of the 1960s. Black Americans remain an underrepresented and impoverished racial caste even in the twenty-first century. In that sense the movement and the need for it never really ended — even if it disappeared from the mainstream media. Consider how little changed in the aftermath of the movement's climactic period. In 1977, despite the earlier passage of the Civil Rights Act and the Voting Rights Act, in the eleven southern states there were still zero black senators and only two black congressmen. Though 20 percent of the population, blacks were only 3 percent of elected officeholders. Unemployment among black youths remained as high as 34 percent.

The share of black children attending de facto segregated schools only dropped from 76.6 percent in 1968 to 74.1 percent in 2010. In 2010 a study conducted by UCLA on the topic of segregation found that 74 percent of blacks still attended majority non-white schools; 38 percent attended intensely segregated schools — those with only 0 to 10 percent of whites enrolled; and 15 percent attended "apartheid schools," where whites make up 0 to 1 percent of the student body. By contrast, white students typically attend school where three-fourths of their peers are white. The criminalization of the black body has also proceeded without respite. Today the United States has the highest incarceration rate in the world — mostly based on low-level drug offenses — much higher than even in Russia and Cuba. However, black males in America have an incarceration rate eight times higher than the rate of Cuba, the next worst country on this ignominious list. And as the publicity about police violence toward blacks has demonstrated, and the Black Lives Matter movement has proved, the US is far from done with its racial problems.

———

> We have just lost the South for a generation.
> — President Lyndon B. Johnson after
> signing the Civil Rights Act of 1964

President Johnson is said to have spoken the words above to an aide after he signed the Civil Rights Act. LBJ, a Texan, had known that his pushing for black civil rights would alienate southerners and drive them into the Republicans' arms. And so it came to pass. After the limited successes of the civil rights movement, white America lashed out and turned against the causes of black activists. When schools attempted busing programs to comply with court orders to integrate schools, white parents — especially in the North — fought back, attacking black students and protesting until the programs were shut down. There was also a Republican renaissance, as the GOP rode white backlash to victories in five out of six presidential elections after 1968. The solid Democratic South transformed into the solid Republican South over the course of just eight years, between 1964 and 1972. The Old Confederacy would be a conservative Republican base.

Black Americans remain uniquely poor and oppressed among America's many minority groups, with the possible exception of Native Americans living on reservations. What the 1950s–60s movement did not do was address the massive wealth inequality and black subjection to police violence that continue to characterize urban black communities. America is just about as segregated now as it was in 1960. Officially, Jim Crow is dead, but the concept lives on in

31

NIXON'S DARK LEGACY

He was corrupt. He was petty, angry, and resentful. He was also one of the most astute politicians in the annals of the American presidency. Time after time he overcame obstacles and defeats to rise again. His genius, ultimately, was this: He envisioned a new coalition and knew how to channel white resentment over the civil rights and antiwar movements into political triumph. This was his gift, and his legacy. Americans today inhabit the partisan universe that Richard Milhous Nixon crafted. Republican leaders to this very day speak Nixon's language and employ Nixon's tactics of fear and anger to win massive white majorities in election upon election. Indeed, though Nixon eventually resigned in disgrace before he could be impeached, the following half century remained rather kind to the Republican Party. Only three of the next eight presidents were Democrats, leaving Republicans to reign over the White House for a majority of the post-Nixon era.

For all that, Nixon remains an enigma. Though he crafted a lasting conservative majority among American voters, he also supported popular environmental and social welfare causes. He secretly bombed Laos and Cambodia and orchestrated a right-wing coup in Chile but also reached out to the Soviets and Chinese in a bold attempt to lessen Cold War tensions and achieve détente. A product of conflict, Nixon operated in the gray areas of life. Though the antiwar activists, establishment liberals, and African Americans generally hated him, Nixon won two presidential elections, cruising to victory for a second term. He was popular, far more so than many would like to admit. Although the 1960s began as a time of prosperity and hope, they produced a president who operated from and exploited anxiety and fear, and in doing so found millions of supporters. Nixon was representative of the

Richard Nixon, August 1974

dark side of American politics, and no one tapped into the darkness as deftly as he did. The key to his success was his ability to rally what he called the "silent majority" of frustrated northern whites, most of whom traditionally were Democrats, and angry southern whites in what came to be known as his southern strategy. It was cynical, and it worked.

White Backlash: Nixon's Southern Strategy

Southern racists didn't disappear in the wake of the civil rights movement; they simply rebranded as Republicans and expressed their intentions in less overtly racial language. Nixon, ever the consummate politician, knew this and set out to form a new American Republican majority, both for the campaign year of 1968 and for the future. The seeds of a new conservative ascendency had been in place for quite some time. In 1948 some southern Democrats bolted the party and ran then-governor Strom Thurmond of South Carolina for president as a "Dixiecrat" on a ticket dubbed the States' Rights Democratic Party. In 1964 many in the Deep South supported the Republican Barry Goldwater — this in a region so Democratic for so long that it was known in the party as the solid South — in his presidential bid against the incumbent, Lyndon B. Johnson. Yet it was Nixon who effectively discerned these symptoms of Democratic weakness and crafted a conservative electoral coalition that has remained in place ever since.

During the 1968 presidential campaign, a young number-crunching political strategist, Kevin Phillips, explained a new southern strategy to Nixon. The bottom line was that Nixon needed to win over southern Democrats to the Republican side and to essentially give up any attempt to win the black vote. As a result the Republicans would abandon civil rights indefinitely. Phillips told Nixon that the election would be won on "the law and order / Negro socio-economic revolution syndrome." In other words, Nixon was being successfully urged to run on "law and order" in response to the massive urban riots that had so spooked northern whites and to say the same things that southern Democrats had long been mouthing about race, although in less overtly racist language.

Nixon was from California and knew he didn't have to speak as coarsely as Strom Thurmond. Instead he used coded, but equally apocalyptic, language to win over fearful whites. "As we look at America, we see cities enveloped in smoke and flame," he said in his 1968 acceptance speech at the GOP convention. Still, he declared, in the tumult there was the quiet "voice of the great majority of Americans, the forgotten Americans — the non-shouters; the non-demonstrators . . . they are not guilty of the crime that plagues the land." What he meant, below the biblical eschatological imagery, was that he would be the candidate for a "silent majority" of whites — folks furious about inner-city riots, crime, hippies, and a civil rights movement that most felt had gone too far, too fast.

In taking particular aim at the rioters, Nixon ignored official government reports that blamed the disorder on racism and entrenched poverty; instead he tied the maelstrom to a defiance of law and order. The year before his first term started, Nixon said the riots were "the most virulent symptoms to date of another, and in some ways graver, national disorder — the decline in respect for public authority and the rule of law in America. Far from being a great society, ours is becoming a lawless society." The jab against Johnson's Great Society, which in considerable part sought to help poor black populations in urban centers, was not lost on his enthusiastic listeners. Nixon had flipped the script, changed the paradigm. The real victims, the real minority, consisted not of blacks and other historically oppressed groups but working-class, white males! In a national address in 1969, Nixon plainly and forcefully unveiled his most famous phrase — *silent majority*. " I would be untrue to my oath of office," he declared, "if I allowed the policy of this Nation to be dictated by the minority who [oppose the Vietnam War] . . . and who try to impose [their views] on the Nation by mounting demonstrations in the street. . . . And so tonight — to you, the great silent majority of my fellow Americans — I ask for your support." Protest, in short, was no longer patriotic. Not in Nixon's America.

Behind the national discourse and Nixon's successful alignment of political sentiment was a staggering degree of cynicism. The president and company knew exactly what they were doing, exactly how they were manipulating white voters. Nixon adviser John Dean would later state that he "was cranking out that bullshit on Nixon's crime policy before he was elected. And it was bullshit, too. We knew it." More damning were the reflective comments of another key Nixon aide, John Ehrlichman:

> The Nixon campaign in 1968, and the Nixon White House after that, had two enemies: the antiwar left and black people. You understand what I'm saying? We knew we couldn't make it illegal to be either against the war or black, but by getting the public to associate the hippies with marijuana and blacks with heroin, and then criminalizing both heavily, we could disrupt those communities. We could arrest their leaders, raid their homes, break up their meetings, and vilify them night after night on the evening news. Did we know we were lying about the drugs? Of course we did.

It was vital, according to the Nixon team, to demonize black activists, especially advocates of black power. The chief of staff, H. R. Haldeman, explained, "The whole problem is really the blacks. The key is to devise a system that recognizes this while not appearing to." Consider it racism-lite.

Still, it worked. The parties were sorted, once and for all, by race. In 1960 about 60 percent of blue-collar workers voted Democrat; in 1968 roughly 30 percent did. As for African Americans, in 1960 more than 30 percent voted Republican; in 1972 just 10 percent did. Of course there were still far more whites than blacks in the United States, and Nixon played the numbers effectively. Haldeman saw the racial polarization and understood the numbers game sufficiently to advise Nixon: "must learn to understand the silent majority . . . don't go for Jews and Blacks." And a memo to Nixon from a member of his administration urged that he indirectly use this message in campaigning: "Today, racial minorities are saying that you can't make it in America. What they mean is that they refuse to start at the bottom of the ladder the way you [the average middle-class American] did. They want to surpass you. . . . They want it handed to them."

Turning this strategy into electoral sound bites required that Nixon make his point without mentioning race. He spoke directly to white resentment, but took it only so far. Many Nixonian Republicans ditched the Confederate battle flag and removed the N-word from their public vocabulary. Nixon would substitute crime, drugs, and welfare for more overt racist tropes popular in the South.

Nixon's pick for vice president, Spiro Agnew of Maryland, used coarser language and served as the attack dog of the 1968 campaign and the administration. He once had damned the "circuit-riding, Hanoi-visiting, caterwauling, riot-inciting, burn-America-down type of black leader." Furthermore, throughout the campaign, Agnew used racial slurs such as "Polacks" and "fat Jap."

There was more than just coded language and white resentment behind Nixon's victories. Indeed, the Republicans spent twice as much as Democrats on radio and TV advertisements, demonstrating, even then, the power of money in politics. In 1968, Nixon won his first term by beating, barely, the Democratic candidate, Vice President Hubert Humphrey. With former governor George Wallace of Alabama running an outwardly racist third-party campaign, 57 percent of American voters opted either for Wallace or Nixon. Only 42.7 percent went for the candidate of the once-ascendant Democrats. Indeed, Humphrey received a shockingly low 35 percent of the white vote in 1968, and Republicans would win a majority of whites in nearly every presidential election in the proceeding fifty years.

To win over whites, especially in the South, President Nixon had to placate the more overt racists in the country. He had his attorney general, John Mitchell, slow the pace of school desegregation, he refused to terminate federal funding for segregated schools, and he tapped a southerner, Clement Haynsworth of South Carolina, for the Supreme Court, though his nomination was blocked in the Senate. Nixon would also rail against court-ordered desegregation measures such as forced-busing programs. It all worked like a charm. The solid South became the Republican South, and, in 1972, Nixon would win a second term in a landslide. He was a vicious political infighter, as reflected by his characterization of his campaign battles and his administration's tactics: "getting down to the nut cutting." And indeed he would.

The Last Liberal or the First Conservative?

Nixon, especially when compared with later Republican presidents, was in many ways a moderate conservative. He was pragmatic, caring more about victory than ideology. He recognized the popularity of certain liberal government programs and went along with them, at least for a while. All this has led many historians to debate whether Nixon was the first conservative of a new era or the last liberal of a bygone, FDR-initiated era. There is some evidence on both sides of the scale, but ultimately Nixon was no liberal.

On the liberal side, Nixon would propose a guaranteed minimum income, the Family Assistance Plan, for all Americans as a substitute for welfare programs. No Republican after Nixon would dare to countenance such massive social spending. Then again, he knew it wouldn't pass and used the plan as little more than a tactical move to protect his left flank, even advising Haldeman to "make a big play for the plan, but make sure it's killed by Democrats." And it was. Conservative Republicans loathed the proposed government spending, but the liberals felt the Nixon proposal was not generous enough. The measure was stillborn, just as Nixon had hoped.

Nixon would sign a fair amount of liberal legislation from 1969 to 1972, but it must be remembered that most of this was pragmatic, a nod to a still-Democrat-dominated Congress. Nonetheless, some of Nixon's achievements seem strange for a Republican president. In his first term he extended the Voting Rights Act, funded the "war on cancer," increased spending for the national endowments for the arts and humanities, and signed the Title IX measure, banning sex discrimination in all higher education that received federal funds. In his first term federal spending per person in poverty rose by 50 percent and total government outlays for social protections more than doubled. His labor secretary, George Shultz, even established the "Philadelphia Plan," which called for affirmative action hiring programs for construction union members employed on government contracts. At one point Nixon called for a comprehensive national health insurance plan. Though he personally cared very little about the environment, he knew that most Americans did. Thus he created the Environmental Protection Agency (EPA) and sanctioned the first official Earth Day. Other environmental protections included the Occupational Safety and Health Administration (OSHA), the Clean Air Act of 1970, and the Endangered Species Act of 1973.

Some of these measures so frustrated conservatives that Patrick Buchanan, one of the more ideological members of his team, warned Nixon that some within the party felt that conservatives were "the niggers of the Nixon administration." On race, the Nixon administration was far from liberal, intervening to curtail desegregation measures in southern school districts and successfully nominating two conservatives to replace liberal icons on the Supreme Court. The appointments of those judges would set the stage for the later dismantling of civil rights legislation. On busing, Nixon opposed court orders and, as previously mentioned, instructed his Department of Justice to slow the pace of integration. As he told Ehrlichman, "I want you personally to jump" on the DOJ "and tell them to knock off this crap. I hold them . . . accountable to keep their left-wingers in step with my express policy" of doing the minimum integration required by law. In 1972, Nixon called for a moratorium on busing measures and made his opposition to the court orders a touchstone of his reelection campaign that year.

Ultimately Nixon's occasional leftward moves were purely tactical. He hoped, eventually, to shift government in a more traditionally conservative direction. He was only waiting for his moment. Nixon funneled much government spending to local control — so-called devolution — which allowed conservative areas to maintain covert racialized policies in spending. Nixon also railed against supposedly undeserving welfare recipients and reframed John F. Kennedy's call to serve the country by urging Americans, in his second inaugural address, to ask "not just what will government do for me, but what can I do for myself?" It was the perfect mantra for a population that writer Tom Wolfe and others called the "Me Generation," one that represented a shift from public service to private profit that would only strengthen with time. After his overwhelming electoral victory in 1972, Nixon began to move rightward. He proposed a budget that slashed government programs and called for the end to urban renewal projects, hospital construction grants, and the Rural Electrification Administration. He cut spending on milk for schoolchildren, mental health facilities, and education for students from poor families.

Nixon's ultimate goal was to work the governmental system and then bring the liberal welfare state crashing down in due time. He sought to reorient American politics away from social spending and racially affirmative policies and toward more conservative government orthodoxy. He wouldn't see his dream realized while he was president — mainly because he was forced to resign over the Watergate scandal — but his successors would achieve most of his goals. In that sense he was, indeed, the "first" conservative, the vanguard of a new Republican ascendancy.

Unexpected Détente: Nixon and the World

Nixon's practicality can best be seen in foreign policy, always his first love. Here Nixon was as savvy an actor as ever. What he had planned was a massive realignment of global affairs, an opening to a relationship with China and the Soviet Union, and some progress in lessening Cold War tensions. In his plans, Henry Kissinger, his national security adviser and eventual secretary of state, was a key player. Kissinger and other "realists" believed that pure national interests, not human rights or even political ideology, should drive US behavior in foreign policy. This posture was framed as the "Nixon Doctrine," the belief that the United States should first consider its own strategic interests and shape commitments accordingly. Gone would be the more moralistic instincts in foreign policy. The team of Nixon and Kissinger would personify the power of the "imperial presidency" — the centralization of foreign-policy power in the executive branch. Nixon would conduct most foreign affairs in secret, using back-channel communications and evading official channels in the State Department. He had, after all, little use for "elitist" experts.

Nixon's first bold move was to reach an agreement with Soviet premier Leonid Brezhnev to lessen tensions over Cuba. The United States would promise not to invade and the Soviets would cease building a submarine base and refrain from supplying Fidel Castro with offensive missiles. The problem was that this deal, like much else in his foreign policy, was reached in secret and thus had no legal standing. Nevertheless, it was a sign of limited rapprochement with the Soviets. Nixon also understood that international communism was far from monolithic, and that the Soviets and the Chinese were becoming increasingly hostile toward each other. As such, Nixon famously decided to "go to China," meet Mao Zedong, and open a relationship between the two countries. Probably only Nixon could have pulled this off. A Democratic president would have been eviscerated from the right and condemned as soft on communism. The longtime Cold Warrior Nixon, however, faced little opposition to his China policy. As he frankly told Chairman Mao, "Those on the right can do what those on the left only talk about." Mao nodded and replied, "I like rightists!"

Months later in 1972, Nixon would head to Moscow and put the final touches on the first stage of the Strategic Arms Limitation Treaty (SALT). The treaty was largely symbolic and did not meaningfully reduce the stocks of nuclear weapons, but it was a start and another step in the direction of détente. Nonetheless, despite his limited successes, Nixon did little to change the long-term arc of Cold War tensions. After Nixon, less adept politicians, especially hawks in his own party, would dismantle détente and revitalize the arms race and tensions with Moscow.

One could argue, moreover, that Nixon and Kissinger were veritable war criminals. They secretly dropped a staggering number of bombs on Cambodia and Laos during the Vietnam War, killing tens of thousands and destabilizing both societies. Congress was not informed. Nixon also prolonged the war unnecessarily and increased the bombing of Hanoi. As a result, huge numbers needlessly died on all sides. Furthermore, the US president and Kissinger supported a military coup in Chile to keep an elected socialist president from holding office. The resulting US-backed government would torture its own people and "disappear" — secretly kill — tens of thousands of dissidents. The coup occurred on what many Latin Americans refer to as the "other 9/11" — September 11, 1973. Finally, in Central Asia, Nixon supported Pakistan — to please its ally, China — in its brutal suppression of its Bengali separatists. Though the experts at the State Department warned him of what might happen, Nixon — true to form — conducted his policies in secret and backed Islamabad. It's estimated that Pakistan, with America's blessing, killed perhaps a million Bengalis in the ultimately unsuccessful war.

What, then, is the historian to make of Nixon's foreign policy? Perhaps little except this: it was his and his alone. Nixon, along with Kissinger, did as he pleased. Sometimes, given Nixon's astute understanding of foreign affairs, that meant dividing the two main communist global powers, China and Russia. Nixon's foreign policy would also open up bilateral negotiations between the United States and the two other countries, contributing to a limited détente. It could also, however, be a brutal realpolitik — secretly bombing civilians, backing coups, and suppressing foreign separatists. But nowhere was Nixon's obsession with secrecy and victory at all costs more on display than at home, in what came to be known as the Watergate scandal.

The World of Watergate

Well, when the president does it, that means that it is not illegal.

— Richard Nixon in a 1977 interview

It began, apparently, with the break-in and attempted wiretapping of the Democratic Party's offices in the Watergate complex in Washington, DC. But that wasn't the half of it. Nixon may not have personally ordered the break-in or even known it was about to happen; the crime was in the cover-up, as it often is. Besides, the real story was this: From start to finish, the Nixon administration was one of the most corrupt, sneaky, vindictive, and win-at-all-costs presidencies in history. Illegality was the hallmark of Nixon and his team. What would ultimately bring Nixon down was the existence of secret tape recordings of every conversation in the Oval Office, tapes that exposed the secrecy and corruption with which Nixon operated with his famously insular staff. The tapes revealed Nixon's pettiness and bigotry. In one rather banal example Nixon and Haldeman had the following conversation in 1971 about the TV host Dick Cavett:

Haldeman: We've got a running war going on with Cavett.
Nixon: Is he just a left-winger? Is that the problem?
Haldeman: Yeah.
Nixon: Is he Jewish?
Haldeman: I don't know. He doesn't look it.

The tapes revealed many such ugly conversations but mainly depicted a man who was always at war with his enemies and saw himself as the perpetual embattled victim. Public enemy number one was the Democrats. So it was that members of the Committee to Re-elect the President (aptly known by the acronym CREEP) would conduct a break-in at the Watergate Office Building. The burglars were caught and arrested. From there unfolded a cover-up of drastic proportions that would ultimately end the Nixon presidency.

Nevertheless, the Nixon team's level of subterfuge, secrecy, and illegality always transcended Watergate. For example, what Attorney General John Mitchell referred to as a program of "White House horrors" was expansive and prevalent both before and after the break-in. In 1971, when Nixon was told by Haldeman that the Brookings Institution think tank might have classified files on Vietnam that might embarrass the previous administration of Democrat Lyndon Johnson and the Democrats more broadly, Nixon ordered a break-in and theft, as documented later in the so-called Watergate tapes. "Goddamnit, get in there and get those files," he ordered. "Blow the safe and get it!" In another incident, when Rand analyst Daniel Ellsberg leaked the Pentagon Papers, Nixon had his underlings break into Ellsberg's psychiatrist's office in an attempt to find embarrassing files that could be used to blackmail him. The list goes on. Nixon discussed infiltrating antiwar groups with undercover agents and selling ambassadorships. CREEP would also harass and embarrass Nixon rivals by organizing fake rallies in the opponents' names and thereby generating mountains of unpaid bills — an example of what CREEP member Donald Segretti called "ratfucking." In addition Nixon tried to plant a spy in the Secret Service detail of George McGovern, his 1972 Democratic opponent for the presidency, and ordered surveillance on Ted Kennedy to unearth dirt on the Massachusetts senator.

Nixon's first vice president, Spiro Agnew, was indicted in Maryland for receiving bribes in return for political favors, and he resigned in October 1973, replaced by Gerald Ford. The corruption went further still. Attorney General Mitchell controlled a secret fund of more than $150,000 to be used against the Democratic Party, specifically for forging letters, stealing campaign files, and leaking fake news. Nixon also promised to offer executive clemency if the Watergate burglars were imprisoned, and Ehrlichman was ordered to pay them $450,000 in hush money. Nixon and Kissinger had the FBI tap telephones in order to gather intelligence on political enemies, placing illegal wiretaps on thirteen government officials and at least four journalists. And this litany of malfeasance is far from comprehensive.

Just six days after the Watergate break-in went public, Nixon, in a conversation captured by his office taping system, discussed damage control and the cover-up with Haldeman. In 1973 and '74, the entire edifice of corruption and cover-up came crashing down. Nixon was forced to appoint a special prosecutor to investigate the Watergate affair, Archibald Cox. However, when Cox turned up the heat and began investigating Nixon and calling on him to turn over the Oval Office tapes, the president ordered the attorney general to fire him. When Elliot Richardson refused to do so, Nixon fired him; when Richardson's deputy, William Ruckelshaus, also refused, Nixon fired him. The dismissals went down in US history as the "Saturday night massacre." Eventually the third in line, Robert Bork — whose nomination to the Supreme Court by President Ronald Reagan would fail in the Senate years later — agreed to fire Cox. Still, Nixon's efforts to block the release of the tapes failed. Both a congressional investigatory committee and the Supreme Court demanded the tapes be turned over. What these tapes revealed ruined Nixon.

The president's advisers believed that Congress had the votes to impeach, convict, and remove him, so Nixon resigned. Despite all the illegality, he would never stand trial or serve a day in prison. His successor, Vice President Gerald Ford, upon becoming president immediately pardoned Nixon and left in place all the structures, institutions, and power bases that had allowed his perfidy to flourish. As such, nothing happened to stop future corruption in the Oval Office. Ford announced that "[o]ur Constitutional system worked," but it was unclear that it had. Nixon almost surely would not have been caught if it wasn't for the tapes and his blatant abuses. The Watergate committees narrowly focused their investigation on the break-in and cover-up, not paying attention to the broader corruption of Nixon's administration or the imperial presidency that remained in place.

———

President Richard M. Nixon was a complicated man, a truly singular figure. He was defined by mistrust, opportunism, and secrecy. Both at home and abroad he played the part of a master tactician, placing politics above principles at every turn. Although his backers found much to praise in his actions, more often than not he subverted democracy both at home and in other countries. Before Nixon and Watergate, most Americans trusted their federal government. That ended with Nixon's resignation. As the extent of Nixon's crimes and abuse gradually came to light, many Americans lost faith in the entire system. They blamed both sides — Democrat and Republican — and took to seeing all politicians as crooks. Thus, though Nixon never achieved the conservative dream of destroying Franklin Roosevelt's social welfare state while president, he did unintentionally usher in the requisite rightward shift in American politics.

As the people lost faith in the ability of the federal government to do good, to improve life and accomplish great things, they ended up endorsing more conservative ideologies. Democrat Jimmy Carter would be elected president, largely because of the Watergate scandal, slightly more than two years after Nixon's resignation, but the humble Georgian would serve just a single, embattled term. Republicans in the twenty-eight years after Carter's 1980 defeat would own the presidency for all but eight years. This reorientation toward the right was, perhaps, the defining legacy of Nixon. He crafted a world of shadows, a more sinister view of government and the gradual empowerment of the executive branch that has by now seemingly resulted in a breakdown of the founders' hopes for separation of powers. There could have been no Reagan, or George W. Bush, without the example and accomplishments of Nixon. There also couldn't have been a Donald Trump, and that is something worth reflecting upon. Tricky Dick lost the battle — Watergate — but he may ultimately have won the war for America's soul.[28]

32

CARTER'S CAGE OF CRISIS

There would never have been a Democratic president in 1977, certainly not a President Jimmy Carter, were it not for Watergate, Richard Nixon's disgrace, and the public backlash against Tricky Dick's Republican Party. Indeed, after the fall of Lyndon B. Johnson, a new era of Republican ascendancy had begun. Often remembered as one of America's most feckless and uninspiring presidents, Carter in reality was neither as successful as his supporters had hoped nor as ineffective as his opponents later claimed. He was, ultimately, a transitional figure and a product of the 1970s, which were increasingly politically conservative although heavily colored by cultural liberalism, especially among the young. Though later portrayed by the right as a hopelessly left-wing liberal, Carter was actually quite pragmatic and became the first of the three Democratic presidents who served between 1977 and 2017 to tack toward the right. In that sense, one could argue that Carter reflected and affected the prevailing conservative winds and started the country down the road toward the "Reagan Revolution" and a long-term rightward trend in American politics.

A Georgia peanut farmer, naval academy graduate, and evangelical Christian, Carter was a complicated, multifaceted figure and supposedly a figurehead of the "new" — post-civil-rights — South. He was an intelligent, inherently decent man, but given the inflation and unemployment of the era — much of which was beyond his control — he seemed doomed to be a one-term president. He could not stem the tide of economic stagnation as the United States emerged from its anomalous postwar affluence. Indeed, in retrospect the American economic expansion that followed the Second World War could not have continued without interruption. However, telling the truth about this inevitable phenomenon was not popular among a populace that had grown spoiled and expected unlimited perpetual growth. Carter tried to rein in that impossible expectation and for his trouble was voted out of office.

If not quite a tragic figure, Carter was, to some extent, treated unfairly by the voters, punished for crises and downturns not wholly of his doing. Then again, few remember that it was Carter who first shifted toward economic austerity and increased military spending and deployments in the Middle East. It is odd that the legacy of a man who seemed so committed to peace should be the onset of what would become a forty-year, ongoing crusade for American dominance of the Greater Middle East. It is ironic, too, that a president later remembered as too liberal should be the first in many decades to call for a balanced budget and initiate monetary policies that emphasized austerity in more traditionally conservative ways. Though their personalities could not have been more different, Carter and his successor as president, Ronald Reagan, pursued policies not totally dissimilar to each other. Indeed, we could argue that Carter was the first in a line of three centrist Democratic presidents who would abandon the social program spending boom that had defined liberalism ever since Franklin Roosevelt's 1933 inauguration. It could be said, then, that Carter was the first conservative president of a Republican-dominated era.

The Carter Anomaly: The Election of 1976

Carter was a long-shot candidate in the 1976 presidential election, a virtual unknown, but he was the beneficiary of a tragedy that had occurred half a dozen years earlier. The politician whom many Democrats wanted as head of the party ticket in 1976 had announced in September 1974 that he would not run. Senator Edward M. Kennedy, a figure of the traditionally liberal consensus, had seemed destined to one day carry the torch of his assassinated brothers, John and Robert. However, his presidential prospects were crippled because the national public never fully forgave him for the so-called Chappaquiddick incident: Late one night in July 1969, the senator drove a car off a bridge in Chappaquiddick, Massachusetts, then swam away. He did not report

Jimmy Carter, president from 1977 to 1981

the accident to authorities until hours later. Left behind in the automobile was Mary Jo Kopechne, a former worker in Robert Kennedy's campaign, who drowned there.

With Ted Kennedy not in the race, Carter gained the Democratic nomination with almost 40 percent of the popular vote in the primaries, defeating Jerry Brown, George Wallace, Mo Udall, Henry M. Jackson, Frank Church, and others.

The former Georgia governor bested his Democratic rivals including some other state-level politicians and, eventually, Republican president Gerald Ford largely because voters saw him as being outside the Washington establishment, with which, after Watergate, Americans were increasingly disgusted. From his election on, presidential candidates would run with and win with just such an "outsider" image.

The Republican Nixon had only recently, in 1972, trounced the Democrat George McGovern in one of the great landslides in American electoral history. It seemed unlikely then, at least until the Watergate scandal, that a Democrat would win in 1976. But times had changed. Americans, by and large, no longer trusted the federal government or establishment figures. The level of citizens who expressed faith in that government had dropped from 75 percent in 1964 to 25 percent in the late 1970s. What Americans wanted, in 1976, was someone new and fresh. They thought they had found that in the farmer from the tiny rural town of Plains, Georgia.

Gerald Ford had become vice president when Nixon's vice president, Spiro Agnew, resigned in disgrace in 1973 and then became president when Nixon resigned in disgrace in 1974. He had never won a nationwide election, and his campaign against Carter was shaky from the start. Though he confidently exclaimed that the "long national nightmare [of Watergate] was over," most of the populace wasn't so sure. And when Ford's first act as president was to preemptively pardon Nixon he may have sealed his own political fate. As the editors of *The New York Times* wrote, "The pardon may be the final blow to [the people's] faith in America." Carter, the Cinderella-story candidate, rode that loss of faith in Washington, and particularly in the Republican Party, straight into the White House.

The 1976 election was a major coup for the Democrats, who picked up dozens of seats in the House and Senate, introducing a large freshman class dubbed the Watergate babies. The status quo, ostensibly, was the enemy of Carter and the young Democratic lawmakers. In style, if not always in substance, Carter would project an agreeable, more accessible personality. Seeking to distance himself from the "imperial presidency" of Richard Nixon, Carter even exited his limousine and walked among the people to the White House following his inauguration. In explaining the phenomenon of his out-of-nowhere victory, the new president said, "Our people were sick at heart, wanted leadership that could heal us, and give us once again a government of which we could feel proud." At first, it seemed, Carter was just the man for this disillusioned moment. In addition to his man-of-the-people inaugural walk, Carter would seek to present a less regal presidency, ditching the Prussian-style uniforms Nixon insisted that his White House guards wear and even ending the tradition of playing "Hail to the Chief" upon his arrival at official events.

Carter's morals and devoted Christianity also appealed to a nation becoming ever more religious. He was an evangelical churchgoer and a Sunday school teacher. Yet he was less forceful in his Christianity than a later host of Republicans who hailed from the growing religious right. As the journalist Robert Scheer noted after conducting a *Playboy* magazine interview with the then candidate, Carter was "a guy who believes in his personal God and will let the rest of us believe whatever the hell we want." Carter's tolerance and lack of ideological dogmatism reflected his leadership style as well. He actually boasted he lacked ideology or fixed political positions, in contrast with the public proclamations of Nixon and Johnson. At election time in 1976, at least, Carter seemed just what the people desired: an honest, politically flexible outsider. Nevertheless, he had his weaknesses. Carter was seen from the outset of his term as bland and wonkish — certainly not inspiring.

For all the strengths that he did possess, and the short-term weakness of the disgraced GOP, Carter barely squeaked by to victory — probably a reflection of Americans' rightward shift. He received just 50.1 percent of the popular vote in an election for which just 54.8 percent of voters — the lowest percentage since 1948 — turned out. Thus the new president hardly possessed a strong mandate to govern. Indeed, neither of the major-party candidates in the '76 election seemed to excite voters. Both were weak public speakers. In fact, the liberal Democrat Eugene McCarthy, who ran for president as an independent in 1976, labeled Carter an "oratorical mortician" who "inters his words and ideas behind piles of syntactical mush." Nonetheless, the "Man from Plains" entered office in January 1977 intent on broad systemic reform and with a goal to reinvest Americans' trust in the presidency. As such, throughout his campaign, Carter had repeatedly proclaimed, "I'm Jimmy Carter and I'm running for President. I will never lie to you." That, of course, remained to be seen.

The Great Malaise: The Domestic Carter

Carter was far less progressive in domestic affairs than either LBJ or John Kennedy, and certainly less than FDR. During his lone term,

the president consistently waffled between traditionally liberal policies, and — partly as a response to shifting popular will as well as his
own fiscal conservatism — by the time he left office he had edged the
nation to the right.

President Carter inherited an economy in near free fall. Over-
spending and borrowing for the Vietnam War, domestic oil shocks
caused by Mideast nations' embargoes in response to US support
for Israel, and the expanding economic competition of other, growing nations combined to cause the nightmare of "stagflation" — the
once-thought-impossible combination of high inflation and rising
unemployment. Carter never managed to overcome this economic
downturn, and that failure ultimately doomed his hopes for reelection.

The new president tried everything and even changed course on
the economy. After calling for more typical liberal stimulus spending, he shifted after 1978 to more anti-inflationary policies such as
spending cuts and balanced budgets. Neither effectively solved the
deep-seated problems, at least while Carter was in office. Toward the
end of his term, a desperate Carter would appoint Paul Volcker to
head the Federal Reserve Board, and Volcker took drastic anti-inflationary actions, choking spending, aggravating unemployment, and
causing a recession. Eventually, however, the measures worked and
inflation was significantly reduced, but it wasn't until the assumption
of the presidency by Ronald Reagan that Volcker's harsh measures
bore fruit, and the Republicans were quick to take credit. Timing was
never on Carter's side.

To the approval of liberals, Carter granted a limited pardon to
Vietnam draft evaders. He also fought hard for environmental protection and saw the necessity to craft an energy policy that would make
the United States less dependent on fossil fuels. He even had solar
panels placed on the White House roof (which Reagan promptly
removed). His national energy policy, largely crafted in secret, was
eviscerated by corporate lobbyists and had little tangible effects. On
energy, Carter was ahead of his time, but he misread the pulse of
American life. He appeared on national television to speak truths that
the gas-guzzling consumerist American people simply didn't want to

hear. "Tonight I want to have an unpleasant talk with you about a problem unprecedented in our history. With the exception of war, this is the greatest challenge our country will face during our lifetimes," he said, adding, "The energy crisis has not yet overwhelmed us, but will if we do not act quickly." However right and prescient Carter proved to be, the public didn't take kindly to his call for cutbacks in energy consumption and resented his paternalistic tone.

Carter took right-leaning positions on a host of other issues. A fiscal hawk by nature, he eschewed liberal spending and promised a balanced budget, something neither Republican Nixon nor Republican Ford had called for. He also proclaimed the limits of government to do great things and improve life. In one decidedly illiberal speech he asserted, "We have learned that more is not necessarily better, that even our great Nation has its recognized limits, and that we cannot answer all problems nor solve all problems. We cannot afford to do everything." This caution was a far cry from the liberal utopianism of LBJ's faith in his Great Society to transform American life and end its social and economic ills. Though Carter did initially call for stimulus spending and universal health insurance, he was never able to square these standard liberal policies with his own penchant for balanced budgets and the international economic crisis he weathered throughout his term. As his adviser Stuart Eizenstat later recalled, "One always knew that [Carter] wanted to spend as little money as possible, and yet at the same time he wanted welfare reform, he wanted national health insurance." This proved to be an impossibility, especially in a time when a majority of citizens had no stomach for increased taxes and higher federal spending. Carter could never find a stable middle ground.

Furthermore, with increased foreign competition eviscerating the Rust Belt and decreasing power among unions, even the overall rising standard of living under Carter was offset by ballooning inflation and increased unemployment. Furthermore, as unions lost clout and high-paying manufacturing jobs left the country, a new income gap rose between the rich and the rest. As working-class wages decreased by 13 percent in the 1970s and '80s, the compensation of CEOs rose by nearly 400 percent. A new Gilded Age kicked off during the

Carter years and has only worsened since. Labor union weakness and America's gradual shift to a service economy meant stagnant wages, fewer benefits, and fewer hours of pay for workers. For this, Carter had no effective answer.

Carter also began the trend of economic deregulation that would define the 1980s and '90s. "It is a major goal of my administration," he said, "to free the American people from the burden of over-regulation." This process placed the American economy on the road to the unregulated hyper-capitalism that would eventually produce the 2008 economic crash. When the imminent failure of Chrysler, one of America's top employers, added to the economy's woes, many on both the left and the right were reluctant to back intervention despite the potential dire consequences of not doing so. One could hardly imagine FDR or LBJ shrinking from bold action to save Chrysler's 250,000 employees. US representative Ron Paul of Texas voiced a common sentiment among conservatives when he asserted that "[i]n a nation that is sinking in a sea of debt, it is irresponsible for this Congress to be considering a measure that will add millions to that debt." On the left, unexpectedly, consumer advocate Ralph Nader agreed: "Mismanagement at the company has been incredible, why should a subsidy solve Chrysler's problems? Let them go bankrupt." Eventually, the feds provided $1.5 billion in relief for Chrysler, but only at the expense of a weakened union, which was forced to accept a wage freeze and, eventually, wage cuts.

Again Carter took to the airwaves to chastise profligate Americans, stating, "In a nation that was proud of hard work, strong families, close-knit communities and our faith in God, too many tend to worship self-indulgence and consumption. Human identity is no longer defined by what one does, but by what one owns." America's biggest problem — more detrimental than inflation or energy issues — was a "crisis of confidence," he declared, and once again Americans resented his brutal honesty and his calls for personal cutbacks in spending. And though he never used the term, pundits dubbed it the "malaise" speech. It won him few popularity points in the long term.

Other limits to Carter's purported liberalism manifested in his momentous deregulation of the airlines. Indeed, his very rhetoric circumscribed his view of what government could accomplish. To the horror of his liberal base, Carter proclaimed in his second State of the Union address, "Government cannot solve our problems. . . . It cannot eliminate poverty, or provide a bountiful economy, or reduce inflation, or save our cities." Such pessimism was a far cry from the boundless faith in government that infused the presidencies of Franklin Roosevelt and his immediate successors in the Democratic Party. Indeed, according to the historian and former JFK adviser Arthur Schlesinger, if Roosevelt had believed these things "we would still be in the Great Depression." But here again, Carter reflected the new national mood, one mistrustful of government. He promised much less than Americans expected and made perhaps the fatal error of asking Americans to economically sacrifice, the kind of plea that rarely has proved to be a political winner.

Carter's personal attributes further held him back and doomed grand endeavors such as his energy plan. He refused to work closely with House Speaker Tip O'Neill, a fellow Democrat, and never developed close relationships with Congress. Instead Carter relied on his small campaign staff from Georgia, refused to delegate, micromanaged, and occasionally displayed the arrogance so often inherent in loners and workaholics. He also alienated many on the left, especially the Congressional Black Caucus, with his fiscal conservatism and inherent distrust of unions — possibly a reflection of his upbringing in the notoriously labor-unfriendly South.

Beyond the domestic political problems caused by economic woes and Americans' negative reactions to his chastising speeches, Carter was plagued by uncontrollable international events and criticism of his foreign policy. He would turn out to be the victim of tumultuous times in the international arena.

Schizophrenic Inconsistency: Carter and the World

Jimmy Carter is often remembered as particularly weak on foreign policy — soft on the Soviets and paralyzed by an inability to force revolutionary Iran to release hostages taken from the American embassy in Tehran. Much of this criticism is wildly unfair. In fact, Carter had few options in ending the hostage crisis and was much more bellicose toward the Soviet Union, and supportive of increased military spending, than is now remembered. Carter may have failed in his foreign policies, leaving office with the Cold War frostier than ever and the world an arguably more dangerous place than he had found it, but this was certainly not because he was too soft or anti-military.

Carter was elected, purportedly, on a promise to re-inject morals and a concern for human rights into America's tarnished, post-Vietnam foreign policy. He announced in 1978 that "[h]uman rights is the soul of our foreign policy, because human rights is the very soul of our sense of nationhood." In some ways, especially early in his term, he attempted to decrease worldwide tensions and practice a rights-based foreign policy. At root, Carter was a Wilsonian internationalist idealist, at least in theory. He initially promised to cut aid to nations with poor human rights records, though he continued to back the brutal, but anti-communist, shah of Iran. He also canceled the neutron bomb program — a radiation weapon system designed to kill people while inflicting less damage on buildings and other infrastructure — and announced in his inaugural address: "We will move this year a step toward our ultimate goal — the elimination of all nuclear weapons from this earth." To that end he negotiated the SALT II treaty with the Soviets to place limits on the total number of missiles and deliver systems for nuclear weapons that each power could possess.

In two other diplomatic coups, Carter officially recognized the People's Republic of China, although this move upset conservative backers of the previously recognized Taiwan regime. Then, after many days of forced and closed negotiations, he negotiated the Camp David Accords, which brought peace between Israel and its archenemy, Egypt. Israel even agreed, under pressure, to return the conquered Sinai Peninsula to Egypt. Carter also signed an agreement to eventually return the Panama Canal to Panamanian control. This too raised the ire of conservative opponents — notably Ronald Reagan, who was particularly hawkish about the canal.

In the end Carter failed to reduce tensions with the Soviets, and détente would die on his watch. Part of this was due to Soviet moves: placing new intermediate-range missiles in Eastern Europe and backing and using Cuban proxies in Angola and Ethiopia. Furthermore, new groups of American Cold War hawks — such as the alarmist Committee on the Present Danger — criticized Carter's "cult of appeasement" and sought to increase bellicosity toward the Soviet Union. As for the SALT II treaty, it died in the Senate in the face of newly hawkish opposition from nearly all Republicans and a significant number of Cold Warrior Democrats.

Matters truly worsened when the Soviets invaded Afghanistan under what was in a sense a policy of defensiveness and insecurity rather than of inherent aggression — the Kremlin acted mainly to prop up a friendly communist regime. The United States had contributed to Soviet woes before the invasion by using the CIA to back Islamist rebels seeking to overturn the Afghan government, arming jihadists who would later coalesce into al-Qaida and the Taliban movements. In response to the Soviet invasion, the CIA only increased support, sending arms and cash to various rebel Islamist groups in an attempt to turn the Afghanistan War into the Soviets' Vietnam. Carter and his advisers overreacted and came to incorrectly believe that the Soviets had the intent and capacity to move through Afghanistan to conquer the Persian Gulf. Fearing a threat to American control of Mideast oil, Carter took serious steps to counter the Soviets. He embargoed grain shipments to Russia, reinstituted selective service, and led an international boycott of the 1980 Olympic Games in Moscow.

Carter also took to using alarmist rhetoric, referring to the Soviet invasion and purported threat to the Persian Gulf as the "most serious threat to peace since the Second World War." He proclaimed what came to be known as the Carter Doctrine, announcing that the United States would use military force to oppose any threat to Mideast oil in the Persian Gulf. In his 1980 State of the Union address, Carter said that "[the Middle East] contains more than two-thirds of the world's exportable oil. . . . Let our position be absolutely clear: An attempt by any outside force to gain control of the Persian Gulf region will be regarded as an assault on the vital interests of the United States of America, and such an assault will be repelled by any means necessary, including military force." Soon Carter would even call for the creation of a new US military command for the Mideast, later known as USCENTCOM. Thus, it was Carter's overreaction that set the stage for a perpetual US military presence — and several wars — in the Greater Middle East.

However, it was events in Iran that most embarrassed the Carter administration. For this there was an important backstory. The United States had long meddled in Iranian affairs, using the CIA to overthrow a democratically elected government that threatened to nationalize Iranian oil. In the place of Prime Minister Mohammad Mossadegh, the United States backed the brutal dictatorial regime of the shah. Few Americans knew or thought much about American actions in Iran, but Iranians never forgave Washington for these transgressions. Thus, when a 1979 revolution overturned the shah's regime, and Washington refused to turn over the shah (being treated in the United States for cancer) to the new Islamist revolutionary government, a crowd stormed the US embassy in Tehran and took the staff hostage. Carter had few options to force the hostages' release, and negotiations failed for more than a year. Eventually Carter allowed himself to be talked into a harebrained military rescue mission that ended in disaster and with several American deaths. In a final insult to Carter, the Iranian government waited until Reagan's 1981 inauguration to release the hostages, a delay that contributed to Carter's electoral defeat and fed the later (not wholly accurate) perception among Americans and others that a tougher and more bellicose Reagan was responsible for ending the Iran hostage crisis.

Carter's foreign policy never lived up to his human-rights-oriented rhetoric. It was Carter, not Reagan, who first increased US military spending, began the shadow war with the Soviets in Afghanistan, and buried the policy of détente. Carter may not have intended an increase in Cold War tensions, but he did allow himself to be pushed in a more combative and pugnacious direction by newly resurgent hawks in his administration and, especially, on Capitol Hill. Far from the dove he was pejoratively labeled as — then and now — Carter actually escalated America's military buildup and helped usher in the last, but quite combative, phase of the Cold War.

———

Some justifiable conclusions about Carter: that his failings as president were largely the results of personal style and a troubled era of global strife and economic downturn, much of it inherited. And that, despite later assertions from Reagan Republicans, his shortcomings stemmed not from his being too liberal but often more from his halfhearted attempts to shift rightward. One can, in fact, sense the end of liberal, optimistic, big-government politics in the Carter administration as much as, or more than, in the Nixon administration. After Carter, conservative positions on economics and cultural matters became ascendant and mainstream. In many ways they remain so, despite the contemporary grassroots resurgence of the progressive left.

The record must be corrected to reflect that Carter, not Reagan, began the national shift toward smaller government, austerity, the end of détente, and increased tensions with both the Soviet Union and Iran. We live in the political space created during the Carter administration, and have for some fifty years. Most of all, Carter's stillborn presidency demonstrated that being inherently decent is not enough to weather hard times or win popular support, that Americans don't take kindly to hard truths or demands for cutbacks in energy consumption, and that this country remains, at root, a center-right nation — more conservative than the rest of the industrialized Western world.

In times since, Republicans have trotted out the specter of a feckless Carter to scare voters rightward, and it works! Carter's legend of incompetence, more than his actual complex presidency, has stuck, demonstrating once again that perception is often more powerful than reality. In this way, Carter was a tragic figure in American history. He taught Republicans how to win and showed Democrats how to lose. They're both doing so still.[29]

33

THE REAGAN REVOLUTION

It was no accident. Indeed, candidate Ronald Reagan knew exactly what he was doing. It was August 1980, at the height of presidential election fever. Visiting Mississippi, once a symbol of the solid Democratic South, Reagan chose the Neshoba County Fair for a key campaign speech. To beat incumbent President Jimmy Carter, he would have to turn the Deep South Republican. The fair was in the same county as Philadelphia, Mississippi, and only seven miles from that town, forever associated with the murder of three civil rights activists, one black and two white, just sixteen years earlier. It was a bold move by Reagan. Stepping up for the occasion, he railed about big government and thundered in ever-so-coded language: "I believe in states' rights." In a state that still proudly flew the Confederate Battle Flag, no doubt the mostly white crowd of some fifteen thousand knew, and loved, the racial undertones of such a statement.

The states'-rights mantra had long amounted to little more than a justification of racism by another name. The only right many states tended to focus on was their right to suppress black voting and maintain the segregation of public life. Reagan's performance at the fair was an insult to the memory of the once-vibrant civil rights movement. And it was understood as such.

The tactic worked. Reagan all but swept the South in the 1980 race — among Southern states, only West Virginia and Georgia went for the Georgian who occupied the Oval Office — and the region has essentially remained Republican ever since. The Sunbelt, that vast southern expanse from Florida to California, would prove to be a stronghold of Republican loyalty for decades to come. Though President Richard Nixon inaugurated the Republicans' southern strategy, it was Reagan who perfected it.

Ronald Reagan, president from 1981 to 1989

The presidency of Reagan, like that of many of the chief executives of the United States, was complex. He was undoubtedly conservative and had run to the right of his primary opponents in 1980. Political ideology aside, he was an astute politician, willing to compromise and never so doctrinaire as liberals feared. On foreign policy he could shift from hawk to dove on a dime, exuding toughness but also, at times, demonstrating restraint. He cut taxes and some social programs but was smart enough not to dismantle the highly popular Social Security and Medicare programs, held dear by liberals before and afterward. Though far more ideological than Dwight Eisenhower and even Nixon, he was at root a pragmatist. For the left, he was ultimately something much scarier than those two earlier Republican presidents: a charming, effective, and highly popular figure of the right. He bent with the prevailing winds and harnessed their energy in continuing the gradual rightward policy shift that had been occurring since the end of the presidency of Democrat Lyndon B. Johnson.

By the time he left office in 1989, he had not quite transformed Washington, but he had nudged it further to the right. The game had changed during his tenure, and Franklin D. Roosevelt's old liberal coalition was more fractured than ever. Democrats sensed trouble in Reagan's peculiar popularity and would rarely run a zealously liberal presidential candidate over at least the next thirty years. After the tumult of the 1970s, white America had indeed grown more conservative, or at least more cynical. Faith in the transformative power of federal intervention was replaced by a sense that government was "the problem." Sick of the identity politics and the countless causes of the late 1960s and early 1970s, many had grown nostalgic for traditional values and gradually had turned more socially conservative. America hadn't quite abandoned the Democrats, per se, but it greatly weakened their political grip. Henceforth increasingly more conservative candidates ran for local and national office on the GOP ticket. The Republican Party, quite certainly, was revolutionized by Reagan.

Though he clearly was a conservative, Reagan is difficult to nail down. He slashed taxes and some social programs yet left others untouched and even raised taxes on one occasion. He was a remarried divorcé who voiced the values of the evangelical right. (His first marriage, a union of eight and a half years with actress Jane Wyman, had ended in 1949.) He benefited greatly from support of the right-wing Christian group Moral Majority but shied away from its demand that abortion be outlawed. He was a Cold Warrior who promised to bury détente but later negotiated substantial nuclear reductions and oversaw a thaw in the dangerous conflict with the Soviet Union. He was elected as a hawk's hawk but rarely put American soldiers in harm's way, instead using airpower and local proxies to kill hundreds of thousands. Indeed, decades later, President Barack Obama would adopt a formula of Reagan-like "restraint."

When it comes to Reagan, what he did is often less sweeping than what he allowed and eventually made possible. He implemented a rightward sea change that would carry both parties in a more conservative direction, often with tragic results. One cannot understand America's present without grappling with the realities of its Reaganite past.

Reagan was never simple and rarely consistent but always confident. Throughout his two terms we can track the widening political gap between truth and fiction, the reality of limitations and the
fantasy of the "more" culture. Reagan won two elections and control
of his own legacy for one major reason: he told Americans what they
wanted to hear, consequences be damned.

A Republican Tide? The Election of 1980

Reagan won the 1980 election by portraying Carter — who had already
shifted rightward — as weak on national security and hopelessly
liberal in economics and on various cultural issues. He built a winning
coalition that rivaled FDR's liberal alliance. First came his hard-core
base — white southerners and an increasing vocal and powerful religious right. The organizing potential of evangelicals was impressive.
In 1979–80 alone the famous Baptist minister Jerry Falwell, a leader of
the burgeoning movement, raised some $100 million for the causes of
Moral Majority, which he and associates had founded. That alone was
more money than the Democratic National Committee raised for the
entire election of 1980. So it was that Reagan and other Republicans,
who traditionally were unconcerned about abortion, learned to speak
"pro-life" language, although they did not actually do much about the
issue itself. The abortion debate also motivated Reagan's advisers to
put devout Catholics on his campaign team. Add to this two other
key, longtime constituencies — corporate interests and national security hawks — and the Reagan coalition looked fearsome. But it was
a new, different constituency — white, northern, ethnic blue-collar
workers sick of what they perceived as liberal excesses — that would
remake the picture. With these voters on board, Reagan could hardly
lose. Some of these supporters, voting Republican for the first time,
came to be called "Reagan Democrats."

In addition to his political team-building, Reagan's personality was
a plus. He had been a famous movie actor and even at almost seventy
years of age looked healthy and fit. Unsurprisingly, then, Reagan
with his soothing baritone voice proved an effective communicator.

He seemed everything President Carter was not. Most of all, Reagan exuded self-confidence and extraordinary optimism. His own daughter admitted that his boundless buoyancy and cheerfulness were "enough to drive you nuts." But it was the struggling economy and Carter's seeming inability to rejuvenate it — though this was often out of his control — that sank the incumbent president once and for all.

Reagan campaigned against the government with a vigor rarely seen. "Government," he would say, "is like a baby, an alimentary canal with a big appetite at one end and no sense of responsibility at the other." He promised deregulation and local control over social programs. He even vowed to dismantle the Department of Energy and the Department of Education, though he didn't ultimately do so. Reagan cloaked these harsh positions in restrained, populist sound bites. He would ask audiences during his campaign against Carter: "Are you better off than you were four years ago?" And he fed Republican crowds a favorite line: "A recession is when your neighbor loses his job, and a depression is when you lose your job, and recovery is when Jimmy Carter loses his."

Although Reagan defeated Carter by almost 10 percentage points in the popular vote and took a lopsided victory in the Electoral College, he hardly had the mandate he claimed. He gained only 50.7 percent of the popular vote in a three-way race (independent candidate John B. Anderson captured 6.6 percent), and only 52.8 percent of Americans of voting age cast ballots, surpassing 1976 to again be the lowest such figure since 1948. Thus it was less than 27 percent of eligible voters who actually chose Reagan. Clearly a majority of Americans had not voiced support for the indelible transformation the candidate planned for the governmental system.

A gender and racial gap was growing. Women were far less likely than men to support Reagan. Almost all minorities generally voted Democratic. The great fault lines of American political life were expanding and hardening.

Republicans won control of the Senate in 1980, despite Democrats maintaining a majority in the House. Key Democratic liberals lost their congressional seats, including Senator George McGovern, who had been the 1972 presidential candidate, and Senator Frank Church, who had led hearings on excesses in the areas of national security and intelligence operations. Even if Reagan's "revolution" wasn't total, it was profound. Democratic Speaker of the House Tip O'Neill, lamenting the damage done to his party, observed that a "great tidal wave hit us from the Pacific, the Atlantic, the Caribbean, and the Great Lakes." If Reagan seemed unsophisticated on policy issues, it hardly mattered. As Bill Moyers, a former top aide to Lyndon Johnson, put it, "We didn't elect this guy because he knows how many barrels of oil are in Alaska. We elected him because we want to feel good."

Critics, with some justification, saw Reagan as more show than substance. Nonetheless, they underestimated the extent of his political acumen. He ran on the mythology of America and on the nation's limitless horizons. He urged Americans to "believe in ourselves and to believe in our capacity to perform great deeds, to believe . . . we can and will resolve the problems which now confront us." "Why," he asked, "shouldn't we believe that? We're Americans!"

Patriotic pageantry was another Reagan tactic. Michael Deaver, a top Reagan aide, would later describe Reagan's successful 1984 reelection campaign by saying, "We kept apple pie and the flag going the whole time," and that could well be applied to Reagan's entire tenure.

Reagan would earn his legendary nickname of the Great Communicator by seamlessly explaining complex issues in simple, plain language. Speaker O'Neill praised the former actor's skills in politics, saying that Reagan "might not be much of a debater, but with a prepared text he's the best public speaker I've ever seen."

Reagan's communications team was a smooth-running machine. Top aides would start each morning with the "line of the day," a single theme that would infuse all presidential business and public relations for the coming hours. "We had to think like a television producer," White House spokesman Larry Speakes explained, because favorable public exposure for the president on TV would consist of only "a minute and thirty seconds of pictures to tell the story, a good solid sound bite." With a Hollywood star in the Oval Office it seemed an unbeatable communications strategy. In the aftermath of Reagan's

1980 victory, *The Washington Post*'s Haynes Johnson declared that "it was clear to all the wise men in Washington what historic shift had occurred. A Reagan Revolution . . . had altered the American political landscape with profound implications for the nation and the world." That remained to be seen.

Reaganomics: How to Craft an Oligarchy

The newly inaugurated president, who in large part had won the election by berating Jimmy Carter about the nation's financial woes, knew he would live or die on the state of the economy. It received immediate attention as Reagan set out, it seemed, to restructure the whole system. He focused on three main areas: increased military spending, lower income taxes, and deregulation of the financial system and other facets of the vast federal bureaucracy. All of this was grounded in Reagan's interpretation of newly popular "supply-side economics." Theoretically, so went the thinking, lower taxes would stimulate economic growth once individuals and corporations had more cash in hand. Thus, federal tax revenue would not fall and might actually rise because of increased incomes stemming from greater entrepreneurial spirit. The problem turned out to be that the theory didn't work as advertised.

Probably a majority of economists were skeptical of supply-side theory — which came to be known as Reaganomics — and many claimed Reagan's ideas were unrealistic, a "have your cake and eat it too" delusion. Could Americans be made to believe that lower taxes and simultaneous raises in military spending would have no negative consequences? When he was competing for the Republican presidential nomination, George H. W. Bush, now the vice president, had complained about Reagan's "voodoo economics." With Reagan in office and trying to implement his economic plan, many Americans were on the fence regarding the supply-side notion. In addition, the Democrats still held the House. By March 1981 it was unclear whether Reagan had the votes to push through his tax-cut bill.

Then on March 30 a deranged young man nearly killed the president when he fired six shots at him. A ricocheted bullet lodged in Reagan's left lung. Through it all, the president seemed to handle his fate with grace, courage, and humor. Just before surgeons began to operate, Reagan quipped to them: "Please tell me you're all Republicans." His popularity soared in the aftermath of the assassination attempt. Thus the passage of Reagan's ambitious tax bill was virtually assured. House Speaker O'Neill would admit as much, declaring, "Because of the attempted assassination the president has become a hero. We can't argue with a man as popular as he is." There was more to it than sympathy votes for a wounded president. Reagan knew how to work the Congress, and work it he did. During the first hundred days, some of which he spent in recovery, Reagan met with 467 members of Congress, and, though he rejected large changes to his tax bill, he proved amenable to compromise. O'Neill admitted he had underestimated the man and complained of "getting the shit whaled out of me!"

Reagan promised to cut income taxes 30 percent over three years and eventually managed to lower the top income tax bracket from 70 percent to 28 percent (though he would marginally raise tax rates before then). The comprehensive budget bill also cut social spending — in food stamps and public assistance — and canceled a Carter-era jobs program that had provided work for three hundred thousand people. This particularly irked some liberals, especially when such frugality was juxtaposed with the expensive clothing that Nancy Reagan wore to public functions. The first lady attended the 1981 inaugural balls in an ensemble that reportedly cost $25,000. For the 1985 galas, the cost of her outfit was said to have almost doubled, to $46,000.

After President Reagan cut some 350,000 Americans from the rolls of Social Security disability payments, a wounded Vietnam veteran and Medal of Honor recipient, Sergeant Roy Benavidez, testified before Congress in June 1983 that the "administration that put this medal around my neck is curtailing my benefits."

All told, Reagan ushered in $140 billion in social spending cuts in his first three years alone. New restrictions reduced the number of children eligible for subsidized school lunches by half a million. And by lowering the highest federal tax bracket to 28 percent, Reagan had created an economy in which, according to reporter and author Donald L. Bartlett, "In 1988, a school teacher, factory worker, and billionaire can all pay 28% [in taxes]." Reaganomics seemed to affect the "two Americas" very differently, and its excesses could appear quite coarse. For example, in 1981 Reagan's Agriculture Department changed regulations to classify condiments such as relish and ketchup as vegetables in free school lunches, thus saving money on fresh produce. That same week the White House ordered $209,508 worth of china with the presidential seal embossed in gold. Regressive taxation and inequality seemed triumphant.

That was the point, according to Reagan administration Budget Director David Stockman. Unlike the cozy rhetoric employed by other supply-siders, Stockman's assessment was harsh and clear. He knew that tax cuts would never sufficiently increase productivity and thus government revenue. He knew there would be deficits, and he welcomed them, knowing that legislators would then come under pressure to cut domestic spending rather than take the politically unpopular step of raising taxes. Stockman called it the "starve the beast" strategy. He explained that the beast is big government and it should be starved by cutting taxes and reducing revenues so programs have to be cut back. (Years later, Stockman would disown Reaganomics.)

Reagan tended to soften Stockman's tone in his own public pronouncements, but even the president could seem heartless, as in a television interview where he claimed that the "homeless . . . are homeless, you might say, by choice."

Many working- and middle-class Americans went along with the deep cuts to poverty-reduction programs. They had been hammered time and again by conservatives with the message that welfare was bankrupting the nation and most of its recipients were unworthy. This was simply false. Welfare, such as it was, accounted for only 8 percent of government outlays in 1986, compared with 32 percent for defense.

In addition to cutting taxes and slashing certain aspects of the social safety net, Reagan also deregulated various industries and federal agencies. "Government," he repeatedly said, is "not the solution, it's the problem." The consequences of Reagan's deregulation bonanza were severe at times. The lack of oversight encouraged risky behavior on Wall Street and ushered in a savings-and-loan crisis. The federal government had to bail out key financial institutions in what became the costliest financial scandal up to that point in US history.

In addition to deregulating the financial sector, Reagan also loosened environmental restrictions. He believed the environment was not in serious danger and ignored scientific evidence of global warming, setting a precedent for Republican orthodoxy for decades to come. His administration cut research funding for renewable energies by some 90 percent. And why not? Just after he took office, twenty-three oil industry executives contributed $270,000 to redecorate the White House. As Jack Hodges, the Oklahoma City–based owner of Core Oil and Gas, bluntly put it, "The top man of this country ought to live in one of the top places. Mr. Reagan has helped the energy business."

Reagan had a particularly nasty habit of appointing officials who were hostile to the very government agencies they led. His secretary of the interior, James Watt, believed that protecting the environment was far less important than Christ's imminent return, divided people into two categories — liberals and "Americans" — and vowed to "mine more, drill more, cut more timber." To lead the Occupational Safety and Health Administration (OSHA), Reagan chose a Florida businessman, Thorne Auchter, whose construction company had regularly been fined by OSHA. Auchter proceeded to cut OSHA inspections by more than 20 percent. A Reagan appointee who was the first ever female head of the Environmental Protection Agency believed that the EPA regulated businesses too aggressively. With such appointees atop these agencies, Reagan created a self-fulfilling prophecy in which government did appear broken and inherently problematic.

Reagan, though once the president of the Screen Actors Guild, a labor union, was a veritable union buster. When tens of thousands of air traffic controllers threatened to strike for better pay and benefits, Reagan gave them a forty-eight-hour ultimatum to return to work. Only 38 percent returned to the job, and the president followed through, firing eleven thousand others and sending military controllers to fill the gap.

Reagan single-handedly destroyed the controllers' union and sent an unmistakable message to many others. Greatly demoralized, organized labor was on the retreat during the 1980s as membership rates and the number of annual strikes plummeted to record lows.

Reaganomics' consequences were mixed but mainly negative. After an initial recession and increasing unemployment in 1981–82, the economy would essentially right itself and growth would return. Inflation did stabilize, largely thanks to the tight-money schemes of the Carter-appointed head of the Federal Reserve, Paul Volcker, whose harsh austerity measures may have caused a recession but did level out inflation over time. Unemployment averaged 9.7 percent during what Democrats labeled the "Reagan recession," the highest rate since the Great Depression. In the long run, however, the painful Volcker medicine cured runaway inflation. Nevertheless, when Reagan left office in 1989 he left the new president, his former vice president, with an economy in which one-quarter of children still lived in poverty.

A growing economy is not necessarily a healthy economy, and Reaganomics no doubt did some structural damage. Lower taxes and greater military spending turned out just as you might suspect. During Reagan's two terms the national debt tripled. His administration never balanced a budget in eight years. Federal debt as a percentage of GDP jumped from 33 percent in 1981 to 53 percent in 1989. Reagan adviser David Stockman admitted in late 1981 that "[n]one of us really understands what's going on with all these numbers."

Even more concerning was that income inequality — the gap between the rich and the poor — was on the rise during the Reagan years. House Speaker O'Neill saw the problem and fired a salvo of dissent. "When it comes to giving tax breaks to the wealthy in this country," he said, "the president has a heart of gold." During Reagan's tenure, the income of the top 20 percent of families rose by an average of $10,000 per year, whereas for the bottom 20 percent wages slowly declined. In 1980 CEOs earned an average salary forty times higher than a factory worker's. By 1989 they were making *ninety-three times as much.* CEOs of major corporations saw their average salaries quadruple between 1980 and 1988, from $3 million to $12 million annually. Such excesses bordered on the absurd. The Reagan tax cuts only aggravated the inequity. The taxes that stayed put, like the Social Security payroll tax, were often highly regressive, with most of the weight falling on low-income people. This only contributed to rising economic inequality. The *Forbes* 400 list saw tripling of the net worth of the richest Americans.

Corporate leaders would pay Reagan back in spades. During the 1984 election campaign political action committees (PACs) favoring the GOP raised $7.2 million, compared with other PACs raising just $650,000 for the Democrat presidential candidate, former vice president Walter Mondale. Reagan won in a near-record landslide. Shaken by this defeat, the Democratic Party began a rightward shift of its own, with "New Democrats" — such as southern governor Bill Clinton and Missouri's US representative Richard Gephardt — in the vanguard. Democrats, the insurgents realized, would need to start sounding like Republicans if they hoped to ever win again. For the Democratic Party this began the long streak of neoliberalism that remained dominant for decades to come.

It mattered little that Mondale was correct in many of his assessments and predictions. The former vice president accurately noted that Reaganomics, if continued, would hollow out the middle class, making the rich richer and the poor poorer. Indeed, in his acceptance speech at the Democratic National Convention, Mondale clamored, "Four years ago, many of you voted for Mr. Reagan because he promised you'd be better off. And today the rich are better off. But working Americans are worse off, and the middle class is standing on a trap door." While it wasn't true that all working Americans were worse off in the increasingly prosperous '80s, Mondale's warning was a prescient harbinger.

Nevertheless, most Americans were attracted to Reagan's "Make American Great Again" rhetoric and the ubiquitous, soothing 1984 Reagan TV advertisement popularly known as "Morning in America." The ad, carefully produced by experts in Radio City Music Hall, featured Norman Rockwell–like suburban nostalgia and patriotic pageantry. The ad's effectiveness demonstrated that most

Americans were captivated by Reagan's unflinching positivity. During his reelection campaign, Reagan even co-opted the decidedly anti-war anthem "Born in the USA" by Bruce Springsteen and played it at rallies for audiences who clearly knew only the chorus and not the verse lyrics. Springsteen reacted angrily to the misappropriation of his song, saying, "You see in the Reagan election ads on TV, you know, 'It's morning in America,' and you say, well, it's not morning in Pittsburgh. It's not morning above 125th Street in New York [Harlem]. It's midnight and there's, like, a bad moon rising." Decades later, the musician deftly summarized what had occurred: "This [when Reagan used the song and even directly praised its "message of hope"] was when the Republicans first mastered the art of co-opting anything and everything that seemed fundamentally American, and if you're on the other side, you were somehow unpatriotic." Through it all, though, the outcome in 1984 seemed a fait accompli.

Reaganomics may have eventually killed the inflation monster, but it didn't seriously reduce poverty. In 1989, 31.5 million Americans lived below the poverty line. The number of homeless Americans doubled in the Reagan years, from two hundred thousand to four hundred thousand. What's more, despite the supposedly miraculous Reagan-induced economic turnaround, overall increases in real per capita income averaged only 2 percent per year, much more modest than during the immediate postwar Good Old Days, and not much greater than growth had been in the late 1970s. The highest increases, of course, were among the wealthiest economic quintiles. Even the federal minimum wage remained stagnant, at $3.15 per hour, through-out Reagan's tenure. By the late 1980s some 14 percent of Americans lacked health insurance, and the corporate interests backing Reagan would hardly countenance any legislative action to improve these rates. When he left office, the United States was the only developed nation in the West without universal health coverage.

The real wages of working people, meanwhile, were stalled, and the fastest-growing occupations tended to be low paying and in the service sector. Farm foreclosures rose. Due in part to foreign compe-tition, the United States shifted from being one of the world's largest creditors to the world's largest debtor. All this contributed to the growth of a consumerist culture in the 1980s. The president encouraged such behavior, stating in 1983, "What I want to see above all is that this remains a country where someone can always get rich."

It seemed that young, upwardly mobile professionals, "yuppies," had become the role models of the Reagan era. A best-selling memoir/business-advice book was published under the name of a young real estate magnate, Donald Trump, and it became a symbol of the yuppie culture. The consumerist values manifested even in popular films, such as Oliver Stone's 1987 *Wall Street*, in which a high finance tycoon famously declares, "Greed is good." It seemed that onetime socially conscious and liberal baby boomers had become increasingly conservative and obsessed with the accumulation of wealth. According to one report, a third of all Yale seniors graduating in 1985 applied for jobs at First Boston Corp., a leading Wall Street investment house. These developments represented a dramatic change from the progressive activism of the 1960s–70s.

Race was a factor in economic inequality. References to cutting the social welfare assistance of black Americans were generally coded in the Reagan years as cuts in "unearned" benefits. Reagan regularly denounced "welfare queens" — meaning inner-city unwed black mothers — and exaggerated the magnitude of welfare fraud. The New Deal and Great Society programs — such as Social Security and Medicare — that he left undamaged are broadly associated with huge, mostly white segments of the population. African Americans resented Reagan's relative disinterest in the urban issues of crime, poverty, and unemployment. It seemed northern urban blacks faced a perfect storm of declining manufacturing jobs, de facto segregation, failing schools, and rising street crime. In 1985 a series in the *Chicago Tribune* described the situation:

> The existence of an underclass is not new. . . . What appears to be different . . . is the permanent entrapment of significant numbers of Americans, especially urban blacks, in a world apart at the bottom of society. And for the first time,

much of the rest of America seems to be accepting a permanent underclass as a sad, if frightening, fact of life.

Reagan also took no serious action to support school integration, and
resources for inner-city schools remained inadequate.

African Americans were particularly hard hit during the 1981–82
recession, with unemployment reaching 19 percent in their community. Even as the economy stabilized, black unemployment seemed
fixed at twice the rate of whites. While a 1983 poll demonstrated
that 46 percent of whites believed the economy was improving, only
17 percent of blacks agreed. There was a distinct sense in the black
community that Reaganomics didn't serve African Americans.

Reagan's was not a diverse administration. He had topped Carter
by substantial margins in capturing the vote of whites and the vote
of men in 1980, and the president would serve and appoint white
men to a considerable degree. It was in the courts that Reagan built
a lasting conservative legacy. In eight years he appointed 368 district
and appeals court judges, nearly half the national total on the bench,
the vast majority of them conservative white males. Just seven were
black and fifteen were Hispanic, for a combined 6 percent of the
total of appointees. Reagan also placed three Supreme Court justices
during his tenure, including the reactionary Antonin Scalia, an "origi-
nalist" who believed the Constitution must be taken literally in its
eighteenth-century context. With these high court and district court
appointments, Reagan launched a long-lasting change in the judiciary. He ensured there would be little or no federal action to support
proactive school integration, affirmative action, or other racially
tinged causes. Instead, Reagan's approach was punitive and based on
"law and order." According to Reagan and most of his judicial appointees, crime, not underlying poverty and segregation, was the problem.
It was thus unsurprising that the number of incarcerated Americans
doubled to nearly one million during the Reagan era.

There were other complaints about Reagan. He wasn't a particularly hard worker, it seemed. He refused to hold early staff meetings,
needed naps, and called it quits by 5:00 p.m. There were rumors that

he would doze off in cabinet meetings. He once even failed to recognize his own secretary of housing and urban development at a public function, despite the man being the only black cabinet officer. Few in the public knew of these shortcomings, and it is doubtful that most Americans would have cared had they known: Reagan's popularity remained high. O'Neill characterized the president as "most of the time an actor reading lines who didn't understand his own programs," someone who "would have made a hell of a king."

Sometimes it even seemed that Reagan could hardly separate fact from fiction. He repeatedly told a patriotic yarn in public speeches about a World War II bomber pilot who decided to stay with a trapped crew member rather than eject from the burning plane. "Never mind, son, we'll ride it down together," Reagan recounted the pilot telling the injured man. The problem is this event never happened, except, fittingly, in a World War II film, *A Wing and a Prayer*, starring Don Ameche and Dana Andrews. The president — whose own military service was Stateside churning out training and propaganda films mainly in Culver City near his California home — on occasion falsely claimed he had helped film the liberation of Nazi death camps in Europe. Reagan seemed to lack any self-awareness or contrition concerning his falsehoods; he kept repeating them.

President Reagan also demonstrated a lack of leadership and empathy during the growing AIDS epidemic. By the mid-1980s he had cut AIDS funding and had publicly mentioned the disease only once. Indeed, it wasn't until a friend of his, the actor Rock Hudson, died of AIDS in October 1985 that Reagan showed any real interest in, or curiosity about, this fatal disease. Though he appointed a government investigator on the issue, Reagan was loath to take that expert's recommendation to support broader sex education in schools or encourage the use of condoms. It's easy to see why. Reagan's evangelical base saw AIDS as a "gay plague" because a significant portion of its victims were homosexual. Such sentiments were on display even in Reagan's inner circle. His director of communications, Pat Buchanan, insensitively wrote in 1983: "The poor homosexuals; they have declared war on nature and now nature is exacting an awful retribution." In the end

Reagan's sluggish response to AIDS ensured that on this issue, too, the United States would fall behind the nations of Western Europe, where sex education and birth control were readily available and AIDS infection rates far lower.

On public policy in general, Reagan was no wonk and was hardly the ideologue that liberals had seen in their nightmares. However, his willingness to compromise, negotiate, and reach across the aisle made him effective and thus, in a sense, a greater danger to liberalism. As early as 1980, an analysis in *The Washington Post* admitted that "[Reagan] is not one to let principles over-ride flexibility, and everyone who knows him concluded that he's a nice guy, a happy secure person who likes himself and other people." As mentioned earlier, Reagan was smart enough not to harm the sacred cows of Social Security and Medicare. He even inched leftward on immigration, passing a reform act that gave "amnesty" — a temporary path to citizenship — to millions of undocumented workers. Such flexibility on immigration would become anathema to future rightward-leaning Republicans. In the near future Republicans would move right, and Democrats left, on immigration and a number of other issues. Reagan's domestic legacy, then, proved to be his ability to achieve conservative goals while maintaining broad public support and the veneer of civility. His GOP successors proved far less amenable to compromise, and it was Reagan who made possible the rigid sorts of later years.

All told, Reaganomics and Reagan's domestic program as a whole were probably more popular than they should have been. Inflation did level off and persistent unemployment finally fell, but Reagan's policies never achieved what he had promised. As the historian Gary Wills noted, "Supply-side economics was supposed to promote savings, investment, and entrepreneurial creativity. It failed at all three." Reaganomics never did serve all Americans. It was never meant to, despite all the promises to the contrary. Working-class Americans without a high school degree saw their weekly wages decrease by 6 percent. Overall, median family incomes, which had steadily risen since the 1940s, began to fall in the Reagan years and would do so for decades afterward. Perhaps the best indictment of the domestic Reagan comes from the Republican strategist and Nixon adviser Kevin Phillips. Reviewing the 1980s, he labeled the decade "a capitalist blowout" that had ushered in a "second Gilded Age." "By several measurements," he continued, "the US in the late 20th century led all other major industrial countries in the gap dividing the upper fifth of the population from the lower — in the disparity between top and bottom." So it remains today, a grim epithet about American "exceptionalism."

Hubris, Restraint, and Secrecy: Reagan and the World

Ronald Reagan's foreign policy is difficult to characterize. It had such paradoxes, contradictions, and reversals. Reagan was the Cold War super hawk who labeled the Soviet Union an "evil empire" but also the first president to meaningfully decrease the nuclear arsenals of the two superpowers. He was the Iran hawk who talked tough in the Middle East but rarely put American lives at risk and demonstrated diplomatic practicality. He was a president who heavily lauded America and its ostensible democratic values but also funded, armed, and supported paramilitary death squads and vicious military juntas. These contradictions raise important questions: If Reagan was so focused on US military potential, then why did so few American servicemen fight and die in combat on his watch? If the Soviets were truly evil, then why open diplomatic channels with Soviet leader Mikhail Gorbachev? If democratic values were so paramount a consideration, then why empower Central American right-wing despots? There are no easy answers, and though it may seem unfulfilling, it must be understood that Reagan's foreign policy was actually all of these things at once, the hubris and practicality, the militarism and the diplomacy.

Improvisation was a key characteristic of Reagan's foreign policy. As in the domestic sphere, he followed little dogma and proved flexible. Still, a focus on toughness and saving face was seen throughout. Reagan entered office on a wave of anti-Soviet hawkishness that he had helped build and encourage. He announced he would end the détente policies of Presidents Nixon, Ford, and Carter and roll back, rather than simply contain, global communism. This was dangerous rhetoric indeed, carrying the possibility to provoke local bloodshed and raise the threat of a general nuclear exchange. Reagan, at almost every turn, chose policies that projected American confidence and power, rather than American values. He seems to have truly despised the communist movements of the world and to honestly have desired the demise of the ideology. However, this doesn't mean Reagan actually wanted war with the Soviets — he did not. The president didn't really believe that the United States, or anyone, could win or survive a nuclear war. Nonetheless, he would risk war and rattle the national saber to project confidence and demonstrate American will.

He entered office with the profound sense that there was "good" and "evil" in a rather binary world and that the United States and Soviet Union were on opposite sides of that divide. His profligate defense spending and modernization were a direct provocation and a warning to the Soviets. And the Kremlin genuinely feared Reagan, taking his hyperbolic rhetoric at face value. It was thus that a NATO training exercise, Able Archer 83, caused the Soviets to think they actually were under nuclear attack. Were it not for the sensibility and courage of individual military officers in Russia, the counter-mobilization might have caused a general conflagration. Able Archer was, perhaps besides the Cuban Missile Crisis and the Yom Kippur War, the closest the two superpowers came to nuclear war.

Reagan also raised alarm in Russia with his military spending. He spent $2 trillion on defense during his presidency, a 34 percent increase over the already rising Carter budgets. He called for a six-hundred-ship navy, reinstated development of the B-1 bomber, secured funding for the B-2 bomber and new cruise missiles. He also enthusiastically backed his Strategic Defense Initiative (SDI) — mocked as "Star Wars" by opponents — a harebrained, probably fantastical scheme to use lasers and other technological means to intercept and destroy Soviet nuclear missiles. Even though many scientists firmly believed Star Wars to be ineffective, Reagan pressed on. And when American Sovietologists explained that SDI could actually increase the threat of war by convincing the Soviets that the United States, now able to defend itself, might seek a first strike, Reagan pressed on anyway. Even when it later spoiled near deals on nuclear disarmament and détente with Gorbachev, Reagan would not relent.

Unlike Presidents Harry Truman and Lyndon Johnson, Reagan sought to turn back the communist tide without the intervention of major American military forces. His Reagan Doctrine, such as it was, stipulated that the United States would back anti-communist insurgencies and uprisings the world over, especially in nearby Latin America. These proxies, when armed and funded, would do America's dirty work to check the Soviets. Reagan would thus fight Soviet proxies in Afghanistan and Angola and across Central America.

Nevertheless, with two exceptions — Lebanon and Grenada — Reagan did not expose US soldiers to much combat or danger. Neither was a very prudent or necessary intervention and likely caused Reagan to avoid interventions in his second term. When he sent US Marines into the maelstrom of Lebanon's bloody sectarian civil war, it was unclear what they were supposed to accomplish. However, once American air and sea power began to intervene on certain sides of the multifaceted conflict, US servicemen became targets for attack. For years after, Hezbollah militias would take American hostages in Lebanon whenever possible. In such a climate an Iranian-backed Hezbollah militia would bomb the US embassy and marine barracks in Beirut in 1983, killing hundreds of American marines and diplomats. Reagan didn't even know how or against whom to respond, and in a surprising but sensible move quietly withdrew the marines offshore to their ships. A Democratic president would undoubtedly have been portrayed as weak for withdrawing, but Reagan's hawkishness was such that he faced little backlash.

The tiny island of Grenada posed absolutely no threat to the United States but — two days after the marine barracks bombing — Reagan decided to invade and overthrow its new left-leaning government. The official explanation was that Grenada's new government was building military airstrips for Cuba or the Soviets and that due to the recent coup somehow a few hundred American medical students were at risk.

Of course they were not, and Grenada vociferously guaranteed their safety throughout the crisis. What the rapid — but surprisingly clumsy — military victory did do was build confidence in America's military, helping to overcome the embarrassment and caution induced by Vietnam. Thus the military doled out thousands of medals and patriotic fervor rose in the United States. Image, as always, was everything.

The United States would also arm and back paramilitary death squads in Nicaragua to fight an elected leftist government, and the United States would back a right-wing junta in El Salvador known to kill progressive priests and nuns. The Nicaraguan counter-revolutionaries, known as the Contras, would murder hundreds of thousands, including women and children, throughout the 1980s. One of Reagan's National Security Council consultants admitted that "Death Squads are an extremely effective tool, however odious, in combating revolutionary challenges." Reagan seemed to have a genuine hatred for Nicaragua's Sandinista-controlled government. His determination to back the Contras would lead to his administration's biggest scandal.

One thing that did unite Reagan's foreign policy was his penchant for secrecy and the use of proxy forces rather than conventional military forces. Congress, still shaken by the Vietnam War, had no stomach for an American war in Nicaragua. Thus, in the Boland Amendment, Congress forbade any aid to the Contras or deployment of military advisers. However, key members of Reagan's team, especially in the National Security Council, persisted. Though Reagan later denied any direct knowledge, America would eventually illegally, and secretly, sell weapons to Iran — even though Washington backed Iraq in the ongoing war between the two Middle Eastern powers — to encourage the release of American hostages held by Iran's Hezbollah proxies in Lebanon and route the profits through Israel into the hands of the Contras. This was strictly illegal and particularly embarrassing since Reagan had repeatedly declared he would never negotiate with terrorists. Furthermore, it was certain to upset Iraq, which Reagan and Carter before him had long supported in its war with Iran.

Had another politician, especially a Democrat, been in the Oval Office, what came to be called the Iran-Contra scandal may well have ended in impeachment. But Reagan was popular and notionally hawkish and also inspired loyalty in his subordinates. The NSC officials who carried out the policies swore to investigators that they had acted in what they saw as the national interest and had taken care not to involve the president. Admiral John Poindexter, the national security adviser, testified, "We kept him [Reagan] in ignorance so that I could insulate him from the decision and provide some future deniability for the president if it ever leaked out."

In the end few of those implicated in Iran-Contra would be punished, and Reagan's successor, President George H. W. Bush, would pardon those who were. Reagan denied any knowledge of the actions that generated the scandal. There was no smoking gun, but it stretches the imagination to believe that Reagan truly had no involvement. Indeed, in a secret memo to Poindexter, Reagan had written, "I am really serious. If we can't move the Contra package before June 9, I want to figure out a way to take action uni-laterally to provide assistance." Reagan, for his part, claimed not to remember key facts and not to know about the arms-for-hostages program. His daughter Maureen would later assert that "[w]hat he doesn't remember is whether he said yes the day before it was done [the Iran-Contra deal] or was told it was done yesterday, and that's the only thing. He cannot remember and there are no notes on that." Part of the reason there were no notes is that NSC staffers had preemptively destroyed thousands of related documents. Iran-Contra ultimately hurt Reagan's popularity, but it didn't meaningfully change his policy or seriously tarnish his legacy.

In Iran, in Central America, and in Africa, Reagan's purported democratic values clashed with the reality of American policy. To get a sense of the gap between Reagan's rhetorical picture of America as a "shining city upon a hill" and the reality of his anti-communism in geopolitics, we need only look to South Africa. The president vetoed an attempt by Congress to impose economic sanctions on the brutal, white supremacist apartheid regime. South Africa, after all, was fiercely anti-communist, so its human rights record was beside the point for Reagan. Congress finally overruled his veto in 1986. Many

African Americans would never forgive Reagan for his support of South Africa.

Still, neither hubris nor bumbling singularly characterized Reagan's policy. There was never enough consistency for that. He was neither all hawk nor all dove. His flexibility was best demonstrated in his remarkable second-term turnaround on relations with the Soviet Union. Much of the credit for reduced tensions and increased engagement between the two superpowers must ultimately lie with Gorbachev, then the new Soviet premier. Independent of Reagan's threats, increased defense spending, and proxy wars, Gorbachev realized the need for reform of the Soviet economy and society. He called for greater political openness and greater economic liberalization. He even eased the Soviet grip on the satellite states in Eastern Europe. Both Gorbachev and Reagan wanted to end the Cold War, but it was Gorbachev who made it possible. He inaugurated such a change in the Soviet Union that he presented Reagan the perfect partner. Thus Gorbachev deserves most of the credit.

Nonetheless, it was Reagan who had to choose, against the advice of most of his advisers and intelligence agencies, to actually engage and partner with Gorbachev. He did so with an enthusiasm that surprised nearly all observers. The breakthroughs were significant in the course of Reagan's three summits with Gorbachev, encouraging a Cold War thaw and the first ever actual reduction in each side's nuclear arsenal. During their second meeting, in Iceland, Reagan's advisers were horrified and shocked by how close the president and the premier came to sealing a deal to eliminate all nuclear weapons. Only Reagan's insistence on maintaining his Star Wars initiative scuttled additional movement toward a total disarmament deal. Perhaps only a hawk like Reagan could have gotten away with such compromise and diplomacy, and just as "only Nixon could go to China," only Reagan could explore peace with the Soviets. Either way, Reagan deserves credit for this volte-face.

All in all, Reagan's foreign policy was improvised, inconsistent and contradictory. Reagan the hawk must bear the responsibility for hundreds of thousands of lives lost in American-backed proxy wars.

Still, Reagan the restrainer — unlike Truman, John Kennedy, and LBJ — largely avoided costly conventional military conflicts. Reagan the spendthrift would shower money on the Pentagon. Still, Reagan the deal maker would repeatedly choose diplomacy over war with the Soviets. Reagan the triumphalist would unnecessarily and somewhat farcically invade the tiny island of Grenada. Reagan the pragmatist would quietly retreat from an ill-advised intervention in Lebanon. Reagan's contradictions could be viewed, alternately, as his downfall and his saving grace in global affairs. His was an administration of tough talk, posturing, and anti-communist adventuring, but it was also one of restraint, compromise, and flexibility. Reagan the statesman should be neither canonized nor dismissed. He proved, as would many succeeding presidents, that an American leader could on the one hand be a peaceable deal broker and on the other hand be a war criminal. The latter characterization has been applied to Reagan by some scholars, analysts, and foreign and domestic foes for several reasons, including aggression against Grenada in violation of the Geneva Conventions, an allegedly illegal attempted assassination of Libyan leader Moammar Gadhafi, and causing the deaths of countless innocents by illegally supporting Contra death squads.

There are few binaries, and almost no dogmatic certainties, in American foreign policy. Reagan was living proof.

———

America remains a center-right country when compared with other Western nations. It was Reagan who moved the definition of acceptable conservatism toward the right. There could have been no President George W. Bush, and thus no Iraq War, without Reagan. There could have been no President Donald Trump without him. Reagan normalized the abnormally right-wing agenda he championed and created the space for conservative populists to ultimately hijack the GOP in later years. Reagan the legend has proved more persistent than Reagan the man. So powerful, so popular, and so canonical is the memory of his presidency that even Democratic President Barack Obama would fess up to having admiration for the once-seen-as-radical Reagan.

Lost in today's Reagan nostalgia is the hard truth that his dereg-ulation, social benefits cutbacks, and spendthrift defense budgets ensured that the United States would fall ever further behind other industrialized nations on key indices of health, education, and income equality. Reagan's optimism, bordering on the delusional, set the tone for decades of unsustainable fiscal policy. Indeed, Reagan, defying the Republicans' historical restraint on budgets, was the first in a long line of GOP executives who ran up immense deficits and exploded the national debt. Reagan and his successors rarely paid any political price for this and other counterintuitive policies. On a range of issues, from the economy to culture to national security, Reagan Republicans seemed cloaked in Teflon, immune to injury. Never-ending proxy war, never-ending debt, and an ever-widening income inequality — all of these germinated in the Reagan wave of 1980. So much so, in fact, that when the party tacked ever farther right in the intervening decades, the fortieth president would appear moderate, or even liberal, on these and other issues.

Many academics and liberals would consider such an analysis to be inherently factual. But that misses the point. The American people, by and large, don't care. They relish fantasy, suspend reality, and avoid hard choices whenever the opportunity is presented. Jimmy Carter told Americans harsh truths — for example, on energy policy — and called for individual belt-tightening and self-restraint. Reagan, on the other hand, told the populace that it could have it all, the biggest and best of everything: limitless growth, credit, military power, and consumable fossil fuels. It doesn't matter if Carter was "right" on some of these issues. He lost. In that sense, the very fact of Reagan's victory is the story. Americans got Reagan and later Bush, Bush II, and Trump because these men, as presidential hopefuls, adhered with the populace's desires more than its objective realities. Reagan reflected as much as affected the national mood. He was America's candidate, America's president. And if unchecked, his political descendants may well be America's demise.[30]

34

BUSH THE ELDER – STRUGGLING IN REAGAN'S SHADOW

His vice president was everything Ronald Reagan was not. The Hollywood actor in chief had far less political qualification "on paper" than his 1980 Republican primary opponent, George H. W. Bush. Though Reagan oozed optimism and soothed the American people with his confident, digestible rhetoric, he was certainly no policy expert or Washington insider. Bush was both. He was a man born of privilege, scion of a prestigious, wealthy family and son of a Republican US senator from Connecticut, Prescott Bush. However, the mid-twentieth century was different from our own time; it was an era when affluence and social standing didn't obviate a sense of duty to country and family honor. Bush, like so many thousands of the other members of the American aristocracy, volunteered for the US military in response to the Japanese attack on Pearl Harbor.

Not yet nineteen, he would become the youngest pilot in the US Navy at that time, eventually flying dozens of combat missions in the Pacific theater. In September 1944 he was involved in an action that won him the Distinguished Flying Cross. In the words of the citation, "Bush pressed home an attack in the face of intense antiaircraft fire. Although his plane was hit and set afire at the beginning of his dive, he continued his plunge toward the target and succeeded in scoring damaging bomb hits before bailing out of the craft." He was the only member of the three-man crew to live through the incident. Afterward, survivor's guilt bled through his letters home.

At war's end Bush entered Yale. After moving to Texas and finding wealth and respect in the oil industry, he followed his father into politics. He won a House seat in the 1960s, then lost a race for the US Senate, unable to shake his eastern establishment image with

George H. W. Bush, president from 1989 to 1993

Texas voters. In the 1970s he was appointed ambassador to the United Nations, director of the Central Intelligence Agency, and head of the Republican National Committee (RNC). After Bush's 1980 defeat in a bitter presidential primary battle with Reagan — in which the Texan declared that his opponent, a supply-side theory advocate, was proposing "voodoo economics" — the Gipper chose Bush as his running mate. They stood together at the helm of the executive branch for eight years, though Bush tended to work behind the scenes, overshadowed by Reagan's big personality.

Though no doubt a conservative, Bush harked back to the yesteryears of northeastern centrist, "country club" Republicanism. By 1980, and especially by the time of his successful 1988 run for the presidency, Bush's credentials and tone made him an anachronism in a party vaulting rightward and increasingly in the grip of southern whites and evangelical Christians who focused on social and cultural values. Bush tried to fit into the mold that his political base required, but he was always a fish out of water. His entire time as vice president and president, from 1981 to 1993, was, in a sense, defined by his battles with the increasingly dominant right wing of his party.

Bush was hardly less conservative, for the most part, than Reagan, but the earlier president, with his soaring rhetoric, charm, and (usually unfulfilled) promises, was more successful in holding the Republican coalition together. Bush never really found the knack for it. It probably cost him a second term.

Although George H. W. Bush can be viewed as perhaps the last of the relatively centrist Republican presidents, he was no friend to liberals. When he was president his domestic policies were rather comparable to Reagan's, and, at least on the domestic front, he was never much of a bipartisan coalition builder. He sought, just as his predecessor had, to destroy what remained of the liberal consensus. As a result, the opposition party moved rightward, and increasingly conservative "New Democrats" — including one Bill Clinton — would emerge and ultimately defeat him. He was stronger on foreign policy, where he was relatively cautious and methodical in his approach, than on domestic policy. Nonetheless, he was an avowed interventionist and threw US troops into some unnecessary adventures. After his death in the second decade of the twenty-first century, he was canonized by nostalgic Democrats and Republicans alike. Some dubbed him "the best one-term president" in US history. This was an overstatement, undoubtedly, but one can understand the sentiment. Looking back at his presidency from thirty years on, Bush 41 does appear to be a moderate and decent leader and a gentleman. Still, a close look at the actual substance of his administration complicates this image and deflates many of its myths.

Decent Man, Nasty Campaign: The Election of 1988

Bush may have had a high-bred pedigree and a genteel image seemingly from an earlier era, but he was undoubtedly highly ambitious and willing to practice hard-nosed, even harsh politics. He knew he would have to tack right in the 1988 Republican primaries to best his two insurgent opponents, Senator Bob Dole of Kansas and Pat Robertson, the Christian televangelist. The race seemed tight at first, but Bush, as Reagan's anointed successor, won the day. At the Republican National

Convention, Bush sought to balance his personal moderation with the increasingly right-wing penchant of his base. He delivered an acceptance speech that at times sounded Reaganesque. Though he called for transforming America into a "kinder and gentler nation," he adhered to Reagan's supply-side economic dogma, which many liberals and others had denounced as an expression of a regressive, trickle-down practice that benefited only those at the top. "Read my lips: no new taxes," he bellowed. Finally, to shore up his position with the religious right, he named as his running mate the undistinguished, at times buffoonish, Senator Dan Quayle of Indiana, a darling of the evangelicals.

Bush's Democratic opponent was Governor Michael Dukakis of Massachusetts, who won the nomination after Senator Joe Biden of Delaware, caught up in a plagiarism scandal, and Senator Gary Hart, caught up in an infidelity scandal, dropped out of the contest. Dukakis was a proud technocrat and a forerunner of the New Democrats — more centrist than their forebears — but was both uninspiring and still far too traditionally liberal to win in a center-right country in which the "L-word" had become a pejorative. Still, that was unclear at the time. On the heels of the Democratic National Convention, Dukakis held an unprecedented 17-point lead in some public opinion polls over Bush.

Then the "gentleman" went on the attack. Bush held his nose and waded deep into the rancorous culture wars. Less than a decade earlier, Bush had held far more liberal views on abortion and the proposed Equal Rights Amendment for women, but by the 1988 campaign he had jettisoned those liabilities and unapologetically flip-flopped on both issues. He hired some of the most ruthless campaign consultants available, notably Lee Atwater and Roger Ailes, the latter a future Fox News media mogul. Before the first debate with Dukakis, Ailes gave Bush some vicious advice. As governor, Dukakis had supported the repeal of state laws against sodomy and bestiality. Ailes whispered in Bush's ear: "If you get in trouble out there, just call him an animal fucker."

After holding a focus group with swing voters in New Jersey, Atwater and company flooded the market with attack ads that implied

Dukakis was somehow un-American. Americans were told that the governor had vetoed a law requiring teachers to lead their class in the Pledge of Allegiance (a genuine First Amendment issue); once called himself "a card-carrying member of the ACLU" (a free speech matter itself); opposed the death penalty (as had most 1960s–70s liberals and most voters in the Western world except Americans); and, finally, had overseen a program that gave a weekend furlough to a convict, Willie Horton, who failed to return and then raped and stabbed a Maryland woman. Atwater was, in his own words, determined to "strip the bark off the little bastard," Dukakis.

The Willie Horton scandal hurt Dukakis the most. The Bush campaign conveniently ignored the fact that many states had similar furlough laws, that Dukakis's Republican predecessor had signed Massachusetts's legislation into law, and that Reagan, when he was California governor in the 1960s, had overseen a similar program. This was a time for political war, not nuance. The most disturbing, controversial, but effective TV ad run by Bush supporters lingered on a close-up photo of Horton, an intimidating-looking black man, in what was obviously a race-based message to voters. Bush was uncomfortable with the ad, though his more conservative, newly evangelical son, George W. Bush, thought it useful. And it was indeed effective in moving toward Atwater's stated goal: "By the time we're finished, they're going to wonder whether Willie Horton is Dukakis's running mate." The final nail in the Democrat's coffin came when he refused during a televised debate to support the death penalty even in a hypothetical case in which his own wife had been raped and murdered. It was an admirable stand, one that was ideologically defensible, but his intellectual courage won Dukakis few votes.

The opinion polls rapidly shifted, and in the end Bush won with a slim 53 percent of the popular vote but a commanding 426–111 majority in the Electoral College. Still, Americans were disgusted and uninspired with both candidates. A paltry 50.1 percent of eligible voters turned out, this time the lowest participation rate since 1924. In other words, just over 25 percent of Americans actively supported the new president. Lower turnout, then as now, favored the Republicans, especially with particularly low participation by the poor and minorities — traditionally liberal voters in a country that despite the Reagan Revolution still counted more registered Democrats than Republicans. When Bush entered the presidency in January 1989, he hardly had massive public backing.

Qualified, Confident, and Sometimes Competent: Bush and the World

Ronald Reagan had shocked the nation, and the world, with his stunning turnaround on Cold War policy in regard to the Soviets. He proved his conservative detractors wrong: Premier Mikhail Gorbachev was a solid, actually monumental, partner. To his credit, Bush would mainly continue the Reagan relationship with Gorbachev and work to bring the Cold War to a bloodless and, hopefully, permanent end. From the unexpected fall of the Berlin Wall to the withdrawal of Soviet troops from Eastern Europe and, finally, to the eventual disintegration of the Soviet Union and resultant independence of the various Soviet republics, Bush proceeded with caution, competence, and restraint. The result was more nuclear limitation treaties and a relatively peaceable end to a half-century standoff, surely the world's most persistent of the twentieth century. Bush even convinced Gorbachev to stand aside and allow Germany not only to reunite but also to join NATO! The catch was, as Bush was obliged to prudently promise, the United States agreed not to trample on the Soviet Union's grave or expand the inherently anti-Russian NATO alliance any further. His successors would blatantly break that gentlemen's agreement and extended NATO membership right up to the borders of Russia, including into the former Soviet Baltic republics. This would prove decisive in the later hardening of tensions between the West and a circumscribed Russian Federation. The result was a veritable Cold War 2.0.

In Central America, Bush was far less responsible. Panamanian strongman Manuel Noriega — an alleged CIA asset — had proved a useful partner so long as left-leaning movements held or contested power in nearby Guatemala, Nicaragua, and El Salvador. By Bush's term, however, the socialist Sandinistas of Nicaragua fell from power and suddenly Noriega became a liability. His drug trafficking — which had previously been overlooked even amid the crack cocaine crackdown in the United States — and the killing of a few American troops by Noriega's security forces gave Bush the "justification" necessary to invade the tiny country. It unfolded like old-school imperialism. Tens of thousands of US paratroopers dropped on the narrow isthmus in the largest American combat action since Vietnam. Noriega was captured and his diminutive military quickly beaten, at the cost of some two dozen American lives. It was an utterly unnecessary, if popular, "patriotic display" for the US, a display that killed hundreds of Panamanian civilians.

In the most serious international challenge that Bush weathered, on August 2, 1990, Saddam Hussein's formidable Iraqi army invaded and quickly conquered its tiny but oil-rich neighbor, Kuwait. This proved awkward for Uncle Sam. Perhaps half the world's oil flowed through the Persian Gulf, mainly from Iraq, Iran, Kuwait, and Saudi Arabia. Iraq's threat to bordering Saudi Arabia was thus taken seriously. Bush seemed keen on military intervention from the start, but there were problems. Saddam was fresh off an eight-year aggressive war with Iran during which the US had supported him and even provided him vital satellite-based intelligence. Furthermore, just days before the invasion, the US ambassador to Iraq — in an epic gaffe — told the Iraqis that the United States "had no opinion on Arab disputes such as your border disagreement with Kuwait," a comment seen by the Iraqis as a US declaration that it would ignore an invasion of the neighboring country. It's understandable, then, why Saddam was soon surprised by the forcefulness of the American and international response.

Without a declaration of war, Bush quickly dispatched a hundred thousand troops to protect Saudi Arabia. This would soon alienate Islamist veterans of the 1979–89 war with the Soviets in Afghanistan — including Osama bin Laden — who offered to defend Saudi Arabia against the Iraqis and thus prevent an apostate occupation by Westerners of Islam's two holiest sites. Those chickens soon came home to roost for Washington. It seems that Bush had decided on war from the first, but he waited until after the November 1990 midterm elections before seeking UN and US Senate approval for military action. He didn't have to do as much, based on earlier precedent, but he chose to. The UN quickly passed the resolution, and Bush then sent his effective secretary of state, James Baker, on the road to form a representative international coalition. He did so in dramatic, and impressive, fashion — even signing on key Arab states such as Syria, Egypt, and Saudi Arabia, and thereby lending local, Muslim legitimacy to American military action.

It was all over in six weeks. One can plausibly argue that Bush could have dislodged Saddam through means other than outright invasion and, had he done so, saved tens of thousands of Iraqi lives. In the minds of most, his prolonged "turkey shoot" air bombardment of fleeing Iraqi troops on the "highway of death" was excessive. US casualties were remarkably light, with 148 deaths. Iraqi fatalities, by some estimates, would reach up to thirty-five thousand soldiers and three thousand civilians, levels seen as disturbing by much of the world. Bush was soon horrified by images of the massacres and called an end to the war after just one hundred hours. While some burgeoning hawks, especially neoconservatives, thought the United States should seize Baghdad and overthrow Saddam, Bush prudently limited American objectives to the expulsion of the Iraqi army from Kuwait.

At that point, even Secretary of Defense Dick Cheney supported Bush's restraint, though the future vice president would later enthusiastically repudiate this early opinion. The Bush decision, in hindsight, undoubtedly represented the prudent course, as invading and then occupying sovereign nations historically has proved messy, lengthy, and bloody. Nonetheless, after the US military commander, Norman Schwarzkopf, hastily and unilaterally agreed to armistice terms that allowed Saddam to keep his helicopters in the air, Bush's position deteriorated publicly when those craft killed thousands of restive Iraqi Shiites and Kurds, groups long repressed by Saddam's Sunni-dominated regime. Many on the American political right, including Bush's son, the future president, soon came to believe that the senior Bush should have "finished the job" and driven to Baghdad. This lingering feeling and brutal sanctions that would result in some five hundred thousand Iraqi children's deaths would prove to be the crucial, tragic outgrowths of an otherwise "neat" victory in the Persian Gulf.

Reagan's Third Term? The Last Gasp of Republican Centrism

Frustrated liberals at the time joked that Bush's administration was little more than "Reagan's third term," more of the same and an extension of increasingly right-wing policies. In a sense it was. Bush initially doubled down on Reaganomics, and he too appointed a highly controversial and conservative Supreme Court justice and expressed scant concern for minorities' civil rights (they weren't part of his electoral base, after all). On the other hand, Bush often proved more practical and less enthusiastic about Reagan's "voodoo economics." Furthermore, on the environment and a few other issues, Bush was far more liberal or centrist than either his old boss or the party faithful. This, and his willingness to practically shift course on supply-side dogma, earned him the permanent animus of many far-right, and increasingly powerful, conservatives. It may have cost him the next election.

Bush's postwar popularity, as is often the case, quickly diminished. A serious recession in 1990–91 was persistent and raised unemployment to 7.9 percent by June 1992, the highest rate in a decade. Large companies, such as AT&T and General Motors, fired tens if not hundreds of thousands. Many companies moved their manufacturing overseas into lower-cost, non-unionized areas, and it seemed that the Japanese were buying up more and more American businesses. Former Massachusetts Democratic senator Paul Tsongas even joked that the "Cold War is over, and Japan won." Of course, the recession wasn't solely Bush's fault; rather, it was the fallout, expected by many economists, from Reagan's high-deficit, low-tax, high-military-spending proclivities. Huge parts of the US population — especially urban blacks and rural whites — lived in desperate poverty, and overall income inequality had exploded.

In a genuine attempt to stem the recession, Bush forever angered — betrayed, said some of his erstwhile supporters — his conservative base, both in the populace at large and on Capitol Hill. He increased domestic spending in a decidedly liberal Keynesian stimulus package; authorized a taxpayer bailout of the crumbing savings-and-loan industry, another Reagan-era scandal; and finally, unforgivably to the political right, backed out of his campaign pledge of "no new taxes," raising rates in order to lower deficits and slow the ballooning national debt. During "Reagan's three terms," after all, the federal debt had jumped from 32 percent of the gross domestic product to 50 percent.

Bush's moves may have been practical, perhaps even an absolute necessity, but they unleashed a congressional Republican rebellion. Some decided, then and there, not to back him in the 1992 election. House Minority Whip, and future Speaker, Newt Gingrich, by then a force on the Hill, walked out of a White House meeting with bipartisan legislative leaders just before Bush was to announce a plan designed to avoid an income tax increase. Bush later chastised Gingrich, complaining, "You're killing us, you're just killing us."

On environmental issues Bush had some success and, like President Richard Nixon, proved willing to cross the aisle when he deemed a bill important enough. He would claim, accurately, that environment issues should "know no ideology, no political boundaries. It's not a liberal or conservative thing we're talking about," though history has shown that much of Congress would not agree with that sentiment. Bush's support of the cap-and-trade compromise on greenhouse gas emissions, whereby companies had limits on output of such emissions but could trade excesses among themselves, turned out to be highly successful. This key element of what became the 1990 Clean Air Act lowered acid rain emissions by some three million tons in its first year. It was a rare, genuine, bipartisan accomplishment — though, predictably, it alienated dedicated deregulators in the Reagan coalition.

If Bush showed only minimal interest in African American or other race-based civil rights, he did secure the passage of the landmark Americans with Disabilities Act (ADA), undoubtedly the most significant civil rights legislation since the late 1960s, which guaranteed various federal protections for over forty-three million Americans.

President Bush surely considered his appointment of Clarence Thomas, a conservative black judge, to replace the esteemed first black justice, the liberal Thurgood Marshall, as a civil rights achievement. This was debatable. In the aggregate Thomas moved the court further rightward and was a long-stated opponent of most federal civil rights legislation. Additionally, the then forty-three-year-old Thomas had limited judicial experience, having served just more than a year on the DC circuit appeals court. His one major qualification, it seemed, was being both an African American — nominated for a seat vacated by a black judge — and a rare black conservative. He was extremely right-wing. As Reagan's head of the Equal Employment Opportunity Commission (EEOC), he had opposed affirmative action and other civil rights programs.

Then, one day before the Senate Judiciary Committee confirmation vote, a leaked FBI interview with law professor and reluctant whistleblower Anita Hill, a thirty-five-year-old black former employee of Thomas at the EEOC, hit the media. She listed a litany of examples of Thomas' long-standing sexual harassment of her during her tenure at the commission. The judiciary committee chairman, Senator Joe Biden, already knew about the charges but had chosen to move forward anyway — at least until the FBI report went public. Biden reluctantly called Hill to testify. Thomas was furious and called the hearings and allegations a "high-tech lynching for uppity blacks," suddenly and ironically bringing race into the picture despite his long-standing opposition to racial protections.

Hill was treated horribly by a room full of male, mostly white and middle-aged or elderly senators. Her character was immediately impugned by Republican lobbyists and judiciary committee members themselves. The hearings quickly shifted to a focus on her character, rather than her accusations against Thomas. In the end Biden let Hill down. He once asked Thomas whether the judge thought Hill had made the whole thing up, and then decided not to extend the hearings and seek testimony from other women who also allegedly suffered sexual harassment at the hands of Thomas. It was not the prominent senator's finest moment. In the end the Senate confirmed Thomas by a highly partisan vote of 52–48, the narrowest margin in the history of Supreme Court nominations.

The next year Los Angeles exploded in a fit of racial angst and violence. The immediate impetus was the shocking acquittal of four city police officers who had been caught on tape brutally beating a prostrate black suspect with their nightsticks. Relations between the mostly white police force and black Angelenos had long been strained. At the height of Reagan-era prosperity, 20 percent of residents of South-Central Los Angeles, then predominantly black, remained unemployed. Rather than address persistent poverty, the Los Angeles mayor ordered Police Chief Daryl Gates to cut "criminality" to improve the city's image during the 1984 Olympics. Thousands were arrested, mostly for nonviolent offenses, during indiscriminate police sweeps. More severe was Gates's ongoing Operation Hammer, a crack-focused response to the spreading cocaine epidemic of the late 1980s. The stated purpose of Hammer was to "make life miserable" for gang members, but the ultimate outcome was unending police raids that resulted in twenty thousand arrests in the second half of the decade.

The civil violence that sprang up after the acquittal of the four policemen abated only with the arrival of the California National Guard and US Marines. The riots left fifty-one (mostly blacks) killed, thousands more injured, and $700 million in property damage. More persistent, and influential, was the significant loss of trust in the police by urban blacks, and a chasm, nationwide, between blacks and whites in how they viewed the riots. Bush may have appointed a black Supreme Court justice, but clearly grievous problems from America's original sin of racial caste and inequality had not disappeared.

Liberalism Betrayed: Bush, Clinton, and the Election of 1992

Single-term presidents are more uncommon than it may seem. In the twentieth century only William H. Taft, Herbert Hoover, Gerald Ford, Jimmy Carter, and George H. W. Bush failed to be reelected. In the immediate aftermath of the Persian Gulf War, in the spring of 1991,

Bush's approval rating was through the roof, and he looked unbeatable. Just a year later, with the economy lingering in what was really a Reagan-induced recession, and Bush's own base frustrated with his tax hike and overall centrism, the president's public approval ratings hit a pathetic 35 percent. The incumbent faced a rare and serious challenge from the right wing of his own party, with Reagan communications director and culture warrior Patrick Buchanan unsuccessfully facing off against the president. Even after its candidate lost, the Buchanan wing of the party never fully embraced Bush in the 1992 contest. In a speech nominally endorsing Bush at the Republican National Convention, Buchanan threw gasoline on the fire of cultural conflict. Sounding very different from the establishment president, Buchanan declared war on liberals and Democrats, even implying that they weren't "real" Americans. "My friends," he said, "this election is about more than who gets what. It is about who we are. . . . There is a religious war going on in our country. It is a cultural war . . . critical to the kind of nation we will one day be." Though Bill Clinton, Bush's opponent in the general election, was a neoliberal New Democrat, far more conservative than almost all the Democratic liberals of the past, Buchanan portrayed him and his wife, Hillary, as radical, godless leftists. He told an impassioned convention audience that "the agenda that Clinton & Clinton would impose on America — abortion on demand . . . homosexual rights, discrimination against religious schools, women in combat units . . . is not the kind of change America needs." Piling on, Republican National Committee chairman Richard N. Bond gave a TV interview in which he claimed of the Democrats, "These other people are not the real America."

Despite these alarmist, exaggerated attacks from the right-wing base, Bill Clinton refused to play into his opponents' hands. He would not make the same mistakes — those of honesty and principle — that Dukakis had made four years earlier. During the campaign, Governor Clinton even made a show of flying back to Arkansas to oversee the execution of a man so mentally impaired that he asked prison guards to save the dessert from his last meal so he could eat it later. Clinton then permanently alienated civil rights icon Jesse Jackson when, appearing before the Rainbow Coalition, he chose to denounce a rapper named Sister Souljah, who had emotionally asked in the wake of the Los Angeles riots "[i]f black people kill black people every day, why not have a week and kill white people?" Clinton avoided the obvious nuance and hyperbole in the rapper's remarks and chose — in what was forever dubbed his "Sister Souljah moment" — to use the occasion to distance himself from traditional liberals.

Clinton was a natural politician, arguably one of the best in modern American history. He knew what won elections — "kitchen table" issues — and fiercely counterattacked on the economy. He portrayed the privileged Bush — juxtaposed with his own rise from poverty — as out of touch with the daily financial struggles of average Americans. Clinton, on the other hand, "felt their pain," or so he claimed. The Democrat's campaign was a slick public relations machine with laser focus. In the campaign's "war room," a sign on the wall read, IT'S THE ECONOMY, STUPID. It was, indeed. Clinton would ride to victory on this economic wave, aided, significantly, by the surprisingly potent self-financed third-party campaign of billionaire Ross Perot. Perot hammered Bush about the rising deficits and national debt and virulently opposed the president's proposed North American Free Trade Agreement (NAFTA), which Clinton would later support; Perot thereby stole deficit-hawk Republican votes from Bush, allowing Clinton, the Democrat, to run as a beacon of fiscal conservatism. The president was cooked. Clinton took 43 percent of the popular vote to Bush's 38 percent, with Clinton aided further by the 19 percent who fled into Perot's arms. Clinton had no mandate, and he knew it. His 43 percent portion of the popular vote was the lowest received by a winning presidential candidate since Woodrow Wilson. His election was not a triumph of liberalism, but a slick piece of political work almost wholly disjointed from any meaningful ideology.

So who exactly were the Clintons? Well, Hillary Clinton — a lawyer and activist — was a favorite target for conservative attack dogs. According to Buchanan, she was a "radical feminist." She was hardly that. Hillary Rodham began her political life as a strident Republican. As a youth she canvassed for Richard Nixon over John Kennedy, then backed Barry Goldwater for president in 1964, considering herself a "Goldwater Girl." At Wellesley College she served as president of the Young Republicans. Eventually, however, her principled opposition to the Vietnam War and growing yet still moderate feminism drove her to sign on with the Democrats. Indeed, Hillary Clinton would gradually shift rightward during her time as First Lady, then as US senator from New York, and finally as a two-time presidential candidate. Yet all that lay in the future.

Bill was a forty-six-year-old charmer who had risen to become a youthful, unlikely governor of Arkansas. He has been described as a "bridge between the Old Democrats and the New." As a southerner he could appeal to the party's traditional base, but as a once-progressive, well-educated professional, he could also connect with the identity politics of the new base. All the while Clinton was, as the historian Jill Lepore astutely labeled him, "a rascal." During the primaries there were reports of alleged infidelities, and shady real estate transactions came to light. He never really admitted to much, circumventing questions and equivocating time and again. He managed to survive — he would ultimately prove to be the ultimate political survivor — and squeaked into the highest office in the land. In the process he would become the undertaker for progressive hopes and dreams. Liberalism, as Americans had known it, was dead by 1992. If Reagan and Bush knocked it down, the New Democrat, Clinton, drove the fatal stake in its heart. This would become ever so apparent during his proceeding two terms.

———

George H. W. Bush, the forty-first president, seems, in retrospect, a transitional figure wedged between the "Eisenhower Republicans" of old and the growing influence of neoconservatives and evangelicals who would come to dominate the party. Not that Bush was a martyr or an inclusive bipartisan leader; he was not. He appointed advisers more ruthless than he and ran dirty election campaigns. His administration was tarnished by a poor economy in recession, though it must be said this was more an outgrowth of Reagan's dogmatic adherence to trickle-down economics. Bush, though far less vicious than his Republican successors, was no benefactor of the liberal social welfare state, nor did he concentrate much on persistent issues of racial and economic inequality. Ultimately, his was merely a kinder, gentler — perhaps less doctrinaire — version of Reaganomics. On his watch, hardly anything substantive was done to slow soaring income inequity as, continuing the trend that had been the case since the early 1970s, the poor generally got poorer and the rich richer.

Bush, like John Kennedy before him, had always preferred, and felt most comfortable in, foreign affairs. After all, much of his career had prepared and suited him for global policy. Even here, however, Bush's term was a mixed bag. He waged "Grenada 2.0" — the ludicrously unnecessary invasion of Panama — and probably killed many more fleeing Iraqi troops than was necessary in the Persian Gulf War. Then again, he carefully, and deftly, worked with Russian premier Gorbachev to finish the work he and Reagan had begun, ushering in an astonishing, bloodless end to the Cold War. That monumental and dangerous affair certainly could have gone another way. And though his leadership during the Gulf War was uneven, he demonstrated presciently prudent restraint, limiting US and coalition goals to the expulsion of the invading Iraqi army from Kuwait while eschewing a hasty march toward Baghdad and regime change. His son George W. Bush would prove far less judicious in 2003.

On the surface Bush and his opponent in 1992, Bill Clinton, seemed polar opposites. One was a war hero, the other evaded service in Vietnam. One was born into wealth, the other suffered poverty in tiny Hope, Arkansas. Bush was, at root, an establishment Yankee; Clinton southern-born and -bred. Bush was reserved, awkwardly professional, and at times stiff; Clinton was smooth, played the saxophone, and had smoked marijuana — though he claimed never to have inhaled. Still, politically, Clinton was not totally unlike his predecessor. Neoliberalism, a cheap, facile imitation of conservatism, defined Clintonianism. The eight years that followed Clinton's victory over Bush in 1992 proved — on a policy scorecard — hardly divergent from the last three terms. The old consensus forged by Franklin Roosevelt and Lyndon Johnson was finished, defeated decisively in the many battles of the transitional 1980s. In the following decades the culture wars divided Republicans and Democrats ever further, but on foreign and fiscal policy there proved to be barely any light between two increasingly corporate parties beholden to Wall Street and the arms industry. The consequences, for Americans and the world, would prove tragic indeed.[31]

35

BILL CLINTON, THE NEW DEMOCRAT

He was bright, he knew the details of domestic policy in and out, and he was a natural politician. William Jefferson Clinton, the "man from Hope," Arkansas, grew up poor and rose to spectacular and unexpected heights. But he was also deeply insecure and obsessively needed to be liked, and ultimately it was unclear just what, if anything, the man believed in. Although Bill Clinton dreamed of being a great president, in the vein of John F. Kennedy and Franklin D. Roosevelt, his abundant ambition was not enough to produce that result. But whatever his failures as a leader and a person, he reached voters, "felt their pain," and, on the surface at least, seemed to possess a common touch, an everyman empathy that drew multitudes to him. Having grown up among black people in Arkansas, he seemed particularly comfortable around African Americans, leading the famed novelist Toni Morrison to dub him "the first black president." In time she, and many of her fellow African Americans, undoubtedly came to regret those words as Clinton's rather conservative New Democrat policies proved to be disastrous for most blacks in the United States.

Clinton loved politics; he was known to talk endlessly into the night about the intricacies of policy. However, that mastery did not extend to his abilities as a boss. He had an awful temper, often lashed out at staff, and seemed ill disciplined and out of his depth early in his first term. Many staff members found him self-pitying, narcissistic, and laser-focused not on values or issues but on opinion polls, his own political standing, and reelection. Clinton was perhaps America's first permanent campaigner president, setting the tone for his copycat successors in an age of tribal political partisanship. He was good at it too. A master of media "spin" and carefully crafted talking points, it was no accident that he would quickly be nicknamed "Slick Willie."

Bill Clinton, president from 1993 to 2001

Perhaps the depth of his character flaws was no more severe than that of presidents before him —think of JFK's scandals with medication and women — but Clinton occupied the Oval Office at a time when the media was far less likely than in earlier generations to defer to authority figures and look the other way. He was under a microscope for eight straight years, and what the public found was often disturbing. His personal foibles and dubious character traits were perhaps best summarized by Michiko Kakutani of *The New York Times* at the end of the second term. "In his adolescent craving to be liked," Kakutani wrote, "and the tacky spectacle of his womanizing, Mr. Clinton gave us a presidency that straddled the news pages and the tabloid gossip columns." How accurate that assessment was!

The ascendant political right — in Congress, the conservative media, and the pulpits of evangelical mega-churches — absolutely loathed the man, and even more so his ambitious wife, Hillary. Republicans exaggerated and cried wolf, depicting the Clintons as extreme leftists out of touch with middle ("real") America and, indeed, even unpatriotic. They stifled the president at nearly every turn, at least when he attempted even marginally liberal policies. Yet just as often the conservatives sided with him, forming alliances of convenience as Clinton showed his centrist and even right-leaning true colors. Indeed, it would be apparent, in hindsight, that the forty-second president was the first outright neoliberal chief executive, tacking right time and again and paving the way for the rise of neoconservative Republican power.

Perhaps it should have been little surprise that Clinton never lived up to his idols, JFK and FDR, or managed to bolster the standing of the flailing Democratic Party. After all, in a three-way race, Clinton earned only 43 percent of the popular vote in winning his first presidential term in 1992. This meant that 57 percent of Americans voted for the Republican George H. W. Bush or third-party candidate Ross Perot.

Clinton was truly a new breed of Democrat. More interested in winning than liberal dogma, he read the tea leaves of the Reagan Revolution and decided to undercut his conservative opponents by taking right-facing positions. Did he really believe that such once-Republican policies were in the nation's best interest? Or did he just do what was necessary to win? The question will undoubtedly be argued forever. What's certain is Clinton did not occupy the liberal ground once traveled by George McGovern, or even Jimmy Carter. He was a corporate Democrat, one who deftly convinced all parties in the waning Democratic coalition that he was "on their side" while often selling them out soon afterward. This went for blacks, Hispanics, gays, union workers, and the very poor. Clinton even spoke differently depending on his audience, managing, despite his inconsistent policies, to win the adoration of many of those he would abandon once in the White House.

Whereas Republicans were once seen as the "big money" party, Bill Clinton carried thirteen of the seventeen most affluent congressional districts in the 1996 election. Was liberalism dead? Maybe. It was, no doubt, at least in remission. The canny Clinton could stymie the Republicans, to their utter frustration, but he was more often than not the slave of the conservative majority on Capitol Hill and the white conservatives in an increasingly right-leaning populace. The least among the American people, theoretically the beneficiaries of the political left, did not gain from the Clinton years. The rich became richer, the poor poorer, and through a slew of neoliberal policies Clinton managed to cede victory to the prevalent ideas of the conservative right. The consequences were often severe.

Clinton at Home: Neoliberalism Ascendant

Clinton ran as a centrist in 1992 but depicted himself as more fiscally conservative than GOP rival George H. W. Bush and promised to "end welfare as we know it." He sometimes sounded as though he had co-opted the right's message and its favorite talking points. Still, early in his first term, Clinton attempted two relatively liberal actions: health care reform and ending the military's ban on gay members. He was rebuked on both counts. In the arena of health care, Republicans, more-conservative Democrats, and powerful insurance industry lobbyists counterattacked, ran millions of dollars' worth of negative ads, and ultimately killed the liberal dream of universal medical insurance that had existed at least since the administration of Harry Truman. The defeat was a political embarrassment to the First Lady, whom Clinton had tapped to lead the endeavor. More worrisome were the stark outcomes. Some thirty million Americans had no health care coverage at all, and US infant death rates and other key health indices were at deplorable levels. Nearly all other industrialized countries had full coverage for their citizens and superior health outcomes.

When Clinton sought to end the ban on gays serving in the military, once again he ran up against a congressional coalition, this time one joined by senior military officers including Chairman of the Joint Chiefs Colin Powell. Their fierce opposition spooked the president, who agreed to a compromise policy known as "don't ask, don't tell." Under a spectacularly vague statute, service members were not to reveal their sexual preference and military leaders were not to inquire. Still, an admission of homosexuality or discovery of a gay sexual act would still lead to dismissal from the military. In the following years more than ten thousand gays were discharged from the service, a disproportionate number of whom filled the paltry, but vital, ranks of linguists and foreign area experts. In the wake of the terror attack of September 11, 2001, the military would desperately miss those troopers. Then, in a final abandonment of gays, Clinton signed the Defense of Marriage Act, a federal law that allowed states not to recognize out-of-state same-sex marriages and defined the institution, from a federal perspective, as a union between "one man and one woman." The number of Democrats who supported or acquiesced to such discriminatory legislation demonstrated the prevailing and persistent social conservatism of the times.

After the debacles involving gays in the military and health care, and after Republicans swept to victory in the 1994 congressional midterm elections, Clinton went fully neoliberal, abandoning almost every traditional liberal cause. Over the complaints of unions and manufacturing workers, he would sign the North American Free Trade Agreement (NAFTA), which Bush had negotiated. Indeed, as pro-labor elements had feared, many companies would move to the cheap-labor environments of Mexico and elsewhere. Additionally, Clinton supported the racially charged crime bill that Democratic senator Joe Biden had shepherded through Congress. Defended with academically debunked charges — which Hillary Clinton repeated — about the existence of young "super-predators" in the inner cities, the crime bill was a disaster for the urban poor, especially blacks. The legislation delivered a blow to opponents of the death penalty (it limited appeals and decreased the time between conviction and execution), eliminated federal parole, encouraged states to take similar steps, and instituted "three strikes" programs (whereby a third felony conviction automatically led to life imprisonment), harsh mandatory minimum sentences, and even new disparate sentencing guidelines for certain classes of narcotics. Specifically, possession of crystalized, or crack, cocaine, associated with users in poor, black urban areas, carried one hundred times the criminal sentence as similar possession of powder cocaine, associated with affluent white users. The results were disastrous. About a million more Americans entered prison, a majority of them black and Hispanic, and the US incarceration rate soon led the entire world by far.

Clinton would also follow through on his promise to gut welfare. In the insultingly titled 1996 Personal Responsibility and Work Opportunity Reconciliation Act, Clinton ended the core poverty-reduction program of the already sparse social safety net, Aid to Families with Dependent Children (AFDC). New limits were imposed on the working or unemployed poor. Benefits were cut after two years, lifetime benefits were capped at five total years, and the impoverished without children could receive only three months' worth of food stamps. The ultimate result was to help increase income inequality, keep wages stagnant, and limit opportunities for the poor.

The president is also remembered as an economic wizard, and, indeed, the economy did improve during the Clinton years as the United States emerged from the early 1990s recession that happened under Bush. The reasons for this were varied. First, a tech boom in Silicon Valley jump-started markets at the high end. The Dow Jones tripled from 3,600 to 11,000 during Clinton's eight-year tenure. Then Clinton raised, ever so slightly, the top federal tax bracket to 39.6 percent (still much lower than the Eisenhower-era rate of 90 percent and the Nixon administration rate of 70 percent) and made modest cuts to various social programs. Though the tax change was moderate, the Republicans, as a bloc, balked. Clinton's budget and corresponding tax legislation passed by only 2 votes in the House, and Vice President Al Gore had to break a 50–50 tie in the Senate to win approval for the package. Not a single Republican crossed the aisle. The long-term economic results, though unclear at the time, were mostly positive. Increased revenue and slight spending cuts created a budget surplus for the first time in many years, and during Clinton's tenure the federal debt decreased by some $500 billion. Had they not hated the president so viscerally and irrationally, the ostensible deficit hawks of the GOP might have been pleased.

Still, amid low unemployment, a stock market boom, and seeming prosperity, the gains of the "roaring '90s" were highly uneven. In keeping with a trend since the early 1970s, working wages were stagnant. The vast majority of the income gains was seen by the super rich. That shouldn't have surprised classical liberals. Indeed, Clinton, in pursuing a strategy for victory in increasingly fiscally conservative America, had long sought to distance himself from "tax-and-spend" liberals. He had even caustically needled his staff with the declaration, "I hope you're all aware we're the Eisenhower Republicans. We stand for lower deficits and free trade and the bond market. Isn't that great?" It was true. Not only was Clinton not the fiscal leftist that the conservatives accused him of being, but his economic policy would most certainly have been squarely Republican in nature just a generation earlier.

The statistics of the economic "boom" were disturbing to those concerned with income disparity and inequality. Though dot-com stocks soared and unemployment dropped to 4.1 percent by 2001, Americans without a college degree or without a high school diploma suffered from stagnant or falling wages in this period. Furthermore, middle-class insecurity seemed to be on the rise. The new jobs created were generally nonunion, low-wage, service-sector jobs that lacked benefits. In many families, both parents now had to have jobs or one or both of the adults had to hold more than one job just to maintain a previous standard of living. The average American worked longer hours in the 1990s yet earned the same or less in real wages than he or she had in the 1970s. This was by no means an equally shared economic "recovery."

As the rich got ever richer, especially in the non-manufacturing tech and financial sectors, a pervasive cultural worship of the very rich became widespread. This tendency has been common throughout US history: American citizens — at least when compared with their more socialist and labor-centric Western European cousins — have been inclined to admire, rather than resent, the rich. New York City provided a telling case study. From 1992 to 1997 half of the increase in income came to those working in the financial sector, even though those employees accounted for just 5 percent of workers in the city. The number of city residents classified as middle class, meanwhile, steadily decreased. The trends of the Clinton years, in a very real sense, were little more than a continuation of those in the Reaganomics era. In 1980–2005 the top 1 percent of earners received more than 80 percent of all income increases, doubling their share of the national wealth.

CEO wages, meanwhile, skyrocketed. In 1965 the average CEO earned twenty-four times as much as a standard worker. By 1999 the average CEO made more than three hundred times more than his — these executives usually were men — average worker. As for the working class and the chronically poor, they languished, earning less and, in many cases, seeing their benefits fade or vanish as Clinton strangled welfare. Between 1990 and 1998 the number of Americans who filed for bankruptcy increased by 95 percent, a high percentage of cases due to unaffordable medical bills and related out-of-pocket expenses. When Clinton began his second term with a sense of economic exuberance, there were still 36.5 million Americans below the poverty line. Many in the underclass — perhaps "undercaste" is a more appropriate word — were black or Hispanic urban residents. National recoveries and new jobs rarely touched their inner-city neighborhoods.

Such racial disparities remained a standard facet of American life 129 years after the Emancipation Proclamation and nearly three decades after the Civil Rights Act. Unemployment rates for Clinton-era urban minority youths were five times higher than those of white youths. In 1998 black unemployment held firm at 9.9 percent, more than twice the national average. All this income inequality was hardly unavoidable. It was a conscious choice, a product of deliberate economic policies delivered by dogmatic elite Republicans and their corporate New Democrat allies. Clinton, supposedly the "first black president," sold out minorities and the very poor for a simple reason: They voted at lower rates than affluent Americans, had no disposable income to contribute to reelection campaigns, and had few or no viable alternatives to voting Democrat. The conservatives, after all, weren't selling any financial policies that the indigent would buy. When it came to the poor, then, Clinton, while professing to "feel their pain," could aggravate their condition without suffering any political penalty. He, and his inflexible, angry, Republican opposition (and sometimes allies), just about completed the Reagan Revolution.

The Hazards of Liberal Interventionism: Clinton and the World

Clinton's first, and perhaps only, love was domestic policy. "Foreign policy is not what I came here to do," he complained in response to the global affairs that had the nasty habit of embroiling him. The president, having been the governor of a small southern state and never having worked at the federal level in any significant way, had little experience with the world at large. He was most definitely far less qualified for making foreign policy than his 1992 opponent and presidential predecessor, George H. W. Bush. Clinton never clearly articulated a coherent doctrine or model for international affairs, usually being reactive rather than proactive on such issues. With the Cold War over and no clear superpower rival, Clinton, and certainly more liberal doves, hoped to reduce defense spending and reallocate the "peace dividend" to social programs or middle-class tax cuts. It was not to be. The president, spurred on by global and domestic pressure, and afraid to suffer the Democratic political disease of "looking weak," eventually submitted to "mission creep" and a form of unipolar liberal interventionism. As a consequence Clinton set the stage for more aggressive neoconservative successors who held bolder, more flagrant plans for American power projection.

Throughout his eight-year term, in foreign affairs Clinton always seemed to do too little, too late, or to overreach, overpromise, and get bogged down in indefinite missions. More often than not he simply failed. In 1993–94 the president tried to mimic Jimmy Carter and broker Mideast peace. With help from Norwegian negotiators in Oslo, Clinton helped broker an end to the Palestinian uprising known as the First Intifada, convinced the Palestine Liberation Organization's Yasser Arafat to recognize the state of Israel, and influenced Israeli prime minister Yitzak Rabin to grant a small measure of autonomy to Palestinians in the isolated, occupied West Bank and Gaza Strip. It was all supposed to be a starting point for later negotiations and a two-state solution, but this never unfolded — mainly due to Israeli intransigence and resulting Palestinian terror attacks. So despite his place in the well-publicized photo of Rabin and Arafat shaking hands on the White House lawn in 1993, Clinton accomplished very little in the way of achieving lasting Arab–Israeli peace. It was all over soon after the ceremony when a Jewish extremist assassinated the relatively moderate Rabin.

In Somalia, where the United States was conducting a "humanitarian" military mission ordered in the last days of the Bush administration, Clinton fell victim once again to mission creep, along with bad luck. When he agreed to widen the mission from famine relief to commando operations against warlords, of whom there were plenty in Somalia, he greatly increased the potential for disaster. It struck on October 3, 1993, when two US Army Black Hawk helicopters were shot down by Somali militiamen. Eighteen American troops were killed, and video images of an American special operator's body being dragged through the streets of Mogadishu flashed across global media. (There were few comments, of course, on the perhaps thousands of Somalis, including many civilians, who had been killed.) Clinton was torn about what to do next and ultimately hedged. In the short term, he said the right things, and he sent in extra troop support, but — like Ronald Reagan before him in Lebanon — he quietly withdrew the troops soon after. A burgeoning Saudi Islamist jihadi and onetime US ally in the Soviet–Afghan war, Osama bin Laden, took notice and claimed a victory of sorts. Kill a few American troops, he surmised, and the US military would turn tail and run.

In Bosnia, Clinton — fearful of another Vietnam, or another Somalia — dithered for two years while Serbs conducted a brutal ethnic cleansing campaign against poorly armed Muslims, often civilians. After a bloodbath at a refugee camp at Srebrenica, and a Serbian shelling of a Sarajevo market, Clinton intervened along with NATO allies. US and NATO warplanes bombed Bosnian Serb positions — maintaining high altitudes to avoid pilot casualties — killing thousands, including civilians, and forcing the Serbs to the negotiating table. An uneasy truce held and thousands of US and allied troops flooded into Bosnia, but, contrary to Clinton's assertion that the deployment would last only a year, American troops remained on the ground. Moreover, many Bosnian Muslims would resent the US hesitance to come to their aid and the resultant deaths of tens of thousands of their people.

Then in 1999, in the same Balkan region, when the Serbian army began forcible removals and killings of the Albanian Muslim majority in the province of Kosovo, the United States and NATO again unleashed a bombing campaign, this time not only on the Serbian army but also on the capital. Thousands died, including hundreds of innocents, and an errant bomb hit the Chinese embassy, killing several staff members and stressing Sino-American relations. The Kosovars won a degree of autonomy, but many Americans doubted that the military intervention had been prudent. Indeed, the insurgent Kosovo Liberation Army was far from an innocent party and exacted bloody postwar retribution on many Serbs in the province. And once again US troops became ensconced in the tiny province. Perhaps most vitally, this second, more aggressive, intervention in the Balkans alienated the Russians, who had long been allied with the Serbs and saw the region as being in their own sphere of influence. By underestimating Russian ambitions and failing to sufficiently negotiate with Moscow ahead of time, the Americans overreached in Kosovo, adding to Russian grievances and later tensions between the US and the still-nuclear-armed former superpower.

Once again, however, the most influential and meaningful Clinton-era foreign-policy crises unfolded in the tense Middle East, specifically around the Persian Gulf. Islamist terrorist attacks on American targets at home and in the region increased. Two embassies in Africa, a US naval vessel in Yemen, and the World Trade Center in New York City all were bombed between 1993 and 2000. Most attacks were claimed by Osama bin Laden's al-Qaida terror network, filled with veterans of the Afghanistan War who had once been on the CIA payroll. The term *blowback* aptly characterized the situation. Bin Laden's attacks should hardly have come as a surprise. He had literally declared war, in writing, on the United States, citing three grievances that he said justified attacks on American targets: the continued US military presence near the Saudi holy sites of Mecca and Medina; reflexive, one-sided US support for Israeli military occupation of Palestine; and strict US economic sanctions on Iraq, still in place after the Persian Gulf War of 1991 and which, he accurately said, had resulted in the deaths of half a million children. His assertions would find agreement among many across the world. Clinton's team, headed by Secretary of State Madeleine Albright, didn't even deny bin Laden's final charge. In a moment of callous honesty, Albright, when asked whether the deaths of all those Iraqi children were "worth it," replied, on air, that "yes, the price, we think the price is worth it." In addition to the crippling sanctions, Clinton continued, even escalated, the Bush policy of regularly bombing Iraqi antiaircraft positions, intelligence headquarters, and other targets in response to supposed Iraqi development of weapons of mass destruction and alleged involvement in a 1993 assassination attempt against George H. W. Bush in Kuwait. Hundreds of civilians were killed in these ubiquitous attacks.

By 2001, Bush I and Clinton had locked Saddam Hussein's regime in a box. Saddam presented no serious threat to US interests, his forces were regularly bombed — especially in 1998–2000 — and, whether or not Clinton intended it, the stage was set for a later US military regime-change invasion of Iraq. Some critics at the time charged that military strikes on a supposedly bin Laden–linked Sudanese pharmaceutical plant, al-Qaida training sites in Afghanistan, Iraqi positions, and Serbian troops in Kosovo represented little more than attempts by Clinton to distract the American public from his ongoing (mainly sexual) personal scandals of the same period. No doubt his affairs, and general domestic policy, did cross to some extent with matters of foreign war and peace. Such intersections have not been rare in American politics.

A Question of Character: Clinton's Scandals

Much about Clinton's soap-opera-like scandals was overblown. They nevertheless dominated media coverage of his administration. This obsessive, almost perverse, focus on Clinton's private life proved, in time, to be both farcical and absurd. Republicans, mimicking the liberal-led investigation of Richard Nixon's Watergate scandal, kept

Clinton under nearly perpetual legal scrutiny during his two terms by using a new law that allowed the appointment of special prosecutors to investigate presidents. For the most part Kenneth Starr, eventually a celebrity as special prosecutor, would uncover very little. Moreover, he probably should never have been appointed. A partisan solicitor general under George H. W. Bush, Starr in private practice had worked in the legal team of one of Clinton's accusers, Paula Jones, and this clearly represented a conflict of interest in terms of his appointment as special prosecutor.

Republican watchdogs first went after a former Clinton real estate deal, dubbed Whitewater, but found mostly smoke and no fire. Regrouping, Starr investigated allegations of sexual harassment brought against the president by a former Arkansas state employee, Paula Jones. After a federal investigation lasting four years and costing $40 million, a judge dismissed the Jones case as a "nuisance." Flailing, Starr shifted attention to allegations that Clinton had, while president, engaged in an extramarital affair with a young White House intern, Monica Lewinsky. The Lewinsky case would dominate the last phase of Clinton's presidency. It turned out that the charges had merit. The president had received oral sex on numerous occasions, even in the Oval Office, from Lewinsky, then proceeded to lie about it under oath; eventually, he would publicly dispute the definition of *is* and equivocate about what constituted *sex*. It was a remarkably juvenile reaction from a sitting president.

Nonetheless, both sides retreated to their familiar battle stations. The Republican majority in Congress filed articles of impeachment. The House would vote to impeach, but in a mainly partisan vote the Senate refused to remove Clinton. That lies about an adulterous affair rose to the level of scandal and illegality of Reagan's Iran-Contra scandal was laughable, but Republican legislators and right-wing Fox News cared not and proceeded with a remarkable lack of self-awareness. Nor were liberals consistent. In fact, many acted hypocritically and embarrassingly. Avowed feminists who had rallied to Anita Hill and fully believed her allegations of sexual harassment against Clarence Thomas now offered full-throated defenses of Clinton. A leading feminist of the day, Betty Friedan, claimed that the president's "enemies are attempting to bring him down through allegations about some dalliance with an intern," adding, "[w]hether it's fantasy, a set-up, or true, I simply don't care." The whole spectacle was symptomatic of a dangerously partisan era as both liberals and conservatives reflexively assembled along party lines regardless of ideological consistency or proper context.

Whatever the negative effects on the republic and the office of the presidency, the Lewinsky affair proved to be a media boon. Fox News had its best ratings to date, and more centrist (like CNN) and patently liberal (like MSNBC) cable news channels also flourished and raked in profits. However, when all was said and done, the Republicans had overreached. Sixty-three percent of Americans disapproved of the attempt to remove the president, and the week after Clinton's impeachment his approval ratings hit a new high of 73 percent. (Years later, Newt Gingrich, House speaker from 1995 to 1999 and a ringleader of the impeachment faction, admitted he was having an extramarital affair with a congressional aide twenty-three years his junior while he was pressing for the impeachment of Clinton.) If the Moral Majority had seemed to gain traction and influence in preceding years, the public response — ultimately a lack of concern — regarding Clinton's affair and lies demonstrated that a more permissive cultural environment had now arisen.

Was Clinton, as the First Lady would later claim, the victim of a "vast right-wing conspiracy"? Yes and no. Republican legislators and pundits no doubt exaggerated Clinton's crimes and the severity of his character failures. They had shown no such concern when President Reagan's staff illegally and secretly sold arms to Iran, laundered the profits through Israel, and funded Contra death squads in Nicaragua. Still, perhaps Americans should expect their president to be truthful under oath and demonstrate mature judgment. Clinton's scandals were neither as serious as the right clamored nor as slight as the left insisted. More than simply a "right-wing conspiracy," the obsessive coverage of Clinton's personal life reflected the times — and not in a flattering way.

The wide exposure, to the detriment of policy and international matters, reflected Americans' growing obsession with celebrity, scandal, and sex. The media statistics were genuinely embarrassing. In a single week in March 1994, the big three TV networks over the previous three months ran 126 stories about Whitewater and other alleged scandals, compared with 107 on bloodshed in Bosnia, 56 on tensions in the Mideast, and 42 on health care reform. Media had, once and for all, morphed into an institution geared toward entertainment over information. As for the populace of the United States, Americans had allowed themselves to be overtaken by voyeurism fed by the indefensible actions of the president and the self-serving ways of his conservative detractors. When it came to the Whitewater, Paula Jones, and Monica Lewinsky affairs, there were no adults in the room.

———

Bill Clinton was many things, his administration an exercise in cognitive dissonance. He was notionally a Democrat but oversaw a shrinking federal debt and several years of budget surplus after his Republican predecessors had produced the opposite. The economy of the late 1990s boomed, but its beneficiaries were hardly representative of the nation at large. The president cut welfare, imprisoned hundreds of thousands of often black citizens, and helped send manufacturing jobs overseas or across the southern border. The candidate who had promised universal health care and the right of gays to serve in the military failed miserably on the former and abandoned the latter, even signing legislation that barred marriage between loving same-sex adults. Perhaps, in part, because of the economic downturn and the international turmoil that occurred under his successor, George W. Bush, many Americans later would pine for the simpler, affluent (for some) era of Clinton, sex scandals and all; however, much of this happy memory was illusory.

Clinton left office a popular president, but he had hardly empowered the Democrats writ large. His anointed successor, Vice President Al Gore, would not win the presidency — though he won the popular vote — and Bush the Elder's more conservative son ascended to power. Nevertheless, Clintonianism lived on in the spirit of many congressional copycat centrists then dominant on the Hill, and, most distinctly, in his wife, the ambitious, jaded, and relentless Hillary Rodham Clinton. Her own rise, first to the US Senate and then grasping at the very height of American power, would, in many ways, define the "liberalism" of the era to come. The tribal, partisan culture wars hardly abated when Bill left power, and the Clintons, peculiarly, remained the favorite scapegoat of the right. Americans as a whole possessed only the illusion of improvement after eight years of Bill and Hill. The aspirations and dreams of liberalism — once the consensus force in American politics — were ditched by the Clintons in the name of power and money. It would take many more years of domestic and international disaster, and a new, insurgent, progressive generation to strike back and contest ownership of the true mantle of liberalism. The outcome of that story remains uncertain.[32]

36

BUSH II AND THE BIRTH OF FOREVER WAR

George W. Bush's presidency forever changed the lives of millions at home and around the globe. (I, as a career army officer, was one of those affected.) Were it not for him, there would never have been long wars in Iraq and Afghanistan. The profound policy decisions of Bush prove the importance of presidential agency, the power of a single man to forever alter history. Bush had run, in the 2000 election, on a platform of "compassionate conservatism" — a softening, of sorts, of the Republican dogma that had characterized the culture wars of the 1990s. He had even criticized the military interventionism of his predecessor, President Bill Clinton, and eschewed "nation-building" missions around the globe. Yet Bush would be one of the most zealous, and polarizing, conservatives in presidential history and would unleash American military might on an unprecedented scale. On his watch, it can be said without exaggeration, the United States shifted from covert to overt imperialism.

So weighty were Bush's decisions, especially in foreign policy, that even his "liberal" Democrat successor, President Barack Obama, would end up doing little to dismantle the invigorated national security state or lessen the momentum of perpetual war that reigned during Bush's two terms, from 2001 to 2009. Empire abroad and militarism at home was the new American way. No one, it seemed, could alter that reality. The profound, yet surprisingly effective, cynicism of twenty-first-century conservatism transformed the political and cultural landscape of the United States. In such a time Bush was more symptom than cause of America's ills. Nevertheless, this man and his team of scoundrels demonstrated the contingency of history and the power of individuals' decisions to drive history in one tragic direction or another. And to think: Bush's election would never have occurred

President George W. Bush on the USS *Abraham Lincoln* in 2003. (Photographer's Mate 3rd Class Tyler J. Clements / US Navy)

if the United States had truly been a representative democracy of "one man, one vote."

Election's Long Detour: Neoconservatives Ascendant

For decades resurgent Republicans and conservatives of various stripes had trumpeted the importance of localism and states' rights over federal power. It had long seemed suspicious, a cover for dog-whistle racism and the dismantling of the social safety net. Yet never was the prevailing conservative philosophy shown to be so hypocritical as when five right-leaning Supreme Court justices invoked federal power to hand a presidential election to a like-minded candidate. And that's exactly what happened over three dozen days at the end of 2000.

George W. Bush — President George H. W. Bush's son and a former alcoholic turned born-again Christian — had run a dirty campaign in winning a tough GOP primary contest with Senator John McCain, the prominent Vietnam veteran and former prisoner of war. He would face off with Bill Clinton's relatively lackluster vice president,

Al Gore, in the 2000 general election. They both were privileged men, were from wealthy families, and held Ivy League pedigrees. Bush was a legacy and C student at Yale and later attended Harvard Business School before leading a group that bought the Texas Rangers baseball team and eventually becoming governor of Texas. Vice President Gore, a former member of the House and Senate, was the son of a prominent senator from Tennessee and had spent much of his youth in Washington, DC.

Bush campaigned on standard Republican policies of tax cuts, arguing that the Clinton-era budget surpluses were "not the government's money" but "the people's money" and even called for the partial privatization of Social Security. He also advocated drilling for oil in the Arctic National Wildlife Refuge in Alaska. As for foreign policy, he ironically, given his later proclivity for starting wars, criticized Clinton's use of the military for "nation-building" in Haiti, Bosnia, and Somalia. In one debate Bush asserted that he would "be very careful about using our troops as nation-builders. I believe the role of the military is to fight and win war. . . . I don't want to be the world's policeman." Nevertheless, both he and Gore promised increased defense spending despite the absence of a genuine global threat to US security.

Neither candidate was particularly inspiring. Bush struck many as unsophisticated, uninformed, and prone to gaffes. He had proclaimed "Our priorities is faith" and "Families is where our nation finds hope, where wings take dreams." Gore was portrayed by the media as overconfident and condescending. He was variously described as "stiff," "wooden," and "pompous." The Democrat was initially predicted to win in a landslide but squandered his advantages; among other things, he presented an off-putting image by rolling his eyes and audibly sighing during debates. Furthermore, he distanced himself from the incumbent president, fearing — despite Clinton's 60 percent job approval rating — that the Lewinsky affair and other character questions would taint his campaign. This would be a grave mistake.

In the end only 55.6 percent of eligible voters turned out. Gore beat Bush by a margin of some five hundred thousand votes, but due to third-party candidates Ralph Nader of the leftist Green Party and

Patrick Buchanan on the right, neither received a majority of votes. Besides, the peculiar US Electoral College system overrode the will of the people as expressed in the popular vote. Bush carried every southern state, including Gore's home state of Tennessee, and every Mountain and Plains state except New Mexico. Gore took just about all of the Northeast, the mid-Atlantic, and the West Coast. The outcome of the election, under the Electoral College, would turn on the swing state of Florida.

Initially, the major media outlets announced that Gore had won Florida, and thus the election. Then, early the next morning, most networks reversed themselves and gave the state to Bush. It was all rather confusing and uncertain. Either way there was an extremely close contest in Florida. The first "final count" showed that Bush led by a paltry 1,784 votes out of 5.9 million cast in the state. For the next thirty-six days, partisan political and legal disputes unfolded before Americans knew who would be their new president. Democrats insisted on a manual recount, and they had a point. In Palm Beach County, more than three thousand voters — mostly Democratic-leaning elderly Jews — mistakenly voted for the far-right Pat Buchanan because of confusing and non-uniform ballot cards. Other statewide ballots failed to register because of "hanging chads" — incomplete punches in the paper ballots. Worse still, thousands of African Americans were incorrectly labeled as felons, thus, under Florida's draconian law, blocking them from voting. Nearly all would have cast a vote for Gore.

None of this mattered given the strengths and discipline of the Bush legal team, spearheaded by Papa Bush's effective former secretary of state, James Baker. Florida's governor was none other than Bush's brother Jeb, and its secretary of state was the highly partisan Republican Katherine Harris. The state legislature was Republican-dominated. However, on November 21 the Florida Supreme Court unanimously approved the Gore team's request for a manual recount. Only then did Florida Republicans — traditionally champions of states' rights — appeal to the federal Supreme Court. By that point Harris had stopped the recounts; Bush's lead was only 537 votes. In a 5–4 vote along partisan ideological lines, the US Supreme Court ordered a final halt to the recounts and essentially declared Bush president.

It was a major blow to the credibility and supposed independence of the courts. All five justices in the slim majority had been appointed by either Ronald Reagan or Bush senior. The decision conflicted with the conservative majority's many recent rulings in favor of federalism and states' rights. The key, and most eloquent, voice of dissent on the court flowed from John Paul Stevens, a Republican appointed by President Gerald Ford. "Although we may not know with complete certainty the identity of the winner of this year's presidential election," he wrote, "the identity of the loser was perfectly clear. It is the nation's confidence in the judge as an impartial guardian of the rule of law." And so it was. The court's decision would be monumental.

Compassionate Conservatism: A Contradiction in Terms?

Bush, in the campaign, had promised to follow a path of "compassionate conservatism" that diverged from the hyper-partisan culture wars over gay marriage, abortion, and school prayer that had characterized Republicanism for decades. In the end, however, he proved to be one of the most doctrinaire conservatives in the history of the American presidency. Admittedly, his position on immigration was rather centrist and starkly different from that of later Republican legislators and presidents. And, sure, he did break with previous conservative calls for the abolition of the federal Department of Education. Still, he ultimately did little to make US border policy more humane, and his No Child Left Behind Act served only to punish low-income schools and embattled teachers and to gear primary education to standardized test-taking at the expense of the arts and humanities. Furthermore, the feds never released the funds necessary to bolster poorly performing schools. It was no accident that critics took to joking that the *money* was the only thing "left behind" in the bill.

Bush also hewed to the long-discredited principles of Reaganomics. He squandered the Clinton-era budget surpluses with a massive tax-break giveaway to the super rich and even amplified Bill Clinton's war against financial regulation. This, combined with the later expenditure of trillions of dollars on hopeless foreign wars, led to enormous federal debt and deficits and, eventually, the massive financial crisis of 2008–09, the worst since the Great Depression. Huge taxpayer-funded bailouts of corporations resulted, in some cases benefiting companies that had engaged in criminality; meanwhile, the wages of working people continued to stagnate. Bush also cut the social safety net, relying instead on the ineffective "generosity" of what he called "faith-based organizations." That policy was stillborn, and the poor grew ever poorer. But when Bush tried to partly privatize Social Security — a highly popular program — the people, and their congressional representatives, balked. It was yet another policy failure for the administration.

In the 2004 election, Bush abandoned "compassionate conservatism" and played the religious and culture card. He specifically ran against gay marriage and abortion, thereby gaining even more of the evangelical vote than he had in 2000. His opponent, longtime US senator John Kerry of Massachusetts, was yet another privileged son of wealth and largesse. Both he and Bush reportedly belonged to the secretive and exclusive Skull and Bones Society while they were Ivy League students. Kerry, though, unlike Bush — who had avoided combat duty by serving in the Texas Air National Guard under circumstances that were highly controversial when he ran for reelection as president — was a decorated navy veteran of the Vietnam War, albeit one who famously turned against that war. It seemed Bush would be unable to play up his own national security "toughness" against such an opponent. Still, he did. Karl Rove, Bush's sneaky and ruthless political adviser, helped Bush wage one of the dirtiest smear campaigns in modern memory. They attacked Kerry's war record, even parading disgruntled veterans of Kerry's "swift boat" teams who claimed that the onetime naval lieutenant hadn't truly earned his many medals. It was an embarrassingly low blow, but it worked, and the term *swift boating* entered the political lexicon. Some, though, said the election turned on whom the average American would rather "have a beer with." Kerry seemed stiff and aloof. Bush, despite his decades of teetotaling Christianity, was pictured as a congenial drinking companion by many voters.

Some of the painful consequences of Americans' choice made themselves known when a Category 5 hurricane hit the New Orleans region in 2005. Undoubtedly, hurricanes and other storms are worsened and made more common by human-caused climate change, a theory accepted by some 98 percent of accredited scientists . . . but not by then president Bush, who in early 2001 had pulled the United States out of the international Kyoto Protocols, meant to tamp down global carbon emissions. Bush would become the most prominent in the long line of Republican "climate deniers" that followed.

In New Orleans local and federal officials had failed to fully heed professional warnings about the effects of a catastrophic storm. Levees broke, over a thousand people died, and most of the city was quickly submerged. Bush had earlier gutted the personnel and funding of the Federal Emergency Response Agency (FEMA) and placed an unqualified political appointee — who had previously been the legal counsel of an Arabian-horse organization — to lead the agency. FEMA was inept, and Bush didn't visit the disaster area for many days. The president came across as aloof and unsympathetic when he declared that his FEMA director, whom he nicknamed Brownie, had done "a heck of a job." The sound bite defined Bush's track record of domestic failure.

Wars of Choice: America's Imperial Endgame

Beyond the crushing effects that the September 11, 2001, terrorist attacks inflicted on the American psyche, the tragedy advanced the agenda of leading US "neocons." In September 2000 a prominent neoconservative think tank, aptly named the Project for a New American Century (PNAC), had published a report concluding that without a "catastrophic and catalyzing event" — a "new Pearl Harbor" — it would be difficult to implement the organization's proposals for military modernization and "transformation." The 9/11 attacks provided that "new Pearl Harbor," precisely the catalyst for the increased military spending and the eventual invasion and regime change in Iraq that PNAC had long championed. The core signatories of PNAC's statement of principles formed a veritable who's who of senior figures in Bush's administration, including future vice president Dick Cheney, future defense secretary Donald Rumsfeld, future undersecretary of defense Paul Wolfowitz, and future UN ambassador John Bolton. All would lend passionate support for Bush's disastrous 2003 invasion of Saddam Hussein's Iraq. The neoconservative aspiration for American military intervention and hegemonic power in the Greater Middle East did not begin as a response to the tragedy of 9/11. Rather, a vocal minority of DC policy makers had long dreamed of US empire, a Pax Americana of sorts. The ascendance of a pliant president combined with an unprecedented act of terrorism provided the perfect storm necessary for these zealots to implement their imperial schemes.

The 9/11 attacks were an outgrowth of ill-advised American foreign policies in recent decades. The Central Intelligence Agency had backed Arab jihadis waging expeditionary war against the Soviets in Afghanistan in the 1980s. Osama bin Laden, a scion of a Saudi construction magnate, was one prominent "Afghan Arab" within the US orbit. After the Afghan rebels and their less effective Arab allies forced the Soviet Union out of Afghanistan, the West had a resentful, and still angry, group of opponents on its hands. By 1998, bin Laden and his newly formed al-Qaida terror group had turned on the United States and literally declared war on America. As stated earlier, bin Laden gave three main justifications in the declaration. The United States, according to bin Laden, had militarily occupied Saudi Arabia (true), starved hundreds of thousands of Iraqis with sanctions (true), and long reflexively backed Israel at the expense of stateless Palestinians (true). This does not justify the attacks that brought down New York's Twin Towers, heavily damaged the Pentagon, and killed nearly three thousand American civilians, but the United States was far from being without fault in its dealings in the region.

Bush's response was profoundly pivotal. He mistakenly treated the attacks as a declaration of conventional war rather than an isolated criminal incident. Within three days, while the ruins of the World Trade Center still smoldered, he pushed through, and Congress rubber-stamped, an open-ended Authorization for the Use of Military

Force that sanctioned the president to wage war on any organization, individuals, or nation-state that *he* deemed had been complicit in the 9/11 attacks. Only one member of Congress, Representative Barbara Lee of California, dissented and voted against the bill, presciently and courageously declaring, "As we act, let us not become the evil that we deplore." Death threats and character assassinations were her thanks at the time.

CIA operatives and military special operations forces quickly toppled the Taliban regime in Afghanistan that had harbored bin Laden and al-Qaida. Because the United States didn't seal the Pakistani border, bin Laden escaped. Afterward, Washington's quick decision to pivot from counterterror to nation-building led to a never-ending military mission in an unwinnable war that continues to this day. What's more, before the mission in Afghanistan was even half complete, the Bush team shifted the focus to its favored target from the start: Saddam's Iraq.

The neocons who authored and signed the 2000 PNAC statement of principles had hankered for an invasion and occupation of Iraq for many years. In fact, on 9/11 itself, Rumsfeld sent a handwritten instruction to his staff to "sweep up" everything "big and small" in the aftermath of the attacks to see if Iraq could be blamed and then attacked. For the next year, the Bush administration, spearheaded by the extraordinarily hawkish Vice President Cheney, lied, equivocated, and fabricated evidence to falsely link Saddam to al-Qaida, even though the two were sworn enemies, and wrongly assert that Iraq possessed a vigorous program for weapons of mass destruction. No WMDs were ever found, and soon enough the US military — though it quickly defeated Saddam's army — became bogged down in a deadly insurgency and sectarian Iraqi civil war. (This development could easily have been predicted if Washington had consulted regional experts.) Thousands of US troops, and hundreds of thousands of local civilians, would die in the maelstrom unleashed by Bush's aggressive war of choice.

Then in 2006, after purportedly antiwar Democrats swept the midterm elections and took control of both houses of Congress, Bush confounded nearly everyone. Rather than downsize the US military presence, the president demonstrated his unilateral control of foreign policy and "surged" nearly thirty thousand additional troops into Baghdad and the surrounding regions within Iraq. Bush appointed a new, allegedly "intellectual," military leader, General David Petraeus, to command the renewed effort in Iraq. Within a year violence did indeed decrease, but the alleged purpose of the surge — a power-sharing government agreement between factions and sects — never came to pass. For all its efforts, the US military failed in its purported mission. Nevertheless, Petraeus, and Bush, declared the surge a victory. It was anything but. Violence had, in fact, decreased due to three factors unrelated to the new "strategy" and troop infusion.

First off, the 2006 civil war had run its course. Once-integrated neighborhoods and towns were ethnically cleansed of Shiite, Sunni, or Kurdish minorities. After this bloody work was done, all sides settled into fortified camps. Additionally, Shiite nationalist insurgents led by Muqtada al-Sadr called a unilateral cease-fire with the US military to reorganize the militia and strategically pivot to electoral politics. Finally, the American army cynically bribed Sunni former insurgents in western Iraq to turn on al-Qaida and paid those former insurgents, who had American blood on their hands, to switch sides. In the short term this lowered violence and US casualties. In the long run the Sunni fighters on the US payroll were never (as had been promised) folded into the Shiite-dominated Iraqi security forces. Many would later switch sides again, in 2014 joining the jihadi bastard offspring of the US invasion and fracturing of Iraq: Islamic State, or ISIS.

What did it all mean? Well, simply put: tragedy. Bush left office not only with the American economy in ruins but with the bloodied US military overstretched in chasing terrorists from West Africa to Central Asia. American victories were literally nonexistent, and Islamist terror outfits grew exponentially. Bush had given the greatest victory possible to bin Laden, turning al-Qaida and its ideology from the Islamic fringe to the mainstream. US military men and women literally couldn't kill the insurgents as fast as these foes were now recruited. The wars would continue, bequeathed to Barack Obama in 2009, with no end in sight. Bin Laden, by the way, still lived. One could argue, in fact, that he had won.

———

Donald Trump, his coarse ego, and his ascendance to the presidency proved to be the best thing that could have happened for George W. Bush's legacy. It was amazing, and disturbing, to watch liberal mainstream media pundits pine for the "presidential" character and values of Bush in the wake of Trump's 2016 election. It has been said, accurately, that most Americans are ignorant of their own history. Beyond that, Americans barely know their quite recently lived present. Bush's presidency was one of the most disastrous ever. He was responsible for huge numbers of military and civilian deaths, both American and foreign. His policies of torture, rendition, enemy detention, drone assassination, and domestic surveillance forever stymied civil liberties at home and sullied the reputation of the United States abroad. The world, and America, would never be the same. Bush nudged domestic politics rightward and laid the groundwork for forever war abroad. No amount of relative politeness or sentimental painting of veterans' portraits during retirement can absolve Bush of his war crimes and disastrous legacy.

When George W. Bush gracefully handed power to Barack Obama in January 2009, he bequeathed his ultimately disappointing successor a dangerous and shattered world and an economy in free fall. Bush's ruinous tenure ought to have forever discredited trickle-down economics at home and neoconservative interventionism abroad. That it fundamentally did not demonstrated the persistence of militarism, imperialism, racism, and hyper-capitalism in America's troubled history. These national "original sins" had been perpetuated by one American president after another and a generally complicit Congress, a condition that laid the groundwork for the buffoonish Bush to take American empire and economic inequity to the next level. The people, more powerless and apathetic than ever, bore the consequences. So did millions abroad who were never even consulted. Perhaps that was the real tragedy.[33]

37

THE OBAMA DISAPPOINTMENT

Barack Hussein Obama. That a man with a black Kenyan father and a name derived from African and Islamic etymology was elected president of the United States seemed profound. America's legacy of chattel slavery and racial apartheid was such that only a decade and a half before the 2008 election Tupac Shakur would rap that Americans "ain't ready to see a black president." Nonetheless, Obama won — with authority — over his Republican opponent, Senator John McCain of Arizona. By carrying traditionally Republican states such as Virginia, North Carolina, and Indiana, Obama appeared to have forged a new Democratic coalition. Perhaps more important was the claim of some of his admirers that he inaugurated a new "post-racial" America. That would turn out to be wishful thinking.

Without the utter, historical failure and by then unpopularity of the George W. Bush administration, due largely to the 2007–08 financial collapse and the intractable, unwinnable Iraq War, a man with Obama's name and skin color would never have been elected in 2008. Indeed, it might have taken many more decades to elect a black president. Such is the contingency of history. Seen in this light, Obama was as much anomaly as transformational. Never as progressive as his rhetoric, always the astute — and ultimately mainstream — politician first, and often fearful of appearing "weak" or providing ammunition for his intransigent Republican opposition, President Obama proved disappointing for liberals and tragic for the Greater Middle East.

Tribal America: Party Over Country and More of the Same

Obama entered the spotlight and rose to national celebrity almost overnight. A last-minute choice to deliver the keynote address at

the Democratic National Convention in 2004, the then little-known
Illinois state senator, running for the US Senate at the time, delivered
a thunderous and articulate address. This new, young face of color
inspired the audience with his call for unity in a time of partisan division. Those who divide the nation into red states and blue states are
incorrect, he said, declaring, "We are one people, all of us pledging
allegiance to the stars and stripes, all of us defending the United States
of America." The speech was indeed excellent. Yet, as Obama's later
tenure as president would illustrate, the young state senator himself
was wrong: there were and are two Americas — the people, and especially their elected representatives, are tribal and divided. The result
for the Obama presidency was often stalemate, infighting, and rightward moderation of even Obama's most modest "liberal" legislation.
In other words, the forty-fourth president's domestic policy was fated
to be more of what had come before.

Obama entered the presidency at the nadir of what was dubbed the
Great Recession, America's worst economic collapse since the Great
Depression. Decades of right-wing, hyper-capitalist, free-market
orthodoxy — combined with fiscal deregulation, much of it stemming from President Bill Clinton's policies — had set the stage for
that collapse. Nonetheless, it was Obama who was expected to pick up
the pieces and who would have his legacy judged by his response to
the fiscal free fall. As a relative newcomer and an ostensible outsider
among the party's New Democrat leaders, Obama had a profound
opportunity to forever transform the American economy and stanch
the growing economic inequality plaguing the nation. That this
was not to be became clear when the new president appointed an
economic team spearheaded by Wall Street–friendly Clinton administration veterans such as Timothy Geithner and Lawrence Summers.
Rather than nationalize banks, "bust" monopolies, and pass a true
New Deal–style public works and massive stimulus program, Obama
— partly due to partisan opposition, it must be admitted — settled
on a modest stimulus, weak financial regulations, counterintuitive
tax cuts, and a taxpayer-financed bailout of the criminals atop the
nation's largest corporations. None of the company executives were

punished, most received "golden parachute" bonuses, and America's flawed, radically rightist economy remained in place.

Next, though he had been warned by his staff that it was politically unpalatable, Obama decided to move for health care reform, a goal long sought by liberals. Democratic presidents from Harry Truman to Lyndon Johnson to Bill Clinton had tried to achieve something approaching universal health care coverage for the citizenry but had failed in the face of fierce Republican opposition and the well-funded lobbying efforts of the lucrative private insurance industry. Obama meant to succeed where his predecessors had failed. Nonetheless, precisely because of his obsession with getting *something* passed in Congress, the president failed to seriously alter America's broken health care system. Realizing that Republican opposition, and Americans' fear of the bogeyman of "socialized medicine," remained strong, Obama never seriously considered the single-payer, universal coverage system prevalent and successful in most of the Western world. Though European single-payer, government health care systems cost far less than the American employer-based system, and though health outcomes in the privatized US system lagged behind those of its industrialized peers, Obama decided that only a hybrid compromise had any chance of passing Congress. Perhaps he was right, but the new president did seem to fold rather quickly, and utterly failed to sell the logic of single-payer, universal coverage directly to the American people as both cost-effective and inherently moral.

Republican opposition to Obama's eventual plan, the Affordable Care Act (ACA) — rapidly, if pejoratively, dubbed "Obamacare" — was vehement and cynical. The ACA, after all, kept in place the employer-based system (almost unique to the United States) and was even based on *Republican* models and plans, such as the Massachusetts system under Mitt Romney (who in 2012 would run against Obama) and a 1989 recommendation of the conservative Heritage Foundation. In a staggering bit of political chicanery, Republicans — including former governor Romney — who had once championed such plans unapologetically flip-flopped into fierce opposition as soon as the ACA took on an Obama and Democratic flavor. Luckily for Obama and the Dems, the party had won slight House and Senate majorities in 2006 and 2008 as the electorate reacted to the failures of Bush. Thus, the chief executive and his party had enough votes to get the ACA compromise passed although nearly no congressional Republicans supported the legislation. To get the ACA through, however, Obama had to eliminate its most progressive aspects, including the "public option" to purchase insurance from the government and public funding for birth control and abortions. So it was that a watered-down health care bill — only modestly improving on what already existed — barely squeezed by in Congress. Ultimately, millions of Americans were left still uninsured.

If Obamacare was a tactical "success," it seemed a strategic failure. The Republicans rallied in opposition to so-called socialized medicine and ran against the bill in 2010, 2012, and 2014, scoring major electoral victories in Congress. No doubt the "old guard" Republican leadership in the House and Senate had been intransigent from the start. After all, the GOP leaders had put politics before country from the first, with Senate Minority Leader Mitch McConnell literally stating that his party's top priority in 2009 was to ensure Obama would be "a one-term president." Still, this was nothing compared with the racialized, populist furor of the grassroots tea party movement that arose in opposition to the ACA and Obama's modest economic stimulus plan that was meant to save capitalism as it existed. Republicans swept control of the House in 2010, took the Senate back soon afterward, and ensured that Obama would achieve no further major legislative achievements. Stagnation, intransigence, and filibuster would epitomize Obama's second term.

Left without any real legislative options, Obama was forced — under questionable constitutional circumstances — to address the nation's worst problems through a series of modest executive orders. As such, he provided minor protections to undocumented immigrants who had spent most of their lives in the US while at the same time deporting a record number of undocumented immigrants at the nation's borders, a practice that earned him the nickname "deporter in chief" among progressives. Worse still, even amid escalating gun violence and the uniquely American epidemic of mass shootings, notably the execution of first- and second-graders and others at Sandy Hook Elementary School in Connecticut, Obama could not pass a single piece of basic, commonsense gun control. As Republicans closed ranks, rejected any limitations on the widely misunderstood Second Amendment, and cashed in on massive donations from the National Rifle Association lobby, the president could again only issue a few limited executive orders. Nothing, however, stopped the epidemic of mass shootings in a country with more guns per capita than any other place in the world. That lawless Yemen was a distant second ought to have been instructive.

The United States also suffered a racial implosion under the first black president, and the racial harmony that had been hoped for proved to be out of reach. Highly instrumental in the public unrest was the vastly increased use of cell phone cameras and YouTube and other branches of social media, allowing widespread and almost instantaneous dissemination of images that caused outrage. Depictions of brutality by militarized police, specifically police killings of a string of unarmed young black men, helped launch a new grassroots civil rights movement named Black Lives Matter. BLM, often critical of the centrism of Obama, was a true grassroots movement, rising as names such as Trayvon Martin, Michael Brown, Eric Garner, Tamir Rice, and Freddie Gray resonated. In response to the almost totally peaceful BLM-influenced nationwide protests, a newly empowered white supremacist backlash appeared. Blandly titling itself the "alt-right," this extremist movement built upon a sense of white victimization. Epitomized by the massacre of Bible study worshippers in a historically black church in Charleston, South Carolina, at the hands of a young white radical named Dylann Roof — who had consumed news from alt-right sources — newly powerful and overtly extreme groups of white supremacists seemed here to stay.

Far from inaugurating the post-racial America of popular fantasy, Obama's presidency, and the backlash against it, ushered in a new age of reinvigorated racial combat sure to extend well past his second term. And while the dog-whistle politics of the Republican

Party no doubt fanned the flames of racist fire, the American people — especially hateful, insecure whites — bore equal responsibility for what followed.

Obama the Superficial: The Inertia and Expansion of the "Terror" Wars

It is highly unlikely that Obama would have defeated the Democratic favorite, Hillary Clinton, in the primaries of 2008 or the veteran senator and war hero John McCain in the general election had it not been for the widespread opposition to Bush's foolish, dishonest, and illegal invasion of Iraq. By 2008 that country was fractured, unstable, violent, in the midst of stalemated civil war, and a haven for Islamist jihadism. Whereas Clinton had taken the then (she thought) politically expedient decision to vote in favor of the Iraq invasion, Obama had, at the time, seemed to oppose the war.

Then again, it was easy for him to do so. As a lowly and obscure state senator in a safe Chicago district, he knew he would pay no political price for rowing against the prevailing nationalist tide. Thus he made a critical speech before the invasion that he later used to burnish his antiwar credentials and separate himself from Clinton. Still, Obama's speech wasn't, instructively, against all wars, but rather — as he termed it — against "dumb wars." Furthermore, had Obama been a national figure, it's likely he would have voted right along with the former First Lady and her mainstream Democratic colleagues. That Obama, as president, proved to be a standard interventionist and even expanded the post-9/11 "forever wars" further bolstered this supposition.

It took him nearly three years, but Obama as president did pull nearly all American troops out of Iraq. Hiding behind the politically and militarily popular myth that George W. Bush and General David Petraeus's 2007–10 "surge" — which Senator Obama had rightly opposed — had been successful, the new president was able to do so despite mostly Republican opposition. In truth, the Iraqi civil war had taken only a temporary pause, and Sunni jihadism had hardly disappeared. On the contrary, Petraeus had simply shortsightedly bought their temporary allegiance. Once the Americans were gone and the cash stopped flowing, the al-Qaida franchise in Iraq rose again like the mythical phoenix and went back to war in both Iraq and the nearby, by then war-torn Syria under the banner of the newly christened Islamic State. By 2016, as Obama prepared for an undoubtedly lucrative retirement, US troops were back in Iraq battling the Frankenstein's monster of Islamist jihadism that the American invasion had helped create.

In what he would absurdly refer to as the "good war" in Afghanistan, Obama sold out the tiny antiwar movement and tripled US troop levels in his own Bush-like "surge." American and Afghan casualties soared, but the Taliban was never defeated and the corrupt, US-backed Kabul-based regime still lacked legitimacy. Though he had promised *his* surge would be temporary and that all troops would withdraw by the end of 2014, more than ten thousand remained in-country in 2016. By that time some twenty-three hundred US military deaths had not changed the prevailing facts on the ground in this most unwinnable of wars: The Taliban controlled more of the country than at any time since 2001, the Afghan central government was financially broke and politically ineffective, and casualties in the Afghan security forces were massive and unsustainable. The war was essentially lost, though Obama would never admit it. Indeed, by the end of his second term he preferred not to mention the "good war" at all.

In 2011, in opposition to a series of venal, authoritarian — usually US-backed — regimes, a series of "Arab Spring" protests spread across the Mideast from Tunisia to Libya to Egypt to Yemen to Bahrain to Syria. The movement seemed to spring from the grass roots but was complicated and multifaceted from the start. There were, indeed, early signs that though the dictatorships were abhorrent, Islamist jihadis were quickly infusing, and soon dominating, the armed rebel groups and protesters. Obama, for his part, was unsure how to respond. His humanitarian-interventionist conscience leaned toward moral and physical support for the varied oppositions, but his caution and practicality led him away from decisive action in either direction. In the end Obama — cheered on by his militarist advisers such as Secretary of State Hillary Clinton — chose the worst of all roads: indecisiveness, inconsistency, and sometimes ill-considered intervention.

The inconsistency was obvious from the start and increased the popular notion on the Arab street that US policy was infused with hypocrisy. While Obama eventually called for the rulers of Egypt, Tunisia, Yemen, Libya, and Syria to step down, he turned a blind eye to Saudi Arabia's military suppression of Shiite majoritarianism in nearby Bahrain. Furthermore, in 2015, when a vaguely Shiite militia movement, the Houthis, overthrew the Saudi-backed transitional government in Yemen, Obama quietly provided vital diplomatic and military support for a US-backed Saudi terror war on Yemen. Saudi planes, fueled by US Air Force aircraft, unleashed a brutal bombing campaign that killed tens of thousands. The US uttered not a peep as a Saudi starvation blockade led to the deaths of nearly one hundred thousand civilians, created millions of refugees, and unleashed the world's worst cholera epidemic on Yemeni civilians. Washington, it seemed, supported democracy so long as it did not upset its oil-rich Persian Gulf State "partners." Clearly, there were limits to the "humanitarian" piece of Obama's humanitarian-interventionist proclivities.

Obama's worst move during the Arab Spring — a move that, to his credit, he later called a "shit show" and the "worst mistake" of his presidency — came in Libya. There, a brutal dictator, Moammar Gadhafi, had ruled for decades, suppressing free speech and also choking any hint of violent Islamism. He had even unilaterally given up on his feeble nuclear weapons program — probably out of fear of an Iraq-style regime-change invasion by Bush — and cooperated with the CIA to fight Libyan Islamists. When a rebellion broke out in 2011–12, though Washington knew little about the country or the rebels' dynamics, Clinton pressed Obama to intervene to "save" the rebellion from a supposed bloodbath. Soon enough, US, French, and British planes were pummeling the Libyan army. The rebels rode to victory, committed many atrocities of their own, and eventually sodomized with a bayonet and executed the captured dictator. Gadhafi was gone, but what was to come next? Obama had no plan and few ideas.

Within a year, varied militias and thousands of jihadis divided the country up into competing fiefdoms. Civil war resulted and raged on through the end of the Obama presidency. Worse still, the massive depots of the Libyan army's arms were carried south and west by various ethnic and religious militiamen, fueling growing insurgencies in Mali, Cameroon, Niger, and Nigeria that would soon "require" the deployment of US troops in restive West Africa. Libya had, indeed, been a debacle.

The most bloody, tragic, and regionally dangerous rebellion and civil war broke out in Syria in 2011. There too an authoritarian strongman, Bashar al-Assad, had ruled, stifling free speech and democracy but protecting minority communities and suppressing jihadism. It was clear early on that the most numerous and effective rebels were Islamists, often allied with the al-Qaida franchise the Nusra Front, and even Islamic State. Though he hesitated, equivocated, and wavered, Obama was eventually convinced to supply the mythical, phantom "moderate" rebels with arms and cash. Nearly all of it ended up in the hands of the very violent Islamists that the United States was purportedly fighting in the "war on terror." In reality, the United States — pushed in this direction by Israel, the Persian Gulf States, and US neoconservatives — was more interested in checking Iran and Russia, which had long backed Assad, than in the defeat of transnational jihadism or the well-being of the Syrian people.

When Assad allegedly used chemical weapons on his own people, killing perhaps a thousand — and thereby crossing what Obama had foolishly said was a "red line" — it seemed Washington would be obliged to militarily strike the Syrian regime. Obama, tempered by the Libya "shit show," balked. This probably was prudent, but rather than sell the downsides of intervention and expanded war to the American public in an honest way he took the political path and punted "authorization" for the strikes to a Congress he knew full well had no stomach for another war. As such, rather than insist that Congress reauthorize or declare war in the dozens of locales where the United States was involved in combat, Obama limited the supposed and constitutionally mandated need for congressional approval to the Syria case alone. Nonetheless, when Islamic State — which the United States had helped catalyze and indirectly supported in the Syrian civil war — suddenly conquered large swaths of Syria and Iraq in 2014–15, Obama felt obliged to go to war. US troops, though in modest numbers, hit the ground in Syria and (once again) Iraq, and US planes pummeled Islamic State and nearby civilians. Ultimately Obama would hand this mess over to his successor in 2017.

Obama, though he had lambasted Bush for his domestic civil liberties abuses and use of indefinite "terrorist" detention at the Guantanamo Bay base in Cuba, turned out to be an equally oppressive "war president." As the National Security Administration whistleblower Edward Snowden would reveal, the United States had secretly and illegally imposed — and Obama had silently continued — a massive domestic surveillance program that violated the privacy of countless American citizens. Instead of starting a major policy shift and giving a medal to Snowden, Obama continued and expanded his veritable war on leakers and the press in general. In fact, Obama — the onetime constitutional law professor — used the archaic, controversial, World War I–vintage Espionage Act to prosecute leakers and whistleblowers more times than all his presidential predecessors *combined*. And though his Justice Department (only just) decided not to indict any media outlets themselves for publishing leaked material, Obama's overall press suppression policy opened the door for more hawkish successors to do just that, in a major threat to the First Amendment itself.

What's more, Obama the "peacemaker," who had ludicrously been awarded the Nobel Peace Prize almost entirely on the basis of conciliatory speeches he had given, proved to be the veritable "assassin in chief." Indeed, partly as what he saw as an alternative to massive military occupations and counterinsurgencies, Obama violated foreign airspace sovereignty across the region and conducted exponentially more drone-strike executions than even George W. Bush. The administration, and its military, then regularly undercounted the many thousands of civilians killed as "collateral damage" in these strikes. Allegedly holding "Terror Tuesday" meetings with his national security staff throughout his administration, Obama would choose people for assassination and order their executions. This was done, ostensibly, in secret, but it was — probably purposefully — the worst-kept secret in the world. It was all so Orwellian. At one point Obama publicly made an absurdly macabre joke when he threatened to unleash a Predator drone on the pop group the Jonas Brothers if any of its members dared to "make a move" on the president's two young daughters, who were avid fans. That a Nobel Peace Prize recipient who had run on an antiwar platform would so boldly joke about a brutal assassination program that he simultaneously claimed did not exist was perhaps the ultimate symbol and manifestation of a morbid and ghoulish era.

In two related incidents, which registered only briefly in the US media or public consciousness, Obama unilaterally used aerial drones to assassinate two US citizens in Yemen. The targets were the Islamist firebrand cleric Anwar Awlaki — admittedly an al-Qaida sympathizer — and his teenage son. Though there was no independent judicial review of the case against the Awlakis, and absolutely zero constitutionally mandated due process besides internal, classified legal "memos" within the Obama Justice Department, the drone-launched assassinations went forward. The incidents were distressing, even if the senior Awlaki was the terrorist mastermind he had been alleged to be; they were indicative of the logical extension and end state of drone warfare combined with the evaporation of domestic civil liberties. If, some progressive activists asked, notoriously cautious "no-drama" Obama was capable of assassinating American-born citizens, to what lengths would a more extreme, militarist-interventionist president go to in the future as the United States waged its "forever wars"? The prospect was indeed haunting.

If Obama was ultimately disappointing in his generally militaristic, inconsistent, and interventionist foreign policy, he had some limited successes. Less overtly bombastic, and more informed, than Bush, Obama wisely — at least after the failure of his Afghanistan "surge" — lowered overall troop levels in the Greater Middle East. US casualties decreased and the overstretch of the army and marine corps eased. The downside was related to the very decrease in casualties: By keeping to a modest level the number of flag-draped coffins shipped home, Obama managed to squelch dissent and war opposition while simultaneously escalating and expanding America's never-ending wars throughout a broad swath of territory from West Africa to Central Asia.

One admirable decision was Obama's willingness to engage with Iran, avoid military escalation — or the regime-change invasion of neoconservative fantasies — and negotiate a settlement that avoided war and halted, if only temporarily, Tehran's nuclear program. In a multilateral agreement known as the JCPOA (Joint Comprehensive Plan of Action) the United States, France, Britain, Russia, China, and Iran had forged a deal to freeze Tehran's nuclear program in exchange for reducing international sanctions against Iran. It was a profound exercise in diplomacy and war avoidance. This was Obama at his (rare) very best. Nonetheless, congressional opposition — mainly, of course, from hawkish Republicans — ensured that the agreement was essentially framed as an executive order. Thus, when an Obama-hating successor, Donald Trump, took office in 2017, it was all too easy for the new president to unilaterally withdraw from the deal and ensure a new war-scare crisis with Iran. Such were the limitations and dangers of the tribally partisan atmosphere in Washington, DC, and the reign of imperial presidents.

When Obama left office, the American warfare state, and the military-industrial-congressional-media complex that enabled it, remained firmly in place. Though he had tried to close Guantanamo Bay's purgatory-like detention center, it remained open. US troops were bombing and occupying even more countries, at least two dozen from West Africa to Central Asia. The wars had escalated in Africa; significant numbers of troops remained on the ground in Iraq, Afghanistan, and Syria. Libya had been destroyed by US intervention. Osama bin Laden was dead, killed under secretive and questionable circumstances in Pakistan by navy SEALs in May 2011, but his ideology and its more radical outgrowth in Islamic State were more powerful and prevalent than ever. The American people were still under massive surveillance, and the war on leakers and the free press

President Barack Obama in the White House situation room on May 1, 2011 (White House photographer Pete Souza)

was in full force. The United States, in sum, remained an empire — it had expanded in its imperial fantasies, in fact — and had been led, it turned out, by just another emperor. That Obama, the coolheaded, handsome, articulate leader that he was, had seemed the polite emperor mattered rather little to the American troops and exponentially larger totals of foreign civilians that continued to be killed. By 2016 American empire was a way of life.

———

Truly profound are the ironies and paradoxes of history. Elected while espousing a somewhat liberal agenda, President Obama proved mostly a centrist in the Clintonian New Democrat mold. He naively sought to work with Republicans, compromised and tacked rightward as a result, and achieved little of substance for the progressive cause. What's more, elected as an opponent of the Iraq War though a cheerleader for the "good war" in Afghanistan, Obama may have altered the tenor of Bush's wars but overall only escalated and maintained the forever wars, adding his own flavor but submitting to the inertia of interventionism. As such, he left North Africa, the Mideast, and Central Asia in worse shape than he had found them.

Matters got only stranger. Though he had been a constitutional law professor, he flouted civil liberties, stretched the Constitution, spied on the citizenry, and even executed an American citizen and his son via aerial drones, absent any transparency or legal due process. Furthermore, Obama knew about but chose to keep secret and maintain the Bush-era mass surveillance state that Edward Snowden eventually exposed. That Obama was so undoubtedly highly educated and informed on topics of constitutional law implies — disturbingly — that the man *knew better* but, in the interest of hoarding executive power and seeking political expediency, went forward anyway with this range of civil liberties violations. This was a strange legacy, indeed, for the man elected on a platform of "Hope and Change," elected as the anti-Bush, as a "transformational" figure.

Such is the disappointment and tragedy of the Obama years. His own Beltway centrism, interventionism, and political opportunism, combined with the combative obstructionism of the tribal conservative opposition, ensured that Obama's presidency would be mostly a failure. One expected as much from the unapologetic, and buffoonish, neoconservatism and imperialism of the George W. Bush team. That Obama was hardly better was far more discomfiting, challenging one's capacity to believe in meaningful progress at all.

Most striking and significant were the moral shortcomings and failures of the American populace, defects that became apparent as the Obama years ground to a close. That so many Americans fell for phony conspiracy theories about Obama's supposed foreign birth, Muslim faith, and even *Manchurian Candidate*-style treason, and joined a growing movement characterized most of all by white backlash, demonstrated clearly that the first black president was an anomaly. If the emotional reaction to the Bush years was for Americans to take a chance on Obama, the even more emotional riposte to a black presidency was the reinvigoration of white supremacy and the election of Donald Trump in November 2016. Sick of the establishment style of Obama, the Clintons, and the entire mainstream pool of both parties, voters chose to "blow up" the system and support a true outsider in the celebrity billionaire and reality TV star Donald Trump.

Perhaps that's the final rub: if there could have been no Obama without Bush, there most certainly would never have been a President Trump without establishment, black Barack Obama as his predecessor. The shame and the consequences belong not only to a broken political system but also to the people, to us Americans.[34]

Epilogue

A ONCE, ALWAYS, AND FUTURE EMPIRE

There is a widespread belief that American history is best viewed in a linear context. The United States, the narrative goes, began as a flawed experiment in democracy — replete with slavery and bigotry at the start — but has gradually and consistently improved into a more perfect union, a millenarian nation on its way toward serving as an example for the world, a "City on a Hill." Minorities, according to this notion, may have once been oppressed but have gained equal rights and equal protection under the law; America might have conquered Indian and Mexican land but has long since set aside its imperial ways. As such, both at home and abroad, the United States, though still imperfect, is a force for good in the world.

It's a comforting narrative, but inconsistent with reality, with the facts and arc of our history. Progress, such as it is, has been wildly inconsistent and halting since the Anglo colonization of the eastern coast of North America. Take the plight of African Americans. Theirs has been a history of false starts, dreams deferred, and hopes enlivened only to be dashed. Consider, for example, that more blacks were US House members and senators in 1877 than in 1967. In the wake of the Civil War, the reforms of Reconstruction launched African Americans into positions of power they would not regain for nearly a century. During this time, northern whites abandoned them to the whims of southern bigots, and the result was Jim Crow — systemic segregation, a parallel apartheid system in the American South. A further example is that blacks finally saw their voting rights protected by the 1965 Voting Rights Act — which required the federal government to carefully review electoral procedures in the former Confederate states — only to find many of those protections stripped away by a reactionary Supreme Court early in the twenty-

US Army National Guard staff sergeant in a battle zone in Afghanistan, 2012 (Lt. Benjamin Addison / US Army)

first century. Clearly, there's very little that is progressive or linear in the journey of black Americans.

Taking such a broad view of American history further, we can cogently argue that the United States couldn't even be considered a true democracy until 1965, when many blacks finally received the right to vote more than 240 years after slaves first arrived on these shores and almost two centuries after the Declaration of Independence was written. Still, few citizens think in or frame their country in those terms. Furthermore, America still runs a parallel system of governance for its remaining colonies, which Washington euphemistically labels territories. In the conquered islands of Puerto Rico, American Samoa, Guam, and many others, the residents have no representation in Congress or say in the election of the presidents, who hold the power to send them off to fight and die in foreign wars. *These* people represent the victims and refuse of America's second empire.

That, indeed, is the key point. The United States was imperial from the very moment when a band of English aristocrats in search of precious gold landed at Jamestown in what is today Virginia. Since that day in 1607, America has never ceased to be a settler-colonial empire in the vein of czarist Russia, British South Africa, and modern Israel. Its manner of empire may well have changed, but its reality never meaningfully altered as the United States proceeded through three distinct phases of imperialism. First, from 1607 to 1897, British colonists, and then self-styled Americans, displaced and destroyed countless native peoples, eventually spreading what they perceived to be a superior way of life from the Atlantic to the Pacific Oceans — another take on the phrase *from sea to shining sea*. America's relationship with conquered native peoples proceeded through phases of displacement, genocide, containment, and finally confinement on often barren reservations. This legacy system remains today in what must be considered a series of internal colonies similar to South African bantustans and to Palestinian enclaves in the West Bank and Gaza Strip. In addition to overrunning outmatched natives, the United States also drummed up a war on false pretenses and proceeded to conquer the northern third of Mexico, even occupying its capital and forcing a regime change of its government.

In phase two, 1898–1945, with the frontier "closed," Native Americans safely confined, and a truncated Mexico firmly in its place south of the Rio Grande, expansionist Americans sought colonies across the seas. After starting another war under false pretenses in 1898, this time with imperial Spain, the United States snatched the massive Philippines, Cuba, Puerto Rico, and a slew of Pacific islands. Finding the strange inhabitants of these lands too brown and too "barbaric" to integrate into coequal states, the United States ruled them first as direct colonies and then as unequal territories and commonwealths. It is instructive, indeed, that occupying American troops took to calling the indigenous peoples of these islands "niggers," borrowing this slur from the nation's original sins of slavery, racism, and internal colonization and apartheid. That transition was seamless and continued well into the next, third, phase of American empire, in which Arabs and Muslims were quickly labeled "sand niggers" by many Americans sent to fight wars in the Greater Mideast.

After emerging from the Second World War relatively unscathed — at least in comparison with war-ravaged Europe and Asia — the United States sought global hegemony in phase three of its imperial journey, from 1946 to the present. Rather than retreat behind its ocean boundaries, America remained militarily deployed abroad while politicians crafted a veritable national security militarist state at home. Although technology, particularly in transportation, obviated the need for physical control and direct governance of old-style colonies, the United States — far from eschewing empire — spread its imperial tentacles over the world. In the name, alternately, of fighting communism, spreading democracy, and protecting human rights globally, the US military constructed, occupied, and operated from an empire of bases. Two decades after the 9/11 terror attacks had justified ever more blatant expansion, the US military controlled eight hundred bases in eighty countries, on every inhabited continent. The US warfare state had unashamedly divided every square inch of the globe into discrete military commands overseen by generals and admirals who often serve in the manner of Roman proconsuls. At the time of this writing, America, rather than offering a peaceful example to the world, is at war in at least seven countries. Post–World War II justifications and enemies may have changed from red communists to brown terrorists, but the outcomes have remained remarkably consistent.

In all phases of American imperialism the empire has inevitably come home, often poisoning any hope for meaningful democracy, meritocracy, or equality within US borders. The racism and white supremacy necessary to wage wars of conquest, plunder, and extermination against Indians and Mexicans not only stemmed from but also added to existing currents within the expanding nation's borders. Anti-immigrant nativism and xenophobia catapulted back to the homeland from American occupation and colonial suppression across the seas. Systems of mass surveillance perfected in the Philippines set the stage for a similar program meant to squelch dissent during the World Wars and morphed into today's tech-savvy digital bugging of American life. Imperial counterinsurgency abroad informed the internal repressive tactics of the later "war on drugs," waged mostly within America's internal colonies of impoverished black and brown neighborhoods and native reservations.

During phase three of the American empire, the results of this imperial "coming home" have been immense. Permanent "terrorist" detention at Guantanamo, torture, prisoner abuse at Abu Ghraib, the

Patriot Act, illegal rendition, and National Security Agency wire-tapping, unthinkable to many Americans before 9/11, are modern outgrowths of a consistent American imperial structure and history. Perhaps the most disturbing outgrowth of late-stage US empire is the phenomenon of militarized "warrior cops," equipped with surplus army equipment and clothed in camouflage fatigues, policing poor communities of color like occupied territory. These law enforcement personnel, which include a disproportionate number of military veterans, have transported counterinsurgency and conventional warfare tactics into the internal colonies of America — forgotten spaces full of forgotten, and forsaken, people.

The vast majority of this imperial history unfolded long before Donald Trump arrived on the national scene. It is a legacy of empire bequeathed to generations of Americans by their forefathers across the centuries. Men — and the top leaders have *always* been men — from every major American political party have built, expanded, and maintained this dual structure of internal and external imperialism. Empire is perhaps the only truly bipartisan national endeavor. Furthermore, class, that most unspoken of American maladies, has often been at the root of American systems of oppression. The division of the working class along ethnic and religious lines, and then the suppression of the remaining class-conscious activists, helped make the imperial machine palatable in the first place. That an outspoken, buffoonish, *billionaire* businessman came to rule, to serve as de facto emperor of the American imperial complex on the back of his claims to represent working-class people and "Make America Great Again" is indicative of the power of class co-option and racial subjugation. Supporters of Donald Trump, deplorable though they might be in the eyes of their opponents, when viewed in context are inherently American.

Trump in Context: Reflections of America's Dark Side

President Trump is no aberration. No doubt the election of a shady real estate magnate, tabloid playboy, and reality-TV-star-turned-xenophobic-populist was a profound matter. That said, much of the Trump effect is a modern-day reflection of America's historical trends and baggage. In fact, with just a touch of difference, the coalition that elected Trump is a standard alliance of four distinct interest groups and peoples that put Republicans in office for decades and maintained American imperialism and internal oppression long before that political party had even been founded. These are anti-taxation (usually hyper-wealthy) libertarians, foreign-policy hawks with imperial proclivities, intolerant brands of evangelical Christians, and racist xenophobes. The genius of Trump, then, was not unlike that of Ronald Reagan or Richard Nixon before him. All managed to appeal to these wide and seemingly dissimilar and contradictory groups and pull them under a big tent, despite subsequently governing mainly in the interests of wealthy elites. The main glue, of course, was in racial appeals to white identity that held together, first, the southern Democrats of the 1830s to the 1950s and then a transformed southern-dominated Republican Party from the 1960s to the present.

In the area of domestic policy, Trump's defense of white supremacist violence, harsh oppression of immigrants and refugees, reflexive support for militarized cops, and refusal to act to tamp down a national epidemic of gun violence seemed to many progressive-minded Americans to be uniquely heinous. In reality, Trump and his supporters have simply rebranded older forms of racism, nativism, and homegrown militarism that had long been crucial links in American society. As in earlier administrations, lines between what constitutes domestic and foreign policy are blurred under Trump. Barbed wire along the southern border with Mexico has a direct link with the walling and wiring off of adjacent neighborhoods by the US military in Baghdad.

Trump's massive tax cuts, statistically highly skewed to benefit the very rich, were far more consistent than anomalous. The massive income inequality that results from this tax revision and regular cuts to social welfare programs may be reaching record levels but is a standard aspect of American economics and not unlike the prevailing situation during the Gilded Age of 1877–1914. The president's call for a Muslim ban, which finally morphed into a travel ban against a

select group of Muslim-majority countries, also has plenty of historical precedent. The Chinese Exclusion Act; the 1924 Immigration Act
that limited migration from Slavic, Jewish, and Asian communities;
and massive internment of Japanese Americans during World War II
are only a few of the antecedents of Trumpian policy and procedure.

In the realm of foreign policy, Trump has, it must be said, spoken
and tweeted in ways that are out of step with the traditionally expansionist foreign-policy-hawk wing of his coalition's quartet. His calls
for the end of "dumb" wars and missions in the Middle East no
doubt appealed to many in a war-weary public and demonstrated an
earthy if uninformed common sense. Still, his lack of follow-through
on this front — whether due to his own dishonesty or the influence
of the wildly hawkish advisers surrounding him — demonstrates
the prevailing power of the national security structure, or what his
supporters term the "deep state." In practice Trump has only increased
the scale of US bombing and worldwide military deployments and
even brought America to the brink of war with states as separated and
diverse as Iran and Venezuela.

Nevertheless, we should not let self-styled liberals or Democratic
partisans off the hook. Their manufacturing of and obsession with
"Russiagate" — the so-far-unsubstantiated claim that the Trump
campaign colluded with Vladimir Putin and Russian intelligence
to win the 2016 US presidential election — has heightened a new
Cold War and, given the long, sordid history of *American* meddling
in foreign elections, illustrated the obtuseness of the "liberal" class.
Trump then expanded Cold War 2.0 to include a growing China by
waging foolhardy economic warfare against Beijing. Finally, Trump's
right-wing authoritarian ambitions have not only spread to a number
of foreign countries but also built upon the precedents set by former
American presidents Nixon, Franklin and Theodore Roosevelt,
William McKinley, and even Andrew Jackson. Taken as whole and
in proper context, then, Trump is an all-American president, and his
promise to "Make America Great Again" is little more than a recasting
of regular calls to return to the whiter, more oppressive, less equal
United States of the past.

The American Future: Republic or Empire, Democracy or Oligarchy

In the light of the correct, if discomfiting, facts, we must conclude that America carries the baggage of four dark historical themes. These are genocide, racism, hyper-capitalism, and empire. Today's Thanksgiving myths to the contrary, English colonists and later self-branded Americans never seriously considered coequal coexistence with indigenous peoples. Through the spread of diseases (sometimes purposefully), wars of conquest, policies of confinement, and cultural attacks on native ways of life, the United States devastated American Indians. By 1890 these First Peoples were nearly extinct.

Racism, which began in the form of color- and caste-based chattel slavery, not only poisoned but also pervaded the American experiment. For more than half of its history, Anglo-American society built itself largely on the literal and figurative backs of black slaves. When the obscenely bloody American Civil War brought de jure slavery to an end, de facto slavery — both economic and social — continued for a century in the guise of a structural system of apartheid segregation. Even today, black poverty and a massive black–white wealth gap, as well as police suppression and institutional racism, continue to maintain a permanent African American underclass. Furthermore, regular appeals to "law and order" throughout American history ensured that black and brown people have filled the nation's prisons, culminating in today's structure of mass incarceration in which more blacks are in some phase of the modern correction system than were slaves in 1861.

Capitalism, which reached its most extreme form on America's shores, also characterized the development and progress of the United States. Generations of historians, pondering the socialism and social democratic and labor parties that developed in the Old World of Europe and across the Global South, have been befuddled by the question of why there has been no widespread socialism in America. Though there are no easy answers, some have noted that a peculiar American strain of hyper-individualism, purposeful racial and ethnic divisions of the working class, and pervasive attacks on labor unions combined to halt the influence of even mild forms of collectivism and social welfare in this country. Gilded Age wealth inequality mirrored colonial-era aristocracy and set the stage for today's record degree of income disparity. American taxation has always — with one brief exception, from the 1930s to the 1960s — been exceptionally low and regressive, slanted from the first to benefit the super rich.

Empire, by now, should speak for itself. Throughout its history the United States has maintained a dual-track system of imperialism. Black urban ghettos and southern sharecropping communities, to say nothing of Indian reservations, served and serve as monuments to internal empire. Conquered native and Mexican lands in North America and captured Spanish Pacific and Caribbean colonies personified external empire for centuries. Since the Second World War, expeditionary US military basing and historically unprecedented interventionism characterized modern foreign empire. This legacy of empire has always "come home to roost" in varying forms of nativist xenophobia, militarized policing, and the squelching of internal dissent and civil liberties. Empire, for America, has always been a way of life.

In spite of it all, hope — however weakened — for a truly democratic, inclusive, and peaceful America remains. The immense power of the military-industrial complex and corporate oligarchs and their misguided xenophobic and racist foot soldiers has, no doubt, only made that American dream seem more distant than ever. Nonetheless, history has consistently demonstrated the potential power of motivated people to shut down the system and force positive change. That change, that progress, is more unlikely than ever to come from the three foundational institutions formed by the US Constitution.

The executive branch has seized so much power — especially in foreign affairs — that presidents, sometimes not even elected by a plurality of the voters, operate more like dictators than servants of the people. The legislative branch, the Congress, is stalemated by tribally partisan division, is veritably owned by well-funded lobbyists, and long ago ceded its constitutionally mandated duty to declare war and oversee foreign affairs. As such, the people's purported representatives cannot be counted on to roll back empire either at home or abroad. The courts, especially the Supreme Court, have become highly politicized and increasingly dominated by archaic, reaction-ary, conservative "originalists" who interpret the Constitution as though it and they were in an eighteenth-century time capsule. After a brief spell of progressive, activist decisions from 1954 to 1971, the courts have rolled back minority protections and affirmative action and even — in the infamous Citizens United decision granting free speech protection to corporations — handed over political power to the wealthiest slice of Americans. Furthermore, these unelected judges have refused to weigh in on the legality of US imperial policy and presidential war-making abroad.

Change, reform, and revolution must explode from the grass roots, from organized people power. The precious, highly lauded institu-tions of American representative democracy have failed the people yet again. Only new collectivist bodies, egalitarian citizen groups, can wield the power to demand a new path for the nation. The odds are stacked against them, no doubt. Those who control the current system count on citizen apathy, reinforce it even, and know they cannot continue indefinitely to hold the reins without it. The owners of this country — the corporations and their proxy politicians — fear a cross-class, multicultural movement by poor and working people more than anything. Power rightfully *belongs* to the people, was promised to them by America's very founding document. After all, the preamble to the Constitution stipulates that the government exists to serve not the states, the rich, the corporations, or the military, but the American people. They can seize control of their collective destiny if they have the courage and the will to take it.[35]

ENDNOTES

1 Ira Berlin, *Many Thousands Gone: The First Two Centuries of Slavery in North America* (2000); Edmund Morgan, *American Slavery, American Freedom: The Ordeal of Colonial Virginia* (1975).

2 Peter Silver, *Our Savage Neighbors: How Indian War Transformed Early America* (2008); Jill Lepore, *The Name of War: King Philip's War and the Origins of American Identity* (2009); Alan Taylor, *American Colonies: The Settling of North America* (volume 1 of *The Penguin History of the United States*, ed. Eric Foner) (2001).

3 Fred Anderson, *Crucible of War: The Seven Years' War and the Fate of Empire in British North America, 1754–1766* (2000); Taylor, *American Colonies.*

4 Alfred Young and Gregory Nobles, *Whose American Revolution Was It? Historians Interpret the Founding* (2011); Edward Countryman, *The American Revolution* (1985); Gary B. Nash, *The Unknown American Revolution: The Unruly Birth of Democracy and the Struggle to Create America* (2005); Woody Holton, *Forced Founders: Indians, Debtors, Slaves, and the Making of the American Revolution in Virginia* (1999).

5 Young and Nobles, *Whose American Revolution Was It?*; Countryman, *The American Revolution*; Nash, *The Unknown American Revolution*; John Shy, *A People Numerous & Armed: Reflections on the Military Struggle for American Independence*, revised edition (1990); Jill Lepore, *The Whites of Their Eyes: The Tea Party's Revolution and the Battle over American History* (2010).

6 Young and Nobles, *Whose American Revolution Was It?*; Countryman, *The American Revolution*; Nash, *The Unknown American Revolution*; Joseph Ellis, *The Quartet: Orchestrating the Second American Revolution, 1783–1789* (2015); Merrill Jensen, *The Articles of Confederation* (1940); Woody Holton, *Unruly Americans and the Origins of the Constitution* (2007).

7 Charles A. Beard, *An Economic Interpretation of the Constitution of the United States* (1913); Saul Cornell, *The Other Founders: Anti-Federalism and the Dissenting Tradition in America, 1788–1828* (1999); Countryman, *The American Revolution*; Ellis, *The Quartet*; David C. Hendrickson, "Escaping Insecurity: The American Founding and the Control of Violence," from *Between Sovereignty and Anarchy: The Politics of Violence in the Revolutionary Era*, ed. Patrick Griffin, Robert G. Ingram, Peter S. Onuf, and Brian Schoen (2015); Woody Holton, *Unruly Americans and the Origins of the Constitution* (2007); Pauline Maier, *Ratification: The People Debate the Constitution, 1787–1788* (2010); John M. Murrin, "A Roof Without Walls: The Dilemma of American

National Identity," from *Beyond Confederation: Origins of the Constitution and American Identity*, ed. Richard Beeman, Stephen Botein, and Edward C. Carter II (1987); Nash, *The Unknown American Revolution*; Peter S. Onuf, "Epilogue," from *Between Sovereignty and Anarchy*; Robbie J. Totten, "Security, Two Diplomacies, and the Formation of the US Constitution," *Diplomatic History* 36, no. 1 (January 2012).

8 Gary B. Nash, "African Americans in the Early Republic," *OAH Magazine of History* 14, no. 2 (Winter 2000); Nash, *The Unknown American Revolution*; Gordon Wood, "The Significance of the Early Republic," *Journal of the Early Republic* 8, no. 1 (Spring 1988); Gordon Wood, *Empire of Liberty: A History of the Early Republic, 1789–1815* (2009).

9 John M. Murrin, "The Jeffersonian Triumph and American Exceptionalism," *Journal of the Early Republic* 20, no. 1 (Spring 2000); Peter S. Onuf, "The Revolution of 1803," *Wilson Quarterly* 27, no. 1 (Winter 2003); Gordon Wood, *Empire of Liberty: A History of the Early Republic, 1789–1815* (2009).

10 Alan Taylor, *The Civil War of 1812: American Citizens, British Subjects, Irish Rebels, and Indian Allies* (2010); Wood, *Empire of Liberty*.

11 Daniel Walker Howe, *What Hath God Wrought: The Transformation of America, 1815–1848* (2007); Wood, *Empire of Liberty*.

12 Alfred A. Cave, "Abuse of Power: Andrew Jackson and the Indian Removal Act of 1830," *Historian* 65, no. 6 (Winter 2003); Lacy K. Ford Jr., "Making the 'White Man's Country' White: Race, Slavery, and State-Building in the Jacksonian South," *Journal of the Early Republic* 19, no. 4 (Winter 1999); Howe, *What Hath God Wrought*; Jill Lepore, "People Power: Revisiting the Origins of American Democracy," *New Yorker* (October 2005); Seth Rockman, "Jacksonian America," in *American History Now*, ed. Eric Foner and Lisa McGirr (2011).

13 Rodolfo Acuna, *Occupied Mexico: A History of Chicanos* (1988); Howe, *What Hath God Wrought*.

14 James M. McPherson, *The Battle Cry of Freedom: The Civil War Era* (1998).

15 David W. Blight, *Race and Reunion: The Civil War in American Memory* (2001); Eric Foner, *A Short History of Reconstruction* (1990); Jill Lepore, *These Truths: A History of the United States* (2018); Richard White, *The Republic for Which It Stands: The United States During Reconstruction and the Gilded Age, 1865–1896* (2017).

16 Robert V. Hine and John Mack Faragher, *The American West: A New Interpretive History* (2000); Lepore, *These Truths*; Patricia Nelson Limerick, *The Legacy of Conquest: The Unbroken Past of the American West* (1987); White, *The Republic for Which It Stands*.

17 Jackson Lears, *Rebirth of a Nation: The Making of Modern America, 1877–1920* (2009); Lepore, *These Truths*; White, *The Republic for Which It Stands*.

18 Stephen Kinzer, *The True Flag: Theodore Roosevelt, Mark Twain, and the Birth of American Empire* (2017); Lears, *Rebirth of a Nation*; Lepore, *These Truths*.

19 George Herring, *From Colony to Superpower: US Foreign Relations Since 1776* (2008); Lears, *Rebirth of a Nation*; Lepore, *These Truths*; Michael McGerr, *A Fierce Discontent: The Rise and Fall of the Progressive Movement in America* (2003).

20 Steve Fraser and Gary Gerstle, *Ruling America: A History of Wealth and Power in a Democracy* (2005); Gary Gerstle, *American Crucible: Race and Nation in the 20th Century* (2001); Lepore, *These Truths*; Howard Zinn, *The Twentieth Century* (1980).

21 Fraser and Gerstle, *Ruling America*; Steve Fraser and Gary Gerstle, eds., *The Rise and Fall of the New Deal Order, 1930–1980* (1989); Gary Gerstle, *American Crucible: Race and Nation in the 20th Century* (2001); Ira Katznelson, *When Affirmative Action Was White: An Untold History of Racial Inequality in Twentieth-Century America* (2005); Ira Katznelson, *Fear Itself: The New Deal and the Origins of Our Time* (2013); David M. Kennedy, *Freedom from Fear: The American People in Depression and War, 1929–1946* (1999); Lepore, *These Truths*; Zinn, *The Twentieth Century*.

22 Gerstle, *American Crucible*; Herring, *From Colony to Superpower*; Katznelson, *Fear Itself*; Kennedy, *Freedom from Fear*; Lepore, *These Truths*; Zinn, *The Twentieth Century*.

23 Michael C. C. Adams, *The Best War Ever: America and World War II* (1994); Gerstle, *American Crucible*; Herring, *From Colony to Superpower*; Kennedy, *Freedom from Fear*; Lepore, *These Truths*.

24 H. W. Brands, *The Devil We Knew: Americans and the Cold War* (1993); Gerstle, *American Crucible*; Kennedy, *Freedom from Fear*; Lepore, *These Truths*; James T. Patterson, *Grand Expectations: The United States, 1945–1974* (1996); Zinn, *The Twentieth Century*.

25 Brands, *The Devil We Knew*; Gerstle, *American Crucible*; Lepore, *These Truths*; Patterson, *Grand Expectations*; Zinn, *The Twentieth Century* (1980).

26 Brands, *The Devil We Knew* (1993); Gregory A. Daddis, *Withdrawal: Reassessing America's Final Years in Vietnam* (2017); Gerstle, *American Crucible*; Lepore, *These Truths*; Patterson, *Grand Expectations*; Zinn, *The Twentieth Century*.

27 Gerstle, *American Crucible*; Lepore, *These Truths*; Patterson, *Grand Expectations*; Zinn, *The Twentieth Century* (1980).

28 Gerstle, *American Crucible*; Lepore, *These Truths*; Patterson, *Grand Expectations*; Bruce Schulman, *The Seventies* (2001); Zinn, *The Twentieth Century*.

29 Gerstle, *American Crucible*; Kevin M. Kruse and Julian E. Zelizer, *Fault Lines: A History of the United States Since 1974* (2019); Lepore, *These Truths*; James T.

Patterson, *Restless Giant: The United States from Watergate to Bush v. Gore* (2005); Schulman, *The Seventies*; Zinn, *The Twentieth Century*.

30 Brands, *The Devil We Knew*; Gerstle, *American Crucible*; Kruse and Zelizer, *Fault Lines*; Lepore, *These Truths*; Patterson, *Restless Giant*; Zinn, *The Twentieth Century*.

31 Brands, *The Devil We Knew*; Gerstle, *American Crucible*; Kruse and Zelizer, *Fault Lines*; Lepore, *These Truths*; Patterson, *Restless Giant*; Zinn, *The Twentieth Century*.

32 Gerstle, *American Crucible*; Kruse and Zelizer, *Fault Lines*; Lepore, *These Truths*; Patterson, *Restless Giant*; Zinn, *The Twentieth Century*.

33 Kruse and Zelizer, *Fault Lines*; Lepore, *These Truths*; Patterson, *Restless Giant*.

34 Kruse and Zelizer, *Fault Lines*; Lepore, *These Truths*.

35 Kruse and Zelizer, *Fault Lines*; Lepore, *These Truths*.

BIBLIOGRAPHY

Acuna, Rodolfo. *Occupied Mexico: A History of Chicanos* (1988).

Adams, Michael C. C. *The Best War Ever: America and World War II* (1994).

Anderson, Fred. *Crucible of War: The Seven Years' War and the Fate of Empire in British North America, 1754–1766* (2000).

Beard, Charles A. *An Economic Interpretation of the Constitution of the United States* (1913).

Berlin, Ira. *Many Thousands Gone: The First Two Centuries of Slavery in North America* (2000).

Blight, David W. *Race and Reunion: The Civil War in American Memory* (2001).

Brands, H. W. *The Devil We Knew: Americans and the Cold War* (1993).

Cave, Alfred A. "Abuse of Power: Andrew Jackson and the Indian Removal Act of 1830." *Historian* 65, no. 6 (Winter 2003).

Cornell, Saul. *The Other Founders: Anti-Federalism and the Dissenting Tradition in America, 1788–1828* (1999).

Countryman, Edward. *The American Revolution* (1985).

Daddis, Gregory A. *Withdrawal: Reassessing America's Final Years in Vietnam* (2017).

Ellis, Joseph. *The Quartet: Orchestrating the Second American Revolution, 1783–1789* (2015).

Foner, Eric. *A Short History of Reconstruction* (1990).

Ford, Lacy K. Jr. "Making the 'White Man's Country' White: Race, Slavery, and State-Building in the Jacksonian South." *Journal of the Early Republic* 19, no. 4 (Winter 1999).

Fraser, Steve, and Gary Gerstle, editors. *The Rise and Fall of the New Deal Order, 1930–1980* (1989).

Fraser, Steve, and Gary Gerstle. *Ruling America: A History of Wealth and Power in a Democracy* (2005).

Gerstle, Gary. *American Crucible: Race and Nation in the 20th Century* (2001).

Hendrickson, David C. "Escaping Insecurity: The American Founding and the Control of Violence." From *Between Sovereignty and Anarchy: The Politics of Violence in the Revolutionary Era*, ed. Patrick Griffin, Robert G. Ingram, Peter S. Onuf, and Brian Schoen (2015).

Herring, George. *From Colony to Superpower: US Foreign Relations Since 1776* (2008).

Hine, Robert V., and John Mack Faragher. *The American West: A New Interpretive History* (2000).

Holton, Woody. *Forced Founders: Indians, Debtors, Slaves, and the Making of the American Revolution in Virginia* (1999).

———. *Unruly Americans and the Origins of the Constitution* (2007).

Howe, Daniel Walker. *What Hath God Wrought: The Transformation of America, 1815–1848* (2007).

Jensen, Merrill. *The Articles of Confederation* (1940).

Katznelson, Ira. *When Affirmative Action Was White: An Untold History of Racial Inequality in Twentieth-Century America* (2005).

———. *Fear Itself: The New Deal and the Origins of Our Time* (2013).

Kennedy, David M. *Freedom from Fear: The American People in Depression and War, 1929–1946* (1999).

Kinzer, Stephen. *The True Flag: Theodore Roosevelt, Mark Twain, and the Birth of American Empire* (2017).

Kruse, Kevin M., and Julian E. Zelizer. *Fault Lines: A History of the United States Since 1974* (2019).

Lears, Jackson. *Rebirth of a Nation: The Making of Modern America, 1877–1920* (2009).

Lepore, Jill. "People Power: Revisiting the Origins of American Democracy." *New Yorker* (October 2005).

———. *The Name of War: King Philip's War and the Origins of American Identity* (2009).

———. *The Whites of Their Eyes: The Tea Party's Revolution and the Battle Over American History* (2010).

———. *These Truths: A History of the United States* (2018).

Limerick, Patricia Nelson. *The Legacy of Conquest: The Unbroken Past of the American West* (1987).

Maier, Pauline. *Ratification: The People Debate the Constitution, 1787–1788* (2010).

McGerr, Michael. *A Fierce Discontent: The Rise and Fall of the Progressive Movement in America* (2003).

McPherson, James M. *The Battle Cry of Freedom: The Civil War Era* (1998).

Morgan, Edmund. *American Slavery, American Freedom: The Ordeal of Colonial Virginia* (1975).

Murrin, John M. "A Roof Without Walls: The Dilemma of American National Identity." From *Beyond Confederation: Origins of the Constitution and American Identity*, ed. Richard Beeman, Stephen Botein, and Edward C. Carter II (1987).

———. "The Jeffersonian Triumph and American Exceptionalism." *Journal of the Early Republic* 20, no. 1 (Spring 2000).

Nash, Gary B. "African Americans in the Early Republic." *OAH Magazine of History* 14, no. 2 (Winter 2000).

———. *The Unknown American Revolution: The Unruly Birth of Democracy and the Struggle to Create America* (2005).

Onuf, Peter S. "The Revolution of 1803." *Wilson Quarterly* 27, no. 1 (Winter 2003).

———. "Epilogue." From *Between Sovereignty and Anarchy: The Politics of Violence in the Revolutionary Era*, ed. Patrick Griffin, Robert G. Ingram, Peter S. Onuf, and Brian Schoen (2015).

Patterson, James T. *Grand Expectations: The United States, 1945–1974* (1996).

———. *Restless Giant: The United States from Watergate to Bush v. Gore* (2005).

Rockman, Seth. "Jacksonian America." From *American History Now*, ed. Eric Foner and Lisa McGirr (2011).

Schulman, Bruce. *The Seventies* (2001).

Shy, John. *A People Numerous & Armed: Reflections on the Military Struggle for American Independence*, revised edition (1990).

Silver, Peter. *Our Savage Neighbors: How Indian War Transformed Early America* (2008).

Taylor, Alan. *American Colonies: The Settling of North America*. Volume 1 of *The Penguin History of the United States*, ed. Eric Foner (2001).

———. *The Civil War of 1812: American Citizens, British Subjects, Irish Rebels, and Indian Allies* (2010).

Totten, Robbie J. "Security, Two Diplomacies, and the Formation of the US Constitution." *Diplomatic History* 36, no. 1 (January 2012).

White, Richard. *The Republic for Which It Stands: The United States During Reconstruction and the Gilded Age, 1865–1896* (2017).

Wood, Gordon. "The Significance of the Early Republic." *Journal of the Early Republic* 8, no. 1 (Spring 1988).

———. *Empire of Liberty: A History of the Early Republic, 1789–1815* (2009).

Young, Alfred, and Gregory Nobles. *Whose American Revolution Was It? Historians Interpret the Founding* (2011).

Zinn, Howard. *The Twentieth Century* (1980).

INDEX

ALSO AVAILABLE FROM **TRUTH TO POWER BOOKS**

 SUNLIGHT EDITIONS

T2P BOOKS // TRUTHFUL NARRATIVES = BETTER UNDERSTANDING

"Margaret Kimberley gives us an intellectual gem of prophetic fire about all the US presidents and their deep roots in the vicious legacy of white supremacy and predatory capitalism. Such truths seem more than most Americans can bear, though we ignore her words at our own peril!"
—CORNEL WEST, AUTHOR OF RACE MATTERS

PREJUDENTIAL

BLACK AMERICA
AND THE PRESIDENTS

MARGARET KIMBERLEY

T2P BOOKS // TRUTHFUL NARRATIVES = BETTER UNDERSTANDING

"This moving and sprightly book is filled with backstories from America's struggle for religious freedom that I'll bet you have never heard before . . . a brilliant scholar's telling insights on the right way for church, state, and society to interact."
— E.J. DIONNE JR., AUTHOR OF CODE RED AND WHY THE RIGHT WENT WRONG

SOLEMN
REVERENCE

THE SEPARATION OF CHURCH
AND STATE IN AMERICAN LIFE

RANDALL BALMER

T2P BOOKS // TRUTHFUL NARRATIVES = BETTER UNDERSTANDING

"[A] nuanced, open-minded, de-politicized discussion of our post-#MeToo world."
—REFINERY29

HAD IT
COMING

Rape Culture Meets #MeToo:
Now What?

ROBYN DOOLITTLE

ALSO AVAILABLE FROM TRUTH TO POWER BOOKS

👁 EYEWITNESS MEMOIRS

T2P BOOKS // TRUTHFUL NARRATIVES = BETTER UNDERSTANDING

"This short, powerful book should be required reading for anyone who has ever wondered what it's like to be an ordinary citizen living in a war zone." — PUBLISHERS WEEKLY

WHEN THE BULBUL STOPPED SINGING

LIFE IN PALESTINE DURING
AN ISRAELI SIEGE

RAJA SHEHADEH

NEW INTRODUCTION BY
COLUM McCANN

T2P BOOKS // TRUTHFUL NARRATIVES = BETTER UNDERSTANDING

One of three books people "should read to understand what happened in Vietnam."
— THE MARINE CORPS GAZETTE

WAR OF NUMBERS

AN INTELLIGENCE MEMOIR OF THE
VIETNAM WAR'S UNCOUNTED ENEMY

SAM ADAMS

FOREWORD BY
COL. DAVID HACKWORTH

NEW INTRODUCTION BY
JOHN PRADOS

T2P BOOKS // TRUTHFUL NARRATIVES = BETTER UNDERSTANDING

"Hope finds a prominent presence in what so many think is a hopeless, endless conflict."
— KIRKUS

NATIONAL JEWISH BOOK AWARDS
FINALIST

FRIENDLY FIRE
A MEMOIR

How Israel Became Its Own Worst
Enemy and the Hope for Its Future

AMI AYALON

WITH
ANTHONY DAVID

INTRODUCTION BY
DENNIS ROSS

THE WOMAN WHO INSPIRED
AN AFRICAN #METOO MOVEMENT

TOUFAH

Toufah
Jallow

with Kim Pittaway

ALSO AVAILABLE FROM **TRUTH TO POWER BOOKS**

 DOCUMENTARY NARRATIVES

T2P BOOKS // TRUTHFUL NARRATIVES = BETTER UNDERSTANDING

"Investigative journalism at its relentless and compassionate best." — *KIRKUS REVIEWS*
"Methamphetamine was a huge part of this case . . . A horrible murder driven by drugs."
— *PROSECUTOR CAL RERUCHA*
"A gripping read." — *PEOPLE MAGAZINE*

THE BOOK OF MATT

THE REAL STORY OF THE MURDER OF MATTHEW SHEPARD

STEPHEN JIMENEZ

NEW INTRODUCTION BY
ANDREW SULLIVAN

 T2P BOOKS // TRUTHFUL NARRATIVES = BETTER UNDERSTANDING

"A book that is both a history and a sports classic." — *DETROIT FREE PRESS*
"One of the most compelling sports biographies [ever]. A must-read."
— (starred review) *BOOKLIST*

HARD DRIVING

THE WENDELL SCOTT STORY

The American Odyssey of
NASCAR's First Black Driver

BRIAN DONOVAN

FOREWORD BY
JOE POSNANSKI

"A gripping, moving tale."
— EVAN THOMAS, AUTHOR OF *IKE'S BLUFF*

IKE'S MYSTERY MAN

THE SECRET LIVES OF ROBERT CUTLER

The Cold War, the Lavender Scare, and
the Untold Story of Eisenhower's First
National Security Advisor

PETER SHINKLE

FOREWORD BY
CHARLES KAISER